To Elizabeth Asprooth Cragan and Vicki Lynne Fitzgerald,
with love and affection

Vice President, Editor in Chief: Paul Smith
Series Editor: Karon Bowers
Editorial Assistant: Leila Scott
Marketing Manager: Kris Farnsworth
Editorial Production Service: Chestnut Hill Enterprises, Inc.
Manufacturing Buyer: Megan Cochran

Congress Cataloging-in-Publication Data

F.
nding communication theory : the communicative forces for
/ John F. Cragan, Donald C. Shields.

iographical references (p.) and index.
9587-3
ion—Philosophy.   I. Shields, Donald C.   II. Title.

97-28099
CIP

f America
2   02   01

Understanding
Communicatio
Theo

The Communica
for I

John F. Cragan
Illinois State University

Library of

ragan, Joh
Underst
human actio

p.
Includes bib
ISBN 0-205-
1. Communica
P90.C73 1997
302.2—dc21

ted in the United States
9 8 7 6 5 4 3

Bost

J. Coates

Contents

Preface

We began teaching university courses in 1967. Of the courses we have taught since then, the communication theory class—whether at the undergraduate or graduate level—has proved to be the most difficult. The communication theory class repeatedly challenges us to present theories in new and dramatic ways. As we near the twenty-first century, the newest challenge is to demonstrate the use of communication theories for solving real-world problems. We have come to believe that the core of your professionalism as a future graduate in communication will center on the communication theories that you know. It is the purpose of *Understanding Communication Theory: The Communicative Forces for Human Action* to teach you the essential, discipline-based, communication theories and to illustrate their important contribution to society. The knowledge contained in this book will arm you with many useful communication theories. In turn, these theories will allow you to function professionally as a respected member of our society. We believe that, when you finish this book, you will be proud that you have selected communication as your field of study. We know that it makes us proud to present you with the way we teach communication theory.

The communication discipline comprises a unique body of communication theories. Those theories justify the discipline's valued place in the academy. They have been developed and validated through grounded research by scholars in our discipline. We believe it is important for you to see them in one place. We also believe it is important for you to learn them, or to refresh your memory of them, in one class. Hence, the communication theories included in this book represent the communication discipline's core theories.

We classify, analyze, and evaluate forty-two core theories by means of a metatheoretical blueprint introduced in Chapter 1. We use this blueprint to direct the organization of the entire book. The metatheory allows us to classify communication theories into five types: general communication theories, contextual communication theories, communication microtheories, special communication theories, and symbiotic (interdisciplinary) theories. General communication theories provide a powerful, rich, "why" explanation of communication across six traditional communication contexts that leads to prediction about and control of communicators communicating in a medium. The basic concept of each general theory identifies a fundamental communicative force that accounts for human action. Chapters 2–7 present the six general communication theories. In Chapter 2, we present Information Systems Theory. It explains the communicative force of *information-sharing* that gives order and structure to human organizing when optimized. In Chapter 3, we present Rational Argumentation Theory. It explains the communicative force of *argument-making* that provides the basis for rational decision-making. In Chapter 4, we present Symbolic Convergence Theory. It explains the communicative force of *fantasy-chaining* that creates symbolic realities containing meaning, emotion, and motive for human action. In Chapter 5, we present Uncertainty Reduction Theory. It explains the communicative force of *social information-sharing* that ignites, maintains, and sometimes destroys personal relationships. In Chapter 6, we present Narrative Paradigm Theory. It explains the communicative force of *storytelling* that bestows the value–justification for human action. Then, in Chapter 7, we present Diffusion of Innovation Theory. It explains the communicative force of innovation diffusing-talk that enables the adoption of new ideas and products for social change. Communication scholars have grounded these six general theories to the observations of communicators communicating in a medium through literally thousands of studies. We identify the major attendant research and provide numerous syntheses of research showing the use of these theories to solve real-world problems.

Chapters 8, 9, and 10 present twenty-three contextual communication theories that explain communicators communicating within the medium of one of our discipline's six traditional contexts. These contexts are interpersonal, small group, public speaking, organizational, mass, and intercultural communication. In each content area, we explain the important contextual theories. Then we unify the contextual theories (3 to 4 per context) with the six general communication theories. In this way we provide an integrated understanding of communication as it occurs within each context. Just as we do with the general communication theories, we demonstrate the real-world application of each of the contextual theories. As you can see, this book stands or falls on the validity of the assertion "There is nothing more practical than a good communication theory."

In Chapter 11, we present a baker's dozen (13) of communication microtheories. Communication microtheories are valid, powerful, useful, and important theories as they explain a narrow band of communication that spans the six traditional communication contexts. Typically, communication microtheories emphasize a basic concept such as lying, a message concept such as speech organization, a dynamic concept such as the content versus relationship dimension of language, a communicator concept such as communication apprehension, a medium concept such as the laws governing the obsolescence of communication technology, and an evaluative concept such as sexism in language.

There is not enough space in this book to present important special communication theories that have been developed in our discipline (such as how to write a press release) or important symbiotic theories that have been developed in other disciplines (such as social penetration theory in psychology, symbolic interactionism in sociology, or social exchange theory in economics). It's our belief that you have learned the special theories in courses such as public relations, persuasive communication, and news reporting. Similarly, we believe that the symbiotic theories are best learned from "the horse's mouth" by taking courses in those minors and cognate areas that interest you or in the context-based courses of our discipline such as interpersonal, persuasive, and organizational communication. Of course, during the semester, your professor may add special theories or symbiotic theories as she or he sees fit.

In Chapter 12, we conclude the book with a metaphorical review of communication theories. Here, we conceive of communication as a field of flowers, our theories as flowers, and the future communication graduate as flower sellers. We do this to help you remember what you have learned and to view the study of communication theory as pleasurable. We know this book will enable you to understand communication theories. We trust it does so in an enjoyable way.

We believe in team research. This book is certainly the culmination of a team effort. First, we want to thank the more than two thousand college students at Illinois State University and the University of Missouri who have helped us immensely. Their criticism of our teaching has allowed us to develop the content contained in this book. Second, we'd like to thank the nearly two thousand communication scholars whose contributions to programmatic lines of research undergird this text. When we joined the communication discipline in the 1960s, there were not enough indigenous communication theories to fill a textbook. Today, there are more than enough. Third, the comments of the following reviewers helped us in finalizing the manuscript: Kenneth D. Frandsen, University of New Mexico; Ferald J. Bryan, Northern Illinois University; John E. Crawford, Arizona State University; J. D. Rayburn, II, Florida State University; H. L. Goodall, Jr., University of North Carolina, Greensboro; and Alan Cirlin, St. Mary's University. Fourth, we'd like to thank the Allyn and Bacon team who encouraged us to undertake this project and worked closely with us to completion. To Carla Daves, Joseph Opiela, Paul Smith, Andrea Geanacopoulos, and Kathy Rubino, our heartfelt thanks. Finally, we thank our extended families and most especially Elizabeth Asprooth Cragan and Vicki Lynne Fitzgerald, to whom we dedicate this book.

JFC
DCS

About the Authors

JOHN F. CRAGAN AND DONALD C. SHIELDS received their Doctor of Philosophy degrees from the University of Minnesota. They have taught and researched for more than twenty-five years at their respective universities. This book is the ninth text they have written together. Their last book, *Symbolic Theories in Applied Communication Research*, received the National Communication Association's 1995 Applied Communication Annual Book Award. Professors Cragan and Shields have published scores of scholarly articles in national and international communication journals. In addition, they have consulted for numerous public and private organizations. Their teaching specialties are communication theory, small group, organizational, and applied communication.

C h a p t e r 1

Introduction to Communication Theory

A communication metatheory empowers us to classify, anatomize (dissect), and evaluate communication theories.

Chapter Outline

In this book, we examine the core communication theories. These core theories are "the tools of our trade." The core theories let us understand, describe, explain, evaluate, predict, and control human communicative behavior. For example, theories help us interpret language and symbols. They pinpoint the communicative forces that prompt human action. They point to future actions and explicate past actions. They enable us to predict and control our future communicative interactions. Theories tell us many things. For example, some theories tell us why one speech is successful and another is not. Others tell us why some problem-solving groups reach productive, efficacious decisions and others do not. Still others tell us why some people respond to novel ideas more quickly than others do. The core communication theories bind us together as players in the field we call *communication*.

By reading this book, you will learn how core communication theories explain human action. Along the journey to understanding, you will come to know a great deal about the communication discipline that you have chosen as the foundation for your professional life and career. We see our job as that of trail guides. We'll point out interesting objects. We'll identify known landmarks. Finally, we will keep you from straying too far from the beaten path. As your guides, we will, from time to time, stop along our journey. At those stops we'll sometimes offer suggestions to help you proceed along the next portion of the trail. At other times, we'll highlight some point of interest. Still other times, we will check the trail to see how far we have come.

Overview

In 1973, we began teaching the communication theory course on our respective campuses. We used an eclectic approach. In hindsight, we would say we naively tried to teach the whole of the communication curriculum in a single course, including parts borrowed from linguistics, psychology, sociology, social psychology, and economics. At the same time, we lacked good landmarks that would help us find our way along the trail to understanding the core communication theories. In particular, we lacked guidelines that would allow us to identify the core theories of our discipline. We lacked a taxonomy that would allow us to sort out and classify theories. We lacked a standard by which to judge one theory as more important than another. Finally, we lacked rules of thumb that would indicate whether one theory deserved more course attention than another. The course for which we designed this book bears little resemblance to those early efforts.

We now ask several questions that identify the landmarks that help us locate our core theories:

1. What knowledge makes us unique in the academy as communication professionals?
2. What kinds of communication theories provide that knowledge?
3. Do all communication theories explain all communication contexts and episodes?
4. Just how many communication theories are there?
5. What criteria can help sort out and classify communication theories?
6. How do people make use of communication theories?
7. How many communication theories should I know?

The remainder of this chapter answers these questions. It sets out the criteria used to select the theories included in this book. We trust that, as you complete this journey, you will be able to answer the question we most often ask of candidates who seek positions in our respective communication departments: "Tell me about your five favorite communication theories and how you would use them." We trust this book will help you answer such questions.

Professor Shields teaches at the University of Missouri–St. Louis. He is a native of the "Show Me" state. He often tells stories about his Great Uncle Fred, another native Missourian, who had fought in France in World War I. Fred's favorite question—"Will this dog hunt?"—related to the use, benefit, or value of some idea. Seldom did a holiday dinner pass without Uncle Fred asking, "What are you learning at that school that is practical?" Don would answer something like, "How to get through dinner without offending anyone!" Fred would roar with laughter. For Fred, Don had demonstrated that the dog could hunt. For us, with kudos to Don's Great Uncle Fred, nothing is more useful than a good communication theory.

We suggest that you ask a similar question: "Will this book hunt?" Will it allow you to classify communication theories? Will it show how theories explain human communicative action? Will it demonstrate their use in solving real-world problems? Will it help you control your future communicative encounters? If this book does not hunt, then we will have failed in our major objective.

All along the trail to understanding communication theory, we plan to interact with you. We believe it will help you understand the most important benefit of completing a course of study in your chosen discipline. That benefit concerns your having learned to recognize, classify, evaluate, and use communication theories. We promise not to preach too much. We promise not to talk down to you. Finally, we promise to show you the trail signs. You will learn to recognize, separate, and store communication theories in a convenient toolbox for ease of use. *Toolbox* is a another name for the metatheory whose presentation comprises the heart of this chapter. A metatheory is a framework for classifying, describing, and detailing differences in theories. We will present the metatheory on up the trail in this chapter.

We, too, have read our share of boring textbooks. We recall more than one author's promises of textual excitement and content importance. We also recall the many times our naive hopes had been dashed by the middle of Chapter 2. Nevertheless, we can assure you that we've spent many years as trail guides at the academy in preparation for writing this book. Literally thousands of our students have listened to the lectures that refined its content. On the other hand, you might want to know that we wrote our first book in 1970 to help pay off our college loans. Your acceptance of this book will help prepay our assisted living at Hazy Acres Retirement Manor. We don't want to burden our families; nor do we want to burden you with a boring book.

Defining Communication Theory

Members of the academy generally hold that a theory is a set of concepts and relationship statements that enables one to understand, describe, explain, evaluate, predict, and control things (phenomena). Theory-makers are puzzle-solvers. Humans naturally invent theories. We cannot resist solving puzzles. Puzzle-solving is in our nature. That's why we say that theories are *why explanations* of puzzling phenomena. The explanation is the solution to the puzzle.

We can quickly illustrate what we mean. In the 1800s, tens of thousands of people died from postsurgical infections. What puzzled physicians was why? Trying to solve this puzzle produced a why explanation called *germ theory*. The theory said that dirty operating instruments and dirty hands spread germs that infected a wound. The theory also said that if surgeons sterilized their instruments and kept their hands clean, and the wound clean, it would reduce the number of postoperative infections. Surgeons, of course, still use this theory today.

In the field of communication, we have many puzzles that call forth why explanations or theories to explain and solve them. The initial puzzle in our discipline concerned why were some public speeches effective and others not? Today's puzzles concern many things. Why do some groups reach quality decisions and others do not? Why do some organizations command the strong allegiance of their employees while others appear to lack a common symbolic identity? Why do information systems break down? How can they be made more effective and efficient? Why do some interpersonal relationships wane and end and others thrive and regenerate? The many communication theories introduced in the chapters to follow provide solutions or answers to such puzzles. Accordingly, we define a *communication theory* as a set of concepts and relationship statements that helps to describe, explain, evaluate, predict, and control communication events.

A communication *concept* is formed when a name or label is given to a set of like things. Once the name or label is given to like things, the set forms a class of objects. For example, a letter contains a *salutation* (chosen from the class of greetings like *dear, dearest, my incredible hulk*), a *body* (comprised of a class of objects known as content, such as information, ideas, points, materials), and a *farewell* (chosen from the class of available closes like *sincerely, yours truly, love and kisses, your incredible hulk*). *Relationship statements* tell how the concepts fit together: the salutation opens the letter, the body presents the letter's content, and the farewell ends the letter.

The three most common forms of relationship statements contained in theories are "either . . . or," "and," and "if . . . then." For example: **If** you exhibit *stage fright* (a theoretical concept in theater), **then** you will not become the *lead* (another theoretical concept) in the *school play* (a third theoretical concept). All communication theories use relationship statements such as "and," "either . . . or," and "if . . . then" to link theoretical concepts. It is the linkage between theoretical concepts that helps provide, in whole or in part, a description, explanation, evaluation, or prediction of the human actions stemming from communicators

With all the variables in communication, these theories MUST be more complex than "germ" theory!

(people) communicating (talking, writing, listening, viewing) over time in a medium (the substance in which a theory functions, propagates, and travels).

Of course, although all communication theories fit the above definition, this is not to say that all communication theories possess the same concepts. Nor is it to say that all communication theories contain the same relationship statements. Nor is it to say that all communication theories provide the same kind of description, explanation, evaluation, and prediction. Nor do all communication theories provide the same amount of control of future events. Just as different theories explain different things in the academy as a whole, so too, in communication, different theories explain different things. Additionally, some theories explain more things than others (their explanation exhibits wider scope), and some theories explain things better than others (their explanation exhibits more power). Sorting out such differences requires a special vocabulary—a major landmark along the trail—known as a *communication metatheory* (a theory of theories). But, we get ahead of ourselves. There are a couple of sites to visit before we reach that ford in the river.

Defining Communication

It's time to stop and highlight a point of interest. Notice that we have yet to define *communication*. The reason is that each communication theory intrinsically yields its own definition of communication.[1] For example, by using a semiotic linguistic theory, Liska and Cronkhite (1995, p. 22) defined communication as "the exchange of certain types of signs" (a kind of I'll trade you my two stop-signs for three loading-zones and a yield-right-of-way explanation of communication). With the six general communication theories presented in Chapters 2–7, you will see rather quickly that each one provides a different way of defining communication. You will see communication defined respectively as information, argument, chaining fantasies, question-asking and disclosing, storytelling, and the talk of diffusing novel ideas.[2] We repeat, theories drive the definition of communication. They do so by providing the lens through which we observe communicators communicating over time in a medium.

By the end of the journey—your completion of this book—we will have introduced you to forty-two communication theories. As you shall see, these forty-two theories come in varying sizes and shapes. And, of course, each comes with its own unique definition of communication. Again, definitions of communication derive from communication theories; not the other way around. You cannot define communication in the absence of a stated or implied communication theory. Of course, if this is not your first course in communication, you already know that communication textbooks often define communication early in the text. You may have noticed, depending upon the course, that some definitions appear more communicator-centered, others more message-centered, and still others more medium-centered. For example, McLuhan (1964) offered the view that the medium is the message. Consequently meaning is in the medium. Such a view differs from Watzlawick, Beavin, and Jackson's (1967) point that meanings are in people's interpretation of the content and relationship dimension of the message. As well, both viewpoints differ from Verderber's (1978) stance that meaning exists in the source who picks the words to create the message that is then decoded by the receiver. The reason for the variance is that each author, either explicitly or implicitly, adopted definitions derived from different communication theories. Respectively, they are Media Law Theory (Chapter 11), Relational Control Theory (Chapter 11), and Information Systems Theory (Chapter 2).

However, we digress from our point and detour from our main trail: Theories drive definitions of communication. But, you needn't take your trail guides' word for it. Take a rest-stop. Think of your definition of communication. Write it down. Then return to it at the end of the book. At that time, see if you can identify the communication theory from which you implicitly derived your recorded definition. If by then you can, we would take that as a sign that you have successfully completed your journey to understanding communication theories.

Three Levels of Communication

Up ahead is another point of interest. Here, we would ask you to stop and think about several levels of communication. Level 1 is actual communication—the ordinary talk that goes on every day. Level 2 is theorizing about actual communication—explanations of the recurring regularities spotted in everyday talk. Level 3 is metatheorizing about communication theories—discussing the possible similarities and differences in the theories that explain everyday talk. Each level possesses its own unique vocabulary. It's important and fun to sort out these levels. You do it every day.

Actual Communication (Level 1)   An example of Level 1 communication is represented by the ordinary dialogue contained in **Table 1-1** (column one). Note that Professor Cragan is meeting Paula, an adult-learning student, for the first time. The conversation is face-to-face.

[handwritten margin note: actual words]

This brief introductory conversation represents communicators (Dr. Cragan and Paula) communicating (talking) over time (the duration of the conversation) in a medium (face-to-face). The dialogue is typical of the communication phenomena about which we theorize. So, the question becomes, have you taken a course in interpersonal communication? If yes, then you already know one or more communication theories that describe, explain, and make predictions about this kind of communicative episode. The interpersonal theory is Uncertainty Reduction Theory (presented in Chapter 5). Like all general communication theories, it provides us with a Level 2 vocabulary to help us theorize about Level 1 communication such as that between Professor Cragan and Paula.

Theorizing about Communication (Level 2)   Level 2 communication provides a discrete theoretical vocabulary for carrying on a professional discussion and analysis of Level 1 communication. The vocabulary is discrete because it is unique to the theory developed or chosen to explain the Level 1 communication. For example, Uncertainty Reduction Theory explains how the force of social information-sharing reduces uncertainty about the communicators and ignites interpersonal friendships and relationships. One of its theoretical concepts is *information-seeking* and that may occur by *question-asking* and *reciprocal self-disclosure* (telling each other things about yourselves). Question-asking and reciprocal self-disclosure give us two other theoretical concepts. In the dialogue reported in **Table 1-1** (column two), Dr. Cragan asked questions and gave information and Paula gave information and asked questions. Together, they made reciprocal self-disclosures. Information-seeking (question-asking) and information-giving (self-disclosure and reciprocal self-disclosure) are among Uncertainty Reduction Theory's communication con-

[handwritten margin note: labels the actual words (so that we can create/apply the theories in level 3)]

TABLE 1-1. Levels of Communication about a First-time Conversation with an Adult-Learning Student

LEVEL I Actual Communication	LEVEL 2 Theorizing about Actual Communication	LEVEL 3 Metatheorizing about Communication Theories
Communication phenomena such as a first-time classroom conversation: ↓	*We do so by using a communication theory like Uncertainty Reduction with such technical concepts as:* ↓	*We do so by using a communication metatheory like the one introduced in this book to classify, anatomize, and evaluate theories.* ↓
"Hi! I'm Dr. Cragan. What's your name?"	Information-giving/seeking	URT is a general communication theory
"Paula."	Information-giving	
"I see a ring. Are you married?"	Information-seeking	
"Yes. I'm coming back to school."	Information-giving	URT explains the effects of optimizing uncertainty reduction across contexts
"Do you have children?"	Information-seeking	
"Yes. Two. Alice and Todd."	Information-giving	
"I have two also, Katie and Keary; and Katie has two, Kyle and Connor."	Information-giving	
"So you're a grandpa?"	Information-seeking	URT explains the force of social information-sharing on human action
"Yep."	Information-giving	
"That's nice. I like grandpas!"	Information-giving	

[handwritten annotation: URT - Uncertainty Reduction Theory]

cepts. The relationship among these concepts explains the regularities (repetitive elements) going on in the actual communication occurring at Level 1. Of course, the theory predicts that as we optimally answer questions and make disclosures we reduce uncertainty and increase *liking* between communicators. Here we see a relationship statement that brings in yet another theoretical concept (liking). Such a relationship statement is an example of Level 2 communication about the "connectedness" of the theory's concepts—the statement tells us the link, or how the concepts fit together.

As scholars, if we decide to talk about Uncertainty Reduction Theory as a whole and compare it to other communication theories, we need a Level 3 metavocabulary. That Level 3 metavocabulary will allow us to classify and compare communication theories (just like we needed a theory to describe, explain, and evaluate actual communication).

[handwritten margin note: classification, creation, application of theories using level 2 (and 1) info.]

Metatheorizing about Communication Theories (Level 3)   A metavocabulary that allows us to classify and compare communication theories occurs at Level 3 of communication. Such a metavocabulary is called a *communication metatheory* (see **Table 1-1,** column three). Let's return to our example, and briefly process Uncertainty Reduction Theory using Level 3 communication.

Social information-seeking (eliciting social information) through specific communicative behaviors such as *question-asking* (What's your name?) and *reciprocal disclosure* (I have two grandsons.) are among the initial or *basic concepts* of URT. The *metaconcept* called a *basic concept* represents Level 3 metavocabulary. You will discover from Chapter 4 that *uncertainty reduction* itself is one of URT's *evaluative* theoretical concepts. Did the conversation between Professor Cragan and Paula reduce their uncertainty? When that question is answered affirmatively or negatively, you have used URT's evaluative concept known as *uncertainty reduction*. The notion of an *evaluative theoretical concept* also represents a Level 3 metaconcept. Does Uncertainty Reduction Theory spawn other theories? That question is itself a Level 3 communication question because *heuristic* is an evaluative metatheoretical concept that concerns the ability of a theory to foster other ideas or to foster spin-off theories. In the remainder of this chapter, we present our metatheory's *metaconcepts* that will help you classify, compare, and evaluate communication theories.

[handwritten margin note: heuristic— 1. aiding or guiding in discovery 2. designating an educational method by which a student is stimulated to make his/her own investigations and discoveries.]

The Communication Metatheory (TCM)

The Communication Metatheory (TCM) provides the topographical map needed to classify, compare, and evaluate communication theories.[3] TCM organizes the various theoretical explanations of communicators communicating over time in a medium. We use TCM consistently as our sole way of looking at the forty-two communication theories included in this book.

By way of foreshadowing exactly where the trail to understanding communication theories will take us, we first use TCM to classify, then to compare, and finally to evaluate communication theories. For example, we identify and classify the core communication theories presented in this book by first using TCM's five *classifying elements* (Is a particular theory a general, contextual, micro, special, or symbiotic theory?). Then we compare the theories by using TCM's *anatomical elements* (origin, roots, and assumptions; communicative force and paradigm; theoretical technical concepts; modeling and relating concepts; and the theory–method complex). Finally, we evaluate the theories by using TCM's *evaluative elements* (power and scope; heuristic and isomorphic theories; elegance and parsimony; validity and utility; and withstanding the critics). *[handwritten: similar appearance but different "ancestry"]*

[handwritten margin note: parsimony - undue sparingness]

This may be a good time to stop on our journey and consider some background on classifying communication theories. In the mid-1960s, as students at the University of Missouri—Kansas City, one of our professors, Lee Thayer, organized the first and second interdisciplinary conferences on communication theory in 1965 and 1966. He invited dozens of scholars from across the academy and from around the world to these conferences.[4]

Thayer (1965, 1967) identified the purpose of these conferences as seeking a common core of interdisciplinary communication theories. His thinking epitomized the status of the discipline at that time just as in the early 1970s interdisciplinary thinking epitomized how we structured our first courses in communication theory.

Suffice it to say, after thirty years of concentrated work by discipline-indigenous communication theorists, we no longer need to seek out interdisciplinary theories to have sufficient material to teach a course in communication theory. We can now write a communication theory book presenting our discipline's core theories. Indeed, the goal is to find ways to teach you the theories that you really need to know within the allotted length of the text. While growing up, Professor Shields (then Donnie) spent Sundays at the Baptist church. He fondly recalls singing the doxology, "Blessed Be the Ties That Bind." For us, the ties that bind the discipline together are our core communication general, contextual, and microtheories.[5]

The act of choosing a classification typology is not a simple decision. By typology, we mean the systematic classification of theories into types that have traits in common. The mere act of choosing a typology puts us beyond Level 3 communication and moves us up to Level 4 because we are of necessity comparing one metatheory with another. At the fourth level of communication, we would be engaged in *meta*metatheorizing (that is, talking about metatheories). To expect you to gain the competence to *meta*metatheorize and talk about and compare competing communication metatheories is beyond the central concern of this text. *Meta*metatheorizing strays too far from the beaten path on our journey to understanding communication theories.[6] Consequently, we'll stick to the Level 1, Level 2, and Level 3 aspects of the trail. That's why TCM is the only communication metatheory we present in this book.

The Classifying Elements

The suggested classification typology, or means of grouping theories with traits in common, allows you to identify and classify communication theories within five categories: general, contextual, micro, special, and symbiotic (interdisciplinary) theories (see **Table 1-2**). This typology is not static or closed. Theories live, die, evolve, and change. As well, new theories arise and others, like Power Rangers, morph into different classifications.[7]

General Communication Theories   For our purposes, a *general communication theory* is a valid, powerful, why explanation of communicators communicating over time in a medium that holds across the traditional contexts of interpersonal, small group, public speaking, organizational, mass, and intercultural communication. In addition to its context-free status, a general communication theory is not time-bound. By "not time-bound," we mean that a general communication theory explains communication among the Colonial Puritans in the same way that it explains today's communication and predicts the type of communication that will occur in the future. The metaconcept that describes the explaining of past-events condition is the word *postdictive*. Conversely, by "not time-bound" we mean that as a general communication theory it will explain and forecast communication in the future, just as it does today. The metaconcept that describes this explaining future-events condition is the word *predictive*. Another identifying characteristic of a general communication theory is that its basic concept locates and names a fundamental communication interaction or communicative force that accounts for human action. For example, Diffusion

TABLE 1-2.   Classifying Forty-Two Core Communication Theories

General Theories	Contextual Theories	Microtheories
Information Systems Rational Argumentation Symbolic Convergence Uncertainty Reduction Narrative Paradigm Diffusion of Innovation	*Interpersonal Communication* Constructivist Coordinated Meaning Management Dialectical Relationship Face Management *Small Group Communication* Decision Emergence Role Emergence Functional Decision-Making Adaptive Structuration *Public Speaking* Neo-Aristotelian Burke's Dramatism Vid-Oral Image Restoration *Organizational Communication* Weick's Organizing Unobtrusive Control Artistic Ethnography Organizational Assimilation *Mass Communication* Spiral of Silence Agenda-Setting Cultivation Effects Uses and Gratifications *Intercultural Communication* Anxiety/Uncertainty Management Face Negotiation Cross-Cultural Adaptation	*Basic Concept Emphasis* Information Manipulation Interpersonal Deception Compliance-Gaining/Resisting *Message Structure Emphasis* Action Assembly Speech/Communication Accommodation Expectancy Violation *Communication Dynamic Emphasis* Relational Control Marital Communication *Communicator Attribute Emphasis* Communication Apprehension *Medium Structure Emphasis* McLuhan's Media Law *Evaluative Emphasis* Muted Group Feminist Genre Habermas's Critical

of Innovation Theory names and explains the communicative force of diffusing innovation talk on social change.

Already it's time for another rest stop to ponder where we are. Here, we need to tell you that the communication discipline does not have a single universal explanation of all communicators communicating over time in all media. Indeed, no discipline in the academy has a universal theory to explain all relevant phenomena. Even physicists still search for a universal theory to explain all of the universe and the microcosm of quantum physics. At this time, no single physical theory explains both. However, every discipline possesses a half-dozen or so general theories that explain major aspects of the phenomena within their purview. In communication, we feel fortunate to have a half-dozen general theories that explain the impact of six communicative forces on human action across contexts. As well, we feel fortunate to have twenty-three contextual theories that explain communication within specific boundaries. Finally, we feel fortunate to have a baker's dozen of microtheories that explain a narrow band of communication phenomena across contexts. Let's continue up the trail and look in detail at what we mean by contextual theories.

Contextual Communication Theories   Contextual communication theories explain communication within the confines of what we call the traditional medium, contexts of interpersonal, small group, public, organizational, mass, and intercultural communication. You are most likely to have already studied several contextual theories in the courses you have taken in communication. TCM recognizes two types of contextual communication theories. *Type 1 contextual theories* use one or more theoretical concepts that by definition tie them forever to the context. For example, Gerbner's Cultivation Theory (presented in Chapter 10) uses a mass media concept, *television,* that forever limits his explanation of the symbolic creation of reality to that context. Likewise, the Functional Decision-Making Theory and Role Emergence Theory (both presented in Chapter 8) permanently reside in the small group context. They exhibit concepts that limit their scope of explanation to decision-making small groups. On the other hand, *Type 2 contextual theories* (such as Burke's Dramatism Theory, presented in Chapter 9) are fermenting and evolving as we write and may become broader in scope as they prove out by way of grounding research across contexts. We illustrate twenty-three contextual theories in Chapters 8, 9, and 10. However, the list is not exhaustive. The number of contextual communication theories is also in flux. As we write, scholars are developing new theories and conducting research that improves the ability to generalize from the existing Type 2 contextual theories. So, in the years to come, this list may change. Can you recall the ways we've indicated the list might change?

Communication Microtheories   Communication microtheories are valid, useful, and important. It is not too far a stretch to say that microtheories are to communication what quantum physics is to physics. Microtheories tend to explain communication at the subatomic level. Like general theories, communication microtheories explain an aspect of communication across contexts—they too are context-free. However, microtheories tend to concentrate on only a single aspect of communicators communicating. That aspect may be a particular unit of communication. It may also be the message. As well, it may be the medium. Additionally, it may be the attributes of a communicator. Finally, it may be a narrow way of evaluating communication. For example, Expectancy Violation Theory and Communication Deception Theory (presented in Chapter 11) are two well-developed microtheories supported by extensive research programs. However, TCM classifies them as having microtheory status because they explain, at this time, a very limited number of communication phenomena. Respectively, the two microtheories explain incongruent nonverbal message behaviors and those message behaviors known as lying. Similarly, our communication microtheory category includes critical theories such as Muted Group Theory, Feminist Genre Theory, and Habermas's Critical Theory. These latter theories achieve microtheory status because they concentrate on revealing a narrow, important, but heretofore unseen structural flaw (their special evaluative metaconcept) present across the communication contexts. As well, our communication microtheories often concern single or simple combinations of communication constructs that describe an attribute of a communicator. A good example is Communication Apprehension (anxiety) that occurs in all contexts. Other microtheories highlight intrinsic tensions in communication, called the communication dynamic. Relational Control Theory and Marital Communication Theory are good examples. Then, too, a microtheory may highlight aspects of a medium in detail. McLuhan's Media Law Theory is representative.

Special Communication Theories   Bormann (1980) indicated that *special communication theories* are "how-to-do-it" theories that advise the communication practitioner about preparing certain types and forms of communication in the agreed-on style of the day. You were first introduced to these special theories in your undergraduate communication courses like public speaking, newswriting, public relations, video editing, and political communication. You learned such things as how to conduct a job interview (Stewart & Cash, 1988), run a political rally (Shields & Cragan, 1981), use news teasers and bumpers to improve the processing and memory of TV news and commercials (Cameron, Schleuder, & Thorson, 1991; Schleuder, White, & Cameron, 1993), shoot a coherent film sequence (Kraft, Canto, & Gottdiener, 1991), put together an issues management program for an organization (Ewing, 1979), or organize a persuasive speech following the five steps in Alan Monroe's (1962) motivated sequence pattern.[8]   *(creating lesson plans)*

   In addition, you may have taken an applied communication course or a seminar in legal communication or health communication. In such courses, you learned such special theories as how to present opening and closing arguments to juries or how to conduct diagnostic interviews with patients. Literally scores of special communication theories exist. New ones arise all the time. For example, Babrow (1992) and colleagues (Ford, Babrow, & Stohl, 1996) recently offered an applied health communication theory, called Problematic Integration Theory, to explain the role of comforting and supportive communication in the treatment of illnesses. We do not have the space in this book to present and explain even a representative sample of the special theories relevant to all the communication context courses. Nonetheless, we would stress that the special theories are useful theories. You should know and frequently use them if you plan to work or train as a communication practitioner.

Symbiotic (Interdisciplinary) Theories   *Symbiotic theories* flow from allied disciplines like linguistics, English, economics, management, political science, psychology, social psychology, and sociology. They often exist in a close relationship with theories from the communication discipline. This relationship exists on a continuum ranging from common ontological assumptions to cooperative interdisciplinary research on the same theory. For philosophical reasons (a psychology professor receives more training in cognitive dissonance than a communication professor) and lack of space (page limitations set by the publisher), we do not present such symbiotic theories as Classical Learning Theory from psychology, Social Judgment Theory from psychology, Social Penetration Theory from social psychology, Symbolic Interactionism Theory from sociology, Generative Grammar Theory from linguistics, or Exchange Theory from economics. Instead, we focus on the theories that grow on the communication tree of knowledge (see **Figure 1-1**).

   Of course, a working knowledge of the symbiotic theories comes from taking cognate courses and minors in the allied disciplines. Although we briefly mention a number of symbiotic theories in Chapters 8, 9, and 10, we would refer you to books and classes in their discipline of origin for a more complete analysis than you will get from this book.

here—a particular theory of reality.

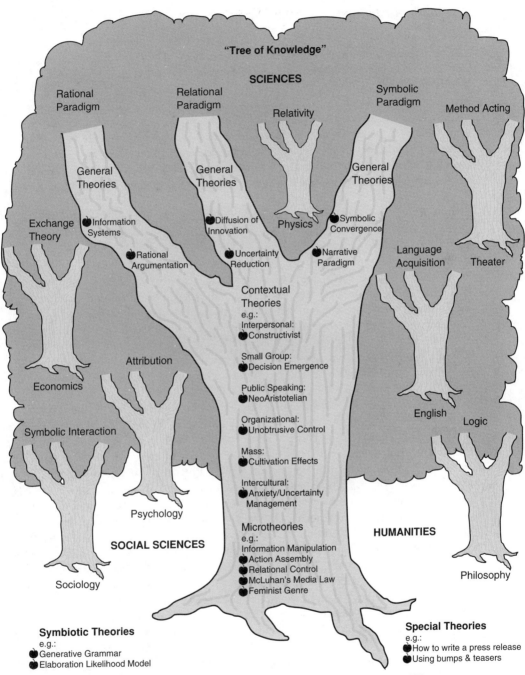

The figure depicts the "Tree of Knowledge" with labels including:

SCIENCES

Rational Paradigm · Relational Paradigm · Relativity · Symbolic Paradigm · Method Acting

General Theories · General Theories · General Theories

Exchange Theory · Information Systems · Diffusion of Innovation · Physics · Symbolic Convergence · Language Acquisition · Theater

Rational Argumentation · Uncertainty Reduction · Narrative Paradigm

Contextual Theories
e.g.:
Interpersonal:
● Constructivist

Small Group:
● Decision Emergence

Public Speaking:
● NeoAristotelian

Organizational:
● Unobtrusive Control

Mass:
● Cultivation Effects

Intercultural:
● Anxiety/Uncertainty Management

Economics · Attribution · English · Logic

Symbolic Interaction

Microtheories
e.g.:
Information Manipulation
● Action Assembly
● Relational Control
● McLuhan's Media Law
● Feminist Genre

HUMANITIES

Psychology · Philosophy

SOCIAL SCIENCES

Sociology

Symbiotic Theories
e.g.:
● Generative Grammar
● Elaboration Likelihood Model

Special Theories
e.g.:
● How to write a press release
● Using bumps & teasers

"The Communication Metatheory allows you to see our discipline's Theory 'Tree of Theory Knowledge' and the Academic Forest."

FIGURE 1-1. Theories Growing on the Communication Theory Tree of Knowledge

posit
1.-put into position,
place
2 - lay down or
  assume as
  a fact/basis
  of argument
  (postulate)

Anatomical Elements

✱ basis on which chapters 2-7 are organized.

The Communication Metatheory (TCM) enables you to explain communication theories. It also posits the anatomical metatheoretical concepts that will help you understand communication theories. These anatomical metaconcepts enable you to anatomize or dissect a theory. They depict a communication theory's: origin, roots, and assumptions; communicative force and paradigm; theoretical technical concepts; way of modeling and relating concepts; and theory–method complex. These metatheoretical concepts provide a complete anatomy of any communication theory. We use these metatheoretical concepts consistently throughout the book. In fact, the next six chapters use the metatheoretical concepts to present general communication theories in detail. We also use these metatheoretical concepts to describe the contextual and microtheories presented in subsequent chapters, although in a less rigorous way.

Origin, Roots, and Assumptions

By *origin,* we mean the source of a theory, that is, its place(s) of creation and its creator(s). *Roots* are a theory's antecedents, ancestors, and bases of support. *Assumptions* are what theories accept as true without proof. Mapping the genealogy of a theory is aesthetically pleasing in and of itself, if you have been in the business of theorizing as long as we have. However, the activity provides more than pleasure. We report on the origin and roots of the general theories in detail and reference the origin of the other theories presented in this book. In this way, you can see who developed a particular communication theory and how. For example, among the theories we discuss, several are "kissing cousins" of Claude Shannon's (1948a, 1948b) Mathematical Theory of Communication. These include Information Systems Theory, Uncertainty Reduction Theory, Diffusion of Innovations Theory, Weick's Organizing Theory, and Anxiety/Uncertainty Management Theory.

Every communication theory possesses, either directly or indirectly, three types of assumptions: ontological, epistemological, and axiological. *Ontological* assumptions concern the nature of humankind. Are humans good at heart or base? Are humans logical or emotional? Are humans active or passive? The answers to these questions affect the makeup of a given theoretical explanation. *Epistemological* assumptions concern how we know what we know. Such assumptions concern the nature of or grounds for knowledge. Do we get knowledge from invention or discovery? Does knowledge come from direct experience or can it come vicariously? Do we ground theories intuitively, empirically, or experimentally? The answer to these questions is all of the above when you consider the communication discipline as a whole. Nonetheless, theorists and theories differ regarding what constitutes the grounds for knowledge claims. *Axiological* assumptions concern the values implied by or implicit in theories. Does a theory assume the goodness or the evil of progress or technology? Does a theory reinforce a sexist, racist, or corrupt power structure? Again, the answers to these questions affect the makeup of a given theoretical explanation.

We carefully identify and discuss the assumptive systems of the core general theories. As well, we often highlight the assumptive systems of the communication contextual and microtheories. However, there is not space to describe the assumptive system of every theory presented in this book. Nonetheless, we ask you to remember that communication theories possess epistemological, axiological, and ontological assumptions. Please accept them as if they were true while learning and using the theory.

Communicative Force and Paradigm   We call the fundamental human interactions—such as information-sharing, argument-making, fantasy-chaining, social information-sharing, storytelling, and diffusing innovation talk—communicative forces. *Communicative forces* account for human action. When a journalist alleges, "the pen is mightier than the sword," he or she is claiming that the force of communicative interaction on the affairs of humans is greater than the force of military interaction. The metaconcept of force or interaction is the ordinary beginning place for theorizing in all disciplines. For example, physicists identify four fundamental forces or interactions that occur in the universe that account for all of the motion between bodies: electromagnetic, gravitational, and strong and weak nuclear forces. Communication theorists do not study the physical interactions or forces that affect the motion of bodies. Rather, we study the communicative interactions or forces that affect human action, which prompts the question, how many communicative forces are there?

Types of Forces.   Scholars have developed and grounded general communication theories to explain the interaction effects of at least six communicative forces on human action. At this time, it would be speculation to guess at how many more could potentially be discovered (**see Table 1-3**). These forces and the theories that explain them are the subjects of the next six chapters of this book.

Again, it's time for another rest stop. Here, we stress that the name of a given general communication theory's basic concept and the name of the communicative force that accounts for the human action reflect one another. For example, Information Systems Theory's basic concept is information and the force that accounts for human action is information-sharing. We know that if we were to find a new communicative force then we would need a new communication theory to explain it. As well, we know that if a single communication theory could explain all of the communicative forces then it would be a *universal theory* as opposed to a general theory that explains only one communicative force. Intriguingly, we already possess general communication theories that explain human action by drawing together a single explanation that accounts for two communicative forces. These are Symbolic Convergence Theory and Narrative Paradigm Theory. We'll visit them on the trail to understanding communication theories in Chapters 4 and 6, respectively.

TABLE 1-3.   Communicative Forces for Human Action

Force	Interaction Effect
1. Information-sharing	Gives order and structure to human organizing when optimized
2. Argument-making	Conveys conviction of rational decision-making
3. Fantasy-chaining	Creates symbolic realities with meaning, emotion, and motive for action
4. Social information-sharing	Ignites, maintains, and sometimes destroys personal relationships
5. Innovation-diffusing talk	Enables adoption of social change
6. Storytelling	Bestows the value justification for human action

Nonetheless, communication researchers, like physicists, continue to search for a universal theory to tie together all of the forces that account for human action in a single, comprehensive explanation. In the future, you may well contribute to the building of such a theory.

Let's rest a few more moments and read some trail signs. Sometimes, both scholars and students confuse the issue of not having a universal theory by concluding that we do not have good general theories (Berger, 1991; 1992). We cannot stress too much that a universal theory differs from general theories. The quest for a universal theory to explain all of communication is noble. However, at this point, we must emphasize that it is our general communication theories, our contextual communication theories, and our communication microtheories that interest us. Together they provide the core theories necessary to explain the breadth of communication phenomena.

Paradigm is a much used and much maligned word. As a metacommunication term it sometimes means the defining example or case (Bormann, Cragan, & Shields, 1996). At other times, mirroring Kuhn (1970), it means the way in which a scientific collectivity thinks about and conducts their research. For example, consider the statement, "Following the logical-positivist exemplar of scientific explanation, we rejected the Null hypothesis." The statement reflects the way in which some members of the scientific community think about and practice research. Elsewhere, we used the word *paradigm* to mean a clustering of communication theories, like constellations in the sky (Cragan & Shields, 1995). For us, each star cluster represented a group of like-theories. The criterion that led to the clusters involved the idea that theories emphasize one of three different ontological presuppositions and one of three different types of social science facts.[9] For fun, like shepherds lying in the fields at night, we named the sets of like-theories using three metaconcepts: rational paradigm (think of it as Libra), relational paradigm (think of it as Scorpio), and symbolic paradigm (think of it as Sagittarius). In this book, we continue to distinguish communication theories by the paradigm that gives them shape.

Types of Paradigms.   Theories cluster into paradigms based on the predominant kind of social scientific fact (material, social, or symbolic) they seek to explain. Material facts are things you can know through your five senses, for example, tables, speeches, and smiles. Social facts are entities created through societal interaction, for example, couples, roles, and organizations. Symbolic facts are the creations of our verbal expressions, for example, ideologies, worldviews, and corporate visions. Theories also cluster into paradigms based on the different ontological presuppositions to which they adhere (Cragan & Shields, 1995). Typically, these ontological presuppositions include allegiance to one of the following viewpoints regarding the establishment of meaning:

1. Humans join in meaning through rational–logical thinking as they communicate in a medium over time;
2. Humans create social structures as they communicate in a medium over time and derive meaning from the roles they play within those social structures; or
3. Humans create reality symbolically as they communicate in a medium over time and derive meaning from those symbolic creations.

Adherence to the first ontological presupposition casts subsequent theory-building within the rational paradigm. Adherence to the second places the resultant theory-building in the *representations of* =

relational paradigm. Likewise, adherence to the third situates the ensuing theory-building in the symbolic paradigm.

Rational Paradigm.   Communication theories within the rational paradigm exhibit an ontological presupposition that humans join in meaning through reasoning or rational–logical thinking as they communicate in a medium over time. Also, the basic concepts of rational communication theories predominantly name material facts. In other words, the substance of their concepts comes from naming material objects. For example, Information Systems Theory is a rational paradigm theory. It assumes that information exchange occurs rationally, as in the statement, "people strive for clarity of expression." Also, Information Systems Theory views *information* as a material fact. You can demonstrate its existence through the senses. You can see information in the form of such material objects as a letter, report, or term paper. As well, the theorists using Information Systems Theory ontologically view the communication process as rational. *(creative (emotional, intuitive ?)*

Relational Paradigm.   Communication theories within the relational paradigm exhibit the ontological presupposition that humans use communication to create social structures. Such theories presuppose that people then play the roles manifest in those social structures. Thus, organizational communication theorists talk about superiors and subordinates acting in certain ways. Small group communication theorists talk about leaders and followers fulfilling certain communicative functions. Likewise, interpersonal communication theorists talk about friends and lovers exhibiting certain communicative behaviors. In addition, relational theories hold in common basic concepts that relate to social facts. Thus, Bormann's (1990) Role Emergence Theory exhibits a basic concept that is a social fact called *group role.* Thus, Role Emergence Theory is said to exist within the relational paradigm. Once you use social science procedures to identify and capture a social fact, it then becomes available for consideration by the senses. For example, it's now easy to see that the United States has a president, a congress, and a supreme court because we've accepted the social science procedures that enable us to identify such societally created entities.

allow for context of past/future

Symbolic Paradigm.   Communication theories arrayed in the symbolic paradigm presuppose that humans create reality symbolically through their communicative interaction. The basic concepts of symbolic paradigm theories name and explain symbolic facts. For example, Fisher's Narrative Paradigm Theory's basic concept, *narration,* is a value-laden story that only exists in language. Likewise, Bormann's Symbolic Convergence Theory's basic concept, *fantasy theme,* conveys reality symbolically through an artistic, imaginative, human expression such as "Remember the Alamo!" As well, the theorists using such theories ontologically view the communication process as symbolic. For example, Burke (1966), in proposing his Dramatism Theory (presented in Chapter 9), assumes that humans are symbol-using animals. Symbolic facts are the newest objects of interest in the communication discipline. Often, intricate procedures are required to identify symbolic facts. However, once identified, and once you get used to them, they too become ordinary, just like social concepts such as group role or cultural malaise appear ordinary. **Table 1-4** summarizes how communication theories differentiate by paradigm type. This is a good time to take a rest and review it.

see also: pg 105

Theoretical Technical Concepts   Here, we arrive at a new landmark that points to TCM's ability to dissect the theoretical concepts of theories. We need TCM because every communication theory possesses a set of discrete technical terms. Technical terms relate one to

See Assignment # 1 (View pg. 322 for more info.)

TABLE 1-4.   How Communication Theories Differentiate by Paradigm Type

	Rational Paradigm	Relational Paradigm	Symbolic Paradigm
Type of Reality Accepted:	Material reality	Material reality and social reality	Material reality, social reality, and symbolic reality
Ontological Presupposition:	Humans join in meaning about the material world through rational–logical thinking as they communicate	Humans create social structures and derive meaning from the roles they play within those social structures	Humans create reality symbolically and derive meaning from those symbolic creations
Primary Type of Fact Observed:	Material facts	Social facts	Symbolic facts
How Facts are Observed:	Directly by the senses by defining the material facts	Indirectly through operational definitions of social facts	Indirectly through operational definitions of symbolic facts
Types of Facts Considered:	Material facts	Social facts and material facts	Symbolic facts, social facts, and material facts
Types of Theoretical Concepts Considered:	Basic concepts, structural concepts, and evaluative concepts	Basic concepts, structural concepts, and evaluative concepts	Basic concepts, structural concepts, and evaluative concepts

another. Typical general communication theories exhibit from ten to thirty technical concepts. TCM helps us distinguish among them. Some technical concepts do one thing, others do something else, and still others do another thing. TCM initially represents a theory's concepts as either basic, structural, or evaluative. It also allows fine gradations to be made regarding basic and structural concepts. Each theoretical concept possesses a unique technical definition, as opposed to an ordinary language definition. Just what are technical concepts?

Technical concepts are the formal terms for like-things that cluster into a new category of things. For example, Scottish Collie, German Shepherd, and Irish wolfhound, despite the isolation of their geographic origin, cluster into a theoretical concept in biology called *canine.* Technical concepts serve as the building blocks of theories. In a theory, each concept is discrete. As well, each concept exhibits a specific technical, as opposed to a pedestrian or everyday, definition. Following Cragan and Shields (1992, 1995) and Shields and Preston (1985), TCM classifies the technical concepts of communication theories using three metaconcepts: basic concepts, structural concepts, and evaluative concepts.

Basic Concepts.   A theory's basic concept denotes the unit of analysis that you must learn to observe when using a particular communication theory. Following Pearce, Cronen, and Harris (1982), we define the unit of analysis (basic concept) of any theory as the foundation datum that can account for human action from the perspective of the given theory. The basic concept is the primary kind of communication "stuff" that you must learn to identify to locate that foundation datum. Depending on the communication theory, the basic "stuff" goes by such names as information, argument, fantasy theme, self-disclosure, story, persuasive appeal, and so forth. Also, a general communication theory's *basic concept* names the communicative force that accounts for human action. All general communication theories name such a force. Many other communication theories do, too.

Associative basic concepts are the subparts of a theory's basic concept. An atom contains subatomic particles (neutrons, electrons, and protons). Likewise, a given communication theory's basic concept contains subparts or subclasses of the basic concept called *associative basic concepts.* For example, if a geologist offers a theory that rocks form through the force of pressure, fire, and water then she or he must identify the theory's basic and associative basic concepts. In this case, rocks (the basic concept) and metamorphic, igneous, and sedimentary rocks (the associative basic concepts) comprise the list of basic and associative basic concepts. Metamorphic, igneous, and sedimentary are subclasses of the basic concept, rocks. Communication theories also possess basic and associative basic concepts. For example, in Chapter 7, we shall see that Diffusion of Innovation Theory's basic concept, *diffusing innovation talk,* includes subclasses such as *awareness talk* and *advocacy talk.* They illustrate the metaconcept of associative basic concepts.

Structural Concepts.   The *structural concepts* of communication theories provide the blueprint or design for the form or superstructure of the observed communication. They bring the specific aspects of Level 1 communication into focus. Structural concepts help frame the basic and associative basic concepts (Cragan & Shields, 1995). There are four types of structural concepts. The first type describes the *message structure* of the communication. The second type details the theory's *communication dynamic structure.* The third type depicts the theory's *communicator structure,* that is, the special names for and attributes of the communicators identified by the theory. The fourth type indicates the nature of the *medium structure* within which the communication functions, propagates, and travels.

Message structure concepts dress up and flesh out a theory's basic and associative concepts. They allow you to give form to talk. For example, *Emplotment* is a message structure concept of Narrative Paradigm Theory (presented in Chapter 6). *Act, scene, agent, agency, purpose,* and *attitude* are the structural concepts of Burke's Dramatism Theory (presented in Chapter 9). *Arguments* go together to form a *case,* two of the message structure concepts of Rational Argumentation Theory (presented in Chapter 3). *Fantasy themes* go together to form a *rhetorical vision,* two of the message structure concepts of Symbolic Convergence Theory (presented in Chapter 4). *Social information* is subclassified into *memory organization packets,* a message structure concept of Uncertainty Reduction Theory (presented in Chapter 5).

Communication dynamic structure concepts refer to a deep structure tension or war that is present in any theory. The war concerns the message's underlying form, mold, or cast. For example, with Symbolic Convergence Theory the war occurs between righteous, social, and pragmatic fantasy themes. We overheard three students, engaged in actual Level 1 communication. They were discussing their Fall schedules. Student 1 said, "I picked classes that would help me understand the feelings of others." Student 2 said, "I picked classes that would help me get a job in public relations." Student 3 said, "I scheduled classes to learn from the top published scholars in the department." Let's take a rest stop and theorize at Level 2 about this communication. By using Symbolic Convergence Theory (SCT), we can classify these statements based on SCT's dynamic structure. We would conclude that the statements show, respectively, a social or humane approach to taking classes (understand others' feelings), a pragmatic or expedient approach to taking classes (prepare to get a job), and a righteous or correct approach to taking classes (to learn the most one can learn). We gain such theoretical insights into the students' statements by applying SCT's communication dynamic concepts, the warring righteous, social, and pragmatic master analogues. Having used SCT's concepts to examine the statements at Level 2, we can now metatheorize about SCT and compare it to other communication theories at Level 3. By looking at the regularities displayed by a number of communication theories, we conclude that SCT's warring master analogues are but one example of a feature displayed by all communication theories. At the metatheory level, this common feature is called *communication dynamic.* Of course, each theory will present concepts with their own names and technical definition that indicate the war undergirding their communication dynamic, just as SCT sees the war in competing *righteous, social,* and *pragmatic master analogues.*

Communicator structure concepts identify and characterize the communicators who communicate over time in a medium. For the most part, each communication theory uniquely names the communicators and ascribes certain attributes to them. The originators of Symbolic Convergence Theory named the communicators *fantasizers.* Their attributes include the *propensity to fantasize.* The originators of Uncertainty Reduction Theory gave several names to the communicators. These include *cointeractants, strategic communicators,* and *targets.* Their attributes include *self-monitoring* and *degree of shyness.* With Rational Argumentation Theory the communicators are *arguers, audience,* and *critic,* and the attributes include *degree of argumentativeness.* With Information Systems Theory the communicators are *senders, receivers,* and *observers.* Finally, with Narrative Paradigm Theory the communicators are *storytellers* and *audience.*

Medium structure concepts specify the nature of the substance within which communication functions, propagates, and travels. These metaconcepts (functions, propagates, and travels) represent the three senses of medium. $Medium_1$ is the sense of the general communication theory *functioning* (working) within the six traditional contexts of interpersonal, small group, public speaking, organizational, mass, and intercultural communication. One of the important characteristics of a general communication theory is its ability to function (work) by explaining the human action that results from communicators communicating in all six communication contexts. $Medium_2$ is the sense of a substance in which communication propagates, prospers, and grows. Here, medium is just like the nutrient medium (yeast) in which a pharmaceutical biologist grows penicillin or the cultivated soil in which a midwestern farmer grows corn and beans. For example, Diffusion of Innovation Theory explains that innovations spread through diffusion talk. However, an innovation diffuses (propagates) quite differently given authoritative, collectivist, or individualist communities. The words *authoritative, collectivist,* and *individualist* identify the different substances that may nourish the diffusion of innovation process. $Medium_3$ pertains to the channel through which the communication flows or travels, such as sound, light, or electrical waves; or books, films, and television; or face-to-face, e-mail, or mail-mail. For example, Diffusion of Innovation Theory notes that interpersonal and mass media communication channels together provide the critical mass necessary for the diffusion of an innovation.

Evaluative Concepts.　Physicists study the interaction of forces in nature (gravity, strong and weak nuclear, and electromagnetic) on the movement of bodies (e.g., planets and tides). Chemists study the effects of various chemical interactions. Cell biologists study the quality and effects of cell development and division on living things. All scientists are concerned with how their theories allow them to explain the *quality* and *effects* of interaction. The same is true of communication scientists who work with communication theories. They develop communication theories to explain the interaction effects of communicative forces on human action.

The *evaluative concepts* of communication theories allow you to make assessments or judgments about the quality and outcomes (interaction effect) of communicators communicating in a medium. By outcomes we mean that the communicative interaction identified by the theory did in fact occur, that is, did the communicative force under study have its predicted impact on human action. Quality refers to a theory's evaluative concepts that denote the degree or grade of excellence of the communication. All general communication theories possess evaluative concepts. Many contextual and microtheories do, too. With Narrative Paradigm Theory, you would determine the *narrative probability* and *narrative fidelity* of the stories you hear. Do the stories hang together (narrative probability)? Do they ring true (narrative fidelity)? With both Information Systems Theory and Uncertainty Reduction Theory, your task is to assess the degree to which *uncertainty reduction* (an evaluative concept) occurs. With Diffusion of Innovation Theory, you would evaluate to see if there was *adoption,* if it occurred at a faster *rate* than anticipated, and if the consequences of the adoption were good or bad. We'll see other examples of evaluative concepts as we explore each theory.

Modeling Theories and Relating Concepts　Hawes (1975) stressed that a theoretical model *re*-represents a theory or part of a theory. As theorists *re*-represent a theory, they do so by using two- and three-dimensional graphic displays. In the next chapter, we present the discipline's first *models* of the communication process. They detail Shannon's (1948a) depictions of a message encoded from a source, down a noisy electronic channel, to a receiver. Of course, a correction (feedback) device assists the whole process.

It's time for a brief rest stop to point out a detail of his particular landmark. Models hold some characteristics in common with the definition of communication. You cannot model communication without a theory in mind, just as you cannot define communication without a theory. We assure you that all models *re*-represent a communication theory (Level 2 theorizing). As such, they enable the theorizer to focus on actual communication and to depict it from the viewpoint of the theory. In other words, the model (Level 2 communication) *re*-represents communicators communicating over time in a medium (Level 1 communication). If you like, this might be a good time to extend your stop. During it, you can draw your concept of the communication process. We suggest you keep it in the same place you earlier wrote your definition of communication. Then, on completion of the book, we suggest you return and identify the communication theory on which you based your model. If at that time, you can, we will again take it as a sign that you successfully completed the trail to understanding communication theories.

In this book, we offer our unique Level 3 metamodel to depict Level 2 theories. The metamodel presents the theoretical technical concepts of communication theories. It does not *re*-represent the elements of communication. Our metamodel names and classifies the common technical concepts of communication theories. It does so by using six interrelated metaconcepts. We let you visualize each metaconcept within its own VENN-type circle. **Figure 1-2** illustrates TCM's six metaconcepts: basic, message structure, communication dynamic structure, communicator structure, medium structure, and evaluative. We will use this metamodel to display the unique technical concepts of each of the general communication theories presented in Chapters 2–7. In other words, we will use the metamodel to display a given theory's basic concepts, its four types of structural concepts, and finally its evaluative concepts.

Please read the metamodel from the smallest VENN circle (basic concepts) to the largest (evaluative concepts). By following our demonstrations of the metamodel in Chapters 2–7, we would invite you to use it to display the technical concepts of the other communication theories presented in Chapters 8–11 of this book. Of course, in the area outside of the VENN-type circles, the metamodel also reminds you to consider a theory's other anatomical elements: origin, roots, and assumptions; communicative force and paradigm; model and relationship statements; and theory–method complex.

Every communication theory characterizes the relationship among its concepts. At the metatheory level, *relationship statement* is a metaconcept that alerts you to look for a theory's implied or explicit statements of the nature of the relationships among its concepts. Shields (1981) observed that "*relationship statements* tell how the concepts of a theory tie together and provide the link as to how the theory can go beyond description and provide a why explanation of human events and action" (p. 7). We previously indicated that the three most common forms of theoretical relationship statements are "and," "if . . . then," and "either . . . or." You will discover that the concepts presented for each theory rely on them regularly. Theoretical relationship statements also provide a description of a theory's prediction of human action stemming from communicators communicating over time in a medium. Of course, if the predicted relationship holds then you have the tools at hand to control your future.

It's time to stop and view the sights at another scenic lookout. Here, we want to highlight two characteristics of relationship statements. The first characteristic is that they vary in form. Just as some science fiction humans "morph" to become Power Rangers, relationship statements morph into different forms for expressing the relationship among theoretical concepts. The different forms for expressing relationship statements are: mathematical, axiomatic, and ordinary language. The second characteristic is that relationship statements express the nature of the regularity of interaction between theoretical concepts using descriptors like *law, rule,* or *principle.*

Form for Expressing Relationship Statements.   Isaac Newton published his *The Mathematical Principles of Natural Philosophy* in 1687. In it he expressed his three laws of motion, the universal law of gravitation, and a few other laws in rigorous, logical, axiomatic style. His axiomatic style followed in the tradition of the ancient Greek mathematician, Euclid, the inventor of geometry.[10] The impact of Newton's work on modern theorizing cannot be overstated. The idea that a few covering laws of motion let Newton explain and

The Anatomical Parts of a Communication Theory: The Types of Theoretical Concepts

Key:
Bold Caps = Names for the Various Kinds of Theoretical Concepts

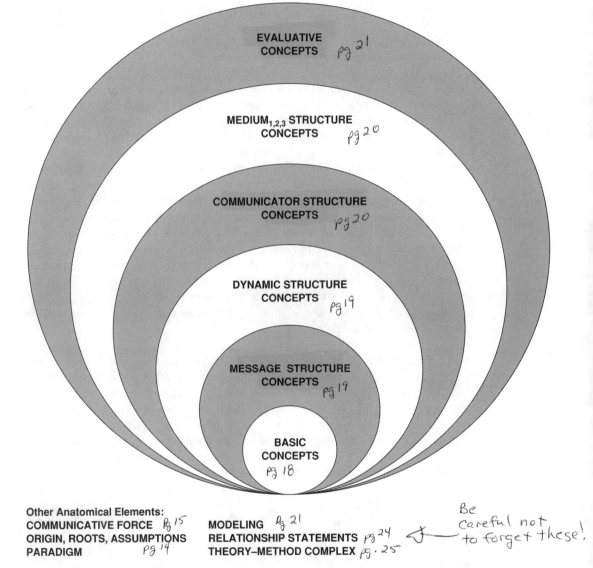

Other Anatomical Elements:
COMMUNICATIVE FORCE *Pg 15*
ORIGIN, ROOTS, ASSUMPTIONS
PARADIGM *Pg 14*
MODELING *Pg 21*
RELATIONSHIP STATEMENTS *Pg 24*
THEORY–METHOD COMPLEX *Pg. 25*

Be careful not to forget these!

ONE FUNCTION OF A COMMUNICATION METATHEORY: To let you compare theories. This part of TCM reminds you to view a theory's basic, structural, and evaluative concepts and its other anatomical parts. TCM's quite a toolbox!

FIGURE 1-2.

predict all the motion among objects in the universe captivated the imagination of philosophers and scholars in all disciplines. You are quite familiar with Newton's Law of Gravitation as expressed in ordinary language:

> *Every material particle in the universe attracts every other material particle with a force that is proportional to the product of the masses of the two particles and inversely proportional to the square of the distance between their centers; the force is directed along a line joining their centers.*

The mathematical formula expressing this relationship statement is: $F = m_1 m_2 G/d^2$, where if m_1 and m_2 are any two point masses, separated by a distance d, and G is the gravitational constant, then F is the gravitational force of attraction (Isaacs, 1990). Undoubtedly, the most well-known mathematical expression of a relationship statement is Albert Einstein's $E = mc^2$, where mass is said to equal energy by substituting the number 1 as the constant, c.[11]

A number of communication theorists, following Newton and Euclid, developed their communication theories in the axiomatic form or style. They did so by presenting axioms, postulates, and theorems. As we shall see in Chapter 5, Uncertainty Reduction Theory provides an exemplar treatment of the axiomatic statement of theoretical relationships.[12]

Of course, you can recast all ordinary language theoretical relationship statements either mathematically or axiomatically. However, we are trying to teach communication theories as efficiently and painlessly as possible. Those of you who are not initiated into formal logic or mathematics might find the trail too difficult and troublesome no matter what the benefits envisioned on arrival at the destination. Consequently, we will translate all mathematical and axiomatic statements into ordinary language so that you can stay focused on understanding the communication theories.

whew! :)

Nature of Relationship Regularity.   Recall that theoretical relationship statements express the nature of the regularity between theoretical concepts. They do so by using adjectives like *law, rule,* or *principle.* For example, acting as philosophers of communication science, Berger (1977) and Chaffee and Berger (1987) stressed the need to search for determinant regularities among communication concepts. Discovering such regularities would mean the identification of communication laws. Other philosophers of communication science, such as Cushman (1977), stressed the need to search for the rules that guide us toward goal attainment and regulate human action. Discovering such rules would acknowledge our nature as purposeful, choice-making animals. Still other philosophers of communication science, such as Farrell (1987), would view human communication as a highly creative, often idiosyncratic, even fleeting and ephemeral phenomenon. However, at the practical level we suspect even Farrell would admit to the necessity of the search for principle-based recipes for training in the communication skills that lead to artistic communication.

At times, scholars assume that adherence to a particular philosophy of communication science makes it possible to characterize other scholars as scientists looking for laws, social scientists looking for rules, or humanists looking for principles. It is also true that people looking for laws often view themselves as scientists. As well, people looking for rules often view themselves as social scientists. Similarly, people looking for principles often view themselves as humanists. Such distinctions are well and good. However, they become

Avoid these classifications

problematic when used to characterize theorists and theories. Bormann (1980), Cragan and Shields (1995), and Shields and Cragan (1975) have cautioned against using such distinctions to classify communication theorists and communication theories.[13]

We view the regularity between a theory's concepts as best exemplified by a continuum with laws at one end, rules in the middle, and principles at the other end. This view contrasts markedly with those philosophers of communication science who would depict laws, rules, and principles as discrete metaconcepts that serve as major discriminating attributes of theories and theorists.[14]

Rocks, eroded from a cliff by wind and water, lack choice about whether or not to conform to the law of gravity. However, humans choose whether or not to conform to the probability-based laws, rules, and principles that govern communicators communicating in a medium. The amount of free choice granted humans does far more than any preassigned label to determine whether or not a theory's relationship statements indicate an underlying probability-based law, rule, or principle.[15]

Theory–Method Complex   A theory is mere armchair speculation until researchers ground its concepts to observable phenomena. As a consequence, theories possess an attendant method. Poole, Seibold, and McPhee (1985) labeled this attendant method the *theory–method complex*. Poole (1990) defined the complex as "an interdependent whole in which methods shape theory and vice versa" (p. 238). He noted that, for any theory, the complex exhibits "a characteristic mode of explanation used by the theory, a characteristic mode of inquiry or research strategy, and typical methodological techniques" (p. 238). As we present the six general theories in Chapters 2–7, we will focus on the initial links between theory and method. Such initial links involve a series of qualitative procedures unique to each theory. Such qualitative procedures help you identify how the basic concept of a given theory is manifest in communicative interaction.[16] We will present each qualitative method as we introduce the respective general communication theories. Space limitations preclude our introduction of the qualitative procedures for each of the contextual communication theories and communication microtheories presented in Chapters 8–11. Nonetheless, as Poole, Seibold, and McPhee (1985) observed, all communication theories link to a unique method that forms a theory–method complex. By understanding that complex, you can then use the theory as a communication scholar or practitioner.

We have just passed by TCM's anatomical elements. They enable you to depict a theory's origin, roots, and assumptions; communicative force and paradigm; theoretical technical concepts; modeling and relating concepts; and theory–method complex. The anatomical elements also help you identify the unit of communication analysis and the structure of a given communication theory. As well, they help you understand that communication theories differ, not in their anatomical elements, but only in the technical concepts they use to explain communication phenomena. Another way of saying this is that all theories look alike at the metatheoretical level (Level 3), but differ at the theoretical level (Level 2).

Summary.

Evaluative Elements

At this point on the trail to understanding communication theories, we are nearing another set of metatheoretical concepts. Although the exact number of evaluative metatheoretical concepts is arbitrary, we selected those that scholars indicate should provide you with the tools necessary to assess the impact of a communication theory. Their use will help you answer Great Uncle Fred's question, "Will this dog hunt?" Our evaluative metaconcepts encompass a theory's power and scope, heuristic and isomorphic, parsimony and elegance, validity and utility, and ability to withstand the critics.

Power and Scope   *Power* evaluates a theory's ability to magnify phenomena. *Scope* deals with the breadth of communication phenomena explained by a theory. These two evaluative metaconcepts help in determining if a communication theory is a general theory, a contextual theory, or a microtheory. A communication theory is a general theory when its power provides a why explanation of communicators communicating in a medium and its scope allows it to do so across the six classical contexts. Bormann (1990) noted that he had developed a general communication theory called Symbolic Convergence Theory and a contextual communication theory called Role Emergence Theory. Symbolic Convergence Theory is both more powerful and broader in scope than Role Emergence Theory. Its power allows it to explain a great deal of communication. Its scope extends across a number of contexts including the six traditional ones. Thus, Symbolic Convergence Theory allows you to generalize its explanation of the communicative force of fantasy across the domain of human communication phenomena. Conversely, Role Emergence Theory is bound to the small group context. Its scope is limited. Even within that context, you can only use it to generalize about role emergence in problem-solving groups. Thus, its power is further limited. In Chapter 11, we introduce a communication microtheory that centers on a single construct, *communication apprehension*. The theory exhibits limited power because it concerns only one communicator attribute. However, it is broader in scope than a contextual theory, and as broad in scope as a general theory, because it generalizes that attribute to all communication situations and contexts.

Heuristic and Isomorphic Theories   A theory is *heuristic* if it suggests new directions for research, raises interesting questions that stimulate further inquiry, or leads to the creation of spin-off theories. By definition, general communication theories are heuristic. For example, each has spawned repeated attempts to ground the theory in different communication contexts. Additionally, some general theories are more heuristic than others because they have generated investigations that led to the development of spin-off theories. In communication, Uncertainty Reduction Theory and Anxiety/Uncertainty Management Theory represent first and second generation spin-offs of Information Systems Theory. *Isomorphic* refers to the ability to map the structures of theories from one discipline to another or from one context within a discipline to another context. General Systems Theory, developed in biology in the 1920s in reaction to the closed systems of physical mechanics, is clearly one of the most isomorphic (similar in form) theories in the academy. Every discipline claims an indigenous systems-like theory. Such theories resemble Von Bertalanffy's (1968) biological, open systems theory. Information Systems Theory (see Chapter 2) is isomorphic in its elaboration to General Systems Theory. As well, it is our discipline's most heuristic theory in terms of its adoption by other disciplines.

Elegance and Parsimony   A theory exhibits *parsimony* if it is stated economically in simple mathematical or ordinary language form. As a rule, axiomatic theories lack the quality of parsimony. A theory exhibits *elegance* when its explanation provides a rich expression, pleases aesthetically, appears as opulent, looks refined, or seems tasteful. Ideally, a theory would be simply stated (parsimonious) and provide an aesthetically pleasing (elegant) explanation of communicators communicating in a medium. However, the ideal is not easy to attain. For example, Diffusion of Innovation Theory (Chapter 7) misses on the elegance standard by labeling the last people to adopt an idea as "laggards," a highly value-laden theoretical concept. Additionally, Anxiety/Uncertainty Management Theory (Chapter 10) falls far short on the parsimony standard given its ninety-four axioms.

pg 20

interpersonal
small group
public speaking
organizational
mass
intercultural

Validity and Utility   The concepts in a communication theory need to be tied to observables through grounding research. The *validity* of a theory concerns the degree to which it is supported by observables, logically derived, internally sound, efficacious, and falsifiable. A *supportable* general communication theory exhibits research that grounds its concepts to the observables of communicators communicating in the six medium$_1$ contexts. Usually, such grounding requires a systematic program of research and years of effort. The general communication theories presented in Chapters 2–7 boast numerous grounding studies. A theory is *logically derived* when it is internally consistent and logical relationships exist among its concepts. In Chapter 5, we discuss the logical consistency of Uncertainty Reduction Theory's Axioms 3 and 7 and Theorem 17. A com-

dfn → munication theory is *efficacious* if it predicts future human actions or explains past actions in a postdictive fashion. The efficacy of a theory allows you to control your future by predicting what will happen. If you don't want it to happen, then change the way you communicate. Finally, a valid communication theory should meet a falsification test. A theory is *falsifiable* if it is capable of being subjected to a research study that might disprove it. All of the communication theories presented in this book fulfill the falsification criterion.

A communication theory exhibits *utility* when it provides some benefit or service to the real world. The question is often asked, "What is the practical value of this theory?" Here, we're back to Great Uncle Fred's question, "Will this dog hunt?" One place to find utility is by applying the general, contextual, and microtheories to solve real-world problems in family, health, legal, or political communication. Another place to find utility is to use the predictive capacity of theories to control your future.

In *Understanding Communication Theory,* we use the utility standard often. Throughout the book, we will review applied studies that demonstrate the use of communication theories to benefit the real world. For example, we demonstrate the use of Diffusion of Innovation Theory (Chapter 7) to guide the dissemination and acceptance of new ideas and products and to drive political campaigns. Similarly, we demonstrate how to use the Functional Decision-Making Theory of small group communication (Chapter 8) to avoid faulty decision-making through the competent performance of key communication behaviors. Again, throughout the book, we place a premium on the hunting ability of our communication theories.

Withstanding the Critics   An important part of assessing a theory's acceptability involves the academy's process of peer review. This review takes two forms. One form furthers theoretical development. The process entails blind peer review of research by the referees of our professional journals. The second form embodies the open, collegial, debates that occur between theorists and critics.[17] Such debates appear in scholarly meeting papers, refereed journal articles, scholarly books, textbooks, and on occasion in splashes in the popular press. Sometimes, a communication theory or theory-building research program does not survive the gauntlet of blind peer review and open collegial dialogue.[18] Then the theory or program loses the esteem of the members of the academy. You too should be skeptical of such a theory's claims of power, scope, validity, and utility.

Communication professionals belong to a number of professional associations. These include the National Communication Association, the International Communication Association, and the Association for Educational Journalism and Mass Communication. Such associations sponsor academic journals edited by communication professionals. The editors publish articles that meet the standards of a blind peer review process. That's why academics hold research published in journals such as *Communication Monographs, Communication Theory, Human Communication Research,* and *Journalism Quarterly* in such high regard. However, surviving the peer review process does not provide a theory with immunity from further criticism. In addition to publishing research, scholars regularly criticize a communication theory in journal-length articles. Likewise, theorists respond and defend their theories within the pages of the professional journals. The marketplace of criticism and defense strengthens communication theories. To illustrate the critical process, we will synthesize the major criticisms and responses for each general communication theory reported in Chapters 2–7. We ask you to consider both the criticisms and the responses. Then, you can make your own informed judgment as to each general communication theory's ability to withstand the critics. Of course, we believe the general communication theories, as well as the contextual and microtheories presented, have withstood the gauntlet of criticism.

Summary

We began this chapter by defining communication theory as a why explanation of phenomena. We noted that with communication the phenomena tend to be communicators communicating over time in a medium. We next discussed the levels of communication. These included the actual communication level, the theory level, and the metatheory level. We then introduced The Communication Metatheory (TCM). It allows you to classify theories as general, contextual, micro, special, or symbiotic. It then allows you to dissect theories and identify their anatomical elements. It also allows you to evaluate and compare theories. As a whole, the chapter presented a detailed explanation of TCM. **Box 1-1** provides you with a detailed summary, "Understanding TCM in a Nutshell."

✳ WORTH REVIEWING SEVERAL TIMES

BOX 1-1 Understanding TCM in a Nutshell

Why a Communication Metatheory?: Communication theories (Level 2 talk) are why explanations of the phenomena occurring at Level 1 talk (actual communication). You cannot define communication without specifying, either directly or indirectly, a communication theory. Metatheories (Level 3 talk) help us classify, evaluate, and compare communication theories.

TCM Defined: The Communication Metatheory (TCM) is a theory of theories that allows you to classify, anatomize (flesh out or dissect), and evaluate communication theories.

TCM's Classifying Elements: TCM's classifying typology allows you to identify and classify communication theories within five categories. *General communication theories* provide a rich, valid, why explanation of communicators communicating in a medium. Their explanation holds across the six traditional communication contexts. Each general theory's basic concept locates a fundamental communicative interaction or communicative force that accounts for human action. *Contextual communication theories* explain communication within the confines of the six traditional contexts: interpersonal, small group, public speaking, organizational, mass, and intercultural communication. There are two types of contextual communication theories. *Type 1 contextual theories* contain one or more theoretical concepts that bind them forever to a given context. *Type 2 contextual theories* may become general communication theories as research grounds the theory across the six contexts. *Communication microtheories* are valid, useful, and important, as they explain a narrow band of communication that goes across the six traditional communication contexts. Typically, communication microtheories emphasize a basic message structure, communication dynamic, communicator structure, medium structure, or evaluative concept. They are low in power regarding their ability to explain communicators communicating in a medium. *Special communication theories* are how-to-do-it theories that provide advice to the practitioner about preparing certain types and forms of communication. *Symbiotic communication theories* come from the allied disciplines. They share, in common with a given communication theory, certain ontological assumptions about how the human mind works, or how humans function in society, or how humans create and use language. Again, TCM provides five categories for classifying communication theories: general, contextual, micro, special, and symbiotic (interdisciplinary) theories. **Table 1.2** uses this typology to classify the six general, twenty-three contextual, and thirteen communication microtheories included in this book.

TCM's Anatomical Elements: TMC offers nine anatomical elements to flesh out or dissect a communication theory. *Communicative force* is the fundamental communication interaction that occurs between communicators and accounts for human action. The six known communicative forces are information-sharing, argument-making, fantasy-chaining, social information-sharing, storytelling, and diffusing innovations talk. The *origin* of a communication theory identifies the creator and the place of creation. A communication theory's *roots* point to its antecedents and ancestors. The *assumptions* of a theory are what it accepts as true without proof. Assumptions are of three kinds. *Axiomatic assumptions* are the values implicit in the theory. *Epistemological assumptions* describe how you know what you know from the perspective of the theory. *Ontological assumptions* characterize how you should view the nature of humans from the theory's point of view. *Communication paradigm* (rational, relational, and symbolic) is a metatheoretical term that identifies a cluster of communication theories that has developed like constellations. They do so through the commonality of their ontological metatheoretical presuppositions and the primacy of one of three types of social science facts (material,

Continued

BOX 1-1   *Continued*

social, or symbolic). *Theoretical concepts* are the set of discrete terms that comprise or make up a theory's technical vocabulary. There are three types of theoretical concepts. *Basic* concepts identify a theory's primary unit(s) of communication analysis. With general theories, the basic concepts point to and name the communicative force that accounts for the fundamental communicative interaction occurring between communicators. *Structural concepts* frame the basic concepts. There are four types of structural concepts. *Message structure concepts* dress up and flesh out a theory's basic concepts. *Communication dynamic structure concepts* label the deep structure tension or conflict present in the theory. *Communicator structure concepts* name and identify the communicators and their attributes. *Medium structure concepts* specify the nature of the substance within which communication functions, propagates, and travels. Communication functions in the six traditional contexts (called medium₁). Communication propagates in a *medium₂* substance such as a free and open society. Communication travels by a *medium₃* means of conduction such as air, light, wire. A communication theory's *evaluative concepts* allow you to make assessments and judgments about the quality and outcomes (interaction effects) of communicators communicating in a medium. *Modeling communication theories* is the act of re-representing a theory through other materials. TCM re-represents the elements of communication theories using six interlocking VENN-type circles within a box referring to the other anatomical elements. *Theoretical relationship statements* indicate how a theory's concepts fit together. The relationship between theoretical concepts can be expressed *mathematically, axiomatically,* or through

ordinary language. The nature of the regularity of the interaction among the concepts can be expressed as a *law,* a *rule,* or a *principle.* The *theory–method complex* describes the interlocking relationship between a communication theory and its unique qualitative method. The qualitative method allows a researcher to identify actual communication that represents the structural concepts of a given theory.

TCM's Evaluative Elements: TCM offers nine metaconcepts that will help you evaluate the merits of a communication theory. They are power and scope, *heuristic* and *isomorphic,* elegance and parsimony, validity and utility, and withstanding the critics. *Power* evaluates a theory's ability to magnify phenomena. *Scope* deals with the breadth of the communication phenomena explained and the breadth of contexts in which the theoretical explanation holds. *Heuristic* deals with a theory's ability to raise interesting questions, spin off new theories, and stimulate further research. *Isomorphic* refers to a theory's ability to apply to more than one context or more than one discipline. *Parsimony* lets you evaluate a theory's degree of economy and simplicity. *Elegance* characterizes a theory's aesthetic qualities. *Validity* concerns how well a communication theory is grounded to observables. It also concerns whether the theory is logically derived, internally sound, efficacious, and falsifiable. *Utility* allows you to judge a theory's ability to solve real-world problems. A theory is also evaluated to determine its ability to withstand criticism. *Withstanding the critics* points to a theory's ability to pass the standards of a peer review process and stand up against published criticism. TCM helps you judge whether or not the dog (theory) can hunt!

Finally, we would ask you to place yourself in the shoes of Corey, our newest communication graduate. We will see Corey again in other chapters. Corey is speaking at a first job interview. Let's listen in and see how Corey makes this chapter work to advantage (see **Figure 1-3**).

"I stand prepared by the Communication Theory Tree of Knowledge. TCM allows us to compare theories and pick those that will help us solve our corporate problems such as segmenting markets, diffusing innovations, and building our all important corporate vision."

FIGURE 1-3.   Communication Graduate Job Interview

Corey could do all this after reading Ch. 1 ??

Chapter 2

Information Systems
Theory (IST)

*The force of information sharing creates order, structure,
and control for coordinated human action.*

Chapter Outline

Information Systems Theory (IST) is our first landmark on the trail to understanding communication theory. It is appropriate to stop and rest for a while as we point out its essential features. Developed in the 1940s and extended in the 1970s, 1980s, and 1990s, IST is our most heuristic communication theory. Much like the spin-off products of the U.S. space program, IST has spawned a number of offspring. Derivative theories include Uncertainty Reduction Theory (Chapter 5), Weick's Theory of Organizing (Chapter 9), and Anxiety/ Uncertainty Management Theory (Chapter 10). We will encounter these theories farther along the trail to understanding communication theory. Also, IST's kissin' cousin, Diffusion of Innovation Theory (Chapter 7), is on the trail ahead. Some of our colleagues have indicated that they admire our fortitude in presenting IST as the initial general communication theory explained in this book, because the trail around this landmark theory is pretty rough going. Nonetheless, because we're all fresh and excited about our journey, we think IST provides the perfect point from which to begin the journey. Once you grasp this theory, many parts of the trail ahead will already seem familiar to you.

IST explains the communicative force of information-sharing that creates and maintains human systems. We begin by viewing IST as a general communication theory. We sketch its power and scope. Then, we trace its origin and roots and discuss its primary assumptive system. Next, we introduce IST's theoretical concepts. We explain how to find its basic concepts, see its structural concepts, and use its evaluative concepts. Then, we report on IST's usefulness. We show IST's use to explain human action and benefit the real world. As well, we discuss its ability to withstand critical scrutiny. Finally, we present our chapter summary, "Understanding IST in a Nutshell."

IST: Viewing the General Communication Theory

IST belongs in the rational paradigm of communication theories. IST assumes a material reality that works in consistent, ordered ways. It assumes that you can identify and follow the flow of information through systems analysis. IST was the first communication theory to use the metatheoretical lens of systems theory. It asks you to think of communication as occurring within a system. In our words, the system is communicators communicating within a medium. IST views information as a communicative force that creates order, structure, and control for coordinated human action. As you know, energy in its varied forms is the force behind motion in the universe. So too, information is one of the six communicative forces for human action. Unlike classical physics, however, human systems are open, not closed.

In physics, the second law of thermodynamics states that energy in the form of heat moves from a hot source to a cold source. Once the heat is in a cold source it is in a degraded form. It cannot be retrieved. In such a state of heat loss, the measure of how much heat is unretrievable is called *entropy*. In the closed systems of classical physics, entropy is always increasing and cannot be reversed. Eventually, the universe will suffer a heat death (Spielberg & Anderson, 1987). Increases in entropy mean increases in randomness and disorder. If you put an ice cube in a hot cup of coffee, the temperature of the hot coffee and the cold ice cube will eventually randomize into a state of equilibrium. Classical physics theory argues that eventually all the heat in the suns of the universe will burn out. The result will be an equalized temperature throughout the universe. At this point, all energy will be in a degraded form of heat. Energy will be unavailable to keep the universe alive.

Although death through degraded heat awaits as the fate of the universe, that is not what happens with open human systems. Human systems exhibit very permeable boundaries in which information acts as a *negentropy*. Negative entropy is an order-creating force (Wiener, 1948). With IST, the communicative force flows from communicators (senders, receivers, and observers) communicating (sharing syntactic, semantic, and pragmatic information) by presenting messages (information bits) propagated through a medium (closed, open, or mixed system).

Sketching Its Power and Scope

IST is a general communication theory. It explains how optimized information in communication systems creates order, structure, and control. It also explains that the flow of information creates and maintains communication systems. IST possesses three distinct threads: Machine-to-machine communication, people-to-machine-to-people communication, and people-to-people communication. With the machine thread, the resultant communication systems are more closed. With the human thread the resultant communication systems are more open. The people-to-machine-to-people thread falls somewhere in the middle.

Information systems are everywhere. They are ubiquitous. We live in the Information Age, the Cybernetic Age, and the Computer Age. IST provides the explanatory power behind communication technology. The Internet is a communication frontier, the Star Wars of the twentieth century. IST enabled its creation. The fact that, with your personal computer, you can search your library at school and download information is made possible by IST. This is an example of people-to-machine-to-people communication. The fact that you can surf on the Internet and, via voice computer chip, talk to others in your interest group is due to IST. Sometimes machine-to-machine communication assists people-to-people communication. IST's explanatory power in explaining machine-to-machine communication is law-like and highly mathematical. The scope of its machine applications crosses the boundaries of computers, facsimile machines, telegraphy, telephony, radio, television, and so forth.

Most communication departments today offer a course in communication technology. Often this course is quite technical. It may even include rudimentary programming skills. Returning from developmental leave, Professor Shields proved the old adage wrong—old dogs *can* learn new tricks. He taught the Introduction to Information Technology course at the University of Missouri–St. Louis. The course allows communication and mass communication majors to learn such technical terms as LAN, WAN, bridge, server, gateway, router, CPU, CD-ROM, CD-I, DVI, and so forth. If you already know a programming language like BASIC or COBOL you have felt the power of IST. It is *the* theory of a computer science major. Hence, it displays isomorphism.) pg 26

The modern television, radio, and newspaper newsrooms all require the electronic journalist to be literate about information technology. Although, at its inception, the machine-to-machine thread appeared fairly exotic and esoteric, the discipline has now come full circle. As students of communication we regularly integrate human communication and machine communication. IST is also the most interdisciplinary of our indigenous communication theories. Biologists, chemists, economists, physicists, psychologists, and sociologists use it. It is one of the theories that communication scholars bring to the table when contributing to the research conducted by interdisciplinary teams. IST has proven itself as possessing isomorphic characteristics. " scope "

With the inception of the machine-to-machine version of IST (Shannon, 1948a; 1948b), other versions began to appear. One speculated about IST's ability to create order, structure, and control in human communication systems (Weaver, 1949). If you've taken an introductory public speaking course, you probably know many of IST's important concepts. For example, in public speaking you learned that the communication process could be viewed as *source, message, channel, receiver,* and *feedback.* If you've taken a small group communication class, you have also used IST to order, structure, and control the flow of information. You did so when you followed any of the various agenda systems or used information generation techniques like brainstorming. Also, if you have taken an organizational communication class then you also know about IST. For example, you may have conducted an audit whereby you studied information flow in the organization. You probably studied the flow of information through the formal and informal channels of the organization. You may have found overloaded bulletin boards, unread e-mail, and tardy memorandums. If such was the case, your recommendations probably dealt with improving the structure and order of the organization through improved information flow. IST is used so widely that you may already know its theoretical concepts even though you have never known its formal name.

Tracing Its Origin and Roots

For the origins of IST, we must go back to the time of World War II and discuss the contributors to the field of communication engineering. With the outbreak of World War II, the government brought together a number of professors and engineers to help in the war effort. Norbert Wiener, a professor of mathematics at MIT, worked on improving the command and control of artillery pieces. Wiener helped improve the efforts to shoot down enemy planes. He did so by using self-correcting feedback messages from the artillery piece to itself. Wiener worked out the mathematics of an automated feedback system suitable to the design of self-regulating information systems. Wiener's mathematical theory of communication concerns the circular causality of feedback in which A causes B, B causes C, and C causes A, so that A causes itself (Krippendorff, 1986; Rogers, 1994; Wiener, 1948).

Wiener's feedback control system meets our definition of an information system. It treats messages as continuous information flows that self-correct and provide order, structure, and control of the communication system. As a student of communication, you are now quite familiar with this feedback circularity. When a speaker modifies his or her presentation in light of an audience's reactions, such an instantaneous adjustment is due to the self-correcting nature of feedback. Robotics machines in manufacturing plants also provide dramatic evidence of the value of Norbert Wiener's information system theorizing.

During World War II, Claude Shannon, an electrical engineering graduate of MIT working at Bell Laboratories, served as a calligrapher devising coding systems for the sending of secret information and code-breaking systems for decoding the enemy's secret information. Shannon had taken courses in mathematics from Norbert Wiener. Using Ludwig von Bertalanffy's (1968) biological systems theory, first developed in the 1920s, Wiener and Shannon collaborated unofficially on the development of two now famous works: *Cybernetics* and "The Mathematical Theory of Communication."[1] Shannon's mathematical theory appeared first in two issues of the *Bell System Technical Journal* (1948a, 1948b). This mathematical theory dealt with the syntactical problem of optimizing the amount of information that could flow through a given channel capacity when transmitted from a source to a self-correcting receiver. The theory operationalized information as an *information bit.* An information bit is a unit of information that could be sent nearly error free over a noisy channel. It was sent by an appropriate processor called an encoder. It was received by another processor called a decoder that contained a self-correcting feedback device. The encoder, noisy channel, decoder, and self-correcting feedback device comprised the communication system. Shannon's theory provided the world with a mathematical formula for determining the maximum amount of information bits that could be sent nearly error free through any given channel with a minimum of power. As a practical matter, his theory proved that AT&T could keep its existing telephone lines and not have to upgrade its lines to improve service.

Shannon's (1948a, 1948b) seventy-five or so theoretical concepts provided a nearly complete vocabulary for modern IST. The impact of his theory has been great. Nearly every college graduate knows the major concepts of the theory (information source, message, encoder, signal, channel, noise, decoder, receiver, destination) regardless of his or her major.

Shannon's ideas rapidly diffused beyond the pages of the *Bell Technical Journal.* This was due largely to an imaginative, cheerleading article by Warren Weaver. Weaver (1949), a Ph.D. in civil engineering who had worked with Shannon in the war effort, published a nonmathematical description of the theory in *Scientific American.* In it he expounded the implications of the theory for all of communication, including human communication. Wilbur Schramm, of the University of Illinois, the first academician in the country to be called Professor and Dean of Communication, also served as editor of the University of Illinois Press (Rogers, 1994). Schramm literally slapped Shannon's initial two articles from the *Bell Technical Journal* and Weaver's single article from *Scientific American* between two covers into a classic text. Schramm published the work under the same name as Shannon's original articles, *The Mathematical Theory of Communication* (Shannon & Weaver, 1949). Oddly, because every entry in the book was a reprint of a previously published piece, with only some minor editing and the inclusion of minor additional notes, Schramm would have been most correct to list himself as editor of the work. Instead, Schramm chose not to do that. As a result, however, he left the world with the false impression that the book was a co-authored, equally conceived and executed, work. A bigger problem resulted. Scholars in the discipline began to call the theory the Shannon and Weaver mathematical theory of communication. Such attributions then left the false impression on thousands of students that Shannon and Weaver had collaborated when they did not. As well, it left the false impression that Weaver somehow had something to do with Shannon's development of the theory, when he did not. Nonetheless, this milestone book simultaneously launched Shannon's theory for the efficient transfer of information from machine-to-machine and Weaver's analogue to explain human-to-human communication. Four decades passed before the machine-to-machine and human-to-human theoretical lines of research again merged in our discipline through the work of Scott Poole (Poole & Jackson, 1993).

The view that information is something measurable led directly to the creation of IST. IST developed rapidly in the 1950s, 1960s, and 1970s. We discuss IST's grounding research later in the chapter as we look at its ability to explain human action. For now, suffice it to say that information systems engineers expanded the mathematics of Shannon's theory to allow for the mathematical measurement of more than syntactic information. Several scholars pro-

future (almost present)

vided formulae for measuring the semantic and pragmatic dimensions of communication in the transmission of information (Conant, 1979; Hyvarinen, 1968; Jumarie, 1990). Today, others work on true artificial intelligence. They seek to expand the interactive communication of humans and machines. In addition, Scott Poole (Poole & DeSanctis, 1992; Poole & Jackson, 1993) and a group of researchers at the University of Minnesota developed Adaptive Structuration Theory (AST). AST explains computer-assisted group information-sharing. Their research on part machine and part human cyborg groups explains the processing of information. Thus, we have come full circle, back to where Shannon (1948a, 1948b) and Wiener (1948) started. We discuss AST in detail in Chapter 8.

Accepting Its Assumptive System

Let's take a brief rest stop. Recall from The Communication Metatheory (TCM), presented in Chapter 1, that all theories possess assumptions that relate to being (ontological), knowing (epistemological), and valuing (axiomatic). Recall also that it is best to accept them as true in order to explore a theory's explanatory power. IST's assumptions are (1) humans are information sharers; (2) the amount of information in a message is proportional to the amount of uncertainty in a communication event; (3) error-free information-sharing is impossible; (4) information systems tend toward chaos; and (5) optimized information creates order, structure, and control in a system.

Humans Are Information Sharers   This is an ontological assumption. It concerns the nature of human beings. To understand it, consider this question. Do you take more pleasure in keeping a secret or in sharing a secret? IST views humans as compelled to give and seek information. This compulsion to share is true of individuals, groups, and organizations. Due to our nature, we devote much of our lives to seeking and giving information. Sharing information appears to be an inherent part of our makeup. As a species, we get angry when someone will not engage in information-sharing. For example, if you sleep through class you know that you can ask a classmate for the lecture notes. You do so out of a real expectation that he or she will share them with you. To not share the information is not to be social and not to be a team player.

Humans crave receiving + sending of info. (? feeling of connectedness Maslow)

   As humans, we have created machines in our own self-image. Such machines create, share, and store information. Indeed, the hallmark of the twentieth century is our invention of information machines. With such machines, we now send and retrieve information at the speed of light. This fact tells us rather pointedly that information-sharing is one of our innate, dominant activities. Some humans become addicted to information-sharing and retrieving. We spend hours on the Internet, or staring at CNN news, or repeatedly checking e-mail, voicemail, and mail-mail. Others among us roam the hallways seeking organizational gossip.

The Amount of Information in a Message Is Proportional to the Amount of Uncertainty in a Communication Event   This is an epistemological assumption. There are ways of proving and knowing it. Claude Shannon's (1948a, 1948b) great insight was perceiving a relationship between information and uncertainty. Another was his derivation of a mathematical formula to express that relationship. If someone shares the name of the president of your college or university with you, have you received new information? Only if you do not

how we know what we know, nature/grounds for knowlg

already know it. Shannon said the same thing. He defined information as the reduction of uncertainty about something. As information-sharers we seek information that we don't know and give information that others don't know.

It's time for a rest stop to highlight Shannon's definition of information. In a deck of fifty-two playing cards, how many questions requiring a yes or no answer would you optimally need to ask to know a specific card drawn from the deck? The answer is 5.7 questions on average. It's a mathematical certainty. 5.7 is the log to the base 2 of 52. You pick the card, and we'll identify it within six questions. Tell your friend it's the Queen of Diamonds. Remember, don't tell us. First question: Is it a black card? You say no. We have now reduced our uncertainty by 50 percent. We went from not knowing the card you chose out of fifty-two to now not knowing the card you chose out of the twenty-six remaining. Second question: Is it a heart? You say no. We again have reduced our uncertainty by 50 percent because the only other possibility is that the card is a diamond. We've gone from not knowing the card you chose out of twenty-six to now not knowing the card out of the thirteen diamonds that remain. Third question: Is it a seven or below? You say no. We again have reduced our uncertainty by roughly 50 percent and know that it must be an eight or above. Fourth question: Is it a ten or below? You say no. We now know it is a face card. Fifth question: Is it a queen or below? You say yes. Again we have reduced uncertainty by 50 percent. Sixth question: Is it a jack? You say no. We now know it is the Queen of Diamonds.

Communication systems analysts code talk to optimize machine-to-machine communication. They do so by operationally defining a *bit* of information as a 50 percent reduction in uncertainty. They do this by using binary digits like 1 and 0 to represent a "yes" or a "no" response, respectively. In human-to-human communication most of us are inefficient information-sharers. Nonetheless, we recognize a good informative speech, or a good lecture, or good directions. We know the good ones from the bad ones because good messages optimize the information that we need to know. They do so in a clear, organized, and straightforward manner.

Error-Free Information-Sharing Is Impossible   This is an ontological assumption. It says that neither humans nor machines get things perfectly right. Physicists tell us that a perpetual motion machine is impossible to build because energy is lost to friction. The same is true of information systems. *Noise* is the name Shannon (1948a) gave to the friction that affects message transmission. Noise is always present in a channel whether the communication is people-to-people, machine-to-machine, people-to-machine, or machine-to-people. There are many sources of noise. These include channel, source, receiver, coding, and decoding noise.

Allow us to illustrate the above point. As we share our information about communication theories with you, errors occur. We make syntactical mistakes. These are mistakes in coding. We make semantic mistakes. These are mistakes in meaning. We make pragmatic mistakes. These are mistakes in tone. Some mistakes come from us (the message), some from the encoder (our computer), some from the publisher's transference (channel) of our text to the published page (the decoder). Professor Cragan is an error-prone receiver of written information because of dyslexia. His eyes often transpose letters and words. Sometimes the problem manifests itself randomly. Professor Shields likes to say that Professor Cragan spends many a night pondering the meaning of the word *doG*.

A quick way to understand the likelihood of error in communication is by playing the communication relay game. Take a group of seven people and send six of them out of the room. Have the first look at a picture and describe it to a second person. In turn, have that person describe it to the third, and so on until the seventh person. Then show the rest of the group the picture. Many translation errors will have occurred.

A similar translation problem exists in machine-to-machine or machine-to-human communication. "Isabel es me esposa" is a correct Spanish sentence. It may be translated into English as Isabelle, Elizabeth, or Betty is my wife or spouse. Imagine the difficulty of error-free translation of a whole book from Spanish to English and then back to Spanish again. Writing code for machine communication exhibits a similar problem. Noise causes errors inherently. That is why cryptographers and program analysts take great care to build in sufficient redundancy to reduce error.

Information Systems Tend Toward Chaos   Again, this is an ontological assumption. It says it is the nature of humans and machines to wear, break down, and fall apart. This tendency toward chaos makes information a two-edged sword. On the one hand, information reduces uncertainty, thereby creating order. On the other hand, when information exceeds channel, encoding, or decoding capacity, we get a situation called *information overload*. Once again chaos ensues. The chaos aspect is like a constant remake of the Goldilocks story in which the porridge is either too cold or too hot. More than that, however, our need for information always tends to exceed the capacity of the sender, channel, and receiver. Do you think there will ever be a computer built with adequate storage capacity? Or a television built with too many channels for the available frequencies? Or a library built with enough Nexus–Lexis terminals?[2] All complex information systems tend toward chaos. That's why Shannon's mathematical theory concerned the optimization of information within channel, source, and receiver capacity. Shannon knew that it is the nature of information systems to exceed capacity.

evaluative - concern values Pg 14

Optimized Information Creates Order, Structure, and Control in a Human System   This is an axiomatic assumption. It says that optimized information is valuable. When physicists first looked to the heavens, they found an apparently ordered universe that looked like a heavenly version of a perpetual motion machine. It came as a surprise that an insidious thing called entropy—a measure of a system's tendency toward randomness—was eventually going to shut down the universe. In physics, entropy is always increasing. It can never be reversed. IST, as first conceived by Shannon (1948a, 1948b), ran the physics problem in reverse. Shannon saw a chaotic world of symbols and signals and thus a situation of maximum entropy or complete randomness. He set about the task of reducing uncertainty by providing information. Thus, in Shannon's theory, entropy decreases. When it reaches zero no information is exchangeable. The physicist's view of entropy and Shannon's view of information are mirror images. The oddity is that the mathematical formula to measure the physicist's entropy and the mathematical formula to measure Shannon's information are similar. Scholars have engaged in much debate about this oddity (Finn & Roberts, 1984; Griffith, 1989). Nonetheless, with IST, information exists only in the presence of the reduction of uncertainty. Moreover, information only reduces uncertainty when it is optimized in terms of source, channel, and receiver capacity. Thus, only optimized information creates order, structure, and control. **Figure 2-1** illustrates the inverse, curvilinear, relationship between increasing information, optimization, and time.

In human-to-human communication, only optimized information reduces uncertainty and creates order. To illustrate this point, think of giving an informative speech about scuba

in between stages cause the tension/ flux that produce need for change which requires communication

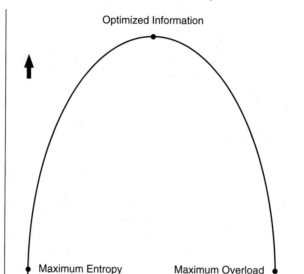

Uncertainty Reduction from Increasing Information

Optimized Information

Maximum Entropy   Maximum Overload

Increasing Information over Increasing Time ➡

**FIGURE 2-1.   Optimizing Information: Curvilinear
Nature Over Time**

diving. To do so, you would want to determine the amount of uncertainty that exists. What does your audience already know about the subject? Of all the information that you could convey, you must select the optimal amount. Then, you must present it with appropriate re-dundant statements. Finally, you must adjust your talk based on the feedback you receive. In short, you must first balance between predictability and uncertainty. Then, you must bal-ance between novelty and redundancy. You must do it all within the capacity of the chan-nels (slides, voice, public address system, handouts, hearing) you are using.

IST: Introducing the Theoretical Concepts

As we indicated, IST is among our most difficult landmarks on the trail to understanding communication theory. It may well take several rest stops to help you understand it. This is a good place to relax and recall some important points from Chapter 1. For example, recall that TCM stipulated that all general communication theories exhibit basic, structural, and evaluative concepts. As you observe communicators communicating through the lens of IST, you will see information-sharers giving and receiving information in a medium. **Figure 2-2** displays IST's anatomical parts, highlighting its basic, structural, and evaluative concepts.

Figure 2-2 draws on TCM's framework of six Venn diagrams to organize IST's con-cepts. The small inner circle contains IST's most basic concept, information. TCM then

Viewing IST's Anatomical Elements

Key:
Bold Caps = The Communication Metatheory's Metaconcepts
Caps + Small Case = IST's Theoretical Concepts

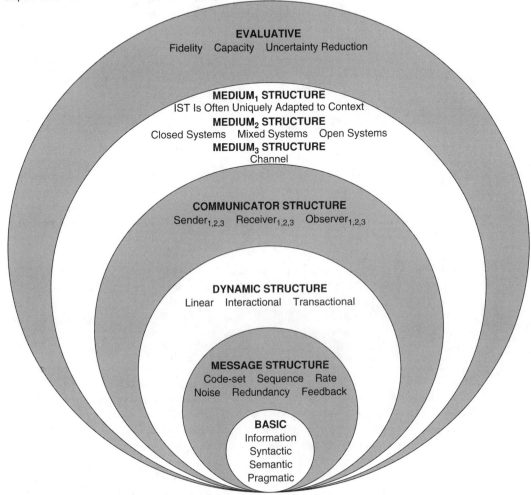

EVALUATIVE
Fidelity   Capacity   Uncertainty Reduction

MEDIUM$_1$ STRUCTURE
IST Is Often Uniquely Adapted to Context
MEDIUM$_2$ STRUCTURE
Closed Systems   Mixed Systems   Open Systems
MEDIUM$_3$ STRUCTURE
Channel

COMMUNICATOR STRUCTURE
Sender$_{1,2,3}$ Receiver$_{1,2,3}$ Observer$_{1,2,3}$

DYNAMIC STRUCTURE
Linear   Interactional   Transactional

MESSAGE STRUCTURE
Code-set   Sequence   Rate
Noise   Redundancy   Feedback

BASIC
Information
Syntactic
Semantic
Pragmatic

Other Anatomical Elements:
COMMUNICATIVE FORCE   **MODELING**
ORIGIN, ROOTS, ASSUMPTIONS   **RELATIONSHIP STATEMENTS**
PARADIGM   **THEORY–METHOD COMPLEX**

EXAMPLE OF PRAGMATIC INFORMATION: "There once was a lady from Niger, who smiled as she rode on a Tiger. They returned from the ride with the lady inside, and the smile on the face of the Tiger" (Monkhouse, 1873).

FIGURE 2-2.

highlights IST's message structure concepts such as code, sequence, and feedback. TCM also allows you to see IST's dynamic structure concepts. These concepts reveal the tension among the three types of information systems. They are linear, interactive, and transactional.

SUMMARY OF WHAT'S TO COME

Next TCM points up IST's communicator structure concepts of sender, receiver, and observer. Then, TCM points towards IST's three types of media. Medium$_1$ reflects the traditional communication contexts of interpersonal, small group, public speaking, organizational, mass, and intercultural communication. IST, as a general communication theory, explains a broad band of communication across these contexts. Medium$_2$ concerns the substance in which a theory propagates and grows. IST propagates best in open and mixed communication systems. It does not do well in closed systems, because no new information can enter them. Medium$_3$ includes the channel in which the communication (information) travels. The channel that conducts information may be air, light, or wire. The final circle of the VENN diagram displays IST's evaluative concepts. They are adequacy, timeliness, fidelity, capacity, equivocation, and uncertainty reduction.

Finding Basic Concepts

To use IST, you must first identify and code its basic concepts. With IST you must find information and then understand it at three levels of meaning. Four technical terms—information, syntactic meaning, semantic meaning, and pragmatic meaning—serve as IST's basic and associative basic concepts. Each represents the communication phenomena you must recognize and find to use IST. *STEP ONE?*

Initial Basic Concept   Again it's time for a rest stop. Recall from our discussion of TCM that a general theory's basic concepts fall within two subclasses: an initial basic concept and the associated basic concepts. An initial basic concept is the primary communication unit that is singled out for analysis. With general communication theories, the initial basic concept also identifies the communicative force that affects human action. IST's initial basic concept is information. Information-sharing is the communicative force.

Information.   Drum (1956) asked a very simple question: What is information? Information is the initial thing you must find in human communication when using this theory. If you cannot find a piece of information, or a bit of information, then you cannot theorize by using IST. Rest assured, however, that information is everywhere. With a little practice, you can find it. In intentionally created information systems, information is whatever the communicators in the system choose to call it. Information can be a character like a letter of the alphabet, a sentence, a paragraph, an idea, a concept, a picture, a memorandum, or a whole body of material like a speech, an article, a book, or an annual report. *Information* is data, knowledge, or opinion that reduces the uncertainty of at least one of the participants in a communication episode by providing something they did not already know.

It is important to operationalize what is meant by information in the communication system under observation. Shannon (1948a, 1948b) operationalized the definition of information by calling it an information bit (binary digit) that reduced uncertainty by 50 percent once it was transmitted to a receiver. Let's see if we can illustrate this point in ordinary language. What would we likely conclude as authors of this book if you answer "No!" to the question, "Did you learn anything when you read Chapter 1?" From the perspective of IST, we can only conclude two things. The first is that Chapter 1 contained no new information. You knew everything we said. You displayed no uncertainty. There was no uncertainty to reduce. If that is not the case, the second thing we could conclude is that we constructed our message in such a way that no information was transferred. In other words, you didn't understand what we said. Your feedback, in this second instance, tells us that we failed to reduce your uncertainty. If this is the case, we would ask you to reread Chapter 1.

Ritchie (1991) stated that information has a receiver component. By receiver component, he meant that a message must be recognized as a message and it must be understood. As Shannon (1948a) put it, "the fundamental problem of communication is that of reproducing at one point either exactly or approximately a message selected at another point" (p. 379). Shannon solved this problem at the syntactic level of meaning in relatively closed communication systems. As you shall see, others have been working since then to solve the problem at the levels of semantic and pragmatic meaning. They are working to do this in both machine and human communication in relatively closed, open, and mixed communication systems.

Associated Basic Concepts   Information theorists regard information transmission and reception as occurring at three levels: syntactic, semantic, and pragmatic.[3] These three levels of information comprise IST's associative basic concepts. As Morris (1938) observed in his theory of signs, *syntactics* deals with the relationship of symbols one to another as in the statement, "i before e except after c." Likewise, the syntactic rules of word choice and sentence structure allow the twenty-six letters of the alphabet to form words and statements in the English language. *Semantics* deals with the relationship between symbols and their meaning. *Pragmatics* deals with the emotional effect of language in use. When you communicate with another, you convey pragmatic meaning about the relationship between sender and receiver. For example, at the syntactical level, the word *pig* is an acceptable noun in the English grammar. At the semantic level it may be understood to be a hoofed animal. However, in the expression "that cop is a racist pig," emotional responses may occur between the sender and receiver due to the pragmatic level of communication (Bormann, 1980). The statement at the bottom of **Figure 2-2** illustrates information at a syntactic (limerick), semantic (news of the ride), and pragmatic (smiling lady versus smiling Tiger) levels.

Syntactic Information.   *Syntactic information* deals with the universe of symbols that comprise the elements of a given grammar plus the rules for constructing proper statements. The twenty-six-letter alphabet and the rules for combining letters into words and words into sentences is the domain of syntactic information. The Morse Code is an early example of converting a human language code, the alphabet, into an electrical impulse code and transferring that code through wire over a long distance. The Morse Code consisted of a dot, a dash, a letter space, and a word space. Morse optimized his coding system by assigning the most frequently used letters of the alphabet short duration symbols. Then, he assigned the least frequently used letters long duration symbols. As a result, the letter "e"—the most frequently used letter of the alphabet—is a single dot. Conversely, the letter "q," an infrequently used letter, is a dash, dash, dot, dash. Shannon's mathematical theory of communication optimized the amount of information sent down any given channel using a coding system of binary digits. Recall that Shannon operationally defined a bit of information as that information that provided a 50 percent reduction in uncertainty. Although Shannon (1948a) indicated that the specific mathematical proofs reported only dealt with syntactic information, Weaver (1949) argued that the theory could be adapted to deal with the semantic and pragmatic levels of information. Indeed, in machine-to-machine, human-to-human, and machine-to-human communication, coding systems for semantic information and pragmatic information now exist.

Semantic Information.   *Semantic information* refers to the meaning of words and their comprehension in sentence form. Chomsky (1957) illustrated that a sentence with syntactic information need not convey semantic information. A Chomsky-like example would be the sentence, *Odorless aromatic thoughts snore loudly.* Here you see a sentence that provides syntactic sense but semantic nonsense. Developing semantic codes to explain and evaluate the process of communication is difficult. However, much has been done. In machine-to-machine and human-to-machine communication a number of semantic codes exist. Programs exist that translate instantaneously English to French or French to Italian. The thesaurus on your word processor uses a semantic code. It allows you to find words of similar meaning. As well, the "key word" program available on-line in the library allows you to find references pertaining to specific content areas.

examples of developed semantic codes

In human-to-human communication, codes exist that allow you to track the transfer of meaning between people. They also allow you to describe the overall communication process that has occurred. The small group and organizational contexts provide ready instances of the use of such coding systems. For example, Robert Bales's (1950) Interaction Process Analysis (IPA) coding system allowed him to code twelve kinds of information (communicative acts) in a decision-making group. He coded for such acts as "asks for or makes suggestions" and "asks for or gives information." The ability to code such semantic information occurring over time allowed Bales to model the group communication process as exhibiting three phases: orientation, evaluation, and control. Fisher (1974) reported the use of a more complex coding system to study group communication. He looked at the types of information contained in communicative acts, interacts, and double interacts. He indicated that decision-making groups go through four phases: orientation, conflict, emergence, and reinforcement. Goldhaber and Rogers (1979) reported on a coding system for classifying communication in an organization. The system is called the International Communication Association (ICA) Audit. The audit called for the retrieval of three types of information: descriptive, evaluative, and policy. This coding system centered on the flow of communication within the organization when conceived as an information system much like Shannon's. For example, this elaborate audit allowed one to "determine the amount of information underload or overload associated with major topics, sources, and channels of communication" (Goldhaber & Rodgers, p. 8).

Pragmatic Information.   *Pragmatic information* concerns the relationship dimension of messages. Pragmatic information connotes the degree of connection and affinity between communicators. It concerns the psychological and social effects of information exchange. You are familiar with the nightly news reporter's question of the crime victim: "How does it feel to lose all your worldly possessions?" It remains for researchers working with IST to evolve machine-to-machine programming or artificial intelligence software that conveys a personality dimension. However, the goal is to have a machine capable of feeling such as Lt. Commander Data on *Star Trek: The Next Generation.* Nonetheless, much progress has been made in the use of IST to develop coding systems relevant to the pragmatic dimension of communication in human-to-human communication.

[handwritten margin note: more recent advances in developing coding systems for pragmatic information.]

Ethnographic researchers specializing in conversational analysis have developed coding schemes that capture the pragmatic dimension of information (Beach, 1989; Millar & Rogers, 1976, 1987). The conversational analysts search for recurring patterns in the creation and resolution of interactional problems. They now code semantic and pragmatic meaning simultaneously as they model the flow of information in everyday conversations.

Seeing Structural Concepts

[handwritten margin note: SUMMARY OF WHAT'S TO COME]

Again, it's time for a brief rest stop. Recall from TCM that the structural concepts of all communication theories relate to message, communication dynamic, communicator, and medium. At its simplest, IST explains that communicators communicate with information in some medium. IST contains message structure concepts (code-set, sequence, rate, noise, redundancy, and feedback), dynamic structure concepts (linear, interactive, and transactional), communicator structure concepts (sender, receiver, and observer), and medium$_{1,2,3}$ concepts (contextual media, type of communication system, and channel).

Message Concepts   Recall that TCM specified that all communication theories contain message structure concepts that dress up and flesh out a theory's basic concepts. As indicated in **Figure 2-2,** IST's message structure concepts are code-set, sequence, rate, noise, redundancy, and feedback. In order to illustrate the linkages of these concepts, we would ask you to think of this book as a message. With this message, we are trying to explain communication theories accurately and efficiently. Our code-set is the written English language. We assume you can decode our meaning because you are familiar with and understand that code-set. If you have problems decoding our words, you can consult a code-decipher book—any good dictionary. We sequenced our message by chapters. Our sequence flowchart asks you to learn general communication theories first. It then asks you to learn contextual communication theories. Finally, it asks you to learn about communication microtheories. The rate at which we present the material is roughly 10,000 words per chapter. In a semester, we anticipate you can cover the information presented in this book at the maximum rate of a chapter per week. We built redundancy into our chapters through the use of chapter outline previews, chapter summaries, and "In a Nutshell" boxes. We did so in the hopes of overcoming the effects of noise that might distract you from and distort our message. The weakest part of our message is the slow feedback loop. It will be three years before we can correct any errors you or your professor may discover in this book. Similarly, it will be three years before we can clarify any part of the message that is ambiguous. Together, such associated basic concepts comprise IST's message structure. Let's now examine them one by one.

Code-set.   A *code-set* is a discrete set of symbols that both senders and receivers know how to encode and decode. Any (every) information system need(s) one to work. The written English language, the spoken English language, American Sign Language, court-reporting shorthand, Morse code, and all our machine languages such as COBOL, assembly, FORTRAN, C-plus-plus, and Pascal are examples of code-sets. Cryptography (secret writing code-sets) conceals the meaning of important messages to all but the intended receiver(s). DNA is said to contain a code-set that contains all the information necessary for human development.

Sequence.   A *sequence* is a continuous or connected series. A fundamental notion of IST is the idea of information traveling as a stochastic process. A *stochastic* process occurs when a system gives rise to a sequence of symbols to which the laws of probability apply. The sequence may be extremely simple like the head or tail of a tossed coin. Conversely, the sequence may be extremely complex, like the sequence of musical notes in a Wagnerian opera or the sequence of letters and words that make up this chapter. A stochastic process is said to be *ergodic* if the probability laws that characterize it remain constant for all parts of the sequence. Without the assumption of ergodicity, or at least an approximation thereto, it is difficult to apply information measures to a sequence of symbols. You can readily appreciate the troubles that would ensue in predicting a head or a tail flip if the bias of the coin changed in an erratic manner between tosses.

Information is sequenced or structured to optimize the amount of information that can travel given the capacity of a given channel. Systems analysts write flowcharts containing decision trees that sequence what the machine is to do given an event. In other words, with Shannon's mathematical theory of communication, the events (symbols) in a code-set possess a certain probability of following another. As indicated, "e" is the most frequently used letter and the English language is 50 percent redundant. Such a high redundancy means that if we deleted randomly 50 percent of the letters on this page, you could still reconstruct it and understand it. The six bits of information (questions) it takes to solve the card you picked from the deck of fifty-two is an example of sequencing based on statistical probability. Each yes or no decision reduced uncertainty by 50 percent.

This sort of sequencing occurs all the time in human-to-human communication (McLaughlin, Cody, & Rosenstein, 1983; Cody & McLaughlin, 1985). However, human-to-human sequencing is not ordinarily as disciplined as Shannon's mathematical formula. If you sought to optimize the fewest bits of information you would need about a potential date named "Pat," how many yes–no questions would you need to ask to reduce your uncertainty to a level where you would date Pat? Assume that the channel of communication to reduce your uncertainty about Pat is the Internet. One possible list might include: gender, race, religion, age, height, weight, occupation, education, hobbies, political affiliation, criminal record, marital status, and so forth. You would arrange these elements in some sequence, thereby developing a decision tree. You would then use that decision tree progressively to reduce your uncertainty about whether or not to date Pat. Electronic operators ask questions of you to reduce uncertainty when you phone the general number of a corporation or university.

Decision trees aren't limited to interpersonal conversations. Small group theorists have produced sequencing decision trees called "agenda systems." A well-known one is John Dewey's five steps of reflective thinking. It helps reduce progressively a group's uncertainty about how to reach consensus. Computerized agenda systems form the basis of Group Decision Support Systems (GDSS). Indeed, given IST's sequencing concept, it is possible to conceive of an outline developed for a multimedia presentation and a storyboard developed for a video shoot as decision trees. In both instances, they sequence and thus optimize the flow of information in the respective tasks.

Rate.   *Rate* deals with the amount of information per unit of time that can be delivered in any given communication channel. The rate is limited by channel capacity, the amount of noise in the channel, the kind of coding sets used, and the communication system's encoding and decoding capacity. You have experienced the message concept of "rate" as you used your e-mail. The faster you typed, the greater the number of errors. Nonetheless, given the redundancy of the English language, it is possible for the person receiving your e-mail message to reconstruct it in most instances. Let's say you typed the sentence: "lease arive homz for dinar bye 7 p." In all likelihood, the receiver of this message could reconstruct it, understand it, and get home on time (assuming the hour is correct). If you are talking to someone across a busy street then you intuitively know you must slow your speaking rate and repeat many phrases in order to be understood. One way of optimizing the rate of information sent per second is by the use of compressed speech. Many software programs use compressed speech. They must be decompressed before copying to your hard disc. CNN covers news around the world in thirty minutes. *USA Today,* the newspaper, regularly summarizes key stories for quick scanning. People often speak faster than receivers listen. That's why good professors build redundancy into their lectures and courses. However, the need for redundancy reduces the amount of information that can be conveyed in a class period or a semester.

Noise. Oddly enough, *noise* is a form of extraneous information that causes a loss of intended information. Cherry (1966) called noise "the destroyer of information." He noted that it "sets the ultimate upper limit to the information capacity of a channel" (p. 176). As we indicated above, the noisier the channel the slower must be the rate of communication. As well, the noisier the channel the greater the need for redundancy in the code-set. Finally, the noisier the channel, the greater the need for corrective feedback from the receiver. There are many sources of noise. Sender noise may occur when a person speaks English with an accent. Dyslexia may lead a receiver to distort messages. And, of course, all channels have a certain level of noise inherent to them. Inherent channel noise distorts messages. We've noticed, however, that today's student possesses a high tolerance for noise. We've seen our students talk on the phone, watch a TV soap opera, and listen to a CD while composing a paper on the computer. At our age, we cannot walk and chew gum at the same time, much less write this book while listening to the radio. Our old receivers exhibit a low tolerance for noise.

Redundancy. *Redundancy* is the inherent or necessary repetition of syntactic, semantic, or pragmatic information that maintains message fidelity. IST posits three kinds of redundancy. Redundancy$_1$ refers to the repetition of sequences in word and sentence formation in language. Redundancy$_2$ refers to the need to repeat code to transmit a message through a noisy channel. Redundancy$_3$ occurs with human communication and is the repetition of statements required to insure that something is understood. In order to optimize the flow of information in any channel—either human or machine—you must assess how much redundancy needs to be present. As redundancy is added, the amount of information transferable in a given period of time is reduced. In the information systems of large organizations, the quantity of distortion, deletion, and substitution leads to the repetition of the same message in different channels: memorandum, e-mail, bulletin board, face-to-face meetings, and so forth. In particular, such repetitions occur regularly whenever new information alters the way an existing system works.

Feedback. *Feedback* is corrective information from a receiver. Feedback helps stabilize and regulate information systems by providing either negative or positive responses to information. "The document is saved" is a positive response from your computer to you. As previously indicated, Norbert Wiener (1948) invented the concept of feedback. He viewed feedback as an important part of self-regulating information systems. This component of the message helps make information more accurate and provides order, structure, and control in human-made communication systems. In human communication, the ability to coordinate, give, and read nonverbal and verbal cues makes humans excellent feedback users. Nonetheless, there is a high error rate and lots of room for strategic and accidental ambiguity in the feedback messages. Learning to be an empathic listener takes training and practice in interpersonal, group, and public communication.

Dynamic Concepts   Again it's time for a rest stop. Let's reflect on where the trail to understanding communication theories next takes us. Recall that TCM posited a deep structural tension that varies with each theory. In other words, a tension exists either in the deep structure of the system the message is in or in the structure of the message itself. In the case of IST, the war that occurs deals with the nature of the three different types of information systems: linear, interactive, and transactional. This tension is so fundamental in IST that it effects directly how we define communication, how we model the communication process, and in turn how we structure the message itself.

Linear Dynamic.   A *linear information system* is a relatively closed system that is designed to send information directionally from sender to receiver with little opportunity for the receiver to provide feedback. The sender is primarily responsible for defining what constitutes information. Also, the sender intentionally structures the message sequentially knowing that there will be little opportunity for feedback correction. In other words, the message will be transmitted as a onetime serial action. Such linear communication systems require much preplanning to insure that the information is understood by the receiver. Many examples of such linear information systems exist and exhibit high utility in our society. For example, pharmaceutical companies must include a package insert called a *label*. The label describes the drug, indicates the dosage, warns against certain drug combinations, and enumerates its potential side effects. Drug companies spend millions of dollars each year conducting market research that pretests such labels. They do so to insure the information is correct, accurate, and clear. If you have ever put together an "assembly required" present while playing Santa Claus on Christmas Eve then you know how difficult it is to create clear directions on a package insert.

Advertising agencies also spend thousands of dollars pretesting their print, audio, and television ads. They do so to increase the probability that their messages will be received as intended. And, of course, we know that your last, good, public speech was marked by audience analysis and message sequencing preparation. This preplanning allowed you to present an optimized message given the requirements of time, the channel, and the audience.

Interactional Dynamic.   An *interactive information system* is still a rather closed system like the linear one. However, the interactional system does allow the receiver to communicate with the sender. Particularly, the receiver can help control the sequencing of the information. In interactive systems, the receiver can select the information he or she wants. However, the receiver can never retrieve information that is not already stored in the system. By putting this book in CD-ROM format, you could select information sequenced in different ways. You could read the text. You could listen and watch us lecture. You could play an interactive theory game. However, you could not retrieve more information than that contained in the CD-ROM. The same is true of interactive computer games. Even a public speech followed by a question-and-answer period does not allow the receiver to get more information than the speaker has prepared. The speaker's repertoire of ideas limits the amount of information. The speaker can select from the repertoire, but he or she cannot change it. The speaker can only alter the rate and redundancy of the information. Only transactional information systems create information.

Transactional Dynamic.   A *transactional information system* is one in which the sender and receiver co-create, work out, and develop information. A transactional information system is relatively open. However, it is not so open that it loses its defined boundaries. Scholars often distinguish machine-to-machine communication and human-to-machine communication from human-to-human communication. They do so through the argument that the latter type is truly transactional. When we model a transactional communication system using IST, we do not label the participants as senders and receivers or speakers and audience. Instead we talk about communicators communicating in a medium in which they are simultaneously senders, receivers, and observers. Problem-solving groups exhibit synergistic qualities. They create information by their transactions that was not present when the communication started. This type of communication system leads us to look at information as a process rather than a product. As a result, it becomes much more difficult to determine the beginning and ending of a piece of information. Fisher (1978) talked about the need to look for double and triple "interacts" as the units of communication analysis when viewing information in a transactional communication system (p. 218). Conversational analysts discuss the need to identify complex "communication episodes." Poole (1983) suggested looking at the multiple sequencing of communicated messages. Whatever the unit of analysis for coding, the discipline has been making valuable progress describing transactional information systems and predicting the type of information generated. These inroads have been made thanks to the development of coding systems that capture the semantic and pragmatic dimensions of information.

Communicator Concepts   Again, let's take a short rest stop. Recall that TCM posited that every communication theory possesses its own unique names for the communicators communicating in a medium. Thus, the communicator structure concepts of IST uniquely identify who are the communicators. Three concepts—sender, receiver, and observer—name the communicators from the perspective of IST. These concepts identify the communicators who are transferring, exchanging, creating, and evaluating information in a communication system.

Sender.   A *sender* is viewed differently given the warring information systems that comprise IST's communication dynamic. In the linear system, the $sender_1$ is simply an information source that sends coded, sequenced information via a signal down a noisy channel to a destination that retranslates the signal back into the message (Shannon, 1948a). In an interactive system, the $sender_2$ still designs, structures, and encodes the information, but the receiver interacts more actively in terms of error correction and feedback. Here, the receiver can even help design or specify the information that is received. In a transactional system the communicators act simultaneously as *sender₃*, receiver, and observer who transmit, receive, and co-create information.

Receiver.   In linear machine-to-machine and human-to-machine information systems, the *receiver* is a passive receiver and storer of information. As well, in human-to-human communication, linear models conceive of receivers—audiences, listeners, or viewers—as docile and inactive in the reception and storage of such information as advertising, news broadcasts, phone mail, newspapers, and books. For IST, this is *receiver₁*. In an interactive machine-to-human communication system the receiver has the opportunity to sequence information through requests and decision tree prompts such as a key word index in a reference search. For IST, this is *receiver₂*. Cable TV, satellite TV, and the Internet now allow receivers to "surf" and select information. Nonetheless, the creation and volume of the available information is still largely controlled by the sender. In a transactional system, the communicators become simultaneous senders, receivers, and co-creators of information. For IST, this is *receiver₃*.

Observer.   IST's third communicator concept is observer. An *observer* is a detached monitor interested in improving the accuracy and flow of information within the communication system. In highly closed, machine-to-machine communication systems, the observer provides correction messages to overcome errors in the transmission. Here, the observer itself is often a machine. For IST, this is *observer₁*. In human-to-machine communication, a correcting device provides error messages about inaccurate data entry and prompts regarding requests for information. For example, the observer built into the computer even helps us log on correctly so that we can use a system. As Shannon (1948a) stated, in a communication system there is "an observer (or auxiliary device) who can both see what is sent and what is recovered (with errors due to noise). This observer notes the errors in the recovered message and transmits data to the receiving point over a 'correction channel' to enable the receiver to correct the errors" (p. 408). For IST, this is *observer₂*. In an interactional system, the observer is frequently a human who monitors your use of machine-to-human communication. For example, with some positions in the modern organization, such as an insurance company, this person may point out that most of your time on the system involved the playing of computer games. Such an observer₂ may also tell you your e-mail is unopened and your error rate for processing insurance applications is 30 percent higher than the average underwriter. In a truly transactional information system, the observer functions as a referee, coach, mediator, or facilitator. For example, a group facilitator may work with a transactional decision-making group involved in long-range planning for a corporation (Frey, 1995). In interpersonal communication, the observer may be a marriage counselor or a labor negotiation mediator. In a large organization, the observer may be a market researcher or communication consultant. For IST, this is *observer₃*. As well, in a transactional system a person or a machine may function simultaneously as a sender, receiver, or observer.

Medium Concepts   You're probably becoming familiar with the pace along the trail to understanding communication theories. Yes, it's time for another rest stop. Recall that TCM stressed three senses of medium. Medium₁ is the sense of a general theory functioning in the six traditional contexts of interpersonal, small group, public, organizational, mass, and intercultural communication. Medium₂ is the sense of a substance in which a theory propagates, prospers, and grows. Medium₃ is the sense of communication traveling by way of a channel. For example, communication is transmitted or carried by words on the printed page, light waves, sound waves, or electrical waves. Of all the communication theories presented in this book, IST most heavily emphasizes all three senses of medium.

Medium₁.   IST is unique among our core general theories in that its developers have generated unique forms of IST applicable in each of the six contexts. This morphing is much like light passing through a prism and breaking into the color spectrum. Nearly every public speaking textbook discusses speaker, message, channel, receiver, noise, and feedback as the organizing concepts of the communication process. When such texts describe how to inform the public, the advice mirrors IST in both its linear and interactive modes. In the interpersonal context, Berger and Calabrese (1975) created an exact analogue of IST that they call Uncertainty Reduction Theory (see Chapter 5). An example of the application of IST to small group decision-making is provided by Fisher and Ellis (1990). Organizational communication textbooks nearly uniformly define organizational communication as an information-sharing system.[4] Schramm (1954) adapted IST to explicate the process of human communication, emphasizing the channel of the mass media. Berlo (1960) adapted Shannon's theory by offering a *source–message–channel–receiver* model of public speaking. Berlo's SMCR Model fleshed out the characteristics of each concept in human terms. Brissey (1961) and Goetzinger and Valentine (1962) conducted early studies grounding IST's concepts to observables. Soon, scholars applied IST to the areas of interpersonal, small group, organizational, and intercultural communication. Ayres et al. (1973), Berger and Calabrese (1975), and Salem and Williams (1984) applied IST to interpersonal communication. Fisher and Hawes (1971) and Fisher, Drecksel, and Werbel (1978) applied IST to group communication. Bormann, et al. (1969), Davis and O'Connor (1977), and Weick (1979) applied IST to organizational communication. In the mass communication context, Watt and Krull (1974) developed an information theory measure for television programming and Basil (1994) applied IST to television viewing. Hansen and Hansen (1991) applied IST to heavy metal lyrics. Gudykunst (1985) applied IST's derivative theory, Uncertainty Reduction Theory, to intercultural communication. IST, as used in mass communication, is also called *agenda-setting* and *gatekeeping* (DeFleur & Ball–Rokeach, 1989). In the context of intercultural communication, Gudykunst (1988) adapted Uncertainty Reduction Theory (presented in Chapter 5), itself an IST derivative theory, to explain the force of social information-sharing in cross-cultural communication. We discuss these theories in detail in later chapters.

Medium₂.   Just as corn grows in the medium of soil and germs grow in cultures, information only truly grows in an open system. A communication system can only slow entropy by exchanging information. It does so through its permeable boundaries and by the interactions and transactions of its transceivers (senders and receivers). However, information systems exhibit characteristics similar to those of a pack mule. They can be overloaded with too much information. You know that you can consume more food and liquids than your body can safely process. Truly open information systems act in the same way. The more open they are the greater their vulnerability to information overload. The problem is that in highly open information systems, transceivers cannot encode and decode the available information fast enough. Therefore, information systems must restrict the flow of information.

Shannon (1948a) identified three senses of medium as propagation: closed, open, and mixed communication systems. Intriguingly, information needs to be optimized in each. His mathematical theory of communication explained how to transfer syntactical information through the medium of a closed, noisy channel. However, at the semantic and pragmatic levels, in mixed to open communication systems, information can take on a life of its own.

Medium$_3$.   From the inception of Shannon's theory, theorists recognized that all channels exhibit a capacity. In a given amount of time, a channel can only carry so much information. As well, theorists noted that the flow of information within any given channel must be optimized. However, because information systems tend toward chaos, channels seem to be overloaded constantly. Indeed, the hallmark of the twentieth century may well be the increasing channel capacity of various communication systems. We've gone from twisted pair, 2X, copper telephone lines with a channel capacity of 19.2 kilobits per second to OC-48 fiber cables with a channel capacity of 2.4 billion gigabits per second. Nonetheless, the students at our respective universities still have trouble getting time on the Internet because of end-of-semester, worldwide traffic jams.

Human transceivers are natural born simulcastors and simulreceivers. We try to encode and decode the same message in two different channels, sound waves and light waves. Indeed, if we broadly construe our conception of communication, we simulcast in five channels corresponding to the five senses: touch, see, hear, smell, and taste. To make matters worse, as transceivers in an intentional communication system, we can send mixed messages. For example, we can send one message using a verbal code and a contradictory message using one (or more) nonverbal code(s). Shannon (1948a, 1948b) would remind us that each channel has its own capacity and transmission rate. Again, of all the communication theories presented in this book, the medium$_3$ view of channel is most important to IST, although Media Law Theory (presented in Chapter 11) rivals it.

Using Evaluative Concepts

During this rest stop, let's return again to TCM. Recall that a theory's evaluative concepts let you make assessments and judgments regarding the quality and outcomes of communicators communicating in a medium. Also recall from Chapter 1 that all scientists are concerned with explaining the outcomes of the fundamental interactive forces that they study. The botanist is interested in the interaction effects of bees pollinating flowers. They predict that a significant loss of the bee population would have catastrophic effects on the pollination system. With IST we evaluate the quality and outcomes of information flowing within human organizations. The variations in closed, open, and mixed information systems require the use of IST's evaluative concepts. The control of quality information in modern organizations is always a top priority.

Quality and Outcomes   By *outcomes* we mean that the communicative interaction identified by the theory did in fact occur. The question to ask is did the communicative force under observation have its predicted impact on human action? In IST's case, was clear, optimized information shared that reduced uncertainty and created order and structure in the social system? *Quality* refers to IST's evaluative concepts that denote the degree or grade of excellence of the communication within the system. IST's primary evaluative concepts are fidelity, capacity, and uncertainty reduction.

Fidelity.   *Fidelity* is the degree to which an information system optimally reproduces the essential characteristics of its information without distortion, deletion, substitution, or addition. At the syntactic level of meaning in machine communication, fidelity is strictly an electrical engineering problem. Shannon worked it out in 1948 by mathematically optimizing the amount of information sent at a distance over time with high fidelity. In human-to-machine communication, at the semantic level, the structuring of high-fidelity information is assessed through a stochastic process of the yes–no decision tree, as in doing a reference search on the Internet. In human-to-human communication it is much more difficult to create high-fidelity messages. In the medium$_3$ of transmitted e-mail or voice mail, you must analyze what information needs to be included in your message and how to optimize it so that the receiver will have the information they need, but no more. In organizations, in which information often tends to be transmitted serially across, down, or up the chain of command, distortions, deletions, substitutions, and additions—at the syntactic, semantic, and pragmatic levels of meaning—often occur. The idea of ambiguous information, created for strategic reasons, also complicates the assessment of fidelity.

Capacity.   *Capacity* concerns the amount of information that transceivers can send, receive, and store, as well as the amount of information that a given channel can handle. The children's rhyme, "There was an old woman who lived in a shoe; she had so many children she didn't know what to do," gets at this notion of capacity, information overload, and optimized information. Any communication context exhibits an inherent capacity for information-sharing that potentially can be overloaded. A simple business meeting illustrates the point. In a one-hour meeting of fifteen people, how much information can be shared? The meeting agenda attempts to answer this question by stipulating blocks of information (topics) to be covered. Moreover, the agenda sequences the order in which the topics will be covered. However, each agenda item can be linear, interactional, or transactional. If one item is a "tell" issue such as "Cars cannot be parked in Lot C because of repaving," then it can be handled rather quickly. Nonetheless, if there is channel redundancy, with slides of alternate parking locations and maps of temporary traffic flow requirements, that agenda point would obviously take more time. As well, questions about the short-term parking problem in an interactive situation would then add more time. Finally, a transactional communication system, in which the meeting participants would help find locations for alternative parking, would add even more information and take up more time. Our point is that there is an inherent limit on capacity for every context in which communicators are communicating in some medium.

Uncertainty Reduction.   *Uncertainty reduction* is the optimized sharing of information at the syntactic, semantic, and pragmatic levels. The concept is sometimes studied under the label *information adequacy*.[5] At the syntactic level in machine-to-machine communication,

Shannon used a stochastic method to provide an operational definition of the process of uncertainty reduction in the transmission of information from a sender to a receiver. Almost all human-to-machine communication produces a decision tree for interaction that is stochastic in form. For example, let's think about planning your career with an interactive software program. It would guide you using a series of prompts that called for your yes–no responses. Where you go next would be based on your previous choice. In human-to-human communication, at the semantic and pragmatic level of meaning, researchers and theorists have developed a number of coding systems that classify and track bits of information over time. These help assess the degree of uncertainty reduction in a communication transaction. However, as Ritchie (1991) indicated, in human-to-human communication systems, Shannon's operational definition of uncertainty reduction might not be the only or even the best way to describe this process. As we shall see later in this chapter, a number of stagic models exist that explain uncertainty reduction in human communication. Many of these models show even more dramatically than Shannon's formula that an inverse curvilinear relationship exists between increases in information and uncertainty reduction.

[handwritten margin note: "Newer, better theories exist re: uncertainty reduction"]

IST: Working with Its Qualitative Method

Using IST to study communicators communicating in a medium requires several things. At the outset, it requires an operational definition of what constitutes information. Then, it requires a coding system. The coding system enables you to observe, track, and study the flow of information over time. Shannon operationally defined information as a single character of the alphabet. He coded each character using binary digits. However, coding at the semantic and pragmatic level of meaning requires larger chunks of the material facts that we call information. Communication scholars now code information in various ways. These include the units you know as words, themes, phrases, sentences, and paragraphs. They even code whole communication episodes in which several people's contributions to the transaction make up the bit of information.

[handwritten margin note: "increasing complexity of functionality of coding"]

Information Flow Analysis (IFA)

Let's stop and emphasize a point of interest. TCM posited that every theory possesses a unique qualitative method as part of its theory–method complex. IST's qualitative method is Information Flow Analysis (IFA). Unlike the other general theories presented in this book, IST's users adapted IFA uniquely to each of the six traditional communication contexts. Nevertheless, each adaptation contains the three basic elements of IFA: coding, tracking, and modeling.

Coding   Regardless of where the information flow occurs, you must determine the types of information you hope to code. Also, you must identify the communication system you plan to examine. As well, the chosen (or developed) coding system should account for the syntactic, semantic, and pragmatic levels of meaning. If it does not then you cannot track the flow of information at that level. Similarly, the type of communication system will determine the size (small or large) of the selected information bit. **Table 2-1** illustrates a coding system for conversations.

TABLE 2-1. Illustrative Coding System for Conversations (Transcription Conventions)

Symbol	Name	Function
1. [ ]	Brackets	Indicate beginnings and endings of overlapping utterances.
2. =	Equal Signs	Latching of contiguous utterances, with no interval or overlap.
3. (1.2)	Timed Pause	Intervals occurring within and between same or different speaker's utterance, in tenths of a second.
4. (.)	Micropause	Brief pause of less than (.2).
5. :::	Colon(s)	Prior sound, syllable, or word is prolonged or stretched. More colons indicate greater prolongation.
6. .	Period	Falling vocal pitch or intonation. Punctuation marks do *not* indicate grammatical status (e.g., end of sentence or question).
7. ?	Question Mark	Rising vocal pitch or intonation.
8. ,	Comma	A continuing intonation, with a slight upward or downward contour.
9. ↑↓	Arrows	Marked rising and falling shifts in intonation.
10. °°	Degree Signs	A passage of talk noticeably softer than surrounding utterances.
11. !	Exclamation	Animated speech tone.
12. -	Hyphen	Halting, abrupt cut off of sound, syllable, or word.
13. *cold* or _____	Italics	Vocalic stress or emphasis.
14. OKAY	CAPS	Extreme loudness compared with surrounding talk.
15. > <	Greater than/ Less than Signs	Portions of an utterance delivered at a noticeably quicker (> <) or slower (< >) pace.
16. hhh	H's hhh ye(hh)s	Audible outbreaths, possibly laughter. The more h's, the longer the aspiration. Aspirations with a superscripted period indicate audible inbreaths. H's within parentheses mark within-speech aspirations, possibly laughter.
17. ((noise))	Scenic Details	Transcriber's comments (e.g., gestures, nonspeech sounds).
18. ( )	Parentheses	Transcriber is in doubt as to word, syllable, or sound. Empty parentheses indicate indecipherable passage.
19. pt	Lip Smack	Often preceding an inbreath.
20. hah heh hoh	Laugh Syllable	Relative closed or open position of laughter.
21. $	Smile Voice	Laughing talk between markers.

Adapted and reprinted with permission of *Western Journal of Speech Communication* from Beach (1989, *53*, 89–90).

Tracking Tracking the flow of information in a communication system may be carried out in real time or after the fact (post hoc). Real-time tracking involves direct observation or retrieval by recording or videotaping. Whatever the case, you must code the information. Conversational analysts often code using a system developed by Gail Jefferson. Her coding system permits the coding of both semantic and pragmatic information (Atkinson & Heritage, 1984, pp. ix–xvi; Beach, 1989; Jefferson, 1978, 1991, 1996). Others, like Rogers and Farace (1975) developed a coding system designed to emphasize the pragmatic dimension of language as described by Ruesch and Bateson (1951) and Watzlawick, Beavin, and Jackson (1967). Fisher (1974) reported a coding system that allowed the tracking of thirteen different types of semantic information as it occurred over time in decision-making groups. Such coding systems enable the description of the phases or stages of development of communication over time. For example, Fisher's (1974) tracking study allowed him to describe the four phases that problem-solving groups follow: orientation, conflict, emergence, and reinforcement.

Post hoc tracking is done primarily through the use of account analysis, recall, and diaries. Flanagan's (1954) Critical Incident Technique (CIT) is an example of a coding method used to collect and classify *re*-remembered communication events. A respondent is simply asked to recall some important event such as, "when I was jealous" or "when my supervisor thought well of me." Responses (accounts) can then be coded into categories and used to analyze the patterns of the flow of information in a given communication setting, context, or system. Diaries are another form of self-reporting. They allow us to trace the flow of information in a communication episode. For example, Nielson uses the diary or log technique to determine the viewership of television programs during ratings weeks.

Modeling   As we saw in Chapter 1, communication scholars typically work with two kinds of models. At times, they work with models of the theoretical concepts of specific theories. At other times, they work with models of the process of communication in particular communication systems as seen through the lens of a specific communication theory. **Figure 2-2** is an example of the first type of model. It shows the relationship between the concepts of IST. Here, we want to discuss the second kind of model. **Figure 2-3** contains two of the models of communication systems that Shannon presented, one linear and one interactive. He did not present a model of his mathematical theory of communication.

At present, no single model of information processing exists that can *re*-represent the communication process in all settings, contexts, or systems. That's the main reason IST, like light through a prism, breaks into different colors (idiosyncratic coding systems) for different communication systems. As well, each new communication system often leads to a different model. In the body of literature called *communication studies,* hundreds of models of various communication systems exist.

Briefly Illustrating IFA

Frankel (1989) reported a classic IST study. His research problem concerned information flow in a midwestern poison control center. The center received roughly 60,000 emergency phone calls each year. Frankel's problem was Shannon's problem, only at the semantic and pragmatic level. Namely, Frankel wanted to optimize the transfer of information in a noisy, interactive system. The poison center's medical operators needed to reduce uncertainty by eliciting two kinds of information. They needed clinical information so that a diagnostic solution could be offered. Then they needed bureaucratic information called a case history. Both types of information allowed the operators to complete the center's incident report. Of course, the information needed to be accurate. Frankel used the coding system contained in **Table 2-1.** He coded the real-time audio and video transcriptions of the phone calls and the operator's completion of the incident report form.

Frankel found that the documentation required to complete the incident report created overload. The length of the incident report consumed up to 50 percent of the conversation

Shannon's FIG. 1: Schematic diagram of a general communication system
(Shannon and Weaver, 1949, p. 5)

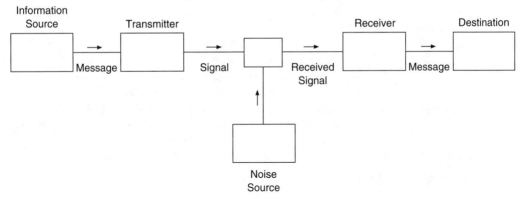

Shannon's FIG. 8: Schematic diagram of a correction system
(Shannon and Weaver, 1949, p. 37)

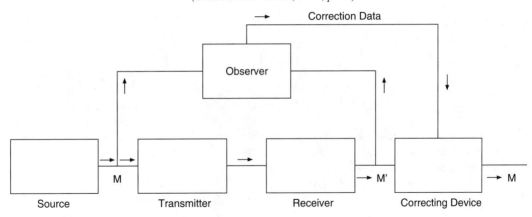

Key: M = Message; M' = Distorted Message

FIGURE 2-3.   Two of Shannon's Models of Communication Systems

From *The Mathematical Theory of Communication* by Claude E. Shannon and Warren Weaver. © 1949 by the Board of Trustees of the University of Illinois. Used with the permission of the University of Illinois Press. These figures also appear in the *Bell System Technical Journal,* 1948, Vol. 27, 379–423, at pages 381 and 409, respectively.

time. As well, completion required an additional fifteen minutes of operator time after the call. Just the post-call reporting meant that each operator was unavailable about seventy-five minutes per eight-hour shift. In turn, this meant that the average emergency caller waited in a phone-holding queue for an average of ninety seconds. Such a wait can be truly traumatic if your child is convulsing. Frankel revised the form into an optimal pattern or sequence for eliciting information. Then he trained operators to receive both types of information efficiently.

IST: Observing its Usefulness

We've now reached our final rest stop on this part of the trail to understanding communication theories. Recall that TCM posited utility as its primary evaluative metaconcept. It's again time to think of our test question, "Will this dog hunt?" As we indicated in the earlier discussion of IST's power and scope, the theory explains the distinct strains of machine-to-machine, human-to-machine, and human-to-human communication. We then noted that linear, interactive, and transactional communication systems use information at respectively the syntactic, semantic, and pragmatic levels of meaning. IST's impact is demonstrated by the marvelous information systems we see and use every day. Now, we will present several examples illustrating IST's use to explain human action and solve real-world problems.

Explaining Human Action

Let's continue our rest stop. Recall that a communication theory validly explains human action when its concepts have been tied to or grounded in directly observable phenomena. A researcher usually grounds a theory's concepts by analyzing communication episodes to determine if the phenomena the concepts represent appear in the communication. The grounding of IST began almost immediately on the release of Shannon's treatises (1948a, 1948b). For a time, it served as the dominant theory for interpreting communication data. For example, Schramm (1954) adapted IST to explicate the process of human communication emphasizing the channel of the mass media. Berlo (1960) adapted Shannon's theory by offering a *source–message–channel–receiver* model of public speaking. Berlo's SMCR Model fleshed out the characteristics of each concept in human terms. Brissey (1961) and Goetzinger and Valentine (1962) conducted early studies grounding IST's concepts to observables. Soon, scholars applied IST to the areas of interpersonal, small group, public speaking, organizational, and intercultural communication.

Ayres, et al. (1973), Berger and Calabrese (1975), and Salem and Williams (1984) applied IST to interpersonal communication. From this effort grew Uncertainty Reduction Theory, which we will visit in Chapter 5. Also, a derivative line of research in the interpersonal context focused on an IST evaluative subconcept called "perceived understanding."[6] This research program examined the role of the perceived understanding of information in relational development, maintenance, and de-escalation. One outcome of the research established several semantic and pragmatic communicative behaviors as essential to instilling perceived understanding in another. These included appearing at ease, helpful, and smiling; being cooperative, patient, and modest; offering emotional support; showing respect, and sounding relaxed and reassuring (Cahn & Frey, 1990). Fisher and Hawes (1971) and Fisher, Drecksel, and Werbel (1978) applied IST to group communication. In Chapter 8, we'll visit an IST derivative theory applied to the small group context called Decision Emergence Theory.

Timmis (1985) applied IST to evaluate the stylistic elements of public speakers by way of auditor responses. Bormann, et al. (1969), Davis and O'Connor (1977), and Weick (1979) applied IST to organizational communication. We'll visit Weick's Organizing Theory in Chapter 10. IST explains the communicative force of information-sharing that creates order, structure, and control for coordinated human action. In the arena of organizational communication, O'Reilly and Anderson (1980) found that information in the form of supervisor feedback during performance reviews increased an employee's trust in a supervisor. In a related fashion, ICA audit data analyzed by Spiker and Daniels (1981) and Daniels and Spiker (1983) indicated a positive relationship between information adequacy to reduce uncertainty and job relationship satisfaction with co-workers, supervisors, and top management. Likewise, Kogler–Hill, Bahniuk, and Dobos (1989) found that sending and receiving "adequate information contributed to the prediction of [the] academic success" of faculty (p. 30).

Explaining the force of information-sharing using IST involves a three-step process. First, a researcher must code the information. Then, the researcher must chart the flow of information through a communication system. Finally, the researcher must evaluate that information flow so that it may be altered if necessary. For example, Kurke, Weick, and Ravlin (1989) examined the problem of information loss during serial transmissions in organizations. They found that serial reconstruction techniques helped minimize information loss in such systems. Similarly, Frandsen and Millis (1993) reviewed the functioning of feedback-processing mechanisms to improve information flow in complex systems. Such problems abound in every organization. IST is the theory of choice for solving them.

In the mass communication context, Watt and Krull (1974) developed an information theory measure for television programming. Basil (1994) applied IST to television viewing. Hansen and Hansen (1991) applied IST to heavy metal lyrics. Gudykunst (1985) applied IST's derivative theory, Uncertainty Reduction Theory, to intercultural communication. We'll visit Gudykunst's Anxiety/Uncertainty Management Theory in Chapter 10.

Benefiting the Real World

Gerald Miller and his associates at Michigan State University conducted a four-year National Science Foundation study of the use of videotaped testimony in legal proceedings. They used IST to guide their research. They found that jurors retained more of the central trial-related information when they watched videotaped rather than live testimony.[7]

In the 1970s, communication scholars belonging to the International Communication Association (ICA) developed and standardized a coding system for tracking and describing the flow of information in an organization. Brooks, Callicoat, & Siegerdt (1979) and Goldhaber and Krivonos (1977) reported that the ICA Communication Audit took a picture of eight key communication variables: (1) amount of information needed; (2) actions taken on information received; (3) timeliness, accuracy, and usefulness of information; (4) sources of information; (5) channels for sending and receiving information; (6) quality of communication relationships; (7) formal and informal communication networks; and (8) outcomes of communication, including organizational effectiveness and individual satisfaction.

Between 1971 and 1974 the ICA auditors studied sixteen different organizations. The organizations indicated that the audit improved the effectiveness of organizational communication and information flow. The audit served as the basis for redesigning these organizations' information systems. Redesigning helped eliminate overload and increased the efficiency of information flow within and between organizational departments (Brooks, Callicoat, & Siegerdt, 1979; Goldhaber & Rogers, 1979). Bahniuk, Kogler Hill, and Darus (1966) reported an ICA-type audit of 418 organizational workers to measure information adequacy. They found that information adequacy related to power and network (mentoring) connections in organizations. They concluded "that information power-gaining adds substantially to career success" and the finding "supports the contention that employees who understand how to manage uncertainty in an organization gain more personal power and career success" (pp. 374–375).

Vivian Sheer and Rebecca Cline (1995) used IST to study the physician–patient interview system in the cardiac ward of a hospital. Among patients, they found three important types of information uncertainty in the preinterview condition: illness uncertainty, medical setting uncertainty, and physician relational uncertainty. Their postoperation analysis of these cardiac patients supported their prediction. They found that information adequacy is a valid predictor of uncertainty reduction. They provided a number of practical suggestions regarding how a physician could reduce such uncertainties. The means concerned insuring information adequacy at the semantic and pragmatic levels of meaning.

Withstanding the Critics

IST has served the discipline well (Broadhurst & Darnell, 1965; Conant, 1979; Ritchie, 1986, 1991). However, many writers of contemporary communication textbooks reify and echo a set of stock criticisms of IST (Griffin, 1994, 1996; Littlejohn, 1996; Mortensen, 1972; Trenholm, 1991). Their criticisms anchor the distortion of one of the most important communication theories of the twentieth century. The major stock criticisms are: (1) IST is not a general communication theory; (2) IST is only a linear theory; and (3) IST uses an inappropriate mechanistic metaphor.

IST Is Not a General Communication Theory   Critics usually support this criticism by claiming that Shannon's mathematical theory does not deal with meaning and only applies at the syntactic level of information transmission. In addition, the criticism posits that Shannon only viewed information as the transmission of Markov-like yes–no decisions. Furthermore, he did not operationalize a definition of information that would include the use of all information by either machines or humans. In other words, Shannon missed the semantic and pragmatic levels of information.

Such criticisms are much like disparaging a hog for not being a horse: "You can't ride it and it won't go fast." It's true that Shannon's mathematical theory provides proofs of channel capacity at the syntactic level. It's also true that Shannon defined a bit of information as a 50 percent reduction in uncertainty. However, Shannon is not the only information systems theorist contributing to the development of IST. As we stated earlier in the chapter, others have routinely operationalized the semantic and pragmatic levels of information mathematically.[8] As well, Broadhurst and Darnell (1965) and Ritchie (1991) noted that Shannon's real insight concerned optimizing information. They went on to indicate that we need not be bound to Shannon's operational definition for transferring information in one type of closed communication system when viewing other open communication systems at the semantic and pragmatic levels.

IST Is Only a Linear Theory   This criticism is made possible by communication textbook writers who reprint only *one* of the models in Shannon's (1948a, 1948b) articles.[9] The criticism is that the model is linear with no feedback from the receiver. In addition, critics portray the receiver as only a catcher of the message who can never interact with the pitcher. As we indicated earlier in the chapter, this linear model is not a model of Shannon's mathematical theory. It is a model of a phone system. Finally, in Shannon's original article he presented another model of a communication system that included his concept of *observer* functioning in his syntactical theory as a continuous feedback component (see **Figure 2-3**). To us, it appears as unfair for communication scholars to accuse a Ph.D. in electrical engineering from MIT, whose major professor was Norbert Wiener—the developer of continuous feedback devices for electrical systems—of forgetting to include the concept of feedback in his theory and model of the system he was theorizing about. Of course, as we indicated earlier in the chapter, some machine and some human communication systems do reflect the linear transfer of information (fax machines, advertising, and pharmaceutical product labels). IST does explain information flow in linear communication systems. However, it also explains information flow in interactional and transactional communication systems.

IST Uses an Inappropriate Mechanistic Metaphor   This criticism exhibits two parts. The first is that mechanistic means linear, serial, sequenced, and cause-to-effect thinking. As we saw, there is an intrinsic war in the communication dynamic of IST about the action–interaction–transaction elements of the theory. With the mechanistic criticism, the critics merely reflect their view that the transactional position is correct. Yet, we know that some communication systems are linear. Moreover, we know that IST does not treat all communication systems as linear. So, the criticism misses the mark. The second criticism is aesthetic in nature. It objects to the use of such physical science terms as *source, transmitter, channel, receiver,* and *feedback* to describe human communication (Fisher, 1978; Trenholm, 1991). This criticism further states that the mechanistic metaphor obscures important aspects of human communication that occur at the pragmatic level (Ritchie, 1991). There is no denying that humans exhibit an emotional response to machines. Some of us fear computers. Others among us love our cars. Still others are beguiled by any electronic or mechanical contraption. Nonetheless, a rose by any other name is still a rose. It's OK to rename feedback using the term "empathic listening" just so long as we keep IST's technical and operational definitions for the phenomena described. Regardless of their feelings about the use of a mechanistic metaphor, scholars routinely code, track, and model the use and flow of information in human communication systems at the semantic and pragmatic levels. For example, conversational analysts code, with machinelike precision, the most emotional exchanges of interpersonal intimacies in dyadic dialogues. They use IST to do so. cause–effect

As you can see, IST's critics have missed the mark. Study after study demonstrated that IST is a useful theory that explains the force of information-sharing on creating order, structure, and control for coordinated human action. With both the criticisms and responses at hand, we leave it to you to make an informed judgment about whether or not IST withstands the critics. We believe it does, as all viable core general communication theories must. When you get to the end of the trail to understanding communication theories, we believe you can use IST with confidence. We wish you happy hunting.

Summary

In this chapter, we introduced you to Information Systems Theory (IST). IST allows you to explain the communicative force of information-sharing on human action. We began by viewing IST as a general communication theory capable of being understood through the lens of

TCM. We sketched IST's power and scope, traced its origin and roots, and discussed its primary assumptive system. Then, we introduced IST's theoretical concepts (see **Figure 2-2**). We looked at its basic concepts, structural concepts, and evaluative concepts. Next, we introduced and illustrated how to work with IST's qualitative method, Information Flow Analysis (IFA). Then we reported on IST's usefulness. We showed IST's use to explain human action and benefit the real world. Then, we discussed its ability to withstand critical scrutiny.

By now, you should be familiar with IST. Corey is now a communication graduate on-the-job. Corey's Chapter 1 job interview got high marks. In **Figure 2-4,** Corey is using IST to good advantage. If you do not yet feel comfortable with IST, we suggest you review the detailed chapter summary contained in **Box 2-1,** "Understanding IST in a Nutshell."

"This is the Information Age and Information Systems Theory (IST) guides the optimizing of information. We owe a debt of gratitude to the pioneering spirit of Claude Shannon. His work made our new communication audit software possible."

FIGURE 2-4.   Communication Graduate On-the-Job

BOX 2-1 Understanding IST in a Nutshell

IST Defined: The Information Systems Theory is a general communication theory that explains how information may be optimized in an open, closed, or mixed communication system to create order, structure, and control.

Origins: IST concerns three distinct strands of communication systems: Machine-to-machine systems, human-to-human, and machine-to-human systems. IST began with the need to solve certain communication problems with the outbreak of World War II. Norbert Wiener and Claude Shannon of MIT followed Bertalanffy's system thinking to create a cybernetic feedback theory and a mathematical theory of communication. Wilbur Schramm, of the University of Illinois, introduced their work to departments of communication in the early 1950s.

Assumptions: (1) Human beings are information-sharers; (2) The amount of information in a message is proportional to the amount of uncertainty in a communication event; (3) Error-free information-sharing is impossible; (4) Information systems tend toward chaos; and (5) Optimized information creates order, structure, and control in a system.

Basic Concepts: *Information* is the basic unit of analysis for IST. Information is data, knowledge, or opinion that reduces the uncertainty of at least one of the participants in a communication episode. Information may be a character of the alphabet, a sentence, a paragraph, an idea, a picture, a nonverbal cue, a communication episode, or even a report or a book. IST's associative basic concepts are the syntactic, semantic, and pragmatic levels of information. *Syntactic information* deals with the identification of the universe of symbols that comprise the elements of a given grammar plus the rules for constructing proper statements. *Semantic information* refers to the meaning of words and their comprehension in sentence form. *Pragmatic information* concerns the relationship dimension of messages and connotes the degree of connection and affinity between transceivers.

Structural Concepts: IST possesses message, dynamic, communicator, and medium structural concepts. The message structure concepts are code-set, sequence, rate, noise, redundancy, and feedback. A *code-set* is a discrete set of symbols that the transceivers and observers know how to encode and decode. Information is *sequenced* or structured to optimize the amount of information that can travel given the capacities of channel and transceivers. *Rate* deals with the amount of information that can be delivered per unit of time in any given communication channel. *Noise* is a form of extraneous information that causes a loss of the intended information. *Redundancy* is the inherent or necessary repetition of syntactic, semantic, or pragmatic information that maintains message fidelity. *Feedback* helps stabilize and regulate information systems by providing either negative or positive responses to information. The dynamic structure concepts of IST are linear, interactive, and transactional systems. A *linear information system* is a relatively closed system that is designed to send information from sender to receiver with little opportunity for feedback. An *interactive information system* is still a rather closed system that allows the receiver to send both positive and negative feedback or in some cases directly sequence the information of the sender. A *transactional information system* is relatively open. Its transceivers (and sometimes observers) transmit, exchange, and co-create information. The communicator structure concepts are sender, receiver, and observer. In both linear and interactive information systems, the communicators are designated as senders who initiate information transfer, receivers who get information, and observers who evaluate the quality of the information and transmit new messages to correct it. In transactional systems all communicators are transceivers, that is, simultaneously senders, receivers, and observers. The medium concepts in which information propagates are closed, open, and mixed communication systems, but only in an open system does information-sharing lead to the generation of new information.

Continued

BOX 2-1   *Continued*

Evaluative Concepts: IST's main evaluative concepts are fidelity, capacity, and uncertainty reduction. *Fidelity* is the degree to which an information system optimally reproduces the essential characteristics of its information without distortion, addition, deletion, or substitution. *Capacity* is the maximum amount of information that transceivers and channels can encode, transmit, receive, and store. *Uncertainty reduction* is the optimized sharing of information at the syntactic, semantic, and pragmatic levels.

Chapter 3

Rational Argument Theory (RAT)

The force of rational argument justifies conviction and spurs human decision-making.

Chapter Outline

Rational Argumentation Theory (RAT) is our second landmark along the trail to understanding communication theory. You should be familiar with it. You have received informal training in RAT since childhood. RAT permeates Western thought and the American educational system. If you debated in high school or college, or studied philosophy, you have received formal training in this theory. As a college graduate entering the workplace, your employer will expect you to know RAT. Our society follows RAT in report-writing, business presentations, or participation in problem-solving teams.

RAT explains the communicative force behind rational decision-making. We begin by viewing RAT as a general communication theory. We sketch its power and scope, trace its origin and roots, and discuss its primary assumptive system. Then we introduce RAT's theoretical concepts. We explain how to find its basic concepts, see its structural concepts, and use its evaluative concepts. Next we report on RAT's usefulness. We show RAT's use to explain human action and benefit the real world, and discuss its ability to withstand critical scrutiny. Finally, we present a Chapter Summary, and review, "Understanding RAT in a Nutshell."

RAT: Viewing the General Communication Theory

RAT belongs within the rational paradigm of communication theories. RAT assumes a material reality that works in consistent, ordered ways and that you can know that reality through reasoned analysis. RAT views rational argument as a force that justifies conviction and spurs people to action as we make decisions. With RAT, the communicative force flows from communicators (arguers) communicating (arguing) by presenting messages (arguments) propagated through a medium (argument field).

Sketching Its Power and Scope

RAT is a general communication theory. It explains the rational bases for human decision-making. RAT views arguers as risking their convictions as they make reasoned arguments to each other. The risk comes from having to modify your convictions as you hear superior arguments. RAT presupposes that in the competition of rational arguments the fit arguments will survive. In other words, the constant comparison and contrast of arguments within the marketplace of ideas will sort out quality arguments.

RAT recognizes some forms of argument as unique to some communities. Nonetheless, it presupposes a minimum rationality acceptable across the myriad of communication contexts. Core to our ideal of a democracy is the notion that the liberally educated person communicates (argues) rationally and evaluates issues critically. RAT explains these processes. For example, RAT explains the conviction that arises when an attorney makes a case, a senator makes a speech, or a professor presents a lecture.

The ability to use RAT is one of the hallmarks of an educated person. When employers advertise an opening for a person with "communication skills," they typically mean that they want someone who can analyze a situation, find the problem, and solve it. As well, they want someone who can create messages steeped in rational argument. RAT is the dominant theory in argumentation and debate classes. It is a mainstay theory that explains decision-making in group discussion and small group communication classes. You may be familiar with RAT from those classes.

RAT possesses great power and scope. It explains the communication of liberally educated citizens making decisions in a democratic society. However, this theory exhibits a problem similar to that of quantum physics. Classical (Newtonian) physicists viewed matter and energy as operating rationally. Following Newton, classical physicists held that the laws of motion and thermodynamics could and would be discovered. Many were discovered. Yet, anomalies arose. For example, physicists learned that the speed of light is a constant. Einstein found that mass equals energy. Others began observing the subatomic world of photons, leptons, and quarks. They found that the latter entities did not appear to behave in a rational way (Stehle, 1994). Another way of saying this is that the motion of the subatomic entities could not be explained by invariant laws (mathematical functions). The subatomic world could only be explained by the use of rules and recipes (statistical probability).

In a similar fashion, communication scientists began noticing that some people in some contexts and in some societies appeared to act like quarks, leptons, and photons. In other words, some people did not act entirely rationally. For example, in the mid-1990s, David Koresh's Branch Davidians of Waco, Texas appeared as such a community. The Branch Davidians appeared to shun society, live communally, and practice a unique brand of religion, mingling the spiritual with the worldly. As well, other communication scientists discovered that some rational arguments exhibited a characteristic called field-dependency. Field-dependency means that some arguments are valid to some people, or in some domains, but not to other people or in other domains. In other words, some communities accept some arguments as valid that other communities do not. Thus, although such a community's communication remains rational in a broad sense of the term, the members of some communities of arguers exhibit unique rules and recipes regarding what constitutes evidence and reason for conviction. A quick way to understand field-dependency is to recall that hearsay evidence is not allowed in a court of law, but then note that it is used all the time in ordinary society. In other words, although past examples of criminal behavior are usually disallowed in court, such data would constitute valid rational evidence for deciding not to hire a baby-sitter. Similarly, your friends might find it peculiar if you based your actions today on what you dreamed last night. Yet, for a Freudian psychologist, your dreams constitute valid evidence for explaining your behavior.

Tracing Its Origin and Roots

RAT developed some 2500 years ago as an approach to rational decision-making. Its roots grew in the fertile soils of rhetoric, dialectic, and logic in ancient Greece. These areas of inquiry concerned, respectively, finding arguments that would persuade others, seeking truth through the procedure of posing questions and providing answers and counterarguments, and testing an argument's formal validity.

Rhetorical, Dialectical, and Logical Roots   In its rhetorical form, those using RAT seek to discover the available means of persuasion. This means that, through the rhetorical canon of invention, you can determine the crucial questions that an argumentative case considers. For example, in a murder trial in the early law courts, it was necessary to show several things.

First, it was necessary to show that someone died (produce a body). Next it was necessary to show that a known person did the killing (produce a witness or confession). Then it was necessary to show that the murder was intentional (premeditated and not accidental). Finally, it was necessary to show that the accused had motive (a reason for committing the crime).

Rhetorically, as outlined by Aristotle in *The Rhetoric* (1960), the resources of the arguer consisted of inartistic and artistic proofs. Inartistic proofs are the proofs at hand, which included such things as witnesses' statements, contracts, deeds, and oaths. Artistic proofs are the proofs that needed to be invented. The invented proofs included ethical proofs (called *ethos*), emotional proofs (called *pathos*), and logical proofs (called *logos*). Regarding the artistic forms of proof, RAT exhibited an early bias favoring conviction through the use of logical argument. RAT initially viewed appeals to emotion (pathos) and speaker qualities (ethos) as suspect. More recently, RAT tempered this bias by accepting, albeit for some adherents regrettably, the use of emotional and ethical appeals if steeped in reasoned argument. Theorists thought these additional appeals necessary because of human foibles and frailties (called the degraded base of the audience). In other words, the proponents of RAT came to the realization that audiences reached decisions for ethical and emotional reasons, as well as rational reasons (Wenzel, 1987).

The dialectical arena, the counterpart of rhetoric, portrayed communicators arguing on a coequal footing to arrive at reasoned decisions. Here, the parties made an honest effort to examine all facets of an issue and to tease out the best arguments in a cooperative endeavor. Those developing the dialectical approach offered various rational procedures. These procedures included syllogistic disputations, school debates, and discussions. RAT posited that following such procedures would lead to the discovery of truth. Beginning in the 1960s, the theorists developing RAT concluded that both the rhetorical invention process and the dialectical truth-seeking procedures exhibited an epistemic attribute (Scott, 1967). In other words, the use of RAT's rhetorical and dialectical procedures provided a way of knowing.

Aristotle and other ancient logicians sought to develop appropriate criteria for evaluating the merits of arguments. They viewed arguments as products. In other words, arguments were a commodity with known characteristics just like apples, pears, and olives. The early logicians developed ideal syllogistic forms for testing the validity of conclusions. Such validity tests concerned the logical structure of an argument. Argument constructions—like "if–then," "either–or," "not–unless," "some–all," "any–every"—allowed for the making of inferences about any (and every) subject. For example, if you are late then your food will be cold, or if you are late then you will miss the plane. Were you late? If so you ate cold food and missed the plane. Later in the chapter, we will introduce some of the available systems for checking the validity of arguments. For now, it is sufficient to understand that logic, when viewed communicatively, posits an arguer examining a product (argument) for validity by engaging in a conversation with him- or herself.

Persuasion and Conviction Roots   Cox and Willard (1982) traced the history of RAT's development in America from the publication of *The Principles of Argumentation* (Baker, 1895). Baker's description of argumentation continued the "war" of rational argument in rhetoric (persuasion), dialectic, and logic. For Baker, pure conviction stemmed solely from appeals to the intellect. For him, persuasion came from appeals to the passions and prejudices of the audience. Cox and Willard (1982) labeled this distinction a *dualism*. They traced the duality through the popular textbooks in debate and argumentation into the 1960s. Meanwhile, in Europe, the logician, Stephen Toulmin (1958), developed the concept of *field-dependent* and *field-invariant* arguments. At the same time, Perelman and Olbrechts–Tyteca (1969) developed the notion of an *ideal audience*. These scholars sought to move argumentation theory away from a speaker-centered theory, with its degraded view of the audience, to an audience-centered theory. They did so by putting the audience on a more equal footing with the arguer.

Modern Transformation Roots   In the United States, a group of scholars, centered at or with ties to the University of Illinois, initiated a dialogue that helped to critique, refashion, and reconstruct what is now modern Rational Argumentation Theory.[1] The dialogue centered on what is an argument? Is it a process, a procedure, or a product? Are there different senses of argument? Is it the thinking up of an argument? Is it argument as an entity? Is it having an argument? Is it a way of knowing? Are ordinary language intrapersonal, interpersonal, and public arguments anything like the formalized arguments allowed in school debates, deliberative discussions, deliberative bodies, and courts of law? Is the essence of an argument to be found in rhetoric, dialectic, or logic?

Wenzel (1980, 1987, 1990), reacting to the scholarly discussions and critiques, and the general refashioning of the concepts in RAT as a result of those discussions, recognized the dynamic fusion of the modes of argument—rhetoric, dialectic, and logic. He viewed their fused state as a coherent whole central to RAT. It is this fused or unified system of rational argument in decision-making that we present in this chapter.[2]

Accepting Its Assumptive System

Let's pause by the side of the trail for a moment, and reflect on an important point of The Communication Metatheory (TCM). As we indicated in Chapter 1, all theories possess assumptions that relate to being, knowing, and valuing. You will grow familiar with this drill. Here, we describe and explain the major assumptions of RAT—not for the purpose of trying to persuade you that this theory is "correct"—but only to indicate what you must assume to explore its explanatory power. RAT asks you to assume that communicators communicating within a medium essentially make rational argument that justifies conviction and human action. RAT's assumptions are (1) humans naturally make argument; (2) arguments occur over questions of fact, value, and policy; (3) the competition of rational arguments in open discourse enables the discovery of truth and the generation of new knowledge; (4) arguers and arguments function rhetorically (as process), dialectically (as procedure), and logically (as product); (5) humans prefer rational proof over other types of proof; and (6) arguments grow and prosper in distinct medium$_2$ soils—an invariant field and a dependent field.

Humans Naturally Make Argument   This is an ontological assumption that concerns the nature of humans. RAT views humans as reason-giving animals. You can readily see this in your own behavior. Think about your past answers to such questions as: Why did I sleep through the alarm? Why was my term paper late? You can also see this behavior in answering the preschooler's question, "Why don't cows fly like birds?" Indeed, RAT assumes that our nature compels us to justify past actions, as well as our choices of future actions, with reasoned, rational argument. Canary et al. (1995) found that the amount of rationality (minimal to full) expected varies with the setting and the importance of the topic. However, they discovered that even simple conversational topics require minimal rationality.

Arguments Occur Over Questions of Fact, Value, and Policy   This is an epistemological assumption concerning how we know what we know. A statement that asserts that something exists is a *question of fact.* Examples include: "There are 20,000 students at our university" or "a half-million Americans lose their lives each year due to inadequate medical care." Arguers agree on standards of measurement and then apply them to resolve questions of fact. A *question of value* asserts that something is good, just, virtuous, proper, admirable, or valuable. Conversely, a question of value also asserts that something is bad, unjust, invirtuous, dishonorable, or invaluable. For example, value questions might include: "Is sex before marriage sinful?" "Is preemptive war justifiable?" "Is killing in self-defense moral?" "Is a therapeutic abortion murder?" In order to resolve questions of value, arguers need to agree on criteria for making a judgment and then apply the criteria. A *question of policy* calls for a course of action to be taken: "Should the number of credit hours required for a major in communication be increased?" "Should we have a national program of health care?" "Should we have federally-funded day care?" "Should there be competency testing for professors?" Each policy question contains hidden questions of fact and value, which the arguers must answer before they can resolve the larger question of policy. For example, if a company is considering a policy of parental leave, planners must of necessity examine questions of fact ("What is meant by parental leave?" "Who can qualify for parental leave?"), and questions of value ("How can we develop a program of parental leave without discriminating against nonparents?") before implementing the specific new program. As we shall see in discussing the associated basic terms or the basic term rational argument, arguers use six types of argument to resolve questions of fact, value, and policy.

The Competition of Rational Arguments in Open Discourse Enables the Discovery of Truth and the Generation of New Knowledge   This is an epistemological assumption. RAT assumes that arguers, alternately making and criticizing arguments, will discover truth and arrive at better decisions. As well, by engaging in truth-seeking procedures and processes, arguers will discover new knowledge. For example, the dialectical discussion technique called brainstorming leads to the generation of new ideas (new knowledge). Our government and legal systems assume that the procedure of debating both sides of a policy issue or legal case creates the new discovery of who is guilty or at fault and the reasoned discovery of the best decision. Although such forums as congress and the courts lack perfection, they outperform the alternatives of mob rule and happenstance.

Arguers and Arguments Function Rhetorically (as Process), Dialectically (as Procedure), and Logically (as Product)   This is an epistemological assumption. Here, an *argument* is conceived as manifesting itself in three ways. Argument$_1$ is the inventive putting together of evidence and reasoning to convince a person (argument as process). Argument$_2$ is a dialectical method such as discussion, debate, or trial that will create good decisions (argument as procedure). Argument$_3$ is a formal structure capable of submission to examination for its material and structural validity (argument as product). Experience indicates that we do each of these every day. In other words, we use argument in each of its three senses. Take, for example, the right-to-die issue, as present in physician-assisted suicide. At one moment, you may create and give a classroom speech trying to justify the correctness of Dr. Jack Kevorkian's medical practices since 1991 (argument as process).[3] At another moment, you may participate in a group discussion and find yourself examining both sides of the question to determine the appropriateness of euthanasia (argument as procedure). At still another moment, your professor could diagram the various arguments for and against Dr. Kevorkian on the board. She or he could then examine the use of evidence and reasoning and evaluate whether or not a sufficient case had been made to support or deny Dr. Kevorkian's actions (argument as product). Each of these rational activities is normal. Each is expected in our daily life.

Open market for argument

Humans Prefer Rational Proof Over Other Types of Proof   This is an ontological assumption. RAT assumes that the rational evaluation of pro and con arguments is the preferred means for making decisions, solving problems, and managing disagreements. Also, RAT assumes that the conviction gained through reason is more enduring than the other kinds of proof. As well, RAT assumes that the conviction gained through reason is more ethically defensible than decisions that come from other kinds of proof. The Athenians held open-air trials before the full senate. Accused people brought witnesses to testify as to their character. They also brought family members and children to cry over their potential loss if convicted. At the same time, the accused would provide a reasoned defense. The accused hoped to win on the merits of the rational arguments, but offered emotional and ethical forms of proof to satisfy the vagaries of the crowd who stood in judgment. We continue such practices in our courts, academic halls, and places of business to this day. We assume a natural presumption in favor of rational arguments. It is part of our democracy's social contract to set aside our prejudices and emotions, keep our tempers under control, and reason together for the greater good. This principle commits us to the rejection of "might makes right" when making choices.

Arguments Grow and Prosper in Two Media—An Invariant and a Dependent Field
This is an epistemological assumption. RAT assumes some forms of argument and some types of evidence are common (invariant) to all human collectives. At the same time, RAT allows that some data sets and reasoning processes are unique (dependent) to some fields. *Field,* as used here, refers to such domains as medicine, law, or religion. Because most arguments are invariant, RAT assumes that people from various subfields can understand and evaluate, for example, most of the arguments made in this book even though it is written for communication students. Conversely, the reasoning process of Chaos Theory (a theory that explains the predictability of entropy within chaotic systems) is difficult to follow and judge for most nonphysicists. This is because the chaos arguments are field-dependent. Similarly, the evidence and reasoning used by the Catholic Church to establish sainthood is difficult for non-Catholics to follow and evaluate. This is because it is also field-dependent, especially the reasoning regarding what constitutes a miracle. It takes training in theological arguments to make the case for sainthood.

RAT: Introducing the Theoretical Concepts

This looks like an ideal place for a rest stop. Recall that TCM enables us to examine a theory's basic, structural, and evaluative theoretical concepts. RAT—like all core general communication theories—exhibits basic, structural, and evaluative concepts with their attendant technical definitions. As we observe communicators communicating through the lens of this theory, we see arguers creating, using, and evaluating rational arguments. In the flow of actual argumentative discourse, it may appear difficult to see the different concepts. Nonetheless, experience dictates that the best starting point is to begin with the most elemental parts of RAT and then build an ever more complex description of arguers arguing in a medium. **Figure 3-1** displays RAT's technical concepts.

Finding Its Basic Concepts

This part of the trail affords a good opportunity to continue our rest stop. This is only the second time that we have put TCM to work. Recall that here is where we flesh out the anatomical parts of a general communication theory using the VENN diagram. We'll be repeating this process completely for the general theories. We'll use it in an abbreviated form for the contextual and microtheories presented in Chapters 8–11. Seven technical terms—rational argument, sign, cause, example, analogy, authority assertion, and dissociation—serve as RAT's basic concepts. Each represents the communication phenomena undergirding RAT. To become proficient in the use of RAT, you need to practice recognizing and making argument.

Initial Basic Concept   Recall that TCM posited that a general theory's basic concepts fall within two subclasses: the initial basic concept and the associated basic concepts. Again, an initial basic concept is the primary communication unit that is singled out for analysis. RAT's initial basic concept is rational argument.

Rational Argument.   A rational argument is the initial thing you must find in human communication when using this theory. If you can't find a rational argument, then you cannot theorize by using RAT. Rest assured, however, that rational arguments are everywhere. With a little practice, you can find them. An assertion is a claim without proof, such as I'm 5'7" tall. An argument is a claim with proof, such as according to the measurement, I'm 5'7" tall. However, RAT's developers provide a technical definition of a rational argument. A *rational argument* is a reasoned, supported claim. Toulmin (1958) defined a rational argument as movement from acceptable data (evidence) through a warrant (reasoning process) to a claim (conclusion). His data, warrant, and claim concepts serve as the subparts of RAT's technical definition of rational argument. Ziegelmueller, Kay, and Dause (1990) stressed that an argument may be thought of as the smallest complete unit of proof. Following Toulmin (1958), they also noted that it consists of three associated elements: the data, the reasoning process, and the conclusion. Thus, as we shall explain in detail below, a rational argument entails three subparts (data or evidence, warrant or reasoning, and claim). To make a complete rational argument requires all three subparts. At the bottom of **Figure 3-1,** we present a rational argument exhibiting a claim (Am I in love?) and data (can't sleep, roses, and so forth). How one gets from such material facts (can't sleep and roses) to the claim (in love) is an inferential leap (reasoning).

   Data—sometimes called evidence—consists of facts, lay or expert opinion, and objects or materials. Facts include anything verifiable through direct observation, experience, statistical procedures, or the scientific method. Opinion is personal testimony. Normally, lay or ordinary opinion is not accepted as evidence and what is accepted as expert opinion

Viewing RAT's Anatomical Elements

Key:
Bold Caps = Metatheory Concepts
Caps + Small Case = RAT's Theoretical Concepts

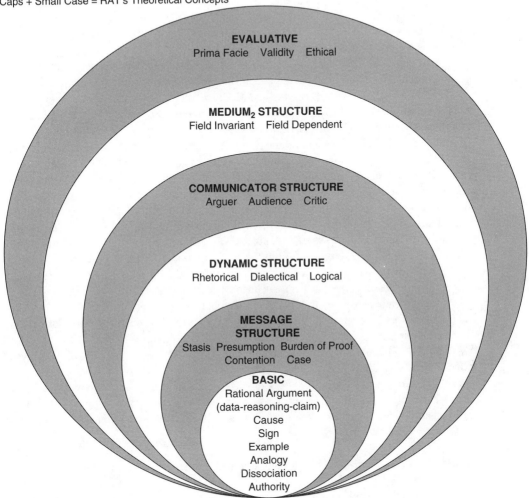

EVALUATIVE
Prima Facie   Validity   Ethical

MEDIUM₂ STRUCTURE
Field Invariant   Field Dependent

COMMUNICATOR STRUCTURE
Arguer   Audience   Critic

DYNAMIC STRUCTURE
Rhetorical   Dialectical   Logical

MESSAGE STRUCTURE
Stasis Presumption Burden of Proof
Contention   Case

BASIC
Rational Argument
(data-reasoning-claim)
Cause
Sign
Example
Analogy
Dissociation
Authority

Other Anatomical Elements:

COMMUNICATIVE FORCE	**MODELING**
ORIGIN, ROOTS, ASSUMPTIONS	**RELATIONSHIP STATEMENTS**
PARADIGM	**THEORY–METHOD COMPLEX**

EXAMPLE OF A SIGN ARGUMENT: "First a smile, then a note, then coffee, we talked for hours, then roses; I can't sleep, I daydream in class, the signs are everywhere, am I in love?"

FIGURE 3-1.

may vary—as we shall see—by different argumentative fields. Lay testimony is generally not acceptable data because the lay person has no special training or practice that would qualify him or her as an acceptable expert. On the other hand, expert opinion, from a person with the knowledge, training, or practice to make him or her an authority, is considered valid testimony and is accepted as data or evidence. Artifacts (objects or materials) that might constitute data include such elements as the results of DNA tests, the presence of lipstick on your collar, and the existence of laws, goals, and contracts. In order for a rational argument to be accepted (by arguers, critics, and audiences), the argument must start from *acceptable* data. If the data is questioned, then new arguments must be formed for and against the accuracy of the data. These tests of data (evidence) will be presented later in this chapter as we discuss RAT's evaluative terms.

Reasoning. Aristotle classified reasoning as of two types. Deductive reasoning moves from a general statement to a specific conclusion. Inductive reasoning moves from specific events or examples to a general conclusion. More recently, a dispute has arisen among argumentation scholars as to whether or not one should classify the various ways to make inferential leaps in reasoning and, if so, how best to do it (Willard, 1983, 1989, 1990). Regardless of the heated nature of the dispute, textbooks on argumentation usually contain classifications and discussions of the forms of argumentative reasoning central to RAT.[4] Typically, argumentation texts include discussions of one or more of the following classes of argumentative reasoning: (1) reasoning through types of argument (sign, cause, example, analogy, authority, dissociation); (2) reasoning through formal argument structures (the logical syllogism and the rhetorical syllogism); and (3) reasoning through informal argument models such as the Beardsley (1950), Canary, et al. (1995), Perelman and Olbrechts–Tyteca (1969), or Toulmin (1958) schema. For example, *reasoning*, within the Toulmin model for the layout of argument, is called the *warrant.* We'll illustrate the formal and informal models later in the chapter. We'll discuss the types of argument as the associated basic concepts of RAT.

Claim. Again, a rational argument is movement from acceptable data, through a warrant, to a claim. Quite simply, a *claim* is a conclusion drawn through reasoning from data. There are four general classes of claims: designative, definitive, evaluative, and advocative. *Designative* and *definitive claims* center on questions of fact (respectively, is it correctly classified or correctly defined), *evaluative claims* center on questions of value, and *advocative* claims center on questions of policy. Questions of fact, value, and policy, as it turns out, are the three general classes of questions (sometimes called propositions) over which rational arguments occur (Brockriede & Ehninger, 1960). We discussed these above as part of RAT's second assumption.

Associated Basic Concepts

A rational argument comes in six forms. Each form represents a special kind of rational argument. Thus, RAT's associative basic concepts are sign, cause, example, analogy, authority assertion, and dissociation. These comprise the types or special kinds of argument that you can make. The statement at the bottom of **Figure 3-1** illustrates a special kind of argument called *sign argument.*

Argument from Cause.   A *causal argument* is made when you claim that one event or condition is *always* the result of a preceding event or condition (Cragan & Shields, 1972). In other words, you are using *causal argument* when you claim that a prior thing, "A," always leads to a subsequent thing, "B," and that without "A" then "B" could not exist. Let's see if we can quickly illustrate the process of making a causal argument: "Without money, I cannot buy food." Here, the subsequent event (buying food) cannot occur without the preceding event (having money).

Argument from Sign.   A *sign argument* is made when you claim that one event or con- dition indicates the presence of a subsequent event or condition (Cragan & Shields, 1972). You are using *sign argument* when you claim that a prior thing, "A," points to the presence of a subsequent thing, "B." Again, we can illustrate this rather quickly. For example, a sign argument is represented by the following statement: "It's cloudy; it's going to rain." The prior thing (cloudy) indicates the subsequent thing (rain). Much of empirical medicine uses sign reasoning as the physician looks for symptoms that point to a particular claim or con- clusion, namely a specific disease.

Argument from Example.   An *argument from example* is made when one or more single item(s), such as a fact, incident, or aspect, is put forth as representative of all of a group or type (Cragan & Shields, 1972). Indeed, you are using *argument from example* when you make a claim from sampling. Let's again illustrate. An argument from example based on sampling would be made as follows: "I've examined the ACT scores of 5 percent of the 1500 members of the entering class and discovered their scores are above average. I con- clude that the student body at my school is above average on their ACTs."

Argument from Analogy.   An *argument from analogy* is made through the inference that if two or more things agree in some respects they will probably agree in others (Cragan & Shields, 1972). You are making *argument from analogy* when you compare the known el- ements of two systems and find similarities. On finding similarities, you then conclude that the known elements of the two systems are so much alike that the unknown elements of the second system are like the known elements of the first. For example, the following state- ment presents an analogy: "Learning how to argue is just like learning how to ride a bike; once you learn you never forget." The first four types of arguments help you make inferen- tial leaps in reasoning. You make arguments using deductive reasoning when you argue from cause and sign. You make arguments using inductive reasoning when you argue from example and analogy. Cause, sign, example, and analogy comprise the most common forms of inferential leaps (warrants) in reasoning.

Argument from Dissociation.   Across the years, RAT's theory builders expanded the list of argument types to include argument from dissociation. *Dissociation* is the disengaging or breaking up of one idea from another. An example of dissociation is the following: "We're tired of merely paying lip service to the teaching of communication theory with stu- dents not seeing any practical use for them. We think students can understand communica- tion theories and use them to advantage." As you may have guessed, once your trail guides made this argument from dissociation, we began writing this book.

Argument from Authority Assertion.   Across the years, RAT's theory builders also ex- panded the list of argument types to include argument from authority assertion (Cragan & Shields, 1972). *Argument from authority assertion* occurs when you let an authority make the argument for you. For example, you may say, "The surgeon general says that cigarette- smoking is hazardous to your health." The authority, the surgeon general, based this claim on the sign argument that cigarette-smoking increases the likelihood of cancer, heart disease, and other serious medical afflictions. We discussed evidence or data from authority above.

Whatever the authority's claim, rest assured that it, too, represents argument from sign, cause, example, analogy, or dissociation. A typical authority assertion is contained in the following: "How do you know that?" "The Bible told me so!"

The six different types of argument (cause, sign, example, analogy, dissociation, and authority assertion) allow you to reason from data to a claim. In other words, they allow you to make a rational argument. **Table 3-1** contains an everyday argument. Can you find the policy question and questions about fact and value? Do you see the occurrence of data, warrant, and claim?   *conclusion*   *evidence*

reasoning process

Seeing RAT's Structural Concepts

Again, it's time for a brief rest stop. Recall from TCM that the structural concepts for all general communication theories sort out by concepts related to message, communicator, communication dynamic, and medium. At its simplest, RAT explains that communicators communicate with arguments in some medium. RAT contains five message structure concepts (contention, case, stasis, presumption, and burden of proof), three communication dynamic structure concepts (rhetorical, dialectical, or logical), three communicator structure concepts (arguer, audience, and critic), and two medium$_2$ concepts (field-invariant and field-dependent).

Message Concepts   Recall also from TCM that all general communication theories contain message structure concepts that dress up and flesh out a theory's basic concepts. As indicated in **Figure 3.1,** RAT's five message structure concepts are contention, case, stasis, presumption, and burden of proof.

Contention.   A *contention* is a statement of premise that is supported by a number of arguments. In other words, when using RAT, communicators typically combine several rational arguments to form a larger unit of proof called a *contention.* For example, quitting smoking is not all sweetness and light (contention): It will increase irritability, reduce the powers of

TABLE 3-1.   Viewing an Argument about Household Chores

Spouse 1:
"In regards to cleaning and household chores, there have been numerous occasions when we've discussed how we are going to keep the apartment up and in good condition to the degree that I feel it should be kept."

Spouse 2:
"I feel that since two days a week I don't go to school I feel obliged that I should do things around the house. Since you work forty hours a week, and [my] having those two extra days that [I] could get things done [that we can't do] at night because we're both too tired by then.

"So, on those days in order to alleviate stress on you and on our weekend activities I would try to do the laundry and daily vacuuming or dusting, whatever it may be. And, of course, since I'm at home it's easier for me to do the dinner.

"But, if I wasn't at home, if I was working the same amount as you, we would have a separation of household chores as when we did prior to my coming back to school."

(Dialogue derived from Canary, et al., 1995, p. 189.)

concentration, and lead to weight gain. Just as a number of arguments are combined typically to form a contention, a number of contentions typically go together to form a case.

Case. A *case* is an organized set of contentions with supporting arguments whose goal is to be *prima facie,* that is, believable on first hearing. When an attorney presents a legal brief to the court, he or she has presented a case that outlines the major contentions. Typically, you would use RAT to develop your message by ordering your contentions around certain *stock issues.* We discuss some typical stock issues in the next section. Regardless of the situation, an arguer is trying to make a good case that speaks to the important issues, meets the audience's expected *burden of proof* (that is, establishing claims through reasoning and evidence), and provides justification for changing from the *status quo* (the present system). In courts of law, school debates, and deliberative bodies like legislatures the word *case* is used technically to mean just such an organized set of arguments. **Table 3-1** presents a *prima facie* argument—contentions forming a case—about household chores.

Stasis. In *stasis,* assertion meets denial. It is the nexus of the argument (as product) as it tells you the issues over which arguers clash when considering questions of fact, value, and policy. Roommates intuitively understand *stasis* when, like Neil Simon's *The Odd Couple,* they quibble over whether the house is clean. Similarly, when critics look at an argument to examine its worth, *stasis* will occur over the argument's formal and material validity. If there is no *stasis,* or clash, there is no need to make an argument or have an argument. In formalized fields like law, congress, and business organizations, what constitutes *stasis* has been codified into what are called *stock issues.* Stock issues—like the Aristotelian special topics or *topoi* from which they are derived—serve as the primary, indivisible, and inherent components of argument and point up the areas of concern that need to be discussed in developing the message structure of the case (Ochs, 1969; Wiethoff, 1981). Several sets of stock issue, message development patterns are available. For example, one set of *stock issues* that calls for a change from the *status quo* includes ill, blame, cure, and cost (Hultzen, 1958). An arguer is expected to create arguments from sign, cause, example, analogy, authority assertion, and dissociation to contend that there is a problem with the current system (ill) that is due to some structural flaw (blame) that requires a new program of action (cure) that is affordable (cost). In the subfield of small group discussion, similar systems have been developed to produce rational group decision-making. The most famous is the procedure adapted from John Dewey's (1910) five steps of reflective thinking (Cragan & Wright, 1995). In public speaking, Alan Monroe's (1935) "motivated sequence" serves as an outline for organizing arguments that would make the case for change (Comeaux, 1993; Ehninger, et al., 1986). Other stock issue patterns for arranging contentions to make a case that denies the *status quo* include comparative advantages (Brock, et al., 1973; Cragan & Shields, 1970) and criteria (Chesebro, 1968). Although such stock issue typologies are useful for locating what generally constitutes *stasis* in a given case, all cases tend to have unique characteristics centering around questions of fact and value that create new points of *stasis* (Ehninger & Brockriede, 1963; Warnick & Inch, 1994).

Presumption. *Presumption* is a bias in favor of what currently exists or is believed true. It tells the arguers who must prove first. Our American court system allows the accused to occupy the ground of presumption. In other words, an accused is presumed innocent until proven guilty. In all instances, the one who seeks change lacks presumption and must prove first. If your college or university is on the trimester or quarter system, that way of setting the academic calendar is the *status quo.* The existing system is said to occupy the ground of presumption. It's like the children's game "King of the Hill." Those who would advocate change to a semester system have the burden of throwing King Presumption (the existing trimester system) off the hill. In everyday conversations, the statement, "That's the way we've always done it" tells the arguers what possesses presumption. The person that risks change or advocates change possesses the burden of proof (Ehninger & Brockriede, 1963).

Burden of Proof.   The *burden of proof* is the risk of proposing change. It is the burden placed on that member of the controversy who will lose (due to presumption) if nothing is done. Because presumption favors what is, the person who asserts change must accept the burden to make argument to justify change. In a court of law, presumption rests with the accused (his or her status is "innocent"). Hence, the prosecutor accepts the burden of proof to make a case against the accused. In a deliberative body like congress, stock issues such as ill, blame, cure, and cost become good starting points for making contentions (arguments) that would meet the burden of proof of the arguer who proposes change. Developing this set of arguments would then constitute the *case* for change. Of course, once the burden of proof is met, a *prima facie* case is said to have been provided. Once a believable case is presented, the other arguers who previously held presumption must now repel the *prima facie* case. Repelling a prima facie case is called the burden of rebuttal. You would repel a prima facie case with rational arguments (data, reasoning, and claims flowing from sign, cause, example, analogy, dissociation, and authority assertion) of equal weight (Ehninger & Brockriede, 1963). We discuss *prima facie* as an evaluative concept of RAT later in the chapter.

Dynamic Concepts   We are creatures of habit. That means that we want to take a rest stop. We do so to remind you of the importance of knowing the communication dynamic structure concepts of a theory. Recall that TCM emphasized that all general communication theories exhibit multiple deep structures to communicative messages. Recall also that there is tension as to the choices of which deep structure the message should follow. The tension is similar to the deep structure tension or dynamic among Freud's psychoanalytic concepts *id, ego,* and *superego,* or Berne's psychological concepts of *parent, adult,* and *child.* Of course, you've already learned the dynamic tension of IST (Chapter 2) with its different dynamic structure concepts, *linear, interactional,* and *transactional* information systems. RAT's communication dynamic structure concepts concern whether the argumentative form of the message follows a rhetorical, dialectical, or logical dynamic. Wenzel (1990) was the first scholar to note that rhetoric, dialectic, and logic formed the three modes of the dynamic structure of RAT.

Rhetorical Dynamic.   The *rhetorical dynamic* concept is the argument-as-process deep structure (Wenzel, 1987). Here, argument is viewed as a naturally occurring human activity in which people attempt to gain conviction and influence others by the use of rational reasons. This argument-as-process dynamic is used to convince others to solve problems, enhance relationships, and coordinate group activity. In rational societies children acquire a bias in favor of the use of rational argument over other types of appeals for gaining conviction. Thus, if a three-year-old child throws a tantrum, we often put her or him in "time-out" until she or he calms down and can reason. The rhetorical dynamic is often loose and free-form. The rules of what constitutes a prima facie case often go unstated in the rhetorical dynamic process. Nonetheless, there must be some implicit rules or those operating in the rhetorical mode of RAT could not have an argument. At a minimum, you will know that some unstated argumentation rule has been violated when someone says, "you're not playing fair."

Dialectical Dynamic.   The *dialectical dynamic* concept is the argument-as-procedure deep structure. Here, argument is viewed as a formalized procedure that will lead to conviction. There are a number of formal procedural systems for the making of argument. These include the rules of legal procedure, Robert's *Rules of Order* for meetings, rules for school debates, and agenda systems for conducting problem-solving discussion. Such procedures, when put in place, insure that the best argument or decision emerges. Such procedures also insure that the decision emerges in a fair and open way. As we've stated, the dialectical dynamic of RAT serves as the cornerstone of a literate, free society. As Thomas Jefferson once said, "Ignorance and freedom can not long co-exist." An implicit "ought" undergirds the dialectical mode. In other words, people in a democracy need to know (ought to know) the procedures for making dialectical argument.

Logical Dynamic.   The *logical dynamic* concept is the argument-as-product deep structure. Here, an argument is examined in terms of its formal and material validity to insure that "correct" conclusions have been reached via the use of valid evidence and reasoning. The logical dynamic is the mode in which the critic—detached observer—functions. The critic reformats the naturally occurring argument so that it can be compared to idealized logical forms in order to assess if it is fallacious or sound reasoning. *[handwritten: le. BIRT statements in a debate?]*

[handwritten: ? as in legality of evidence]

Communicator Concepts   Again, this point on the trail to understanding communication theories affords a good opportunity for a brief rest stop. Recall that TCM specified that communicator structure concepts identify or name the communicators from the perspective of a particular theory. Three technical terms (arguer, audience, and critic) comprise RAT's communicator structure concepts. These concepts depict the communicators who are communicating by way of argument.

Arguer.   An *arguer* is a person who is willing to set forth reasoned claims and risk confrontation of those claims by others. This is a risk because the rational confrontation may lead to disconfirmation or modification of the claim held by the arguer (Darnell & Brockriede, 1975). Discerning the appropriate means for making and confronting reasoned claims is what RAT is all about. RAT provides the agreed-on ground rules for arguing. With those ground rules, arguers agree as to what constitutes data and reasoning and what makes a good case. Arguers must agree upon the ground rules. Agreement is needed because, as Feyerabend (1975), Kuhn (1970), and Rasmussen (1974) have indicated, it is difficult for people to argue satisfactorily if they possess distinctly different worldviews, paradigms, or frames of reference. Your mother may have told you, "Don't discuss politics or religion at family gatherings." She did so because, like most families, she did not believe your family had ever agreed to accept common ground rules for pleasantly risking their convictions when arguing these subjects. Finally, an arguer is committed to making choices (decisions) on the basis of the outcome of rational argument (as opposed to fights, *ad hominen* attacks, wars, emotional appeals, and so forth). It is this agreed-to rule that causes the arguer to risk his or her convictions as a result of engaging in argument.

Audience.   *Audience* is the person or persons the arguer is trying to convince. The audience may be a single arguer functioning as self-critic, a judge in a courtroom, the person with whom one is arguing, fellow arguers as in a deliberative body like congress, or a real or idealized audience. In any of these instances, once the audience has agreed to the arguer's claim or claims then the argument, debate, discussion, trial, or deliberation has ended. The choice can be made, the decision rendered, the vote taken, and so forth.

The question arises, what is the best way for the arguer to build a compelling argument? Perelman and Olbrechts–Tyteca (1969) maintained that an arguer should build his or her case based on the ideal audience in a given field. Thus, a physician writing in the *New England Journal of Medicine* would provide the kind of proof, through his or her arguments, that the best physicians in the medical area under discussion would have to have in order to be convinced. Across the years, the scholars developing RAT moved the audience concept closer to the definition of arguer and thereby placed arguer and audience on equal footing (Cox & Willard, 1982).

Critic.   RAT's third communicator concept is critic. A *critic* is a detached observer who has no immediate interest in the outcome of the argument or case. A critic is assumed to be in a superior position to assess and draw conclusions about the validity of the arguments being made (Scott, 1990). In the rhetorical mode of argumentation, the critic analyzes public argument and offers judgments as to their validly. In the dialectical mode, such as a business discussion group, the members of the group who seek the best, fairest, or truest way to do something serve as the critics. You'll recognize the dialectical critics when someone says, "Let's let Inez and Ismail speak." In the logical mode, the critic is a person who examines the formal and material validity of the arguments. A courtroom judge functions in the logical mode when he or she holds arguments inadmissible.

Medium Concepts   You are probably thinking about taking another rest stop. So are we. Let's take one. During it, we will remind you that TCM specified that all general communication theories explain communication across the medium$_1$ contexts of interpersonal, small group, public speaking, organizational, mass, and intercultural communication. It is their ability to work in these contexts that qualifies such theories as general communication theories. Recall, also, that each core general communication theory often possesses a unique sense of medium. That is, a theory's technical terms name a substance in which the theory propagates or grows. TCM specified such a substance with the metaconcept called medium$_2$. RAT's medium$_2$ concepts are field-invariant and field-dependent. Both field-invariant and field-dependent are examples of a medium$_2$ propagating substance. Unlike Information Systems Theory (Chapter 2), RAT posits no specialized role for the medium$_3$ metaconcepts of how arguments are conducted by air or light waves.

Field-Dependency.   Toulmin (1958) first posited *field-dependency* as an important concept. In a vague way, the field-dependency concept refers to such entities as academic disciplines like physics and economics, professions like medicine and law, cultures like Eastern and Western, and subcultures like African American and Italian American. RAT posits such fields as exhibiting special characteristics that resemble an electromagnetic field. After Toulmin introduced the field-dependency concept, communication scholars began providing an operational definition of what constitutes an argumentative field. Warnick and Inch (1994) summarized this effort. They indicated that an argumentative field is created over time by humans with a common set of shared goals. Each argumentative field exhibits some unique rules, norms, and standards for acceptable evidence and reasoning. As well, each argumentative field specifies the type of overall case that is required to answer questions of fact, value, and policy. Let's see if we can illustrate the field concept. Your experiences with the different requirements for term papers illustrates the presence of certain term paper fields. Term papers, as opposed to essays, possess their own rules for making a case and the use of evidence. For example, beware of plagiarism, use primary sources, document your sources, use a consistent bibliographic form, and so forth. Other examples of your familiarity with argumentative fields abound. For example, you probably have noticed a difference in what is acceptable argument on campus as compared to what is acceptable argument at your part-time job. Such distinctions illustrate field-dependency.

Field-Invariant.　*Field-invariant* arguments hold true regardless of the $medium_1$ context in which they occur or $medium_2$ field in which they propagate. Field-invariance is a very good thing. Field-invariance allows most of us to recognize, comprehend, and use arguments in most situations in which we find ourselves. Field-invariance keeps us from having to know a different theory of rational argument for each argumentative field in which we travel. Field-invariance keeps RAT from fragmenting into separate microtheories for every special and applied context. The *field-invariant* concept allows you to accept the existence of standards for constructing and evaluating arguments regardless of the subfield of argument. Let us illustrate the point. You know that the standards for acceptable evidence in law and politics differ—certain reasons are acceptable in one field and not the other. For example, law courts exclude *ad hominem* argument, but the political arena accepts it as a means of determining fitness for office. Nonetheless, in the main, lawyers and politicians exhibit the capacity to follow most of the arguments made in each other's fields. They exhibit this capacity because the argumentative fields that form the core of a democratic society—law, politics, education, commerce, and industry—contain about an 80:20 ratio of field-invariant to field-dependent arguments. On the other hand, cultlike groups such as the Waco Branch Davidians or esoteric disciplines like quantum physics probably display a 20:80 ratio of field-invariant to field-dependent arguments. You need not worry about RAT's usefulness as you function professionally and as a citizen in our democratic society. RAT is the general theory that explains the communicative force of the rational arguments you will be building, using, and judging in your decision-making.

Using Evaluative Concepts

During this rest stop, let's again return to TCM. Recall that a theory's evaluative concepts let you make assessments and judgments regarding the quality and outcomes of communicators communicating in a medium. Recall from Chapter 1 that all scientists are concerned with explaining the outcomes of the fundamental interactive forces that they study. The cell biologist specializing in oncology is interested in the interactive effects within cells that cause them to become cancerous and grow at rapid and uncontrolled rates. With RAT we evaluate the quality and outcomes of arguments in terms of their effects on decision-making and conviction. One of the greatest expectations of a college graduate is that her or his convictions are the outcome of the rational decision-making process. RAT explains and evaluates this most important human communication activity.

Quality and Outcomes   By *outcomes* we mean that the communicative interaction identified by the theory did in fact occur. The question to ask is did the communicative force under observation have its predicted impact on human action? In RAT's case was an ethical, valid *prima facie* case made and did it effect conviction? *Quality* refers to RAT's evaluative concepts that denote the degree or grade of excellence of the communication. RAT's primary evaluative concepts are *prima facie,* validity, and ethical.

Prima Facie.   *Prima facie* is an evaluative concept that states the standard of proof required for conviction or adherence to an argument. It is a Latin idiom borrowed from the legal field of argument meaning 'on its face' or 'on first seeing.' Vancil (1993) noted that a *prima facie* case supports each stock issue "with argument and evidence at a level that would be accepted by a reasonable person unless and until the arguments and evidence are refuted" (p. 234). Scott (1960) argued the *prima facie* case needs to be internally consistent and adequate in terms of the types of arguments (sign, cause, example, analogy, and dissociation) present. As this evaluative concept moves across various fields of argument, RAT transforms the concept of *prima facie* into a case that would be acceptable by an idealized audience comprised of the members of a field (Perelman & Olbrechts–Tyteca, 1968).

Recall the requirements for proving murder in the early Greek courts: death, murder, opportunity, and motive. It is the same today in our legal system. The judge may (and sometimes does) rule that the prosecution lacks a *prima facie* case and set the accused free without him or her ever having to make a defense.

In the argumentative field of college textbook writing a prospective author must present a *prima facie* case in a document called a prospectus. This case must be made before a publisher will offer a contract to produce a book. In the prospectus (case), the author must identify several things. These include the market for the book by type of course and size of the student body. Then, the prospective author must review existing textbooks and describe their strengths and weaknesses. The prospective author must also position the proposed book among them. The poorest positioning is a "me too" book. Next, the prospective author must provide a detailed outline of the proposed book. In that outline, the author must identify its unique features, and indicate why it will be superior to existing textbooks. Next the prospective author must demonstrate his or her expertise to write the textbook. Here, the prospective author presents such evidence as scholarly articles published, previous textbooks written, and classroom experience in teaching the book's contents. Finally, the prospective author must predict the book's length and provide a feasible time line for completion. This case (prospectus) is usually sent to the potential publisher's acquisitions editor. The acquisitions editor then sends the prospectus (case) to reviewers called "blind referees." Such blind referees are peers who do not know who sent the prospectus. These reviewers judge whether or not a *prima facie* case has been made. If the referees say no to the book prospectus, then the case (prospectus) is rejected. The prospectus is rejected because it did not present a *prima facie* case. Because the prospectus was not evaluated as having established a *prima facie* case, the book is then rejected by that publishing house.

When students negatively evaluate a professor, it is often on the grounds that the professor failed to provide the ground rules (spell out the burden of proof) for completing a term paper that is acceptable (*prima facie*). In golf parlance, the student does not know what constitutes "par" for the term paper let alone what constitutes a "bogey" or an "eagle."

Validity. *Validity* is an evaluative concept that concerns each argument's soundness. The validity evaluative concept reminds you to do several things when evaluating arguments. First, engage in evidence testing. Second, evaluate the flow of reasoning from the data to the claim. Third, check for fallacies in the reasoning. As used in RAT, validity is an elaborate evaluative concept and space does not permit us to provide more than an overview.

You should be familiar with evidence testing because you live in a literate, democratic society. The first test of evidence incorporates direct observation to see if the "fact" is present. For example, you and another arguer can determine directly if your department offers courses in argumentation and debate. Unobservable facts are another story. For example, if we wanted to know the average salary of communication graduates, then we might use survey statistics to find out. Another evidence testing procedure is inferential statistics, such as the correlation between two events. For example, a correlation lets you determine the relationship between smoking and cancer. Courses in research methods delineate the various tests of statistical evidence. Finally, much of the evidence from which you reason is authoritative, that is, reported to you by some source. Here, you need to test the acceptance of the source. Usually such tests include the source's expertise, objectivity, recency, and completeness. Let's see if we can illustrate how a source might be tested. Walt Garrison, a former Dallas Cowboy football player, served as spokesperson for the National Tobacco Institute. He did so after gaining notoriety in advertisements for a national manufacturer of snuff. One might question Garrison's acceptableness as a source by arguing that a snuff-using, retired football player does not have the expertise or objectivity to talk to the American people about the benign effects of nicotine as the active drug in tobacco. You will encounter such evidence testing a lot in your career. Rest assured that as a college-educated person in our society, others will judge your ability to evaluate the evidence you include in your professional reports. They will also evaluate the evidence you use in your social and political arguments.

Once data or evidence is presented and accepted, one must test the strength of the reasoning from that data to a claim. Recall that there are five types of arguments for field-invariant reasoning. These included argument from sign, cause, example, analogy, and dissociation. Just as with evidence, there are questions to ask that help you interrogate each form of reasoning. With a sign argument one first asks, "What is the reliability of the sign?" "Does the sign point continuously to that which it signifies?" The medical community, for example, often informs the lay public of the signs of an impending heart attack. The symptoms (signs) include chest pain, numbness in the left arm, sweatiness, and dizziness. We want to emphasize, that, with aging, such signs are no small issue to your trail guides. Yet, you also know that 25 percent of heart attacks are silent heart attacks (no symptoms precede the event). As well, an aging individual can sometimes panic and manufacture all the symptoms. Finally, you know that such symptoms may just point to indigestion. So, reasoning by sign is tricky business. Ferreting out reliable signs to use is an important task in any argumentative field, but especially important for medicine because it deals with life or death. We remind you that the key sign of someone who is not choking on their food at a restaurant is: "Are they talking." If not, the other signs—choking, gagging, and bulging eyes—all tell you to apply the Heimlich maneuver.

One can reason fallaciously either by accident or by purpose. Fortunately, there is a system for formally detecting the fallacies present in reasoning. However, determining the formal validity of arguments is a complex activity. The list of fallacies that can occur is lengthy. Unless you've taken a course in logic or a course in argumentation, you've probably not taught yourself how to evaluate arguments for formal validity. The rules for the proper construction for categorical syllogisms (all A are B) and disjunctive syllogisms (either A or B is true) and conditional syllogisms (if A then B) are important to know, but not teachable in the context of this book. Later in the chapter, we provide the example, "John is a monkey," to illustrate the test of the fallacious undistributed middle term for categorical syllogisms. Other types of commonly discussed fallacies are non sequitur, tautology, and ad hominem. A *non sequiter* occurs in reasoning when the conclusions do not follow from the premises. A *tautology* occurs when the argument is circular, such as "women are mortal because they die." An *ad hominem* fallacy occurs when an arguer attacks the maker of the argument as opposed to the argument. For example, "You dirty rat! How can I believe you?" Larson (1986) indicated that one of the strategies for deceptive advertising is to look for formally valid syllogisms whose premises are materially false: "If you are seeking a world-record fish, you should use Trilene line" (p. 158). He noted that you can detect quite easily the conditional nature of this syllogism, yet you know that lots of brands of fishing line will catch large fish.

Ethical. *Ethical* is an evaluative concept that tells you to examine the nature of the arguer and her or his argument. When arguers use arguments to deceive, slander, tell falsehoods, spread misinformation, and misdirect people from important issues, we speak of them as behaving unethically. If they are well-known leaders, such as Senator Joseph McCarthy (R–WI) in the 1950s, we call them demagogues. Although ethics, like some arguments, is often field-dependent—that is, what is ethical may vary in medicine, law, politics, and interpersonal relationships. However, the field of ethics exhibits certain constants that provide a field-invariant code when arguers are arguing for purposes of problem-solving. In general the code specifies rationality, fair play, objectivity, honesty, accuracy, and so forth. Brockriede (1972) used a romantic metaphor to characterize this ethical code and indicated that arguers should act as lovers and not as seducers or rapists.

RAT: Working with Its Qualitative Method

As with all theories, we remind you that it is difficult to find material, social, or symbolic facts initially. The process of discovering and identifying a theory's basic and structural concepts is not pedestrian. It takes training and practice—in the use of the unique qualitative method associated with each general theory— to observe and count the respective communication facts systematically and reliably. With RAT, as with the other general theories, you need to use a qualitative method to assist in uncovering and finding the basic and structural concepts as they appear in communication phenomena.

Argument Layout Analysis (ALA)

Let's stop and look at a point of interest. TCM posited that every theory possesses a unique qualitative method as part of its theory–method complex. RAT's qualitative method is Argument Layout Analysis (Brockriede and Ehninger, 1960). Not all communication is an argument. However, you will know an argument is occurring when you find data, reasoning, and a claim. To help you recognize an argument, RAT's developers have offered both formal and informal models for the layout of argument.

Formal Argument Models   Several formal models allow you to construct valid arguments and reconstruct human talk to check the logical validity of reasoning. One system uses logical and rhetorical syllogisms. The ancients developed idealized, logical syllogisms for testing reasoning, as in the syllogistic Law of Identity (all A is B). Example: "All people are mortal, Julie is a person, therefore Julie is mortal." The conclusions of properly constructed syllogisms provide certain truth. A nonvalid syllogism of this type would be: "All monkeys have two legs, John has two legs, therefore John is a monkey." This latter syllogism is invalid due to the error (fallacy) of the undistributed middle term. A disjunctive syllogism takes the form: "Either you study or you will fail the exam; you did not study; therefore you failed the exam." A conditional syllogism is of the "If–then" construction: "If you get a college degree, then your earning power will increase; you're going to get a college degree; your earning power will increase."

Aristotle gave us enthymemes—rhetorical syllogisms—whose premises are only probably true and that appear in a truncated form in which the major premise or the conclusion is called forth by the audience (McBurney, 1936). Like syllogisms, enthymemes come in categorical, conditional, and disjunctive varieties. A categorical enthymeme might simply read: "Julie is mortal." That claim would be tested by supplying the major (All humans are mortal) and minor (Julie is a human) premises. In the form of an enthymeme, such constructions are incomplete, allowing the listener or reader to supply the missing part(s). A class in argumentation may well devote a week or more to the examination of logical and rhetorical syllogisms and the procedures for checking their validity. Such study of syllogisms is not outmoded. Our system of jurisprudence routinely uses categorical syllogisms to rule by precedent. Similarly, the favored approach to demonstrating scientific knowledge—the testing of hypotheses through "If–then" statements—is in essence the use of conditional syllogisms.

Informal Argument Models   If you dislike building and verifying arguments syllogistically and enthymatically, other structures allow you to assess the correctness of the reasoning process. Beardsley (1950) offered the "general model for practical argument analysis," Toulmin (1958) provided a "model for the layout of argument," Perelman & Olbrechts–Tyteca (1969) developed a "schema for classifying and evaluating types of rational arguments," and Canary, et al. (1995) offered a "model of minimally rational argument." Some people have called the Toulmin Model, and others like it, "a syllogism lying on its side." Such models break RAT's basic concept, rational argument, into its constituent parts of data (evidence), warrant (reasoning), and claim (conclusion). The Toulmin Model adds "backing" for the reasoning process, reservations (exceptions) to the claim, and qualifiers (such as *probably*) to the claim. Many practitioners find such later layout systems easier to use than the syllogistic model (Warnick & Inch, 1994).

Briefly Illustrating ALA

Brockriede and Ehninger (1960) introduced the discipline to the Toulmin Model for constructing, describing, and evaluating argument. The Toulmin Model is routinely used to explain the reasoning process of rational argument in communication courses from public speaking to small group communication. The Toulmin Model contains six parts—three indispensable concepts (data–warrant–claim) and three associative concepts (backing for the warrant, reservation to the claim, and qualifier to the claim). The *warrant,* and the materials that comprise its *backing,* become the reasoning process that gets you from data to claim. Let's look at the previously introduced argument by example about ACT scores using the complete Toulmin Model:

> *Data:* A sample of the entering class's ACT scores were above average.
>
> *Warrant* (Reasoning): The entering class is representative of the student body.
>
> *Backing for the Warrant* (Reasoning): The theory of large numbers says that a sample drawn correctly from a population allows one to generalize to that population.
>
> *Reservation to the Claim:* Unless this entering class is unique from other classes; then
>
> *Qualifier to the Claim:* Probably,
>
> *Claim:* The student body's ACT scores are above average.

ALA allows you to check the thoroughness of any argument or to construct any argument.

RAT: Observing Its Usefulness

We have now reached our final rest stop on this part of the trail to understanding communication theories. Recall that TCM posited utility as its primary evaluative metaconcept. It's again time to think of our litmus test question, "Will this dog hunt?" As we indicated in the earlier discussion of RAT's power and scope, the theory explains the force of rational argument on reaching conviction in decision-making. It has been the theory of choice to explain rational decision-making for 2500 years. As well, much organized research undergirds the development and grounding of RAT. The American Forensics Association, comprised of communication professionals interested in argumentation, provides several outlets for the presentation and discussion of argumentation research and theory-building. The American Forensics Association publishes a journal, *Argumentation and Advocacy* (formerly, *Journal of the American Forensic Association*), which contains studies on argumentation. It meets jointly each year with the National Communication Association and sponsors programs concerning argumentation. It also coordinates debating tournaments for intercollegiate competition and cohosts with the National Communication Association an annual, weeklong symposium on argumentation for communication scholars and students. This organized research activity has generated numerous studies that both ground RAT across Type 1 media and demonstrate the real-world usefulness of competently performing the communication skills derivative of RAT. In this section, we overview the research that grounds RAT, provide some examples of RAT's usefulness in the real world, and respond to RAT's critics.

Explaining Human Action

Scholars ground the concepts in theories by analyzing communication episodes to determine if the concepts appear in the communication. In the past one hundred years, scholars have conducted scores of studies to ground RAT's technical concepts to observables. In recent examples, a number of scholars found the various types and forms of argument in the communication of people talking in a number of situations and contexts. For example, Black (1994) examined the force of rational argument as speakers gave public addresses. Van Eemeren, et al. (1995) reported on the force of rational argument among school students using ordinary language. Heath (1988) examined the use of rational argument among organizations promoting public policy issues. Bantz (1981), Dunbar (1986), and Wiethoff (1981) examined the force of rational argument among organizations and people embroiled in public controversy. Benoit and Lindsey (1986), Condit (1987), Hollihan, Riley, and Freadhoff (1986), and O'Rourke and Manuto (1994) studied the use of rational argument by participants in judicial, deliberative, and religious domains. Allen and Burrell (1992) and Hirokawa (1985) studied the effects of rational argument on participants in dyadic conversation and small group discussion. Infante, Chandler, and Rudd (1989) and Infante, Myers, and Buerkel (1994) studied the force of rational argument on family and organizational disagreements. Putnam and Geist (1985) studied the effects of rational argument on the bargaining and negotiation process. Other recent examples support the grounding of RAT's concepts across a number of Type 1 media. In the cross-cultural or intercultural medium, for example, Hazen (1989) noted that the role of argument, reasoning, and logic in Japan versus the West is one of degree, not kind. Jensen (1992), in his summative study of rhetorical writings of such Asian cultures as Taoism, Confucianism, Buddhism, and Hinduism, concurred with Hazen's conclusion. Jensen found, and thus grounded cross-culturally, such rational argumentation concepts as: dialogue with opponents; evidence and reasoning from authority, analogy, and comparisons; gathering information and intellectual insights; deductive reasoning and problem-solving; using hypothetical-deductive reasoning and logic; and even engaging in formalized dialectical disputation and debate. Gan (1994) examined RAT's contributions to the development of journalistic science in China. Whaley and Babrow (1993) codified the various perspectives on argument by analogy. Garlick (1993) reported on the field-dependency of acceptable arguments about minorities. The study noted, however, that spokesperson race and gender did not influence argument evaluations, demonstrating that some arguments are field-invariant. Pfau and Burgoon (1989) studied comparative attack (issue and candidate) message strategies in political campaign communication. They found generally that campaign communication issue attack messages exert more change in attitudes and vote intention than character attack (*ad hominem*) messages.

Other studies demonstrated RAT's use as a means for justifying decisions and inducing convictions in several field-dependent media. Benoit (1991) investigated the arguments advanced in briefs, oral arguments, and the Court's opinion in the U.S. Supreme Court case of *Miranda v. Arizona*. He found that the supreme court adopted claims and arguments from the briefs of the winning side to justify their decision. In the general populace, people not trained in the making of rational argument accepted stronger arguments over weaker arguments. For example, Allen and Burrell (1992) presented liberal arts college undergraduates, not formally trained in RAT, with the arguments used in the final round of the National Debate Tournament. These students selected the arguments they evaluated as superior. The results indicated that the naive students selected the same arguments as the trained judges at the tournament. Thus, the trained judges and the untrained students agreed that the stronger arguments were used by the team that won the debate and the weaker arguments were used by the team that lost. Infante (1982) and Infante, et al. (1984) found that people who can make rational argument are less aggressive than people who cannot make rational argument. Neer's (1994) study of argumentative flexibility and Sanders, Wiseman, and Gass's (1994) study of argumentation training supported Infante's findings that training in argumentation decreases verbal aggression. As well, Sanders, et al. (1992) found that teaching argumentation skills reduced verbal aggressiveness and empowered intercultural students. Anderson, Schultz, and Courtney (1987) viewed training in argument as a new hope for nonassertive women.

Benefiting the Real World

Beginning more than fifty years ago, scholars reported studies that demonstrated the value of using RAT. The studies indicated a relationship between adroitness in using RAT and success in the real world. For example, Brembeck (1949) found that college students trained in RAT improved significantly in critical thinking over a nontrained matched group. Krumboltz (1957) noted that business executives trained as debaters made more money. McBath (1963) reported a survey that indicated that 62.5 percent of government leaders—including members of congress, senators, governors, cabinet members, and supreme court justices—participated in school debate. Of these, 90 percent indicated that their experience had helped their careers either "greatly" or "invaluably."

Other studies appeared that showed training in RAT transferred to other aspects of the real world. Semlak and Shields (1977) found that community leaders—after watching RAT-trained and nontrained people arguing value questions in celebration of our nation's bicentennial—had rated participants with debate experience comparatively higher in analysis, delivery, and organization. Hirokawa (1985) demonstrated that discussion groups who more competently performed the functions of analyzing a problem and assessing the advantages and disadvantages of each proposed solution got higher quality decisions as compared to groups who did not perform these functions well. Infante and Gordon (1987) reported that people with the ability to make argument were perceived as more competent in superior–subordinate work situations. Canary, et al. (1995) reported that "communicators using complex arguments are seen as more instrumentally effective than communicators using simple arguments" (p. 183).

Studies by Chaffee (1978), Drew and Weaver (1991), Lemert (1993), and Morello (1988) exemplified a research program reporting that televised presidential debates inform voters about public policy, candidate qualities, and campaign issues. Johnson and Sellnow (1995) used Ryan's (1982, 1984, 1988) RAT-based elaboration of policy arguments in the rhetoric of accusation and apology. They reported a case study of an organization facing crisis (the Exxon Valdez tanker oil-spill incident of March 23, 1989). They found that Exxon's arguments concerned three subjects. First, Exxon depicted the causes of the accident as human error. Second, Exxon described the nonneed for further regulation. Finally, Exxon stressed the harms of further regulation. Johnson and Sellnow concluded that both forensic (legal) and deliberative (public policy) arguments were intrinsic to organizational crisis communication. We present another theory of image management in Chapter 9.

RAT provides a detailed explanation of the rational decision-making process central to most human action in a civilized society. Without exaggeration, we can say that your mastery of this theory, and the communication skills derived from it, will provide you with both immediate and long-term benefits. In the near future, your research reports should become more cogent and closely reasoned. As well, your oral presentations should be better received by your critical audience of peers and professors. Communication professors, who have spent time acquiring the skills associated with this general theory, testify to the beneficial impact it has had on their careers. Even noncommunication professors celebrate the utility of this theory. Virginia Owen, Dean of the College of Arts and Sciences and Professor of Economics at Illinois State University, maintains that RAT provided the most valuable training for her role as dean that she received in college. If you have had training in argumentation theory, we are sure you are now agreeing with her.

Withstanding the Critics

Across the centuries, scores of critics have contributed to the transformation of the modern RAT. Indeed, a theory about how communicators make decisions through rational argumentation just naturally invites critics into the fray. Since about 1960, communication scholars have engaged in a very healthy discussion about the acceptability of RAT as a general communication theory. Cox and Willard (1982) succinctly summarized these criticisms and Trapp and Schuetz (1990) continued the dialogue.

RAT is Not a General Communication Theory   The first criticism concerns RAT's status as a general communication theory. The critics argue—by the exception rule—that RAT cannot explain human argumentation across either all contexts or argument fields. Toulmin (1958) first made this criticism in his discussion of field-invariant and field-dependent arguments. Luckily, theories are dynamic entities. They possess the capability to change. Thus, Brockriede and Ehninger (1960) and Ehninger and Brockriede (1963) accepted Toulmin's argument and modified RAT. As a result, RAT continued to explain most kinds of argument, and—with some situational adjustment—nearly everything else. You may take comfort in knowing that the studies grounding RAT's technical concepts allow you to generalize its use to all but the most provincial forms of argument, such as those undergirding cults, primitive societies, and uneducated or unacculturated children. Moreover, even in these cases, RAT can identify what passes for argument in such microcontexts.

Creating, Making, and Having an Argument Require Different Theories to Explain Them   We've seen these ideas previously in this chapter. Recall that creating an argument views argument as process, making an argument views argument as product, and having an argument views argument as procedure. The specific criticism is that RAT, as a normative theory, may explain argument as product in a mechanistic, speaker-centered way, but it cannot explain argument as procedure when arguers co-join in a transactional way to make argument as they have an argument (O'Keefe, 1977). As indicated above, Wenzel (1990) provided a mature way out of this trilemma by viewing argument process, procedure, and product as mere variations of the same concept. As Hample (1988) put it: "I hold that we have a single thing with three manifestations" (p. 13).

Two outcomes of this reasoned deliberation contributed to our healthy characterization. First, the reasoned deliberation contributed to modifications in RAT that allowed for explanation of the identified anomalies. Second, the deliberations led some theorists to construct several microtheories of argument which, for them, appeared low on prescription and formula, and high on description and reflexiveness (Balthrop, 1980; van Eemereen and Grootendorst, 1990; Jacobs and Jackson, 1982; Willard, 1983). However, as of this writing, these alternate theories have not replaced RAT in its power and scope of explanation of rational decision-making in democratic communities.

Modern Cognitive Explanations Do Not Support RAT   The third major criticism focused on RAT's delineation of logical argument as separate from emotional or other types of justification for action. Delia (1970) and Hample (1980) maintained that the dualism between conviction and persuasion lacked the support of modern explanations of cognitive processes. What they did not explain away, however, were RAT's research findings (and one's own personal experience) regarding rational argument. Grounded studies and reports of personal experience indicate that people prefer rational argument. Such studies also indicate that people make decisions based on logical arguments. Presently, the cognitivists have yet to link the way they say people "really" think to an alternate explanation of human decision-making in the fields of law, politics, medicine, science, industry, and commerce.

As you can see, RAT's critics have missed the mark. Study after study demonstrated that RAT is a useful theory that explains the force of rational argument on conviction and human decision-making. With both the criticisms and responses at hand, we leave it to you to make an informed judgment about whether or not RAT withstands the critics. We believe it does as all viable general communication theories do. When you get to the end of the trail to understanding communication theories, we believe you can use RAT with confidence. We wish you happy hunting.

Summary

In this Chapter, we introduced you to Rational Argument Theory (RAT). RAT allows you to explain the communicative force behind the human action known as rational decision-making. We began by viewing RAT as a general communication theory capable of being understood through the lens of the Communication Metatheory (TCM). We sketched RAT's power and scope, traced its origin and roots, and discussed its primary assumptive system.

Then we introduced RAT's concepts (see **Figure 3-1**). We explained its basic concepts, structural concepts, and evaluative concepts. Next, we introduced and illustrated how to work with RAT's qualitative method, Argument Layout Analysis (ALA). Then, we reported on RAT's usefulness. We showed RAT's use to explain human action and benefit the real world. Then, we discussed its ability to withstand critical scrutiny.

By now, you should be familiar with RAT. Like our communication graduate on-the-job, Corey, you ought to be able to use RAT to good advantage (see **Figure 3-2**). If you do not yet feel comfortable with RAT, we suggest you review our detailed chapter summary, **Box 3-1,** entitled, "Understanding RAT in a Nutshell."

"Rational Argument Theory (RAT) empowers us with the decision-making capacity to analyze, evaluate, and gain conviction concerning the problems we face, the choices we make, and the roads we take in strategic planning."

FIGURE 3-2.   Communication Graduate On-the-Job

BOX 3-1   Understanding RAT in a Nutshell

RAT Defined: *Rational Argument Theory* is a general communication theory that explains the rational bases for human decision-making. RAT views arguers as risking their convictions.

Origins: The earliest forms of RAT surfaced 2500 years ago in ancient Greece. RAT's roots are in the classical studies of rhetoric, dialectic, and logic. Contemporary scholars with ties to the University of Illinois initiated the dialogue leading to the modern form of RAT.

Assumptions: (1) Humans naturally make argument; (2) Arguments occur over questions of fact, value, and policy; (3) The competition of rational arguments in open discourse enables the discovery of truth and the generation of new knowledge; (4) Arguers and arguments function rhetorically (as process), dialectically (as procedure), and logically (as product); (5) Humans prefer rational proof over other types of proof; and (6) Arguments travel in two media—an invariant and a dependent field.

Basic Concepts: A *rational argument* is a reasoned, supported claim. It is the smallest, complete unit of proof consisting of three subelements: data (evidence), the reasoning process (warrant), and the claim (conclusion). Data or evidence consists of facts, opinions, and materials. Six types of reasoning exist: argument from sign, cause, example, analogy, authority, and dissociation. There are four types of claims: designated, definitive, evaluative, and advocative. Again, RAT assumes that arguments, and therefore claims, center on questions of fact, value, and policy.

Structural Concepts: RAT possesses message, dynamic, communicator, and medium structural concepts. The message structure concepts are stasis, presumption, burden of proof, contention, and case. The *case* is the largest unit of proof and consists of several *contentions* that in turn consist of many arguments that combine to form an answer to a question of fact, value, or policy. *Stasis* is where assertion meets denial. It tells the arguers what they are arguing about. Most field-dependent communities develop lists of stock issues that form their stasis.

Presumption is a piece of argumentative ground that tells the arguers who is responsible for proving one's contentions and case. Usually, the person who seeks change must prove. The person defending the current way of doing things possesses the presumption that no change is needed. *Burden of proof* is the risk of proposing change. It is the burden on that member of the controversy who will lose (due to the saliency of natural presumption) if nothing is done to prove an assertion or claim. One's burden of proof is met when a *prima facie case* is made by presenting arguments comprising *contentions*. RAT's dynamic structure concepts are rhetorical, dialectical, and logical. The *rhetorical dynamic* views argument as a natural human process that influences others. The *dialectical dynamic* views argument as procedures that exhibit well-defined rules for problem-solving. The *logical dynamic* views argument as a product to be examined for its formal and material validity. RAT's communicator structure concepts are arguer, audience, and critic. An *arguer* is a person who is willing to risk confrontation of their claims with others. Of course, arguers must be willing to modify their claims as a result of the argumentative encounter. *Audience* is the person or persons the arguer is trying to convince. The audience may be the arguer, fellow arguers, a third party, or an idealized audience. A *critic* is a detached observer with no interest in the outcome of the argument. The critic is assumed to be in a superior position to make judgments about the argument. An arguer can also function as his or her own objective critic. The medium structure concepts propagating RAT are field-invariant and field-dependent. *Field-invariant* arguments cross all rhetorical communities. *Field-dependent* arguments display unique rules, norms, and standards for acceptable evidence and reasoning.

Evaluative Concepts: RAT's main evaluative concepts are prima facie, validity, and ethical. A *prima facie* case is a standard of proof needed for conviction or adherence to an argument. *Validity* assesses each argument's soundness. *Ethical* refers both to the examination of the ethics of the arguer and his or her use of arguments.

Chapter *4*

Symbolic Convergence Theory (SCT)

*The force of fantasy-chaining provides meaning,
emotion, and motive for human action.*

Chapter Outline

Let's pause here by the trail so that we can talk about our next landmark, Symbolic Convergence Theory (SCT). SCT is indigenous to the field of communication. Ernest Bormann, his students, and colleagues developed SCT in the 1970s and 1980s primarily at the University of Minnesota. SCT explains the force of fantasy themes—for example the idea of your authors as "trail guides leading you along the journey to understanding communication theories"—that groups of people cocreate to fashion their symbolic worlds. SCT is well suited to explain such communicative actions as school spirit, the close camaraderie of Airborne Rangers, and the pride that a good work group takes in its accomplishments. As well, SCT helps explain and predict the direction and actions of participants in political campaigns, social and religious movements, and the culture of organizations.

SCT explains the communicative force behind the creation of a common consciousness (symbolic reality) called a *rhetorical vision*. A rhetorical vision resembles a drama in form and is akin to a viewpoint, ideology, or worldview. The explanatory power of SCT "lies in its ability to account for the development, evolution, and decay of dramas that catch up groups of people and change behavior" (Bormann, 1972, p. 399). We begin by viewing SCT as a general communication theory. We sketch its power and scope, trace its origin and roots, and discuss its primary assumptive system. Then we introduce SCT's theoretical concepts. We explain how to find its basic concepts, see its structural concepts, and use its evaluative concepts. Next, we introduce and illustrate how to work with SCT's qualitative method, Fantasy Theme Analysis (FTA). Then, we report on SCT's usefulness. We show SCT's use to explain human action and benefit the real world. Then we discuss its ability to withstand critical scrutiny. Finally, we present our Chapter Summary, "Understanding SCT in a Nutshell."

SCT: Viewing the General Theory

Symbolic Convergence Theory (SCT) seeks to explain three things: (1) the process of how people come to share (or cease to share) a common symbolic reality; (2) why group consciousness begins, rises, and is sustained, thereby providing meaning, emotion, and motive for action for members of a symbolic community; and (3) the recurring forms of communication indicative of a shared group consciousness.[1]

SCT derives from the symbolic paradigm of communication theories. All theories flowing from the symbolic paradigm adhere to a paradigmatic ontological assumption that humans create a symbolic reality. Theories within the symbolic paradigm allow you to view human communication as a force that spurs people to action, stabilization, or even inaction. The force emanates from the way in which people linguistically interpret events through the use of symbolic facts. In other words, symbolic theories view the motive for human action as contained in the language that people use to depict or describe reality. With SCT, communicative force flows from communicators (fantasizers) communicating (fantasizing) by presenting messages (fantasy themes) propagated through a medium$_2$ substance (group-chaining and/or public-chaining).

Sketching Its Power and Scope

The *Symbolic Convergence Theory* is a general communication theory. Its explanatory power comes from the acceptance of words as vigorous operating forces that attract and repel much like electromagnetic energy. SCT allows you to look at human "talk" and explain the appearance of a common symbolic consciousness among communities of humans. That symbolic consciousness contains shared meanings, emotions, and motives for action. SCT explains how humans come to share a common symbolic reality such as that of the Cold War, Manifest Destiny, or the American Dream.

　　SCT is a general theory of broad scope. As we've indicated, a general theory provides a why explanation of human communication across a broad array of contexts. Scholars have used SCT to explain communication in political campaigns, public speeches, movement rhetoric, small group discussions, organizational cultures, television programs, movies, cartoons, advertising, marketing, and public relations activities. Recall that The Communication Metatheory (TCM; presented in Chapter 1) posited that general theories are not time-bound. In SCT's case, it allows explanation of the impact of the Puritans' vision of salvation and the work ethic (seventeenth century), self-governance and the War of Independence (eighteenth century), Manifest Destiny and the expansion of the frontier (nineteenth century), and the rise and end of the Cold War (twentieth century). Indeed, as a general communication theory, SCT explains new phenomena as you experience them right now. For example, within moments of the April 19, 1995 bombing of the Federal Building in Oklahoma City, correspondents began fantasizing about who was responsible. They created a new reality—filled with characters, plot lines, and scenic description—that provided meaning, emotion, and motive for action. We return to this journalistic reality later in the chapter.

Tracing Its Origin and Roots

SCT began with the work of Ernest Bormann and his students at the University of Minnesota in 1970. It developed as a message-centered theory derived from the systematic observation of symbolic facts. SCT's developers worked to explain how small and large human groups created, used, and in turn became influenced by the symbolic facts known as fantasy themes. SCT's roots, as a means of explaining symbolic consciousness, grew in the fertile medium$_1$ soil of small group communication, public address, and mass and political communication.

　　The theory began by explaining the sharing of fantasy themes in the communication of members of small work groups. Group studies conducted at the University of Minnesota confirmed in a collaborative way Robert Bales's (1970) research at Harvard on group fantasizing (Bormann, 1982b, 1990). Both the Harvard and Minnesota studies found that at certain moments in group problem-solving, members grow excited, become boisterous, and interrupt conversation. The content of the messages created at such moments of fantasy-chaining provided a symbolic explanation of events. The content, a symbolic world filled with heroes and villains, plot lines, and scenic description, formed a new consciousness for the group members (Chesebro, Cragan, & McCullough, 1973).

The researchers then observed the existence of symbolic realities in the rhetoric of larger rhetorical communities. They noted, for example, that exemplar models of public speeches often depicted a vision of reality filled with heroes and heroines, and scenarios and scenes, much like the view of reality created by participants in small group discussions. As well, the content of such speeches often called forth extant visions of reality such as the Puritan view of the nature of a just God (Bormann, 1972, 1985b), or the pioneer's view of Manifest Destiny (Shields, 1981a), or the social activist's view of communism (Ilka, 1977). For the SCT researchers, symbolic facts such as fantasies and shorthand symbolic cues became every bit as important as social facts like roles and networks or material facts like receivers and channels. The emphasis on symbolic facts led to the assumption that the locus of meaning for communication resided in the message (Bormann, 1980; Cragan & Shields, 1981a).

The idea of the dramatic nature of messages also provided a good fit between theory and practice in studies of the mass media and mass communication campaigns. For example, the researchers observed the chaining process in the presentation of mediated symbolic facts in print and electronic media.[2] A number of studies sought to link the fantasy themes portrayed in the media and in mass media campaigns with the resultant symbolic realities of the viewing, voting, and acting audience.[3] The studies that developed and used FTA proved central to the later development of the Symbolic Convergence Theory.[4]

Accepting Its Assumptive System

Again, it's time for a brief rest stop. In our discussion of TCM (Chapter 1), we indicated that all theories assume things about the nature of human beings, how we know what we know, and the values present in discourse. Recall also that a given theory often emphasizes one kind of assumptive system as primary. SCT's assumptions concern how we know what we know when working with the theory (Cragan & Shields, 1995a). SCT's epistemological assumptions are (1) the direct content of the message conveys meaning, emotion, and motive for action; (2) reality is cocreated symbolically; (3) fantasy-sharing creates symbolic convergence; (4) fantasy themes occur in all forms of discourse; and (5) on any subject, at least three deep structures—righteous, social, and pragmatic master analogues—compete as alternate explanations of symbolic reality.

The Direct Content of the Message Conveys Meaning, Emotion, and Motive for Action
This assumption stresses that meaning is in the dramatizing message (Bormann, 1972). It contrasts with some other theories that assume meaning, emotion, and motive for action are in people rather than in words (Watzlawick, Beavin, & Jackson, 1967) or that the medium is the message (McLuhan, 1964). The following illustration should help you understand this assumption. Anita Hill, a law professor and former employee of Supreme Court Justice Clarence Thomas, took the stand at Thomas's 1991, televised Senate Confirmation Hearings.

Hill accused Thomas, in *ex post facto* fashion, of past incidents of sexual harassment. Thomas proclaimed that the whole confirmation process appeared to be "a high tech lynching of an uppity black man." This fantasy theme made headlines in newspapers and national news magazines and filled the columns of syndicated writers. This material indicated that many American men shared the fantasy. Many believed Judge Thomas was being lynched electronically, just as in the past thousands of African American men had been lynched from trees for being too assertive in a white-dominated culture.

Reality Is Cocreated Symbolically   This assumption stresses that the members of a rhetorical community participate in the embellishment and chaining of fantasy themes (Cragan & Shields, 1995a). For example, it is commonplace for work groups to cocreate a symbolic name for their supervisor. On January 1, 1995, Professor Shields's sister, Katheryn, took office as the elected County Executive of Jackson County, Missouri. At the level of material fact there is a person—Katheryn Shields. At the level of social fact, the Honorable Katheryn Shields functions in the role of County Executive (boss). At the level of symbolic fact, such as an inside joke, her work group of predominantly male colleagues on the County Legislature may refer to Katheryn Shields, acting in her role of County Executive (boss), as "Attila the Hen."[5]

Fantasy-Sharing Creates Symbolic Convergence   This assumption indicates that a symbolic fact, initiated by one person, is picked up, embellished, and reconfigured by others and becomes the common consciousness (symbolic interpretation) for the community (Bormann, 1972). A chaining fantasy often links group members in playful dialogue until shared group consciousness results. When single, Professor Cragan's youngest daughter lived and worked in downtown Chicago. At that time, Chicago's only suburban telephone area code was 708. Keary and her downtown womenfriends shared the fantasy theme: "We don't date a 708." Downtown Chicago's area code was 312. That prompted, "312, we'll date you!" These fantasies indicated that the urban women did not date men who lived in the suburbs, who probably still lived with their parents, and who came into Chicago irregularly. Conversely, they would date men who had moved out on their own and had a job and an apartment downtown.

Fantasy Themes Occur in All Forms of Discourse   This assumption indicates that fantasy themes occur in both rational and imaginative language (Bormann, Cragan, & Shields, 1994). The force of fantasy accounts for irrational and nonrational aspects of communication as well as its rational aspects. In other words, fantasy themes may be found in logical arguments as well as myths, stories, anecdotes, and metaphors. For example, a rhetorical community may chain-out and accept the theme, "there are more than 5 billion people on earth," just as they may conclude from that material fact that "the earth is overcrowded and needs population control," or conversely, "new, genetically engineered, agricultural developments will solve the world's hunger problems."

On Any Subject, At Least Three Deep Structures—Righteous, Social, and Pragmatic Master Analogues—Compete as Alternate Explanations of Symbolic Reality   These embedded deep-motive structures underlie and help explain the force of fantasy themes and rhetorical visions (Cragan & Shields, 1981b). For example, in selecting a campus dormitory as an entering student you may have participated in one of three competing alternative symbolic realities: "I want a dorm that enforces quiet-hours so that I can study" (righteous deep structure), versus "I want a dorm that allows me to make a lot of friends" (social deep structure), versus "I want a dorm that's conveniently located close to my classes" (pragmatic deep structure).

Remember, assumptions are just that. They require you to say, "I will act as if these assumptions are true and see what I find." Again, we emphasize that as a general theory of broad scope you should suspend judgment and adopt SCT's assumptive system for the purposes of understanding the theory.

SCT: Introducing the Theoretical Concepts

It's time to pause a moment and contemplate a landmark up ahead. Recall that TCM asks you to examine a theory's basic, structural, and evaluative theoretical concepts. SCT—like all core general communication theories—exhibits basic, structural, and evaluative concepts with their attendant technical definitions. SCT contains four basic, fourteen structural, and three evaluative concepts. As you observe communicators communicating through the lens of this theory, you should see fantasizers creating, using, and evaluating fantasy themes. In the flow of dramatizing discourse, it may appear difficult to see the different concepts of this theory. Nonetheless, experience dictates that the best starting point accentuates the most elemental parts of the theory. **Figure 4-1** displays SCT's theoretical concepts. Again, we discuss each concept separately even though they are interrelated and often occur unseparated as discourse is viewed through the lens of SCT.

Finding Basic Concepts

Four technical terms—fantasy theme, fantasy type, symbolic cue, and saga—serve as SCT's basic concepts. Each represents the phenomena present in communication that you must recognize and find to use SCT. Again, as with the other general communication theories, these basic concepts do not come naked. They will be encapsulated in SCT's structural terms of rhetorical vision, dramatis personae, plot line, scene, sanctioning agent, and the righteous, social, and pragmatic master analogues. Having found communication phenomena representing SCT's structural terms, you may then analyze such symbolic facts using SCT's evaluative terms of shared group consciousness, rhetorical vision reality links, and fantasy theme artistry.

Initial Basic Concept   TCM (presented in Chapter 1) posited that a general theory's basic concepts fall within two subclasses: the initial basic concept and the associated basic concepts. Again, an initial basic concept is the primary communication unit that is singled out for analysis. SCT's initial basic concept is the fantasy theme.

Fantasy Theme.   The fantasy theme, as the primary unit of analysis among SCT's basic concepts, is the initial thing you must find in human communication when using this theory (Bormann, 1972). In other words, the fantasy theme serves as the kind of symbolic fact you must find to use this theory. If you cannot find a fantasy theme, then you cannot theorize using SCT. A *fantasy theme* embodies a dramatizing message depicting characters

Viewing SCT's Anatomical Elements

Key:
Bold Caps = The Communication Metatheory's Metaconcepts
Caps + Small Case = SCT's Theoretical Concepts

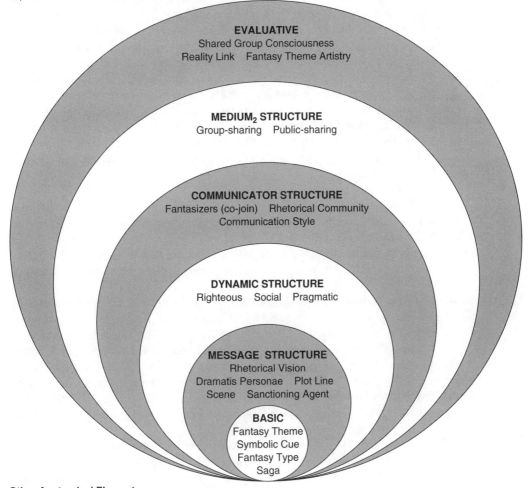

EVALUATIVE
Shared Group Consciousness
Reality Link   Fantasy Theme Artistry

MEDIUM₂ STRUCTURE
Group-sharing   Public-sharing

COMMUNICATOR STRUCTURE
Fantasizers (co-join)   Rhetorical Community
Communication Style

DYNAMIC STRUCTURE
Righteous   Social   Pragmatic

MESSAGE STRUCTURE
Rhetorical Vision
Dramatis Personae   Plot Line
Scene   Sanctioning Agent

BASIC
Fantasy Theme
Symbolic Cue
Fantasy Type
Saga

Other Anatomical Elements:
COMMUNICATIVE FORCE	**MODELING**
ORIGIN, ROOTS, ASSUMPTIONS	**RELATIONSHIP STATEMENTS**
PARADIGM	**THEORY–METHOD COMPLEX**

EXAMPLE OF A FANTASY TYPE: "There's little doubt that failing that discussion assignment is the best thing that ever happened to our small group!" "Yah, we sure fetched good out of evil for the remainder of the semester." "Yah, it made us get our act together."

FIGURE 4-1.

engaged in action in a setting that accounts for and explains human experience. For example, the following statements exemplify fantasy themes representing a larger symbolic reality: "Our house and property are being systematically demolished by a half-dozen young thugs and we stand by helplessly, two women, with no one to assist us . . . The court system is more concerned about the rights of the perpetrator than the rights of the victim" (Tiegen, 1973, 8A). Such dramatizing messages allow two or more people to account for and explain experience by sparking a fantasy-chain or shared interpretive experience. In other words, although the fantasy theme *is* the message, it becomes a part of a community's consciousness through the dynamic process of chaining and sharing.

Groups and other rhetorical communities make sense out of confusing events by creating a consciousness that provides symbolic common ground. Because fantasy theme messages depict reality symbolically they are always slanted, ordered, and interpretive. As well, fantasy themes serve as carriers of the structural concepts (*dramatis personae,* plot line, scene, sanctioning agent) that comprise a rhetorical vision. As the carrier of these structural concepts, a fantasy theme may vary from a phrase, to a sentence, to a paragraph in length. You can recognize a fantasy theme because it exhibits substantive qualities (content), structural qualities (the depictions of the *dramatis personae,* or plot lines, or scenic attributes, or the sanctioning agent), and stylistic qualities (the dramatizing, embellishing, and reconfiguring of fantasy themes).

Associated Basic Concepts   SCT's remaining basic concepts are symbolic cue, fantasy type, and saga. These latter concepts are really merely special categories of fantasy themes. In other words, SCT's basic units of communication phenomena, fantasy themes, work as the carriers of symbolic cues, fantasy types, and sagas. SCT's associated basic concepts are distinguishable from a fantasy theme, per se, due to their use in consistent, repetitive ways in discourse.

Symbolic Cue.   A *symbolic cue* is a shorthand rhetorical indicant or code that stands for a fantasy theme. At your school, the phrase "publish or perish" is a cue to an important professorial fantasy about contributing to the discovery of new knowledge at the university. Thus, a commonly agreed-on, cryptic, symbolic cue triggers the resharing of a fantasy theme (Bormann, 1982c). As the members of a rhetorical community tell and retell a fantasy theme it tends to get shorter and restylized. Eventually the complete theme is called forth by a single word, phrase, or symbol. Symbolic cues can evoke anger, hatred, love, and affection as well as laughter and humor. Among the best evidence that people have shared fantasies is the presence of such inside symbolic cues.

Examples abound of symbolic cues that allude to more elaborate, previously shared fantasy themes. They range from the inside jokes of a work unit (recall "Attila the Hen") to simple symbols such as "U\$A" to characterize the materialistic nature of our country. For example, an "X" on a cap cues one to the fantasy of Malcolm X who gave up his surname, Little, to symbolize all his slave forebears who had lost their African names due to slavery.[6] Most consumer product lines develop a rich fantasy in introductory advertisements. Such a fantasy theme eventually gets reduced to a single symbolic cue in subsequent advertisements. Hence, the Marlboro Man cues the rugged individualist fantasy of the "Old West," the Red Cross cues the Christian help fantasy of the Good Samaritan or Knights Templar, and Nike's "Just do it" cues the active sports participant (and not the couch potato). The symbolic cue concept also makes possible the development and observation of fantasy types and sagas.

Fantasy Type.   When members of a rhetorical community share similarities between the plot lines in different dramas, or the qualities of characters across dramas, or the particulars of scenes, or sanctioning agents across dramas, they may generalize a fantasy type. Bormann (1977) indicated that a *fantasy type* is a stock scenario used to explain new events in a well-known dramatic form. Hence, Watergate, Irangate, and Whitewatergate explain repeated governmental corruption and cover-up using the "gate" symbolic cue as a fantasy type. Fantasy types help to fit the breaking news and the unfolding of experience comfortably into a rhetorical community's existing symbolic reality. A fantasy type often functions as the workhorse of emerging rhetorical visions because it tends to convey meaning, emotion, and motive for action for the members of a rhetorical community more easily than an original fantasy theme might. The phrase, "remember Waco," an important fantasy theme of the armed militia movement of the mid-1990s, was acted out with the bombing of the Federal Building in Oklahoma City on the April 19 anniversary of the FBI raid on the Branch Davidians' compound in Waco, Texas. The fantasy type, remember Waco, exhibited more driving force because of the original "Remember the Alamo" and "Remember the Maine" fantasy types from other times and places.

Rhetoricians often turn to the fantasy type as a rhetorical device rather than dramatizing specific new characters taking action in the here-and-now setting. Rhetoricians who sustain a given rhetorical vision (a composite drama that catches up large groups of people in a common symbolic reality) often use a fantasy type as if it were an archetypal fantasy to portray new experiences and bring them into line with the overall values and emotions of their rhetorical vision. For example, rhetoricians may "fetch good" from the "evil" of a new calamity as in "the lesson of Vietnam," or "the lesson of Oklahoma City," or "the lesson of downsizing" at my company.

Saga. A *saga* is an oft-repeated telling of the achievements in the life of a person, group, community, organization, or nation as in quest stories or the Puritan work ethic (Bormann, 1982c, 1985a). For example, fantasy themes often denote the part of a saga that refers to the genesis of the group, community, organization, or nation. All companies exhibit a symbolic reality that contains meaning, emotion, and motive for action for its members. When preparing to interview for a job, it often pays to know about a company's genesis fantasy. Within that saga is the meaning, emotion, and motive for that company's being. For example, the 3–M Company, in St. Paul, Minnesota, possesses a genesis fantasy that relates to the development of their first product and many noteworthy subsequent products. This saga tells you that if you go to work for 3–M, your mission is to develop or assist in the development and marketing of new products. In addition, the achievement part of the saga relates how the successful 3–M employee first contributes to product development or marketing and then moves from the laboratory or the sales field to the "glass house," that is, the administrative building for top management located in St. Paul, Minnesota. Once there, he or she then manages these products. State Farm Insurance, a Fortune 12 company, possesses a saga cued by the positioning statement, "Like a good neighbor, State Farm is there." The genesis fantasy in the saga centers on the State Farm agent who lives and works in the neighborhood of his or her policyholders. This agent shows civic concern and volunteers to work with many worthwhile charities like the Special Olympics. Being neighborly and involved in the community reflects a major aspect of State Farm's corporate culture. So, if you interview at 3–M or State Farm, or any other company, you need to know the company's corporate saga.

Symbolic cues representative of America's nation–state saga include "the spirit of entrepreneurship," "the great experiment in democracy," and "the power of education to eradicate disease and eliminate poverty" (Shields, 1981e). Organizations also exhibit important sagas just like nation–states. Undoubtedly, your college or university has both a genesis fantasy and one or more achievement fantasies that make up its saga.

Seeing Structural Concepts

Let's again take a brief rest stop. Recall that TCM stipulated that communication theories possess structural concepts that sort out by metaconcepts concerning message, communicator, communication dynamic, and medium. At its simplest, SCT explains that communicators communicate with fantasy in some medium. SCT contains five message structure concepts (rhetorical vision, dramatis personae, plot line, scene, and sanctioning agent), three communication dynamic structure concepts (the warring righteous, social, and pragmatic master analogues), four communicator concepts (cocreating fantasizers, propensity to fantasize, rhetorical community, and communication style), and two medium$_2$ concepts (group-chaining and public-chaining).

Message Concepts   All general communication theories contain message structure concepts that dress up and flesh out a theory's basic concepts. SCT's structural concepts allow you to see the way a rhetorical community dramatizes messages to order the world symbolically. We would remind you that when you find a dramatized message filled with character description, or plot line depiction, or scenic attributes, or sanctioning agent enumeration you have found a fantasy theme. As indicated in **Figure 4-1,** SCT's message structure concepts are rhetorical vision, dramatis personae, plot line, scene, and sanctioning agent.

Rhetorical Vision.   A *rhetorical vision* is a composite drama that catches up large groups of people in a common symbolic reality (Bormann, 1972). Bormann (1985b) noted that a fully articulated rhetorical vision is "a unified putting together of various scripts [fantasy themes and fantasy types] that give the participants a broader view of things" (p. 8). A rhetorical vision contains many fantasy themes that depict heroes and villains in dramatic action within a dramatic scene. Rhetorical visions represent a special type of symbolic fact that helps us "make sense out of what prior to that time [the emergence of the vision] may have been a confusing state of affairs" (p. 5). For example, Bormann, Cragan, and Shields (1996) demonstrated how the Cold War rhetorical vision helped to make sense of the confusing aftermath of World War II. Similarly, Huxman (1996) demonstrated how the Seneca Falls women's rights rhetorical vision helped to make sense of the disparate writings (the enlightenment, transcendentalism, and the abolition of slavery) by three important nineteenth-century women.

Each rhetorical vision reflects a life cycle containing consciousness-creating, consciousness-raising, consciousness-sustaining, consciousness-decline, and consciousness-terminus stages. Rhetorical visions often come steeped in one of three available deep structures that provide motive for action. We will discuss these in the next section on communication dynamic. Rhetorical visions also exist along several continua: pure to mixed deep structures reflective of the communication dynamic; inflexible to flexible in adapting to

[handwritten margin note: USA – we are at war / are at competing / V.'s rhetorical vision / Osama's / followers]

changing circumstances; intense to passive in promoting action; secretive to proselytizing regarding the expansion of the rhetorical community that adheres to the vision; and paranoid to healthy regarding the vision's links to objective reality (Bormann, Cragan, & Shields, 1996).

You already know several important rhetorical visions by name. For example, our forebears expanded the frontier and gained island territories following the plot line of the Manifest Destiny rhetorical vision as offered by Horace Greely: "Go West young man!" Similarly, the Suffragette Movement coalesced around a rhetorical vision concerned with women gaining the right to vote. Likewise, the Civil Rights Movement converged through a rhetorical vision concerned with public accommodation and voting rights. The Right to Life and Choice movements link respectively to competing rhetorical visions centering on the issue of abortion. The remaining message structure concepts flesh out the substructure of a rhetorical vision.

Dramatis Personae.   The *dramatis personae* are fantasy theme depictions of the characters that are given life in the vision (Bormann, 1972). Dramatis personae mirror what we think of as characters in a play or movie, such as King Lear, Forest Gump, Freddie Kruger, Thelma and Louise, or Spike Lee's character in *School Days.* The fantasy themes depicting the characters provide insights into, and descriptions of, the character's human qualities. Dramatis personae fantasy themes may depict frailties or foibles, strengths or weaknesses, virtues or vices, and consistencies or idiosyncrasies. For example, Putnam, Van-Hoeven, and Bullis (1991) identified the rich fantasy themes that teachers and administrators developed to vilify each other during their bargaining negotiations over salary and working conditions. For example, an administrator described one elementary teacher on the bargaining unit as "like a woodpecker on a rotten log back there, her head bobbing up and down. I wonder if she's going to sleep" (p. 95). Such characterizations are also true in movies. For example, the scriptwriters and the director portrayed Ace Ventura, Pet Detective, as the weird but lovable, laughable, heroic persona of some Generation X types. Characters may also be vilified. Students, in some faculty rhetorical visions, receive vilified symbolic characterizations such as "slackers," "frat rats," "deadheads," "sorority Sallies," "computer nerds," and so forth. Of course, the students at our universities, Illinois State University and the University of Missouri–St. Louis, as well as those who have read this book, are the hardworking, career-minded, cyber-surfers who graduate with a thorough knowledge of communication theories and go on to successful careers in this land of milk and honey.

Scene.   *Scene* details the symbolic location of the action portrayed in the vision, such as "behind closed doors" or "in the wild West." As in a play, scene is the setting, the place where the action occurs, the location where the actors and actresses act out their roles (Bormann, 1972). However, the scene in which the heroines, heroes, villains, and supporting players appear may be more than just props and scenery. The scene may exude known fantasy-type qualities such as those implied by the labels "Animal House," "Ghetto," and "Suburbs." Similarly, managers of corporations often work in named scenes that exude a symbolic reality depicting corporate headquarters: "The Taj Mahal" (Upjohn Company), "Mahogany Row" (Goodyear Company), "Hovey Heaven" (Illinois State University), the "Glass House" (3–M and Ford), and the "Ivory Tower" (State Farm). Your college's brochures often highlight known scenes like "Fraternity Row," "the Commons," or "Quad." In some rhetorical visions, scene looms as so important that it influences the qualities attributed to the characters and even the plot lines generated within the vision. The "Land of Opportunity," the "Holocaust," and the "Dark Continent" provide excellent examples of scene-dominated rhetorical visions.

Plot Line.   *Plot line* portrays the action or plot of the vision (Bormann, 1972). It is the undergirding rationale for why the drama is unfolding as it is and for why the characters are acting the way they do. Someone once wrote a treatise on the basic plots of plays. These included love story, conspiracy, good versus evil, adventure, quest, paradise lost, mystery, violation of nature, and so forth. A similar finite universe appears to hold true for rhetorical visions. For example, the symbolic reality of participants adhering to the O. J. Simpson first-degree murder defense, or the Cold War rhetorical vision, or the vision of the armed militia movement, and the rhetorical visions of nearly all religious cults—such as the Branch Davidians, Jim Jones's Guyana, and the Reverend Sung Yung Moon—appear to include a paranoid conspiracy plot line (Cragan, 1975; Goodnight & Poulakos, 1981). In the 1980s and 1990s, the downsizing of U.S. corporations gave rise to many conspiracy plot lines in which workers depicted executives conspiring secretly to eliminate thousands of productive workers from their company.

Sanctioning Agent.   The *sanctioning agent,* for example, God or the Constitution, legitimizes the symbolic reality depicted by the rhetorical vision (Bormann, 1972; Shields, 1981a). In some rhetorical visions the sanctioning agent that justifies its acceptance and promulgation is a higher power, such as God, justice, or democracy. In other rhetorical visions, it is a salient here-and-now phenomenon, such as the atomic bomb, corporate survival, a crucifixion and resurrection, or a governmental action. In still other rhetorical visions, the sanctioning agent may be a moral code, such as the Cadet Code at West Point, or the Code of the West, or one's personal or professional code of ethics.

Thomas Jefferson said that ignorance and freedom can not long coexist. In accord with that plot line, the federal government, through the Morrell Act, donated public lands to provide the monies to establish public, land grant universities (Blum, et al., 1963). Their charges included: (1) to educate the populace to wipe out ignorance; (2) to create new knowledge to further industrialization and scientific advancement; and (3) to engage in public service to bring the applications of the university's research efforts to the people. In short, the desire to train the uneducated (a salient here-and-now phenomenon), invent new knowledge (scientific advancement as a higher good), and apply knowledge to the solution of everyday problems (a moral code) sanctioned the creation of the nation's great public universities. Nearly all of America's Fortune 500 companies have formalized what they call their mission statement. Such a statement invariably depicts the sanctioning agent that justifies corporate behavior in much the same way that the Morrell Act justified teaching, research, and public service as the missions of land grant colleges and universities.

Dynamic Concepts   Again, a rest stop is in order. Recall from TCM that we know that general communication theories exhibit a deep structure undergirding communicative messages. Moreover, there is a tension as to the choices of which deep structure will predominate. SCT's communication dynamic concerns whether the deep structure of a rhetorical vision follows predominantly a *righteous, social,* or *pragmatic* master analogue. In other words, rhetorical visions often compete with one another to explain phenomena (Cragan & Shields, 1981c, 1995a). The adjective "predominantly" indicates the mixed master analogue deep structure of some rhetorical visions. By way of forecast, a rhetorical vision steeped in a *righteous master analogue* stresses the correct way of doing things. A rhetorical vision emanating from a *social master analogue* emphasizes primary human relations focusing on such things as friendship. A rhetorical vision derived from a *pragmatic master analogue* elevates practicality.

Cragan and Shields (1981b, 1981c, 1992) reported several organizational communication studies that grounded the notion that the righteous, social, and pragmatic master analogues comprise the dynamic structure of SCT. In each case, they found competing rhetorical visions reflective of the hypothesized deep structures. In a collaborative fashion, Endres (1989) found the same three-part dynamic structure in the rhetorical visions of unwed mothers. He labeled them "The Down and Out" (righteous), "Making the Best" (pragmatic), and "Yummy" (social) rhetorical visions of unwed motherhood. Endres (1994) also found the key fantasy themes reflective of the warring master analogues of the Knights of Columbus. Mirroring the work of Cragan and Shields (1977, 1978)—with their computer-written, perfect political speech on foreign policy that reflected themes from the righteous Cold War, the social Neo-Isolationist, and the pragmatic Power Politics visions of the United States' involvement in foreign affairs—Endres blended themes from the competing Knights of Columbus rhetorical visions into a public relations campaign that would please the most and offend the least among the membership celebrating the 500-year anniversary of the initial Columbus voyage to the Western hemisphere. As well, McFarland (1985), in a Q-sort study of law professors, found three rhetorical visions, each reflective of the righteous ("Tough, Humanist Scholar"), social ("Caring Liberal Arts Teacher"), and pragmatic ("Teaching Lawyer Activist") deep structure of rhetorical visions.

Righteous Master Analogue.   Rhetorical visions steeped in the deep structure of a *righteous master analogue* depict the correct or moral way of doing things. Righteous rhetorical visions tend to exhibit concerns about right and wrong, proper and improper, superior and inferior, and just and unjust (Cragan & Shields, 1981c, 1992, 1995a). People who make statements such as "abortion is morally wrong," "the death penalty is wrong," "that violates the Constitution," "keep the quality up," or "I didn't learn anything in that class" are using the kind of messages reflective of a righteous vision master analogue.

Social Master Analogue.   Rhetorical visions exhibiting a *social master analogue* portray a humane or interpersonal cast. They tend to emphasize attributes of primary human relationships such as caring, trust, friendship, loyalty, comradeship, family ties, social compatibility, brotherhood, sisterhood, and humaneness (Cragan & Shields, 1981c, 1992, 1995a). People who make statements like "she's friendly, concerned, and understanding," "he's a good soldier—a great team player," "it's a people-oriented company," or "she's a loyal, trusting, friend" provide the kind of messages indicative of a social vision master analogue.

Pragmatic Master Analogue.   Rhetorical visions cast in a *pragmatic master analogue* present an efficient or cost-effective way of doing things. Such visions tend to emphasize efficiency, expediency, utility, parsimony, simplicity, and practicality (Cragan & Shields,

1981c, 1992, 1995a). People who make statements like "whatever it takes to get the job done," "I picked my school because of its low tuition," or "I'm majoring in communication because it teaches me the skills I need to get a job" express messages indicative of a pragmatic vision master analogue.

Recall that, from the perspective of SCT, people through communicative interaction symbolically create their view of reality. Thus, it should come as no surprise that such symbolic realities often diverge, and compete, and even go to war one with another. Some students participate in a pragmatic vision of education that says, "I just want to get a degree in a major that will give me the skills to get a good job." Other students espouse a social vision: "To get the most out of college, I try to meet and get to know my professors and fellow students and involve myself in as many student organizations and activities as possible." Still other students embrace a symbolic reality that is righteous: "I seek out challenging courses and celebrate the difficulty of many of the courses I take. I want to master a body of knowledge and make it my own." Of course, you already know that these three analogues are at war. Imagine the ruckus that would ensue if three students, one caught up in each view, teamed up to rent an off-campus apartment or share a dorm suite. Come to think of it, it seems as if we've all experienced the "roommate from hell" at one time or another in our college years. SCT helps explain theoretically and dramatistically such dormitory conflicts.

Could this be a source of personality conflicts?

Communicator Concepts   Again, it's time for a rest stop on the trail to understanding communication theories. Recall that TCM (Chapter 1) specified that communicator structure concepts name the communicators and their noteworthy attributes from the perspective of a particular theory. In other words, the same names for communicators will not serve to identify the communicators specified in all theories; indeed, every theory uniquely specifies the names of the communicators and details their attributes. For example, recall that in Chapter 2, IST posited the communicators as senders and receivers who engaged in information-sharing. In Chapter 3 RAT posited the communicators as arguers and critics who made arguments to improve decision-making and observers who judged the arguments. With SCT, we have fantasizers who share fantasies to make sense of reality. Because SCT views messages as cocreated through transactional communication, its most important communicator structure concept is *fantasizers,* followed closely by their *propensity to fantasize, rhetorical community,* and the *communication style* exhibited.

Fantasizers.   Recall that one of the epistemological assumptions of SCT is that reality is cocreated symbolically. That assumption stressed that the members of a rhetorical community participate in the embellishment and reconfiguration (chaining) of fantasy themes and, in turn, those chaining fantasies then contain meaning, emotion, and motive for action for the participants. Thus, the concept of audience, so essential to some other general communication theories, is meshed coequally with that of the originator of the fantasy. Consequently, *fantasizers* become the members of a rhetorical community who participate in the creation and sustenance of rhetorical visions (Bormann, Cragan, & Shields, 1996).

Although fantasizers cocreate rhetorical visions, it is nonetheless possible to conceive of a single communicator using fantasy themes managerially to attempt to catch up others. Public speakers do this all the time. Many of their fantasies are now famous, such as Booker T. Washington's "Cast down your buckets where you are," Malcolm X's "the ballot or the bullet," the Reverend Martin Luther King's "I had a dream last night," or President Bush's "thousand points of light." Here, of course, you may be concerned with an attribute of the communicator called the *propensity to fantasize.*

Propensity to Fantasize. Some individuals dramatize more readily than others. The *propensity to fantasize* concerns just such a communicator attribute. Cocreators pick up, embellish, reconfigure, restructure, and evolve fantasy themes into a new shared consciousness for the originator as well as the other participants (fantasizers) more readily than others. From the viewpoint of SCT, for communicators to communicate they must share and chain-out fantasies. The former governor of Alabama, George Wallace, demonstrated a propensity to fantasize. Indeed, one of the here-and-now phenomena that led us to our initial interest in fantasy themes concerned the wild, enthusiastic, crowd reaction Wallace received from a statement made during the height of the anti-Vietnam war protests: "If one of those long-haired hippies lays down in front of my car, I'll run over him!"

Rhetorical Community. A *rhetorical community* consists of and is constituted by the participants in a rhetorical vision who share a common consciousness (Bormann, 1985b, p. 19). We would caution that although vision participation identifies membership in a rhetorical community by definition, a traditionally named grouping such as Americans, Southern Baptists, or Republicans does not by definition mean that all such designees participate in the same rhetorical vision. Thus, a number of people may belong to an organization such as the Knights of Columbus and exhibit participation in distinctly different rhetorical visions flowing from divergent master analogue deep structures (Endres, 1994). The point here is that you must find the parameters of the rhetorical vision and identify those participants who adhere to it to know the membership of a particular rhetorical community. The members of a rhetorical community are known by the fantasies they share.

Communication Style. A *communication style* reflects the broad language use of a community of people engaged in significant discourse for which they understand the rules, customs, and conventions that shape that discourse (Bormann, 1985b, p. 19).[7] With SCT, the communication style reflects a shared sense, on the part of the membership of a rhetorical community, of the kind and forms of communication transactions suitable and appropriate for communicative interaction. To get a ready sense of the meaning of communication style think of locker-room jock talk among a group of male athletes. Then compare it to the style of communication present among the participants at Dorothy Parker's Algonquian Round Table. You should see a decided difference; yet, both styles of communication practice evolved from the conventions, customs, rules, and standards of their respective rhetorical communities. Bormann (1985b) illustrated the concept of communication style by distinguishing among the "recurring form of the Puritan sermon," the transitional form of the revivalists of the Great Awakening, and the "ungenteel style" of preaching of the nineteenth century Evangelical Baptists and Methodists (pp. 22–23). Bormann (1980) illustrated communication style by distinguishing among the *information-centered style* of the adherents to Information Systems Theory, the *authentic style* of adherents to the Palo Alto school of interpersonal communication, and the *persuasive style* of adherents to Rational Argumentation Theory.

Medium Concepts   We're ready for a rest stop. Let's take a moment and recall that TCM specified three senses of medium. Medium$_1$ concerned a general communication theory functioning within the six traditional contexts of interpersonal, small group, public speaking, organizational, mass, and intercultural communication. Medium$_2$ expressed the sense of a substance in which communication propagates, prospers, and grows. Medium$_3$ pertained to the channel through which communication flows or travels, such as sound, light or electrical waves, or books, films, or television, or face-to-face, e-mail, or mail-mail.

Like the other general communication theories presented in Chapters 2–7, SCT works to explain communication in all six of the medium$_1$ contexts. That means SCT explains much of interpersonal, small group, public speaking, organizational, mass, and intercultural communication phenomena. In other words, the force of fantasy is present in each context and its effect on human action has been noted in each context (Cragan & Shields, 1995a). SCT's medium$_2$ concepts consist of group-chaining and public-chaining. Both group- and public-chaining constitute examples of medium as a propagating substance. *Group-chaining* occurs when face-to-face participants grow excited, boisterous, and interrupt one another as they pick up, embellish, and reiterate a specific fantasy theme. Over time, such fantasy themes are repeated, often identified by symbolic cues, and become a part of a group's collective memory. Chesebro, Cragan, and McCullough (1973) confirmed the presence of chaining fantasies as central to consciousness-raising and identity-building in small groups. *Public-chaining* occurs as large groups of people pick up, reiterate, embellish, reconfigure, and reuse the same fantasy themes, symbolic cues, fantasy types, and sagas, and come to participate in a shared rhetorical vision. Bormann (1973) identified this process in his study of Senator Eagleton's (D–MO) withdrawal in 1972 as a vice-presidential nominee of the Democratic Party. Bormann found that the national and local print and electronic media picked up, reiterated, and embellished the fantasy themes centering on Eagleton's past electric shock treatments for depression. The themes chained-out in the media as if the news crews had engaged in face-to-face, small group communication. Cragan and Cutbirth (1984) discovered that the publicly-chaining negative fantasy theme, "I'm no Wimp," contributed directly to Adlai Stevenson, III's gubernatorial election defeat in Illinois. The SCT researchers, in a series of a dozen corroborative empirical studies, confirmed the presence of public-chaining in the consciousness-creating, -raising, and -sustaining of rhetorical visions.[8]

Using Evaluative Concepts

Again, we're due for a rest stop. Recall that TCM specified that all general communication theories posit and define one or more technical concepts that allow you to evaluate communication from the perspective of a particular theory. Also recall from Chapter 1 that all scientists are concerned with explaining the outcomes of the fundamental interactive forces that they study. The meteorologist tells us each evening on a televised weather report that he or she is concerned with the interaction of high-pressure and low-pressure air systems that produce occluded fronts that generate storms. With SCT, we evaluate the quality and effects (outcomes) of fantasy-sharing among the members of rhetorical collectivities and their impact on creating symbolic realities.

Quality and Outcomes   By outcomes we mean that the communicative interaction identified by the theory did in fact occur, that is, did the communicative force under study have its predicted impact on human action? Quality is a feature denoting degree or grade of excellence of the communicative interaction. In SCT's case, were artistic, grounded fantasies shared by a rhetorical community and did they lead to a rhetorical vision that contains meaning, emotion, and motive for human action? SCT employs three evaluative concepts. They are *fantasy theme artistry, shared group consciousness,* and *rhetorical vision reality links.*

Fantasy Theme Artistry. *Fantasy theme artistry* allows you to judge the rhetorical creativity, novelty, and competitive advantage of fantasy themes, symbolic cues, fantasy types, sagas, and rhetorical visions (Cragan & Shields, 1995a). One of Professor Shields's colleagues, Professor Jim Fay, is a renowned artistic director for plays and video productions. Professor Fay likes to say that, "Creativity is difficult to assess in the abstract, but we tend to know it when we see it." The same is true of fantasizing. As we saw within the discussion of communicator structure concepts, some people are better fantasizers than others, that is, they have a higher propensity to fantasize. In other words, highly skilled fantsizers turn ordinary statements into dramatic events. Moreover, we tend to recognize such fantasies when we see them. Uniquely, however, once a great fantasy theme is out in the public domain, it's available for all to use—even those without intrinsic artistic ability. Indeed, once a creative fantasy has chained-out, it can be used to the same effect as when the original creator used it. Who among us hasn't used such fantasy theme statements as, "All talk and no show!" or "Where's the beef?" to accentuate the emptiness of a proposal. Similarly, who among us hasn't said, "Life's a bitch, and then you die!" or "There you go again!" to highlight our frustrated moments. Nevertheless, new, highly artistic fantasy themes are constantly being created. For example, a couple of senior firefighters, whose job it is to suppress fires, recently vilified those fire fighters with a specialty certification in the handling of hazardous materials and High-Rise rescue. They referred to the Hazmat Team with the symbolic cues, "The mop and glow boys" and "The guys in the body bag with a view." Similarly, they vilified the High-Rise Rescue Team as "Dopes on a Rope." Pragmatically, as you study a specific symbolic reality, you may find it difficult to tell if the artistic themes present represent the creative product of one individual or many refiners and polishers. Yet, the resultant creative artistry remains for whoever uses the fantasy theme.

After the novelty of a fantasy theme wears thin, there is a need to redramatize the character, plot line, and scenic attributes of a rhetorical vision to keep the vision alive. With the release of the Academy Award-winning movie, *Forest Gump,* lots of people took the line, "Momma always said, 'Life is like a box of chocolates; you never know what you're going to get'," and refashioned it to fit their symbolic reality. We couldn't wait to talk to one another when one of our colleagues depicted the University as "like a box of chocolates: sweet on the outside with a bunch of nuts on the inside." From our personal experiences, to our lessons in English classes, we are aware of trite sayings and the impetus to avoid them. That's why there are dozens of ways to depict the deviant person engaged in crazy behavior: "she's not well-wrapped," "he's not playing with a full deck," "her elevator doesn't go to the top floor," "he's one brick short of a load," "her lights are on, but nobody's home," and so forth. In other words, fantasy themes possess a half-life and intrinsically wear out. The novelty principle requires that for fantasies to chain-out, and continue to convey meaning, emotion, and motive for action, they must be and remain fresh and creative.

Finally, in regard to artistry in the world of symbolic realities, there is the notion of competitive advantage. Some artistic themes fit our existing views of reality better and gain supremacy for us against their competition. A young police recruit may listen to three experienced law enforcement officers commenting on the job over coffee and donuts. One officer says, "Police need to be aggressive and patrol the street curb-to-curb." The second officer might respond, "Being aggressive is overrated; communication is the key." The third may retort, "Being aggressive does not add anything to my pay. My goal is to stay alive, put in twenty years, and retire." The young recruit must decide over time in which of these three competing symbolic worlds (righteous, social, or pragmatic) she or he wants to live.

Shared Group Consciousness.   *Shared group consciousness* is an evaluative term that reminds you to check for the occurrence of symbolic convergence (Cragan & Shields, 1995a, 1995b). Here, you want to see if a collectivity of people have shared a fantasy theme or fleshed out a symbolic interpretation of reality. Shared group consciousness can be identified by isolating fantasy themes that are created, told, retold, reconfigured, and embellished by the members of a rhetorical community.[9] We overheard a group of mass communication majors sitting around after they had just produced a news program for student television. We present their chaining fantasy in **Table 4-1.** It illustrates a small group engaging in the sharing of their symbolic reality through fantasy-chaining.

Large groups of people also get caught up in chaining public fantasies that produce a shared group consciousness. Collecting and analyzing such chaining fantasies often requires extensive research. Porter (1976) decided to collect and document the chaining public fantasies surrounding "Watergate." She analyzed the White House recordings of the meetings of President Richard Nixon and his closest advisors and researched the public commentary appearing in the popular media. She tracked the various fantasies regarding Watergate as they were told, retold, and refined. Today we have extant some very polished symbolic cues to the symbolic consciousness of the American people regarding this act of

TABLE 4-1.   Student News Producers Engaging in Fantasy-Chaining

Student A: I'm tired of doing TV news stories that contain eight-second sound bites. My stories end up looking just like everyone else's.

Student B: The whole world is tired of talking in sound bites.

Student C: If a person can't explain what they want in eight seconds, we do a voice-over. So, they don't have a choice.

Student A: Politicians are trained to do it. Even the president of the school is requiring his vice-presidents to take a training workshop in media interviews. So you know they're all going to sound the same.

Student D: Well, all the news looks and sounds the same. Haven't you ever channel surfed? The networks run the same stories. They have the same people. They say the same thing.

Student B: That's right! We not only tell them what to think about, we tell them how to think about it.

Student A: And how to say it.

Student C: And what to say.

Student B: That's right. Its agenda-setting gone wild!

Student C: Gone crazy!

Student A: Gone boring—it all looks alike.

governmental corruption and cover-up: "the smoking gun," "the missing tape," "I'm no crook," "Deep Throat," and "Napoleon met his Waterloo and Nixon met his Watergate."

Initially, and rather mundanely, the nightly news reported a burglary at the Democratic National Headquarters in the Watergate Hotel Complex in Washington, D.C. Eventually, the word *Watergate* became the symbolic cue for the entire milieu of fantasy themes regarding this President-approved burglary and cover-up. Today's college generation was not yet born when Watergate occupied the national news and Congressional hearings preempted network programming for weeks. For those not present at the first chaining of the Watergate fantasy, the term may not provide much meaning, emotion, and motive for action. To understand the force of the Watergate fantasy you need to go back and read the original news reports and watch a videotape of the televised hearings.

The need to recreate the experience of first-chaining is true for the understanding of all symbolically created realities. For those not present at first-chaining, it is necessary to reconstruct the communication to understand the shared consciousness. Because of the short half-life of symbolic consciousness, the only way for symbolic realities to live on is through a conscious effort to sustain them. That's why a sorority must require its pledges to learn and share the fantasies surrounding its genesis, its purpose, and its key symbols and rituals. At the wedding reception of Professor Cragan's daughter, Katie, sixty members of the Delta Gamma Sorority, including the bride, stood on their chairs, raised their champagne glasses, and began to sing a song that ended, "Delta Gamma, Delta Gamma, Delta Gamma 'til we die." In unison, they then drank from and threw down their champagne glasses. The force of this fantasy had been kept alive by reliving a sorority tradition begun more than one hundred years ago.

Rhetorical Vision Reality-Links.　*Rhetorical vision reality-links* tie rhetorical visions and fantasy themes to the objective reality of the authentic record and material facts (Bormann, 1982a; Cragan & Shields, 1995a). Sometimes people chain-out fantasies but the resulting rhetorical visions possess few or no reality links. Such fantasies are often labeled gossip, rumor, or paranoid delusions. Journalists know well the problem of undocumented rumor turned chaining public fantasy. For example, in the breaking news of the bombing of the Federal Building in Oklahoma City on April 19, 1995, many news networks picked up and helped chain-out the fantasy that the bombing was the work of Middle-Eastern terrorists. Rush Limbaugh, during his weekday broadcast of "America: The Way it Ought to Be," called for a retaliatory, preemptive, military strike. Days elapsed before the arrest of Timothy McVeigh squelched this chaining Middle-Eastern terrorist fantasy by demonstrating it possessed no link to reality. The arrests of McVeigh and Terry Nichols linked reality to a different fantasy; namely, that America now had "homegrown" terrorists. Similarly, in the summer and fall of 1996, the respective bomb explosion at the Olympics and the midair explosion of TWA Flight 800 off of Long Island led to a number of false chaining fantasies in the media. With the first incident, the FBI falsely suspected, arrested, and accused an Olympic Park Ranger and with the second the electronic media and the Internet swirled with false accusations of a U.S. Navy missile blowing up the plane. Former Kennedy White House Press Secretary, Pierre Salinger, from his home in Paris, became a champion proponent of this missile fantasy. Again, the force of fantasy spurs people to action, but the need for a link to reality helps squelch totally fantastic fantasies.

Once the existence of a shared fantasy is established, the reality-link concept allows for the identification of the people who share the fantasy or vision (see rhetorical community, this chapter). Typically, a researcher using SCT gathers demographic (gender, age, race, income), sociographic (church member, business executive, student, farmer), and psychographic (believes in God, holds family values, patriotic, likes sports) information that helps flesh out the identity of people participating in a symbolic reality. With the arrest and indictment of Timothy McVeigh for the Oklahoma City bombing, people wanted to know about him. It soon became known that he'd fought in the 1990 Desert Storm War, on discharge had joined a Michigan state militia group, and had a history of testing homemade bombs. Then people wanted to know how many others were like him. News reports quickly documented the existence of Armed Militia Patriot chapters in twenty-six states with an estimated membership of 200,000.

Demographically, the Armed Militia Patriot membership appeared as white, middle-class veterans. Sociographically, they appeared as family men, church members, jobholders, Republican voters, and National Rifle Association members who used weekends to dress in fatigues and hold military-style training exercises. Psychographically, they espoused a belief in the Bill of Rights and a fear of government, which they saw as conspiring to take away their right to bear arms. Such graphic characteristics tended to give flesh-and-bones reality to the size of the rhetorical community participating in the vision.

SCT: Working with Its Qualitative Method

We've now come pretty far on our trail to understanding SCT. Let's take another rest stop and rethink what we know about the qualitative methods of theories. Recall that each communication theory possesses its own unique qualitative method that is part of its theory–method complex. As with all theories, we remind you that it is difficult to find material, social, or symbolic facts initially. The process of discovery and identification of a theory's basic concepts is not pedestrian. Training and practice in the use of a theory's unique qualitative method helps us observe and count the theory's respective communication facts systematically and reliably. With SCT, as with the other general theories, you need to use a qualitative method to assist in uncovering and finding the basic concepts as they appear in communication phenomena.

Fantasy Theme Analysis (FTA)

The qualitative method unique to SCT is called Fantasy Theme Analysis.[10] Not all communication is a fantasy theme. However, you will know a fantasy theme by its stylistic, substantive, and structural qualities.[11] Stylistic qualities are directly observable—they are the linguistic dress of a fantasy. Stylistically, you will know a chaining fantasy in a small group when you see it. You will notice that the members pick it up, repeat it, and embellish it. As well, you will notice that members grow excited and boisterous, conversation is animated, and everyone talks over each other (Bormann, 1990). To see an example of a small group fantasy-chaining event, look again at **Figure 4-1.** You will know a fantasy has chained out in the print and electronic media when similar language is used across media and over time, that is, you will know it by its redundancy.

A fantasy's substantive qualities are also directly observable. The substance of a fantasy is its content. An example might prove helpful. We overheard a group of professors offer this fantasy theme characterization: "Our university's president has never seen a window of opportunity he is not willing to jump through." This theme depicts the carpetbagging world of academic administration.

Finally, you will know fantasy themes by their structural qualities, that is, the part of the structural skeleton of rhetorical visions they represent. Do they portray character, plot line, scene, or sanctioning agents, and do they flow from righteous, social, or pragmatic deep structures? The "window of opportunity" theme vilifies a character who has no institutional loyalty. The theme would appear to flow from the deep structure of a social rhetorical vision in which professors participate.

The collecting of fantasy themes that make up rhetorical visions requires lots of work. The symbolic facts contained in speeches, documents and reports, and personal and focus group interviews must be examined to find the universe of fantasy themes of a given rhetorical community. You then need to sift through the universe to first find like themes, and then to place them in categories representing the dramatis personae, plot lines, scenic elements, and sanctioning agents of a rhetorical vision. Of course, in the case of competing rhetorical visions, you must also sift through the themes to find the ones that fit the righteous, social, or pragmatic deep structure view of reality (Cragan & Shields, 1981c, 1995a, 1995b).

Briefly Illustrating FTA

The Cold War spanned the years 1947 to 1990. It exhibited large scope and considerable duration as it dominated the agenda of the superpowers for some five decades. During its life span, the Cold War rhetorical vision led to a number of confrontations, world crises, police actions, limited wars, and side-taking in faraway civil wars and wars of liberation. A composite depiction of the Cold War rhetorical vision would look something like the following:

> *A monolithic, international, communist conspiracy, directed from the Kremlin and set on overthrowing the free world, provides the major obstacle to world peace. The Communists, by exporting conspirators, seek to infiltrate, corrupt, and undermine our democratic institutions. The fight is between the free world and the totalitarian world for the minds and hearts of people. Only the reality of the nuclear age tempers the struggle. American foreign policy specialists must walk a tightrope between avoiding the major error of World War II, appeasement of a totalitarian regime bent on conquest, and the fatal error of the next world war, atomic holocaust. It is a war that we must not lose, but that we can not win without sacrificing millions of humans to nuclear destruction. Thus, the Cold War is a struggle for the hearts and minds of people. It is a war fought, not with guns and bombs, but with words and propaganda. With a strong democratic presence, with an eye toward containment, and with a steadfast resolve, the Communist form of government will eventually implode from within.*

Bormann, Cragan, and Shields (1996) studied Cold War rhetoric as a paradigm case of SCT's structural concept, rhetorical vision. They found that the Cold War rhetorical vision traveled through five stages: Consciousness-creating, consciousness-raising, consciousness-sustaining, consciousness-decline, and consciousness-terminus. They discovered that the formal statements of U.S. President Harry Truman, U.S. Secretary of State George Marshall, British Prime Minister Winston Churchill, and U.S. State Department Official George Kennan created the Cold War rhetorical vision in 1947. These men and the Truman speechwriters fashioned a righteous rhetorical vision that contained a strong missionary, proselytizing, fantasy-type plot line (the struggle for the minds and hearts of people) linked with a strong, international involvement plot line (calling for the containment of communism). The scene became the location of one international crisis after another. Two characters, Democracy and Communism, dominated the scene. The horror of the nuclear bomb sanctioned and promulgated the Cold War rhetorical vision. Throughout its life cycle, vision proponents justified foreign policy initiatives as the need to contain Communism: first through the Berlin airlift; then regarding the maintenance of a peacetime army; then through aid to Greece and Turkey; then through the Marshall Plan for the rebuilding of Europe; then by way of the arms race; then in the Korean police action; then in the support of the Shah of Iran; then in the Cuban Missile Crisis; then in Indochina and Vietnam; and finally with the Star Wars defense initiative and illegal arms sales to the Central American Contras.

The Cold War rhetorical vision proved inflexible and paranoid in its view of an international Communist conspiracy out to enslave the free world. The frustrations of the Vietnam War allowed for the development of a competing social rhetorical vision best exemplified by George McGovern's "Come Home America" acceptance speech for the Democratic nomination for President in 1972. The Cold War rhetorical vision declined further with the surfacing of the Nixon–Kissinger Power Politics rhetorical vision of "A World Restored," and the Carter Administration's social vision of International Human Rights. The Reagan Presidency briefly breathed new life into the Cold War rhetorical vision with its novel "Evil Empire" and "Star Wars" fantasy types, but the Cold War rhetorical vision contained the seeds of its own destruction. Facing such reality-links as the breakup of the Soviet bloc, the fall of the Berlin Wall, the death of the Soviet Communist Party, and the collapse of the Union of Soviet Socialist Republics, the Cold War—as a righteous, inflexible, rhetorical vision—imploded. Indeed, a central fantasy theme of the vision had been that Communism would collapse if it could only be contained for fifty years. It was and it did.

The case study provided the authors with the insight that rhetorical visions exist along several continua. The Cold War rhetorical vision proved to be a righteous, inflexible, proselytizing, paranoid, oxymoronic vision tempered only by the pragmatics of the nuclear bomb. The study allowed the authors to demonstrate that up to twelve rhetorical principles drive the stages of a rhetorical vision. Five principles (shielding, explanatory deficiency, exploding free speech, resurfacing of competitive rhetorical visions, and implosion) apply to those visions that resemble the Cold War. The remaining seven principles (novelty, explanatory power, imitation, critical mass, dedication, rededication, and reiteration) apply to all rhetorical visions.

SCT: Observing Its Usefulness

We've now reached our final rest stop on this part of the trail to understanding communication theories. Recall that TCM posited utility as its primary evaluative metaconcept.

Throughout *Understanding Communication Theories: The Communicative Forces for Human Action,* we dramatize this evaluate metaconcept in the phrase, *Will the dog hunt?* It's again time to begin our answer to that question. As we indicated in the "Origin and Roots" section above, SCT's contributors worked systematically to ground important theoretical concepts and their relationships to observables. Here, we overview the research that grounded SCT, review several exemplar studies that demonstrated SCT's usefulness in solving real-world problems, and examine SCT's ability to withstand critical scrutiny.

Explaining Human Action

A communication theory can explain human action when its concepts have been tied to or grounded in directly observable phenomena. A researcher usually grounds a theory's concepts by analyzing communication episodes to determine if the phenomena the concepts represent appear in the communication. Between 1970 and 1997 more than seventy published studies appeared that used SCT to explain human communicative interaction. As indicated previously, the theory is grounded by research in each of the six traditional communication contexts.

The SCT research team first identified fantasies chaining-out in a small group.[12] Their studies demonstrated that the dramatizing, chaining fantasies held meaning, emotion, and motive for action for the original participants in the communication episode. The SCT researchers also developed a method for identifying, capturing, and analyzing fantasy themes called "Fantasy Theme Analysis" (FTA). Through the use of FTA, the SCT researchers documented the existence of fantasy chaining among large publics.[13] Other SCT researchers studied specific rhetorical visions.[14] Through such studies, the SCT researchers grounded the concept of rhetorical vision and its elements.[15] As well, they grounded such theoretical statements as "rhetorical visions war with each other" and "rhetorical visions reflect a deep motive structure that is typically righteous, social, or pragmatic."[16] Still other SCT researchers demonstrated that those who comprise a rhetorical community with a given symbolic reality or symbolic consciousness may be identified by observable demographic, psychographic, and sociographic characteristics and demonstrated that such observables predict vision participation and behavior.[17] Other SCT studies viewed discursive argument, as opposed to imaginary language, as part of the symbolic consciousness of participants in political campaigns and members of organizations.[18]

Benefiting the Real World

A number of SCT studies provided insights into and solutions for real-world applied communication problems. The researchers demonstrated the usefulness of SCT early in its development and continued to make meaningful applications. For example, Barton and O'Leary (1974) used SCT to help alleviate the crisis of physicianless communities in rural Minnesota. They discovered that, in 1973, 75 percent of small towns in rural Minnesota lacked a practicing physician. Barton and O'Leary faced a clear client problem. They needed to recruit physicians for six rural communities. To do so, they conducted face-to-face field surveys with hundreds of Minnesotans from small towns to determine the dominant fantasy themes about rural life that might attract young graduating medical doctors.

They discovered that the fantasy themes espoused by rural Minnesotans, such as "a quiet, independent life far from the maddening crowd of the Twin Cities" produced negatively chaining fantasies among young medical doctors who viewed that theme as "proving they would be isolated from other medical personnel and worked to death." Barton and O'Leary then fashioned new fantasy themes dramatizing such plot lines as "adjoining rural communities cooperating to provide support services for rural physicians and emergency transportation so that special-needs patients could be transported to large city hospitals for advanced care." Their rhetorical campaign, using such SCT-based fantasy themes, allowed them to recruit physicians for the six rural areas. Their study highlighted the practical benefit of using SCT to solve real-world problems. The study demonstrated that fantasy themes could be discovered, refashioned, and used in a public relations campaign to recruit physicians for rural practices successfully.

Cragan, Shields, Pairitz, and Jackson (1978, 1981), in a study funded by the National Fire Protection and Control Administration, developed a model for recruiting public fire education officers. Their research differentiated successfully the heroic persona of a public fire education officer from other types of firefighters. They isolated key attributes (graphics characteristics) that distinguished firefighters participating in a public fire education rhetorical vision from two competing visions. They identified several statistically significant characteristics: art or photography as a hobby, high scores on two tests of creativity, and more years of formal education. They recommended that fire chiefs use the two creativity tests and a customized SCT-based inventory in their assessment of potential recruits. This study demonstrated that SCT could be used to find personnel who possessed the appropriate heroic personae for a given job.

Cragan and Shields (1992) conducted an SCT-based study of an organization in which they, in conjunction with a national advertising agency, recreated the corporate symbolic reality for a major Fortune 500 company that had experienced a corporate buyout and subsequent downsizing and restructuring. Their task was to invent a new corporate name and identity, develop new markets for products, and develop new advertising themes and sales stories. Using SCT, they conducted scores of focus group and personal interviews, and did phone and mail surveys to hundreds of customers to capture the discrete rhetorical visions held by the corporation's customers. They successfully repositioned the company, segmented its marketplace into five distinct buying types, and developed hot button fantasy themes keyed to each market segment for national media ads and sales stories. The study marked the second time that Cragan and Shields had segmented the marketplace for a Fortune 500 company (Bush, 1981). This line of research demonstrated the use of SCT to create new symbolic realities or refashion old symbolic realities for companies. As well, it demonstrated SCT's real-world benefit in segmenting markets to target sales campaigns.

Vasquez (1994) studied Blooming Grove Academy, a private school that needed to recruit more students to remain economically viable. Vasquez did a Fantasy Theme Analysis of the school's public relations literature and conducted personal and focus group interviews with administrators, parents, students, and teachers. To assist in the identification of the competing righteous, social, and pragmatic fantasy themes, Vasquez developed an SCT-based phone survey that contained fifteen fantasy themes—five from each rhetorical vision.

He phoned the parents and created an index of vision participation. He concluded that the school's public relations messages should stress righteous themes so that newly recruited parents would blend in with the predominantly righteous parent base of Blooming Grove Academy. His study provided more grounding evidence of SCT's use for matching people to organizations. For example, organizations with a highly righteous culture can use SCT to find employees with a righteous work vision.

Lee and Hoon (1993) designed a concurrent validity study using profile, word, and fantasy theme analysis to examine the media-based rhetorical vision of men and women managers in Singapore. They sought to use SCT to explain the low participation of women in upper-level management positions as due to the symbolic reality in which the media portrayed men's and women's participation. Their study revealed that the media portrayed different visions for men and women managers. The Singapore media profiled women managers as in their thirties, usually married, mostly well educated, and mostly working in the service sector, advertising, or banking. The media depicted the communication style of these women as people-centered, sociable, and helpful. The media reported that such women exhibited a zest for life, displayed family-oriented lifestyles, and appeared interested in community and social work. As well, the media indicated that these women read, traveled, listened to music, and enjoyed plays and dances (pp. 530–532).

On the other hand, the Singapore media profiled men managers as in their thirties, mostly of unknown marital status and educational level, but working in manufacturing. The media portrayed their communication style as people-centered, innovative, and outgoing. The media depicted these men as interested in outdoor sports such as squash, golf, swimming, and tennis. Finally, the media noted their interests as including art collection, music, reading, and traveling (pp. 530–532).

With the qualitative fantasy theme analysis complete, the researchers turned to a quantitative validation of the respective visions of men and women managers. The word analysis of prevalent fantasy theme adjectives indicated that the media portrayed the men managers as: *able, challenging, amiable, aggressive,* and *proven* (pp. 532–533). Conversely, the word analysis of prevalent fantasy theme adjectives indicated that the media portrayed women managers as: *charming, cautious, assertive,* and *tough-willed* (pp. 532–533). Adjectives describing both groups included: *hardworking, confident, lucky, successful,* and *dreamers.* However, except for the adjective *hardworking,* used 48 percent of the time to depict men managers and 35 percent of the time to depict women managers, the frequency nod for *confident, lucky, successful,* and *dreamers* went overwhelmingly to the men managers.

The fantasy theme analysis of the media's portrayal of the rhetorical vision of women managers also revealed clear differences. For men managers, the media depicted the most frequent themes in the rhetorical vision (in descending order) as follows (pp. 536–538): management style ("it is people who make a difference" or "management philosophy is human respect"), working experience ("years of experience" or "track record"), struggles ("overseas posting"), and desire to improve oneself ("career path crammed with courses" or "learning on the job").

For women managers, the most frequent themes in media's rhetorical vision of managers (in descending order) included (pp. 534–536): role conflicts/dilemmas ("when work at the office is over, work at home begins" or "torn between family and a demanding job"), men's attitude ("male subordinates a problem" or "invidious comments from coworkers"), reason to work ("bring home more bacon" or "financial independence"), supportive husband ("a supportive husband is an important factor" or "a husband who helps out in domestic chores"), supportive mother/maid ("a strong-minded mother who encouraged" or "most employ at least one maid"), and male mentor ("a mentor is vital for success").

In short, Lee and Hoon concurrently validated that "the mass media depicted different rhetorical visions for the women and men managers" and that "each portrayed a distinctive view of social [symbolic] reality" (p. 540). They went on to note that "the intent of the articles was to provide 'role models' for the young professionals, especially for the young aspiring women executives" but that "readers who get caught up in the depiction of 'reality' may develop a set of expectations, which can serve as a filter to influence their interpretation of daily experiences . . . [that] can possibly limit the career expectations of women" (p. 540). This study demonstrated how SCT may be used to frame symbolic facts and provide a feminist critique of organizations. In Chapter 11, we present two communication microtheories—Muted Group Theory and Feminist Genre Theory—that, when combined with SCT, would help to overcome the sexist stereotyping faced in Singapore. For example, Huxman (1996) combined SCT with Feminist Genre Theory to provide a feminist critique of the roots of the emerging rhetorical vision that converged in the nineteenth century to form the Women's Movement.

Withstanding the Critics

Could this be seen as spin-doctoring?

Theoretical advancement in communication is dependent on good criticism. In this section, we present the four major criticisms of SCT and respond to them. The four criticisms are: (1) SCT is not a general theory; (2) SCT is Freudian-based; (3) SCT's insights are researcher dependent; (4) SCT is merely a category system.[19] Bormann (1982b), Bormann, Cragan, and Shields (1994), and Cragan and Shields (1995a) provide extended responses to these criticisms.

SCT Is Not a General Theory   Critics (Mohrmann, 1982a, 1982b) contended that SCT is not a general theory by arguing that fantasy chaining is true of small groups but is not demonstrable in the case of mass publics. To make this criticism stand, the critics simply ignored the line of studies that grounded the sharing of group fantasies by large mediated publics, including: Bormann (1973), Cragan and Shields (1977, 1978), Nimmo and Combs (1982), Rarick, et al. (1977), and Shields (1981f).

SCT Is Freudian-Based   Mohrmann (1982a, 1982b) made much of the fact that Robert Bales, a Freudian psychologist at Harvard, used a Freudian definition of fantasy in his studies of fantasy chaining in small groups (Bales, 1970) and that therefore SCT must be Freudian and not an indigenous communication theory. Although Bales is indebted to Freud, SCT is not. The clearest way to see that SCT's theoretical concept of fantasy theme is not Freudian is to examine the SCT studies to see if there are Freudian interpretations in the grounded research. As Hyde (1980) pointed out, a truly Freudian analysis must contain such psychoanalytic concepts as Oedipus complex, castration, phallus, primal regression, and transference. A reading of the technical definitions of SCT's concepts and their use in both basic and applied research indicates that no such Freudian concepts are used.

SCT's Insights Are Researcher Dependent   Mohrmann (1982a, 1982b) argued that the insights found in the SCT studies did not flow from the use of the theory; rather they flowed only from bright people doing good work. Although it is awkward for us to say that SCT researchers are not bright, we submit that if a researcher's basic unit of analysis is not a fantasy theme then he or she would have no reason to look for fantasies as well as no way of knowing how to identify a fantasy. Although a rose is a rose, it still must be classified as something with like qualities (genus, species, smell, shape, texture) to identify, count, and analyze it. In other words, all systematic research needs theoretical concepts with technical definitions. As we indicated in Chapter 1, to sort out raw phenomena, one must have an implicit or explicit theory. The SCT researchers did, and they have used the theory scores of times. Indeed, as we noted previously, sometimes the theory highlights failed fantasies and dying rhetorical visions.[20]

SCT Is Merely a Category System   Black (1980), Farrell (1982), and Hart (1986) called SCT a mere taxonomy with a cookie cutter mentality producing the same predictable analysis from study to study. Of course, such a characterization is not a criticism at all; rather, it is high praise. Accurate taxonomies, such as the periodic table of elements in chemistry, are important, so long as they are accurate and the critics never indicted SCT's taxonomy as inaccurate. As well, "cookie cutter" merely represents an inartistic description of what a theory really is. Systematic investigation, the ability to generalize across cases, and the replication of findings requires a "cookie cutter" method that will serve as a template so that theories can be grounded and become general in scope. SCT's grounding crosses the interpersonal, small group, public speaking, organizational, mass, and intercultural communication contexts.

As you can see, SCT's critics have missed the mark. Study after study demonstrated that SCT is a useful theory that explains the force of fantasy-sharing on meaning, emotion, and motive for action by the participants in a rhetorical vision. With both the criticisms and responses at hand, we leave it to you to make an informed judgment about whether or not SCT withstands the critics. We believe it does, as all viable core general communication theories must. When you get to the end of the trail to understanding communication theories, we believe you can use SCT with confidence. We wish you happy hunting.

Summary

In this chapter, we introduced you to Symbolic Convergence Theory (SCT). SCT allows you to explain the force behind the creation of a common consciousness or symbolic reality. We began by viewing SCT as a general communication theory capable of being understood through the lens of The Communication Metatheory (TCM). We sketched SCT's power and scope, traced its origin and roots, and discussed its primary assumptive system. Then we introduced SCT's theoretical concepts (see **Figure 4-1**). We explained its basic concepts, structural concepts, and evaluative concepts. Next, we introduced and illustrated how to work with SCT's qualitative method, Fantasy Theme Analysis (FTA). Then, we reported on SCT's usefulness. We showed SCT's use to explain human action and benefit the real world. Then we discussed its ability to withstand critical scrutiny.

By now you should be familiar with SCT. Like our communication graduate on-the-job, Corey, you ought to be able to use SCT to good advantage (see **Figure 4-2**). If you do not yet feel comfortable with SCT, we suggest you review our detailed chapter summary, "Understanding SCT in a Nutshell," presented as **Box 4-1**.

"Symbolic Convergence Theory (SCT) allows us to see the various rhetorical vision segments of our customers so that we can position our products correctly in our advertising campaign."

FIGURE 4-2.   Communication Graduate On-the-Job

BOX 4-1   Understanding SCT in a Nutshell

SCT Defined: *Symbolic Convergence Theory* is a general communication theory explaining the appearance of a common symbolic consciousness that contains, among participants in a rhetorical community, shared meanings, emotions, and motives for action.

Origin: SCT developed as a message-centered communication theory derived from the systematic observation of symbolic facts. The theorists first observed the sharing of fantasy themes in small group communication, then in mediated communication, and lastly they observed the sharing of fantasies among the members of large rhetorical communities.

Assumptions: (1) Meaning, emotion, and motive for action are in the content of the message; (2) Reality is created symbolically; (3) Fantasy-sharing cocreates symbolic convergence; (4) Fantasy themes occur in all forms of discourse; and (5) Three master analogues (righteous, social, and pragmatic) compete as explanations of symbolic reality.

Basic Concepts: A *fantasy theme* is the basic unit of analysis for SCT as it embodies a dramatizing message depicting characters engaged in action in a setting that accounts for and explains human experience. Symbolic cues, fantasy types, and sagas are special derivations of fantasy themes. A *symbolic cue* is a shorthand, rhetorical indicant that stands for a fantasy theme (such as "publish or perish" is a cue to an important professorial fantasy). A *fantasy type* is a stock scenario used to explain new events in a well-known dramatic form (such as Watergate, Iran-gate, and Whitewater-gate repeatedly reference governmental corruption and cover-up). A *saga* is the repeated telling of the achievements in the life of a person, group, community, organization, or nation.

Structural Concepts: SCT possesses message, communicator, dynamic, and medium structural concepts. The message structure concepts are rhetorical vision, dramatis personae, scene, plot line, and sanctioning agent. A *rhetorical vision* is a composite drama that catches up large groups of people in a common symbolic reality. A rhetorical vision contains many fan-

tasy themes that depict heroes and villains in dramatic action within a dramatic scene. Each rhetorical vision reflects a life cycle containing consciousness-creating, -raising, -sustaining, -declining, and -terminus stages. Rhetorical visions exist along pure-to-mixed, inflexible-to-flexible, intense-to-passive, secretive-to-proselytizing, and paranoid-to-healthy continua. Other structural concepts flesh out the substructure of a rhetorical vision. The *dramatis personae* are fantasy theme depictions of the characters in the vision. *Scene* details the symbolic location of the action portrayed in the vision (such as, "behind closed doors"). *Plot line* portrays the action or plot of the vision. The *sanctioning agent* (e.g., God or the Constitution) legitimizes the symbolic reality depicted by the rhetorical vision. The dynamic structure concepts are the warring righteous, social, and pragmatic deep structures of visions that provide motive for action. *Righteous* visions depict the correct or moral way of doing things, *social* visions portray a humane or interpersonal way, and *pragmatic* visions present an efficient or cost-effective way. The communicator structure concepts are *fantasizers* who co-join in dramatizing, a *rhetorical community* made up of the adherents to a rhetorical vision, and *communication style* or the broad language use of a rhetorical community of people. The media$_2$ that propagate symbolic convergence are small group-chaining and public-chaining.

Evaluative Concepts: *Fantasy theme artistry* prompts one to judge the rhetorical novelty, consistency, and creativity of fantasy themes, symbolic cues, fantasy types, and sagas. *Shared group consciousness* reminds those using SCT as their theoretical lens to check the communication of a rhetorical community to see if symbolic convergence has occurred. Shared group consciousness can be identified by isolating fantasy themes that are created, told, retold, reconfigured, and embellished by the members of a rhetorical community. *Fantasy theme reality-links* tie rhetorical visions and fantasy themes to the objective reality of the authentic record and material facts. They remind those using SCT to assess the sense-making capacity of fantasy themes and rhetorical visions.

Chapter 5

Uncertainty Reduction Theory (URT)

The force of social information-sharing creates, stabilizes,
and sometimes destroys interpersonal relationships.

Chapter Outline

It is again time to pause by the trail to understanding communication theories. Here, we want to talk about our next landmark, called Uncertainty Reduction Theory (URT). URT is our first general communication theory that stems from the relational paradigm constellation of communication theories. Recall from The Communication Metatheory (TCM) that theories reflective of the relational paradigm explain social facts. URT explains the social fact known as an interpersonal relationship. URT evolved within the discipline beginning in the mid-1970s. Charles Berger, then of Northwestern University, along with several colleagues and students, built the line of research that supports it. URT explains the communicative force of social information-sharing on the development of interpersonal relationships. You should not have much difficulty comprehending URT. Just like Information Systems Theory, URT looks at information-sharing. However, URT limits itself to a special kind of information called *social information*. In other words, URT looks at the kind of information that is shared by people involved in relationships.

We begin by viewing URT as a general communication theory. We sketch its power and scope, trace its origin and roots, and discuss its primary assumptive system. Then we introduce URT's theoretical concepts. We explain how to find its basic concepts, see its structural concepts, and use its evaluative concepts. Next, we report on URT's usefulness. We show URT's use to explain human action and benefit the real world, and discuss its ability to withstand critical scrutiny. Finally, we present our Chapter Summary, "Understanding URT in a Nutshell."

URT: Viewing the General Theory

URT exists within the relational paradigm of communication theories, and assumes a social reality about relationships that can be known through the sharing, disclosing, and receiving of social information. In turn, such sharing increases the predictability of facts, beliefs, attitudes, and behaviors attributed by you to others and by others to you. URT views such social information as a force. The force of social information-sharing enables relationship development and maintenance. It does so by providing increased and optimized certainty and predictability to human actions in relationships. With URT, communicative force originates in communicators (social information-seekers and -givers) communicating (sharing social information) messages (biographical material, beliefs about activities, attitudes) propagated through a medium (cultural or social context).

Sketching Its Power and Scope

We've traveled a good distance on our trail to understanding communication theories. Let's extend our rest stop to highlight an element of TCM. Recall from Chapter 1 that TCM uses two metaconcepts called *power* and *scope* to assist you in differentiating communication theories. Uncertainty Reduction Theory is a general communication theory. Thus, it is a theory of broad scope. It explains a broad band of communication known as relationship-building communication. As well, it explains relationship communication as it occurs across the six traditional communication contexts of interpersonal, small group, public speaking, organizational, mass, and intercultural communication. URT explains how the force of social information-sharing reduces uncertainty about self and others. It also explains the force of social information-sharing on reducing uncertainty about the direction of interpersonal relationships. In other words, social information-sharing lets you know where a relationship is going. URT's power derives from its programmatic line of research. That line of research has grounded the theory through the establishment of lawlike relationship statements between its concepts. Berger and Calabrese (1975) argued that "when strangers meet, their primary concern is one of uncertainty reduction or increasing predictability about the behavior of both themselves and others in the interaction" (p. 100). Uncertainty concerns both our ability to predict how interactants (self and others) will behave and to explain their actions (Berger & Calabrese, 1975). Uncertainty reduction, therefore, involves proactive predictions and retroactive explanations about the behavior of the interactants. The need for uncertainty reduction, however, is not limited to the original reactions between two strangers. Berger (1979) indicated that "the communicative processes involved in knowledge generation and the development of understanding are central to the development and disintegration of most interpersonal relationships" (p. 123). Indeed, URT posits that both the creation and maintenance of interpersonal relationships is due to the use of social information to reduce uncertainty. Furthermore, URT allows both predictions about and explanations of your own and another's relationship behavior.

The first grounding research for URT centered on the use of social information to reduce uncertainty between strangers in initial interpersonal communication encounters. Subsequent grounding research extended the theory to explain the force of social information-sharing throughout the stages of interpersonal relationships, and extended the scope of URT's explanatory power across a number of communication contexts. URT looks at both the quantity and quality of social information needed to reduce uncertainty. URT acknowledges that an optimal degree and amount of social information exists and that you can develop competence in the sending and receiving of social information. As well, URT allows you to use social information about the interaction situation to reduce uncertainty.

Of the core general communication theories receiving chapter-long treatment in this book, URT is the only one that relies on an axiomatic format to present the relationships between its key concepts. Recall, from the discussion of TCM in Chapter 1, that the axiomatic format means that the form of the theory is presented as axioms, postulates, and theorems much as a geometry textbook explains plane and solid geometry. You may recall from geometry that "the shortest distance between two points is a straight line" or that "the square of the hypotenuse of a right triangle is equal to the sum of the square of the two sides." Recall that the axiomatic format differs from the mathematical relationship format and the ordinary language format.

Berger and Calabrese (1975), in their initial presentation of URT, outlined seven axioms and twenty-one theorems. Since that time, other contributors have added new axioms and new theorems. At this writing, ten axioms and more than thirty theorems comprise an axiomatic rendering of URT. However, just as we stripped away the mathematical structure of Information Systems Theory and presented it to you in ordinary language, we are going to do the same with URT's axiomatic structure. We will again follow the elements of TCM to explain URT in an accessible fashion.

URT, through its axioms, posits an interrelationship among uncertainty and the following technical concepts: amount of communication, nonverbal affiliation expressiveness, information-seeking, intimacy level of communication content, reciprocity, similarity, liking, shared communication networks, deviance, and incentive value. In general, URT's contributors see these concepts as interacting. The line of reasoning goes as follows: When two strangers meet, these ten concepts either contribute to or diminish the reduction of uncertainty. Consequently, the concepts either add to or take away from the stability of a relationship.

Berger and his associates sought to explain and predict the communicative process that creates and maintains stable relationships. They posited social information-sharing as the means by which strangers develop relationships. Strangers, of course, naturally possess both a high level of uncertainty about meeting someone new and an innate need to reduce that uncertainty. Strangers in initial interactions begin by asking safe biographical questions of each other. What's your name? What's your major? What's your classification? If the strangers respond to each other by smiling, making eye contact, head-nodding, and using other kinds of nonverbal affiliative expressive behaviors, then these are taken as signs that the initial high levels of uncertainty have been reduced. As more and more personal disclosures occur, eventually the number or amount of questions asked decreases. The decrease in disclosure over time, of course, is in keeping with what we know about information—of which social information would be a specific type—from IST, presented in Chapter 2. IST would predict that in long-term relationships, in which people have exchanged information over time, there may be very little seeking of new information. For example, if you have a current social partner, you probably no longer need to ask them biographical questions, such as, "Do you have any sisters?" Nor do you need to ask them belief questions about activities, such as, "Do you believe it's important to go to church?" Similarly, you already know the answers to some attitude questions, such as, "Do you like your Mother?" We have just talked through the relationship statements regarding social information-sharing that URT presents as Axioms 1, 2, and 3.

Next, Axiom 4 expresses the view that if you are uncertain as to who a person is, you are not likely to disclose information of an intimate nature to them. On the other hand, if you know them and trust them you are likely to disclose social information of an intimate nature. In addition, according to Axiom 5, you will disclose intimate social information at a rate that is reciprocal to the rate, amount, and kind of information disclosed to you. Such reciprocity will, of course, decrease as you get to know the person. The more you perceive others to be different from you, as in "you're from Venus and he or she is from Mars," the more uncertainty you will exhibit. Conversely, according to Axiom 6, the more similarities (you both like Wagner, opera, and violins) that exist between the two of you, the more that uncertainty will be reduced.[1]

Berger and Calabrese (1975) established a close relationship between uncertainty reduction, discovered similarity, and liking. They found that as people reduce uncertainty and discover similarities they start liking each other (Axiom 7). Another way to reduce uncertainty about other people is to talk to their friends and family. Axiom 8 indicates that networking (talking) with another's family and friends reduces uncertainty further, thereby stabilizing and maintaining the relationship (Berger & Gudykunst, 1991).

Research by Kellermann and Reynolds (1990) offered two more axioms. Axiom 9 predicts that increases in deviant behavior will produce increases in uncertainty, while Axiom 10 indicates that the incentive value attributed to a self-serving relationship will increase the need for uncertainty reduction. These axioms mean that if a new friend starts acting in bizarre ways then that behavior will increase your uncertainty about the relationship. The incentive value means that if the person engaging in deviant behavior is your boss then your incentive value to continue the relationship is higher. In such a case, you are more likely to engage in behaviors to reduce uncertainty rather than behaviors that end the relationship.

Tracing Its Origin and Roots

The origin of URT stems directly from the 1970s work of Charles Berger and his students at Northwestern University. Berger and Calabrese (1975) published the theory's first formal statement. Since then, a number of scholars have reported research findings and offered state-of-the-art summaries of the theory.[2] URT's research program, like those of the other general communication theories presented in Chapters 2–7, is extensive.

Berger (1987) noted that "the idea that uncertainty is a function of the number of alternatives present in a situation and their relative likelihood of occurrence is, of course, taken directly from information theory" (p. 41). Although Berger relies heavily on IST's establishment of a relationship between information and uncertainty, he and his research associates have developed several insights that are unique to URT. As we saw in Chapter 2, Shannon's (1948a, 1948b) original formulation of IST dealt with the problem of sending information down a noisy channel to a receiver and determining if it had been sent correctly. URT reverses this process and views communicators as highly uncertain receivers who actively seek information in order to create order (reduce uncertainty) in their interpersonal world. Consequently, a great deal of URT and its grounding research centers on communication activities—passive, active, and interactive—that help the receiver acquire the necessary social information to reduce uncertainty so that a stable, liking relationship can be created and maintained. Early studies dealt with uncertainty reduction among strangers (Berger & Calabrese, 1975). Later studies examined developed relationships (Parks & Adelman, 1983). More recently, those grounding the theory have adopted the vantage point of the sender of social information and begun to offer insights into how to influence others (Berger, 1995a, 1995b).

Another insight that gives URT its unique status as a stand-alone, general communication theory that is analogous to but distinct from IST is the presupposition that humans invent explanations that allow them to understand and predict their own and other's behavior. In other words, humans inherently seek the reduction of uncertainty. In addition, the theory presupposes that the human tolerance for uncertainty varies from person to person and from communication situation to communication situation.

URT also exhibits roots connecting it to social psychological research and theory. The relationships among the concepts presented in the initial seven axioms were supported by a number of social psychological, attributional research reports affixing specific causes to interpersonal behavior.[3]

Accepting Its Assumptive System

Again, it's time for a brief rest stop. Recall that TCM posits that theories possess ontological, epistemological, and axiological assumptions that relate to being, knowing, and valuing. In order to help you understand URT, we feel it is important to discuss its assumptions (two ontological and three epistemological). These assumptions must be accepted as if they were true to explore URT's explanatory power. URT's assumptions are (1) humans display an innate need to reduce uncertainty about themselves and others; (2) humans desire stable, predictable relationships with others; (3) social information-sharing is goal-directed; (4) increased social knowledge produces stability in relationships; and (5) many sources of uncertainty exist.

Humans Display an Innate Need to Reduce Uncertainty about Themselves and Others
Berger (1988), Berger and Calabrese (1975), and Berger, et al. (1976b) stressed this ontological assumption. Kellermann and Reynolds (1990) argued that this assumption "rests on the belief that the primary concern of interactants is predicting and explaining cointeractants' behavior" (p. 8). In other words, humans are driven as a species (it is our nature) to create order. URT presupposes that this ontological motive is present in interpersonal communication. URT assumes that, as humans, we want to know what we are going to do and what others are going to do as we engage in communication situations. Further, we want to explain why we said what we said and why the other person said what he or she said. It is as if humans engage continuously in the invention of little theories—that is, we provide attributions—to explain what we said and others said in communication settings. Let's see if we can illustrate this point. Think about how novel but frustrating it can be to communicate with children under five years of age. For example, it is often difficult to predict what they will say or explain away what they do say. Art Linkletter, a 1950s and 1960s television personality, made a career out of a show segment entitled, "Kids say the darnedest things."

Humans Desire Stable, Predictable Relationships with Others   Berger and Calabrese (1975) turned to Goffman (1959) to support this ontological assumption and concluded that "people prefer to have smooth-running interpersonal relationships" (p. 103). They repeated Goffman's assumption that by nature people contribute to and assist each other in an encounter "so that each performer can maintain 'face' " (p. 103). Cupach and Metts (1994) offered a similar, detailed, communication-based explanation of how facework is maintained or lost in close relationships. Additionally, they demonstrated how facework relates to URT (see especially, pp. 42–43). For Cupach and Metts, appropriate facework is cocreated and negotiated by the cointeractants until Goffman's "working consensus" evolves into a smooth-running interpersonal encounter. It is this cointeracting, negotiating, social information-sharing process that reduces uncertainty and stabilizes the relationship (pp. 96–97). In Chapter 8, we introduce Face Management Theory.

Social Information-Sharing Is Goal-Directed   With this third ontological assumption, Berger (1995a, 1995b), Berger, Karol, and Jordan (1989), and Berger and Kellermann (1994) indicated that goals serve as desired end-states. As humans we set and try to meet our goals. URT presupposes that interactants use social information-sharing strategies to meet their goals. In some communication situations, manipulative goals arise in which a sender of social information tries to gain influence over a target. Typically, such manipulative goals arise with compliance-gaining, affinity-seeking, terminating relationships, and the like.[4] Of course, this is not to say that goal metamorphosis may not occur during the communication situation. Furthermore, even nonmanipulative, relationship-building communication is goal-directed in that people set out (plan) to learn more about another individual. Berger and Kellermann (1994) articulated the available goal-directed strategies for creating and maintaining interpersonal relationships.

Increased Social Knowledge Produces Stability in Relationships   This is an epistemological assumption. It deals with how we give and get social knowledge. Common, everyday adages such as "ignorance is bliss," "spice makes nice," and "familiarity breeds contempt" expose the fact that information is a two-edged sword (see Chapter 2). Thus, although optimized social information is needed to achieve goals, it is not necessarily all the information that could be exchanged. We've all experienced the feeling of disclosing more social information than appropriate in many communication situations. As well, we've experienced the feeling of disclosing social information at the wrong time. Nonetheless, the opposite case, in which you might clam up and present no social information, is equally chaotic. Hence, this epistemological assumption says that to create and maintain relationships a certain amount of social information is necessary. The amount of social information-sharing is tempered only by the recognition that there is a point of diminishing returns. The crux of the matter is to determine a sufficient range or optimal amount of social information to share.

Many Sources of Uncertainty Exist   Berger and Calabrese (1975) noted that uncertainty in interpersonal relationships relates to uncertainty about predicting and explaining actions. Furthermore, deviant communication (lying, betraying confidence, changing values, illicit sexual affairs) often serves as a continuous source of uncertainty even in ongoing relationships (Planalp & Honeycutt, 1985). Berger (1995b) listed several additional sources of uncertainty. For example, uncertainty springs from concerns about the communication competency of the message producer and receiver. As well, uncertainty flows from not knowing if the goals that one hopes to achieve in the communication transaction will be met. Additionally, uncertainty comes from doubts about the plans constructed to achieve those goals. Also, uncertainty evolves from not knowing the emotional state of the receiver. Finally, uncertainty develops from not knowing another's beliefs on some topic. All of these sources provide support for the epistemological assumption that many sources of uncertainty exist.

URT: Introducing the Theoretical Concepts

Again, we've reached a point in the trail where we can stop and examine a landmark. Uncertainty Reduction Theory—like all general communication theories—exhibits basic, structural, and evaluative concepts. By observing communicators communicating through the lens of this theory, you should see cointeractants seeking and giving social information. They do so to predict and explain behavior, reduce uncertainty, and develop a liking, stable relationship. Berger, et al. (1976b) stated: "If the interacting parties are unable to describe, predict, and explain each other's behaviors and beliefs with some degree of accuracy they will not achieve interpersonal understanding" (p. 154). **Figure 5-1** displays URT's major concepts. Using TCM, we present the theory's basic, structural, and evaluative terms.

Finding Basic Concepts

To use URT it is necessary to find, identify, and code its initial and associative basic concepts. URT's initial basic concept is social information of which there are at least three subtypes. URT's associative basic concept is social information-seeking; again, there are three subtypes.

Initial Basic Concept   Once again, this is an ideal spot along the trail to understanding communication theories to take a rest stop. Recall from TCM that a general theory's basic

Viewing URT's Anatomical Elements

Key:
Bold Caps = The Communication Metatheory's Metaconcepts
Caps + Small Case = URT's Theoretical Concepts

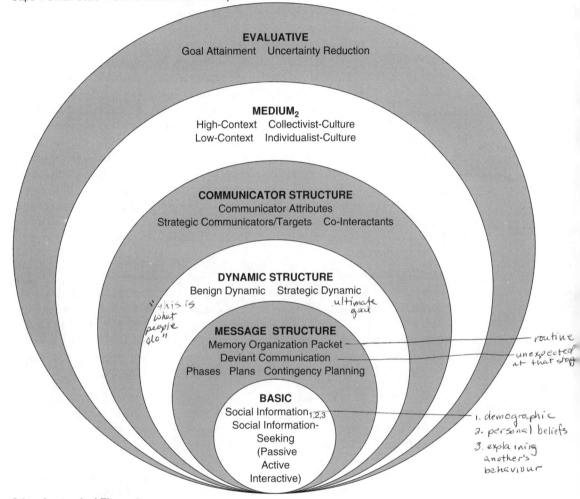

Other Anatomical Elements:

COMMUNICATIVE FORCE	**MODELING**
ORIGIN, ROOTS, ASSUMPTIONS	**RELATIONSHIP STATEMENTS**
PARADIGM	**THEORY–METHOD COMPLEX**

EXAMPLE OF SOCIAL INFORMATION-SEEKING: "If you like me so much, how come you've never invited me home to meet your family?"

FIGURE 5-1.

concept stipulates the communicative force for human action. As well, an initial basic concept is the primary communication unit that is singled out for analysis by a particular theory. URT's initial basic concept is social information.

Social Information.   Social information is the tabular term for the various types of inter-personal information exchanged by interactants in social situations. It is the initial thing you must find in human communication when using URT. If you cannot find a piece of social information and distinguish it from information, per se, then you cannot theorize by using URT. Recall that with Information Systems Theory information is data, knowledge, or opinion that reduces the uncertainty of at least one of the participants in a communication episode. With URT, the communicators begin as strangers in a context of interpersonal uncertainty. They seek specialized knowledge that is called social information. Berger, et al. (1976b) specified three levels of social knowledge: descriptive statements (demographic data), statements of personal beliefs on issues, and statements that explain another's actions or beliefs. Berger and Calabrese (1975) indicated that these are the three kinds of social information that communicators seek from one another in order to create and maintain a stable relationship. Berger (1995a, 1995b) stipulated that these three kinds of social information are also necessary if you hope to succeed at social influence. Recall that URT assumes that people strive to reduce uncertainty about self and others so that they can predict and explain behavior and thus create interpersonal order. For purposes of discussion, we use subscripts to distinguish the three kinds of social information. You should think of them as if you were climbing a mountain trail to get a better view of this theory. The first type of information is relatively easy. The next type is more difficult. The final kind is quite hard. So it is with giving and eliciting the three kinds of social information.

Social Information$_1$—*Demographic Data.*   In *Dragnet* reruns on television, Sergeant Joe Friday wants "the facts—just the facts!" We suspect that the sort of information included in Sgt. Friday's "facts" is better known to you as demographic and sociographic information. Demographic information includes such social information as biographical data, such as birthday, age, location of birth, country of citizenship, and occupation. Sociographic information includes such social information as attends class regularly, works out, goes to church, watches soap operas, goes to concerts, and so forth.

Social Information$_2$—*Personal Beliefs.*   The ability to know another person's core beliefs, attitudes, and vital interests is often difficult social information to acquire. People hold beliefs, opinions, and attitudes that they hesitate to share with strangers. Even low-level beliefs and attitudes, or peripheral beliefs and opinions are often not disclosed in most communicative situations. The expression, "It's hard to get to know people," possesses a sizable kernel of truth. Disclosing beliefs and attitudes involves a great deal of risk-taking. Professor Shields might find it risky to disclose to other faculty that he views the Dean of the College as "Prince Machiavelli in baggy pants." On the other hand, he discloses the latest precocious adventure of his nephew, Phil, to anyone who will listen. Moreover, sensitive beliefs are hard to disclose. What strong beliefs do you know that your roommate holds? How did you learn such social information? Does knowledge of those beliefs allow you to predict and explain your roommate's behavior? Such questions lead us to our discussion of the third kind of social information.

Social Information$_3$—*Explaining Another's Behavior.*   Acquiring or giving social information at the third level is hard. If you disclose information to others it means that they know enough about you to explain your behavior. Conversely, if others disclose such information to you, it means that you know enough about them to explain their behavior. Professor Shields's knowledge of his Dean is less than Professor Cragan's knowledge of his spouse (Elizabeth). This difference is due to the amount of social information sought and gained over the years. The difference is also due to our respective motivations to predict and explain behavior. John wants to continue his stable relationship with Betty. Don lacks interest in knowing, other than professionally, his Dean. After more than thirty years of marriage, John has acquired much social information about the attitudes and beliefs that Betty holds. Knowledge of such social information has made life predictable. For example, he always reads the sports page first. Elizabeth likes the front page. Similarly, he always squeezes the toothpaste from the bottom of the tube. Elizabeth likes toothpaste on demand. As well, John just unplugs the curling iron when he finds it still heating. Elizabeth doesn't like to be reminded that she forgot to unplug it.

Associated Basic Concept   URT's remaining basic concepts are social information-seeking and its three subtypes. The subtypes are passive, active, and interactive social information-seeking. In essence, URT's associate basic concepts reflect the potential strategies available to elicit social information about a communicator.

Social Information-Seeking.   In stark contrast to IST—which depicts communicators actively sending information to create order—URT views communicators actively seeking social information in an effort to reduce uncertainty. In URT, *social information-seeking* concerns the goal-directed communication activities designed to reduce uncertainty about another through the acquisition of social information. In its initial presentation in 1975, URT did not contain this basic term, but later research and theorizing produced the three broad categories of social information-seeking behavior for reducing uncertainty: passive, active, and interactive.[5]

Passive Social Information-Seeking.   Berger (1987) describes passive strategies as those in which "the uncertainty reducer gathers information about a target through unobtrusive observation" (p. 46). A typical passive strategy is unobtrusive observation without interaction. Unobtrusive observation involves viewing from afar a target who is engaging in informal social interaction and conversations with other people (Berger & Douglas, 1981; Berger & Perkins, 1978). The kinds of social information elicited through such unobtrusive observation include gender, age, general appearance, manner of dress, appropriateness of social behavior, conversational fluency, nonverbal expressiveness skills, and social affiliations. Any or all of these unobtrusively gained types of social information might cause your feelings of uncertainty to lessen and increase your feelings of similarity and liking. Berger and Bradac (1982) labeled the passive preference for informal social observation "the Matthew effect." They did so because Berger's eight year-old son could recognize the importance of such an environment for gaining important social information about targets.

Active Social Information-Seeking.   Berger and Bradac (1982) indicated that active social information-seeking strategies involve "those ways of gaining [social] information which require the observer to do something to affect the response of the actor but do not involve direct contact between the observer and the actor" (p. 18). One such strategy is asking third-parties about the target. Hewes, et al. (1985) found that about 30 percent of all social information is gained from third-party sources. Parks and Adelman (1983) found that people involved in romantic relationships who used the social network of their partner's friends and relatives demonstrated lower levels of uncertainty. They also reported that such romantic partnerships were less likely to experience dissolution than nonnetworking romantic partners. Such research indicates that networking reduces uncertainty and contributes to the maintenance of social relationships.

Another active strategy, according to Berger (1987), entails "manipulations of the interaction environment" (p. 46). A typical manipulation would be to ask your special friend to go to your parents' house for the weekend. You extend this strategic request so that you can observe her or him in your family situation. Conversely, you may be at college and your special friend is at home. So you invite her or him to campus for the weekend. Again, you extend this strategic request so that you can observe him or her interacting with your college friends. Another variation might be to have your roommate go for coffee with a target person. Of course, you may find that your roommate then asks the target out on a date. At any rate, all three active or manipulative strategies allow you to use your family, friends, and roommates to elicit third-party disclosures about what they think of your special someone. Such strategies also allow you to observe your friend in environments that you know and can control.

Interactive Social Information-Seeking.   Berger (1987) indicated that interactive social information-seeking concerns "direct, face-to-face contact between the information seeker and the target" (p. 46). Seeking interactive social information involves question-asking, self-disclosures, and using affiliative communication behaviors (pauses, vocalizations, paralinguistic cues) at appropriate times to relax the target and lead them to feel at ease with you. In a series of studies, Berger and Kellermann (1983, 1989) and Kellermann and Berger (1984) found that persons engaging in information-seeking employed more positive nonverbal behavior than interactants not engaged in information acquisition. The choices of question-asking, self-disclosure (in the hopes of the target's reciprocation), and nonverbal and verbal relaxing techniques (aimed at putting the target at ease) seemed to be tempered by a tension concerning social appropriateness and efficiency. A trade-off appeared to exist between the efficiency of question-asking and its perception by the target as socially inappropriate. On the other hand, actively presenting self-disclosures in the hopes of fostering reciprocation and employing relaxing techniques in the hopes of generating social information appear more socially acceptable. However, they are not as efficient in reducing uncertainty as question-asking.

Baxter and Wilmot (1984) reported data from the study of 181 people involved in either a platonic or romantic relationship. Through a qualitative and quantitative investigation they discovered that interactants used a repertoire of fifteen separate "secret tests" designed to reduce uncertainty and reveal information about the partner's level of commitment to the relationship. The repertoire of fifteen strategies reflects URT's passive, active, and interactive strategies for seeking social information. Additionally, their research indicated that women reported the use of more secret test strategies than did males. The repertoire of "secret tests" is contained in **Table 5-1.**

Seeing Structural Concepts

Here a brief rest stop appears in order. Recall that TCM specified that the structural concepts for all general communication theories relate to message structure, communication dynamic, communicator structure, and medium structure. At its simplest, URT explains

TABLE 5-1. Repertoire of "Secret Tests" in Relationships

1. Direct questioning: "How do you feel about me?"

2. Asking third parties: "I asked his friend what my romantic partner thought of me."

3. Escalating touching: "By touching her I found out if she was ready for our relationship to go beyond being friends."

4. Self-disclosure with the hope of reciprocating disclosure: "I was having trouble getting him to open up about his family, so I told him about my family."

5. Public presentation: "She invited me to her family's home for a week and her mother started treating me like her son. I got scared."

6. Joking about the seriousness of the relationship: "My boyfriend jokes about the number of children we'll have to see if I'm serious about marriage. I'm not yet; but it's OK that he keeps pushing me."

7. Who initiates contact: "I'll sometimes wait for a long time to see if she'll call me. The length of time it takes tells me something about how serious she is about our relationship."

8. Self put-down: "My boyfriend really gets down on himself sometimes to see if I will compliment him and tell him how much I think of him."

9. Hinting: "I flirt with him a lot in letters and wait to see what his reaction is to my flirting."

10. Forcing choices: "My girlfriend called me during spring break and wanted me to drive 500 miles to pick her up. It was just a test to see how much I cared about her."

11. Physical separation: "Our separation while I was at school showed how much we cared for each other."

12. Rule deviation: "He will test how much I love him by showing his worst side to me."

13. Creating jealousy #1: "I talked about my other boyfriend in his presence to see if he would get jealous."

14. Creating jealousy #2: "I tested her limits by going out with another woman and making sure she saw me."

15. Fidelity checks: "I would intentionally leave him alone in my room with my roommate; then return and ask, 'What have the two of you been up to?' If he acted embarrassed, then I knew he had been unfaithful or was at least thinking about it."

(Adapted from Baxter & Wilmot, 1984, pp. 182–188.)

that communicators communicate with social information in some medium. URT contains five message structure concepts (message organization packets, deviant communication, phases, plans, and contingency plans), two dynamic structure concepts (benign and strategic), three communicator structure concepts (cointeractants, strategic communicators/targets, and communicator attributes) and two medium$_2$ concepts (high-context collectivist culture and low-context individualist culture).

Message Concepts   Recall that TCM specified that all general communication theories contain message structure concepts that dress up and flesh out a theory's basic concepts. As indicated in **Figure 5-1,** URT's message structure concepts are message operation packets (MOPs), deviant communication, phases, plans, and contingency. Let's continue our rest stop and look at the linkages of these concepts. Part of learning a language concerns knowing more than just a vocabulary and how to put words into sentences. It means knowing what to say and when to say it. Message Organization Packets help us know what to say. What is said at the initiation of a relationship is not what is said as a relationship matures. There are different message organization packets for that. Using MOPs out of sequence illustrates deviant communication. The technical concept associated with the maturation of relationships is phases. In other words, relationships go through their ups and downs and they go through a beginning, middle, and an end. Plans, along with MOPs, help you move through the phases of relationships. Contingency plans help you continue your goal-directed purposes when plans meet resistance.

Memory Organization Packet.   URT asks you to view relationship communication as highly ritualized and routine. Much like Information Systems Theory, URT posits a somewhat fixed linguistic sequencing of many communication interactions. Such sequencing is best understood as a memory organization packet. A *memory organization packet* is a knowledge structure that organizes conversational scenes or topics (Schank, 1982; Kellermann, 1991; Kellermann, et al., 1989). Thus, MOPs are routine but flexible scripts or chunks of potential conversational behavior that may be called forth by the interactants (Kellermann, et al., 1989). In other works, a conversational MOP tends toward universality and provides a means for pursuing or developing talk on any topic. Kellermann (1991) indicated that the most universal MOP contains six generalized acts. *Get facts* such as, "Where are you from?" *Discuss facts* such as, "What's there to do in your hometown?" *Evaluate* such as, "Do you like it there?" *Explain* such as, "Why or why not?" *Future goals* such as, "Do you want to return to your hometown when you graduate?" Finally, you seek to know the *enabling condition* such as, "Can you find a job there?"

Another MOP with which we are all familiar is what Kellermann (1991) called the "informal initial conversation MOP" (pp. 388–389). For example, "Hi! My name's Don. What's your name?" "How are you?" "What's your major?" "Do you follow the school basketball team?" "Are you going to the game tonight?" "Isn't it exciting watching them play?" "Maybe I'll see you there." "Catch you later. Bye."

URT posits that social information-seeking is highly standardized. MOPs provide the standardization. We use memory organization packets with their clear, well-understood scripts to gather nonthreatening biographical demographic information first (What's your name? Where are you from?) before we gather sociographic information (Are you going to the game tonight? Would you like a cup of coffee?) or attitudinal information (Isn't it exciting watching them play? Don't you just love Mocha Java?).

Deviant Communication.   Again, like Information Systems Theory, URT requires the proper sequencing of conversational MOPs. The reason is that major violations of these standard, routine scripts increase uncertainty. In routine social interactions, a typical second or third question is usually "How are you?" If you reply at any more length than "I'm fine," or "I'm OK," or "I'm fair," then you deviate from the content of the standard MOP. Similarly, if in the initial conversation with a stranger you ask him or her to tell you his or her annual income, then his or her level of uncertainty about you will increase. This increase in uncertainty occurs because she or he would see you as having violated a standard MOP. Information about a person's income or net worth is generally not disclosed until much later in a relationship. Such deviant communication increases uncertainty. In fact, Kellermann and Reynolds (1990) found that as deviant communication behavior increases, the level of uncertainty increases, and a decrease in intimacy occurs. Planalp and Honey-cutt (1985) and Planalp, Rutherford, and Honeycutt (1988) demonstrated that deviant communication behavior (improperly sequenced MOPs) in developed relationships increases uncertainty. They also found that many ongoing relationships became more distant (or were terminated) as the result of deviant communication events (improperly sequenced MOPs). Again, not all communication works to decrease uncertainty in relationships. Deviant communication often increases uncertainty (Berger, 1986).

Phases. Relationships involve a developmental process that occurs over time. Interpersonal communication scholars consistently view relationship formulation and maintenance as occurring stage-by-stage or phase-by-phase. A *phase* is a specific length of time (beginning –middle–end) in a developmental relationship. Each phase is characterized by unique social information exchanges. As relationships progress from one phase to the next, they are characterized by an increasing level of intimacy between the interactants from stage to stage. For example, two social psychologists, Altman and Taylor (1973, pp. 136–142), proposed a four-phase model (orientation, exploratory affect, affective exchange, and stable exchange) for relationship development. Altman and Taylor noted that interactants disclosed different levels of intimate information at each stage until a stable stage (a state that occurs in only a few relationships for most people) is reached. Likewise, two communication scholars, Knapp and Vangelisti (1992) described a five-stage model of the development of relational intimacy (initiation, experimenting, intensifying, integrating, and bonding). Berger and Calabrese (1975) indicated that developing relationships go through three phases: entry, personal, and exit. The central idea in these stagic accounts of message structure is that the disclosure of social information is not random and haphazard, as it at first might appear, but is quite ordered. In the initial and early stages of a developing relationship humans tend to disclose safe biographic information. Next, as uncertainty is reduced, people disclose safe sociographic information about activities. Then, as uncertainty about the riskiness of disclosure is reduced still further, they disclose more intimate psychographic information pertaining to their beliefs and attitudes.

Plans. As relationships develop, goals emerge for continuing the relationship, engaging in joint activities, and eliciting more intimate information. A *plan* is a hierarchically organized, goal-directed blueprint or knowledge-structure for achieving an objective (Berger, 1995a; Berger & diBattista, 1992, 1993; Berger, Knowlton, & Abrahams, 1996). Of course, as we shall see in the communication dynamic section of this chapter, as the information-seeker clarifies future goals and formulates plans he or she has moved from the domain of the benign use of social information to reduce uncertainty to the social influence domain of using information to meet his or her social goals. Plans are hierarchically ordered on the basis of what Berger and diBattista (1993) and Berger, Knowlton, and Abrahams (1996) called the *hierarchy principle*. Here, abstract actions necessary for goal achievement are located toward the top of a hierarchy and more specific actions are "nested beneath them" (p. 113). They explain: "A plan to persuade one's parents to allow one to go to the movies might include such abstract elements as a general strategy, for example, asking for something larger first, and when the large request is denied, making a smaller request" (p. 113). Lower order message plan elements might then include the use of less abstract message plans such as the argument to persuade a parent to grant permission to go to the movies because "I cleaned my room without being told to." Thus, the hierarchy principle of message plans posits that "when individuals experience goal failure, their first response is to alter lower level message plan elements rather than the more abstract elements that require more cognitive resources for their modification" (Berger, Knowlton, & Abrahams, p. 133).

Contingency Planning.   Berger (1995a, 1995b) and Berger and Gudykunst (1991) indicated that with goals come contingency plans to help the information-seeker achieve her or his goals. *Contingency plans* refer to the repertoire of alternative actions that the information-seeker will pursue if his or her goal is initially blocked. Another way of saying this is that strategic communicators develop contingency plans to help them when their initial plans meet resistance. For example, if a college student asks you to go to a movie and you decline by indicating you have to study, then does the college student have an alternative for the study contingency? Would this social information-seeker then indicate that he or she could begin researching his or her own term paper too, and if you would like he or she could meet you at the library? In such a case, if you decline again by indicating a desire to study at a coffeehouse, does the social information-seeker then have a contingency for asking if you would like to meet him or her at the coffee shop? It appears that some communicators develop complex contingency plans to achieve their social goals more effectively and competently than others (Berger & Bell, 1988).

Dynamic Concepts   Again, we've reached a point on the trail to understanding communication theories where a rest stop is indicated. Recall that TCM posited that general communication theories exhibit a deep structure that varies with each theory. Moreover, a tension exists either in the deep structure of the system the message is in or in the structure of the message itself. In the case of URT, the conflict that occurs concerns the nature and type of the social relationship: benign versus strategic.

Benign Dynamic.   URT in its initial formulation assumed that strangers meeting in a social situation sought to reduce uncertainty about each other. URT assumed the interactants possessed a benign need to reduce uncertainty, and that they disclosed social information without any ulterior motive beyond getting to know each other. In other words, URT initially presupposed that interactants gently and graciously used their kind dispositions to reduce uncertainty. We all long for such benign social interactions. All of us would like to form acquaintanceships and friendships free from professional and societal entanglements. Oftentimes, vacations provide the opportunity to meet people outside of the work and school environment without ulterior motive. It's exciting and refreshing to be free of all strategic communication other than the desire for new relationship formation. In such encounters, we downplay the potential for strategic communication. For example, Professor Cragan's daughter, Katie, met her future husband, Rob, while on spring break in South Padre Island, Texas. For Katie and Rob, spontaneity and disclosure reduced uncertainty in the total absence of strategic planning for a future relationship.

Strategic Dynamic.   Although we long for an idyllic world of only benign friendships, contributors to URT's research program noted that we sometimes strategically target individuals. Here, we seek to acquire social information to help us meet our goals. To do so according to Berger (1986, 1987, 1995a, 1995b), we use the passive, active, and interactive strategies needed to gain the information that allows us to influence someone socially. On the other hand, we sometimes strategically foil another's attempts to know us. Berger and Kellermann (1989) identified a series of offensive and defensive tactics that strategic communicators use to foil the strategic information-seeking attempts of others. One way to foil strategic information-seekers is to give minimal or ambiguous responses to questions. Another way is to offer negative nonverbal cues. Still another way is to continuously pepper the information-seeker with questions so that we receive more social information than we provide. We all dislike being the target of strategic information-seekers. As our careers develop, however, it becomes nearly impossible to avoid strategic information-seekers. For example, famous people find that nearly all of their social communication situations become strategic. Celebrities regularly speak of the difficulty of forming new friendships once they become famous.

Communicator Concepts   Again, let's take a brief rest stop. Please recall that TCM posited that every communication theory possesses its own unique names for the communicators who communicate in a medium. URT's communicator structure concepts identify the communicators in social information-sharing interaction. URT's three communicator concepts are cointeractants, strategic communicators/targets, and the special case of specific communicator attributes. These concepts label and describe the communicators who exchange social information in an initial or developing relationship.

Cointeractants.   In benign social information-exchange situations, URT views the communicators as coequal seekers and givers of social information. URT calls them *cointeractants.* Each cointeractant engages in the process of reducing uncertainty about the other for the purpose of relationship formation. The cointeractants use and follow memory organization packets (MOPs) that structure their interaction. They try to avoid the use of deviant communication such as out-of-sequence MOPs. Over time, the ordered sharing of social information leads the cointeractants through the stages of relationship formation.

Strategic Communicators/Targets.   In strategic, social, information-exchange situations, there may not be a coequal relationship. This comes about because one of the communicators targets the other for social influence. As well, both communicators may strategically seek information. In such a case, neither individual is a passive target. Given such a strategic dynamic, the competency level of the cointeractants and the passivity of the targets determines the extent to which they share social information and reduce uncertainty (Spitzberg, 1994).

Communicator Attributes.   Let's extend our rest stop. Obviously, every communicator in every communication situation exhibits certain communicator attributes. However, we know from TCM that some theories emphasize particular attributes. Let's see if we can illustrate this point. Obviously, communicator competency is an attribute that effects all communication theories. However, a particular theory may give a specific name to one or more characteristics of communication competency. With URT, several communicator attributes have been identified that affect your competency regarding the sharing of social information. One of the attributes is *self-monitoring,* that is, being aware of your communicative behavior. Another attribute is *communication apprehension,* that is, anxiety about communicating socially. Still another is *shyness,* that is, reticence regarding communicating socially. Yet another is the characteristic of *powerful* or *powerless speech,* that is, your degree of fluency in conveying social information. Socially fluent people are said to exhibit powerful speech. Socially dysfunctional people are said to exhibit powerless speech. A final communicator attribute is *degree of loneliness,* that is, how relationship-starved are you? Each of these communicator attributes effects the cointeractants' abilities to reduce uncertainty through social information-sharing. For example, Berger and Bell (1988) discovered that *shyness* and *loneliness* effected a cointeractor's ability to reduce uncertainty in order to obtain a date. They demonstrated that "persons with certain types of social dysfunction may simply lack the procedural knowledge necessary for obtaining certain social goals" (p. 230). In addition, McCroskey, et al. (1975) reported that highly *apprehensive communicators* cannot reduce uncertainty and are perceived as less attractive because their apprehension leads them to communicate less. On the other hand, according to Douglas (1983) and Gudykunst (1985a), communicators who are high *self-monitors* make better use of social information-gathering strategies than low self-monitoring communicators. As well, high self-monitors are better detectors of deception, and more successful at retrieving social information than low self-monitoring communicators. Haleta (1996) examined the role of language use in uncertainty reduction following Berger and Bradac (1982, esp. p. 51), Friedrich and Cooper (1990), and Ng and Bradac (1993). She found that professors who use powerful speech (hesitation-free) as opposed to powerless speech (hesitations) during initial class meetings reduced student uncertainty about the course.

Medium Concepts Again, it's time for a rest stop on the trail to understanding communication theories. Recall that TCM posited three senses of medium. Medium$_1$ is the sense of the general theory functioning in the six traditional communication contexts of interpersonal, small group, public speaking, organizational, mass, and intercultural communication. Medium$_2$ is the sense of a substance in which a theory propagates, prospers, and grows. Medium$_3$ is the sense of communication traveling by way of a channel. For example, with medium$_3$ communication is conducted, transmitted, or carried by words on the printed page, light waves, sound waves, or electrical waves. URT contains only one sense of a medium$_2$ substance. It is called culture. However, it appears that there are two fundamentally different cultural media that effect uncertainty reduction and social information-seeking and disclosure. One type is labeled a high-context, collectivist culture. Japan, Korea, China, and West Africa are high-context, collectivist cultures. The other type is labeled a low-context, individualist culture. Scandinavia, Germany, and the United States are low-context, individualist cultures.

High-Context, Collectivist Versus Low-Context, Individualist Cultures. Berger and Gudykunst (1991) indicated that high-context cultures make a greater distinction between insiders and outsiders than low-context cultures. Okabe (1983) noted that such cultures prize verbal skills more than low-context cultures. Berger and Gudykunst (1991) reported that people in individualist cultures look after themselves and their immediate family. Conversely, people in collectivist cultures look after people in extended in-groups in exchange for loyalty. URT, because it is a general communication theory, can explain the relation between uncertainty reduction and relationship development across cultures. Nonetheless, it is clear from the research that the preferred communication strategies used to reduce uncertainty differ between collectivist, high-context and individualist, low-context cultures. For example, Gudykunst and Nishida (1984) found that the Japanese used fewer self-disclosures and interrogations than Americans as a means to reduce uncertainty. Nonetheless, the Japanese exuded higher confidence levels than Americans that they had reduced uncertainty. Gudykunst and Nishida indicated that the Japanese used strategies other than those typically used by Americans. For example, the Japanese reduced uncertainty by looking to the definition of the situation. In their high context culture, the situation told them what to expect. However, when unfamiliar with the context, the Japanese do use social information-seeking strategies just like the Americans. Nonetheless, Olaniran and Williams (1995) found that communication across individual and collectivist cultures is made more difficult because collectivist, high-context cultures are more protective of in-group information.

Using Evaluative Concepts

At this point, let's take another rest stop. Recall from TCM that all general communication theories posit concepts that help you evaluate communication from the perspective of a particular theory. Such concepts allow you to make assessments and judgments regarding the quality and outcomes of communicators communicating in a medium.

Also, recall from Chapter 1 that all scientists are concerned with explaining the outcomes (effects) of the fundamental interactive forces that they study. For example, the biochemist studies the chemical interactions in all living organisms. He or she is concerned with such biochemical interactions as *bioluminescence* that explains why glowworms glow and fireflies light. With URT, we evaluate the quality and effects (outcomes) of social information-sharing and its resultant impact on human relationships.

Quality and Outcomes   By outcomes we mean that the communicative interaction identified by the theory did in fact occur. That is, did the communicative force under study have its predicted impact on human action? Quality is a feature denoting degree or grade of excellence of the communicative interaction. In URT's case, were coninteracts reducing uncertainty and attaining their goals through the sharing of social information and did liking increase among the cointeractants as a result of reducing uncertainty? URT's primary evaluative concepts are uncertainty reduction and goal attainment.

Uncertainty Reduction.   It stands to reason that for the effects of social information-sharing to prove out, there must be uncertainty reduction. Likewise, for URT to prove out there must be uncertainty reduction. The question becomes, how to design a way to test for uncertainty reduction so that the effects of social information-sharing can be evaluated? In other words, the question is how to define uncertainty reduction operationally so that it can be measured like a thermometer measures temperature. Clatterbuck's (1979) Attributional Confidence Scale (CLUES) measures a respondent's confidence in knowing the other person across a number of questions. One form of the CLUES Scale contains seven questions; another form contains sixty-five. **Table 5-2** contains the items of the CLUES (CL7 Scale).

Respondents score their answers to the items in the CLUES Scale using from 0 percent to 100 percent for each question. Thus, a number of URT studies operationalized *uncertainty reduction* as an increase in one's score on the CLUES Scale given a period of interpersonal interaction.

Clatterbuck reported a correlation between increased communication and uncertainty reduction in a series of eight studies. Berger and Gudykunst (1991) reported that Berger,

TABLE 5-2.   Items of the CLUES (CL7) Scale

1. How confident are you of your general ability to predict how he/she will behave?
2. How certain are you that he/she likes you?
3. How accurate are you at predicting the values he/she holds?
4. How accurate are you at predicting his/her attitudes?
5. How well can you predict his/her feelings and emotions?
6. How much can you empathize with the way he/she feels about him- or herself?
7. How well do you know him/her?

(Adapted from Clatterbuck, 1979, p. 149.)

Douglas, and Rodgers (1980) had found that one's uncertainty about new acquaintances—as measured by CLUES—decreased significantly over six weeks. Berger and Gudykunst also reported that the 1980 study indicated that the greater the amount of reported communication, the less the uncertainty. Berger and Gudykunst (1991) also reported that a longitudinal study conducted by VanLear and Trujillo (1986) using CLUES had demonstrated significant decreases of uncertainty over time (two weeks) due to the amount of communication. After two weeks, the decrease leveled. Uncertainty reduction had been optimized.

Uncertainty normally decreases as more information is shared by the cointeractants. Eventually fewer questions are asked on the same topics because the interactants have already shared the answers. Even in initial interactions, Berger and Kellermann (1983) and Douglas (1985) found that the number of questions asked by interactants decreased over time. However, as we noted above, not all communication decreases uncertainty. Recall that deviant communication, that is out-of-sequence MOPs, can increase uncertainty.

Goal Attainment.   This evaluative concept relates to the communication dynamic of strategically achieving social influence. Berger (1995a, 1995b) indicated that social influence goal attainment cannot be guaranteed. However, he suggested that several strategies may well optimize goal attainment. These strategies included information-seeking through active and passive strategies, planning, remaining focused on the goal, contingency-planning, plan adaptation, and face-saving framing. The idea is that strategic communicators have goals like getting to know you, making a date, and so forth. With such social influence goals, URT explains not only reducing uncertainty but getting what you want out of the interaction. For example, if your goal is impression management, then you may be strategic in the type of social information you are willing to disclose so that your professional or personal image is maintained.

URT: Working with Its Qualitative Method

Using URT to study communicators communicating social information in a medium (culture) requires at the onset an operational definition of what constitutes social information and a coding system so that the occurrence of the operationally defined information can be observed, tracked, and studied over time. A good deal of URT's research program contributed to the development of its theory–method complex.

Social Information Analysis (SIA)

Let's stop and look at a point of interest. TCM posited that every theory possesses a unique qualitative method as part of its theory–method complex. Recall that the qualitative method unique to Information Systems Theory requires the coding, tracking, and modeling of the flow of information. Because URT is an analogue of Information Systems Theory, we should expect that the qualitative method of URT will mirror the qualitative method of IST. It does. With URT the qualitative method is called Social Information Analysis (SIA).

Berger and his associates developed qualitative procedures for coding and tracking social information. They did so for the purpose of explaining uncertainty reduction in the development of personal relationships and in the achievement of personal social goals. Their coding system allowed them to identify three kinds of social information: demographic data, personal beliefs, and attributing reasons to explain another's behavior. Their coding system placed special emphasis on social information-seeking communication behavior using passive, active, and interactive strategies. They coded passive strategies, such as observation, and active strategies, such as inviting another to known environments. As well, they coded such interactive strategies as question-asking, reciprocal self-disclosure, and nonverbal relaxing techniques. They also developed a coding schema for capturing communication tactics used to avoid giving social information, such as topic-changing, asking questions yourself, and nonverbal disinterest.

The SIA method requires that you first identify social information and the strategies used to acquire it. Next it requires that you describe the communication interaction of people as they exchange social information. To do this, SIA chunks interpersonal conversations into episodes, tracks the flow of information-seeking and information-giving, and evaluates them in terms of amount and quality. Thus, SIA enables you to chart whether such things as the amount of question-asking and type and quality of social information disclosure rises or falls in the course of a five-minute communication episode. It also allows you to provide global ratings of the interactants in terms of such elements as the quality of social information exchanged, self-presentation, impression management, social appropriateness, efficiency, and evasiveness. This sort of coding and tracking eventually allows you to model the entire episode into various phases such as entry, personal, and exit. Additionally, it allows you to characterize communicatively what goes on in each phase. Of course, the measure of uncertainty reduction known as the CLUES Scale also comprises part of URT's theory–method complex.

Briefly Illustrating SIA

Berger and Kellermann (1983) and Kellermann and Berger (1984) conducted two URT studies from a common data base of interactants that illustrate the use of SIA. In each study, the researchers paired the participants into conversational dyads reflecting four subsets: (1) high information-seekers matched with high information-seekers; (2) low information-seekers matched with low information-seekers; (3) high information-seekers matched with low information-seekers; and (4) normal information-seekers matched with normal information-seekers. Berger and Kellermann gave each of the three types of information-seekers (high, low, normal) a different set of instructions. They instructed all high information seekers to discover as much as they could about their conversational partner. They instructed all low information-seekers to find out as little as possible about their conversational partner. Finally, they told all normals nothing about how much or how little they should seek or disclose.

In the 1983 study, judges coded the videotaped conversations for amount of information-seeking, degree of social appropriateness, and the efficiency with which the persons met their information-seeking goal. In the 1984 study, judges coded the frequency and duration of various verbal behaviors (asking questions, verbal prompts, and statements). They also coded the frequency and duration of various nonverbal behaviors (positive head nods, smiles, and forward body lean) and global impressions about the interactants. The judges used a nine-item, bipolar, semantic differential scale to evaluate each interaction. The scale items allowed the judges to assess the degree to which the cointeractants' comments were evaluative–nonevaluative, pleasant–unpleasant, directive–nondirective, or socially appropriate–inappropriate. In the 1983 study, the researchers found 1,128 sequences of questions, answers, and statements in forty-eight five-minute conversations. The questions concerned twenty-three content areas such as education, experiences, biography, health, and so forth. The researchers reported that biographical and other demographic social information-seeking comprised 41 percent of question-asking.

In the 1983 study, Berger and Kellermann reported that the number of questions in these encounters asked by normal and high information-seekers exceeded the number asked by lows, but highs did not exceed normals. In essence, the data indicated that an optimum number of questions occur in a five-minute initial interaction. In the 1984 study, Kellermann and Berger reported that high information-seekers and normals are isomorphic and compatible in their use of almost all relaxation techniques. This finding suggested that an optimal number of relaxation behaviors occurs in a five-minute interaction. Finally, they concluded that a memory organization packet for the encounter intrinsically limited the number of attempts to elicit information. Both studies exhibited a similar cyclical trajectory of interpersonal conversation over time. Kellermann and Berger (1984) labeled this trajectory a "power-up-glide" model (p. 441). By this name they meant that questions are asked initially to power up the exchange of social information in the conversation. Then the conversation glides with exchanges of statements and the reinforcement of disclosure through head-nodding and leaning forward. As the conversation begins to wane or lull, another question is asked to power up the conversation, again.

URT: Observing Its Usefulness

We've reached our final rest stop on this part of the trail to understanding communication theories. Recall that TCM posited utility as its primary evaluative metaconcept. It's again time to think of our litmus question, "Will this dog hunt?" As we indicated in the earlier discussion of URT's power and scope, the theory explains how the force of social information-sharing reduces uncertainty about self, others, and the direction of interpersonal relationships, and enables you to meet social influence goals. Here, we will use some illustrative examples to demonstrate URT's use to explain human action and reduce social influence problems.

Explaining Human Action

Let's continue our rest stop. Recall that a communication theory validly explains human action when its concepts have been tied to or grounded in directly observable phenomena. A researcher usually grounds a theory's concepts by analyzing communication episodes to determine if the phenomena the concepts represent appear in the communication. The grounding of URT began almost immediately on the publication of Berger and Calabrese (1975). Berger and Calabrese (1975) developed URT to explain the initial entry stage of interpersonal interaction. After more than two decades and scores of studies, URT has matured. It has since been used to explain human actions that go beyond the initial interactions of strangers. For example, Parks and Adelman (1983) expanded the scope of URT and demonstrated its utility in explaining developed relationships. Afifi and Reichert (1996) grounded URT as a viable means of explaining and predicting the experience of and expression of jealousy in relationships. Booth–Butterfield, Booth–Butterfield, and Koester (1988) revealed the power of URT to explain the impetus for and process of reducing primary tension in small group communication.

Several scholars explored the value of URT in explaining relationship formation in organizational communication.[6] A number of them found support for Berger and Calabrese's (1975) third axiom—"high levels of uncertainty cause increases in information-seeking behavior" (p. 103)—in their studies of organizational communication. For example, Spiker and Daniels (1981) initially linked uncertainty levels to employee job satisfaction. Putnam and Sorenson (1982) examined equivocal messages in organizations and found a positive correlation between equivocality (uncertainty) and interaction cycles. Lester (1987) studied new employees in organizations and reported that their job success stemmed from uncertainty reduction about what counted for their performance evaluation. Comer (1991) studied active and passive coping designations, and Miller and Jablin (1991) offered an expanded model of URT's active–passive information-seeking process as followed by assimilators into an organization. Miller and Jablin proposed a typology of seven information-seeking strategies: overt questions, indirect questions, third parties, testing limits, disguising conversations, observing, and surveillance. Teboul (1994) tested Miller and Jablin's Newcomer's Uncertainty Typology. His findings linked a newcomer's uncertainty to each category of information-seeking. Teboul also discovered that a newcomer often experiences uncertainty connected with multiple concerns and uses multiple strategies to reduce it. Similarly, Mignerey, Rubin, and Gordon (1995) found that URT's social information-seeking behaviors positively effected the role-making process for newcomers entering an organization.

In the context of mass communication effects research, Dimmick, Sikand, and Patterson (1994) used URT to explain a large part of the gratifications obtained from the household telephone. Walther (1994) and Walther and Burgoon (1992) reported significant uncertainty reduction effects from social information-sharing in computer-mediated communication. As well, Alperstein (1991) examined uncertainty reduction by celebrities in television commercials as they created imaginary social relationships.

A number of scholars also grounded URT in cross-cultural communication research. Gudykunst, Yang, and Nishida (1985) studied developed acquaintance and dating relationships across both the collectivist cultures of Korea and Japan and the individualist culture of the United States. They found that URT explained relationship development in all three cultures. Gudykunst and Hammer (1988) demonstrated that URT accounted for ethnic differences in initial interactions between African Americans and whites in the United States. Gudykunst, Chua, and Gray (1987) wrote: "The present findings also are compatible with earlier inter-cultural research by Ting–Toomey (1981) on Chinese–American friendships, as well as Gudykunst's (1985b) comparison of intracultural and intercultural friendships" (p. 467). Ear-lier in their discussion, Gudykunst, Chua, and Gray noted that the cross-cultural research sug-gested that URT "can be generalized to account for differences in initial interactions between Japan and the United States (Gudykunst & Nishida, 1984), as well as to explain communication in acquaintance, friend, and dating relationships in Japan, Korea, and the United States" (Gudykunst, Yang, & Nishida, 1985, p. 457). They went on to say that such intercultural research as Gudykunst's (1985a, 1985c) "further indicates that uncertainty re-duction theory is useful in explaining communication between people from the United States and other cultures, as well as detailing differences in intra-ethnic and inter-ethnic communication in the United States" (p. 457). Moreover, Gudykunst, Nishida, and Chua (1986) and Gudykunst, Chua, and Gray (1987) concurrently validated the cross-cultural ex-istence of "systematic patterns in uncertainty reduction processes as relationships increase in level of intimacy" (p. 467).

Benefiting the Real World

Olaniran and Williams (1995) studied the real-world problem of foreigners (West Africans) applying for a visa through a Western culture consular service. They field-note recorded thirty-two interviews in which an applicant made a visa application to a Western official in the consular service located in a West African country. As well, they conducted twenty-one post-application interviews with applicants about the experience and the outcome of their application. They reported that applicants whose applications were denied exhibited less competency in using verbal and nonverbal uncertainty reduction strategies. They concluded that the consular interviewers needed training in cross-cultural communication that would show the differences in how collectivist cultures share information as compared to how in-dividualist cultures share information. Conversely, they suggested that the consular service provide information kits on differences in cross-cultural communication to all applicants before the interview rather than just to the successful applicants after the interview.

Hammer and Martin (1992) studied the impact of cross-cultural training for 17 Japan-ese and 123 American managers in an industrial company. They split the sample so that some participated in monoculture training and some participated in monoculture and joint-culture training. All training took place during a three-month period. They found that cross-cultural trainees felt a higher degree of comfort in understanding Japanese cultural patterns as a result of the training positively affecting uncertainty reduction and anxiety reduction as compared to monoculture training alone. Also, they found that cross-cultural training produced a higher degree of technical information exchange.

Kramer (1993) found URT to be a valuable theory for explaining the stress on both the transferee and other employees in the leaving and joining process in 102 job transfer situ-ations. He found that transferees who solicited more feedback about their new job from their supervisors and peers in their old positions reported experiencing less stress and more job satisfaction on their new positions. Conversely, transferees who spent more time with their new supervisors and coworkers seeking information about their new job and work environment experienced less stress and more job satisfaction. The optimum reduction of uncertainty about the new transfer environment came from seeking information about it from both the old and new supervisors and coworkers.

Withstanding the Critics

In the mid-1970s, Berger began developing URT. As we have seen, a number of other communication scholars contributed to the research program that built and grounded this general communication theory. However, URT did not develop without criticism. The three major criticisms of URT are: URT is not a general communication theory, predicted outcome value theory better explains initial relationship formation than URT, and Axiom 3 should be dropped from URT.

URT Is Not a General Communication Theory   Bochner (1978) charged that the theory failed to explain movement from one stage of development to another. As well, he charged that the theory failed to identify the causal mechanisms that led to such change. Conville (1983) claimed that URT only explained processual development within a system and it could not explain a change in "the development of the interpersonal system itself" (p. 195). Trenholm (1991) argued that URT "fails to explain when individuals will act to achieve certainty and when they will seek novelty" (p. 164). Furthermore, she argued that the theory "has little to say about how we perceive others during normal daily interactions when our primary focus is on the task at hand" (p. 164). Stacks, Hickson, and Hill (1991) indicated that real-world testing is difficult and "it has trouble with such questions as to what extent are axioms cultural bound" (pp. 35–36). They concluded that URT is not particularly heuristic and it does not provide a causal model to explain the interaction between other communication events and uncertainty reduction.

These criticisms of URT fly directly in the face of the research reported in this chapter. As we reported, numerous studies extended URT's explanatory power beyond initial interactions. Other studies identified the signs of movement from one stage to another. Specifically, they identified the different kinds of social information sought and disclosed in the respective stages. The studies reported in the section on real-world benefits speak to the application of the theory to day-to-day communication. The subsequent development of Uncertainty/Anxiety Reduction Theory (presented in Chapter 10) demonstrates URT's heuristic value. As well, some of the most exciting studies extended the scope of URT as they showed its organizational, mass, and intercultural communication applicability. We agree with Berger and Gudykunst's (1991) assessment. URT qualifies as a general communication theory because it has been grounded in mature interpersonal communication relationships, small group communication, public speaking, organizational communication, mass communication, and intercultural communication.

Predicted Outcome Value Is the Reason for Forming Relationships, Not Uncertainty Reduction   Sunnafrank (1986a, 1986b, 1990) argued that "uncertainty reduction would not be the primary concern of individuals, but only a means to achieving the more central goal of maximizing outcomes" (1986a, p. 4). Berger (1986) stated: "URT views predicted outcome values as a subset of a much larger set of predictions that are vital to the production of co-ordinated interactions" (p. 37). His implication is that Sunnafrank had the cart before the horse. Kellermann and Reynolds (1990) explained Berger's point. They indicated that pre-dicted outcome values (POVs) are only one type of incentive value and that the act of max-imizing rewards for oneself in the future is only one class of reasons for reducing uncertainty among individuals.

URT's Theorem 17 Has Been Falsified   An axiomatic derivative of Axioms 3 and 7 is The-orem 17: "Information-seeking and liking are negatively related" (Berger & Calabrese, 1975, p. 109). From the beginning, Berger and Calabrese indicated that this is an odd-seeming, "non-commonsensical" deduction. Why should we seek less information about the very people we like. Berger and Calabrese reminded their readers that "one operational indica-tor of information-seeking suggested earlier was the number of questions asked per unit of time. It would seem reasonable to suggest that as a relationship develops through time, there is less need for questions to be asked" (p. 109). As Professor Cragan would say, after thirty-plus years of marriage: "I feel little need to ask social information questions about my spouse. I already know the answer. And to ask a third party about Elizabeth would be an out-of-sequence MOP that would be viewed by her as deviant communication, thereby increasing her uncertainty."

Kellermann and Reynolds (1990), in twelve tests of Theorem 17, found a positive re-lationship between information-seeking and liking. They felt their study had falsified The-orem 17 and called for a modification of Axiom 3 in order to square the axiomatic statement of URT with their findings. The weakness in Kellermann's and Reynolds's reasoning is that Axioms 3 and 7 have been supported by studying communication interaction directly, while the studies they report asked their student–subjects to complete questionnaires on how they thought they might communicate in four hypothetical situations. Hence, the falsification claim is only indirect and awaits further research.

As you can see, URT's critics have missed the mark. Study after study has demon-strated that URT is a useful theory that explains the force of social information-sharing on interpersonal relationships. With both the criticisms and responses at hand, we leave it to you to make an informed judgment about whether or not URT withstands the critics. We believe it does, as all viable core general communication theories must. When you get to the end of the trail to understanding communication theories, we believe you can use URT with confidence. We wish you happy hunting.

Summary

In this chapter, we introduced you to Uncertainty Reduction Theory (URT). URT allows you to explain the communicative force of sharing social information on creating, stabiliz-ing, and sometimes destroying interpersonal relationships. We began by viewing URT as a general communication theory capable of being understood through the lens of The Com-munication Metatheory (TCM). In accord with TCM, we sketched URT's power and scope, traced its origin and roots, and discussed its primary assumptive system. Then we intro-duced URT's technical concepts (see **Figure 5-2**). We explained its basic concepts, structural concepts, and evaluative concepts. Next we introduced and illustrated URT's qualitative method, Social Information Analysis. Then, we reported on URT's usefulness. We showed URT's utility in explaining human action and benefiting the real world. Then, we discussed its ability to withstand critical scrutiny.

By now, you should be familiar with URT. Turn to **Figure 5-2** and see how our communication graduate on-the-job, Corey, is using URT to good advantage. If you do not yet feel comfortable with URT, we suggest you review our detailed chapter summary, "Understanding URT in a Nutshell," presented as **Box 5-1**.

"Uncertainty Reduction Theory (URT) tells us to share and seek information about ourselves and others to improve employee morale and job satisfaction."

FIGURE 5-2. Communication Graduate On-the-Job

BOX 5-1   Understanding URT in a Nutshell

URT Defined: *Uncertainty Reduction Theory* explains human interaction as the force of sharing social information that leads to the creation, stabilization, and sometimes destruction of interpersonal relationships.

Origin/Roots: URT stems directly from the 1970s work of Charles Berger and his associates at Northwestern University. Berger noted that URT is a direct extension of Information Systems Theory (IST) and IST's definition of information as reducing the number of alternatives present in a situation.

Assumptions: (1) Humans display an innate need to reduce uncertainty about themselves and others; (2) Humans desire stable, predictable relationships with others; (3) Social information-sharing is goal-directed; (4) Optimized social knowledge produces stability in relationships; and (5) Many sources of uncertainty exist.

Basic Concepts: *Social information* is the initial type of communication that you must find when using this theory. It comes in three forms or levels. Level 1 social information is *demographic data* such as biographical information (e.g., birthday, age, occupation) and sociographic information that discloses typical activities (e.g., goes to school, works out, goes to church). Level 2 social information concerns one's core beliefs, attitudes, and vital interests. Level 3 social information refers to that kind of information or intimate knowledge that allows you to explain another's behavior or allows them to explain your behavior. URT's associative basic concept is *social information-seeking*. Passive social information-seeking gathers information about another indirectly and unobtrusively (e.g., viewing someone from afar). Active social information-seeking relies on asking others about the target person. Interactive social information-seeking is direct contact (face-to-face, e-mail, telephone, letter contact) with the target. Strategies for getting information directly include question-asking, self-disclosing in anticipation of reciprocation, and the use of affiliative com-

munication behaviors (pauses, vocalizations, paralinguistic cues or prompts).

Structural Concepts: URT possesses message, dynamic, communicator, and medium structural concepts. The message structure concepts are memory organization packet (MOP), phases, and contingency planning. *MOPs* are ritualized, routine scripts that people use to organize conversations and develop topics. People call forth MOPs for use as needed. *Phases* are the specific lengths of time that comprise the various stages (typically four or five) of development that must be traversed in initial, unfolding relationships. Each phase is characterized by unique types of social information exchange. *Contingency planning* refers to the goals that emerge for continuing the relationship, engaging in joint activities, and eliciting more intimate social information. Contingency plans refer to the repertoire of alternative actions that the information-seeker will pursue if their goal is initially blocked. The communication dynamic structure concepts are benign versus strategic dynamic. In the *benign* dynamic, interactants are assumed to possess a desire to reduce uncertainty without any ulterior motive beyond getting to know one another. In the *strategic* dynamic an interactant may target another to acquire information that would help the interactant meet his or her goals. The communicator structure concepts include benign cointeractants and strategic communicators/targets as the communicators. These communicators display several communicator attributes (e.g., competence and self-monitoring) that effect the exchange of social information. The medium$_2$ structural concepts propagating URT are high-context collectivist cultures and low-context individualist cultures.

Evaluative Concepts: URT's primary evaluative concepts are uncertainty reduction and goal attainment. *Uncertainty reduction* is often defined as an increase in one's score on the CLUES Scale. *Goal attainment,* as an evaluative concept, relates to the communication dynamic of strategically achieving social influence.

Chapter **6**

Narrative Paradigm Theory (NPT)

The force of narration (storytelling) contributes the value justification for human action.

Chapter Outline

Your trail guides need a rest. We're not so young anymore and we need to catch our breath. In case you haven't noticed, we've been traveling uphill since Chapter 1. Around the bend is our next point of interest, Narrative Paradigm Theory (NPT). NPT should be easy for you to understand. NPT explains the force of storytelling as it contributes to the value justification for human action. NPT views all humans as primarily storytellers. As you know, all the great religions of the world use parables (stories) to teach religious values. All nation–states and corporations have compelling narratives about who they are and what good they do in the world. As the old industrialist's slogan stated, "As General Motors goes, so goes the country." NPT, like SCT, is an indigenous communication theory developed in the 1970s and 1980s.

NPT allows you to examine "good reasons"—the values that exist in stories that justify human action—to determine if the stories hang together and ring true. NPT is highly compatible with Rational Argumentation Theory, presented in Chapter 3, in that NPT also examines the contribution of argument and evidence to narrative probability (hangs together) and narrative fidelity (rings true). We continue the pattern set in the previous chapters by discussing NPT's power and scope, origin and roots, theoretical concepts, and research applications.

NPT: Viewing the General Theory

The symbolic facts of NPT are value-laden stories. These stories compete as explanations of reality. NPT views all human communication as essentially a narration or story. Therefore, NPT is a general communication theory. It can explain all forms of communication in all contexts.

Sketching Its Power and Scope

NPT's explanatory power derives from its ability to explain and assess the values that are implicit or explicit in stories that call forth human action. This theory argues that humans inherently possess narrative rationality, which allows them to tell good from bad stories, moral from immoral stories, and acceptable from unacceptable stories. NPT allows you to accept a story on the basis of whether or not it hangs together and rings true to your own experiences. NPT is a theory of broad scope because it has been used to explain the power of narrations in personal conversations, small group interaction, presidential speeches, history texts, plays, and even scientific papers. Scholars have used NPT to explain communication in physician–patient interviews, political party platforms, murder trials, the assessment of movies, the coverage of terrorist bombings, the mission of a student health center, the culture of an organization, and so forth. An NPT value analysis of human narration intrinsically demonstrates a struggle between materialistic and moralistic stories in these diverse communication contexts.

Tracing Its Origin and Roots

The origin of NPT grew out of Walter Fisher's (1973, 1978, 1987a, b) work at the University of Southern California beginning in the 1970s. Fisher held strongly to the belief that communication studies needed a theory that could flesh out and identify human values and critically assess their implications. He sought to draw together within NPT both logical reasoning and value reasoning so as to present a more complete assessment of humans' symbolic justification for action. Fisher reviewed the historical roots of poetics, rhetoric, and logic and found that in the writings of the ancient Greeks and Romans close distinctions were not drawn among these activities. As well, he discovered that the ancients placed a premium on values as a component of knowledge and wisdom and he suggested that NPT would return the concept of value to its initial place of importance. Fisher illustrated the importance of value in engendering wisdom. He used the example of our technological knowledge enabling us medically to sustain a brain-dead life, and asks, but should we?

Fisher established that NPT is accessible to the average person. NPT calls for the use of informal argumentation theory, as presented in Chapter 3, combined with value analysis. Thus, Fisher viewed NPT as a real return to the ancient understanding of the interconnectedness of the Greek words, *logos* (logical reasoning) and *mythos* (narrative storytelling). Narrative Paradigm Theory is explained in a number of articles and book chapters appearing since 1978.[1]

Accepting Its Assumptive System

All theories assume things about the nature of human beings, how we know what we know, and the values present in discourse. NPT exhibits ontological, epistemological, and axiomatic assumptions. Again, we would emphasize that a theory's assumptions do not occur in a closed system. As you study each theory you may find additional assumptions and presuppositions. Fisher (1985a, 1985b, 1987a) highlighted five assumptions.

Human Beings Are Storytellers   Fisher (1985b) specifically calls humankind *Homo narrans.* This ontological assumption is in stark contrast to Rational Argumentation Theory's ontological view that humans are essentially rational beings. Quite obviously, human beings must be storytellers from the perspective of this theory because communication is defined by the theory as narration or storytelling. To describe this book from the perspective of NPT, we are offering you a story. Our story is grounded in moralistic and materialistic values reflecting an emplotment that highlights the utility of knowing general communication theories. We escape the trap of having our book viewed solely as a story through the ontological assumption of our own metatheory as presented in Chapter 1. One of The Communication Metatheory's metaassumptions is that human beings are essentially theory-makers and theory-users (*Homo theoreticus*). Thus, NPT is but one theory used to explain communication phenomena. Nonetheless, you should understand that any of our six core general theories of broad scope can explain this book as a communication phenomenon. For example, IST (see Chapter 2) would help you explain this book as a message encoded into a number of information bits and transmitted for your decoding through the printed word. Alternatively, SCT (see Chapter 4) would help you view this book as a rhetorical vision that describes general communication theories in heroic form. In NPT's terms we present a narrative that leads you to understand the communication tree of knowledge (general, contextual, micro, criticism, symbiotic, and special theories), thereby empowering you to further your careers.

All Forms of Human Communication Are Best Viewed as Stories   When viewing human communication through the lens of NPT, all you see are stories. They are everywhere

(Fisher, 1987a). The stories you see may be Aesop's fable of the Hare and the Tortoise, George Washington chopping down the cherry tree, Moses climbing Mount Ararat for the Ten Commandments, Paul Revere's midnight ride urging preparedness, your physics professor's story on black holes, or your psychology professor's story about the war between the id, the ego, and the superego in Freud's psychoanalytic theory. NPT allows you to explain your acceptance or rejection of these stories, your actions on hearing them, and the process by which you evaluated them by using the same theoretical concepts. With the use of NPT, you are empowered to judge which are to be believed (i.e., possess narrative fidelity and coherence) and which are not. As you can see, NPT assumes that everyone—whether philosopher, theologian, historian, physicist, or psychologist—tells value-laden stories.

Through Discourse Humans Use "Good Reasons"—Value-Laden Warrants—For Believing or Acting   NPT assumes that good reasons provide the values that all human beings use in accepting or rejecting stories (Fisher, 1987a). NPT assumes that rational reasoning and evidence are insufficient or incomplete as explanations of people's acceptance of truth, knowledge, and reality. A recent misadventure on the part of Professor Cragan might help emphasize this assumption. Professor Cragan's identical twin grandsons, Kyle and Conner, age four, saw Spielberg's movie, *Jurassic Park,* which dealt with the recreation of dinosaurs from the DNA double helix of dinosaur blood withdrawn from a parasitic insect entombed in amber. The twins asked their grandfather if the story could be true: "Did it happen? Could it happen? Has that ever been done?" Grandpa Cragan responded by telling a story about frog-cloning, in which scientists had produced a new frog by cloning the DNA of an original frog. This story did not have its intended effect. The twins' eyes began to water and Kyle asked, "Are we clones? Is that what identical means?" Conner wanted to know if they were cloned from their mother or their father and how could they be identical since they were not the same person. Dr. Cragan quickly abandoned his advocacy of NPT, suggested the boys ask their grandmother, and promptly took the dog for a walk.

Humans Naturally Possess a Narrative Logic That They Use to Assess Communication   At the heart of this presupposition is Fisher's (1987a) belief that *Homo narrans* inherently evaluates stories and appraises which stories are true. This act of assessing stories to determine truth, knowledge, and reality Fisher called "narrative rationality." He noted that narrative rationality resembles common sense or practical wisdom and, as we shall see, he offered two special tools to assist you in accepting or rejecting stories. NPT would suggest that as you read the above story of Professor Cragan and his grandsons, you would automatically begin to assess it in light of the previous parenting stories you have heard (e.g., Do fathers and grandfathers often shirk their parental responsibilities, especially when they must deal with emotional issues?).

Humans Create and Recreate Reality through Sets of Stories (Accounting and Recounting) That Must Be Chosen among Continually to Live Life to Its Fullest   This presupposition tells you to look for the constant making and remaking of reality by the telling and retelling of stories. As you look at the structure of stories you will find that they are contained in other stories and indeed the deep structure values of all stories, according to Fisher (1987a), flow from two master myths: idealistic/moralistic and materialistic. Professor Shields took great pleasure in telling his nephew, Philly, age five, the story of the Big Bad Wolf and the

Three Little Pigs. Dr. Shields told the story as you know it: The three pigs built houses, the wolf blew down the straw and wooden ones, but the brick house saved them. This idealistic/moralistic story reminds everyone not to take shortcuts, but to build a strong home that will last. His nephew Philly, although listening intently, suddenly jumped up and announced that he was now going to tell the "*true* story of the three pigs." Philly proclaimed that: "The wolf used the ruse of being a neighbor seeking a cup of sugar, and the first two dumb pigs opened the door and lost their life, but the third smart pig—the brains of the family—built his house of brick and survived. But, remember, the wolf is still out there looking for his cup of sugar." Philly then turned and advised his two playmates to: "Smarten up or the wolf may get you!" Philly demonstrated narrative rationality by rejecting the idealistic/ moralistic, shortcut story and retelling the story from a materialistic, wolf-eat-pig world in which only the smart pigs survive. We offer this story as anecdotal evidence for the ontological assumption that all human beings are endowed with narrative rationality and the epistemological assumption that they account and recount reality through storytelling.

As with the other general communication theories of broad scope, it is important not to debate the validity of NPT's assumptive system at this time. Rather, you should proceed as if these axiomatic, epistemological, and ontological assumptions are true. In this way, you can best understand and most readily learn to use NPT.

NPT: Introducing the Theoretical Concepts

At this writing, Narrative Paradigm Theory contains at least thirteen theoretical concepts with their attendant technical definitions. The theory contains three basic (narration or story, logical reasons, good reasons), eight structural (characterization, emplotment, place of presentation, idealistic/moralistic myth, materialistic myth, storytellers, audience, and open democratic society) and two evaluative (narrative probability and narrative fidelity) concepts. Again, we discuss each concept separately, but remind you that they are interrelated and often occur unseparated as discourse is viewed through the lens of NPT. **Figure 6-1** displays NPT's technical concepts.

Finding Basic Concepts

To use NPT, you must be able to identify value-laden stories. Three technical terms—narration (story), logical reasons, and good reasons—serve as NPT's basic concepts. Each represents the communication phenomena you must recognize and find to use NPT.

Initial Basic Concept   Again, a general communication theory's basic concepts fall within two subclasses: the initial basic concept and the associated basic concepts. NPT's initial basic concept is a narration (story).

Narration (Story).   A *narration (story)* is an accounting or recounting of a value-laden symbolic action embodied in words and deeds reflecting sequence, time, and place. The initial thing you must find in human communication when using NPT theory is a story. Again, a story is a depiction or account of actions in sequence, time, and place. If you cannot find a narration (story) then again you cannot explain phenomena by using NPT. There are two

Viewing NPT's Anatomical Elements

Key:
Bold Caps = The Communication Metatheory's Metaconcepts
Caps + Small Case = NPT's Theoretical Concepts

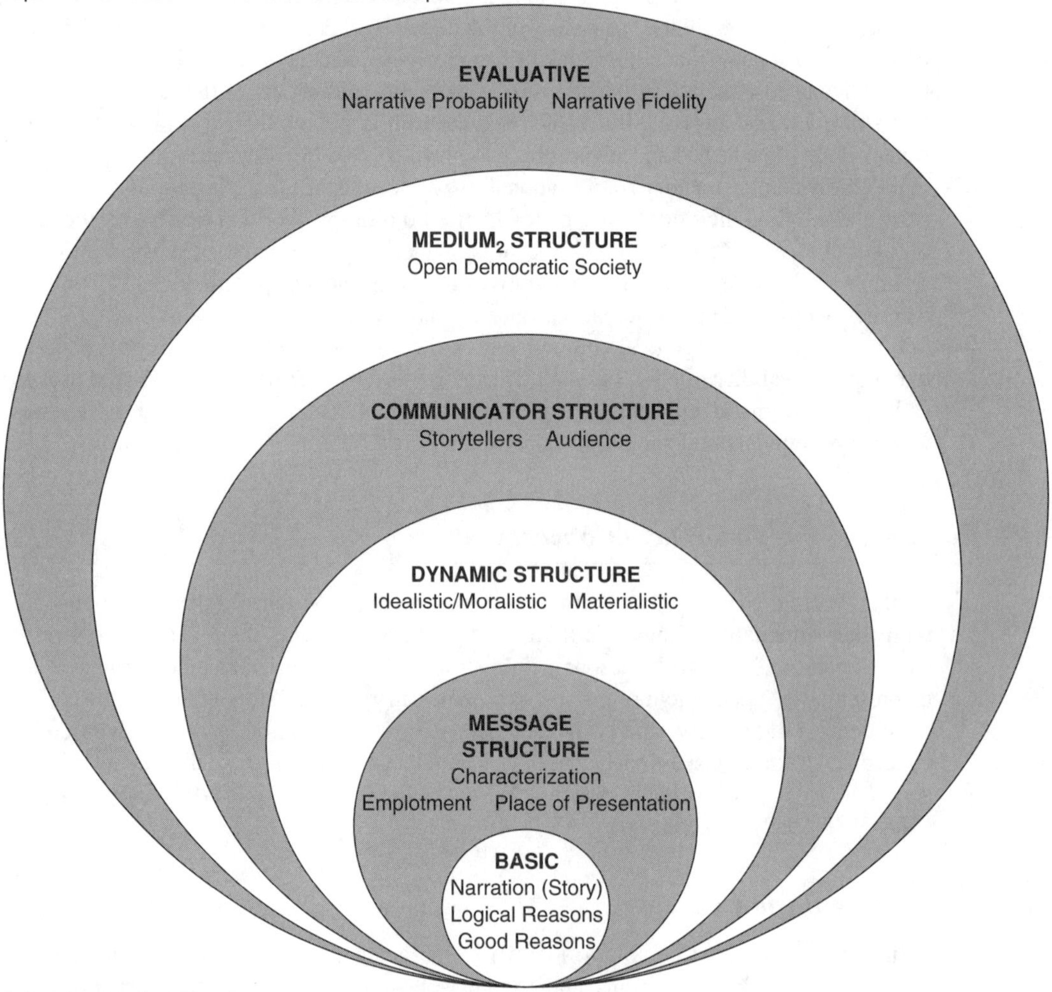

EVALUATIVE
Narrative Probability   Narrative Fidelity

MEDIUM$_2$ STRUCTURE
Open Democratic Society

COMMUNICATOR STRUCTURE
Storytellers   Audience

DYNAMIC STRUCTURE
Idealistic/Moralistic   Materialistic

MESSAGE STRUCTURE
Characterization
Emplotment   Place of Presentation

BASIC
Narration (Story)
Logical Reasons
Good Reasons

Other Anatomical Elements:

COMMUNICATIVE FORCE	MODELING
ORIGIN, ROOTS, ASSUMPTIONS	RELATIONSHIP STATEMENTS
PARADIGM	THEORY–METHOD COMPLEX

EXAMPLE OF VALUE-LADEN STORY: "Horatio Alger, with his qualities of initiative, hard work, thrift, and perseverance, overcame poverty to become a successful entrepeneur. He died a lonely old man."

FIGURE 6-1.

kinds of narration: accounting and recounting, which constitute "the stories we tell ourselves and each other to establish a meaningful life world" (Fisher, 1995, p.170). Accounting and recounting stories take such forms as theoretical explanations, arguments, histories, biographies, dramas, poetry, and novels. Every story has its exposition and provides sequence and values with meaning for those who live, create, or interpret them. Fisher would call our presentation of his theory just such a story (Fisher, 1992). It may help you to know that researchers working with NPT often look at three types of stories: the personal narrative, the case study narrative, and the collective narrative (Clair, Chapman, & Kunkel, 1996).

A Fisher-like story contains reasons that provide warrants for accepting or rejecting the story. NPT focuses specifically on the value-laden warrants contained in a story. For example, a group of college students in a communication theory class conducted interviews with their fellow students about the health service on campus. They collected 90 stories that contained 135 value statements that could be classified into 9 key values held by the students who used the campus health facility (see Cragan & Shields, 1995, pp. 245–251). One value concerned competence: *"I don't know if they are qualified. I heard a bunch of stories about misdiagnosis."* Another value concerned compassion: *"He won't listen to me; he just prescribed medicine. I showed him respect; he could at least listen to me."* Still another value related to time: *"I have a life. Once I waited almost an hour. Waiting and waiting. Finally I saw a nurse. I never did see a doctor."* The statement at the bottom of **Figure 6-1** illustrates another value-laden story.

Associated Basic Concepts   NPT's remaining basic concepts are the associative concepts of logical reasons and good reasons. You have already learned logical reasons because they were presented in Chapter 3 with Rational Argumentation Theory. What NPT does is add "good reasons" or value-laden reasons to provide a complete explanation for people's acceptance of and adherence to a story. RAT explained the force of logical reasons; NPT explains the force of value-laden reasons on human action.

Logical Reasons.   As we indicated in Chapter 3, a rational argument is a reason-supported claim and there are two broad types: deductive and inductive. When a person is telling a story, he or she may give a number of rational reasons as an account for human behavior. As we indicated when reviewing Rational Argument Theory, such reasons stem from the use of argument by cause, sign, example, analogy, authority, and dissociation. Elizabeth Cragan, Professor Cragan's roommate since 1965, taught for a number of years at Kansas City's Our Lady of Guadalupe School. One day, her student, Gabriel, threw a rock through the classroom window. The principal saw the incident and asked him, "Why did you do that?" Gabriel did not respond. He just looked down at the ground and shuffled his feet. The principal continued to ask poor Gabriel why he did this dastardly act, until Gabriel began crying and blubbering, "I don't know. I don't know!" The principal called Gabriel's mother. His mother repeated the same question. Gabriel responded, "I don't know." His mother said, "Wait until your father comes home; perhaps he can find out the reason." His father asked the same question and Gabriel gave the same answer. His father sent him to his room without supper.

The next week, Gabriel was again pitching rocks. Again, a rock went through the classroom window. This time, the principal did not see it, but Elizabeth did. Of course, Elizabeth sent Gabriel to the principal. Gabriel, being a bright, somewhat precocious student, was prepared this time. He knew the question and he was ready. The principal asked, "Gabriel, why did you throw the rock through the school window, again?" Gabriel replied, "I've had a very bad day. I broke my sister's doll this morning and I lost my allowance for the week. My little brother, who sleeps in my bed, had an accident again and I had to change the sheets. Then, I missed the bus and had to walk to school. And there was the rock and I'm sorry, but I just took my frustrations out on the window." The principal said she understood, gave him a glass of chocolate milk, and invited Gabriel to come by anytime and talk out his frustrations. Gabriel had learned an important lesson of NPT—provide accounts that contain logical reasons for your actions.

Good Reasons.   *Good reasons* are the values that are laden in stories. Fisher (1987a) indicated that the values in narratives "determine the persuasive force of reasons and that values may constitute reasons in and of themselves" (p. 138). Good reasons allow the hearer or reader to decide whether or not she or he should act on a story. Stories often exhibit competitive values that the hearer or reader must choose among. Later in this chapter, we will learn the evaluative concepts of NPT as we introduce narrative probability and narrative fidelity.

Fisher's good reasons can best be enumerated in terms of the values that bind a community together. The list of values would start with the ancient Aristotelian virtues of justice, courage, temperance, magnificence, magnanimity, liberality, gentleness, prudence, and wisdom (Aristotle, 1366b, pp. 2–4) and would also include such modern values as freedom, democracy, individuality, self-determination, community, and the pursuit of happiness. As well, the list would include the values generated in the socialization process of a given community of people such as compassion, time, money, and property. Gabriel's final account to explain the rock-throwing incident contained more than just logical reasons; it also contained good reasons (i.e., value-laden reasons) that provided persuasive force for his logical reasons. Finally, these values would coalesce around two master myths—moralistic and materialistic—which we discuss later in the chapter. **Table 6-1** contains the presentation and evaluation of some everyday narratives as offered by Juan and Maria. Can you find both logical reasons and good reasons evident in the narrative?

Seeing Structural Concepts

The structural concepts for general communication theories relate to message, dynamic, communicator, and medium. At its simplest, NPT explains that communicators (storytellers) communicate (accounting and recounting stories) in some medium (an open, democratic society).

TABLE 6-1.   Viewing Two Stories Concerning Future Plans

Maria: "I'm proud of myself for escaping the barrio. It's been difficult but worth it to work my way through school. Yet, I don't feel complete. I want a career, but I also want a family, maybe a boy and two girls. When I think of how my Mother sacrificed for me, it just makes me all teary-eyed. I want to give something back to my own family just as she gave to me. Whatever I am, and I'm talking about my essential qualities, I owe to my Mother. Did I tell you she gave up her nursing career to stay home and raise my three sisters and me? I want to do the same for my children."

Juan: "Well, possessions don't mean all that much to me, you know. Both my parents, who were missionaries, and my church instilled many humanitarian, 'give unto other,' values in me. They taught me to give something back. Recently, I've been thinking about committing myself to a tour in the Peace Corps. I really want to work with teenage runaways in Mexico City. I want to give something back."

(Dialogue derived from Cragan & Shields, 1995, pp. 109–110.)

NPT contains three message structure concepts (characterization, emplotment, and place of presentation), two dynamic structure concepts (moralistic and materialistic myths), two communicator structure concepts (storytellers and audience), and the medium$_2$ structure concept of an open, democratic society.

Message Concepts   Again, message structure concepts dress up and flesh out a theory's basic concepts. As indicated in **Figure 6-1,** NPT's three message structure concepts are characterization, emplotment, and place of presentation. Fisher (1985a, 1985b, 1987a) also allowed for the addition of other useful symbolic, fictive, and narrative structural terms that might be imported from other theories.

Characterization.   *Characterization* is the depiction of the characters present in the narrative. Fisher (1987a) stressed the importance of characterization in narrative: "Central to all stories is character . . . and coherence in life and in literature requires that characters behave characteristically. Without this kind of predictability, there is no trust, no community, no rational human order" (p. 47). Fisher called for a correspondence between the attributes or values given to the actors in the story and the values given to the narrator of the story. This is especially necessary in political campaign storytelling. Fisher (1987a, 1988) indicated that all characterizations of both the actor in the story and the storyteller need to be consistent. Fisher's (1982, 1987a) analysis of President Reagan's speeches revealed that the Reagan character's values of self-reliance, competitiveness, and freedom were consistent with the heroic character in the mythical story of the American Dream to which large numbers of the American electorate adhered.

In support of a candidate for appellate judge, we once collected 200 stories about an idealized judge from registered voters. We then analyzed the values in the voters' stories. We determined that the character of an idealized judge exhibited six major values. Three of the values were consistent with the character of our candidate for the judgeship. Consequently, we featured these three values in all the political messages of the campaign. The three values were competent, fair, and tough-minded (Cragan & Shields, 1990).

Emplotment.   A plot is the action of the characters in a story. You are familiar with many types of plots. There is the conspiracy plot, the good triumphs over evil plot, the love triangle plot, the quest adventure, the pilgrimage, and so forth. Professor Shields often fills his leisure time reading Louis Lamour's western novels. A typical plot offers a rugged, individualistic, humble hero who acts to help a strong-willed woman in time of travail stemming from the greed of the villain. In the end, the villain is vanquished with extreme prejudice and the hero wins the hand of the fair damsel. Just as Professor Shields loves westerns, otherwise interesting individuals on campus gravitate to the typical plot lines of *The Young and the Restless* and *As the World Turns.* In fact, some students schedule classes to allow time to view their favorite soap opera.

Fisher labeled his message structure term for plot, *emplotment. Emplotment* is the action attributed to the story by the storyteller. By using the term *emplotment,* he stressed that all communication is narration and thus has a plot. Take for example the artifact known as a history book. History texts often contain emplotments such as "discovering the new world," "conquering the frontier," "winning the West," or "the age of exploration." Fisher (1995) made a special case that scientific writing is narration and contains transparent emplotments such as Darwin's (1964) survival of the fittest in his treatise *On the Origin of Species* or Watson's and Crick's (1953) proposal of the double-helix model of DNA. Fisher (1995) described the double-helix proposal as "a narrative, a tale of conflict, competing characters, resolution, and a 'happy' ending" (p. 181).

Place of Presentation.   Fisher (1992) offered the concept of place of presentation of a narrative or story. The *place of presentation* is the placement, setting, or location of the community in which a story takes place or occurs symbolically. You will know the place of presentation when you identify the location of the community of people who share common values. Our university community might create a value structure like civility, intellect, morality, harmony, and wisdom. Our family communities may be the place where values such as friendship, pleasure, material success, love, and loyalty are shared. Our political community might adhere to values like political acumen, expediency, self-aggrandizement, and power.

Much like the correspondence demanded between characterization and the character of the storyteller, the place of presentation concept calls for a correspondence between the setting of the story and the setting in which the storyteller is telling the story. In a church, synagogue, or mosque, or at the family dinner table, some stories would be judged as off-color or inappropriate for those settings. *The Andy Griffith Show* can have homespun tales reflective of family values when placed in Mayberry, but those same values as depicted in the *Beverly Hillbillies* become farcical. We risk such tension with the personal anecdotes we offer throughout this book. Some of you, in responding to our text, may deem our anecdotes (family stories) inappropriate to a serious, academic textbook. If such is your reaction, we would offer the simple emplotment that "privilege comes with age."

Dynamic Concepts   Once again, it's time for a rest stop on our journey to understanding communication theories. Here, we need to review our understanding of communication dynamic structure. Recall that all general communication theories exhibit a deep structure tension or conflict that varies with each theory. We saw with IST that the conflict was between the three types of information systems—linear, interactive, and transactional. With RAT, the struggle concerned whether the argumentative form of the message was rhetorical, dialectical, or logical. With SCT, the conflict concerned the clash between righteous, social, and pragmatic rhetorical visions. With NPT, the tension or struggle exists in the deep structure of the story. Specifically, the conflict occurs between two deep structure value systems that compete as the overarching good reasons for audiences to adhere to a story. These two deep structure value systems are the idealistic/moralistic and materialistic value systems that Fisher (1973) first found embedded in the American Dream story of the struggle between the rugged individualist and the egalitarian good Samaritan.

Idealistic/Moralistic Myth.   The *idealistic/moralistic master analogue* myth has roots in the American Dream and concerns brotherhood and sisterhood and emphasizes the egalitarian notion that humans are created equal. The idealistic/moralistic myth stresses such values as charity, love, trustworthiness, justice, and tolerance. Fisher (1987a) offered Dr. Martin Luther King, Jr.'s (1969) famous speech, "I Have a Dream," as an example of discourse flowing from the idealistic/moralistic myth. In that speech, King stressed his fervent belief that Americans of all colors and economic backgrounds could come together and be treated equally. King's use of the idealistic, Gandhi-like approach to nonviolent civil disobedience helped bring down oppressive laws that denied public accommodation, the right to vote, and civil liberties to a large segment of the U.S. populace. The civil rights movement in the 1960s, which focused on the civil rights of African Americans, is only one of many movements for equality that drew their intrinsic values from the idealistic/moralistic myth. For example, the Suffragette Movement brought women the right to vote with the ratification of the Nineteenth Amendment to the U.S. Constitution in 1920. The force for human action contained in the narratives of this movement drew their power from the values of equality and justice endemic to political participation in our democratic society. Indeed, most social movements in the history of the United States—from the formation of unions to gay rights—are anchored by the values present in the idealistic/moralistic myth identified by NPT.

Materialistic Myth.   The *materialistic master analogue* is a competitive myth that celebrates individual achievement through such values as competitiveness, self-reliance, perseverance, tenacity, political acumen, and entrepreneurial spirit. Its roots, as well, reside in the American Dream. This materialistic myth undergirds stories of heroic achievement and accomplishment. For example, the modern American Horatio Alger story can be seen in Bill Gates's building of Microsoft. Gates, a systems operation genius, gave up his schooling at Harvard during the 1970s to contribute to the development of operating software for personal computers. His Microsoft disk operating system (MS–DOS) allowed him to beat all comers in the world of operating systems and become the richest individual in America by 1995 with a personal net worth more than 10 billion dollars. Gates provides but one example in a long series of individual stories that reflect the values intrinsic to part of what Fisher called the American Dream. Other stories include John D. Rockefeller and Standard Oil, Howard Hughes and the Hughes Tool Company, and Henry Ford and the Ford Motor Company. However, such materialistic stories are not limited to capitalist achievements. As U.S. citizens, we also celebrate political and sports achievements. For example, we celebrate Abe Lincoln's rise from a log cabin in Illinois, Harry Truman's emergence from a failed haberdashery in Kansas City, Missouri, Jimmy Carter's ascendance from a small peanut farm in Georgia, and Bill Clinton's triumph over a broken home in Arkansas as heroic examples of the American materialistic myth that anyone can grow up to be president if they work hard and exhibit political acumen, competitiveness, and tenacity. Similarly, George Herman Ruth left an orphanage, Jim Thorpe left a Native American reservation, and Martina Navratolova left her communist homeland to rise to the pinnacle of their respective sports professions, baseball, football, and tennis.

These two master myths—idealistic/moralistic and materialistic—are at war with each other, or at least potentially at war in every story or narration. Think about the grading policy in your class. Should the professor use a Bell Curve and only allow 7 percent of the students to get an A, or should every student have the potential to get an A if they know 90 percent to 100 percent of the material? If you have a small group assignment, should everyone in the group receive the same grade, or should some small group members receive higher grades because they did more work than other members? Fisher (1987a) noticed these warring myths as he read such diverse texts as the political discourse of Ronald Reagan, Ted Kennedy, and Jimmy Carter. He also found these two warring myths in the *Dialogues* of Plato (for example, 1952a, 1952b), in such plays as Arthur Miller's *Death of a Salesman* (1955), and in such novels as F. Scott Fitzgerald's *The Great Gatsby* (1925).

Communicator Concepts The communicator structure concepts of NPT identify the communicators. NPT's communicator structure concepts are storyteller and audience. Because NPT assumes that all communication is narration, then we are either telling a story or hearing/reading and evaluating a story to determine if it hangs together and rings true in light of the previous stories we know.

Storyteller. A *storyteller* is a person who tells stories to account for or recount human action. Thus, all communicators are storytellers. Fisher argued that humans are endowed with the natural ability to tell stories and to evaluate them. He stressed that there must be a characterological coherence between the values present in the story and the characteristics possessed by the storyteller and the attributes of the characters in the story (Fisher, 1985a, 1987a). In essence, there is a kind of storyteller credibility that is revealed by the characterization of the storyteller and the characterization of the storytellers in the story.

To test this view of *storyteller,* allow us to retell a story that Professor Cragan told his children many times. One day, when John was a small boy growing up in the West End of Rockford, Illinois, Mr. Bowman, an African American friend of the family, walked by the Cragan's backyard. John's playmate looked up and called Mr. Bowman a horrible name. Mr. Bowman, shocked and angered by the epithet, went around the block and knocked on the Cragan's front door. He told Mrs. Cragan what had happened and then departed. Soon, Mrs. Cragan was calling to her son: "John Francis Cragan, come here this minute!" Usually when John was called by all three names, he knew he was in serious trouble and might even get a spanking. However, when John came in the house, Mrs. Cragan, in soft tones, explained that the particular epithet was a terrible name to use, that he should never use it again, and that Mr. Bowman was hurt. She suggested quite strongly that John should go immediately to the Bowman's home and apologize.

John left for the Bowman home walking ever so slowly. Reluctantly, he arrived at the Bowman house and knocked on the door. Mrs. Bowman answered and let John into the foyer. Across the living room, in a big chair, sat Mr. Bowman, reading the evening paper. John walked into the living room and said: "Excuse me, Mr. Bowman, but I came to apologize for the mean word that was said to you." Mr. Bowman put down the paper, looked sternly at John, and said, "I'm sorry John, but I do not forgive you." Startled and confused, John ran teary-eyed from the Bowman house. This was the first time he had ever apologized for something and not received forgiveness.

Six years later, John worked as the neighborhood paperboy. He found himself asking Mrs. Bowman why Mr. Bowman still had not forgiven him for being called a bad name. Mrs. Bowman replied, "John, you'll have to take that up with Mr. Bowman." Another six years passed and John returned from college for the holidays to discover that Mr. Bowman had died that week. He rushed to the Bowman house to pay his respects to Mrs. Bowman. As their eyes met, Mrs. Bowman smiled and said, "Mr. Bowman would be pleased to know you're here paying your respects, John. You know words, like a bee, can bring sweet honey or they can carry a terrible sting." John finally understood that Mr. Bowman, by not forgiving, had taught him an important lesson. John had learned that you can say some hurtful things that once said cannot be taken back.

Fisher would say that you as an audience member would automatically begin to judge this story. You would do so by naturally comparing the characterization in this story with what you know of the storyteller (Professor Cragan). For example, you would ask yourself, "Is this story consistent with other stories in this book that inform me about Professor Cragan?" If so, then the story would ring true for you.

Audience.   The second communicator concept of NPT is audience. *Audience* consists of the hearers or readers of stories who evaluate a given story to conclude if it hangs together and rings true to their experience. Fisher adopted Perelman's (1979, 1982) idea of audience. Perelman (1982) wrote that "an argument is as good as the audience that would adhere to it" and concluded that because "the efficacy of argument is relative to audience, it is impossible to evaluate it above and beyond reference to the audience to which it was presented" (p. 140). Fisher (1987a) argued that "a story is as good as the audience that would adhere to it" (p. 97) and indicated that as an audience becomes more open to the free flow of ideas and more competent and sophisticated, then the more compelling the good reasons (values) in a story must be to illicit audience adherence. Fisher would say that all humans are endowed with natural narrativity, but that through education in a free and open society we improve our ability to use and assess stories.

Medium Concepts   In presenting our metatheory in Chapter 1, we identified three types of media. Medium$_1$ refers to the discipline's six most prevalent contexts: interpersonal, small group, public, mass, organizational, and intercultural communication. Fisher and others have demonstrated that NPT explains communication within and across medium$_1$ contexts. Medium$_2$ concerns the substance within which communication grows and prospers. Medium$_3$ pertains to the channel through which communication flows such as air or light waves, books, or film. Here, we emphasize the medium$_2$ sense of NPT.

For NPT, the medium$_2$ concept is an open democratic society. An *open democratic society* is a community of people existing within a free society who willingly and naturally examine ideas. As well, it is an open democratic society in which narrations flourish. Openness promotes the existence of competing stories and freedom provides the opportunity for the audience to enhance their narrative rationality by studying and evaluating the stories competing in the marketplace of ideas. In turn, this testing process improves the quality of life in the community. However, in a totalitarian society stories get corrupted because they lack the "fitness" that comes from competition with competing stories. Audiences in authoritarian societies can be "duped" or controlled when the government controls the media such as in Nazi Germany of the 1940s or Serbia of the 1990s.

From the perspective of NPT, the basis of a liberal education at a university concerns the improvement of your ability to tell and assess stories. Your ability to use characterization, emplotment, and place of presentation relates to your ability to tell stories. With regard to story assessment, ignorance and freedom do not long coexist. For example, in economics, you need to be able to compare the stories of the Keynesian economists with those of the followers of Milton Friedman. In political science, you need to be able to compare the social conservative's call for tough love on welfare with the compassionate liberal's calls for social safety nets. In criminology you need to be able to compare the hard-liner's call for higher penalties, longer prison terms, and eliminating the country club atmosphere of our prisons with the liberal rehabilitationist's call for prevention, treatment, job training, and conjugal visits.

Using Evaluative Concepts

Let's take another rest stop. Recall from TCM that all general communication theories posit concepts that allow you to assess the quality and outcomes of communicators communicating in a medium over time. Also, recall from Chapter 1 that all scientists are concerned with explaining the outcomes (effects) of the fundamental interactive forces that they study. For example, the seismologist studies interaction of earth phenomena such as subterranean heat and pressure from the movement of the continental plates along faultlines in order to predict the intensity, duration, and movement of earthquakes. With NPT we evaluate whether or not a story hangs together and rings true for a given audience.

Quality and Outcomes   By outcomes we mean that the communicative interaction identified by the theory did in fact occur, that is, did the communicative force under study have its predicted impact on human action? Quality is a feature denoting degree or grade of excellence of the communicative interaction. In NPT's case, did the audience accept the values contained in the story because it had narrative prabability and narrative fidelity? NPT's primary evaluative concepts are narrative probability and narrative fidelity. Together with their associated evaluative subconcepts, they provide the necessary tools to evaluate the force of narrative as a justification for human action.

Narrative Probability.   *Narrative probability* concerns the audience's evaluations of a story's coherence: Does it hang together? Is it internally consistent? Is it consistent with previous stories on the same topic that the audience members have heard? And is it consistent with previous characterizations of the storyteller? Fisher (1987a) provided three ways to assess the narrative probability of a story. First, check the story's structural coherence. Here, you would check to see if the story is internally consistent. Second, examine the story for its material coherence. Here, you would check to see if evidence is missing or major arguments are avoided that you know are normally present in other major competing stories. Third, analyze the story for its characterological coherence. Here, you would check to see if the behavior of the characters within the story is consistent and if so is it consistent with what you know about the character of the storyteller.

We often observe a lack of characterological coherence with public figures in our society. Bing Crosby portrayed a warm, genial, compassionate singer and family man in most of his movies and radio and television specials. Yet, one of his sons reported that characterization was all an act. To the son, Bing was mean-spirited and abusive to his children. Similarly, Joan Crawford's daughter unmasked Joan's Hollywood public image depicting her as a cruel "Mommy Dearest." President John Kennedy projected a public image of the loving husband and father, yet privately others have depicted him as a great philanderer. President Reagan's daughter reported that the President had been anything but an ideal father despite his repeated public pleas for a restoration of family values. It is reported that Newt Gingrich, the Republican Speaker of the House of Representatives (1994–1998) and another champion of family values, divorced his first wife as she lay in a hospital bed dying of cancer. Such breaks in characterization are often excused by lines like, "Jesse James was a model citizen except during business hours" and "the Cub Scout leader was a fine role model except for periodic outbreaks as a pederast." Facts about the storyteller that are contrary to the general behavior of the characters in the story destroy a story's material coherence.

Narrative Fidelity.   *Narrative Fidelity* examines the truthfulness of a story. When you use this evaluative concept you are checking to see if the story "rings true" as compared to other stories of the same type. Aside from such a direct comparison of stories, Fisher (1987a) recommended two tests of narrative fidelity: the test of rational reasons and the test of value-laden good reasons. In order to assess rational reasons, Fisher recommended that you, as an audience member, turn to RAT to criticize the rational arguments in the story and to test the evidence in the story. We discussed these tests in Chapter 3 and we will not repeat them here.

What makes NPT unique from RAT are Fisher's (1987a) tests of value-laden good reasons. Fisher offered five questions that provide the basis of his value-testing. They include questions of fact, relevance, consequence, consistency, and transcendent issue. Cragan and Shields (1995, p. 106) report these questions as: (1) *Question of Fact:* What are the values reflected in the story? (2) *Question of Relevance:* Are the values in the story relevant, accurate, and undistorted for the topic the story presents? (3) *Question of Consequence:* What are the outcomes, in terms of yourself and your relations with others in society, when you adhere to the values contained in the narrative? (4) *Question of Consistency:* Are the values in the story consistent with those held by you, by those you respect, and by an ideal audience? (5) *Question of Transcendent Issue:* Even if the story rings true in a particular case, are the values in the story consistent with those of the idealistic/moralistic or materialistic master analogue myths? Fisher (1987a) noted that such tests pinpoint the value-laden good reasons for an audience's acceptance of a story as true or its rejection as false.

In order to assist you in understanding how these questions help you identify the values in stories, we offer a story from the Old West, namely an editorial that appeared in *The Cheyenne Daily Leader,* 1870:

> *The rich and beautiful valleys of Wyoming are destined for the occupancy and sustenance of the Anglo-Saxon race. The wealth that for untold ages has lain hidden beneath the snow-capped summits of our mountains has been placed there by Providence to reward the brave spirits whose lot it is to compose the advanced-guard of civilization. The Indians must stand aside or be overwhelmed by the ever advancing and ever increasing tide of emigration. The destiny of the aborigines is written in characters not to be mistaken. The same inscrutable Arbiter that decreed the downfall of Rome has pronounced the doom of extinction on the red men of America. (As cited in Brown, 1970, p. 184).*

You can see that this story flows from the materialistic master analogue myth as embodied in the distorted version of Darwin's idea of the survival of the fittest. Do you adhere to the values in this story that call for the extinction of Native Americans if they stood in the way of God-fearing Anglo-Saxons? What is the likely outcome, in terms of your own behavior, toward other ethnic and racial groupings in North America if you adopt the values in this story? But this whole story might not be accurate. How does this story compare to others you've heard of the Old West. How does it compare to the stories told of Sitting Bull and the Lakota Sioux in *Dances with Wolves, Little Big Man,* or *Custer's Last Stand.*

NPT: Working with Its Qualitative Method

Using NPT to study communicators communicating in a medium requires special tools. The procedure for identifying a theory's basic, structural, and evaluative concepts is not easy. It takes training and practice in the use of a qualitative method developed specifically for finding a theory's key concepts in everyday communication. Let's again take a rest stop. Now that we have finished examining NPT's theoretical concepts, it's important to remind you that all general communication theories develop a qualitative method so that researchers and theory-builders can ground their theory to observables. In Chapter 2, you learned how to find, code, track, and model the flow of information. In Chapter 3, you learned how to collect and analyze arguments. In Chapter 4, you learned how to find, classify, and analyze fantasy themes, and in Chapter 5, you learned how to gather, code, and track social information. Now it is time to learn how to gather and analyze stories or narrations.

Fisher did not initially provide a method for doing value analysis. However, others did. For example, Vanderford, Smith, and Harris (1992) developed Value Identification in Narrative Discourse (VIND), Cragan and Shields (1995) reported that Flanagan's (1954) Critical Incident Technique (CIT) adapts easily for use in collecting and analyzing stories, and Meyer (1995) provided a means for operationalizing the saliency of the values found in narratives using Content Value Analysis (CVA).

Value Identification Analysis (VIA)

With NPT, Value Identification Analysis (VIA) relies on three primary qualitative methods. One is called Value Identification in Narrative Discourse (VIND). Another useful qualitative method is Critical Incident Technique (CIT). An alternative qualitative method is Content Value Analysis (CVA). Any one of these techniques allows you to identify the values in stories.

VIND   Vanderford, et al. (1992) developed Value Identification in Narrative Discourse as a technique to develop criteria for identifying *terminal values* (values that are ends in themselves) and *instrumental values* (values that allow one to fulfill a terminal value). As part of the criteria for identifying terminal values, they suggested examining the "ought" or "should" statements in a story, the goals appearing in a story, the story's justification for action, and the action being praised or condemned in the story. For determining instrumental values, VIND requires you to focus on the story's plot line and examines the actions that lead to terminal value fulfillment and the actions that block the achievement of terminal values.

Vanderford, et al. (1992) provided seven rules for assessing the values held by the characters in a story. They are the positive and negative labels attributed to characters, the positive and negative emotions felt by characters, the relationship between characters, the evaluative statements about the relationship between characters, evaluation of the storyteller, what the storyteller(s) define(s) as his/her(their) needs, and what part of the story takes up the most time.

CIT   Flanagan's (1954) Critical Incident Technique (CIT) has been adapted for discovering, counting, and analyzing the saliency of values in a number of stories that focus on an issue, or organizational or societal activity (Cragan & Shields, 1995). Flanagan recommended five specific procedures for collecting and classifying critical stories: (1) Identify the critical incident, such as health service, hotel service, communication courses; (2) Collect stories about the critical incident that either had a positive or negative impact on the person (e.g., tell me your best and worst experiences about first dates, or blind dates, or visiting the dentist); (3) Collect self-reported stories of the people who experienced them (not secondhand stories); (4) Analyze the data by reading and rereading the stories and grouping the stories into like categories. In a restaurant study there might be collections of stories about bad food, poor service, obnoxious people at the next table, and so forth; (5) Interpret the categorized stories in light of the general research question of the study.

CVA   Meyer (1995) used Content Value Analysis (CVA) to group stories, as told by subjects, by moral point. These groupings in turn yielded a list of the values present in the narratives. He then operationalized *saliency* as occurring whenever 50 percent of the subjects' stories exhibited the same values. He also used the derived percentages to rank-order the importance of values to the community of subjects.

In summary, CIT is a systematic qualitative method for gathering stories. VIND is a qualitative method for identifying the values present in the stories in order to provide an NPT-based qualitative analysis of the data. Finally, CVA is a content value analysis method for determining the saliency and rank-order of the values held by a community of people.

Briefly Illustrating VIA

Hollihan and Riley (1987b) reported a classic NPT study. They looked at the stories present in a "Tough Love" parents' support group in California that resembles the familiar support groups of Alcoholics Anonymous, Parents without Partners, and so forth. They sought to describe and analyze the narrative produced by the participants in the group and illustrated the use of VIA in doing an NPT-based study.

In analyzing the Tough Love story, Hollihan and Riley attended four consecutive three-hour meetings of one support group. They took notes on the parents' accounts and recounts of their parenting stories. The parents each told essentially the same story with the same characterization and emplotment. The parents' stories flowed from the deep structure of the idealistic/moralistic master analogue myth. Their common story described Tough Love parents besieged by incorrigible children wreaking havoc on the parents' lives. According to the parents, the experts (e.g., teachers, counselors, social workers, and police) on modern society had duped the parents into abandoning strict discipline and spoiling their child (children). As Hollihan and Riley (1987b) report, the moral of this story is: "If parents truly loved their children, they could not let them destroy themselves or their families. They had to be tough. This was the Tough Love story" (p. 17).

Hollihan and Riley pointed out that the Tough Love support group created a unique storytelling environment in that the participants suspended their natural narrative rationality during the session—the audience was nonjudgmental. Thus, the extended storytelling sessions created a powerful, compelling, cohesive story. To the authors, however, the nonjudgmental requirement provided a unique and disarming quality to Fisher's concept of audience in that deception could more easily occur by limiting the free flow of ideas.

Fisher's NPT works best in the presence of an audience that can compare competing stories. When the Tough Love story is told to a larger audience, such as society in general, a clash of narratives occurs. For example, some members of the larger audience, may view the Tough Love story not as an idealistic/moralistic story, but as a corrupt materialistic story in which the parents are unwilling to spend time and money on their children and are self-ishly putting themselves ahead of the needs of younger family members. The Tough Love parents regard critics as participating in a narrative that is best understood through the em-plotment of the Dr. Spock story. In the Dr. Spock story, parents are morally responsible for the care, training, and socialization of their children. Here, parents should provide a home that is nurturing and secure from the havoc of society. The parents are the adults and should possess emotional control over the children while allowing them to engage in youthful out-bursts without fear of reprisal. As Hollihan and Riley found, the Tough Love parents re-garded the Dr. Spock story as a corrupt, materialistic story because it was just a cover for a parenting process that produced hedonistic, live-for-today children who did not respect their parents or contribute to a sense of family. Hollihan and Riley demonstrated the war-ring or competitive clash of the two master analogue myths—idealistic/moralistic and ma-terialistic—and pointed up the danger of self-help groups becoming delusionary as they suspend the judgment of competing stories required by narrative rationality.

NPT: Observing Its Usefulness

Now that you understand the theoretical concepts of NPT, we can introduce you to several significant studies that grounded the concepts of NPT as explaining human action, describe other studies that showed its use in benefiting the real world, and show its potential for with-standing its critics. Fisher (1987a) held strongly to the belief that the most indispensable need in contemporary communication was "for a schema by which values can be identified and their implications critically considered" (p. 105). NPT fills this void as it explains how the force of narration contributes the value justification for human action.

Explaining Human Action

NPT provided a theoretical explanation of human action as Fisher combined his study of the modes of proof in drama, literature, and film (Fisher & Filloy, 1982) with the linkage of his logic of good reasons to his studies of the American Dream (Fisher, 1973, 1982) and his studies of fictive form (Fisher, 1984). In his American Dream studies, Fisher discovered the ongoing conflict between the two master analogue myths of idealistic/moralistic and materi-alistic (Fisher, 1987a). He studied the competing threads of the American Dream in the speeches of Presidents Nixon and Reagan (Fisher 1973, 1982). With the American Dream, as Fisher discovered, Americans appeared to want it both ways. We want to be free, rugged in-dividualists who can go about our life untethered by the rules of bureaucracies. On the other hand, we turn to a higher governmental authority as we seek social and economic justice, re-ligious–gender–racial equality, and a fair distribution of the U.S.'s resources.

More than forty published studies have served to ground NPT's concepts in various com-munication contexts (see Cragan & Shields, 1995, for a review of many of them). For exam-ple, Carpenter (1986) used the evaluative concepts of coherence and fidelity to explain the Japanese acceptance of a U.S. admiral's advocacy of sea power and how this acceptance led to the December 7, 1941 attack on Pearl Harbor. Mackey–Kallis (1991) provided a Fisherian analysis of an eighteen-minute biographical film that preceded Reagan's acceptance speech at the 1984 Republican Party convention. They concluded that the film's reliance on the materialistic master analogue myth of the American Dream provided "a powerful example of mass-mediated political persuasion" (p. 313). Rostek (1992) explained the persuasive power of Dr. Martin Luther King's speech, "I Have Been to the Mountain Top." Rostek argued that the speech's effectiveness came from its narrative consistency. Solomon (1991) examined feminist autobiographies as "sustained narratives" that complemented and supported the public rhetoric of social movements. Aden (1994) grounded the concept of *place of presentation* with his study of place metaphor as used in the *Field of Dreams* motion picture. His study reaffirmed the presence of competing materialistic versus moralistic master analogues and highlighted the competing producerism versus consumerism emplotments associated respectively with the use of place versus machine metaphors (see, especially, pp. 313–315).

Other scholars published studies grounding NPT to organizational communication. Mumby (1987) argued that narratives in organizations provide a principle form of symbolic communication that constitutes ideology and power structures. He stressed that "the everyday use of narrative in organizations is one of the means by which the power structure of an organization is produced and reproduced" (p. 125). Strine and Pacanowsky (1985) characterized the interpretive approach to the study of organizations as capable of being subsumed within narrative theory. For example, they argued that four popular books about organizational life represented narrative stories that shed light on the nature of communication in organizations. Downs, Javidi, and Nussbaum (1988) conducted two studies on the effectiveness of the lectures of fifty-seven professors. In the first study, they reported that the use of humor, self-disclosure through stories, and narrative provided relevancy to the course content and facilitated the explication of course material. In the second study, they found that award-winning professors used more humor, self-disclosure, and narrative (myths, legends, fairy tales, fantasies, personal anecdotes, and storylike descriptions of others' experiences) than nonaward-winning professors. Brown and McMillan (1991) gathered narratives from nursing home employees through interviews. They compared these stories to the official narratives of the nursing home. From this database, they created a new narrative, using fictitious names, but "real dialogue" from their interviews, that captured the official culture of the organization. Brown and McMillan recommended the use of the resultant fictional narrative as an excellent training device for new employees. Sharf and Poirier (1988) advocated a narrative-based training program using literary case studies to exemplify the symbolic and pragmatic aspects of human relationships as a way of improving the practitioner–patient communication of health professionals. The applied outcome of their study was the development of a training course steeped in this narrative program.

Baesler (1995) constructed and tested an empirical measure of narrative coherence and fidelity. He found "Cronbach inter-item *alpha* reliability coefficients of .63 for the ten, nine-point, agree–disagree, Likert items representing Narrative Coherence, and .87 for the twelve items related to Narrative Fidelity" (pp. 98–99), thereby providing "evidence to support Fisher's theoretical claim that the coherence and fidelity of a story are related to persuasive outcomes" (p. 100). Lang, et al. (1995) used cued recall to study empirically the effects of audio versus video narrative structuring of stories. They found that people recalled television messages in narrative form regardless of the audio or picture narrative structure of the story, thereby supporting Fisher's (1985) view of narrative as an "organizing principle of human behavior" (p. 103).

Shadowing Fisher's (1985a, 1985b, 1987a) allowance for the use of argumentation, dramatic, and narrative fiction terms from other communication theories, Katriel and Shenhar (1990) explored the rhetoric of place and settlement at the heart of Israel's nation-building *ethos*. In particular, Katriel and Shenhar analyzed competing narrative dialogues to assess the mythic role of the narratives about Israel's first settlements. Known as *Homa Umigdal* (Tower and Stockade), Katriel and Shenhar found that two fifty-year-old narratives are told and retold on ceremonial and commemorative occasions. They reported that the narratives reflected the deep structural communication dynamic of the idealistic/moralistic and materialistic master analogues. Katriel and Shenhar put it this way: "Israeli discourses of settlement vacillate between an antecedent, moral concern with justification (the right to the land; the virtue of self-sacrifice) and a teleological concern with the consequences of action (the success or failure of settlement operations from a long-term, historical perspective)" (p. 366). A typical emplotment revealed the heroic sacrifice necessary to overcome hardships and triumphantly achieve the nearly miraculous outcome of establishing the settlement. The values present were self-reliance, self-motivation, self-sacrifice, courage, physical prowess, mental endurance, and the pioneering spirit (see especially, pp. 369–370). Katriel and Shenhar contrasted this intrinsic dialogue with the historical story-line of tales of forced, involuntary migration: The Jews' residence is threatened; an evil ruler orders them out; much wandering ensues; haven is found in another land whose ruler has been impressed with the wisdom or accomplishment of a particular Jewish figure. Here, they found that the values presented were those of a victim seeking safe refuge aided by "supernatural miracles and the cunning cleverness of the weak" (p. 369). Katriel and Shenhar then contrasted the traditional Jewish migration stories with the Tower and Stockade stories: "They [the migration stories] are about finding a refuge, not about the making of a place [the settlement stories]" (p. 369). Making a place prompted constructive human action; finding refuge prompted homeless wandering. For Katriel and Shenhar the values present in the settlement narratives helped forge the eventual borders of modern Israel and promoted the settlement of the West Bank.

Benefiting the Real World

Meyer (1995) used NPT to study the values present in the organizational narratives of the members of a government-supported, child care center to gain an understanding of the organization's culture. His Content Value Analysis (CVA) grouped stories by moral point—"people should show concern for others' needs and feelings" or "people should be given flexibility and independence on the job" (p. 215)—that in turn yielded a list of the values (for example, consideration or autonomy) present in the narratives. He defined saliency of the values to the organization operationally as existing when at least 50 percent of the subjects exhibited the same value in the narratives that they told about their work life. The particular values and their rank order identified in this manner included: consideration, organization/planning, timely information, participation in decision-making, discussion of conflict, friendliness, clarity of messages, commitment, autonomy, and authority. Meyer argued that "seeing them listed provides a holistic yet unique view of the organization's culture" (p. 217). Next, Meyer assessed the "points of consistency and inconsistency in the values obtained from member narratives" (p. 218). Here, the warring idealistic/moralistic and materialistic master analogues representing the communication dynamic of NPT surfaced as Meyer uncovered such contradictory values as autonomy versus authority, which he likened to the ongoing clash in American cultural life between individuality and community. Meyer's study demonstrated NPT's usefulness in analyzing the culture of an organization.

Vanderford, Smith, and Harris (1992) conducted a study of AIDS patients at a Veterans Hospital to develop a demonstration model for the ethical treatment of HIV patients. The study was funded by the Department of Veterans Affairs. This year-long study included a database of seventeen HIV patients and eleven resident physicians. The three goals of the study were to: improve treatment quality; bring the values of patients and physicians to a state of congruence; and eliminate unethical physician behavior in the treatment of HIV patients. Using NPT and VIND analysis procedures the researchers used a series of personal interviews to identify patient and physician values and established a training program to bring the values closer together. The researchers discovered two competing emplotments in the respective stories. The patients' stories reflected idealistic/moralistic values like keeping confidentiality, receiving equal treatment, the receipt of adequate information, and the establishment of needed services. The physicians' stories reflected materialistic values such as saving time, providing life-giving treatment, and avoiding disease contraction. The researchers developed a training program and tested it using a pre–middle–post, NPT-based, interview design. The training involved a year-long intervention using fifty-two weekly morning report sessions, seventy plus noon case conferences, and weekly ethics rounds in which a Ph.D. ethicist accompanied the physicians on rounds and provided corrective suggestions. At the completion of the training, the patients felt the physicians were meeting and fulfilling their values about information, individuality, special needs, and equal treatment. As a consequence, patients held their physicians in much higher esteem than before the ethics training intervention. This study demonstrated how to use NPT to provide value-based training in an organization.

Barbara Sharf (1990), a Professor of Communication in the Department of Medical Education at the University of Illinois at Chicago, studied medical interviews for the purpose of improving them for both the physician and the patient. She used NPT to analyze the interview data, which consisted of the patient's mini-ethnographic stories relating the problem and the physician attempting to induce patient cooperation by way of the physician's own narrative. Her case study involved a forty-minute interview between a twenty-eight-year-old, white, male, third-year resident and a forty-eight-year-old, African American male patient who was recovering from neurosurgery on his spine. Sharf's analysis of the videotaped interview revealed that the physician wanted the patient to lose weight and the patient wanted the physician to make a further diagnosis of the pain in his legs, a pain he attributed to the post-surgery electrical treatment he had received. Sharf found that the competing narratives did not "fulfill the criteria of a good story for the other; that is, both lacked sufficient coherence and fidelity to gain the imaginative involvement, let alone active cooperation, of the listener" (p. 227). Sharf recommended that physicians view the physician–patient interview as a coauthored, negotiated narrative so that the patient would feel some emotional ownership of the medical recommendations for the treatment.

Sharf's research pinpoints NPT's ability to improve the efficacy of physician–patient interviews.

Smith (1989) studied the 1984 Democratic and Republican platform statements. These platforms, for Smith, transformed each party's diversity of stories from the primaries into a working coalition for the November election. He found the emplotments of the platforms to be at odds. He noted that the Democratic platform represented the idealistic/moralistic master analogue myth of NPT and the Republican platform was wedded to the materialistic myth. For example, the emplotment of the Democratic platform included such idealistic/moralistic value-statements as: "We need an economy that works for everyone—not just the favored few"; "Higher education should not become a luxury affordable only by the children of the rich"; and "We should support opportunity that promotes fairness instead of widening inequities" (pp. 94–95). By contrast the Republican platform stressed such materialistic values as individual accomplishment and competitiveness: "We need to get the government's hand out of the people's pocketbooks"; "The American people want an opportunity society—not a welfare state"; and "Only sustained economic growth can give credible hope to those at the bottom of the opportunity ladder" (p. 96). Smith's contribution to NPT rests in his observation that storytelling functions as a means of ordering experience and justifying values in pursuit of political action within a democratic form of government.

Solomon and McMullen (1991) used NPT to explain the success of the motion picture, *Places in the Heart.* Their study uncovered the values represented by the clashing values of the idealistic/moralistic and materialistic master analogue myths found in the American Dream as a widow, her laborer (an African American, blind, war hero tenant), and her young children sought to save the family cotton farm. Solomon and McMullen noted that it was necessary for the heroine to abandon her egalitarian, idealistic, family-value structure and adopt successful materialistic, competitive values to win the prize of the first cotton ginned in the county and receive the proceeds necessary to make the mortgage payment. The researchers concluded that central to the movie's success was its retention of the tension between the conflicting thrusts of the American Dream. Their study indicated that you can have NPT-driven movie criticism and emplotment.

Alberts, Miller-Rassulo, and Hecht (1991) used NPT to develop a typology of drug-resistance strategies. Their interview study of thirty-three community-college and high-school students uncovered the narratives (stories) of drug-resistance messages among teenagers that go beyond "just say no!" They demonstrated that controlled substance and alcohol prevention programs need to be developed and implemented separately (that is, their resistance narratives differ). They found that prevention programs need to focus on both decision-making and resistance messages (stories and strategies).

Withstanding the Critics

Since the early 1970s, Fisher and other scholars have been contributing to the development of NPT. A natural counterpart of the process of theory development is theory criticism. Despite the relative youth of NPT, a sizable number of critics have offered challenges to the theory and attacked it using the familiar stock issues of the critic.[2] The criticisms can be summarized under four issues: (1) NPT is not a general communication theory; (2) NPT does not lead to new knowledge; (3) Narrative rationality does not exist; and (4) NPT diminishes rationality.

NPT Is Not a General Communication Theory   Gronbeck (1987) and Megill (1987) said all historical writings are not narrative. Rowland (1987, 1988, 1989) claimed that discursive material could not be analyzed with NPT. Lucaites and Condit (1985) claimed that rhetorical narratives differ from fictional narratives and thus are not subject to analysis using fictional narrative concepts.

Fisher (1988) responded by pointing out that he really uses three meanings of narration: Narration 1 is the simple telling of a story; Narration 2 is a simple category of discourse; and Narration 3 is a conceptual framework for understanding all human discourse. The critics' countervailing views occur only because their criticisms stem from the conceptualization of narration in only its first or second meaning; they ignore its third meaning, which constitutes the general communication theory.

NPT Does Not Lead to New Knowledge   Warnick (1987) argued that NPT was circular and that its insights derived from the practitioner rather than the practitioner's application of the theory. After reading the findings of such studies as Hollihan and Riley's (1987b) analysis of the Tough Love group, Katriel and Shenhar's study of Israeli settlement, and Vanderford, et al.'s (1992) hospital study, it's readily apparent that the theory provided insights that could not be gleaned by even the most perspicacious of atheoretical critics.

Narrative Rationality Does Not Exist   Cali (1993) and Warnick (1987) directly challenged Fisher's ontological statement that we are all storytellers endowed with both the ability to judge the coherence and fidelity of stories and a natural tendency to prefer true and just stories over false and unjust stories. Cali's essay challenges narrative fidelity directly, calling instead for "infidelity" (p. 133) because he asserts that he's found one instance of a successful speech by a cult religious leader, Chiara Lubich (who founded the Focolare Movement), whose narratives did not ring true with the awards audience. Cali's assertion is based solely on the premise that Lubich's historical narrative of the founding and spread of her movement at the occasion of her acceptance of the Templeton Prize in 1977 differs from the narratives found in the exhortations of other recipients like Aleksandr Solzhenitsyn (condemnation of Western Imperialism), the Reverend Billy Graham (meet the challenge of the hour), and Bikkyo Niwano (advance from our limited nationalistic views). However, at no point does Cali provide direct evidence that would support his statement of the "infidelity" of the Lubich narrative, nor that it lacked coherence and fidelity as a historical narrative, nor that it did not possess narrative rationality for those committed to the movement. Indeed, to the extent that NPT subsumes Rational Argumentation Theory for half of its explanatory power, NPT would admit to the field dependency of some arguments. Cali ignores both the existence of field dependency as a major tenet of RAT and NPT's assumption that it extends RAT.

Similarly, Warnick challenged Fisher to show how, if his assumptions of narrative rationality were true, the German people could have been seduced by Hitler's corrupt narrative of

Mein Kampf (1943). Fisher argued that human beings are fallible and they can be falsely seduced by a clever narrative. In other words, NPT exhibits the same field-dependency attributes as Rational Argumentation Theory. However, NPT goes a step further, as Fisher noted. He argued that the best guardian against the field-dependency aspect is a free and democratic society in which good narratives can also propagate. For Fisher, Hitler's Germany was a totalitarian state in which competing stories were neither told nor heard. As you recall, we discussed just such a problem as we introduced NPT's medium$_2$ structural concepts.

NPT Diminishes Rationality   Rowland (1988) and Warnick (1987) accused Fisher of displacing rationality. To make her indictment applicable, Warnick created an unnecessary and unrealistic fight pitting RAT against NPT. The fight is unrealistic because value questions have been an important element of RAT since the inception of its modern version (Baker, 1898). More importantly, as we have seen, Fisher's narrative rationality called for the use of both values and rational reasons for determining the coherence of a story (Fisher, 1987a). Fisher argued that both tests of value and tests of argument comprised his theory. He did not call for something new, but really something old. His NPT stressed the need for returning to the classical definition of *logos,* which required both rational and value analysis. We would add that you don't have to put RAT down to put NPT up, or vice versa. Both dogs will hunt. Indeed, by the time you finish this book, you'll see that we have forty-plus theories that will hunt. As well, we make the point that in the absence of a universal theory that can explain all of communication, we need each one of these forty-plus theories. Ours is a call for academic tolerance so that each theory can mature into a beautiful flower that blossoms in our communication field, as we point out in Chapter 12.

As you can see, the critics of NPT have missed the mark. Study after study demonstrated that NPT is a useful theory that explains the force of narration as the value justification for human action.[3] Nonetheless, with the criticisms and responses at hand, we now leave it to you to make an informed judgment as to whether or not NPT has withstood the critics. We believe it does, as all viable core general communication theories must. When you get to the end of the trail to understanding communication theories, we believe you can use NPT with confidence. We wish you happy hunting.

Summary

In this chapter, we introduced you to Narrative Paradigm Theory (NPT). NPT allows you to explain the communicative force of storytelling as the value justification for human action. We began by viewing NPT as a general communication theory capable of explication through the lens of our metatheory. We sketched its power and scope, traced its origin and roots, and discussed its primary assumptive system. Then we introduced NPT's concepts (see **Figure 6-1**). We explained its basic, structural, and evaluative concepts. Next, we introduced and illustrated how to work with NPT's qualitative method, Value Identification Analysis (VIA). Then, we reported on NPT's usefulness. We showed NPT's utility in explaining human action and benefiting the real world. Then, we discussed its ability to withstand critical scrutiny.

By now, you should be familiar with NPT. **Figure 6-2** illustrates Corey, our communication graduate on-the-job, using NPT to good advantage. If you do not yet feel comfortable with NPT, we suggest you review our detailed chapter summary, "Understanding NPT in a Nutshell," in **Box 6-1.**

"Narrative Paradigm Theory (NPT) tells us that to increase contributions to the Heart Association we need testimonials that stress future well-being stemming from a check-up and a check."

FIGURE 6-2.   Communication Graduate On-the-Job

BOX 6-1   Understanding NPT in a Nutshell

NPT Defined: *Narrative Paradigm Theory* is a general communication theory that explains the force of narration as contributing the value justification for human action.

Power & Scope: NPT's power derives from its ability to explain and assess the values that call forth human action that are implicit or explicit in stories. NPT is a theory of broad scope that explains the power of narrations in personal conversations, public speeches, small group interaction, and mass, organizational, and intercultural communication.

Origin & Roots: NPT grew out of the work of Walter Fisher at the University of Southern California beginning in the early 1970s. NPT draws together logical and value reasoning and discursive and fictive materials from the classical period to modern times to provide a more complete assessment of humans' symbolic justification for action.

Assumptions: (1) Human beings are storytellers; (2) All forms of human communication are best viewed as stories; (3) Through discourse humans use "good reasons"—value-laden warrants—for believing or acting; (4) Humans naturally possess a narrative logic that they use to assess communication; and (5) Humans create and recreate reality through sets of stories (accounting and recounting) that must be chosen among continually to live life to its fullest.

Basic Concepts: A *narration (story)* is an accounting or recounting of a value-laden symbolic action embodied in words and deeds reflecting sequence, time, and place. NPT's remaining basic concepts are the associative concepts of logical reasons and good reasons. *Logical reasons,* following Rational Argumentation Theory (RAT), are reason-supported claims. *Good reasons* are the values in stories that provide value-supported claims.

Structural Concepts: NPT possesses message, dynamic, communicator, and medium structural con-

cepts. The message structure concepts are characterization, emplotment, and place of presentation. *Characterization* is the depiction of the characters present in the narrative. *Emplotment* is the action attributed to the story by the storyteller. *Place of presentation* is the placement, setting, or location of the community in which a story takes place or occurs symbolically. NPT's dynamic structure concepts are the idealistic/moralistic and materialistic master analogue myths vying for primacy in every narrative. The *idealistic/moralistic myth* concerns brotherhood and sisterhood and emphasizes the egalitarian notion that humans are created equal as it reflects such values as charity, love, trustworthiness, justice, and tolerance. The *materialistic myth* celebrates individual achievement through such values as competitiveness, self-reliance, perseverance, tenacity, political acumen, and entrepreneurial spirit. NPT's communicator structure concepts include storyteller and audience. The *storyteller* is the person who tells stories to account for or recount human action. The *audience* is an ideal audience consisting of hearers or readers who evaluate a given story to conclude if it hangs together and rings true to their experience. NPT's medium$_2$ structure concept is an *open democratic society* or community of people existing within a free society who willingly and naturally examine ideas.

Evaluative Concepts: NPT's main evaluative concepts are narrative probability and narrative fidelity. *Narrative probability* concerns the audience's evaluations of a story's coherence: Does it hang together? Is it internally consistent? Is it consistent with previous stories on the same topic that the audience members have heard? and Is it consistent with previous characterizations of the storyteller? *Narrative fidelity* examines the truthfulness of a story, evaluating it to see if it "rings true" to other stories of the same type, and meets the tests of rational reasons and value-laden good reasons.

Chapter *7*

Diffusion of Innovation Theory (DIT)

The force of diffusing innovation talk about new
ideas produces change in social systems.

Chapter Outline

We've reached another good place for a rest stop along the trail to understanding communication theories. Here, let's discuss our next landmark of interest, Diffusion of Innovation Theory (DIT). DIT is the final general communication theory introduced in *Understanding Communication Theories*. DIT allows you to explain the communicative force of diffusing innovation talk that leads to the human action known as "adoption." Individuals and collectives of individuals adopt some new ideas and practices and reject others. DIT explains the process of how new ideas diffuse across and through social systems. DIT also provides a blueprint for designing communication campaigns aimed at the adoption of new ideas, such as new product adoption, changing agricultural practices, practicing safe sex, or electing a political candidate to office. DIT allows researchers to analyze and determine why some communication campaigns fail while others succeed.

DIT: Viewing the General Theory

The early bird gets the worm! Fools rush in where angels fear to tread! This is an idea whose time has come! With DIT, such adages take on serious meaning. DIT provides a rich explanation regarding the wisdom of such adages. DIT fits within the relational paradigm of communication theories. It focuses on social facts. It explains the combined effects of interpersonal and mass media messages on the diffusion and adoption of new ideas in a social system. DIT is a general communication theory that allows you to trace and manage the flow of information about new ideas through a collectivity of people. Like Information Systems Theory (Chapter 1), a mathematical base undergirds DIT.

Sketching Its Power and Scope

We've traveled a good distance on our trail to understanding communication theories. Let's extend our rest stop and recall that TCM provides two metaconcepts called power and scope to assist you in differentiating communication theories. DIT's explanatory power derives from its ability to explain and assess the diffusion of innovations. Valente (1995) defined the *diffusion of innovations* as "the spread of new ideas, opinions, or products throughout a society" (p. 2). Rogers (1995) elaborated: "Diffusion is the process by which an innovation is communicated through certain channels over time among the members of a social system" (p. 5). Both Rogers (1995) and Rogers and Kincaid (1981) characterized diffusion as a two-way, interactive process of convergence (coming to mutual agreement) concerning the acceptableness of an innovation. With this characterization they mirrored the explanation of convergence (Bormann, 1980) offered by Symbolic Convergence Theory (see Chapter 4). As well, DIT is a theory of broad scope. It explains the diffusing process across all of the medium$_1$ contexts of interpersonal, small group, public speaking, organizational, mass, and intercultural communication.

To most easily understand DIT, you need to recognize that the diffusion of innovations occurs in a social system (collectivity of people). Within the social system both mass communication about the innovation and networking between individuals facilitates the diffusion process. Networking communication is especially important as the process approaches the decision to adopt or not to adopt. The members of each network hold certain opinion leaders in high esteem. A change agent who tries to influence a social network must work with and through opinion leaders to increase the diffusion rate for the adoption of a new idea. At the same time, gatekeepers in the mass media determine whether or not to use their medium to spread a new idea. Here again, the change agent must work with gatekeepers to accelerate the diffusion of innovation. After a certain frequency of adoptions, a critical mass is reached. Once a critical mass of individuals receives exposure to and adopts a new innovation then rapid, exponential adoption occurs.

The consequences of a social system's adoption of a new idea may be good or bad. Ideas are not created equal. For example, few among the Allies of World War II considered the adoption of militarist Nazism by the German people a good idea. Many human societies prosper or fail based on the ideas and practices they choose to adopt or reject.

Tracing Its Origin and Roots

The roots of diffusion research grow deep in the fertile soils of anthropology, rural sociology, political studies, marketing, and communication. Everett Rogers (1962) introduced DIT to the communication discipline with his landmark book, *The Diffusion of Innovations*. At this writing, the book—in its fourth edition (Rogers, 1995)—remains the best single source for understanding DIT. Rogers worked with DIT during sojourns as a professor of communication or journalism at Michigan State University, Stanford University, University of Southern California, and the University of New Mexico. He has made a career of collecting and analyzing diffusion research from across the academy. More importantly, he has worked actively to build DIT. He has also actively used DIT to solve social problems worldwide. Rogers (1995) indicated that 3, 810 diffusion studies undergird the research program in the United States. Of those, 27 percent (1,070) were the work of scholars in the fields of communication and marketing communication.

The French sociologist Gabriel Tarde (1903) introduced the modern DIT (Rogers, 1971, 1983, 1994). Tarde suggested that over time the cumulative adoption of a new idea followed an "S-shaped" distribution curve. Tarde also identified early adopters as more cosmopolitan than late adopters. As well, he indicated that opinion leaders could effect adoption in their respective geographic areas.

Rural sociologists in the second quarter of the twentieth century started the systematic study and implementation of DIT. They did so for the purpose of accelerating the adoption of modern farming practices in America. By using the land-grant university extension agent as the change agent, private companies and government officials sought to diffuse new farming practices. Gross (1942) and Ryan and Gross (1943) reported the initial studies of this agricultural diffusion model. They discovered that, in addition to the S-curve, a bell-shaped curve (normal distribution) characterized the adoption process. They also reported that the adopters fell into four categories on that bell curve. The categories included early, early majority, late majority, and laggard adopters. Ryan and Gross found that both mass media messages and messages from the change agents (seed salesmen and county agents) influenced the early adopters. Conversely, Ryan and Gross found that and the opinions of neighbors who had already adopted the new practice influenced the later adopters.

In the late 1930s, The Rockefeller Foundation funded a Columbia Broadcasting System grant proposal. The proposal described the Princeton Radio Research Project headed by the Viennese research methodologist, Paul Lazarsfeld (Rogers, 1994). The radio researchers sought to determine the role of radio in promoting federal farm policies. However, from time to time, these researchers also did other types of studies. Thus, it came to pass that the radio research project piggybacked on a commissioned panel study of the November, 1940, U.S. presidential election (Rogers, 1994). Lazarsfeld, Berelson, and Gaudet (1944), independently of Ryan and Gross, confirmed the role of mass media and interpersonal influences on the adoption of ideas. Their conclusions came from their six-month long, campaign study of 600 Erie County Ohio voters.

Katz and Lazarsfeld (1955) labeled the contributions of both the mass media and interpersonal influence on the adoption, decision-making process "the Two-Step Flow" hypothesis. According to Katz (1957), they hypothesized that "ideas flow from radio and print to opinion leaders and from these to the less active sections of the population" (p. 61).

DIT came directly to the communication discipline in the 1940s. The study of the diffusion of a major, breaking news story in the mass media began with Miller's (1945) treatment of the diffusion of President Roosevelt's death. His research marked the start of a major line of diffusion of innovation research. For example, Sheatsley and Feldman (1964) studied the diffusion of news about the assassination of President Kennedy. They found that 68 percent of Americans became aware of the shooting within thirty minutes. Mayer, et al. (1990) reported that 50 percent of their sample became aware of the spaceshuttle *Challenger* disaster within thirty minutes. Such studies showed the important role of electronic mass media channels regarding the rapid dissemination of major news events. As well, the research line demonstrated that the communication process required for news dissemination differed from the explanation offered by the parsimonious, Two-Step Flow hypothesis.[1] For example, Basil and Brown (1994) reviewed and reanalyzed thirty-four major news diffusion studies and reported their own study of the news diffusion of Magic Johnson's positive HIV test. At the time, Johnson, a perennial all-star, played professional basketball with the Los Angeles Lakers. In their metaanalysis, Basil and Brown confirmed three things. First, people learn of news stories through both the mass media and interpersonal channels. Second, the more personally relevant a news story, the more likely that a person discusses it with others. Finally, the more important the news story, the more likely that both mass media and interpersonal communication spread it. Basil and Brown concluded that, in fast-breaking major news stories, "mass media and interpersonal communication appear to be more interwoven than the Two-Step Flow hypothesis suggests" (p. 317).

Rogers (1995) noted that the 1980s witnessed the reporting of studies of the diffusion of new electronic media technologies such as cable television and e-mail systems. For example, Holmov and Warneryd (1990) studied the adoption and use of facsimile machines in Sweden. LaRose and Mettler (1989) studied the adoption of information technology in rural America. Rogers (1985) studied the adoption of home computers in households in the Silicon Valley. Such studies also confirmed the traditional form of S-curve adoptions. The LaRose and Mettler study demonstrated that the adoption curve for rural America paralleled that of their urban counterparts.

The first DIT study in marketing communication concerned the diffusion of Pfizer's antibiotic tetracycline. Pfizer's researchers conducted the study in Bloomington, Galesburg, Peoria, and Quincy, Illinois. Coleman, Katz, and Menzel (1957) reported that it took eighteen months, beginning in 1955, for 87 percent of the 125 physicians studied to accept the wonder drug as the prescription of choice. The adoptions followed an S-curve cumulative distribution. The researchers discovered that networking played a major role in the adoption decision. For example, they found that physicians who networked with other physicians adopted more quickly than isolated physicians. They also found that, on reaching a critical mass, adoption occurred rapidly as predicted by the S-curve of cumulative adoptions.

In the late 1960s, Bass (1969) introduced a new product marketing diffusion model. Subsequent research revised the mathematical model (Bass, 1980, 1986). His mathematical model allowed for the prediction of adoptions over time. Such major corporations as IBM, Sears, and AT&T have used his model to track new product introductions. The Bass model incorporates both mass media and interpersonal (word-of-mouth) channels within its forecasting variables. The model's predictive capacity regarding the rate of adoption again follows the S-curve of diffusion (Mahajan, Muller, & Bass, 1990).

Accepting Its Assumptive System

Again, it's time for a brief rest stop. Recall that TCM posited that theories reflect assumptions about the nature of human beings (ontological assumptions), about how we know what we know (epistemological assumptions), and about the values present in society (axiological assumptions). Such assumptions provide the perspective from which the theory analyzes communication. We present DIT's assumptions in this section. They include (1) the diffusion of innovation requires communication; (2) humans' propensity to adopt innovations varies; (3) the nature of human social systems (networks) requires change and evolution for survival; (4) the perceived value of an innovation affects its rate of adoption; and (5) more effective communication occurs when the communicators are homophilous.

like SCT

The Diffusion of Innovation Requires Communication   Rogers (1995, p. 17) indicated that, whether diffusion is spontaneous or planned, communication is the essential element of the process. Diffusion cannot occur without communication. The essence of the process involves several things. First, an innovation must exist. Second, an individual or social unit with knowledge of or experience with the innovation must be present. Third, another individual or social unit with the potential to adopt the innovation must be present. Fourth, either an interpersonal or mass media communication channel, or both, must connect the two individuals or units.[2]

Humans' Propensity to Adopt Innovations Varies   This ontological assumption indicates that some people will adopt early. Others will adopt later. Still others will reject the adoption.[3] Bach (1989), Rogers (1995), and Valente (1995) indicated that communication networks—the patterns of who communicates to whom—affect adoption. As well, the complexity of social networks affects adoption. Nonetheless, over time, the frequency of adoptions of a new innovation resembles the normal bell curve of adoption. Again, the cumulative rate of adoption resembles an S-curve (Dodd, 1955).

Let's see if we can illustrate this assumption. Think of the important innovations available for your adoption. Have you purchased a personal computer? If so, when? Were you the first person in your group of friends to purchase one? If so, did others in your group seek your advice about buying a computer? Are you on e-mail? Were you one of the first persons in your network of friends to go on e-mail? If you haven't adopted e-mail, why not? Is it because you don't have the money for a modem? Is it because you're unsure of how it works? Is it because you don't see any value in it for you? As we walk you through DIT, you should see how, within your circle of friends, you may be an innovator, or an early adopter, or in some cases even a rejecter of an innovation. This assumption says that every human being resides at some point on the continuum of adoption.

The Nature of Human Social Systems (Networks) Requires Change and Evolution for Survival   This is an ontological assumption. It says that open human systems naturally change. The assumption implies that closed human systems stagnate and degenerate. The key communicative force for change within an open system is diffusion of innovation talk. To survive, members of a collectivity actively seek, understand, experiment, and eventually adopt new practices. This assumption views change as necessary and inevitable. However, there is a risk to change. The diffusion of innovations, if managed incorrectly, sometimes leads to serious consequences for the social system.[4] Again, think for a moment of your network of friends. Someone usually knows where the live bands play. Someone else knows the latest movies in town. Another knows the latest changes in student loan programs. Still another knows the best deals on off-campus apartments. If your group of friends represents a social collectivity that is not monitoring innovations, then you will soon fall behind the diffusion curve. In such a case, you will be experiencing a *knowledge gap* (Rubinyi, 1989).[5]

The Perceived Value of an Innovation Affects Its Rate of Adoption   This is an epistemological assumption. The adoption of innovations varies with the value system of the social system or communicative network (Menzel & Katz, 1955–1956; Rogers, 1995; Valente, 1995). The adoption of an innovation is not necessarily desirable (Rogers, 1995, p. 12). Relative advantage, compatibility, complexity, trialability, and observability all hasten or slow the rate of adoption. Some innovations appear more appropriate for some situations than others. As well, some diffusing innovations harm nonadopters. For example, cars led to the disappearance of blacksmiths. Diesel locomotives, which could travel great distances without refueling, led to the death of many small communities. Airplanes and automobiles turned our nation's great urban railway stations into mausoleums. Such adoptions of innovations caused economic loss and social upheaval for many people. As well, a destruction of values may occur as a result of the rapid adoption of new technologies. Indeed, most collectivities that actively resist an innovation do so from the desire to protect core community values. The Amish communities of the United States provide an excellent example. Amish people dress in an unadorned manner, travel by horse and buggy, support community activities such as barn raising, and devote much time to teaching their children their religious and social values.

More Effective Communication Occurs When the Communicators are Homophilous
The degree to which one is similar to another (exhibits the quality of homophily) increases the likelihood of interaction (Rogers, 1995). Similar people belong to the same groups and "physical and social propinquity make homophilous communication more likely" (p. 19). Rogers suggested that highly empathic individuals lessen the need for homophily. He also indicated that effective communication increases the appearance of homophily. Because the diffusion of innovation relies so heavily on interpersonal communication channels to effect change, it is not surprising that one of DIT's assumptions centers on interpersonal communication skills. DIT assumes that empathy and perceived similarity are extremely important interpersonal communication skills. They help speed up the adoption of new ideas. In addition, Rogers stressed the importance of the interpersonal relationship that occurs between the change agent and the opinion leaders of an adopting social system.[6]

Let's continue our rest stop, and again look back along our trail. Please recall the suggestion that you suspend judgment about the validity of a theory's assumptions until you understand it and can assess its usefulness. At the same time, to determine the utility of DIT it is important for you to proceed as if these assumptions are true.

DIT: Introducing the Theoretical Concepts

Diffusion of Innovation Theory—like all general communication theories—exhibits basic, structural, and evaluative concepts. DIT contains at least twenty-six technical concepts with their attendant technical definitions. By observing communicators communicating through the lens of this theory, you should see various types of adopters and change agents cointeracting about an innovation. You should also see the sending and receiving of mass media messages about innovation. As well, you should see several types of diffusion talk. DIT contains six basic, eighteen structural, and two evaluative technical concepts that will help you understand the diffusion of innovation process (see **Figure 7-1**). We would characterize DIT as an elegant, as opposed to a parsimonious, theory. We discuss each concept separately. However, remember that the concepts are interrelated. They often occur together when observing diffusing innovation talk.

Finding Basic Concepts

To understand DIT, you first need to understand its six basic concepts. Initially, you must find an innovation. Next you must find diffusing innovation talk of which there are five kinds: awareness, opinion, practice, advocacy, and resistance. These concepts will not necessarily appear "naked." They occur encapsulated in DIT's message structure of the innovation decision-making process. As well, their impact is observed over time through the use of diffusion curves and the assessments of the rate of diffusion. They also come encapsulated in DIT's dynamic structure concepts of spontaneous diffusion versus a planned communication campaign. With DIT, it is the innovation that communicators communicate about in a medium. The success or failure of the diffusion process is then analyzed using DIT's evaluative terms of adoption and consequences.

Initial Basic Concept Once again, this is an ideal spot along the trail to understanding communication theories to take a rest stop. Recall from TCM (Chapter 1) that a general theory's basic concept stipulates the communicative force for human action. As well, recall that a general communication theory's basic concepts disperse into two subclasses. These include the initial basic concept and the associated basic concepts. DIT's initial basic concept is diffusion of innovation. Its associated concepts are the five kinds of diffusing innovation talk.

Diffusion of Innovation. To understand this technical concept you must understand both diffusion and innovation. Rogers (1995) defined *innovation* as "an idea, practice, or object that is perceived as new by an individual or other unit of adoption" (p. 11). New technologies (objects) are easy to see and trace. You can see the adoption of a telephone, television, microwave, personal computer, or cellular phone. Harder to see are new practices such as

Viewing DIT's Anatomical Elements

Key:
Bold Caps = The Communication Metatheory's Metaconcepts
Caps + Small Case = DIT's Theoretical Concepts

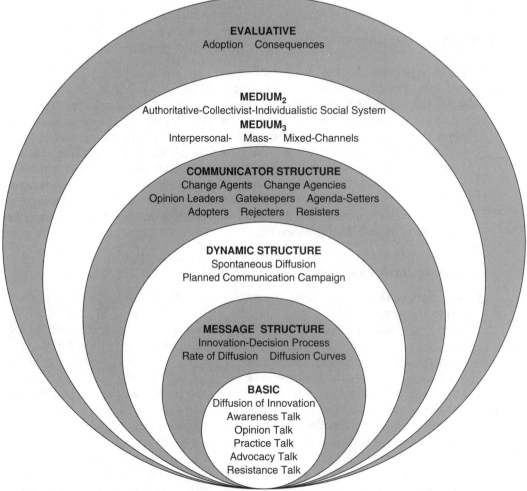

EVALUATIVE
Adoption   Consequences

MEDIUM₂
Authoritative-Collectivist-Individualistic Social System
MEDIUM₃
Interpersonal-   Mass-   Mixed-Channels

COMMUNICATOR STRUCTURE
Change Agents   Change Agencies
Opinion Leaders   Gatekeepers   Agenda-Setters
Adopters   Rejecters   Resisters

DYNAMIC STRUCTURE
Spontaneous Diffusion
Planned Communication Campaign

MESSAGE STRUCTURE
Innovation-Decision Process
Rate of Diffusion   Diffusion Curves

BASIC
Diffusion of Innovation
Awareness Talk
Opinion Talk
Practice Talk
Advocacy Talk
Resistance Talk

Other Anatomical Elements:

COMMUNICATIVE FORCE	**MODELING**
ORIGIN, ROOTS, ASSUMPTIONS	**RELATIONSHIP STATEMENTS**
PARADIGM	**THEORY–METHOD COMPLEX**

EXAMPLE OF INNOVATION DIFFUSION TALK: "I was surfing on the Web last night and found my local newspaper's home page. So, I'm not going to kill trees anymore. I'm just going to use the Internet. You ought to check for your newspaper's home page."

FIGURE 7-1.

recycling, safe sex, and crop rotation. Still harder to see is the adoption of new ideas such as Marxism, feminism, or supply-side economics. Of course, this theory is not about innovation, by itself. It's about the diffusion of innovation. Hence, Rogers (1995) defined *diffu-*

sion as "the process by which an innovation is communicated through certain channels over time among the members of a social system" (p. 10). Given that *diffusion of innovation* is the basic concept, it stands to reason that you are going to look for *diffusion of innovation talk* as communicators communicate in a medium.

Let's continue our rest stop and reemphasize a feature of the basic concepts of general communication theories. Recall that with Information Systems Theory researchers code the syntactic, semantic, and pragmatic information that creates order, structure, and control for coordinated human action. Then, with Rational Argumentation Theory researchers code the types of arguments that lead communicators to reach rational decisions that provide conviction and spur human action. With Symbolic Convergence Theory researchers code the fantasy themes present in human conversations that produce symbolic reality. Then, with Uncertainty Reduction Theory, researchers code the social information used by communicators to build and maintain interpersonal relationships. Finally, with Narrative Paradigm Theory, researchers code the stories that provide the value justification for human action. With DIT, researchers code diffusing innovation talk and explain how, over time, it produces adoption of a new product, idea, and practice that produces social change in society. Just as every day you engage in informing, arguing, fantasizing, exchanging social information, and storytelling, you also engage in diffusing innovation talk. Just ahead, along the trail to understanding communication theory, we detail what such talk looks like.

Associated Basic Concepts   DIT's remaining basic concepts are the associative concepts of awareness, opinion, practice, advocacy, and resistance. The statement at the bottom of **Figure 7-1** illustrates the first four types of diffusion of information talk. Let's examine it closely. The statement, "I was surfing on the Web last night and found my local newspaper's home page," represents talk concerning the awareness of an innovation. The statement, "So, I'm not going to kill trees anymore," represents opinion talk about the use of the innovation. The statement, "I'm just going to use the Internet," represents talk regarding the adoption of the innovation. Finally, the statement, "You ought to check for your newspaper's home page," represents advocacy talk regarding the innovation. From this example, you can see that the communicator is aware of electronic newspapers, holds an opinion about electronic newspapers, has tried the home page, and is at the point of trying to influence someone else to adopt the same practice. Resistance talk is illustrated by the additional statement, "I've heard there are traffic jams on the Internet. You can never depend on it when you need it."

Although DIT's associative basic concepts are discrete, in everyday conversation they often occur piled on top of each other just as they did in the example. On the other hand, with communication campaigns, diffusion of innovation talk often specifies each associative concept and connects each to a particular communication channel. For example, awareness might be on billboards, opinion might be in newspapers, practice might be in television infomercials, and advocacy might be on interpersonal channels. Starosta (1976) has suggested that the more taboo or controversial the nature of the topic the greater the need for interpersonal advocacy talk.

Awareness Talk.   *Awareness talk* is the communicative dissemination of a new idea, practice, or product to people in a collectivity. Awareness of an innovation is required before one can form opinions about it or adopt the idea. Rogers (1995) indicated that the "awareness of an innovation may be expressed in terms of knowledge, persuasion, or a decision to adopt" ⁂

(p. 11). For him, "awareness knowledge" (p. 18), or awareness of an innovation, does not mean adoption, practice, or even opinion. (It simply means awareness.) He described a diffusion of innovation campaign in Cincinnati, Ohio (Star & Hughes, 1950) designed to build public support for the United Nations shortly after its founding in the 1940s. Rogers reported that the campaign failed because it only provided messages at the awareness level. The change agents distributed 60,000 pieces of literature and aired numerous radio commercials that featured the slogan "Peace begins with the United Nations and the United Nations begins with you." The follow-up results indicated awareness of the slogan. However, people had no idea what it meant. The ambiguity of the message precluded people from forming opinions, changing practices, or becoming advocates. Although awareness is insufficient to achieve adoption by itself, as Rogers and Storey (1987) have argued, it is a necessary ingredient. The mass media play an important role in spreading awareness knowledge. However, awareness also spreads through interpersonal channels called "word-of-mouth."

Opinion Talk.   *Opinion talk* is the disclosing of one's beliefs and attitudes toward a new idea, product, or practice to other people in an interpersonal communicative network. With URT, we noted that people hesitate to express their opinions on topics until they are familiar with the person they're talking to. A similar phenomenon happens with DIT. (People don't form an opinion about an innovation until they really know about it.) People want to be sure that the innovation fits their existing social beliefs and values.

Rogers (1995) reported a failed diffusion of innovation campaign representing this phenomenon. Two hundred Peruvian villagers (Wellin, 1955) rejected the innovation of boiling their drinking water despite the efforts of a two-year public health campaign. Interestingly, the Peruvians already boiled water, but they only gave it to the already sick. Consequently, the Peruvians associated warm, boiled water with disease, and cool water with health. The change agent failed to consider the impact of the Peruvians' existing attitudes, beliefs, and opinions about boiled water on the communication campaign.

Practice Talk.   *Practice talk* is the interpersonal sharing, between people in a communication network, of their experiences with a new idea, product, or practice. (In terms of adoption, people talking about their experience with a new idea is a very important part of the diffusion of innovation process.) For example, Rogers (1995) emphasized the importance of opinion leaders, who have adopted the idea, disclosing their experiences and practices to potential adopters. When we worked with a new product innovation for the Upjohn Company, we used teleconferencing focus groups to spread the word. We encouraged respected local veterinarians to share their experiences with a new animal health drug (Bush, 1981). These veterinarians served as opinion leaders as they answered nonusers' questions about the new drug. This peer-selling strategy helped introduce the new product to market. Of course, any opinion-leading interpersonal communication contributes to a new product's adoption rate over time. However, by structuring the interpersonal contacts, we accelerated the rate of adoption.

Advocacy Talk.   *Advocacy talk* is intentional communication designed to persuade others to adopt the innovation. Starosta's (1976) study of the rhetorical influence of the village-level worker in India and Sri Lanka confirmed the importance of advocacy talk (persuasion) on the part of change agents. Recall that in the Christian religion, Christ's Apostles did more than model a Christian lifestyle; they went into the world and preached the gospel.

You may feel so strongly about your religious beliefs that you actively seek out nonbelievers and attempt to convert them. Such are bona fide examples of advocacy talk. Such advocacy talk is crucial to adoption. Again, let's see if we can illustrate this point. Professor Cragan's family shows a history of prostate cancer. His sister, June, is a nurse. She serves as the medical opinion leader for the Cragan family. When physicians developed a new innovation called a prostate-specific androgen test, June got on the phone and used advocacy talk to encourage her three brothers to make appointments to have the test. As it turned out, the test proved to be a lifesaver for one of the brothers. Who serves as the medical opinion leader in your family? What health practices have they recommended to you? If your family lacks a medical opinion leader, you may suffer from a medical knowledge gap that exposes you to unnecessary health risks.

Resistance Talk.   *Resistance talk* is a special kind of DIT talk. Resistance talk occurs when some people, called rejecters, actively oppose the innovation. There are three kinds of resistance talk: denouncing, disembodying, or deflating the innovation (Zelizer, 1995). For example, a surgeon might criticize a new innovation after a patient died. Such criticism represents the resistance talk called *denouncing.* As well, a consumer might talk about a technology as if it could operate without human hands: "The computer is always making errors." This is an example of *disembodying.* Finally, rejecters might deflate a technology by labeling it a "necessary evil" that at best must only be accommodated (Zelizer, pp. 83–88). Such a statement illustrates *deflating* talk.

Seeing Structural Concepts

Here, too, a brief rest stop appears to be in order. Recall that TCM specified that the structural concepts for all general communication theories relate to message structure, communication dynamic structure, communicator structure, and medium structure. At its simplest, DIT explains that communicators communicate about new innovations through awareness, opinion, practice, and advocacy talk. They do so by using mass media and especially interpersonal communication channels. DIT contains three message structure technical concepts (the innovation–decision process, diffusion curves, and rate of diffusion), two dynamic structure technical concepts (spontaneous diffusion and planned communication campaign), seven communicator structure technical concepts (change agent, change agency, opinion leaders, gatekeepers, agenda setters, adopters, rejecters—and their respective attributes), three medium$_2$ structure technical concepts (authoritative, collectivist, and individualistic social systems), three medium$_3$ structure concepts (interpersonal, mass, and mixed channels) and two evaluative technical concepts (adoption and consequences).

Message Concepts   Recall that TCM specified that all general communication theories contain message structure technical concepts that dress up and flesh out a theory's basic concepts. As indicated in **Figure 7-1,** DIT's three message structure concepts are the innovation–decision process, diffusion curves, and rate of diffusion. The adoption of an innovation is a multistage process that occurs across a population. One way the process can be plotted or graphed, and thus depicted, is by an "S-curve" tilted to the right at about 45 degrees. Adoption begins at zero and curves slowly upward forming the bottom of the S. The curve increases its speed sharply as many adopters surface, forming the trunk of the S. Then, the curve tapers and curves slowly to the right as saturation is reached, forming the top of the S. Another way to view adoption is to graph the rate of adoption by means of a population distribution. Here, the adoption curve resembles the normal distribution or bell-shaped curve. Finally, the rate of diffusion can be estimated and tracked by using an estimation measure such as the Bass formula (Mahajan, Muller, & Bass, 1990).

Innovation–Decision Process.   The innovation–decision process includes such elements as knowledge, persuasion, decision, implementation, and confirmation. Rogers (1995) based this stagic model on the five-step model of the rural sociologists presented at the beginning of this chapter. The *knowledge* stage occurs when an individual is exposed to an innovation. Coleman, Katz, and Menzel (1966) argued that a person becomes aware of an innovation either by accident or the active work of a change agent. In other words, a person cannot actively seek out an idea unless he or she knows that it exists. Knowledge might entail more than the innovation, by itself. For example, it is one thing to know of the Internet. It's quite another thing to know how the Internet works. It is still another thing to grasp how the Internet might be put to good use.

The *persuasion* stage occurs when a person forms either a favorable or unfavorable opinion about the innovation. In this stage a potential adopter actively seeks information to form an evaluation. The potential adopter may even seek out change agents and opinion leaders. It is this stage of the process that provides the insight as to why DIT emphasizes the interpersonal channels of communication and not just the mass media channels. The interpersonal channels attract and ignite the critical mass necessary for the further rapid diffusion of the innovation.

The *decision* stage is when "the individual engages in activities that lead to a choice to adopt or reject the innovation" (Rogers, 1995, p. 171). Most people want to try out a new product or practice before adopting it.[7] Even with new ideas, we often try them out on our friends to see how they will react. Professor Cragan's daughter, Keary, recently announced that she had become a vegetarian. After trying the idea for a while, and hearing no resistance talk, she adopted the practice of not eating red meat. She then encouraged her mother to make special vegetarian meals available when Keary came home for holiday dinners. Of course, Dr. Shields wasn't around to pooh-pooh the idea. Dr. Shields would say that Keary had gone beyond the point of advocacy to oppression, but even he is eating fewer four-legged animals these days.

The *implementation* stage is highlighted by practical considerations of how best to make the new innovation work. In this stage, the adopter remains an active information-seeker as he or she adapts and reinvents the innovation for use in his or her life. For example, the microwave oven, initially designed to cook meals rapidly, often serves most homes as a means to warm leftovers and heat water for coffee and tea.

The *confirmation* stage reflects the adopter's desire to verify the wisdom of the adoption. In this stage the adopter actively seeks information to confirm the sagacity of the decision. Recall how many times you have asked your friends to comment on your last new hairstyle or new purchase. You were seeking confirmation for an adoption decision.

Diffusion Curves.   Three types of curves help to explain the diffusion process as it occurs over time: (1) the S-curve of the cumulative adoption of an innovation over time; (2) the normal distribution or bell curve of the frequency of adoption over time; and (3) the curve of relative influence of the mass media and interpersonal communication on adoption. The

S-curve—first suggested by Tarde (1903), algebraically brought to life by Pemberton (1936, 1937), and practically applied by Gross (1942) and Ryan and Gross (1943)—provided a powerful depiction of the cumulative adoption of an innovation over time. **Figure 7-2** displays the S-curve for the adoption of a hypothetical innovation over time.

A key aspect of the innovation S-curve is the point at which critical mass arises and a chain reaction of adoptions results. *Critical mass* is the smallest number of adopters needed to sustain the subsequent wide diffusion of an innovation. Interpersonal communication appears essential to achieving critical mass (Rogers, 1995). Valente (1995) indicated that critical mass sets in for any innovation once 15 percent to 20 percent adoption is achieved. Ironically, contagious diseases also spread in epidemic proportions once 15 percent or 20 percent of a community is infected. Thus, health professionals isolate people with contagious diseases, once outbreaks occur, so that they can prevent their spread reaching a critical mass. If a critical mass is reached, the spread of the disease is uncontrollable.

Figure 7-3 displays the normal distribution (bell curve) of the diffusion of innovations over time for a hypothetical innovation. This curve helps you to see the five major types of innovation adopters. Innovators are the initial 2.5 percent of adopters. Early adopters are the next 13.5 percent of adopters. Early majority adopters are the next 34 percent of adopters. Late majority adopters are the next 34 percent. Laggards are the final 16 percent of adopters (Rogers, 1995, p. 262). **Figure 7-4** displays the normal distribution in terms of these adopter types for a hypothetical innovation. We will revisit these adopter types in the communicator structure section of this chapter. There, we will see that each adopter type possesses distinct characteristics. Hence, over time, adoption of innovations is not random; rather it is systematic by adopter type.

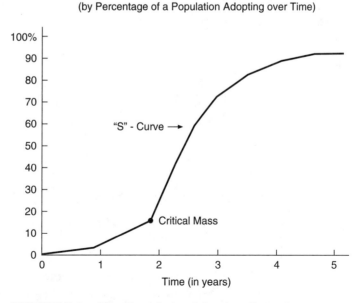

FIGURE 7-2.   **The Cumulative Adoption Curve for a Hypothetical Innovation**

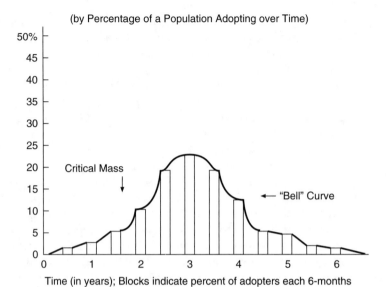

FIGURE 7-3.   The Normal Distribution for a Hypothetical Innovation

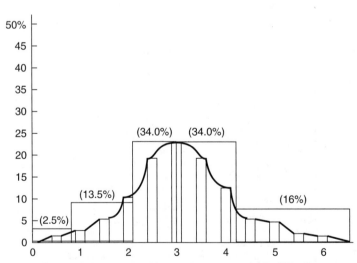

Time (in years); Percentages in parentheses stand for the following adopter types: Innovator = 2.5%; Early adopters = 13.5%; Early majority adopter = 34%; Late majority adopter = 34%; and Laggards = 16%.

FIGURE 7-4.   Adopter Types Superimposed across the Normal Distribution

DIT researchers are also interested in knowing the relative influence of interpersonal versus mass communication messages over time. Bass (1969) worked out the initial relationship. His mathematical forecast model allows the incorporation of estimates of the number of adopters influenced by the mass media and the number of adopters influenced by word-of-mouth. Bass called the estimate of adopters influenced by the mass media, the "coefficient of innovation." He called the estimate of adopters influenced by word-of-mouth, the "coefficient of imitation."

Mahajan, Muller, & Bass (1990) reported a review by Sultan, Farley, and Lehmann (1990) of fifteen marketing studies that had used the Bass predictive forecasting model. Across the fifteen studies, the average mass media influence coefficient (coefficient of innovation) was .03 while the average interpersonal influence coefficient (coefficient of imitation) was .38 (Sultan, Farley, & Lehmann, 1990). **Figure 7-5** provides a visual representation of the relationship between mass media influence and word-of-mouth influence for a hypothetical innovation. Rogers (1995, p. 80) argued that the greater weighting of word-of-mouth communication in the Bass model is consistent with the findings of the vast majority of diffusion of innovation studies. In such studies, the DIT researchers found interpersonal communication to be much more important than mass communication in the adoption of new ideas, products, and practices.

Rate of Diffusion.   *Rate of diffusion* concerns the speed at which new adoptions occur. Edmonson (1961), a cultural anthropologist, used radiocarbon-dated prehistoric pottery to compute its spread around the world during the Neolithic period. He concluded that the use of pottery, and other Neolithic innovations, diffused at the rate of 1.15 miles per year from

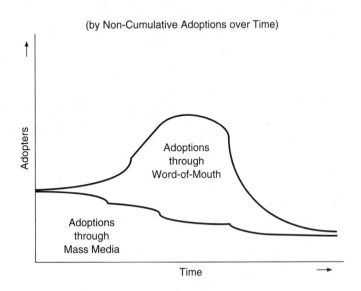

**FIGURE 7-5.   Word-of-Mouth versus Mass Media
Influences for Adoption**

their point of origin. It took more than 10 millennia for pottery to spread around the world. Of course, jet travel and the Internet have dramatically increased the diffusion rate of many ideas. For example, a major news story like the start of the 1990 Desert Storm War against Iraq or the June, 1994, O. J. Simpson slow-motion car-chase diffused in terms of awareness within an hour. As well, the complexity and importance of an innovation affects its rate of diffusion. It took fourteen years for hybrid corn to diffuse across two Iowa farming communities. Of course, the farm belt at the time was wracked by the Great Depression. On the other hand, it took only eighteen months for tetracycline to diffuse across four Illinois medical communities. Additionally, the cost of an innovation affects the rate of adoption. When working with DIT, it is normal to assess the rate of diffusion of a particular innovation and assign a coefficient for it if you are trying to predict its diffusion rate along the S-curve (Dodd, 1955).

Rogers (1995) explained that the rate of adoption of an innovation is affected by five variables: relative advantage, compatibility, complexity, trialability, and observability. *Relative advantage* is the degree to which the innovation is perceived as a better idea than the one it supersedes. For example, Windows 95 is more user-friendly than MS–DOS. *Compatibility* is the degree to which the innovation is consistent with the existing values and past experiences of potential adopters. For example, a college savings plan for one's children fits the esteem with which people in the United States hold higher education. *Complexity* is the degree to which the innovation is perceived as relatively difficult to understand and use. Thus, the more complex the idea, the slower the adoption rate. For example, the home personal computer (PC) became available as the Commodore, Kaypro, or Osborne in the early 1970s. However, only 30 percent of U.S. homes contained a PC by 1993. The reason relates to the PC's complexity. *Trialability* is the degree to which one may experiment with the innovation. For example, you may easily test-drive a car, but it's more difficult to test-take an ocean cruise. *Observability* is the degree to which the results of adopting and using the innovation are visible to others. The benefits of a cellular car phone are visible, but the benefits of adopting a low-sodium diet are difficult to see.

Dynamic Concepts   Again, we have reached a point on the trail to understanding communication theories where a rest stop is indicated. Recall that TCM posited that general communication theories exhibit a deep structure that varies with each theory. Moreover, a tension exists either in the deep structure of the system the message is in or the structure of the message itself. In the case of DIT, there is an intrinsic tension between the spontaneous diffusion of innovations and the planned communication campaign to diffuse innovations.

The Spontaneous Diffusion of Innovations.   Rogers (1995) indicated that the *spontaneous diffusion of innovations* is an unplanned adoption of a product, practice, or idea by a collectivity of people. As we were preparing the final drafts of this chapter, the "grunge look" among male adolescent students appeared to be running its course. For several years, everywhere we looked in class, we saw baseball caps turned backwards, shirttails out, and pants worn loosely, often with the inseam beginning nearly around the knees. From zoot suits to Ivy League, from the greaser look to the preppie look, these kinds of clothing fads fade in and out of our culture. DIT explains that each fad came about through a combination of interpersonal and mass media channels with stylish opinion leaders in the forefront. In other words, each stylistic innovation over time cumulatively produced an S-curve.[8] As well, each stylistic innovation produced a bell curve of innovators to laggards. Were you an early adopter or an active resister to such clothing fads? Professor Shields, not a model for *GQ,* resists changing his clothing style. He argues that he becomes fashionable about every fifteen years.

The mass media regularly report new discoveries in health and science. Many of these discoveries diffuse spontaneously. For example, a twenty-year longitudinal study of the effects of the daily intake of aspirin on heart attacks produced an almost spontaneous diffusion. Males over fifty regularly take an aspirin each day to help lessen the likelihood of heart attack. New scientific discoveries often exhibit either high profit potential or significant societal consequences. In such cases, change agents regularly intervene to accelerate the rate of diffusion. This leads us to our second communication dynamic structural concept, the planned communication campaign.

The Planned Communication Campaign.   Rogers and Storey (1987) indicated that the *planned communication campaign* is intended "to generate specific outcomes or effects on the part of a relatively large number of individuals usually within a specified period of time through an organized set of communication activities" (p. 821). Rogers (1995) explained that the etymology of the word *campaign* goes back to the Latin word *field,* as when Julius Caesar went to the field with a military campaign. As a major or graduate student in communication, you will probably find yourself at the forefront of many communication campaigns designed to gain the adoption of products, practices, or ideas.[9] You may well have taken a course or courses concerned with how to run a political, public relations, or new product introduction campaign. Kendall's (1996) book, *Public Relations Campaign Strategies,* provides a 500-page treatment of how to run public relations campaigns. He discusses the use of marketing, advertising, promotion, publicity, and special events tools. Similar books on political and advertising campaigns also provide a litany of procedures and tactics for accelerating the adoption of an innovation.

Rogers (1995) suggested that DIT's planned communication campaigns are of three types. The first type concerns profit-driven *commercial campaigns,* such as new product introductions. The second type concerns responsibility-driven *societal campaigns,* for example changing your lifestyle to practice safe sex. The third type concerns *idea campaigns* driven by a proselytizing imperative, such as religious revivals, social movements like feminism, and political campaigns. In this chapter, we do not have the space to describe the specific strategies and tactics suitable to each campaign type. However, we are sure you can learn them in such classes as public relations, health communication, political communication, advertising and marketing communication, and the rhetoric of protest or social movements.

Communicator Concepts   Again, let's take a brief rest stop. Please recall that TCM posited that every communication theory possesses its own unique names for the communicators who communicate in a medium. Thus, the communicator structure concepts of DIT identify its communicators. DIT offers seven communicator structure concepts. The first two concepts package nicely as adopters and rejecters with their respective attributes. The next three concepts package nicely as opinion leaders, gatekeepers, and agenda setters. The final set of concepts package nicely as change agents and change agencies. Because DIT explains the communicative force of diffusing innovation talk, its communicators use awareness, opinion, practice, advocacy, and resistance talk. This talk occurs often.

Adopters/Rejecters and Their Attributes.   Among the communicators that emerge during the diffusion of a new innovation are five types of adopters: innovators, early adopters, early majority, late majority, and laggards. Recall that their cumulative adoption rate resembles the S-curve and their frequency adoption rate resembles the normal distribution (see **Figures 7-3** and **7-4**). Also, recall that each group of adopters possesses unique defining attributes. As well, there are rejecters of the innovation. *Innovators,* who comprise approximately 2.5 percent of a given population, are venturesome and willing to try out new ideas at the risk of adverse peer pressure. Innovators are often aware of each other and form friendships stemming from their common risk-taking qualities. Rogers (1995, pp. 166–167) indicated that research supports seven characteristics that provide additional attributes of innovators. These attributes include more formal education, a higher social economic status, and exposure to more mass media channels, interpersonal channels, change agents, and community activities. As well, they are more cosmopolitan. These characteristics also tend to be true of early adopters when compared to late adopters.[10]

Early adopters, who comprise 13.5 percent of adopters, generally command the respect of their peer group. They are more integrated into the local social network than innovators. What DIT calls *opinion leaders, gatekeepers,* and *agenda setters* comprise much of this category (Rogers, 1995, p. 264). Change agents often target the early adopters to accelerate diffusion and increase the likelihood of reaching critical mass. Early adopters feel pressure to evaluate new innovations and reject bad ideas and accept the good ones.

Early majority adopters, who comprise 34 percent of the population adopting a diffusing innovation, tend to be more deliberate than early adopters and less risk-taking. Although not opinion leaders, the early majority communicators tend to be more integrated with the average person in the community. They provide interpersonal linkages that are important to the diffusion process. The early majority communicators live by the old adage, "Be not the first by which the new is tried, nor the last to lay the old aside" (Rogers, 1995, p. 265). The *late majority,* who also constitute 34 percent of adopters, tend to be skeptical of innovations, yet susceptible to peer pressure. They typically wait to see if the bugs are out of the innovation. Often, in the DIT literature, the late majority are called *resisters.* Their friends must convince them of the value of adoption. The *laggards,* constituting 16 percent of adopters, tend to be traditionalists. They believe that if the present system isn't broken then it doesn't need fixing. They also tend to be interpersonal isolates. As well, they attend to mass communication channels less fully. Laggards display suspicion toward change agents and change agencies. The "knowledge gap" associated with DIT pertains to the gulf between laggards (and rejecters) and the innovators and early adopters. The gap often manifests significant social consequences.

Rejecters are people who refuse to make use of the innovation. There are two different types of *rejecters,* active and passive (Rogers, 1995, p. 172). Generally, *active rejecters* have tried the new idea, practice, or product and found that it failed or had negative consequences. They now actively campaign against adoption of the innovation in the community. They typically use one of the three kinds of resistance talk that we discussed under basic concepts. Recall that those three kinds are denouncing, disembodying, or deflating the innovation (Zelizer, 1995). In planned communication campaigns, the change agent estimates the size of the rejecter segment and develops and implements strategies to minimize the impact of resistance talk.[11] *Passive rejecters* simply lack awareness of the innovation or they remain unconvinced of its positive or negative value for them. Like the laggards, the passive rejecters are isolates from both mass communication and interpersonal communication networks and channels.

Identifying the various types of adopters and rejecters involves more than just asserting that an individual meets a "litmus" test. Often, you can identify them by the kind of innovation talk that they use. At other times, more sophisticated techniques may be needed. For example, Kopfman and Smith (1996) used discriminate analysis procedures to specify the attributes of nonadopters of organ donor cards. Fan (1985) developed an "ideodynamic model" of public opinion change to assess the intensity of the arguments offered by adopters and nonadopters. Fan and McAvoy (1989) and Hertog and Fan (1995) employed the ideodynamic model—a mathematical model based on the logistic function's S-curve—to account for "unadoption or change in beliefs from pro to con and back to pro" (p. 548) in studying the diffusion of ideas about HIV transmission.

Opinion Leaders/Gatekeepers/Agenda Setters.   Rogers (1995) indicated that *"opinion leaders* are individuals who lead in influencing others' opinions about innovations" (p. 281). They determine the rate of adoption of an innovation in a system and are the key to reaching a critical mass of adopters. Studies have shown that opinion leaders are not self-nominated; others have named them or characterized them as deserving of the title *opinion leader.* As a group, they attend to both interpersonal networks and mass media channels, are more cosmopolitan, talk more to change agents, are more integrated into the community's interpersonal network, possess higher socioeconomic status, and are more innovative.[12] These opinion leaders act as *gatekeepers* and *agenda setters* for their respective interpersonal communication networks.[13] However, opinion leaders also may function as gatekeepers in mass communication channels, such as assignment editors and opinion page editors (Benton & Frazer, 1976). Then, too, there can be gatekeepers in organizations who control the flow of information and the diffusion of innovation (Rice, 1993).

Change Agent/Change Agency.   The *change agent* or *change agency* is an open advocate of the diffusion of innovation for the planned communication campaign (Rogers & Storey, 1987). Sometimes this is a salesperson for a product, or a public health worker for an organization like Planned Parenthood, or a get-out-the-vote manager for a political campaign. The change agent or change agency is the credible, interpersonal interface who facilitates the flow of information to the hoped-for adopters. Rogers (1995) indicated that it is important that the change agent be able to empathize with the adopters. Sometimes such change agencies as the Environmental Protection Agency, the public health department, or the American Heart Association possess as their sole purpose the diffusion of new ideas within society.[14] In the case of change agencies you need to be cognizant of the need to view the agency systematically as a change agent for the campaign.[15]

Medium Concepts   Again, it's time for a rest stop on the trail to understanding communication theories. Recall that TCM posited three senses of media. Medium$_1$ is the sense of the general theory functioning in the six traditional communication contexts of interpersonal, small group, public speaking, mass, organizational, and intercultural communication. Rogers (1995) and others demonstrated that DIT explains the diffusion of innovations in each of these media contexts. Medium$_2$ is the sense of a substance within which communication grows and prospers. For DIT these medium$_2$ substances represent the different types of social collectives: authoritative, collectivist, and individualistic. Finally, the medium$_3$ concepts pertain to the channel through which communication flows such as air or light waves, books, or film. DIT offers a unique medium$_3$ configuration. The researcher or campaign planner must assess the appropriate interaction effects of mass media *and* interpersonal channels for the diffusion of a particular innovation within a given communication collectivity (Hertog & Fan, 1995; Valente, 1993, 1995).

Medium$_2$: **Authoritative–Collective–Individualistic Social System.**   An innovation appears to propagate and spread differently depending on the type of social system into which the innovation is being introduced.[16] For Rogers (1995) and Rogers with Shoemaker (1971), many formal organizations, with their predetermined goals and prescribed rules and regulations, constitute an *authoritative* social system. With an authoritative social system, relatively few people in the system possess the power, status, or expertise to adopt or reject an innovation. With *collectivist* social systems members take pride in consensus decision-making and open communication among members of the system.[17] Here, the collectivity as a whole decides whether to adopt or reject the innovation. Thus, it should not surprise you to know that O'Keefe, Kernaghan, and Rubenstein (1975) and Barker, Melville, and Pecanowsky (1993) reported that cohesive work groups facilitated the adoption of innovations. However, some individuals may passively adopt a new idea, but not actively advocate its adoption by others in the collectivity.[18] Such passive individuals are harder to spot than the traditional opinion leaders in an individualist social system or the formal power brokers of authoritative organizations (Van de Ven & Rogers, 1988). The *individualistic* social system allows for the individual adoption of innovative ideas independently of other social system members. For example, physicians in private practice, family farmers, and individual consumers represent such individualist social systems.[19] However, Tjosvold and McNeely (1988) found that, in organizations with individualistic, competitive goals, the rate of innovative communication slowed. Apparently, in such social systems, the competition for scarce resources made gatekeepers out of likely advocates.

Medium$_3$: **Interaction of Mass Media and Interpersonal Channels.**   In **Figure 7-5**, we presented a model depicting the relative influence of the mass and interpersonal communication channels pertaining to the diffusion process. Depending on the stage of the diffusion process, mass communication or interpersonal communication contexts may be significant. Additionally, in some stages and some medium$_2$ propagating substances, mixed medium$_3$ channels serve to spread the innovation. Since the creation of the printing press, the mass media channels have been regarded as powerful tools for reaching large numbers of people (see Chapter 10). Particularly for innovators, the mass media channels provide awareness and knowledge of a new idea (Valente, et al., 1994). On the other hand, interpersonal communication provides the persuasive impetus for the actual adoption.[20] Indeed, in the creation of a critical mass of adopters, opinion leaders play a central interpersonal communicative role.[21] However, as Rogers (1995) pointed out, "different communication sources/channels function at different stages in an individual's innovation–decision process" (p. 285). The original Two-Step Flow model of the mass media creating awareness and interpersonal communication spurring adoption fails to explain the stagic diffusion of innovation. As Rogers (1995) put it, "the original Two-Step Flow model did not recognize the role of different communication sources/channels at various stages in the innovation–decision process" (p. 286).

Ironically, innovations in communication technology and marketing techniques now blur the lines between interpersonal and mass communication channels (Woods, 1993). For example, infomercials on television mimic the opinion leader persuasion stage at the interpersonal level. As well, inexpensive how-to-do-it videotapes interact at the decision to adopt and implementation stages of the innovation–decision process. Indeed, on viewing an infomercial on how to cook with a Chinese Wok, you may make a direct purchase. Similarly, after viewing Jane Fonda's workout videotapes, you may adopt a more healthy lifestyle. Thus, the sophistication of modern advertising and information campaigns allows the mixture of mass and interpersonal communication strategies throughout the diffusion process (Valente, 1993; Zhu, et al., 1993).

Using Evaluative Concepts

At this point on our journey to understanding DIT, let's take another rest stop. Recall from TCM that all general communication theories posit concepts that help you evaluate communication from the perspective of a particular theory. Such concepts allow you to make assessments and judgments regarding the quality and outcomes of communicators communicating in a medium. Recall from Chapter 1 that all scientists are concerned with explaining the outcomes (effects) of the fundamental interactive forces that they study. For example, the agronomist studies the interactive effects of soil nutrients such as potassium, phosphorus, and nitrogen on the growth of crops such as corn, soybeans, and wheat. With DIT, we evaluate the adoption and consequences of diffused ideas on society.

Quality and Outcomes   By outcomes we mean that the communicative interaction identified by the theory did in fact occur, that is, did the communicative force under study have its predicted impact on human action? Quality is a feature denoting degree or grade of excellence of the communicative interaction. In DIT's case, at what rate was the idea being adopted and with what consequences? DIT's primary evaluative concepts are adoption and consequences. They provide the necessary tools to evaluate the force of diffusing innovation talk.

Adoption.   Adoption is an evaluative concept of DIT. *Adoption* is "a decision to make full use of an innovation as the best course of action available" (Rogers, 1995, p. 21). Implied in this definition is the idea that a potential adopter may consciously reject the adoption. It is often difficult to identify who has actually adopted an innovation (Coughenour, 1955). Sometimes a person will adopt a product or practice for a short while and then discontinue use. If, for example, adoption is determined as occurring at the point of purchase, then actual adoption, defined as use of the innovation, might be much less. Similarly, a person might buy a NordicTrac Skier, but never use it. As well, a person might buy condoms, but not use them. One of the difficult parts of using DIT is measuring "adoption" accurately. Additionally, it is sometimes difficult to know the unit of adoption. An organization may adopt electronic mail, but that doesn't mean that all members use it, nor does it mean that the ones who do use it use it equally. DIT, of course, tends to view adoption at a social system level. DIT's contributors developed the diffusion curves to sum up adoption by a complete social system like Democrat voters, or members of a medical society, or students. However, even in the case of a social system, there still must be a "unit" that makes the adoption. Again, to measure adoption, this unit must be counted accurately. Finally, the type of innovation complicates the researcher's discernment of true adoption. For example, is the innovation a product, practice, or idea? As we've already emphasized, it's easier to see product than idea use.

Consequences.   Rogers (1995) defined consequences as "the changes that occur in an individual or in a social system as a result of the adoption or rejection of an innovation" (p. 405). Despite the importance of the consequences concept, Rogers reported that only a small part of the DIT research program has focused on the identification of either the benefits or harms of adoption or nonadoption. Let's see if we can illustrate this point. Change agents typically assume that innovations are beneficial. They then hand off the responsibility to evaluate the acceptance or rejection of the innovation to others. Nonetheless, Rogers (1995) provided reviews of some case study evaluations of the consequences of innovations. A major study concerned the effects of snowmobiles on the Lapp reindeer herds in Northern Finland (Pelto, 1973). As you might guess, snowmobile use by Laplander households between 1961 to 1971 had the good consequence of providing faster travel to town. The innovation cut the trip time from three days by reindeer sled to five hours by snowmobile. However, saturated usage led to the depletion of the reindeer herds. In turn, the depletion of the reindeer herds led to high unemployment. Why were the reindeer herds depleted? The Laplanders sold their reindeer to pay for the snowmobiles. As a consequence, their subsistence herder economy went into a tailspin because of unemployment, debt, and cash dependency.

Another consequence of the diffusion of innovation relates to the intrinsically uneven adoption of any new idea. As Rogers (1995) stated: "Usually new ideas make the rich richer and the poor poorer, widening the socioeconomic gap between the early and late adopters of a new idea" (p. 414). This DIT consequence is sometimes called the *knowledge gap*.[22] At other times, this DIT consequence is called the *communication effects gap*.[23]

You may already have experienced the knowledge gap produced by the rapid diffusion of new communication technologies during the late 1990s. If you cannot use electronic mail, write reports with WordPerfect 7.1, search your campus library system with Nexus and Lexis, or comprehend SDCSHIE@UMSLVMA.UMSL.EDU, you may be the victim of a knowledge gap. Furthermore, that knowledge gap may place you at a disadvantage in competing for jobs when you graduate. On the other hand, if you know these things you can immediately contact Professor Shields and ask him questions about DIT. There is little doubt that any knowledge gap between computer and Internet literacy and illiteracy in the twenty-first century will have major worldwide socioeconomic consequences. As the adage goes, if you think education is expensive then check out the cost of being ignorant.

DIT: Working with Its Qualitative Method

Using DIT to study communicators communicating in a medium requires special tools. The procedure for identifying a theory's basic, structural, and evaluative concepts is not easy. It takes training and practice in the use of a qualitative method developed specifically for finding a theory's key concepts in everyday communication. As with all theories, it is difficult to find material, social, or symbolic facts initially. The process of discovery and identification of a theory's basic terms is not pedestrian. It takes training in and practice with the unique qualitative method associated with each general theory to observe and count the respective communication facts systematically and reliably. With DIT, as with the other general theories, you need to use a special qualitative method to assist in uncovering and finding the basic concepts as they appear in communication phenomena.

Innovation Diffusion Analysis (IDA)

Let's stop and look at a point of interest. TCM posited that every theory possesses a unique qualitative method as part of its theory–method complex. Recall that the qualitative method unique to Information Systems Theory required the coding, tracking, and modeling of the flow of information. Recall also that Uncertainty Reduction Theory required the coding, tracking, and modeling of social information. As a kissing cousin of Information Systems Theory, we should expect that the qualitative method of DIT will mirror the qualitative methods of IST and URT. It does. With DIT, the qualitative method is called *Innovation Diffusion Analysis* (IDA).

A working knowledge of IDA helps you first identify the innovation. Is it a product, a practice, or an idea? Then, IDA helps you to focus on awareness, opinion, practice, advocacy, and resistance talk about the innovation. Also, IDA alerts you to examine the spread of the innovation. As well, it tells you to identify the stages of the innovation–decision process, assess the rate of diffusion, and graph the various diffusion curves for a specific innovation. IDA then asks you to examine what the change agent is doing to effect diffusion rates. Finally, IDA alerts you to examine both the number and the consequences of the adoption. In all likelihood, you will follow seven steps when using IDA (Rogers, 1995).

The first step when using IDA is to identify the innovation. This is sometimes an easy task if you are tracking the diffusion of a product like personal computers. It is harder if you are identifying the diffusion of health practices like proficiency in the Heimlich maneuver. It is even more difficult if you are coding and tracking a new idea such as scientific knowledge or awareness of a news event. Just as an immunologist needs to find ground zero in the start of an epidemic, an IDA researcher must determine the beginnings of awareness and opinion formation about an innovation in a given collectivity.

The next steps involve identifying the adopters and rejecters. This includes plotting or modeling their respective communication networks. It also includes determining the effects of mass media versus interpersonal communication on the adoption decision. Other steps relate to tracking the rate of adoption over time and graphing the rate of adoption with a special focus on the point at which critical mass occurs. IDA also involves an examination of the change agent's or change agency's communication strategies for effecting adoption through the formal and informal channels of communication. Sometimes a change agent targets opinion leaders for purposes of accelerating the adoption curve through the point of critical mass. This is especially true if the change agent represents for-profit products and practices. At other times, a change agent targets late adopters and laggards with the purpose of closing the knowledge gap created by the innovation. This is especially true of change agents interested in public health and safety issues. Conversely, a change agent may target messages to counter resistance talk. This is especially important when the resistance talk is comprised of rumor and misinformation about the innovation. Finally, IDA alerts you to evaluate information and innovation diffusion in terms of the various kinds of adoption and the positive and negative consequences of those adoptions.

With IDA, the researcher often uses questionnaire or interview data retrieved from a target population. Such data seeks to answer two questions. First, when did an adopter first learn about an innovation? Second, how did she or he learn about it? One way to retrieve such data is through an individual's recall of when he or she became aware of an innovation, the channels from which she or he heard it, what opinion leaders or other sources of information she or he may have used, and what test-trials she or he may have engaged in before adoption. In short, the researcher asks the famous Watergate Affair question: "What do you know and when did you know it?" At other times, researchers code and track the diffusion of innovation by more direct measures. Such measures may include point-of-purchase electronic data recording or the longitudinal observation of practices.

Finally, DIT researchers typically do frequency counts and content analyses of the various types of information developed by change agents. The researchers want to know such things as the amount and content of direct mail, advertising, and face-to-face meetings used by the change agent. Such data help the researcher assign weights to the variables contained in the various mathematical formulas designed to predict market demand (Mahajan, Muller, & Bass, 1990). As well, IDA researchers often use the critical incident technique, and personal and focus group interviews to help sort the effects of the formal and informal communication channels (information sources) on the adoption decision.

Briefly Illustrating IDA

Thomas Pinelli, of the NASA Langley Research Center, headed up an interdisciplinary research team that included doctors of philosophy in communication, library science, and sociology. Each team member possessed experience in using DIT and IDA. The team conducted a multiyear study entitled, "NASA/DOD Aerospace Knowledge Diffusion Research Project." The project began in 1988 and is continuing at this writing. To date the project team has produced thirty-nine separate reports of their studies. The studies identified and tracked the use of scientific and technical information by scientists and engineers within NASA and the Federal Government, and within the United States and worldwide. These thirty-nine reports appeared in various publication outlets worldwide.[24] This NASA/DOD project used Rogers's diffusion of innovation theory to guide the research design and the interpretation of the data (Holland, et al., 1991; Pinelli, et al., 1994).

The project encompassed four lines of research designed to provide an empirical basis for understanding the aerospace knowledge diffusion process and its implications for NASA. In the first line of research, the project team identified the information-seeking behavior of U.S. aerospace engineers and scientists. In the second line of research, the project team examined the flow of information between industry and government in the aerospace knowledge diffusion process. In the third line of research, the project team identified key adoption issues involved in the academic–government interface with emphasis on the faculty–student relationship. In the fourth and final line of research, the researchers explored the information-seeking behavior of non-U.S. engineers and scientists worldwide (Pinelli, et al., 1993, p. 193).

The research team used DIT's research methods to meet several objectives: (1) identify and track scientific and technical information knowledge; (2) determine early and late adopters; (3) model the formal and informal channels of communication as they relate to the use of scientific and technical information; (4) characterize the type of social system in which diffusion occurs; and (5) develop a change agent program for accelerating the scientific knowledge base of late adopters and laggards in regard to the diffusion of new information.

To date their findings demonstrate the utility of DIT. They found that early adopters of scientific and technical information are scientists. Typically, late adopters are engineers. They discovered that engineers faced with a creative task first sought new knowledge informally. If the knowledge gained appeared insufficient to complete the task, they then turned to the formal channels of communication.

The project team developed a model for depicting the dissemination of federally funded research and development (R&D) information (Pinelli, Kennedy, & Barclay, 1991). Their model identified the formal and informal channels of communication and the opinion leaders and gatekeepers within the collectivity of scientists and engineers of the aerospace industry. Pinelli, Kennedy, and Barclay also discovered that newly hired engineers lacked interpersonal networks within the engineering community. Typically, such isolates lacked awareness of the new knowledge coming from R&D. The project team recommended that change agents (such as librarians) develop and present training classes for engineers and new hires (Pinelli, Kennedy, & Barclay, 1993). The classes concerned how to access the formal and informal channels of communication to acquire scientific and technical knowledge rapidly in real-time from R&D centers worldwide. Finally, the NASA/DOD diffusion research project team conducted comparative cross-cultural studies of U.S., Dutch, Israeli, and Russian engineers and scientists. They found that the international community of scientists and engineers fit the model developed to explain the diffusion of new knowledge in the U.S. scientific/engineering community (Barclay, et al., 1993).

DIT: Observing Its Usefulness

We've reached our final rest stop on this part of the trail to understanding communication theories. Recall that TCM posited utility as its primary evaluative metaconcept. It's again time to think of our litmus test question, "Will this dog hunt?" As we indicated in the earlier discussion of DIT's power and scope, the theory explains how the force of diffusing innovation talk promotes social change. Here, we will provide a review of DIT's grounding research and present several illustrative examples to demonstrate DIT's use to explain human action and promote social change.

Explaining Human Action

Let's continue our rest stop. Recall that a communication theory validly explains human action when researchers tie its concepts to directly observable phenomena. This effort is called grounding. A researcher usually grounds a theory's concepts by analyzing communication episodes to determine if the phenomena the concepts represent appear in the communication. Rogers (1995) marked the grounding of modern DIT as beginning with the Gross (1942) and Ryan and Gross (1943) reports of the study of the diffusion of the hybrid seed corn innovation. As well, Rogers (1995) reported dozens of studies that grounded DIT's concepts to the diffusion of innovation in communication, marketing, education, behavioral change, and information science departments. Again, the results of four thousand studies conducted worldwide demonstrate the value of DIT.

Numerous studies grounded DIT across the six traditional communication contexts. From its inception, the researchers grounding DIT noted both the effects of mass communication and interpersonal communication (dyadic and group) on the diffusion of innovations.[25] Many of the studies highlighted in this chapter reported such grounding. For example, Albrecht and Hall (1991) studied the relational and network conditions conducive to talk about new ideas within organizations. They found that relationships conducive to innovation related talk were characterized by amount of talk ("high content") and role multiplexity ("interwoven relationships"). Nonetheless, Albrecht and Hall found the protection of "personal face" to be an important variable regarding the disclosure of opinion about a new idea. Rice (1993) also examined the network innovation–decision process for computer-mediated communication technologies in organizations.

Grounding for the public communication context is found in the many case studies of strategic campaigns.[26] One interesting innovation in the public communication arena served both to promote democracy and to lessen the knowledge gap for the lower socioeconomic groups of our society. O'Sullivan (1995) and Schmitz, et al. (1995) examined the impact or consequences of the Internet's Public Electronic Network (PEN) in Santa Monica, California. O'Sullivan called the project a study in the diffusion of a teledemocracy experiment. He found the innovation "well-suited for facilitating pluralistic political participation" (p. 93). Schmitz, et al. evaluated PEN's effect on the homeless. They found it useful in bridging "communication gaps between very dissimilar persons" (p. 41).

With regard to organizational communication, Van de Ven and Rogers (1988) indicated that those using DIT often viewed the transfer of new communication technologies in organizations.[27] Kanter (1988) reported on multiple efforts to study aspects of innovation in organizations. She noted strands of research about innovation projects and their rate of diffusion among individuals.[28] Then, she noted strands of research about innovation diffusion success conducted from the standpoint of the organization.[29] Finally, she noted strands of research that centered on the effects of the political, economic, social, and legal environment on organizational innovation diffusion.[30]

Hoffman and Roman (1984) reported on a typical DIT organizational study. They studied the diffusion of innovation contributions of 2,083 supervisors in 96 different organizations. Their study, like that of Beyer and Trice (1978), reported a stagic diffusion model for the dissemination of changed alcohol policies in organizations. Both studies sought to identify the best ways to encourage supervisors to serve as change agents and take constructive action toward subordinates with drinking problems. Cheney, Block, and Gordon (1986) found that the source of organizational innovation varies with the hierarchical (authoritative) versus participatory (collectivist) structure of the organizations. For example, they found that some organizations, such as advertising agencies, attribute a great deal of the percentage of innovative ideas as coming from the group effect of their collectivist environments. Conversely, they found that workers in hierarchical organizations, such as banks, cite top management as the source of most innovative ideas. Wall and McCain (1975) identified structural constraints that predicted the ease or difficulty of adopting a new idea. They studied school district bond issue voting. They found the upscale, early adopters of new ideas more willing to listen to change agents from the school district than late adopters. Woods (1993) used DIT to explain the merchandising of Malcolm X diffusing across the culture with the marketing of the movie, *Malcolm X.*

As well, studies indicated that the mass media context contributed a major focus of the theory.[31] Specifically, a number of scholars examined the process of news diffusion.[32] For example, Deutchmann and Danielson (1960) reported on the rapid diffusion of major news stories via the mass media. They found that people listed radio, television, and newspapers as their initial sources for information about such news events as the launching of the Explorer I satellite and Alaska's statehood. Indeed, as we saw, the mass media served as one of the major steps in the Two-Step Flow hypothesis of diffusion. Of course, Deutchmann and Danielson also reported that two-thirds of the people had been involved in interpersonal conversations about the news. As well, a number of discipline-based studies traced the diffusion of new electronic communication technologies. For example, Carey and Moss (1985) studied the diffusion of new telecommunication technology.

Finally, DIT's contributors worked to explain the intercultural introduction of innovations, including news, U.S. television programs, and technology as intercultural innovation diffusion.[33] DIT, it seems, brought both good and ill in the intercultural arena, particularly in regard to third world, development campaigns.[34] Chan (1994) reported that in third world countries the media themselves develop within the diffusion process. McPhail (1987) examined the impact of such electronic colonialism.

As we indicated early in the chapter, Rogers's (1995) book, *The Diffusion of Innovations,* is the best single source to find reports of the empirical studies that ground DIT's major concepts. The theory itself is so diffused across academia that it is difficult to track grounding studies from a dozen different disciplines. Truly, DIT and Information Systems Theory represent the discipline's most heuristic general communication theories. For example, it surprised us to discover the NASA/DOD knowledge diffusion project, discussed previously. Clearly, the totality of the communication research on the innovation–adoption process provides a richer understanding of the complex interplay of mass media formal channels and informal face-to-face channels in the diffusion of innovations across the six traditional medium$_1$ contexts.

Benefiting the Real World

Hundreds of studies serve as exemplars of the real-world benefits of DIT. Let's look at some of them. Dearing and Rogers (1992) and Rogers, et al. (1995) reported the successful intervention on the part of the citizens of San Francisco in stopping the AIDS epidemic in that city. They detailed the extensive mass media coverage that gay newspapers provided in developing awareness of the epidemic. Then, they documented the effects of the interpersonal networks of the advocates for safe sex. Their findings demonstrated the persuasive power of the peer networks embodied in the STOP AIDS small group campaign. Change agents successfully recruited and used hundreds of highly motivated volunteers who engaged in diffusion talk. Perlof (1991) reported on another successful AIDS communication campaign in Cleveland, Ohio. That campaign focused on the innovative message of sterilizing used needles with bleach by HIV drug users. Schooler, Flora, and Farquhar (1993) developed a diffusion model independently of the lines of research reported in this chapter. Nonetheless, they confirmed that adoption is based on the synergistic use of mass communication and interpersonal communication channels. They introduced their model in a public health campaign to reduce the risk of heart disease.

Schramm (1971) reported on the use of DIT-based campaigns to improve family planning. He studied diffusion talk in such countries as Afghanistan, Columbia, El Salvador, India, Iran, Kenya, Korea, and Uganda during the 1950s and 1960s. He reported on the use of a multiplex of mass media and interpersonal communication channels to foster population control through family planning. Of course, the messages conveyed newly available family planning innovations. Schramm reported many successes, but he concluded that much needed to be done regarding the fine-tuning of the mix of mass and interpersonal channels to achieve family planning in the different cultures. As we have seen, many of the studies reported earlier in the chapter provided much of that fine-tuning.

The third world communication campaigns of the 1950s and 1960s exhibited mixed results. During those times, many failures occurred. Recent DIT research serves to explain the causes of those failures. Part of the answer lies in recognizing that a knowledge gap exists between early adopters and laggards and nonadopters of new innovations. In other words, the people who most need innovative knowledge are often the hardest to reach. Snyder (1990) reported a two-year study of the adoption of an oral rehydration solution to combat the widespread incidence of diarrhea among 1,000 women living in twenty villages in Gambia, West Africa. Snyder found that initial awareness by all women soon gave way to a knowledge gap between rich and poor women. Poor women displayed retention problems. Specifically, they kept forgetting the formula for mixing the rehydration solution out of salt, sugar, and water. However, close monitoring by change agents overcame the retention problem. The change agents created a printed flyer illustrating the steps in mixing the formula. The flyer led to the trial of the innovation becoming a permanent adoption.

Peterson, et al. (1994) reported the positive effect of interpersonal interviews with owner–operator farmers on inducing voluntary actions to improve farm safety. Their structured interviews engendered thematic descriptions (awareness talk) of safety problems as well as thematic descriptions (adoption talk) of ways in which they had improved farm safety. Again, this study highlighted the importance of interpersonal communication about innovation and its effect on persuasive campaigns.

Krendal, Olson, and Burke (1992) designed and tested a volunteer-based, modest, DIT-inspired persuasive communication campaign to foster recycling in a small midwestern city. They compared the outcomes of interpersonal door-to-door contact, a printed educational appeal, and a printed economic appeal in one neighborhood with a control subdivision of houses that received no persuasive message. This study is important because it defined a favorable outcome as adoption by actually recycling, not just awareness of the program. Results were as follows: The control group increased its adoption level from 18 percent to 24 percent, despite not receiving a change agent personal or written message. However, we suggest that you may well assume that, given the five- to seven-day time lapse between the delivery of the message and the pickup, DIT worked spontaneously diffusing news of the program. By the way, those receiving the face-to-face personal message, the printed educational flyer, and the printed economic persuasive flyer increased their participation equally. It went up 15 percent from the recycling levels in existence before the campaign. Recycling levels were already at 18 percent of households and within the range of reaching critical mass. The campaign successfully enrolled sufficient households for the recycling effort to prove cost-effective for the city. Krendl, Olson, and Burke concluded about the equal effectiveness of the different channels that "the **medium** was not the message; the **message** was the message" (p. 34). Sometimes there are ideas whose time has come!

Withstanding the Critics

With the emergence of the modern DIT, hundreds of scholars contributed to its grounding research. However, DIT did not mature without criticism. Rogers (1995) devoted a chapter to a discussion of the criticism. He identified four major challenges to the theory: (1) DIT reflects a pro-innovation bias; (2) DIT blames the individual for nonadoption; (3) DIT research suffers from the recall problem; and (4) DIT promotes a knowledge gap, thereby fostering inequality.

DIT Reflects a Pro-Innovation Bias   Downs and Mohr (1976) claimed that DIT reflected a built-in bias in favor of innovation. They elegantly argued that the word itself is hard to resist. Innovation implies a better idea and who wants to be called a "laggard" or a "rejecter" of new ideas. Also, they argued that change agents promote the pro-innovation bias because they already think the innovation is a good idea. Finally, they argued that the pro-innovation bias is visible in the fact that few sponsored studies have concerned antialcohol, antidrug, and antismoking campaigns. Rogers (1995, pp. 106–114) answered this pro-innovation criticism through five suggestions. He called for more research on the consequences of innovations, more research on innovation resistance campaigns, an examination of the reasons for rejecting an innovation, an examination of the reasons why adopters adopt (rather than assuming their motivation), and an examination of the interaction of the consequences of multiple innovations on a social system. Many of the modern DIT studies incorporated these suggestions to negate this criticism.

DIT is Source-Centered, Not Receiver-Centered   Caplan and Nelson (1973) argued that source-centeredness blames the individual for nonadoption instead of the source. They pointed out that blaming the individual for failure to adopt is like saying that if a shoe doesn't fit there is something wrong with your foot. They noted that the salesman, marketing system, or manufacturer is often at fault rather than the nonadopter. Rogers (1995) suggested several ways to overcome this criticism. First, he suggested the use of larger units of analysis, such as the organization or the social system, in place of the individual as the adopter. Next, he suggested the examination of multiple causes of social problems as opposed to just a change agent's definition of them. Then, he suggested the use of potential adopters to help define the diffusion problem as another means of overcoming this criticism. Additionally, he suggested the inclusion of structural variables, such as who owns and controls the R&D system behind the innovation and measuring its impact in the research design. Again, many of the modern DIT studies have followed these suggestions to moot this criticism.

DIT Research Suffers from the Recall Problem   Menzel (1957) and Coughenour (1965) observed that DIT studies typically only intervene once in the diffusion of innovation process. Additionally, they indicated that recall data is inaccurate, and notoriously so the longer the length of time between the date of adoption and the date of recall. Rogers (1995) offered three suggestions for overcoming this criticism. First, use longitudinal tracking studies. Second, triangulate the point of adoption from recall with other data bases like sales receipts, marketing studies, and the corroboration of other knowledgeable people. Third, pretest the interview instrument for accuracy. Many of the modern DIT studies used such research designs to negate this criticism.

DIT Promotes Knowledge Gaps, Fostering Inequality   McAnany (1984) and others charged DIT with worsening knowledge gaps.[35] Rogers (1995) offered several suggestions to overcome this criticism. Each suggestion provided a strategy to narrow any gap. First, tailor messages specifically to the late adopters and laggards. Second, use the communication channels to which the "have-nots" attend. Third, target the opinion leaders in the have-not groups. Fourth, develop change agents from the membership of the have-not groups. A number of modern DIT studies followed these procedures to negate this criticism (Schmidtz, et al., 1995; Shingi & Mody, 1976).

As you can see, to repeat the indictments of DIT's critics is to miss the mark. Rogers suggested changes, responding to the critics, and later studies incorporated the changes. Study after study has demonstrated that DIT is a useful theory that explains the force of diffusing innovation talk contributing to social change. With both the criticisms and responses at hand, we leave it to you to make an informed judgment as to whether or not DIT has withstood the critics. We believe it has, as do all viable core general communication theories. When you get to the end of the trail to understanding communication theories, we believe you can use DIT with confidence. We wish you happy hunting.

Summary

In this Chapter, we introduced you to Diffusion of Innovation Theory (DIT). DIT allows you to explain the communicative force of diffusing innovation talk on human action. We began by viewing DIT as a general communication theory capable of explication through the lens of The Communication Metatheory. We sketched its power and scope, traced its origin and roots, and discussed its primary assumptive system. Then we introduced DIT's anatomical elements (see **Figure 7-1**). We explained its basic, structural, and evaluative concepts. Next, we illustrated how to work with DIT's qualitative method, Innovation Diffusion Analysis (IDA). Then, we reported on DIT's usefulness. We showed DIT's utility in explaining human action and benefiting the real world. Then, we discussed its ability to respond to critical scrutiny.

By now, you should be familiar with DIT. **Figure 7-6** illustrates Corey, our communication graduate on-the-job, using DIT to good advantage. If you do not yet feel comfortable with DIT, we suggest you review our detailed chapter summary, "Understanding DIT in a Nutshell," presented as **Box 7-1**.

"Diffusion of Innovation Theory (DIT) tells us that we must develop a special new product introduction campaign that links mass media and interpersonal channels of communication to insure that we reach a critical mass of adopters."

FIGURE 7-6.   Communication Graduate On-the-Job

BOX 7-1 Understanding DIT in a Nutshell

DIT Defined: *Diffusion of Innovation Theory* explains the communicative force leading to the human action known as "adoption." DIT explains the process of how new ideas diffuse across and through social systems.

Origin/Roots: DIT's roots grow in the fertile soils of anthropology, rural sociology, political studies, marketing, and communication. The French sociologist Gabriel Tarde introduced modern DIT. He suggested that the adoption of a new idea follows an S-shaped distribution curve over time. Gross (1942) and Gross and Ryan (1943) provided the initial studies of the agricultural diffusion model, incorporating mass media and interpersonal channels. Everett Rogers (1962) introduced DIT to the communication discipline.

Assumptions: (1) Communication must take place if an innovation is to spread; (2) Humans vary in their propensity to adopt new innovations; (3) The nature of human social systems (networks) requires change for survival; (4) The characteristics of innovations help to explain their different rates of adoption; and (5) More effective communication occurs when two or more individuals are homophilous (similar).

Basic Concepts: The *diffusion of innovation* is the initial concept you must understand. An innovation is an idea, practice, or object that is perceived as new. DIT's associative concepts are awareness, opinion, practice, and advocacy talk. *Awareness talk* is the communicative dissemination of a new idea, practice, or product to people. *Opinion talk* is the disclosing of one's beliefs and attitudes toward a new idea, product, or practice. *Practice talk* is the interpersonal sharing of one's experience with a new idea, product, or practice. *Advocacy talk* is intentional communication designed to persuade others to adopt the innovation.

Structural Concepts: DIT's message structure concepts are the innovation–decision process, diffusion curves, and rate of diffusion. *The innovation–decision process* includes such elements as knowledge (exposure), persuasion (forming a favorable or unfavorable opinion), decision (the choice to adopt or not), implementation (making the innovation work),

and confirmation (seeking evaluative information). *Diffusion curves* are of three types: the S-curve of the cumulative adoption of an innovation over time; the normal distribution or bell curve of the frequency of adopters over time; and the curve of the relative influence of mass media and interpersonal communication over time. The *rate of diffusion* concerns the speed at which new adoptions occur. DIT's *communication dynamic* concerns the tension between spontaneous diffusion and the planned communication campaign. The *spontaneous diffusion of innovations* is an unplanned adoption of a product, practice, or idea by a collectivity of people. The *planned communication campaign* involves the systematic introduction of a set of communication activities designed to generate specific outcomes or effects on the part of a relatively large number of individuals. DIT's *communicator structure* concepts are adopters–rejecters and their attributes, opinion leaders–gatekeepers, and change agents and agencies. *Adopters–rejecters* are of five types: innovators, early adopters, early majority, late majority, and laggards. *Innovators* are the 2.5 percent of a given population who are venturesome and willing to try out new ideas immediately despite the risk of adverse peer pressure. *Early adopters* are the 13.5 percent of a given population who generally command the respect of their peer group and are more integrated into the local social network than innovators. Early adopters are usually targeted by change agents to accelerate diffusion and increase the likelihood of reaching a critical mass of adopters. *Early majority* are the 34 percent of a given population who are more deliberate than early adopters and less risk-taking. The *late majority,* who also comprise 34 percent of a given population, tend to be skeptical about innovations, yet susceptible to peer pressure until they are convinced by their friends of the value of an innovation. The *laggards,* constituting 16 percent of adopters, tend to be traditionalists and believe that if the present system isn't broken, then it shouldn't be fixed. Laggards tend to be interpersonal isolates and attend less fully to mass communication channels. There is a "knowledge gap" between the laggards and innovators and early adopters that can often have significant social consequences. There

BOX 7-1 *Continued*

are two different types of *rejecters*. *Active rejecters* have generally tried the new idea, but found that it failed or had negative consequences. They now actively campaign against the idea by denouncing, disembodying, or deflating it. *Passive rejecters* simply are unaware of the innovation or unconvinced of its personal value for them. *Opinion leaders* are people who lead in influencing others' opinions about innovations. Opinion leaders act as *gatekeepers* by passing along or withholding information and as *agenda setters* by identifying the innovations or new ideas that will be passed along. The *change agent or agency* is an open advocate of the diffusion of innovation for the planned communication campaign. DIT's *medium structure* concepts are the medium$_2$ concepts of authoritative, collective, and individualistic social systems and the medium$_3$ concepts of mass communication and interpersonal communication channels. Research indicates that innovations spread differently depending on the type of society into which they are introduced. With *authoritative social systems* innovations are adopted or rejected by the relatively few people in the system who possess power, status, and expertise. *Collective social systems* place pride in open communication that allows for consensus decision-making. The *individualistic social system* allows for the individual adoption of innovative ideas independently of other social system members. *Mass media and interpersonal communication channels* work in tandem to diffuse the adoption of innovations. The complexity of modern advertising and information campaigns allows the mixture of mass communication and interpersonal strategies throughout the stages of the process of adoption of new practices, products, and ideals.

Evaluative Concepts: DIT's primary evaluative concepts are adoption and consequences. *Adoption* is a decision to make full use of an innovation. If an innovation is not adopted it is not diffused. *Consequences* are the changes that occur in an individual or social system as a result of the adoption or rejection of an innovation. What are the benefits, what are the harms, and what are the side effects?

Chapter 8

Interpersonal and Small Group Communication Context Theories

Communication scholars theorize about dyadic communicative interaction and about small group communicative interaction.

Chapter Outline

I. Interpersonal Communication Context Theories
   A.   *Constructivist Theory (CT)*
   B.   *Coordinated Management of Meaning (CMM)*
   C.   *Dialectical Relationship Theory (DRT)*
   D.   *Face Management Theory (FMT)*
   E.   *Unifying the General and Contextual Interpersonal Theories*

II. Small Group Communication Context Theories
   A.   *Decision-Emergence Theory (DET)*
   B.   *Role Emergence Theory (RET)*
   C.   *Functional Decision-Making Theory (FDT)*
   D.   *Adaptive Structuration Theory (AST)*
   E.   *Unifying the General and Contextual Small Group Theories*

III. Summary

On our journey to understanding communication theories, this is an excellent place for another rest stop, perhaps even a campsite. For it is in this chapter that we change the type of communication theory that you need to understand. Recall that The Communication Meta-theory (TCM) offered a classification system that distinguished, among other things, general communication theories from contextual communication theories. This is the first of three chapters that focus solely on contextual communication theories. Contextual theories

208

primarily explain communication within one of the six traditional medium$_1$ communication contexts: interpersonal, small group, public speaking, organizational, mass, and intercultural communication. Recall also that TCM recognized two types of contextual communication theories. Type 1 contextual theories use one or more theoretical concepts that by definition tie them forever to the context. Such theories are context-bound. Type 2 contextual theories begin in a particular context but exhibit the potential to become multicontext theories through research that grounds their explanation of communicative interaction across two or more contexts. Of course, if researchers ground a Type 2 contextual communication theory's explanatory power across all of the contexts, we would call it a general communication theory.

As good trail guides, we should stress that the general communication theories presented in Chapters 2–7 provide rich explanations of a broad band of communication phenomena. In addition, each general communication theory explains that broad aspect of communication within each context. Thus, every general communication theory is used to explain communication phenomena within each context. Nonetheless, in the two main sections of the trail just ahead we present four contextual communication theories that explain aspects of interpersonal communication and four more that explain aspects of small group communication. The four interpersonal communication theories are: Constructivist Theory, Coordinated Management of Meaning, Dialectical Relationship Theory, and Face Management Theory. The four small group communication theories are: Decision-Emergence Theory, Role Emergence Theory, Functional Decision-Making Theory, and Adaptive Structuration Theory. To best understand the communication phenomena in each context, you need to use both the general communication theories and the relevant contextual theories.

Interpersonal Communication Context Theories

Interpersonal communication is among the most recently introduced of the six traditional communication contexts. Jenkins (1961) and Richmond and Buehler (1962) appeared as the first disciplinary scholars to contribute published articles with the words *interpersonal communication* in the title. At the same time, Barnland (1962) called for courses in interpersonal, decision-making, organizational, and societal communication to complement existing courses in public communication "if scholarship supports it" (p. 208). Within ten years, Illardo (1972) reported "an upsurge of interest in the field of interpersonal communication" (p. 1). He offered several reasons for the growth of the new context theories including the novelty of considering "such items as *interpersonal attraction, relationships,* and *personal growth*" (p. 1). Following Illardo's view, we conceive of interpersonal communication as "one-to-one" or "one-to-few" in which the goal is "effective communication as a humanizing force" (p. 2).

Arnett (1981), Hart and Burks (1972), and Johannesen (1971) argued that interpersonal communication flowed from the dialogic traditions of the phenomenologists and existential philosophers such as Martin Buber, clerics such as John Powell, S.J., and humanistic psychologists such as Eric Fromm, Sidney Jourard, Abraham Maslow, Rollo May, and Carl Rogers.[1]

Whatever the specific roots, between 1969 and 1974, a number of scholars introduced the discipline to the nuances of important interpersonal communication concepts. The concepts included ideas such as dialogue, empathy, identity, openness, risk, self-actualization, self-disclosure, shared feelings, transaction, trust, and warmth.[2] Bormann (1980a) noted that those with an interest in interpersonal communication moved the discipline to begin placing the emphasis on the receiver(s) of messages. The interpersonal communication scholars did so as they stressed person-centered, as opposed to information-centered, communication. Kim Giffin, John Keltner, Bobby Patton, and John Stewart were among the early contributors typifying the new emphasis on communicators communicating in a transactional medium in which the receiver played an equal role.[3]

Since 1970, the discipline has developed a number of important general and contextual communication theories that explain interpersonal communication. You are already familiar with two general communication theories—Uncertainty Reduction Theory and Diffusion of Innovations—that began with research in the interpersonal context. We would remind you that each of the general communication theories presented in Chapters 2–7 explains a broad band of communication that crosses each context. Consequently, each general communication theory explains some aspect of communication within the interpersonal context. In the section of the trail just ahead, we introduce four contextual communication theories that also explain aspects of interpersonal communication. Again, to best understand the communication phenomena in each context, you need to use both the general communication theories and the contextual theories.

Constructivist Theory (CT)

Constructivist Theory explains the relationship between *cognitive complexity* and interpersonal communication competency (Delia, O'Keefe, & O'Keefe, 1982). Jesse Delia, of the University of Illinois—who had worked with the psychologist Walter Crockett (1965) while at Kansas University (Delia and Crockett, 1973)—led a research program that developed and grounded CT within the interpersonal communication context.[4]

Delia (1977) indicated that CT uses the concept of *personal construct*—conceived by the psychologists H. H. Kelley (1950) and G. A. Kelly (1955, 1963)—as its basic concept. A *personal construct* is an interpretive scheme that allows a person to make sense out of reality (Delia, O'Keefe, & O'Keefe, 1982). Simple personal constructs may be thought of as bipolar adjectives like friends–foes, relatives–strangers, good–bad, tall–short, obese–anorexic. CT's scholars assume that the presence of one adjective requires a knowledge of its polar opposite, for example the use of *hot* assumes a knowledge of *cold. Interpretive scheme* serves as an associated basic concept of CT. It is akin to an interpretive frame, or way of looking at the world. Personal constructs, as they go together to form an interpretive scheme, range from the simple to the complex. The argument goes something like this: As a person develops and moves from infancy through childhood to adulthood his or her personal constructs become more complex, allowing for finer degrees of differentiation (Delia, O'Keefe, & O'Keefe, 1982). For example, *boy–girl* is differentiated more finely by *boyfriend–girlfriend,* which in turn is differentiated more finely by *fiancé–fiancée.*

The CT scholars embarked on a systematic research program. They placed a major emphasis on the attributes of communicators and the structure of their messages given the presence or absence of cognitive complexity. Through numerous studies they discovered that cognitive complexity consisted of the number (amount), abstractness, and orderliness of personal constructs. In other words, the communicated messages of cognitively complex individuals exhibited greater differentiation. Such people depicted a more organized schema of reality. As well, such people used constructs that fit a greater variety of situations. Let's see if we can illustrate this point. You can see cognitive complexity if you consider that a simple personal construct such as *baby crying–mommy coming* gives way with development to a more structured interpretive scheme to point up the more complex frame of *childhood needs–parenting activities.* The latter more complex schema might include a number of bipolar adjectives such as *dirty face–bathing, meal time–feeding, soiled clothes–washing, school night–homework* that more completely and complexly interpret the world of parental child care.

The central message structure concept of CT is strategy. *Strategy* is an anticipated or actual discourse pattern tacitly selected to meet a communicator's goals (Delia, O'Keefe, & O'Keefe, 1982). The CT scholars determined that cognitively complex people displayed greater propensity to adapt and develop tacit strategies to meet their communication goals than cognitively simple people (Delia & Clark, 1977). In this sense, strategy serves as the organizing scheme for degree of construct differentiation. For example, Gourd (1977) found that cognitively complex people perceived plays differently (they made finer distinctions) than cognitively simple people. Burleson and Samter (1990) found that cognitively complex people rated affectedly oriented communication skills, such as comforting (the ability to make others feel better when they are depressed, sad, or upset), as a more important quality in their friends than cognitively simple people. Burleson and Samter (1996) tied such similarities to attraction in relationships. Burleson and Denton (1992) related such similarities to attraction and satisfaction in marriage. Such findings correspond with the findings of other CT scholars who found that cognitively complex individuals exhibited more person-centered communicative abilities than cognitively simple individuals.[5] O'Keefe (1988, 1990), O'Keefe and McCornack (1987), and Peterson and Albrecht (1996) contributed the message structure concept of message design logics to CT. *Message design logics* concern the form of messages such as rhetorical (cocreated meaning), expressive (regulative), or conventional (instrumental). A rhetorical message is considered the most complex and is designed to achieve harmony and consensus as a goal is met (Peterson & Albrecht, 1996).

Usually, the CT scholars used an instrument developed by Crockett (1965) and refined by Crockett, Press, Delia, and Kenny (1974). The instrument is called the Role Category Questionnaire (RCQ). The RCQ is a two-peer, descriptive task requiring about ten minutes for completion. The procedure goes as follows: A subject is asked to think of two peers about their age, one that they like and one that they dislike. Then, without using descriptions of their physical characteristics, the subject is asked to write down the personal characteristics associated with each peer. The CT researcher then records the number of personal constructs presented in the two descriptions and assesses their quantity, abstraction, and organization (Burleson & Waltman, 1988). Typically, the CT researchers first identified the median number of construct responses for the population of subjects under study. Then they classified each individual subject as cognitively complex or cognitively simple depending on whether the number of constructs each listed placed him or her above the median or below the median of the population studied. In other words, the researchers labeled (evaluated) the subjects scoring in the top half (above the median) of all scores for the population studied as cognitively complex. Then, the researchers labeled (evaluated) the subjects scoring in the bottom half (below the median) as cognitively simple. They then compared the two groups' responses to some independent measure to see if cognitive complexity mattered.

The RCQ procedure is the most important part of CT's qualitative method. It produces the operational definition of cognitive complexity and cognitive simplicity. The use of RCQ continues to generate robust findings in experimental studies that use some form of communication competency as a dependent measure. In general, cognitively complex individuals perform better (and often differently) in such experiments than cognitively simple individuals.

Hale's (1980) study is typical of CT research. She collected RCQ data from a sample of college students. She split her sample following the procedures outlined above. Then, she compared the split samples' communication competency on two tasks. She found that cognitively complex people (those individuals scoring above the median in terms of the number of constructs generated) performed better than cognitively simple people (those scoring below the median in terms of the number of constructs generated) in regard to their communication effectiveness on the tasks. In keeping with the initial receiver perspective of the interpersonal communication context, other CT scholars such as Wilson, Cruz, and Kang (1992) associated cognitive complexity and construct differentiation capacity with the communicative abilities of assuming a perspective and making causal judgments.

CT's real-world benefit comes from knowing that construct differentiation can be taught to enhance a person's cognitive complexity (Sinclair-de-Zwart, 1969, especially, pp. 322–325). It can also be used to identify those who need special communication training. Zimmermann (1994) and Zimmermann and Applegate (1992) applied CT with good results to the study and training of hospice teams' message production effectiveness. For example, Zimmermann (1994) used the RCQ to capture hospice team members' cognitive differentiation about a two-peer, liked and disliked other. She then clustered the captured constructs into five categories: quantity of talk, quality of talk, relevance of talk, clarity of talk, and politeness of talk. As well, she coded the constructs by *other-centered, self-centered, humor,* and *communication style.* She also asked the hospice team members to generate a list of constructs that defined their role with the team. Zimmermann reported that the RCQ differentiated team members who lacked communication skills that addressed the needs of others. As well, she reported that the role differentiation task led to the identification of team members who paid inadequate attention to team tasks. She recommended training to improve person-centered communication for some team members and group-centered communicative interactions for other team members. Peterson and Albrecht (1996) studied nursing teams in hospitals. They reported evidence that a relationship exists between relational patterns of message design logics and perceptions of social support in mixed status (rhetorical versus conventional or expressive) dyads. In general, in situations where the superior is a rhetorical communicator and the subordinate is not, the data indicated that nurses "report the highest levels of perceived social support given and received, the highest levels of trust and relational certainty, and the lowest levels of burnout" (p. 301). So, when on the job, and you find yourself in the position of superior, you should attempt to be a rhetorical communicator engaging in the cocreation of meaning with your subordinates.

Coordinated Management of Meaning (CMM)

Coordinated Management of Meaning is a communication theory that explains how individuals use the pragmatic dimension of language for coordinating contextual meaning and constructing reality. As such, CMM is a kissing cousin of Information Systems Theory (Chapter 2). CMM explains how people cocreate meaning in and through communication.

It centers on the use of semantic and pragmatic meanings to choreograph joint human actions.[6] CMM developed through the efforts of Vernon Cronen and Barnett Pearce and their students primarily at the University of Massachusetts. They began by asking how humans coordinate the meanings of communication. In other words, how do communicators become more than actors milling about a stage engaged in an "unscripted drama" that produces "a cacophonous bedlam with [only] isolated points of coherence" (Pearce & Cronen, 1980, p. 121.)? Their answer was CMM.

CMM asks you to accept six ontological assumptions, as presented by Cronen, Pearce, and Harris (1982): (1) humans create systems of meaning and order even when there are none (that is, human talk creates order out of chaos); (2) humans organize meanings hierarchically (that is, there's a pecking order of meanings); (3) humans adhere to meanings temporally (that is, humans change meanings); (4) humans' meaning systems differ from one person to another (that is, they bring their view of symbolic reality to the interaction); (5) humans interpret behavior in the context of larger and larger meaning systems (that is, they interpret speech acts through the interpretive frames provided by such ideas as life scripts and cultural archetypes); and (6) human communication itself creates a social reality.

CMM also assumes that three kinds of rules (constitutive, regulatory, and authoritative) guide communicative interaction, that is, they "block" or choreograph the play so that communication is not bedlam. Pearce, et al. (1980) indicated that rules establish standards for and habits of behavior. For example, start a letter with "Dear" and stop at a red light. In CMM, rules also help coordinate the pecking order of the various hierarchical levels of pragmatic contextual meaning in communication. *Constitutive rules* specify the established behavior within a given context. For example, kissing in greeting old friends in our culture shows affection; yet, in another culture it may show respect. *Regulatory rules* guide communicative interaction by telling what should happen next. For example, an agenda system for a business meeting reflects the existence of a regulatory rule governing the order of procedure for the meeting. *Authoritative rules* constitute CMM's communication dynamic structure. We explain them later in this section.

CMM views meaning, especially pragmatic meaning, in human interpersonal relationships as cocreated and contextually bound. CMM's basic concepts are *content* (semantic meaning) and *contextual* (pragmatic) meaning. Branham and Pearce (1985) indicated that the hierarchy of meaning is encapsulated in the *context* of communication. They defined contextual meaning as the social information we need to understand content. They differentiated contextual meaning from the *text* or *content* (goals and purposes) of human communication. Let's illustrate their point. For example, the content or the text of communication is reflected in actual conversation between a manager and a subordinate: *"How's your mother?" "She's fine, thank you."* Content provides the semantic meaning. *Context* determines the coordinated pragmatic meaning of this content statement. The context lets the communicators know if the content is reflective of a game of one-upmanship like "the dozens," or is an expression of concern, or is something else.

CMM's message structure concepts are of two types. The first type comprises a hierarchical series of concepts including speech act, episode, relationship contract, autobiographical life script, and cultural archetype. The second type concerns the identifiable patterns of communication over time. The hierarchical series of concepts includes a basic concept—the speech act—and the associative basic concepts of episode, relationship contract, autobiographical life script, and cultural archetype. Together these concepts provide the contexts that frame the pragmatic dimension of language. The concepts that identify the patterns of communication over time are the message structure concepts called repetitive loops. *Repetitive loops* are of three kinds: charmed, subversive, and strange. With repetitive loops, the link between communication text (content) and context becomes an identifiable pattern over time. Cronen, Johnson, and Lannamann (1982) indicated that *repetitive loops* exhibit reflexivity, a communicator attribute of being able to recognize what is happening within the speech act as affected by the episode, relationship contract, autobiographical life script, and cultural archetype. In other words, *repetitive loops* become the patterns of communication that help establish the nature of the relationship. They do so by tying together the semantic and pragmatic dimension of language and the various hierarchical levels of context. An example of a positive pattern that facilitates the coordination of meaning is a *charmed loop*. Charmed loops link the content and context of social rituals like weddings, funerals, anniversaries, and birthdates throughout the five hierarchical levels of act, episode, autobiographical life script, and cultural archetype. If the pragmatic meaning of these is consistent through all levels then the pattern is said to be charmed. The charmed relationship between text and context helps us know the appropriate things to say and do at a funeral or a wedding within our respective cultures. *Strange loop* is the name for an unwanted or destructive repetitive pattern. Branham and Pearce (1985) offered the alcoholic syndrome as a good example of an unwanted repetitive pattern of contextual meaning that occurs between content and the episodic and autobiographic levels of context. The alcoholic says, "I can control my drinking." Nonetheless, episodes of drunkenness contradict this autobiographic self-image. This leads the alcoholic to construct a new image, "I cannot control my drinking." Often, lengthy periods of sobriety lead again to the original autobiographic self-image, "I can control my drinking." Then episodes of drunkenness return.

According to CMM, humans cast the hierarchical concepts and the pattern concepts to achieve or not achieve the coordinated management of communication. In the example of a social inquiry about another's mother, the hierarchy of contextual meaning levels is displayed as **Table 8-1.** Our reading of the coordinated management of meaning by these two people is that the episode reflects two people who are coworkers in a family-operated busi-

TABLE 8-1. CMM's Hierarchy of Contextual Meaning by Type of Meaning System for a Speech Act: "How is your mother?" "She's fine, thank you."

	communication content occurring within a contextual speech act	
Low Level	Speech Act:	personal inquiry; response
	occurring within a contextual episode	
↓	Episode:	professional courtesy
	occurring within a contextual relationship contract	
↓	Relationship Contract:	coworkers
	occurring within a contextual autobiographical life script	
↓	Autobiographical Life Script:	self-image as caring professional
	occurring within a contextual cultural archetype	
High Level	Cultural Archetype:	view of employees as family

ness. In the context of that business, the expectation is high that a worker or manager will inquire about a coworker's loved ones.

Authoritative rules constitute CMM's communication dynamic structure. The authoritative rules represent CMM's communication dynamic as they justify (or don't justify) particular regulatory and constitutive rules. Cronen, Pearce, and Harris (1982) called the authoritative rules *metarules,* because they justify the constitutive and regulatory rules of a given interpersonal relationship, group, or organization. Let's see if we can illustrate authoritative rules. Recall the last time you joined a new organization. Did you ask a common question: *"Why do we do it this way?"* The answer illustrates a metarule. CMM possesses five authoritative metarules: (1) natural necessity (in the nature of things); (2) expert consensus (authorities tell us); (3) community consensus (custom and tradition); (4) unique to self/us (the way I/we do it); and (5) negotiative (open to suggestion). Pearce (1989) labeled the authoritative metarules the *logical forces* (causal, practical, contextual, and implicative) that justify the use of constitutive and regulatory rules in an interpersonal relationship.

CMM's major evaluative concept is communication competency, although its meaning is different than when the concept was employed as a technical concept for Constructivist Theory. With CMM *communication competency* includes the ability to learn and enact the rules of an existing system and to be creative and flexible in changing repetitive patterns. Cronen, Pearce, and Harris (1982), Harris and Cronen (1979), and Harris (1979) identified three levels of communication competency. The first, called *minimal,* is used to classify a person who barely functions in a communicative social system. The second, called *satisfactory,* is used to classify a person whose communicative skills mesh well with the social system's requirements. Finally, the third, called *optimal,* is used to classify a person whose communicative skills exceed the system's requirements. The optimally competent communicator is capable of changing the system by negotiating new communication patterns.

CMM's real-world benefit and value springs from its diagnostic capabilities. You can use CMM's concepts to examine the different communicative relationships in which you or others participate. As a rule, try to identify and reinforce charmed loops and alter strange loops. You can use CMM to identify, use, and change the constitutive and regulatory rules that undergird communication to facilitate the coordinated management of meaning. A number of studies confirm CMM's real-world value. For example, Buchli and Pearce (1974) applied CMM to improving such communicative skills as person-centered listening. Cronen, Pearce, and Harris (1979) and Pearce (1977a, 1977b) used CMM to improve the teaching and studying of interpersonal communication. Harris (1980) and Pearce, et al. (1974) used CMM to facilitate family and counseling therapy. CMM also will help you determine the constitutive and regulatory rules of other cultures. As well, it will help you pinpoint where cultures collide communicatively.[7]

Dialectical Relationship Theory (DRT)

Dialectical Relationship Theory identifies the dyadic (two-person) communication strategies necessary for coping with the dialectical tensions (push–pull) endemic to close personal relationships. The goal is for the couple to "successfully manage over time the dynamic interplay of opposing tendencies" (Braithwaite & Baxter, 1995, pp. 180–181). The tensions arise between the oppositional centrifugal forces that push the relationship apart and centripetal forces that bond or pull it together (Baxter, 1992b). Rawlins (1989) described

DRT as systems thinking about the innate contradictions that affect relationship activity, change, and relationship management.

Baxter (1988, 1992b) indicated that DRT's dialectical tension is a non-Marxist dialectic derived from the early twentieth-century Russian philosopher, Mikhail Bakhtin. For Bakhtin, dialogue between partners served to "fuse their perspectives through interaction but without losing their differential voices" (Baxter, 1992b, p. 331). The dialectic of oppositions in close, personal relationships is multifaceted, continuous, and in constant flux. The oppositions necessitate an ongoing dialogue between relational partners (Baxter & Montgomery, 1996).

DRT's basic concept and unit of analysis is the dyadic speech event, sometimes called the speech genre (Baxter, 1992b). A *dyadic speech event* is a jointly enacted communication event, that occurs over time, by which the fabric of the relationship is woven (Baxter, 1992b; Goldsmith & Baxter, 1996). Baxter and Philpott (1982) also identified such associative basic concepts as distinctiveness, consistency, and consensus. These concepts identify the interactive qualities of dyadic speech events and serve to characterize the various types of social information present in them. *Distinctiveness* refers to the degree to which the social information used to understand is unique to a given couple or is still the product of the individuals who make up the dyad. *Consistency* refers to the degree to which such distinctive social information remains stable across time and circumstance. *Consensus* refers to the extent to which the couple's social information is validated by others.

To ground DRT, the researchers gathered information about dyadic speech events using retrospective self-reports and questionnaires. Then, they analyzed the communicative content by topic or type of talk, by stagic development, and by maintenance strategies needed to cope with dialectical tension.[8] Chronologically, in their program, they developed their communication dynamic structure concepts before developing their message structure concepts. They reversed the order because they needed to know the former to classify the latter.

DRT's dynamic structure concepts come into play even as the relationship begins. They mold the dialogue that occurs in the dyadic speech events. Baxter (1988, 1990) and Baxter and Montgomery (1996) identified six important dialectical contradictions that push a relationship together or pull a relationship apart. There may be more.[9] Here, we provide details on the dialectics researched by Baxter. The first three name the dialectics that affect the relationship from within. These internal dialectics include Autonomy–Connection, Predictability–Novelty (sometimes called certainty–uncertainty), and Openness–Closedness. The next three name the prominent tensions between the couple and the community. These external dialectics include Inclusion–Seclusion, Conventionality–Uniqueness, and Revelation–Concealment. The tensions inherent in the various dialectics constitute the theory's communication dynamic structure concepts. Individually and simultaneously, the pairs present a continuous tension in personal relationships. The irresolvable tensions created by these polar opposites necessitates continuous management over time. They function to explain the cyclical nature of communication in interpersonal relationships (Baxter, 1988, 1990).

Baxter (1990) and Rawlins (1983a) argued that the autonomy–connection dialectical contradiction is the most central to a relationship. The partners in a relationship tend to vacillate between the voices of connection and the voices of autonomy and respond to the demands of one or the other depending on the topic or the activity confronting them (Carbaugh, 1994). The autonomy–connection contradiction produces tension in the following way. On the one hand, as individuals, we want to identify with a partner. On the other hand, we don't want to lose our unique individual identity. For example, Professor Cragan's youngest daughter, Keary, and Professor Shields's only sister, Katheryn, both kept their maiden names on marriage to protect their respective professional identities as a mechanical engineer and an attorney-at-law.

Tension also flows from the openness–closedness contradiction. As humans, we need to disclose social information to achieve intimacy. Nonetheless, that same self-disclosure carries risk and makes us vulnerable as individuals (Rawlins, 1983b). Petronio (1991, 1994) developed a microtheory called Communication Boundary Management that explains how couples regulate this dialectical tension in committed relationships by relying on disclosure boundary management strategies. Examples could include such statements as: "My closet, my mail, and my e-mail are off-limits to you" or "I don't talk about past relationships."[10]

DRT's third dynamic structure concept is embodied in the tension innate to the predictability–novelty dialectical contradiction. A tension exists between certitude and mystery. Too much predictability in a relationship produces boredom. Too much novelty produces chaos, loss of control, and loss of anchor points. Relationship partners count on the repetition of certain routines and roles to provide predictability. Nonetheless, they must balance predictability against the novelty that provides excitement in the relationship.

Baxter (1993) noted that the couple as a unit faces not just each other but the outside world as well. In this case, the same dialectical tensions exist regarding how the couple relates to the larger society. Baxter (1993) renamed the three dialectics as they apply to a couple as a unit relating to society. She called them Inclusion–Seclusion, Conventionality–Uniqueness, and Revelation–Concealment. Inclusion and seclusion concern the desire for privacy and separateness as a couple versus the desire for connectedness with company. Couples tend to "honeymoon" alone. Grandparents enjoy "family" get-togethers. Revelation and concealment concern the tensions of describing your "coupleness" to others. The advantages of "going public" as a couple are offset by dangers. Do you really want to have holiday dinner with the family of your most recent "significant other"? Conventionality and uniqueness concern the pressure for a couple to conform to societal standards. Society's norm typically calls for dating for an extended period before engagement. Then the norm calls for engagement for at least a year before marriage. As well, society's norm calls for marriage before living together or having children. A display of uniqueness by the couple that goes against society's standard makes others uncomfortable. In such a case, tension arises. Does the couple risk the wrath of Mom, Dad, the church, or even Aunt Mabel and Uncle Hays?

DRT's message structure concepts concern the stages in the life cycle of a relationship. As well, they concern the coping strategies available to manage the dialectical tensions. The DRT researchers grounded a number of communication coping strategies designed to help couples secure satisfaction with, commitment to, and maintenance of their close personal relationship.[11] These communication coping strategies help couples manage the dialectical tensions. DRT's message structure concepts include at a minimum the six types of coping strategies. These include selection (or denial), cyclic alteration, topical segmentation, neutralizing moderation, neutralizing disqualification, and reframing (or integration) (Baxter, 1988, 1990). These communication coping strategies help individuals overcome the continuous effects of the dialectical contradictions. Baxter (1988, 1990) reported a study that grounded these coping strategies to the stages of relationships and tied them to specific dialectics. Let's look at the coping strategies in detail.

Selection or *denial* is a coping strategy that manages dialectical contradictions by focusing on one polar element and making it dominant while ignoring or denying the other

(Baxter, 1990; Baxter & Montgomery, 1996). Of course, if you transcend the autonomy–connection dialectic by favoring autonomy, then be aware that the relationship often ends. Conversely, if you opt for the connection side, then be aware that you sacrifice individual identity. Either way you go with the selection strategy, you are not likely to be satisfied with the relationship (Baxter, 1990). *Cyclic alteration* is a coping strategy that separates the bipolar dialectical forces at given points in time by first satisfying one polar opposite and then the other. For example, reserving Saturday night for connectedness and Thursday night for girls- or boys-night-out might satisfy both the need for autonomy and connection. *Topical segmentation* is a coping strategy that allows you to handle the dialectical tension by naming a content or activity that is associated with each pole. For example, Professor Cragan avoids disclosing his views on autonomy and connection by running marathons. Nonetheless, he has indirectly intimated that marathons are an autonomous activity for him. On the other hand, for most couples "dining out" is a connected activity. *Neutralizing moderation* is a coping strategy that enables you to weaken the perceived contradiction by limiting the conversation to trivial small talk rather than dramatizing the breadth of the contradictions contained in the dialectics. *Neutralizing disqualification* is a coping strategy that allows you to avoid the tension of the dialectics by neutralizing the conversation through ambiguity, humor, and topic-switching. *Reframing* or *integration* is a coping strategy that provides a very sophisticated response to the dialectics (Baxter, 1988, 1990; Baxter & Simon, 1993). With it, you transform the dialectics by viewing each as a good and not an evil. Also, with it, you transform the dialectics by finding something you can do in concert that integrates the dialectics. For example, couples could redefine their relationship and define the yen and yang of the contradiction as enabling bonding over disruption. Such redefinition might come from celebrating the view that opposites attract, absence makes the heart grow fonder, in diversity there is strength, on the holidays we're all family, and so forth.[12]

Among the communicator attributes explored are attachment style differences (Simon & Baxter, 1983), displays of affection differences (Rawlins, 1989), and the like. The presence of these attributes varies with where an individual falls on a particular dialectic. For example, connected couples are affectionate. Autonomous couples are distant. DRT's evaluative terms are relationship maintenance, commitment, and satisfaction. How couples manage the dialectical tensions affects each evaluative judgment.

Sabourin and Stamp (1995) presented an intriguing applied study of the dialectical tensions present in the communication of abusive and nonabusive families. They found that abusive families displayed unbalanced management of the dialectical tensions of autonomy–connection and stability–change. As well, the abusive families were more likely to choose the strategy of selection (denial), a strategy often employed by less satisfied couples (Baxter, 1990). Braithwaite and Baxter (1995) reported on the dialectics of *private–public, stability–change,* and *conventionality–uniqueness* that surfaced in their study of long-term couples discussing the renewal of their wedding vows. They found that the ritual of renewal served to "weave together their past, their present and their future commitment" and "enabled them to cope simultaneously with a variety of dialectical oppositions" (p. 193).

Face Management Theory (FMT)

Face Management Theory (FMT) enables you to identify, use, and manage face-saving and face-threatening communicative acts. A *face* is a personally and socially approved identity.

Ho (1976), noting that face is an ancient Chinese concept, stated that "face is never a purely individual thing. It does not make sense to speak of the face of an individual as something lodged within his person; it is meaningful only when his [or her] face is considered in relation to that of others in the social network" (p. 882). Ho's view assumes that face is a communicative interaction phenomenon, not a psychological trait or a sociological role. Face arises through communication when people come into each other's presence. Cupach and Metts (1994) defined face as "the conception of self that each person displays in particular interactions with others" (p. 3).

Goffman (1959) introduced the concept of face to sociology. He elaborated on the concept in subsequent works (1967, 1971). Goffman (1959) said that to observe face is "to study the traffic rules of social interaction" (p. 216). As such, face was not yet a communication concept. Brown and Levinson (1978, 1987) introduced the concepts of positive and negative face as concepts in their social psychology theory of politeness (Brown, 1990). Lim and Bowers (1991) conceived of three dimensions of face identity springing respectively from the human wants of, or needs for, inclusion, affection, and control first introduced by Schutz (1958). Lim and Bowers (1991) described the source of the three types of face identity: *fellowship face* that flows from our needs for inclusion and feelings of solidarity, *competent face* that flows from our needs for affection, recognition, and praise, and *autonomy face* that flows from our need to control our independence. Cupach and Metts (1994) indicated that, in normal circumstances, communicatively competent people mutually cooperate in the maintenance of each other's faces. They posited FMT to explain how we communicatively manage face-threatening situations (Cupach & Metts, 1994).[13]

FMT's basic concepts are face-threatening, face-saving, and face-giving communicative behavior (Brown & Levinson, 1987; Cupach & Metts, 1994; Lim & Bowers, 1991; Tracy, 1991). *Face-threatening* communicative behaviors include those acts that run contrary to the face wants of an individual. *Face-saving* communicative behaviors include those acts that help to avoid face loss or to repair and restore face once it is lost. *Face-giving* communicative behaviors include those acts that promote the face wants of another person.

FMT's major message structure concept is facework. *Facework* includes the activities and strategies that support or deny "the socially situated identities that people claim or attribute to others" (Tracy, 1990, p. 210). There are four kinds of facework: defensive, protective, preventative, and corrective. *Defensive facework* is directed at one's own face as an individual protects his or her self-image, identity, and autonomy. *Protective facework* is directed at the face of another to maintain his or her positive self-image. Praising another's abilities is an example of protective facework. *Preventative facework* involves the disclaimers and hedges that we use to avoid, or minimize, damage to face. Examples would include: *"Hear me out before you get upset"* or *"Hm! Let me see. I don't know."* *Corrective facework* attempts to restore or repair face loss through the use of remedial, fix-it, communication strategies such as apology.[14] Corrective facework is a "ritualized sequence of four moves—challenge, offering, acceptance, and thanks—sufficient to restore the social order [face]" (Metts, 1997, pp. 374–375). A *challenge* upsets the normal maintenance of face, an *offering* is an attempt to repair face, *acceptance* is the receptive approval of restored face, and *thanks* is appreciation for the acceptance.

FMT's dynamic structure concerns the tension caused by the trilemma of trying to meet all three types of face needs—fellowship face (solidarity), competent face (recognition), and autonomy face (independence)—for both ourselves and other people. Meeting these needs becomes problematic in salient communication interactions such as embarrassing moments (Sharkey & Stafford, 1990). For example, you may use self-deprecating humor to repair the damage of another person's faux pas. When a child unintentionally spills her or his milk, you may intentionally spill your drink so the child won't cry. You've repaired the child's competence face, but at the expense of yours.

Another problematic communicative moment may occur during those communication encounters where *power distance* (status) issues are present. For example, if your boss unexpectedly singles you out for praise in the presence of your peers, do you beam or do you become embarrassed. Similarly, you might go for a burger and fries with an exchange student from India. Here, you would work to save face with the exchange student by only eating French fries with your right hand. Ting–Toomey (1988) developed a cross-cultural negotiation theory using FMT as its point of departure. We discuss her Face Negotiation Theory in Chapter 10.

FMT theory requires one overriding evaluative term—interpersonal communication facework competency. *Facework competency* involves effectively supporting and confirming your face and the face of another. As well, it involves saving your face and the face of another when it is lost or damaged by effectively repairing and restoring face. Facework competency is classified into three types: face-maintenance, face-repair, and face-enhancement.

Several facework researchers identified the corrective facework communication strategies used to repair the damage of face-loss that occurs from such embarrassing predicament situations as faux pas, mistake, accident, overpraise, and breach of privacy.[15] For example, Cupach and Metts (1990, 1992) grounded several remedial communication behaviors (avoidance, humor, apology, justification, aggression, empathy, support, and excuse) to the situational predicament events that prompt embarrassment. As well, their research linked or paired certain face-threats with certain face-repair strategies. For example, they found that excuses surfaced more often in mistake situations, justifications in faux pas situations, humor in accident situations, aggression in teasing and ridicule situations, and apology in rule violation situations. Collectively, such studies suggested that apologies may be used effectively in response to most embarrassing predicament situations. On the other hand, justification worked best with faux pas. Cupach and Imahori (1993b) grounded these strategies to both U.S. and Japanese cultures. They found that Americans used humor, accounts, and aggression more than the Japanese. On the other hand, the Japanese used apology and remediation more than Americans. Again, Lim and Bowers (1991) grounded the three types of face—fellowship, competent, and autonomy—to observable reality. They demonstrated that the complexity of many predicament situations requires that you be competent in the simultaneous use of multiple types of facework such as use of tact, praise, and respect.

FMT explains important features of interpersonal communication. We have all experienced face-threats and face-loss. Likewise, we have all tried to save our face and the face of others. The research grounding this theory has occurred in both interpersonal and intercultural communication contexts. (Again, in Chapter 10, we present Ting–Toomey's (1988) application of FMT's role in intercultural negotiations.)

FMT provides some sound advice when it comes to the pervasive but problematic realm of teasing. Alberts, Kellar–Guenther, and Corman (1996) reported that teasing often results in a loss of face. They examined teasing about topics, appearance, romance/sex, abilities, teasing, and identity. They found that the subject or topic of teasing has little to do with effecting negative responses. The trouble comes when intent is misinterpreted and when paralinguistic cues are misinterpreted. However, those of you with a sense of humor, but no *sense* of humor, take heart. Participants most frequently reported neutral responses rather than positive or negative ones. On the other hand, 17 percent of the people studied reported that they have no sense of humor. That's why teasing is especially problematic in the workplace.

Unifying the General and Contextual Interpersonal Theories

Let's slow our pace a bit and take a rest stop. Let's think about how far we've come. We now can see that the six general communication theories explored in Chapters 2–7 and the four contextual theories just discussed provide a unified understanding of interpersonal communication. For example, Information Systems Theory tells us that information-sharing includes both semantic and pragmatic information. It also tells us that we must be careful that inadvertent conflicting messages don't travel actively (linearly), interactively, or transactionally at these levels of meaning. It also tells us that redundancy helps to reduce misunderstanding and optimize the flow of information. As well, we now know that Rational Argumentation Theory leads to better decision-making between interpersonal communicators. It lessens the likelihood that conflicts will escalate into physical and verbal abuse. Finally, it strengthens our convictions. Additionally, we now know that Symbolic Convergence Theory explains how the visions of reality in which we participate sometimes constrain and at other times foster interpersonal relationships. We now know that we must watch our use of fantasies because if we vilify another, they truly do become a symbolic devil in our consciousness. Similarly, we now know that Uncertainty Reduction Theory points to the importance of certain personal disclosures of social information that build trust and liking among interpersonal communicators. It also explains our use of routine scripts (Message Organization Packets) that help us sequence our interpersonal conversations. We also now know that other types of disclosure work to destroy relationships, especially when they escalate uncertainty. Then too, we now know that Narrative Paradigm Theory explains how the stories we tell reveal our idealistic/moralistic and materialistic values. It also provides the tools necessary to tell if the stories hang together (narrative probability) and ring true (narrative fidelity). It allows us to detect deception by others. Finally, we now know that Diffusion of Innovations theory explains the use of awareness, opinion, practice, advocacy, and resistance talk in our interpersonal communication that fosters the diffusion and adoption of new ideas. Then, when we add the four contextual theories, our explanation of the phenomena of interpersonal communication becomes even more complete. For example, Constructivist Theory explains how cognitive complexity improves interpersonal communication competence. It helps us to differentiate thoughts and feelings more completely and allows us to be more empathetic. Then, we now know that the Coordinated Management of Meaning Theory explains how interpersonal relationships are cocreated, but contextually bound by the episode, relationship contract, autobiographical life script, and cultural archetype that we bring to our interpersonal communication. Additionally, Dialectical Relationship Theory identifies and provides us with the strategies necessary to cope with the inherent push-us-together and pull-us-apart dialectical tensions we face in the relationship and with the world at large. It also tells us that such tensions are continuous and require on-going dialogue to manage them. Finally, we now know that Face Management Theory tells us that we must communicate with others so as to protect face (ours and theirs) to reduce embarrassment and foster goodwill. Taken as a whole, the six general communication theories and four contextual theories provide you with a unified understanding of the interpersonal communication context. **Figure 8-1** shows Corey, our communication graduate on-the-job, using one of the interpersonal contextual theories to good advantage.

"I recommend a screening program based in Constructivist Theory so that our employees will be better matched to the communication demands of their jobs."

FIGURE 8-1.   Communication Graduate On-the-Job

Small Group Communication Context Theories

Let's continue our rest stop. While resting, we will introduce the small group communication context. It is the second oldest communication context (public speaking is the oldest). Initially, this context centered on group discussion problem-solving methods. Students, in courses entitled "Discussion," learned a number of special "how to do it" communication theories such as McBurney and Hance's (1939) adaptation of John Dewey's (1910) five steps of reflective thinking, and Coon's (1957) or Osborn's (1959) "brainstorming" systems.[16] In addition, students learned leadership skills based on White and Lippett's (1960) or Sargent and Miller's (1971) studies of democratic, autocratic, and laissez-faire styles of leadership. The communication research conducted during this period mirrored the topics taught in the discussion classroom. For example, Dickens and Hefferman (1949), Keltner (1961), and Larson, C. E. (1971) characterized the research effort as emphasizing problem-solving discussions and leadership skills.

As noted in the overview of the interpersonal context, Barnland (1962) called for courses in decision-making in addition to courses in interpersonal communication. Discussion courses were, of course, ideal for studying decision-making in small groups. Then, beginning in the late 1960s, members of the discipline called for the development of theories to explain small group communicative behavior (Cragan & Wright, 1980). The calls asked for new theories that would explain the communication process of task-oriented groups. As well, the calls asked for new theories that would link communicative interaction behaviors to important group outcomes.[17]

The next twenty years witnessed important developments in small group communication theorizing.[18] Cragan and Wright (1980) reported that Bormann (1969) described a program of group research conducted in cooperative fashion at the University of Minnesota. That program grounded Role Emergence Theory (RET). As a heuristic outgrowth of that same research program, Fisher (1970a, 1970b, 1974) introduced the Decision Emergence Theory (DET). A decade later, Cragan and Wright (1990) reported that Gouran and Hirokawa (1986) had grounded Functional Decision-Making Theory and Poole, Seibold, and McPhee (1985) had developed Adaptive Structuration Theory. Then, Poole and DiSanctis (1990) introduced Adaptive Structuration Theory as an explanation of decision-making in computer-augmented work groups.

The 1990s witnessed the discipline moving beyond the study of task groups in the laboratory. Scholars began studying real-world nondecision-making groups and decision-making groups in natural settings. Works by Frey (1994a, 1994b, 1995) presented important case and applied research studies of these efforts. The contributors to his volumes drew on both contextual and general communication theories to explain small group communication. As well, Cragan, Shields, and Wright (1996) presented a unified theory of small group communication.[19]

Since 1970, the discipline has developed a number of important general and contextual communication theories that explain small group communication. You are already familiar with Symbolic Convergence Theory, a general communication theory that began in the small group context. In other words, its grounding research began in the small group communication context before it expanded to the public and other contexts. SCT explains group consciousness-creating, consciousness-raising, consciousness-sustaining, and

identity-building communication particularly well.[20] As well, the other general communication theories also contribute their respective explanations of communicators communicating within the medium₁ definition of the small group communication context. In this section
of the trail to understanding communication theories, we introduce you to four major context-bound explanations of small group communication: Decision-Emergence Theory, Role
Emergence Theory, Functional Decision-Making Theory, and Adaptive Structuration Theory. Again, to best understand the communication phenomena in each context, you need to
use both the general communication theories and the contextual theories.

Decision-Emergence Theory (DET)

Decision-Emergence Theory (DET) explains the complex communicative process that
problem-solving groups go through in reaching consensus about a decision. DET is the
culmination of more than forty-five years of research into the group decision-making
process. Beginning in the 1940s, Robert Bales conducted a research program at Harvard
University. His works (Bales, 1950, 1970) formed the basis for much subsequent research.
Bales emphasized the communicative acts that comprise the task and social dimensions of
problem-solving groups, the stages that groups pass through in reaching decisions, and the
major roles played by group members as they engage in decision-making.

Communication scholars continued the study of small group interaction in the Bales
tradition. They did so because Bales's studies focused on the communicative acts of group
members that explained the dynamics of a discussion group. The communication researchers demonstrated an interest in these same communicative acts. Crowell and Scheidel (1961) and Scheidel and Crowell (1964) discovered that problem-solving discussion
groups did not, however, traverse in a linear model through the Balesian stages of orientation, evaluation, and control. Rather, they discovered that a group discussion "spiraled"
from the initial orientation to anchor points of agreement on ideas as the group moved toward consensus decisions on different sets of problems.

Fisher's (1968) dissertation at the University of Minnesota, conducted under the direction of Ernest Bormann, formed a part of the Minnesota Studies of Small Group Communication. It provided the database for developing DET. DET explains the structure of the
communicative interaction in groups. Typically, some group members attempt to arrive at
consensus by offering proposals they believe will lead to a decision. Other members comment on those previously introduced proposals. Over time, Fisher observed both changes
in such proposal–response patterns and changes in the kind and amount of communication
that occurred.

Following Crowell and Scheidel (1961), Fisher and Hawes (1971) reported on a qualitative method, Verbal Interaction Analysis, used to identify the basic concepts of DET and
track them through the process of group decision-making. DET's basic concepts include the
act, interact, and double-interact. An *act* is a verbal statement such as, *"I like oysters."* An *interact* is a verbal statement and a verbal response such as: *"I like oysters." "Well, I like oysters, too."* A *double interact* is a verbal statement, a verbal response, and a verbal response
to the response such as: *"I like oysters." "Well, I like oysters, too." "Good, let's order some
for our next group meeting."* Fisher coded such verbal acts and interacts as showing interpretation, substantiation, clarification, modification, agreement, and disagreement regarding

the decision proposal(s) being considered by the group. Fisher's (1980) observation of the distribution of the functions of these acts and interacts over time produced the naming of four distinct phases of group interaction. The four phases (orientation, conflict, emergence, and reinforcement) comprise DET's structural concepts.

Orientation is the initial phase of group decision-making. During the orientation phase, the group answers questions about identity, purpose, and procedures to follow. Fisher (1980) indicated that ambiguity, tentativeness, and the search for insights characterize *orientation.* During orientation members clarify points of information, ask questions, and often quickly agree but are ambiguous and hide their feelings about suggested proposals for approaching the problem. Conflict is the second stage of group emergent decision-making. *Conflict* is "ideational dispute over decision proposals" (Fisher, 1980, p. 146). In the conflict stage, members recognize the direction the group is taking and appear secure in their verbalization of arguments, beliefs, and opinions. Clash is open and direct. The group members offer arguments and evidence to support their positions in this phase. Emergence is the third phase. The hallmark of the verbal interaction patterns of the *emergence* phase is the return of ambiguity, although the function of that ambiguity is quite different. In the emergence phase, the ambiguity is not tentative. Rather, the ambiguity reflects a form of retreat, that is, a modifying of one's opposition from dissent to likely acceptance of the decision proposal.[21] This emergence stage is the longest phase in duration. The emergence phase gradually allows dissenters to come around to the majority's decision so that consensus is reached. Reinforcement is the shortest phase. In the *reinforcement* stage, the group members reiterate their consensus and positively and favorably reinforce their decision. In other words, the group members give themselves a pat on the back for a job well done. Positive, favorable comments comprise more than 50 percent of the verbal communication during this phase. These comments show the group's commitment to the decision, and reflect the group's solidarity in support of it. Laughter and warmth of support for both other group members and the proposal mark this stage.

Poole (1981, 1983a, 1983b) and Poole and Roth (1989a, 1989b) coded the same verbal behaviors as Fisher in a series of studies. They developed a richer and more complex explanation of a problem-solving group's decision emergence. Their studies indicated that although Fisher's four-stage model explained the decision emergence of 20 percent of groups, a more complex, multiple-sequenced explanation provided a better fit to the decision emergence pattern displayed by most groups. Despite this minor disagreement over the number of phases encountered as most groups deliberate about decisions, Cragan and Wright (1995) and Fisher and Ellis (1990) characterized DET as possessing high utility in regard to explaining and teaching the communication processes that occur as problem-solving groups reach consensus.[22]

It's probably time for a rest stop on our journey. While resting, let's reflect on the preceding discussion. See if you can identify DET's communicator structure and its evaluative concepts. We'll give you a clue or two. DET's communicators are the group members who are attempting to reach a decision about the solution to a problem. DET's implied evaluative concepts are finding a solution (reaching a decision) and the workability of that decision (quality of decision). However, the evaluative concept most often used concerns whether or not the group reached consensus on the decision. Thus, DET's explicit evaluative concept is group consensus.

Role Emergence Theory (RET)

Role Emergence Theory allows us to explain the complex process of role formation and leadership emergence and their impact on member satisfaction and productivity. Bormann (1990) defined a small group *role* "as that set of perceptions and expectations shared by the members about the behavior of an individual in both the task and social dimensions of group interaction" (p. 161). Benne and Sheats (1948) first suggested twenty-seven potential roles that group members could play. These clustered into twelve task roles (for example, information-giver, evaluator, recorder), seven maintenance roles (for example, harmonizer, standard-setter, encourager), and eight deviant roles (for example, blocker, aggressor, dominator). Soon thereafter, Kurt Lewin (1951) offered his field theory of small group communication. With his field theory came the concept of a *lifespace* that exists within a group field. It is the sharing of the lifespace within that group field that fosters member interdependence and creates cohesion.[23]

Bales (1950), Bales and Strodtbeck (1951), and Bales and Slater (1955) argued that a group's lifespace contained both a *task* and a *social dimension* respectively within which group members soon specialized in certain kinds of communication. This specialization of certain kinds of communication thereby produced role differentiation such as the *social emotional specialist* and the *substantive task specialist.* The group's members who provided emotional support for the group served as social emotional specialists. Likewise, the group's members who helped the group get its work done served as the substantive task specialists. Soon thereafter, scholars in the communication discipline sought to determine how the lifespace dynamic and role specialization dynamic in groups led to role emergence and role stability. Specifically, they wanted to know how these specializations increased productivity and member satisfaction.

A group of communication scholars, under the direction of Ernest Bormann at the University of Minnesota, set about to develop a grounded explanation of group role formation. Their studies led to the positing and grounding of RET.[24] RET explains how roles form in small task groups. RET's first grounded principle is that "no group has ever been observed by the Minnesota Studies where role specialization did not happen and no such group has ever been reported by other investigators" (Bormann & Bormann, 1988, p. 100). RET's second grounded principle is that "a member's role is worked out jointly by the person and the group" (p. 100). RET's third grounded principle is that people play different roles from group to group depending on the task and the particular idiosyncratic composition of the group (Bormann, 1990, see especially p. 161). RET's fourth grounded principle is that "the group selects its leader by a method of residues" eliminating "members from consideration until only one person is left" (Bormann, 1990, p.205).

RET's basic concept is role talk. *Role talk* is the type of communication suitable for a particular role specialization such as task leader, tension releaser, and critic. Those who use RET to observe problem-solving groups look for specific types of talk that indicate the group members' contributions to a particular role. The number of roles created in a given group, or the number of role functions fulfilled, is idiosyncratic and depends on the size of the group and the complexity of the task.[25] Cragan and Wright (1995) argued that five major roles typically form: task leader, social-emotional leader (lieutenant), central negative (critic), tension releaser, and information provider.

RET's structural concepts accentuate the phases of role emergence and the patterns evident in the process of residues that leads to leadership emergence. Phase 1 of the two-phase process of role emergence is of short duration. Phase 1 results in the group's elimination of nearly 50 percent of its members from consideration as potential leaders. The group eliminates members for various reasons. For example, a member may be eliminated for being too quiet. As well, a member may be eliminated for being too extreme in their opinions. In addition, a member may be eliminated from consideration for leadership because she or he initially assumed the role of tension releaser to help break the primary tension that marks the beginning of the lifespace of any new group. Phase 2 of role emergence usually leads to leadership emergence. However, the phase is complex and may continue throughout the life of a group in that no leader emerges and there is continued conflict over the leadership role and who will fulfill it. Geier (1963), in a study of sixteen task groups, found that only one had an emergent leader who possessed an authoritative style and five groups never solved their leadership problem. Geier reported that after three months people continued to contend for the high status roles.

RET establishes four distinct patterns of leadership emergence (Bormann, 1975). In Pattern 1, the leader emerges with the help of a specialized role called *lieutenant.* A lieutenant is a well-liked member who supports the leader. In Pattern 2, competitors for leadership each receive support from a lieutenant. Pattern 2 encourages the leader contenders to struggle for a longer period of time. This pattern often leads to the losing contender assuming the role of central negative. The group must then work to turn central negative behavior into a valuable commodity such as critic (Bormann & Bormann, 1988). In Pattern 3, external or internal factors, usually unexpected, force a crisis on the group. For example, a particularly difficult group member tends to precipitate an internal crisis. Similarly, an external crisis may call for a person with particular task skills. Typically, the person who possesses the special skills to meet the external or internal crisis emerges as leader. In pattern 4, the struggle for leadership continues throughout the life of the problem-solving group, but no one leader emerges. Instead, leaders emerge for short periods, but are quickly deposed. Often, this pattern is related to issues of race, gender, and ethnicity (Bormann, 1975; Bormann, Pratt, & Putnam, 1978; Cragan & Wright, 1995).

RET's evaluative concepts include role formation, membership satisfaction, and productivity. The utility of this theory is found in its application to the training and development of work teams in professional organizations. Bormann and Bormann (1988) offered scores of suggestions for improving role formation, membership satisfaction, and productivity. They reported that more than 75,000 people have been trained in small group communication using RET.

Functional Decision-Making Theory (FDT)

The Functional Decision-Making Theory explains the relationship between competently performed communication behaviors, called *functions,* and the quality of group decisions. Scholars contributing to FDT's development confirmed that the competent performance of certain key decision-making functions leads to a high quality decision.[26] FDT traces its routes to Irving Janis's (1971, 1972, 1983, 1989) theory of faulty group decision-making caused by "the group-think syndrome." Janis examined seven decision-making groups involved in U.S. policy-making over a period from the 1940s to 1970s. He looked at cases like the aborted invasion of Cuba in 1962 (called the "Bay of Pigs Fiasco"), the Vietnam War escalation, and President Richard Nixon's Watergate cover-up. In five of the cases, Janis found evidence of the group-think syndrome. He concluded that group-think was responsible for the faulty decision-making that occurred. The highly cohesive but faulty groups exhibited group-think syndromes such as the illusion of unanimity, avoidance of disagreement, blocking outside information, forcing group conformity, and rationalizing mistakes. Such group-think syndromes appeared to push the groups to a false consensus. The false consensus developed from the group's decision-making defects. The defects included ignoring alternative ideas, failing to reexamine preferred alternatives, selectively choosing information, proceeding without contingency plans, rejecting expert opinions, and failing to reexamine rejected alternatives.[27]

The communication theorists developing FDT asked a different set of questions than Janis. Janis wanted to know the decision-making faults that caused bad decisions. Conversely, Dennis Gouran, Professor of Communication at Pennsylvania State University, Randy Hirokawa, Professor of Communication at the University of Iowa, and their associates set out to find the communicative functions that caused good group decisions (Gouran & Hirokawa, 1986). In so doing, they offered seven assumptions of the theory. These included (1) motivated group members; (2) nonobvious decision choices; (3) synergistic group resources; (4) task specifiability; (5) available relevant information; (6) a doable task; and (7) instrumental (goal-achieving) communication.

FDT's basic concepts are the problem and the solution to the problem. Its message structure concepts concern the rational decision-making functions that must be performed to reach consensus and maximize the correctness or quality of a decision. The participants in the FDT research program grounded four decision-making functions: (1) understanding the problem; (2) assessing requirements for an acceptable choice; (3) assessing positive consequences of proposed alternatives; and (4) assessing the negative consequences of each proposed alternative (Hirokawa, 1985, 1988). Let's see how they did it. Hirokawa (1985) created fifty-four, four-person groups and randomly assigned each a different agenda system from among reflective thinking, ideal-solution, single-question, and free discussion. He discovered that the type of problem-solving agenda system employed did not predict high quality decisions. However, vigilance in the performance of the four communication functions did. Hirokawa (1988) replicated these findings.[28]

FDT's other message structure concepts are idiosyncratic to whatever agenda system a group may evolve or follow as they solve a problem. However, the agenda must contain agenda points that at a minimum mirror the four functions. FDT's evaluative concepts are *consensus, vigilance* and *quality of decision.* Consensus (group agreement) and quality of decision are self-explanatory. Vigilance may not be as readily understood. Gouran (1982) indicated that *"vigilance* is a quality that individuals and groups sometimes display in processing information" (p. 22). It "reflects a sensitivity to the need for the careful and thorough examination of the information on which a choice rests" (p. 22). FDT underscores the relevance of sixty years of advice about the practice of group decision-making benefiting from the use of a viable, problem-solving agenda system.

Cragan and Wright (1993, 1995) indicated that FDT is important to small group communication because it allows us to rethink the relationship between quality group decisions and problem-solving agenda systems.[29] The theorists developing FDT demonstrated that the sequencing of decision steps takes a back seat to the competent performance of the important decision-making functions as consensus is achieved and the group reaches a decision.

Adaptive Structuration Theory (AST)

Adaptive Structuration Theory, according to Gary Dickson, Scott Poole, and Gerardine DeSanctis (1992, p. 163), explains how work "teams incorporate social technologies into their work." AST then explains the interaction process for such decision-making groups. AST focuses on the structure that is created and recreated through the generative and adaptive rules and resources of the group members. These rules and resources surface as the group members use an automated, computer-based support system to facilitate their movement through the decision-making process. As Poole, Seibold, and McPhee (1986) stated: "Structuration is the process of producing and reproducing social systems through members' application of generative rules and resources (structure)" (p. 247). Poole and his colleagues adapted AST from Giddens's (1976, 1979, 1984) Structuration Theory of Society. They then developed a special Software-Aided Meeting Management (SAMM) system.

Poole and Jackson (1993) argued that "an effective group must maintain a balance between independent thinking and structured, coordinated work. Too much independence shatters cohesion. . . . Too much synchronized, structured work . . . stifles novel ideas" (p. 287). AST accounts for and explains both stability and change within the group system. It accounts for stability because, at the surface level of communication, group members use rules and resources in a consistent way. It accounts for change because group members adapt rules and bring new resources to bear on the problem. In other words, the group is constantly creating and recreating its decision-making system. A number of communication scholars contributed to the building and grounding of AST.[30]

AST's grounding reflects four separate lines of research. One line compared structurational decision-making with less interactive decision-making theory and found AST better able to explain group outcomes like quality of decision and member satisfaction.[31] A second line examined the patterning and repatterning of argumentation in small group decision-making in terms of the group's structuration.[32] A third line of research concerned the development of a multiple-sequenced model of decision-making groups.[33] A fourth line of research involved the use of AST to account for decision-making by human groups working with computer-augmented group decision support systems.[34]

AST in part explains the structure of group interaction by providing an automated group-decision support system environment with features to support and encourage independent, private thinking, and convergent thinking. The group decision support system consists of a network of about ten personal computers and the SAMM software. AST's group-decision support system (GDSS) gives the team members autonomous, user-driven control over the decision-making software because they each have a personal computer. However, in addition to the autonomy feature, AST's GDSS provides automated record-keeping and automated recording of group ideas and actions, and an agenda system for coordinated group problem-solving (Poole & Jackson, 1993). However, AST's supportive, automated structure is not static. As people use it they adapt it, recreate it, and reinvent it for their purposes. Thus, a particular group's structuration is idiosyncratic. Nonetheless, redundant patterns across groups arise.

AST's basic concepts are the talk sequences contained in acts, interacts, and double interacts that represent task process activities, relational activities, and topical focus. These talk sequences occur as the group members use the GDSS system. AST's structural concepts are the structured patterns of group communication. Poole (1983b) identified "three interlocking tracks of group activity interrupted at irregular intervals by breakpoints and serving to accumulate a series of components for task accomplishment" (p. 340). These three tracks of the multiple-sequence model represent the talk that contributes to task process activities, relational activities, and topical focus. Poole and his colleagues discovered these tracks by observing the occurrence of the basic concepts of acts, interacts, and double interacts. AST's evaluative concepts include group productivity, quality of work, membership satisfaction, and group consensus.[35]

AST may well prove to be a just-in-time theory regarding its real-world benefit. As a worker in the twenty-first century, you will find yourself a part of computer-mediated groups. AST provides both the explanation of how such groups make decisions and points to certain principles for improving decision-making through group-decision support systems by way of the features built into the SAMM software. **Figure 8-2** illustrates the structure of the SAMM program provided to each team member.

Unifying the General and Contextual Small Group Theories

Let's slow our pace a bit and take a rest stop. Let's think about how far we've come. We now know that the six general communication theories explored in Chapters 2–7 and the four contextual theories just discussed provide a unified understanding of small group communication (Cragan, Shields, & Wright, 1996). For example, Information Systems Theory tells us that group members share both semantic and pragmatic information actively, interactively, and transactionally. The theory also reveals that group members use redundancy to reduce misunderstanding and optimize the flow of information. As well, we know that Rational Argumentation Theory, particularly the dialectical dynamic, allows group members to make better, more reasoned decisions. The force of argument also increases the group members' convictions that they have made the best decision. Additionally, we know that Symbolic Convergence Theory explains how the force of fantasy-sharing builds identity, creates and raises group consciousness, and contributes to cohesion and commitment. Similarly, we know that Uncertainty Reduction Theory points to the importance of certain personal disclosures of social information that build trust among the group members. Then, too, we know that Narrative Paradigm Theory explains how storytelling discloses the group members' idealistic/moralistic and materialistic values. The theory also makes the assessment of the probability (do the stories hang together) and fidelity (do the stories ring true) of the groups' stories possible. Finally, we know that Diffusion of Innovations Theory explains the use of awareness, opinion, practice, advocacy, and resistance talk in gaining (or failing to gain) commitment to the new idea (solution) and in diffusing it from the group to the world at large. Then, when we add the four contextual theories, our explanation of the phenomena of small group communication becomes even more complete. For example, Decision-Emergence Theory explains the complex stagic process that problem-solving groups go through in reaching consensus about a decision. Role Emergence Theory explains the complex process of role formation and leadership emergence and delineates their impact on member satisfaction and productivity. Additionally, Functional Decision-Making Theory explains the relationship be-

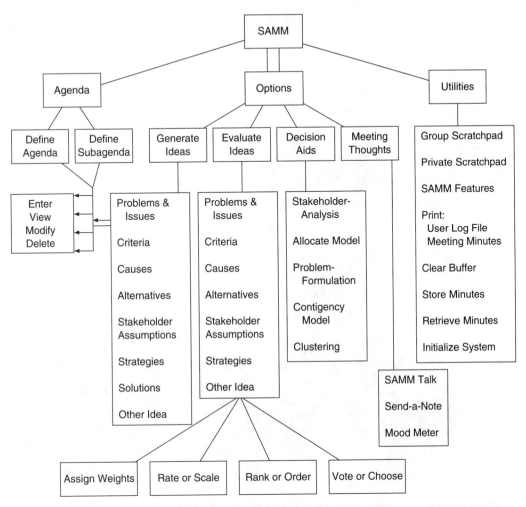

FIGURE 8-2.   The Structure of the Software Aided Meeting Management (SAMM) Program Provided to Each Team Member

From G. W. Dickson, M. S. Poole, and G. DeSanctis (1992, p. 168). "An Overview of the Minnesota GDSS Research Project and the SAMM System," appearing in G. R. Wagner, R. P. Bostrom, R. T. Watson, and S. T. Kinney (Eds.), *Computer Augumented Teamwork: A Guided Tour* (pp. 163–180). Copyright International Thomson Computer Press, 1992. Used with permission.

tween competently performed communicative behaviors, called *functions,* and the quality of group decisions. Finally, Adaptive Structuration Theory explains how work teams augment their work through automated, decision-making technologies such as SAMM. As a whole, the six general communication theories and four contextual theories provide you with a unified understanding of the small group communication context. They enable you to describe, explain, and predict human action in the small group context. They help you to control the common small group outcomes of quality of decision, consensus, group productivity, and member satisfaction. **Figure 8-3** shows Corey, our communication graduate on-the-job, using one of the small group communication contextual theories to good advantage.

"In the weeks ahead, we'll be placing the new SAMM software program on the network to improve the group decision-making of our participatory management program."

FIGURE 8-3.   Communication Graduate On-the-Job

Summary

This chapter introduced you to the communication theories endemic to the interpersonal and small group communication contexts. As well, it provided brief sections unifying the general and contextual theories. The chapter indicated how together the general and contextual theories explain communication within the interpersonal and small group contexts. In the first half of the chapter, we introduced you to four interpersonal communication context theories: Constructivist Theory, Coordinated Management of Meaning Theory, Dialectical Relationship Theory, and Face Management Theory. In the second half of the chapter, we introduced you to four small group communication context theories: Decision-Emergence Theory, Role Emergence Theory, Functional Decision-Making Theory, and Adaptive Structuration Theory.

   Box 8-1, entitled "Understanding Interpersonal and Small Group Communication Context Theories in a Nutshell," presents a synthesized look at the theories.

BOX 8-1   Understanding Interpersonal and Small Group Communication Context Theories in a Nutshell

Interpersonal Communication Context. This chapter introduced four contextual interpersonal communication theories: Constructivist Theory, Coordinated Management of Meaning, Dialectical Relationship Theory, and Face Management Theory. The general communication theories presented in Chapters 2–7 also explain communication within the interpersonal context, but Uncertainty Reduction Theory (Chapter 5) is particularly useful. The communication microtheories presented in Chapter 11, of course, provide a thin-banded explanation of communication in this context. Information Manipulation Theory, Interpersonal Deception Theory, Expectancy Violation Theory, Relational Control Theory, and Marital Communication Theory are most often included in texts on interpersonal communication.

Constructivist Theory (CT). CT explains the relationship between *cognitive complexity* and interpersonal communication *competency*. CT argues that people with *high* cognitive complexity are generally more communicatively competent than people who are cognitively simple.

Coordinated Management of Meaning (CMM). CMM explains how people cocreate meaning in and through communication and use semantic and pragmatic meanings to choreograph joint human action. CMM argues that three classes of rules—constitutive, regulatory, and authoritative—guide communication interaction as communicators cocreate their hierarchically based scripted reality.

Dialectical Relationship Theory (DRT). DRT explains the dyadic communication strategies necessary for coping with the inherent dialectical tensions that are endemic to close personal relationships. DRT posits that the primary dialectical tensions include autonomy–connection, predictability–novelty, and openness–closedness.

Face Management Theory (FMT). FMT explains the communicative rules for maintaining and repairing public face in communicative interaction. FMT argues that facework contains four classes of communicative strategies: defensive, protective, preventative, and corrective facework.

Small Group Communication Context. This chapter introduced four contextual small group communication theories: Decision-Emergence Theory, Role Emergence Theory, Functional Decision-Making Theory, and Adaptive Structuration Theory. The six general communication theories also explain communicative interaction in the small group context, but Rational Argumentation Theory and Symbolic Convergence Theory are especially helpful. As well, the communication microtheories presented in Chapter 11 explain thin bands of communication within the small group context. However, Muted Group Theory is most often emphasized in small group communication texts.

Decision-Emergence Theory (DET). DET explains the complex communicative process that problem-solving groups go through in reaching consensus about a decision. DET argues that over time small groups go through a four-stage communicative process of orientation, conflict, decision-emergence, and reinforcement.

Role Emergence Theory (RET). RET explains the formation of group roles as a product of the perceptions and expectations shared by the group members about the communicative behaviors of an individual in both the task and social dimensions of group interaction. RET argues that people compete for group roles and these roles evolve through a two-stage process of primary and secondary tension.

Functional Decision-Making Theory (FDT). FDT explains the relationship between competently performed communication behaviors and the quality of group decisions. FDT argues that faulty decision-making can be avoided if at least four communication behaviors are performed competently. These four behaviors are understanding the problem, assessing the requirements for acceptable solutions, assessing the positive consequences of each proposal, and assessing the negative consequences of each proposal.

Adaptive Structuration Theory (AST). AST explains how work groups incorporate communication technologies into their work on a group problem. AST posits that small groups create and recreate problem-solving systems through the application of generative rules and resources that incorporate ever-evolving communication technologies.

Chapter *9*

Public Speaking and Organizational Communication Context Theories

Communication scholars theorize about public and organizational communicative interaction.

Chapter Outline

In this chapter we introduce several important contextual communication theories developed to explain communicative interaction in the public and organizational communication contexts. As you recall from Chapter 1, contextual communication theories explain communication within the confines of one of the six traditional medium$_1$ contexts: interpersonal, small group, public speaking, organizational, mass, and intercultural communication. Recall also that The Communication Metatheory (TCM) recognized two types of contextual communication theories. Type 1 contextual theories use one or more theoretical concepts that by definition tie them forever to the context and Type 2 contextual theories begin by describing in a particular context but evolve into a general theory through grounding that demonstrates their explanation of communicative interaction holds, as well, across the other contexts.

In this chapter we present four public speaking context theories: Neo-Aristotelian Theory, Burke's Dramatism Theory, Vid-Oral Theory, and Image Restoration Theory. (Note that Feminist Genre Theory presented in Chapter 11 also is a microtheory about public address.) Then, we discuss four organizational communication context theories: Weick's Organizing Theory, Unobtrusive Control Theory, Artistic Ethnography Theory, and Organizational Assimilation Theory. As well, we encourage you to remember that the six general communication theories presented in Chapters 2–7 also provide rich explanations of public speaking and organizational communication.

Public Speaking Communication Context Theories

Public communication, the speaking of one to many, is the oldest of the six traditional communication contexts discussed in this book. The public speaking context dates back to the public speaking traditions of the Sophists, Plato, Aristotle, Cicero, and Quintilian. Mc-Croskey (1968) noted that this Graeco-Roman tradition gave us a speaker-centered theory for evaluating the persuasive impact of public speeches. However, we tend to center on translations of Aristotle's *Rhetoric* like those offered by Roberts (1954). Thonssen and Baird (1948) characterized Aristotle's *Rhetoric* as "giving effectiveness to truth" (p. 74). Aristotle defined rhetoric as the faculty of discovering in the particular case the available means of persuasion (Cooper, 1932). What differentiates rhetorical from literary criticism primarily is rhetoric's concern with the speaker's effects (both short-term and long-term) on persuasion rather than the literary concern with beauty and permanence (Wichelns, 1925).

In 1806, Harvard University installed a future President of the United States, John Quincy Adams, as its first Boylston Professor of Rhetoric and Oratory. Adams gave his last lecture on July 28, 1809 (Ried, 1988). The chair had been endowed for the purpose of giving lectures on rhetoric about the Graeco-Roman tradition in public speaking. Adams (1810) published his two-volume set of thirty-six lectures on rhetoric, which covered such topics as The General Views of Rhetoric and Oratory, Cicero and His Rhetorical Writings, Deliberative Oratory, Composition and Order, Delivery, Eloquence of the Pulpit, and Judiciary Oratory. By 1914, just over one hundred years later, the teachers and professors of public speaking had formed their own national professional association, The National Association of Teachers of Public Speaking, and published their first professional journal, *The Quarterly Journal of Public Speaking*. Today, the association, of which we are professional members, is called the National Communication Association and the original journal is now published as *The Quarterly Journal of Speech*.

As early as 1915, the founders of the National Association of Teachers of Public Speaking exhibited a scientific concern for the effects of public speaking. Scholars like Winans (1915), Hunt (1915), Woolbert (1917), and Knower (1929) published articles concerning the need for research, the scientific spirit in public speaking, suggestions as to methods in research, and scales for measuring the effectiveness of public speeches. These forebears of the modern theory did not want to take Aristotle at his word; instead, they wanted to test—using the newly created social science research procedures—just what contributed to an effective persuasive speech. Bormann (1980) indicated that since the beginning of the twentieth century scholars have tested the effects of a whole speech on the audience and the effects of specific parts of a speech, such as humor, emotion, or fear appeals. The testing continues. For example, Seibold, Kudsi, and Rude (1993) reported on the short- and repeated-measure longer-term effects, including on-the-job behavior change, of training in sixteen presentation skills.

The concerns of the War Department with propaganda and persuasion made the study of speech-making highly interdisciplinary during World War II. Early persuasion books by Brembeck and Howell (1952) and Minnick (1957) tended to merge the contributions of the researchers in the speech discipline with those in psychology, social psychology, and sociology. In addition, the Neo-Aristotelians took the classical rhetorical canons of *invention* (the ethical, emotional, and logical appeals contained in the speech), *arrangement* (the order of the points of the speech), *style* (the word choice and sentence structure of the speech), *delivery* (the speaking rate, volume level, and timbre of the speaker's voice), and *memory* (whether the speaker memorized, recalled extemporaneously, or recalled from notes) and merged them with the elements of one of Claude Shannon's systems models of the communication process. Thus, the Neo-Aristotelians, such as Berlo (1960) and McCroskey (1968), described the speaking or communication process as involving a source (speaker), sending a message (the speech), through a channel (visual, audio, print), to a receiver (audience).

The merging of the ancient and the modern into the Neo-Aristotelian theory had by the 1970s led authors of textbooks in public speaking and persuasion to emphasize a new receiver-centered, as opposed to the traditional speaker-centered, approach to persuasion. Illustrative texts included Larson's *Persuasion: Reception and Responsibility* (1973), Pfau and Parrott's *Persuasive Communication Campaigns* (1993), and Beebe and Beebe's *Public Speaking: An Audience-Centered Approach* (1991).

Black (1965) gained a measure of fame with his indictments of the Neo-Aristotelian Theory of speechmaking and speech criticism. His attack on the theory helped to legitimize the discipline's embracement of new, non-Aristotelian, theories to explain the effectiveness of speechmaking and aid in its criticism. The new approaches included Bitzer's (1968) rhetorical situation, Burke's (1968) Dramatism, Bormann's (1972) fantasy theme analysis, and Fisher's (1973) conflicting dynamic structure elements of the American Dream.[1] Of course, you've already studied Bormann's fantasy theme analysis and Fisher's competitive strains of the American Dream when you read Chapters 4 and 6. The explanations of communicators communicating in a medium provided by those two general theories exhibit much power when used as recipes for constructing a public speech. With Benoit's (1995a/b) Image Restoration Theory, presented in this chapter, you will see the extension of Bitzer's (1968) rhetorical situation. With Burke's Dramatism Theory, you will see one of the original non-Aristotelian rhetorics popularized within the discipline.

We begin the chapter with what is today called the Neo-Aristotelian Theory (NAT) of public speaking. In the form presented, it is the culmination of 2500 years of contributors to the theory. Of course, Aristotle was among the first.

Neo-Aristotelian Theory (NAT)

Neo-Aristotelian Theory (NAT) is a communication theory that explains the force of persuasive speeches and messages that effect changes in the attitudes, beliefs, values, and behaviors of audiences. As indicated, many people have contributed to the line of research that supports this theory. Since Aristotle, the non-twentieth century contributors have included Cicero, a Roman, with his *De Oratore* (1891), Quintilian, a Roman orator, with his *Institutes of Oratory* (1856), John Whately, an Englishman, with his *Elements of Rhetoric* (1828), and John Quincy Adams, an American, with his *Lectures on Rhetoric and Oratory* (1810). To this roster must be added the twentieth century contributors discussed in this Chapter.

NAT possesses at least three important assumptions. NAT's epistemological assumption is contained in Aristotle's definition of rhetoric, "The faculty of observing in any given case the available means of persuasion" (Aristotle, Roberts' trans., p. 24), which included finding the appropriate inartistic and artistic proofs (Aristotle, Roberts' trans., pp. 22–24). NAT's important ontological assumption is that humans persuade through and are persuaded by communication (Aristotle, Roberts' trans., pp. 19–24). NAT's axiomatic assumption is that the cooperative actions gained through ethical persuasion in the name of truth and justice are good (Aristotle, Roberts' trans., pp. 24–31).

NAT's basic concepts are the inartistic and artistic proofs. The *inartistic proofs* are things that exist that provide proof such as driver's licenses, marriage licenses, deeds of ownership, and contracts for services. However, the most important modes of proof for discovery by a speaker are the *artistic proofs* of *ethos, pathos,* and *logos.* We visited *logos,* or logical proof, as we introduced Rational Argumentation Theory (Chapter 3). We would ask you to reread that discussion to refresh your understanding of *logos. Ethos* is the name given by Aristotle to the forms of ethical proof available to the speaker, that is, the speaker's intelligence, truthfulness, and goodwill toward the audience. Aristotle called *ethos* the most influential element in persuasion, prompting many modern scholars to conduct research on the concept to confirm or deny his assertion. These modern scholars referred to the *ethos* concept as *source credibility.*

Haiman (1949) initiated the social scientific grounding of the dimensions of the classical concept of *ethos.* McCroskey (1993) reported that Berlo and Lemert (1961) reconfirmed Aristotle's *intelligence* and *character* dimensions of *ethos* and added a new dimension called *dynamism.* McCroskey (1966) quantified the *ethos* concept to include the communicator attributes of *authoritativeness* and *character* with *goodwill* reduced to part of the character attribute. Hart and Burks (1972) identified a communicator element of *ethos,* which they named *rhetorical sensitivity,* that applies to both the speaker and the members of the audience.[2] For Hart and Burks (1972), a rhetorically sensitive individual exhibited the following communicator attributes that would heighten the feeling of goodwill toward the audience and the audience's belief in such goodwill: (1) accepts role-taking as part of the human condition; (2) avoids stylized verbal behavior; (3) flexibly adapts; (4) distinguishes relevant information; and (5) accepts diversity in communication styles. Hart and Burks indicated that these characteristics predominate, especially when one views NAT as either interactive between speaker and audience or receiver-centered.

In part two of *The Rhetoric,* Aristotle worked through a catalog of fourteen common emotions—calmness, anger, friendship, enmity, fear, confidence, shame, shamelessness, kindness, unkindness, pity, indignation, envy, emulation—to illustrate emotional or pathetic appeals. Of this list of pathetic appeals, NAT's modern contributors most often studied fear appeals.[3] Pfau and Parrott (1993) and Shields (1993) reported that the fear appeal research showed that a credible speaker would use moderate fear appeals when requesting difficult personal actions, would use high fear appeals when requesting simple social actions, and would direct fear appeals at the audience's loved ones rather than the persuadees, themselves.

NAT's major message structure concepts are arrangement and style. The ancients, like Cicero in *De Oratore,* talked about partitioning the speech into parts that included an *introduction* to arrest attention and arouse interest, a *body* of main points with the strongest first, the second strongest last, and the weakest in the middle, and a *conclusion* that reminded the audience of what had been said and provided an emotional clincher or *peroration* to round out the speech. NAT's modern social science contributors conducted studies that demonstrated the effect of structure, organization, and quality of arguments on messages (Greenberg & Razinsky, 1966; Shields, 1993).[4]

The social science studies confirmed many of the Ancients' message arrangement and stylistic guidelines to persuade receptive, neutral, and reluctant audiences. As a general rule, the social science researchers upheld the classical advice: be organized as opposed to disorganized; mix logical and emotional appeals supported by evidence; place strong arguments first and weak arguments in the middle; make use of counter arguments; use stylistic devices such as metaphors, analogies, similes, and humor; and use climax order to hold audience interest (Shields, 1993).

NAT's communication dynamic structure is the tension produced between a truthful rhetoric and a sophistic rhetoric. Plato, in dialogues such as the *Gorgias* (1871), argued that rhetoric is sophistic and dangerous because it has only the appearance of knowledge and truth and has the ability to make the weaker argument sound stronger and the stronger argument sound weaker. On the other hand, Aristotle stressed that rhetoric need not be sophistic—it can be the counterpart of dialectic. For Aristotle, truth made effective through rhetoric would inherently win out over sophistry and falsehood. Today we still have this controversial dynamic in the sophistic form of the spin doctors of politicians and the manipulated communication of public relations officers. Indeed, in the academy, the communication discipline is periodically challenged to show that it is not sophistic and is seeking truth as all other disciplines do.

NAT posits two communicator structure concepts: speaker and audience. Each exhibits unique communicator attributes: delivery on the part of the speaker and listening on the part of the audience. Cicero, in *De Oratore,* defined *delivery* as the control of voice and body suitable to the dignity of the subject and the style of presentation. In modern times, Norton (1978, 1983) and Norton and Warnick (1976) provided a typology of communicator styles that a speaker could adopt—animated, assertive, attentive, contentious, dominant, dramatic, friendly, open, and relaxed.[5] In addition to communicator style, such modern researchers as Addington (1965), Berlo and Gulley (1957), Bowers (1963), and Gunderson and Hopper (1976) studied the effects of variations in delivery on persuasion and audience perceptions of a speaker's ethos.[6] Shields (1993) reported that these studies indicated that persuasion could be enhanced if the source appeared credible, prestigious, verbally and nonverbally competent, attractive, and prompt, and used an intelligible, conversational, fluent, standard American, animated delivery.

Adams (1938), Ewing (1945), and Nichols (1948) introduced NAT's audience-based communicator attribute called *listening*. Listening is the process of recognizing, understanding, and accurately interpreting messages. As NAT began to view the audience as active as opposed to passive, listening increased in its importance as an audience attribute. Recall that NAT's communication dynamic centers on the tension between persuasion and propaganda. Distinguishing one from the other is in part the audience's responsibility and that responsibility is met by learning to be a critical listener. We spend half of our total communication time listening. Of course, listening is itself a construct and the discipline has witnessed half a century of agonizing about listening. What is it? How does it fit with short- and long-term memory? How is the testing of listening affected by recall and comprehension? How best is it measured? How do we train people to listen? The debate continues as we write this book (Bostrom, 1996; Thomas & Levine, 1996).

Wolvin and Coakley (1985) identified several different types of listening. The two most important are comprehensive listening and critical listening. Comprehensive listening concerns understanding what the speaker intended. Critical listening concerns the critical analysis of the message regarding such issues as source credibility, reasoning, evidence, and emotional appeals. Bormann, et al. (1969) argued that good listening exhibits three central abilities: (1) the ability to overpower distractions such as extraneous noise and the speaker's mannerisms; (2) the ability to structure content and see the main points of the speech and its supporting materials; and (3) the ability to maintain emotional control and not become overstimulated or turned off by the emotional appeals, that is, maintain some kind of objective distance.

Whether you see your future as a practitioner giving persuasive messages or as a consumer receiving persuasive messages, NAT is a two-edged sword. On the one hand, it demonstrates the powerful force of ethical, emotional, and logical appeals on the evaluative concepts of attitude change, behavior change, and belief change. In other words, was there persuasion? On the other hand, NAT empowers you with the skills of critical listening so that you can detect unethical propagandists and demagogues. After all, Parry–Giles (1996) reminded us that even democratic governments engage in covert propaganda efforts. Thus, NAT's final evaluative concept is ethics, just like Rational Argumentation Theory (Chapter 3).

Burke's Dramatism Theory (BDT)

Burke's Dramatism Theory (BDT) explains the cyclical and hierarchical nature of human relations as moving symbolically from order, to pollution, to guilt, then victimhood, and finally redemption. BDT posits that the rhetor describes this purification ritual in dramatistic terms to elicit identification with the audience. Marie Hochmuth Nichols (1952) introduced the discipline to Kenneth Burke's Dramatism Theory (BDT). Burke began his career as a literary critic in the 1920s. Although he lacked formal university degrees, he did teach at the University of Chicago and at Bennington College from 1943 to 1961. Thereafter, he held short-term teaching positions at a number of universities. Burke's theory is in juxtaposition to Aristotle's in a number of ways. Aristotle provided a treatise on how to give an effective public speech. Then, according to Black (1965), scholars turned Aristotle's *Rhetoric* into a cookie-cutter for how to do rhetorical criticism. Burke, on the other hand, provided criticisms of literary works such as Adolph Hitler's *Mein Kampf* (Burke, 1939) in which Burke uncovered Hitler's genocidal motives for the extermination of European Jews. Out of the many criticism applications of BDT has come advice for using BDT in speech-making.

Burke (1966, 1968, 1969a, 1969b, 1970) specified BDT's six ontological assumptions: (1) humans are symbol-using animals; (2) humans invent the negative (that is, thou shall not!); (3) humans' symbol systems separate us from nature; (4) humans are goaded by a spirit of hierarchy that divides us; (5) humans are rotten with perfection (we strive to improve, but always fall short); and (6) humans repeat the purification ritual—order exists, we sin, we feel guilty, we seek penance through mortification or scapegoating, we receive absolution, order returns for a while, pollution sets in, and we repeat the cycle again—throughout life.

BDT employs three basic concepts. *Motive-embedded symbols* are pieces of communication that indicate a verbal action or a specific conduct. For example, a president's "State of the Union" address and a corporation's procedures manual represent a verbal action and a specific conduct, respectively. *Clusters of terms* are groupings of symbols that often reveal, as well as provide, motives when viewed in their totality. For example such a cluster of words as *lady, young lady, girl, dame, matron, gentlewoman, handmaiden, maid, homemaker, housewife, little lady, little old lady,* and *wife* convey a symbolic meaning that we would expect an American feminist speaker to utter with contempt. A *representative anecdote* is a short account of some element of the text (symbols) that stands for all of it, or some document that represents the vocabulary that shapes perceptions such as a constitution (Brummett, 1984; Burke, 1945; Bygrave, 1993; Ewbank, 1996). Burke (1972, pp. 293–304) indicated that speakers often illustrate the "typical, recurrent situations" of life through the use of familiar entities, such as "works of art" that provide "equipment for living." The tragedy of Oedipus, the repetitive dangers portrayed in movie serials like *The Perils of Pauline,* or the entrepreneurial successes of Horatio Alger's heroes are examples of works of art that might serve as representative anecdotes that provide equipment for living.

Burke (1945) believed that you should view symbolic actions like speeches, documents, and novels as dramas. This is so because by nature humans use symbols dramatistically. What Burke (1968) called his *dramatistic hexad* contains BDT's message structure concepts of act, scene, agent, agency, purpose, and attitude. An *act* is what takes place in the drama, that is, the motivated symbolic action. The act is the central term of the hexad and everything else in the hexad flows from and around it. *Scene* is more than just a place where the act occurs; it is the type of place in which the action of the drama unfolds. *Agent* is the character mentioned in the speech who did the act. *Agency* is the means by which the act occurred or how the act occurred. *Purpose* is the ultimate goal of the symbolic act. *Attitude* is a special attribute of the agent that affects verbal action such as an agent's predisposition. Burke (1968) gave several examples of predisposition, such as "the attitude of 'humility' that leads to the act of obedience or the attitude of 'pride' that leads to the act of disobedience" (p. 450). Turned to the task of speech-making, the hexad can also serve as a means of explaining action through speeches.[7]

A number of communication scholars conducted studies to discover the identification strategies used by speakers, whether attorneys, judges, politicians, ministers, or spokespersons for organizations. Typically, these scholars used a ratio analysis of the dramatistic hexad to uncover the identification strategies. For example, Hample (1979) explored how participants in the legal system employed identification strategies to obtain favorable outcomes in cases. Ritter (1985) examined the perjury trial of Alger Hiss and showed how Burkeian identification occurred. Bennett (1978, 1979) viewed trial communication as storytelling and used the hexad as a means for analyzing the lawyers' attempts to produce identification with the jury.[8]

In 1965, we benefited from a short seminar taught by Burke at the University of Missouri—Kansas City. Burke had just completed the *Rhetoric of Religion.* In the seminar, he explained his Iron Law of History that characterizes BDT's dynamic structure concept named the *purification ritual* (also see Burke, 1970, pp. 4–5). The *purification ritual* is an ever-repeating cycle of first order, then pollution, then guilt, then redemption through scapegoating or mortification, and a return to order followed by pollution again contaminating order. Klumpp and Hollihan (1979) used the purification ritual to explain the firing (scapegoating) of Secretary of Agriculture, Earl Butz, for his racist comments to a reporter; they noted that the scapegoating left racism intact in U.S. society. Brummett (1981) examined how scapegoating and mortification operates in presidential campaign rhetoric. Appel (1987) employed the purification ritual to explain the success of former Moral Majority leader, the Rev. Jerry Falwell. Benoit, Gullifor, and Panici (1991) found that the purification ritual explained the evolution of Reagan's defensive discourse in denying any wrongful acts concerning the illegal sale of arms to Iran and subsequent illegal diversion of the money to support the Contras rebels in El Salvador.

The fertile medium$_2$ in which BDT propagates and grows includes two substances. First, BDT grows where there is *hierarchy*. As well, it grows where there is *mystery*. Burke, as we saw with BDT's assumptions, assumes that hierarchy is everywhere, and if not, humans create it. Without hierarchy, the purification ritual would not continue recycling. Similarly, without hierarchy, or the symbolic reconstitution of hierarchies, there would not be mystery. *Mystery* concerns one's lack of knowledge, information, and understanding of those who are not your peers, or those hierarchical orders that have gone before. Indeed, Burke (1969b, pp. 174, 205) characterized mystery as a rhetorical "device" for actively "maintaining cultural cohesion" and "unity of action" among the diverse positions in hierarchies. As well, mystery helps inhibit criticism. The loss of mystery leads to changes in the cultural order or hierarchy. In other words, the loss of mystery leads to pollution. It's like Dorothy going behind the curtain with the Wizard. Lose the mystery; return to Kansas!

Burke's was a "new" rhetoric because he labeled speech-making, not as the art of discovering ethos, pathos, and logos, but as the art of presenting the purification ritual in such a way that identification occurred between speaker and audience. Thus, *identification* replaced persuasion in NAT as the major evaluative concept of the new Burkeian rhetoric. *Identification*—or as Burke (1950/1969b) said, "the use of language as a symbolic means of inducing cooperation" (p. 43)—serves as BDT's central evaluative term.

Burke offered identification as both a means to an end and an end in itself in his new rhetoric (Tompkins, et al., 1975, p. 137). Burke suggested that identification exhibits three rhetorical uses. The first "flowers in such usages as that of a politician who, though rich, tells humble constituents of his humble origins" (Burke, 1972, p. 28). The second involves disparate groups or disputing parties who "join forces against a common enemy" or a politician deflecting criticism of policies because to discuss them "reinforces the claims of the nation's enemies" (p. 28). The third and "major power of identification derives from situations in which it goes unnoticed" (p. 28). Burke suggested the use of the word *we* as his "prime example" of creating identification, as in the expression " 'we' are at war" (p. 28). Burke also suggested that identification with a speech rests in the ratios of the hexad. For example, is the scene dominating the agent? If a speaker describes people "living in a boiling, churning cauldron of poverty" then the scene dominates—it calls forth—the act committed by the agent. If you are a Sorority Sally talking to a Fraternity Freddie, it's relatively easy to achieve identification. On the other hand, how do you achieve identification when talking to G. D. Independent? It's a useful question. You might stress your commonality as majors in the communication department or as struggling graduate students. Such a tactic to induce cooperation would involve the use of an agency dominating over agent ratio.

BDT has proved robust in demonstrating real-world benefits. For example, Elwood, Dayton, and Richard (1995, pp. 272–273) called for training outreach workers in Burke's Dramatism Theory to help improve identification and reduce illegal drug usage. Smith and Golden (1988) reported that the success of incumbent Senator Jesse Helms, against his opponent Governor James Hunt in the 1984 North Carolina senate race, sprang from his use of the soap opera representative anecdote in his television advertisements. Messner (1996) relied on BDT's purification ritual to analyze and criticize constructively the popular, alcohol-inspired, codependency, "road to recovery" literature. Her goal was to use the rhetorician's art to improve the diagnostic capabilities of professional counselors. Coombs, relying on Burke's Dramatism Theory and Image Restoration Theory (presented later in this section), identified five communication strategies for crisis management: nonexistent (denial), distancing (justification), ingratiating strategies (bolstering), mortification strategies (repentance), and suffering strategies (company as victim) (1995).

Other scholars advised those who would challenge the social order. Using the purification ritual, Carlson (1992) explained the rise and fall of the nineteenth century Female Moral Reform Movement. She demonstrated that rhetoric following the purification ritual worked to build identification among the members of a social movement. However, she advised that a movement must be careful in its selection of a scapegoat. Vanderford (1989) employed the purification ritual to clarify the vilification strategies used by the members of the pro-life and pro-choice movements regarding abortion. Griffin (1964, 1969) used BDT's purification ritual to advise that all social movements begin with a resounding "No!" to the existing social order. As well, these scholars advised those who would change the social order to carefully follow the steps of the purification ritual. Cathcart (1978) advised that the movement should be confrontational. Simons, Chesebro, and Orr (1973) cautioned against a movement associating with political campaigns.

Again, it's time for a rest stop on our trail to understanding communication theories to see how far we've come. In reflecting on the competencies to be derived from Burke's Dramatism we would point out that, although you may not want to start a new social movement, you should now see BDT's application to everyday life. BDT works well as a tool for critiquing public speeches and provides a useful guide for inventing an effective public speech.

Vid-Oral Theory (VOT)

Lance Haynes (1988, 1989, 1990), a professor of speech and media studies at the University of Missouri—Rolla, offered a theory of public speaking based on the resurgent orality flowing from our media dominated culture. Haynes posited the Vid-Oral Theory (VOT) of public speaking by drawing together the mass media ideas of Chesebro (1984, 1989), Innis (1972), Gumpert and Cathcart (1985), McLuhan (1964), and McLuhan and Fiore (1967); the conscious awareness ideas of Howell (1982); and the literacy and orality ideas of Ong (1980, 1982).

VOT assumes that a new orality is developing—a complement to the old orality based in writing—due to the mirroring of the electronic media. As Haynes (1990) put it, "we are increasingly bombarded with 'vid-oral' communication, [and] increasingly responsive to and informed by electronically simulated experience" (p. 91). The result is that we are learning "to monitor and respond to the ongoing [media] without conscious interference"

(p. 95). Much like Ong's (1980) view that preliterate humans engaged in decision-making by weighing their experience against myths and stories, new features of vid-oral communication stress both phenomenal (real) experience with mediated experience. Haynes viewed the vid-oral environment as functioning to provide our "experience." He argued that epistemologically we convert personal, interpersonal, and mediated information about events into the "shared knowledge of such events' meanings" (p. 96).

With VOT, the basic concept is the *meaning* or interpretation of reality derived from the process of the vid-oral experience. Indeed, "tradition shared through oral and now vid-oral process may create the most 'real' experience of all" (Haynes, 1990, p. 96). The message structure of a vid-oral speech stresses stories, narratives, anecdotes, and fantasy themes to develop a *subject* as experience. As well, it emphasizes a *style* that will create intimacy with the audience. Haynes argues that Burke's Dramatism Theory (see previous section), Symbolic Convergence Theory (see Chapter 4), and Narrative Paradigm Theory (see Chapter 6) are friendly to the speech development and presentation requirements of VOT.

VOT's communication dynamic structure focuses on the stress arising in speech-making that occurs between the dual constraints of the formal orality based in the written tradition of manuscripts, outlines, and notes and the freedom of orality based in the emergent video tradition of stories, narratives, motive-embedded symbols, representative anecdotes, fantasy themes, fantasy types, and so forth.

One of VOT's evaluative concepts concerns the *altering* of an audience's predispositions. Haynes (1990) indicated that this altering is accomplished by the speaker "simulating experience" through the use of stories, anecdotes, and fantasy themes appropriate to the desired version of reality. This version of reality should accommodate "all relevant facts" (p. 98). Accommodating the relevant facts is accomplished by the speaker's judicious consideration, during preparation, of the various ways the audience's counter-fantasies and counter-stories might affect the interpretation of the facts. Finally, altering predispositions comes by "striving to achieve an intimate relationship with each member of the audience." This *intimate relationship,* another evaluative concept, comes through the speaker's use of memorable narratives, stories, anecdotes, and fantasy themes (pp. 98–100). Thus, *memorable* also serves as an evaluative term.

We've included VOT for several reasons. First, it illustrates the use of principlelike relationship statements among its concepts. Second, it draws together scholarly thinking typically found in mass communication classes to inform the creation of public speaking communication. That linkage also helps us remind you that the traditional communication contexts exhibit a certain artificiality. Finally, we included VOT because it meshes basic concepts from Burke's Dramatism Theory, Narrative Paradigm Theory, and Symbolic Convergence Theory to illustrate their use in the public speaking communication context.

Image Restoration Theory (IRT)

Image Restoration Theory (IRT) explains the image restoration strategies necessary to the repair of the good name of individuals and/or organizations. Developed by William Benoit, a professor of communication at the University of Missouri, IRT posits that several image repair strategies exist that help restore the tarnished image of a person or organization. The strategies include denial, evasion of responsibility, reducing the offensiveness of the act, correcting the wrong, and mortification (self-humiliation).

The theory begins from the presupposition that a public attack on one's image has occurred and an audience perceives that the individual or corporation is responsible. Thus the person attacked, or a spokesperson for an attacked organization, must respond. Image Restoration Theory (IRT) evolved from the study of this special type of epideictic or special occasion speaking, known as apology. You are probably most familiar with some of the famous apologies that scholars have studied, like Bill Clinton's "I Didn't Inhale Marijuana" press conference speech and John Kennedy's "Bay of Pigs Fiasco" speech about an aborted attempt to invade Cuba in 1962. These are just two instances of a long line of apology speeches. For example, Baskerville (1952) studied Richard Nixon's "Checkers" speech that concerned Nixon's attempt to assure the U.S. public that he had not used campaign contributions for personal advantage. Benoit (1982, 1988) reviewed, respectively, Ted Kennedy's "Chappaquiddick" and Richard Nixon's "Watergate" apologies. The Chappaquiddick speech concerned Kennedy's apology for his role in the accidental drowning of Mary Jo Kopecne in an automobile accident. The Watergate speech concerned Nixon's reaction to Congressional charges of presidential corruption and obstruction of justice. (It seems that Nixon was always apologizing for something.) In a similar vein, Brock (1988) studied Gerald Ford's "Pardon Nixon" speech. (It seems that others had to apologize, too, when Nixon was involved.) As well, Benoit, Gullifor, and Panici (1991) studied Ronald Reagan's "Iran-Contra Affair" apology. This speech concerned the illegal funding of a civil war in Guatemala by the White House staff. Benoit and Hanczor (1994) analyzed Tonya Harding's "Olympic Try-Out Attack" speech. Ms. Harding, in a moment of competitive zeal, hired a thug to attack a primary competitor with a night stick. Each of these speeches represented a defense when the person had been attacked. Such attacks were sometimes for cause and sometimes not.

Individuals are not alone in the need to make apologies. Scholars have also noted that corporations engage in apology and image restoration communication. For example, Brinson and Benoit (1996) studied Dow-Corning's "Breast Implant Affair." Benoit (1995a) and William and Treadaway (1992) examined Exxon's "Valdez Oil Spill." As well, Benoit (1995b) analyzed Sears's "Autoparts Scam."

From such grounding studies, scholars offered five primary explanations of how to achieve favorable effects from apology. For example, Rosenfield (1968) developed an analog model for comparing apologia speeches of two speakers facing similar circumstances ("My case was just like her case"). Ware and Linkugel (1973) uncovered four communication strategies (denial, bolstering, differentiation, and transcendence) used in speeches of apology.[9] Ryan (1982) developed a model that called for developing one's apology after a careful comparison of the attack and the defense speeches in similar apologia situations. Benoit (1995a), through a comprehensive study of his own and other's works, pulled together the most complete theory of image restoration. It is the one we will explain in this chapter. Finally, Coombs (1995) offered a symbolic crisis management theory that is similar to Benoit's, but draws heavily on the public speaking theory of Burke and is written from a public relations perspective with an eye for a corporate spokesperson managing a crisis.

IRT articulates two assumptions. The first is that communication is a goal-directed activity. The second is that the maintenance of a favorable reputation is a key goal of communication (Benoit, 1995a). IRT explains the communication process required to restore the tarnished image of a person or organization.

IRT's basic concepts include the particulars of the *attack* on one's image (the substance of the attack talk) and the *response* to the attack. What should the response talk look like? IRT envisions five classes of communication responses suitable to the defeat of the public attack and the restoration of one's image (Benoit, 1995a, 1995b). These response strategies comprise IRT's message structure concepts.

The *first* strategy available to counter the attack is denial. *Denial* is of two types: simple, straight-forward denial ("I didn't do it") or denial and then the blaming of another ("I didn't do it, she did it!"). If the denial communicative strategy is suitable and true, then a person or corporation can restore their image. Subsequent strategies merely allow the person or corporation to minimize damage.

The *second* broad image restoration communicative strategy is evading responsibility. Responsibility may be evaded in any of four ways: provocation ("He hit me first!"); ignorance ("I didn't know the ball hit him!"); accident ("No one is at fault!"); and good intentions ("We were just playing!").

The *third* broad image restoration communicative strategy is to reduce the offensiveness of the act. The offensiveness of the act may be reduced in six ways: bolstering ("Our company's been a good corporate citizen for many years!"); minimization ("There wasn't much damage and it will soon go away!"); differentiation ("We didn't steal the money, it was a computer error!"); transcendence ("Killing the abortion mill doctor was doing God's work!"); attack the accuser ("My accuser is a convicted felon!"); and compensation ("We agree to set things right with the harmed parties!").

The *fourth* broad image restoration communicative strategy is to correct the wrong. For example, tell the aggrieved that we've taken corrective action to see that it won't happen in the future.

The *fifth* broad image restoration communicative strategy is mortification (self-humiliation). With mortification, the person or the corporation confesses, apologizes, and asks for forgiveness—humans can forgive the sinner even when they hate the sin.

Although there appears to be a degree of autonomy in one's choice of an image restoration communicative strategy, the IRT theorists have discovered some general linkages between the type of accusation and the selection of an apology strategy. At the very least in their theory-building, they have provided some good rules of thumb to assist you in your choice-making. For example, Benoit (1995b) indicated that if an individual or company is at fault then it is best to admit the problem quickly, apologize, and set forth how corrective action will be taken. Such a combination of *admittance, apology,* and *correction* served the Atlantic Telephone and Telegraph (AT&T) Company well in regard to the service interruption of its T-1 trunk lines (Benoit & Brinson, 1994). Of course, as Benoit (1995a) indicated, Union Carbide contributed to its image loss by not following such a strategy with their Bhopal, India chemical plant explosion.

A second effective use of these image restoration communicative strategies is to deny wrongdoing by blaming a third party, but still take corrective action. Benoit and Lindsay (1987) concluded that the handling of the strychnine-laced Tylenol affair followed this second combined pattern. Of course, as Benoit (1995a) reported, it didn't do any good for Exxon to use this strategy when they were slow to implement corrective action regarding an Alaska oil spill.

Finally, bolstering is almost always an effective strategy. Shields and Cragan (1981) observed that politicians routinely repair their public image "by stressing their good qualities that have been ignored by the press coverage" (p. 194).

As Coombs (1995) noted, the management of communication crises is an important part of public relations. As a soon-to-be, competent graduate in your present academic work, we would expect you to become familiar with IRT. After all, we wouldn't want you to feel like a deer caught in headlights when a communication crisis occurs and you or your company's public image is attacked. As well, we believe that IRT provides a smooth linkage to the second half of this chapter, the organizational communication context. IRT helps us emphasize that a major communication activity of organizations is public speaking.

Unifying the General and Contextual Public Speaking Theories

Let's slow our pace a bit and take a rest stop. Let's think about how far we've come. We now know that the six general communication theories explored in Chapters 2–7 and the four contextual theories just discussed provide a unified understanding of public speaking communication. For example, Information Systems Theory tells us that speakers must optimize information through the use of multiple channels of communication. For example, IST, when used in this context, tells us that if we exceed six lines per transparency when using an overhead projector as a visual aid, we will increase uncertainty instead of reducing it. As well, we know that Rational Argumentation Theory provides guidelines for producing a prima facie case that would meet the burden of proof in persuading an audience to accept a policy change. As well, we know that the force of argument will strengthen the audience's convictions regarding the wisdom of the proposed policy change. Additionally, we know that Symbolic Convergence Theory explains how a public speaker can select fantasy themes, fantasy types, and symbolic cues that will chain out thereby producing symbolic convergence within the members of a given audience. Similarly, we know that Uncertainty Reduction Theory points to the need for speakers to engage in anecdotal personal disclosures that would reduce the uncertainty that the audience may have about the speaker's character and goodwill. Then, too, we know that Narrative Paradigm Theory suggests the use of value-laden stories that can have a parablelike effect on persuading an audience. Also, NPT warns that the stories you tell must hang together and ring true if they are to be acceptable. Finally, we know that Diffusion of Innovations Theory demonstrates how to coordinate a set of public speeches in conjunction with planned interpersonal communication to expedite the reaching of critical mass in the adoption of new ideas and products.

When we add the four contextual theories, our explanation of public speaking communication becomes even more complete. For example, for centuries, Neo-Aristotelian Theory identified the guidelines or rules for effective public speech construction as the canons of invention, arrangement, style, delivery, and memory. From the beginning, NAT pointed the speaker to the three most efficacious modes of proof: ethos, pathos, and logos. Likewise, we know that Burke's Dramatism Theory offered important principles for speech construction in terms of analyzing an issue by means of the purification ritual of hierarchical order, pollution, guilt, victimization (scapegoating or mortification), and finally redemption. BDT also suggested the use of a hexadic analysis to pinpoint key points of identification with the audience. As well, Vid-Oral Theory returned the public speaking context to the oral tradition of ancient Greece. It stressed the use of vid-oral elements of mediated reality as represented by narratives, anecdotes, and fantasy themes to alter the predispositions of audiences. Finally, Image Restoration Theory outlined a series of rhetorical strategies for repairing the good name of individuals or organizations.

As a whole, the six general communication theories and four contextual theories provide you with a unified understanding of the public speaking communication context. They enable you to describe, explain, predict, and control human action as it is engendered through the activity of public speaking. **Figure 9-1** shows Corey, our communication graduate on-the-job, using a public speaking theory to good advantage.

"With our customers, the product of the video age, we need a new public affairs speakers' training program grounded in oral communication. I'm proposing a pilot-testing of a program using Vid-Oral Theory. Through it, our people will learn how to prepare talks out loud and on their feet."

FIGURE 9-1. Communication Graduate On-the-Job

Organizational Communication Context Theories

The organizational communication context is among the more enduring communication contexts of the twentieth century. The members of businesses and organizations need communication skills. Puls (1917) published the first essay in the *Quarterly Journal of Public Speaking* on "Speech Training for Business Men." By the 1930s Dickenson (1932) and Rogers (1934) had written respectively on "The Influence of the Press in Labor Affairs" and "The Social Justification of the Business Press." In the 1940s, Dickens (1945) introduced small group skills to organizations with "Discussion Method in the War Industry," and Estes (1946, 1951) introduced interpersonal skills with his "Speech and Human Relations in Industry" and "Communication in Industry" articles. In the early 1950s, Cullen (1951), Clark (1951), and Freeley (1953) reported on the outcomes of communication training in the organization with articles entitled, respectively, "Teamwork and Productivity," "Wanted: Skilled Communicators in the Air Force," and "Speech among the Bankers." As well, other scholars applied general communication theories to explain effective organizational communication. For example, Dahle (1954), writing from the perspective of Information Systems Theory, reported "An Objective and Comparative Study of Five Methods of Transmitting Information to Business and Industrial Employees."

Of the six traditional contexts, the organizational communication context appears most adept at drawing on the six general communication theories (see Chapters 2–7 of this book). This context is also adept at using the contextual theories developed initially for the interpersonal, small group, public speaking, mass, and intercultural communication contexts. Indeed, the authors of organizational communication textbooks routinely describe the applications of various general and contextual communication theories to explain organizational communication.[10] As well, since the appearance of works by Pacanowsky and O'Donnell–Trujillo (1982, 1983), Putnam (1983, 1986), and Putnam and Pacanowsky (1983), these same texts regularly report the contributions of the interpretive or ethnographic approach to the study of organizations. As we shall see, the ethnographic approach sometimes relies on extant communication theories and at other times uniquely "discovers" the communication theory or theories at play in the organization.

Interestingly, in this chapter, two of the four context-bound organizational communication theories derive from theories you have already learned and a third, Artistic Ethnography Theory, often draws heavily on existing symbolic theories. For example, Weick's Organizing Theory is an offshoot of Information Systems Theory (see Chapter 2). Unobtrusive Control Theory evolved from a unique organizational adaptation of Burke's Dramatism Theory (presented in the earlier section of this chapter). As well, Artistic Ethnography Theory, which seeks to discover an organization's culture through direct experience, is, in many of its forms, a hybrid offspring of Symbolic Convergence Theory (see Chapter 4), Narrative Paradigm Theory (see Chapter 6), or another theory that is part of the symbolic paradigm constellation of communication theories. Only Organizational Assimilation Theory seems not to be isomorphic to another communication theory.

Weick's Organizing Theory (WOT)

Carl Weick's Organizing Theory (WOT) explains the organizing process as the attempt to reduce the amount of equivocality faced by humans. Weick (1979) assumed that humans organize through communication to reduce equivocality. Here, Weick's *equivocality* and Shannon's *uncertainty* serve as identical concepts.[11] However, Weick (1979) also assumed that humans act in accord with Darwin's notion of the survival of the fittest and strive to find the best strategies for overcoming equivocality/uncertainty, that is, they attempt to share the best kind of information to get their work done. Next, Weick assumed that an organization attempts to optimize the amount of equivocal information, so that it can do work at an optimal level, by identifying appropriate assembly rules and cycles (Weick, 1979). Finally, Weick (1979) assumed that organizing occurs within an open information system requiring the use of positive and negative feedback loops from humans engaged in interacts and double interacts. Thus, feedback loops help identify the assembly rules and cycles that optimize the level of equivocality that organizing humans face.

WOT's basic concept is information equivocality, that is, information that has many levels of meaning due to ambiguity, complexity, and obscurity. Weick (1979) assumed that if we're sure of the meaning of information then we don't talk much about it; instead we turn to routine rules and procedures for handling it. When using WOT to view an organization, one begins with a focus on the highly equivocal information that individuals must talk about in order to reduce that information's equivocality. Thus, WOT's main evaluative term is equivocality reduction which is akin to uncertainty reduction, in Information Systems Theory.

WOT's three major message structure concepts—enactment, selection, retention—form Weick's evolutionary, organic cycle, which can be a loose cycle or a tightly drawn cycle. Bantz (1995) indicated that the enactment, selection, and retention phases of organizing are respectively best characterized as the collective activity of organizations embodied in talking, interpreting, and remembering. People talk to themselves and others about the multiple meanings of equivocal information. Thus, the *enactment* part of the cycle is to recognize the equivocal information present in intrapersonal or interpersonal communication. Once such a recognition is made, then the information must be *interpreted* and acted on. Of course, the *retention* stage allows the organization to turn to its collective memory to see if it has a standard operating procedure (assembly rule) for handling the equivocal information. Studies by Bantz and Smith (1977), Kreps (1980), and Putnam and Sorenson (1982) corroborated the cyclical nature of the handling of equivocality. Another way of saying this is that the researchers demonstrated that people talked more about equivocal than unequivocal information. Of course, this conclusion derives directly from Information Systems Theory's definition of information as that which is new or uncertain (not known).

Because WOT assumes only interacts (interactional) and double interacts (transactional) occur in organizations, it's dynamic structure concepts do not mirror directly those of Information Systems Theory. Weick does not see the same war as IST. Rather, WOT's dynamic comes from framing the organization as an *open, mixed,* or *closed* system. Weick's bias is clearly in favor of the open system, if the organization is going to survive over time. Nonetheless, there is tension, here. Let's see if we can illustrate it. Your body is a living, open system that interacts with its environment, taking in air and fuel and giving off carbon dioxide and other waste products. However, if your body became too open with its environment—as with hemophilia or dyspepsia—you could bleed to death or dehydrate. Similarly, if you became more closed and stopped breathing or eating, you would die.

Based on his research, Kreps (1990) made six recommendations for improving an organization through WOT:

1. *Supervisors should allow adequate time for the processing of equivocal information, including time for discussions on e-mail, impromptu discussions in the hallway and lunchroom, and meetings. For example, does the professor allow you enough classroom time to talk about the case studies you may have been presented with in class?*

2. *The organization must correctly judge the amount of equivocality in a message and optimize the amount of time spent on it. In other words, a simple case study may not take a whole period, and to spend that much time on it may waste your time; on the other hand, if the case is too complex, you may not be able to reduce equivocality in one class period. In the latter case, you will not arrive at an answer, or come up with the wrong answer, or at least not the best answer.*

3. *The organization must register the correct level of the information inputs and route them to the appropriate members. You may know this problem from those classes that use teaching assistants. You may want to talk about the ambiguity and equivocal nature of the information presented in the class, but the TA doesn't appear to know enough to help you resolve the equivocal nature of the information.*

4. *Managers can facilitate adaptation to information equivocality by fostering interaction among organization members about complex problems. In other words, assign groups and task forces to complex tasks and individuals to simple tasks.*

5. *Concentrate less on the individual and more on the interlocking communication of organizational networks and groups. In short, get people in the organization talking together and manage that talk instead of managing the individual. In your classroom, this is a cry for collaborative learning and study groups.*

6. *Develop and implement training programs stressing teamwork, open communication, and group problem-solving skills. In other words, the context theories presented in the interpersonal and group communication contexts should help the members of an organization organize following Weick's model.*

Unobtrusive Control Theory (UCT)

Unobtrusive Control Theory (UCT) explains how organizations exert power over their employees by using corporate identification to foster conformity to company decision-making patterns, policy, and procedures. Its roots are to be found in the Dramatism Theory of Kenneth Burke as adapted to organizations initially by Burke and later by Tompkins, et al. (1975).[12] Here, identification is both a process and an outcome, that is, a means and an end (Tompkins, et al., 1975). The newcomer experience is a process of increasing identification with an organization until he or she sees the organization's interests as his or her own with the resultant feelings of belonging and similarity (Bullis & Bach, 1989, p. 275). The scholars contributing to UCT have indicated that the more an individual identifies with a company's goals, values, and mission then the more likely he or she is to make decisions consistent with the "company line" and follow the company's policies, rules, and procedures.[13]

UCT assumes that decision-making in an organization flows enthymatically (syllogistically) either from the individual's or the company's symbolic structures. For example, *All good employees identify with the company's goals; I am a good employee; I identify with the company's goals.* Because UCT is a derivative of Burke's Dramatism Theory, UCT's basic concepts are the motive-embedded symbols—clusters of terms and representative anecdotes—that identify, respectively, the goals, values, mission, policy, and procedures of the organization and the individual's goals, values, and procedures. UCT's message structure terms are the symbolic structure of the organization and the symbolic structure of each individual member. UCT's dynamic structure concepts concern the tensions between the individual's values–goals–procedures (symbolic structure) and the organization's values–goals–procedures (symbolic structure). UCT's evaluative concept concerns the gaining of unobtrusive control through identification. As well, job satisfaction and commitment serve as evaluative terms indicating the presence or absence of unobtrusive control.

Bullis and Tompkins (1989) provided the major grounding for this theory with their study of the U.S. Forest Service. They found that rangers who identified highly with the Service's symbolic structure followed the Service's rules and procedures. Conversely, those who did not identify did not follow. Also, they found differences over the years as the Forest Service went from a system of inculcating control unobtrusively to a chain-of-command obtrusive control system, that is, changing from decentralized to centralized management. Sass and Canary (1991) reported—from their study of six organizations in California (ranging from a lumber company to a savings and loan)—a high correlation between identification (unobtrusive control), organizational commitment, and job satisfaction.

UCT fits our everyday experience with organizations. You may have encountered a graduate teaching assistant (GTA) who is down in the mouth about your school and criticizes the policies and procedures that he or she must follow in teaching a class discussion section. In this case, the school is exerting little unobtrusive control on this GTA. Conversely, you may have encountered a GTA who is satisfied, committed, speaks fondly of the experience, and appears at ease following the syllabus, presenting lectures, and clarifying the assigned readings. From the perspective of UCT, this latter GTA identifies with the values, goals, and mission of the school and the class. Unobtrusively, the school-as-organization has influenced and controlled such a GTA.

Throughout the 1980s and 1990s, Americans witnessed a number of corporate mergers, buyouts, and takeovers and the resultant downsizing, right-sizing, and reengineering. Clustering terms like *downsizing, right-sizing,* and *reengineering* represent euphemisms for massive corporate layoffs and firings. UCT would predict that the managers of the twenty-first century will be working more independently of company policies and procedures and will display less of a commitment to the company because the Burkeian notion of identification that bonded the individual to the company has been violated and broken. You might ask yourself these questions: To what degree do I identify with the company for which I presently work? What sources of control does it have over me? Can I be fired (exert direct control) if I don't fit in with its procedures? Can it provide me with monetary incentives (indirect control from bribery) to enhance my conformity? Isn't the control that gets me to work for the good of the company attributable to my identification with the symbolic structure of the company (unobtrusive control)?

The simplest way to determine the force of this theory may well be to think about who is the teacher's pet in one of your classes. Then compare that person to the adult learner who commutes from out of town and who must get a passing grade to graduate this semester. Does the teacher's pet see the course in the same way as the adult learner? Who more willingly follows the course's procedures (assignments, readings, attendance)? We submit that the differences may be accounted for by the unobtrusive control stemming from the teacher's pet identifying with the values, goals, and mission of the teacher.

Artistic Ethnography Theory (AET)

Pacanowsky and O'Donnell–Trujillo (1982) were among the first to conceive of the organization as a culture. Bormann (1982) characterized culture as "the sum total of ways of living, organizing, and communing built up in a group of human beings and transmitted to newcomers by means of verbal and nonverbal communication" (p. 50). Jan Kelly (1985), following Bormann (1982, p. 50), indicated that "culture, complete with attitudes, values, norms, and rules, provides a context for organizational sense-making" (p. 45). In other words, the culture is symbolically created and in turn the culture becomes a force for human action. The culture approach to the study of organizations has become quite popular. For example, scholars such as Phillipsen (1976, 1992), Procter (1995), and Trujillo added the concept of symbolizing about *place,* thereby giving meaning to the cultural identity and cultural boundaries of organizations. As the discipline neared the close of the twentieth century, Daniels, Spiker, and Papa (1997) described three broad, interpretive approaches that scholars choose among to view an organizational culture: traditional interpretive, critical interpretive, and ethnographic interpretive.

The traditional interpretive approach relies on a general or contextual communication theory often drawn from the symbolic paradigm constellation of theories to serve as its means of making order out of the data that represents an organization's culture. Here, scholars often select a general communication theory such as Symbolic Convergence Theory or Narrative Paradigm Theory to find an organization's meaningful cultural themes, visions, stories, narratives, sagas, and myths.[14] For example, Mary–Jeanette Smythe (1995) reported an ethnographic study of bodyworkers at a health salon. She assumed the role of participant–observer and listened to their stories following Narrative Paradigm Theory. Then, following Fisher's advice to use the structural concepts that are at hand, she turned to Symbolic Convergence Theory and reported the way the message structure themes in these stories "affected the way these women viewed themselves and their participation in the fitness culture" (p. 259). Even Burke's Dramatism Theory, as adapted to the organization by Tompkins and Cheney's Unobtrusive Control Theory that we just introduced, reflects the traditional interpretive approach to understanding an organization's culture. For example, Gary Ruud (1995) reported his ethnographic analysis of the cultural world of a regional symphony orchestra. Following Cheney and Tompkins (1987), Ruud used Burke's Dramatism Theory's "clusters of terms" to show that the symbolic constructions of "musicians," "board of directors," and "administration" each expressed a particular identity and reflected "cultural symbols of solidarity and division" (p. 201).

The critical interpretive approach uses a critical microtheory (see Chapter 11) to evaluate an organization's culture and make judgments about it. The goal of critical ethnography is to understand and analyze, or as Geertz (1973, p. 26) put it, "to ferret out the unapparent import of things."[15] However, as Goodall (1989) noted: "It should be enough to simply point to the [ethnographer's] story and say, 'Read it, and if it informs and moves you, then it has value.' But that is not enough. Instead ethnographers have to up the ante" (p. 135). They up the ante in terms of uncovering some structural flaw in the culture or some personal flaw in the communicators that allows a controversial element of the culture to continue. As Ronald Wendt (1995) noted, the uncovering of an organization's political tensions and delusions "is the primary function of critical ethnography" (p. 287); or, as Calas and Smircich (1991) noted, such deconstruction points up the biased, cultural communication "in which we have encased our organizational signifiers because it allows for absurdity to appear" (p. 597). For example, Clair (1993, 1994) found absurdity and tension using critical interpretation to examine sexual harassment in the workplace. Della–Piana and Anderson (1995), although they didn't report it as such, found the competitive tensions of Fisher's materialistic and idealistic/moralistic thrusts of the American Dream (see Chapter 6) when they reported that the communication and performances of members of the Lowell Bennion Community Service Center exhibited "the tensions, contradictions, ambiguities, paradoxes, and ironies that exist between a desire to meet individual needs and a commitment to live the principles of social responsibility" (p. 188).

We present the communication microtheories that often serve as the critical lenses for such deconstructions in detail in Chapter 11 when we introduce you to the evaluative microtheories. Also, because we've already presented many of the general and contextual communication theories used by those scholars engaging in the traditional interpretive perspective, we do not detail their use here. However, we do present the ethnographic interpretive approach to cultures. Before we begin however, it is time for a rest stop to reflect on our journey so far, and to make one final point about critical, interpretive ethnography. The scholars using this approach often rely on the convention of storytelling to both capture and encase their data. For example, Goodall (1989, 1991) offered clues about organizational culture by telling detective stories; Pacanowsky (1988a) used story narratives to describe organizations emersed in the crisis of rapid change; Pacanowsky and O'Donnell–Trujillo (1983) viewed stories as cultural performances; Kelly (1985) uncovered recurring stories about bosses, rule-breaking, and meeting obstacles in the cultures of high technology companies; and Wendt (1994, 1995) told dialectically opposing stories to ferret out organizational delusions.

Whether the scholar relies on the convention of straight data reporting, thematic reporting, topical reporting, narrative reporting, or idealized storytelling, the ethnographic interpretive approach uses detailed, participant–observer study to find and report the organizational practices and rituals as communication performances that possess unique meaning for the organization's members.[16] These scholars place a premium on the interpretive ethnographic method's axiological assumption of striving to incorporate multiple views, voices, and perspectives of reality to make sense of data as opposed to the biases of imposing a scholar's view, a preexisting theory's lens, or even an objective, contemplative gaze (Dervin, 1989, 1992). In other words, the goal is to let the data speak for itself and point to the findings and any underlying theoretical perspectives. Robert Huesca's (1995) study of three distinct organizations— a union radio station, a religious radio station, and a nongovernmental radio program producer–distributor contributing to the Bolivian alternative media known as "tin miners' radio"—followed the interpretive ethnography approach. Huesca, by letting his subjects talk to determine the substantive content, found multiple "subject-authored theories of media practice" with the most dominant explanation of the force of the media contributing to the listenership's "committed bonding" with "popular organizations" such as the union. He argued that such bonding stemmed from the themes, topics, and programming of the alternative media.

Let's take a brief rest stop. Recall that in Chapter 1 we indicated that communication theories existed on a continuum from lawlike to ephemeral. Artistic Ethnography Theory (AET) is among the discipline's most ephemeral theories. It reasons that understanding comes from observing the organization, but that it is wrong to impose a preexisting theory on the phenomena. Rather, AET—as spelled out by Pacanowsky and O'Donnell–Trujillo (1982, 1983) and Pacanowsky (1988a, 1988b, 1989), and envisioned by Anderson (1991), Eisenberg (1986, 1990), and Eisenberg and Riley (1988)—is based on the anthropologist Clifford Geertz's (1973) spider-weaving and spiderweb analogies. Geertz introduced the analogies to approach his studies of the Indonesian island and Moroccan highland cultures. AET views culture as resulting from communicative performances that spin a web that binds members together into "the interlocked actions of a collectivity" called an organization (Pacanowsky & O'Donnell–Trujillo, 1982, p. 122). Pecanowsky and O'Donnell–Trujillo (1983) indicated that interactional, contextual, episodic, and improvisational communicative performances bring the organization's culture and reality to life: "*Performances are those very actions by which members constitute and reveal their culture to themselves and others*" (Pacanowsky and O'Donnell–Trujillo, 1983, p. 131). Thus, performances—or as Smythe (1995, p. 256) put it, "talking the talk of the culture"—comprise the basic concept of AET. Indeed, the AET researchers indicated that the five most important communication cultural performances are ritual, passion, sociality, politics, and enculturation. These five performances constitute AET's associative basic concepts.

Ritual performances are the regular, recurring performances of organizational life including personal, task, social, and organizational. A *personal ritual* is some action you perform routinely and regularly such as reading your e-mail first thing each morning. A *task ritual* is the routine work you do on your job such as taking notes in class. A *social ritual* is a regular participatory routine such as "morning coffee" or "casual dress" on Fridays. An *organizational ritual* is a recurring event such as the monthly sales rally, or the annual company picnic. *Passion performances* are the anecdotal stories that organizational members tell that display passion. For example, you probably have an anecdotal story of going through "hell week" or studying for finals that reveals passion for your role in the academic organization. *Sociality performances* are the everyday courtesies, pleasantries, bantering, and discussions that promote cooperation and unity in the workplace. *Politics performances* are the instances of power, control, and influence that occur in organizations. For example, a study group in class might form a power clique (culture) aimed at getting the As. *Enculturation performances* refer "to those processes by which organizational members acquire the social knowledge and skills necessary to behave as competent members" (Pacanowsky and O'Donnell–Trujillo, 1983, p. 143). You demonstrate that you have learned the ropes of being a successful student when you: attend classes regularly, take copious notes, complete assignments on time, and study systematically. In other words, you now know when to study, when to play, the classes you need, and the classes you elect. You know the university's culture and how to be competent within your role in it.

AET has no message structure concepts indigenous to itself; rather the message structure concepts come from the structure of the talk of the members of the organization. IBM talk may differ from fire service talk. Similarly, cop talk may differ from academic talk. In extended fashion, it is fair to say that if the organization under study uses talks and speeches then AET will look at talks and speeches. Or, if the organization under study uses oral histories and written documents then AET will look at oral histories and written documents.

As well, if the organization under study uses operations and procedural manuals then AET will look at operations and procedural manuals. Finally, if the organization under study uses mission statements, sagas, and visions then the AET observer will look at the mission statements, sagas, and visions. By now you should understand our point. Additionally, you should now understand why when using AET you would view an organization's cultural web as the lone message structure concept of the theory, but as an AET ethnographer you cannot say what that web will look like structurally.

As well, AET exhibits no indigenous evaluative concepts due to one of its assumptions, also drawn from anthropology, that the ethnographer should not make judgments about the culture under observation. Rather, in the individual case, AET invites its user to look directly at the communicative interaction occurring in organizations as an anthropologist might study a newly discovered Stone Age tribe. Any underlying communication theory must surface from the native (organizational) accounts and be reported by the ethnographer.

AET does exhibit a qualitative method. Pacanowsky and O'Donnell–Trujillo (1982), for example, invited the communication researcher to observe performances directly and ask the participants why they do what they do. Let's assume for a moment that an AET researcher came to study your class. They would start from the assumption that they knew nothing about the university's organizational culture and they would ask questions like "Why do you take notes? Why is the professor standing? Why does the class last fifty minutes? Why does the professor write things on the wall?" Why does this class mention theory and theories so often? Similarly, you might go to McDonald's and see if you can provide fresh insight into the culture of that organization by observing the ongoing communicative performances. Do you see any underlying communication theory reported in the performances of the participants in the McDonald's culture?

Organizational Assimilation Theory (OAT)

Organizational Assimilation Theory (OAT) explains both the communicative process that mediates the individual–organizational relationship and why newcomers become, or fail to become, organizational members (Bullis, 1993). Consequently, OAT places great emphasis on its communication dynamic of individualization versus socialization concerning whether the employee influences the organization or the organization influences the employee (Hess, 1993; Jablin, 1987). OAT explains the function of communication in the organizational entry, assimilation (anticipatory socialization stage, encounter stage, and metamorphosis stage), and exit processing of employees.[17]

On entry to an organization, the multistage process of assimilation begins. The first stage, or anticipatory socialization, actually includes all that has gone into your training for work since childhood. As a communication major you are more aware than most of the importance of developing good communication skills prior to job entry. Also, most managers view people with part-time work experience as having developed good work and communication habits and contend that they will assimilate more easily than those with no prior experience. OAT points to the job-screening and second interviews as major events in determining whether or not an employee will assimilate successfully. Jablin's (1984) research suggested that job applicants usually have unrealistic, inflated expectations about the organization from which they are seeking employment. Further, he found that the more unrealistic the applicant's expectations, the sooner they would fail to assimilate and leave the organization. This expectation–reality gap is in part caused by recruiters and recruitment literature that dramatize the company as an exciting and prestigious place. Jablin (1984) suggested that you should try to get the most realistic assessment of the company possible and the exact nature of the job you will be required to perform. He indicated that the candidate should seek this information from the job interview, current employees, peers, and parents. In overview, Jablin's research showed that the companies who were the most successful assimilators didn't exaggerate, and their prospective employees didn't over-promise.

The second phase of assimilation is encounter. This is the breaking-in-period during which the rubber first meets the road, the vessel takes its shakedown cruise, the newcomer learns the normal work patterns and thought patterns of the organization. Jablin (1982) argued that the key sources for information needed during the encounter stage were the newcomer's immediate work group and the newcomer's supervisor. These people are important because they serve as translators of the formally stated mission statement, vision, and rules and procedures of the organization. Research has indicated consistently that a newcomer's relationship with his or her initial supervisor has long-term consequences on the success of the individual's organizational career. Furthermore, the more opportunity for interaction with coworkers, and the more such coworkers provide encouraging words, then the more likely the newcomer will assimilate successfully (Jablin, 1987).

Jablin (1984) indicated that "during the metamorphosis stage of assimilation the newcomer attempts to become an accepted, participating member of the organization by learning new attitudes and behaviors or modifying existing ones to be consistent with the organization's expectations" (p. 596). He also pointed out that the newcomer needs to find the organization making some accommodation to his or her unique needs and to his or her desire to influence the organization.

As you may have guessed by now, OAT's communicator concepts are newcomers, coworkers, immediate supervisors, and the formal communication of rules and regulations from upper management. The medium$_2$ in which OAT propagates and grows includes both the supervisor–subordinate dyad, and the coworker small group. Its primary evaluative concept is assimilation, although from time to time it uses other evaluative concepts like satisfaction with the job and commitment to the organization (Jablin, 1987).

DiSanza (1995) reported a study on bank teller organizational assimilation. He noted that assimilation failed to occur for five of the nine bank tellers studied.[18] The failure was due primarily to a systematic contradiction of operations practices that existed in the banking system. In short, the home office trained in one set of procedures and when the new employees arrived at their branch office assignments they had to learn a contradictory set of procedures. This contradiction produced "surprise, disappointment, and disparagement" (p. 213). The tellers were surprised that there were two different sets of training rules and disappointed that the organization was in such disarray. These feelings resulted in their disparagement of both the training school and the branch bank. The DiSanza study points up the importance of an organization's need for consistency and coordination in newcomer assimilation.

Unifying the General and Contextual Organizational Theories

Let's slow our pace a bit and take a rest stop. Let's think about how far we've come. We now know that the six general communication theories explored in Chapters 2–7 and the four contextual theories just discussed provide a unified understanding of organizational communication. For example, Information Systems Theory tells us that organizational members share both semantic and pragmatic information actively, interactively, and transactionally. The theory also tells us that organizations use redundancy to reduce misunderstanding and optimize the flow of information. As well, organizations often audit their communication system to eliminate information bottlenecks, breakdowns, and the overloading of the system. As well, we know that Rational Argumentation Theory, particularly the dialectical dynamic, allows organizational members to make better, more reasoned decisions. RAT is at the epicenter of decision-making in organizations as reflected in everyday business meetings and the trend toward participative management teams. The force of argument increases the organizational members' convictions that they have made the best decision. Additionally, we know that Symbolic Convergence Theory explains how the force of fantasy-sharing builds identity with the corporation, creates and raises organizational consciousness, and contributes to cohesion and commitment. SCT also guides the development of a corporate rhetorical vision and corporate sagas. As well, it has proved useful in segmenting customer markets. Similarly, we know that Uncertainty Reduction Theory points to the importance of certain personal disclosures of social information that build trust among organizational members. It goes far to explain the good and bad outcomes of superior–subordinate communication as relationship-building and non-building. Then too, we know that Narrative Paradigm Theory explains how storytelling reveals the group members' idealistic/moralistic and materialistic values. It points to the need for sacred stories in organizations that depict the organizational values. NPT also makes possible the assessment of the probability (do the stories hang together) and fidelity (do the stories ring true) of the organizations' stories. Finally, we know that Diffusion of Innovations Theory explains the use of awareness, opinion, practice, advocacy, and resistance talk in gaining (or failing to gain) commitment to new product innovations and in diffusing them from the R&D department through marketing to the world at large. DIT guides, predicts, and controls marketing campaigns.

Then, when we add the four contextual theories, our explanation of the phenomena of organizational communication becomes even more complete. For example, Weick's Organizing Theory, a direct derivative of Information Systems Theory, explains that organizing itself is the product of information-sharing. WOT reminds people to optimize the amount of equivocal information so that it can work at an optimum level by identifying appropriate assembly rules and cycles. WOT provides six guidelines for optimizing equivocal information. Unobtrusive Control Theory explains how organizations exert power over their employees by using corporate identification to foster conformity to company decision-making patterns, policies, and procedures. Additionally, Artistic Ethnographic Theory focuses on corporate culture-building. Drawing on the storytelling concept of NPT, AET views organizational culture as the sum product of performances such as ritual, passion, sociability, politics, and enculturation. The relationship between competently performed performances such as the organizational rally and company picnic, relating anecdotal stories like the customer from hell, and so forth comprise the corporate culture. Then, Organizational Assimilation Theory explains the communication process that influences new members and in turn how organizations influences new members. OAT explains how a metamorphosis takes place as the individual becomes assimilated. As a whole, the six general communication theories and four contextual theories provide you with a unified understanding of the organizational communication context. They enable you to describe, explain, predict, and control human action in the organizational context. **Figure 9-2** provides a look at Corey, our communication graduate on-the-job, using a small group communication theory to good advantage.

"Retention on this campus is a problem. We need to do a better job of assimilating students, faculty, and staff. I recommend we begin following the advice provided by Organizational Assimilation Theory. We need to insure that we help each new person travel through the stages of assimilation."

FIGURE 9-2.   Communication Graduate On-the-Job

Summary

This chapter introduced you to the communication theories endemic to the public speaking and organizational communication contexts. As well, it provided brief sections unifying the general and contextual theories relevant to these contexts. The chapter indicated how together the general and contextual theories explain and guide communication within the public speaking and organizational communication contexts. In the first half of the chapter, we introduced you to four public speaking communication theories: Neo-Aristotelian Theory, Burke's Dramatism Theory, Vid-Oral Theory, and Image Restoration Theory. In the second half of the chapter, we introduced you to four organizational communication theories: Weick's Organizing Theory, Unobtrusive Control Theory, Artistic Ethnography Theory, and Organizational Assimilation Theory. **Box 9-1**, "Understanding Public Speaking and Organizational Communication Context Theories in a Nutshell," presents a synthesized look at the theories.

BOX 9-1 Understanding Public Speaking and Organizational Communication Context Theories in a Nutshell

Public Speaking Communication Context. This chapter introduced four theories that explain communication in the public speaking context: Neo-Aristotelian Theory, Burke's Dramatism Theory, Vid-Oral Theory, and Image Restoration Theory. The general communication theories presented in Chapters 2–7 also explain communication within the public speaking context. However, Narrative Paradigm Theory is often singled out in public speaking texts as especially relevant to the creation of imaginative language that conveys values. The communication microtheories presented in Chapter 11 also provide important explanations of communication in this context. For example, Communication Apprehension and Feminist Genre Theory appear regularly in public speaking texts.

Neo-Aristotelian Theory (NAT). NAT explains the force of persuasive speeches on the attitudes, beliefs, values, and behaviors of audiences. NAT argues that rhetorical syllogisms are used to make three important artistic proofs—ethos, pathos, and logos—to persuade audiences.

Burke's Dramatism Theory (BDT). BDT explains the cyclical and hierarchical nature of human relations as moving symbolically from order to pollution to guilt, then victimhood, and finally redemption. BDT argues that the rhetor describes this purification ritual in terms of the dramatistic hexad to elicit identification with the audience.

Vid-Oral Theory (VOT). VOT emphasizes the oral preparation and presentation of talks over the written. It calls for the use of arguments and proofs drawn from the influence of contemporary media. VOT is compatible with the use of Burke's Dramatism Theory, Symbolic Convergence Theory, and Narrative Paradigm Theory as contemporary communication theories that bring the symbols of these vid-oral times to life.

Image Restoration Theory (IRT). IRT explains the image restoration strategies necessary to the repair of the good name of individuals and/or organizations. IRT offers several image repair strategies, such as denial, evasion of responsibility, reduction of the offensiveness of the act, correction of the wrong, and mortification, to restore the tarnished image of the speaker or organization.

Organizational Communication Context. This chapter introduced four organizational communication contextual theories: Weick's Organizing Theory, Unobtrusive Control Theory, Artistic Ethnographic Theory, and Organizational Assimilation Theory. Organizational communication texts often present the general communication theories (Chapters 2–7) to explain communication in the organizational context. However, Information Systems Theory is particularly helpful. As well, the communication microtheories presented in Chapter 11 also explain narrow slices of organizational communication. For example, organizational communication texts regularly report Muted Group Theory and Feminist Genre Theory.

Weick's Organizing Theory (WOT). WOT explains the organizing process as an attempt to optimize the amount of equivocality faced by humans. WOT posits three message structure concepts—enactment, selection, and retention—that characterize the collective activity of organizations as embodied in talking, interpreting, and remembering.

Unobtrusive Control Theory (UCT). UCT explains how organizations exert power over their employees by using organizational identification to foster conformity to organizational decision-making patterns, policies, and procedures. UCT argues that a tension occurs between an individual's symbolic identification and the organization's symbolic identification structure.

Artistic Ethnography Theory (AET). AET explains organizations as cultures. AET critiques the organization as a symbolic place with an identity and boundaries with each organization being a unique symbolic construction.

Organizational Assimilation Theory (OAT). OAT explains the communicative process that mediates the individual–organizational relationship. OAT explains why newcomers become or fail to become organizational members—they complete or fail to complete a stagic process of assimilation.

Chapter 10

Mass and Intercultural Communication Context Theories

Communication scholars theorize about mass and intercultural communicative interaction.

Chapter Outline

I. Mass Communication Context Theories
   A. *Spiral of Silence Theory (SST)*
   B. *Agenda-Setting Theory (AST)*
   C. *Cultivation Effects Theory (CET)*
   D. *Uses and Gratifications Theory (UGT)*
   E. *Unifying the General and Contextual Mass Communication Theories*

II. Intercultural Communication Context Theories
   A. *Anxiety/Uncertainty Management Theory (AUMT)*
   B. *Face Negotiation Theory (FNT)*
   C. *Cross-Cultural Adaptation Theory (CCAT)*
   D. *Unifying the General and Contextual Intercultural Theories*

III. Summary

In this chapter we introduce the more popular communication theories developed to explain communicative interaction in the mass communication and interpersonal communication contexts. As you recall from Chapter 1, contextual communication theories explain communication within the confines of one of the six traditional medium$_1$ contexts: interpersonal, small group, public speaking, organizational, mass, and intercultural communication. Recall also that The Communication Metatheory (TCM) presented in Chapter 1 recognized two types of contextual communication theories. Type 1 contextual theories use one or more theoretical concepts that by definition tie them forever to the context and Type 2 contextual theories begin by focusing on a particular context but evolve into a general theory through grounding research demonstrating that their explanation of communicative interaction holds across contexts. In this chapter, we present four mass communication theories: Spiral of Silence Theory, Agenda-Setting Theory, Cultivation Effects Theory, and Uses and Gratifications Theory. (Also, we treat another mass communication theory, McLuhan's Media Law Theory, in detail in Chapter 11.) Next, in this chapter, we discuss three intercultural communication theories: Anxiety/Uncertainty Management Theory, Face Negotiation Theory, and Cross-Cultural Adaptation Theory. (We treat another theory about intercultural communication, Gile's Speech/Communication Accommodation Theory, in Chapter 11.)

Mass Communication Context Theories

Mass communication research and theorizing evolved in concert with the technological development of writing, printing, and the more recent electronic media of radio, television, and the Internet. McLuhan (1962, 1965) and McLuhan and Fiore (1967) divided all of human history into four epochs: the tribal, the literate, the print, and the electronic age. McLuhan (1973), mirroring much of the speed-of-light discussion of information transfer presented in Chapter 2, noted that "at instant speeds the public begins to participate directly in actions which it had previously heard about at a distance in place or time" (p. 54). Professor Shields, in teaching "Introduction to Communication Technology," has observed his students wide-eyed with wonder as they traveled at the speed of light on the Internet retrieving political speeches even before they were given, viewing the Monet's of the Louvre in Paris, chatting in real-time via print-voice-visual with persons thousands of miles away, and reading the major metropolitan newspapers from their computer screens. McLuhan (1965) forecast that the computer "promises by technology a Pentecostal condition of universal understanding and unity" (p. 80). McLuhan and Powers (1989) said of the global village: "The electric field of simultaneity gets everybody involved with everyone else. All individuals, their desires and satisfactions, are co-present in the age of communication" (p. 94). McLuhan has proved to be a true visionary of the coming of the global village.[1] Nonetheless, technological development has been so rapid and has diffused so quickly in the latter half of the twentieth century, that it is close to outstripping our ability to theorize and ground research about it. We present McLuhan's Media Law Theory (McLuhan & McLuhan, 1988) in Chapter 11.

Lowery and DeFleur (1995) reported on the milestones of "six decades of empirical research on the process and effects of mass communication" (p. xi). The 1930s saw the development of the Magic Bullet Theory, a straightforward explanation of the effect of the movies and radio on communicative human action, which postulated that the effects of these media were direct and immediate. However, Becker and Roberts (1992) cautioned that "in the early days of media research, scholars underestimated the complexity of mass communication and human behavior" (p. 507). In this chapter, we present four theories, which, when combined with a general communication theory like the Diffusion of Innovations Theory

(handwritten margin note: "Strong affects" group of theories that relate to media)

(presented in Chapter 7), present a much richer explanation of how the mass media affect our lives.

Spiral of Silence Theory (SST)

The Spiral of Silence Theory (SST) posits truly powerful mass media (Noelle–Neumann, 1973). SST explains the long-term effect of the mass media on public opinion and human action and inaction.[2] Noelle–Neumann (1983) described the power of the media in this way: "Journalistic preference for findings of 'minimal media effects' has distorted the interpretation of research findings over the years, but today the 'dogma of media powerlessness' is no longer tenable" (p. 157). (Noelle–Neumann is taking issue with the tenets of the Uses and Gratifications Theory, introduced later in this chapter.) SST explains how the mass media works in conjunction with majority opinion to silence minority beliefs on political issues and engender conformity (Noelle–Neumann, 1974). As Herbst (1991) emphasized, Noelle–Neumann's "central argument is that fear of social isolation forces people to assess the opinions of others, so they may conform to what they believe is majority opinion" (p. 227).

Elizabeth Noelle–Neumann (1984, 1991) developed SST over five decades. She directed a public opinion research institute in Germany. She began her career in the Ministry for Popular Enlightenment and Propaganda as an apologist for the Third Reich (Simpson, 1996). Simpson stated that "in 1937 Goebbels's Ministry granted Elizabeth a scholarship to the University of Missouri to study journalism and emerging U.S. techniques for monitoring and shaping public opinion" (p. 152). Although SST is not controversial, its creator, its origins, and its early grounding database are. Simpson (1996) argued forcefully that Noelle–Neumann developed this theory while writing her dissertation on U.S. public opinion and the press at the University of Berlin in 1940. He further argued that Noelle–Neumann and Joseph Goebbels, the Minister for Popular Enlightenment and Propaganda in Nazi Germany, together used the media and SST to create public opinion and silence minority opinion about the activities of the Third Reich, including the Jewish Holocaust.

Recall that The Communication Metatheory, presented in Chapter 1, posited that a medium$_2$ substance helps theories grow and propagate. SST grew and propagated in the fertile soils of a nondemocratic, totalitarian form of government, but since the 1970s Noelle–Neumann has retrofitted the theory for use in more open democracies. Nonetheless, in both cases, the spiral of silence is a top-down accelerating spiral that maintains society by controlling public opinion, not a bottom-up spiral that gradually catches up large groups of people into a common view of reality. In fact, Noelle–Neumann (1983) has argued that, within the field of communication studies, the majority opinion, that the media have minimal effects on the public, has silenced the minority opinion that the media is powerful and has strong long-term effects on the public. As Noelle–Neumann put it: "By 1979, I had begun to think that the long tenure of the minimal effects hypothesis stemmed from the influence of the media on media research" (p. 159).

SST, according to Noelle–Neumann (1991, p. 260), is based on five assumptions: (1) society threatens deviant individuals with isolation; (2) individuals experience continuous fear of isolation; (3) fear of isolation causes individuals to assess continually the climate of opinion; (4) the results of an individual's estimates affect the disclosure or concealment of opinion; and (5) together these assumptions explain the formation, defense, and alteration of public opinion.

SST's basic concepts are public opinion, personal opinion, and mass media. The mass media help forge and maintain a society's public opinion. SST's structural concept is the downward spiral of public opinion that moots minority personal opinion and, with the help of the mass media, produces more and more conformity to the majority public opinion. In other words, each of us is constantly testing public opinion against our personal opinions. If we find that our personal opinions match public opinion, then we tend to speak out; conversely, if we find that our personal opinions go against public opinion, we remain silent. With more and more mass media support of the majority public opinion, we desire conformity and join in the expression of the majority view. Of course, we know public opinion through what we hear, see, and read in the mass media and in talking with other people.

Noelle–Neumann (1984, 1991) reported on the development of several indirect methods for grounding or getting at the fear of isolation and the tendency for speaking up when sharing the majority opinion and remaining silent when in the minority. She developed what she called "the threat test" (1991, p. 266) as part of a six-step method for analyzing public opinion and predicting future changes in it. For example, if you were to have four nonsmokers and one smoker in a group, and one of the nonsmokers stated, "It seems to me that smokers are inconsiderate; they force us to inhale their health-endangering secondary smoke," and then the other group members agreed, would you predict that the smoker would speak up and defend his or her right to smoke or remain silent? Noelle–Neumann (1984, p. 42) tested this situation and found that most smokers remained silent.

The most important communicator attribute in SST is what Noelle–Neumann (1991) called a "quasi-statistical sense" (p. 268) of what the majority view is on any given issue. For example, if two campus speakers were talking about the proliferation of nuclear energy plants and one got booed, who do you think got booed? Noelle–Neumann found that people thought that the speaker supporting the proliferation of nuclear energy got booed. This is her indirect test of the quasi-statistical sense of people knowing what the majority side is and it helps explain the bandwagon effect of mass media that persistently report a majority opinion or present an opinion as a majority opinion. In either case, over the long term, people will gradually gravitate toward holding the majority opinion and fewer and fewer people will speak out against it. Indeed, Yum and Kendall (1995) studied 567 male and female adults and found that when discussing presidential political campaigns there were no sex differences and "that people talk mainly with people in social groups who agree with them" (p. 131).

SST's communication dynamic is the continuous tension between shifting majority and minority opinion on issues that are highly emotionally and morally charged. The force of this dynamic on human action was driven home to us on Sunday night, October 6, 1996, when we watched and heard the incumbent President of the United States, Bill Clinton, speak out and say, "I am not a liberal." In this instance, the standard-bearer for the party of Thomas Jefferson, Andrew Jackson, Franklin Roosevelt, and Harry Truman had denied his and his party's heritage. In this instance, the standard-bearer for the party of workers' rights, civil rights, and women's rights—the right to form unions, the right to vote and use public accommodations, the right to control one's own body—had denied his heritage. In this instance, the same Bill Clinton who as a teenager had admired, looked up to, shaken hands, and proudly had his picture taken with his hero, President John F. Kennedy, at a White House lawn ceremony had denied the politics of that hero. Noelle–Neumann's SST would explain this phenomenon as an example of a majority opinion, reinforced by the media, silencing the minority opinion based on the 1996 polling data that two out of three people would define themselves as conservative; President Clinton was conforming to that majority view, lest he be shunned right out of the White House.

SST also explains how a majority view is formed and why hard-core minorities speak out. Noelle–Neumann (1991) reported on her decade-long study of the nuclear energy plant issue in Germany. She used that research to show how a minority opinion opposing nuclear energy power plants gradually became a majority view with the consistent and persistent help of the powerful mass media. In fact, she stated that in her fifty years of public opinion polling, "I have never found a spiral of silence that goes against the tenor of the media, for the willingness to speak out depends in part upon sensing that there is support and legitimization from the media" (p. 276). In other words, a minority viewpoint can never become a majority viewpoint without the persistent help of the media, which are either naturally sympathetic or authoritatively powerful.

Agenda-Setting Theory (AT)

Becker and Roberts (1992) wrote that "the Spiral of Silence Theory predicts and explains the effect of the media on what people think about some issues. Agenda-Setting Theory predicts and explains the effects of the media on what issues people think about" (p. 517). In other words, Agenda-Setting Theory (AT) argues that people's beliefs about the importance of an issue are related to the amount of space an idea receives in the newspaper and/or the amount of time it receives as reported on radio and television (Weaver, 1984). You should be somewhat familiar with the agenda-setting concept, as it is a concept from Diffusion of Innovations Theory (Chapter 7). Recently, Brosius and Weimann (1996) reiterated the notion of agenda-setting as a component of the two-step flow of diffusing news stories in a survey study of 28,000 East and West Germans. We include agenda-setting as a contextual mass communication theory due to the extensive attention it has received by print and electronic mass communication scholars. Recall that many of the news diffusion studies reported in Chapter 7 also concern agenda-setting.

McCombs and Shaw (1972) reported the landmark study that first grounded Agenda-Setting Theory without tying it to Diffusion of Innovations Theory.[3] They examined the media coverage of the 1968 presidential campaign through a content analysis of the length and duration of stories appearing in *Time, Newsweek, The New York Times,* and newspapers from Raleigh and Durham, North Carolina, and on CBS's and NBC's evening news. With a database of one hundred undecided registered voters they found that the important ideas in the news correlated almost perfectly with what the undecided voters specified as the important issues. In other words, it appeared that the media had influenced what people thought about in the election. As Cohen (1963) first observed, "the press may not be successful much of the time in telling people what to think, but it is stunningly successful in telling its readers what to think about" (p. 13). Rogers, Dearing, and Bregman (1993) reported that 223 studies examined the relationship between the media's agenda and the public's agenda in the two decades since McComb and Shaw's classic study. Rogers and Dearing (1988) reported that such investigations overwhelmingly support the proposition that the mass media influence the public's agenda of important issues. Moreover, the public's agenda once set or reflected by the media's agenda influences the policy agenda of elite decision-makers such as congress and the president; conversely, the elite's policy agenda sometimes affects the media's agenda. Hence, AST's communication dynamic is the tension or conflict between these three agendas.

AT's communication dynamic has become more complex over the years. Initially, AT asserted that the media first selected what is news (gatekeeping) and then established what is important news (agenda-setting) by giving some issues more coverage than others. AT then argued that this media influence or function set the public's agenda about what to think about and what issues to regard as important. Like the Spiral of Silence Theory, which works best with highly charged issues, AT works best in explaining agenda-setting about complex issues of national importance and less well in explaining agenda-setting about the more mundane local issues of everyday living. Recently, AT's communication dynamic has expanded to include the question of who sets the media's agenda. The answer appears to be high-ranking policy-makers, elite publics, serendipitous events, and news beats such as city council meetings, public elections, and Ground Hog Day (Brosius & Kepplinger, 1990; Rogers & Dearing, 1988; Smith, 1987a, 1987b).

The agenda-setting effects of the media have also been studied cross-culturally.[4] For example, Brosius and Weimann (1996) reported a two-phase, three-year study of agenda-setting by the major television networks in East and West Germany. Their content analysis of 118,000 news items, sampled using a time series design twenty-eight times, led to the report of five major issues of relevance to the German TV news viewers. The biggest issues were German Reunification, unemployment, crime, prices, and political asylum for foreigners. They found that "the flow of issues between the media and the public is found to be more complex than a one-step, one-direction flow (media to public)" (p. 575). Indeed, they found that the flow of information was best explained using Diffusion of Innovations Theory (DIT) because the innovation was information. Also, in line with DIT, the biggest intervening variable in moving the issue from the media to the public was the "early recognizers" of issues who took the media's issues to other members of the public through interpersonal communication, but also influenced the media's agenda-setting. They concluded that the most important contribution of their study was reviving the notion of the two-step flow of the diffusion of communication (information).

Cultivation Effects Theory (CET)

George Gerbner and his associates at the Annenberg School of Communications, University of Pennsylvania, introduced Cultivation Effects Theory (CET) to explain the data from a longitudinal study of television violence.[5] Initially, CET posited that heavy exposure to television's consistent and persistent portrayal of images and messages lead viewers to see themselves or the real world as consistent with those mediated portrayals. More recently, the cultivation effect has been grounded with media delivery systems other than television. Gerbner began the ongoing research program in 1967 at the Annenberg School of Communication. The research program was called the Cultural Indicators project (Tapper, 1995). It initially concerned the development of a violence profile of television programs for the Federal Communications Commission (Coffin & Tuchman, 1972/1973; Eleey, Gerbner, & Tedesco, 1972/1973a, 1972/1973b). Gerbner and others continued the reporting of the violence profile for heavy television viewers (Gerbner & Gross, 1976; Gerbner, et al., 1978, 1979a, 1979b, 1980) as part of the research base grounding CET. For example, Gerbner, et al. (1980) reported that heavy viewers became more fearful and distrustful of others than they would otherwise be.

CET began from the assumption, that, over time, heavy viewers come to accept the mediated reality of television as their perception of actual reality. A twelve-year database collected between 1967 and 1979 grounded the relationship between the theory's concepts of heavy viewing and cultivation. Gerbner, et al. (1980), wrote: "Television is the central and most pervasive mass medium in American culture and it plays a distinctive and historically unprecedented role . . . that provides a coherent if mythical world in every home" (p. 14). Gerbner, et al. went on to report that "the more time one spends 'living' in the world of television, the more likely one is to report perceptions of social reality that can be traced to [television]" (p. 14). Later, the CET researchers added the assumption that the process of cultivation was multidirectional and that some subgroups held beliefs that could differ from that portrayed in the television world. As we shall see, the concept of mainstreaming relates to the first assumption and the concept of resonance relates to the second.

CET's basic concepts are *mediated acts of social life* and *real acts of social life.* A mediated act of social life would be a portrayal of police officers on a television show such as *NYPD* and a real act of social life would be observing real police officers in action. CET's communication dynamic is the tension between these two realities. CET's primary structural concepts are *mainstream* and *resonance.* Gerbner, et al. (1980) indicated that "the mainstream can be thought of as a relative commonality of outlooks that television tends to cultivate" (p. 15). Over time, heavy users of television incrementally come to hold a common, homogenized, mediated view of American life that distorts real life. *Resonance,* as a structural concept, occurs when what people see on television is congruent with what they see in real life; in such cases resonance works in tandem with television mainstreaming to complete the cultivation process for the heavy TV viewer (viewing four or more hours of television each day). Thus, resonance produces what Gerbner, et al. (1980) called a double-dose of cultivation. Doob and Macdonald (1979) provided evidence to reaffirm the mainstream and resonance effects. Let's pause a moment and illustrate these concepts. If a female heavy viewer possesses a televised mainstream view of male police officers being brutish and sexist and she is then stopped for a traffic violation by a male police officer who acts in a brutish and sexist manner, then reality resonates with the television mainstream reality and the female heavy viewer sees that life confirms just what she had come to think from television.

CET's lone evaluative concept is *cultivation differential* (effects). The Annenberg researchers developed two indices for measuring the cultivation differential (effects): the Mean World Index and the Perceptions of Danger Index. The Mean World Index deals with questions concerning perceptions of the meanness of the real world like, "Would you say that most of the time people try to be hurtful?" "Do you think that most people would try to take advantage of you?" and "Would you say that most people can be trusted?" The Annenberg studies consistently found that heavy television viewers described the real world as meaner, as more dog-eat-dog, and as a place in which you cannot be too careful. The Perceptions of Danger Index rates how dangerous you think the world is. It asks viewers such questions as: "What are the odds that you'll be involved in some kind of violent act in the next week?" "What percentage of our society is involved in law enforcement?" and "How much crime do you think is occurring on our streets?" Again, heavy users of television exaggerate danger as compared to light users. The heavy users think it is more likely that they will be involved in an act of violence in the next week, they are more afraid to walk the streets, and they think that more people are involved in law enforcement. Also, regarding the demographic attributes of the heavy user communicators, they found that women, the elderly, and children exhibited especially distorted views of the real probability of danger.

Since the development of CET, its use has been expanded to explain the cultivation effects of all types of television programming, as opposed to just violence. Signorielli and Morgan (1990) argued that cultivation research is concerned with "identifying and assessing the most recurrent and stable patterns in television content . . . in attempts to document and analyze the contribution of television to viewers' social reality" (p. 16). This extension of the theory was made possible by a number of grounding studies. For example, Morgan (1982), in a study of sixth- and eighth-graders, found that television cultivated—especially in girls—the mediated notion that men are born to be more ambitious and successful than women. Comstock and Strzyzewski (1990) reported that television produced a mediated reality that portrayed women in traditional nurturing roles and men in traditional authority roles. Oliver (1994) found that reality-based police shows, such as *America's Most Wanted, Cops,* and *Top Cops,* portrayed police officers as predominantly white and criminals as predominantly black and Hispanic and that the suspects were frequently the target of physical aggression by police officers. Such television programs blur the distinction between the television world and the real world, thereby heightening the cultivation effect. Gibson and Zillmann (1994), using an experimental study design, demonstrated the cultivation effect of newspaper news stories. They found that people reading extreme exemplars of car-jackings believed that car-jackings were a significantly more serious national problem than people who read only mild exemplars.

The task of proving the relationship between television viewing and cultivation effects is difficult. First, there is difficulty in using correlation studies to establish a linear relationship between increasing amounts of viewing and cultivation effects (Potter, 1991). Second, as we enter the twenty-first century, there is difficulty in defining what is television due to the many expanding channels of UHF, cable, and direct satellite broadcasting. Perse, Ferguson, and McLeod (1994) found that interpersonal mistrust linked to heavy use of traditional cable channels, but that fear of crime and interpersonal mistrust correlated negatively with the heavy viewing of specialized cable channels. In other words, you get the violence cultivation effect if you watch ABC, CBS, NBC, and Fox, or the traditional cable channels (USA, WGN, Turner Network, HBO, Cinemax, Showtime, and CNN), but you don't get the effect if you watch the nonviolent or less violent Disney Channel, Arts and Entertainment, and the Discovery Channel. From our view, such data would be predicted by the theory.

This is an ideal spot for a rest stop. Although we indicated in Chapter 1 that we would not always review and answer the critics of the contextual and microtheories, CET provides an excellent example of the presence of critical response to such communication theories. For example, Hirsch (1980) argued that CET's assumption of linearity between the cultivation effect and heavy and light viewing didn't hold. Hughes (1980) produced a curvilinear relationship. Potter (1991) also reexamined his own cultivation data and found a curvilinear relationship. Gerbner, et al. (1981) rebutted the criticism by indicating that the Hirsch and Hughes data sets were of extreme groups comprising only 10 percent of the sample and thus were unimportant. Shapiro (1991) found that heavy- and light-viewing college students from suburban and rural backgrounds believed the extent of crime to be more prevalent than it is portrayed on television. Tamborini and Choi (1990) reported similar data for Korean immigrants. The criticism is that CET does not adequately account for the direction of the relationship between television viewing and perceptions of crime. The critics' argument is that once mainstreaming occurs it serves as a new symbolic reality that affects perceptions more than mere viewing and therefore CET must be wrong. That's like saying that clothes keep you warm in winter, but getting hot from too many clothes means that clothes don't keep you warm. The critics miss Gerbner's points of tying the concepts of main-streaming and resonance together. Finally, Potter (1991, 1993) argued that the relationship between heavy television viewing and the cultivation effect is asymmetrical, that is, heavy viewing may be a necessary but insufficient cause for cultivation to occur. In other words, other forces may mediate the effect. Again, the problem is that the critics fail to see that one's beliefs about the world (worldview) created by television become the cultivation effect. Gerbner's very point is that the symbolically created worldview initiated by heavy television viewing then affects one's perceptions of reality. That's why CET is a theory flowing from the symbolic paradigm of communication theories. Tapper (1995) synthesizes the criticisms and in light of them offers a modified model for researching CET. However, it would seem that he's fixing something that may not be broken.

Uses and Gratifications Theory (UGT)

The three preceding mass communication contextual theories each view the audience as being acted on by powerful media. The Spiral of Silence Theory posited all-powerful media creating and sustaining majority public opinion and in turn stifling and silencing minority public opinion. Agenda-Setting Theory posited that the media may not tell people what to think, but they most assuredly determine what people think about. Similarly, Cultivation Effects Theory posited that television produced long-term effects on heavy viewers that made those viewers feel less safe and more fearful of violence and distrustful of people. In stark contrast, the Uses and Gratifications Theory (UGT) assumes that the media has limited effects on its audience because the audience is actually in control of media selection and information-processing. Each particular study may well prove out an effect of the media, but when viewed as a whole the body of research indicates that each effect is but a small part of many explanations of media uses and gratifications.[6] Thus, UGT views the audience as more active and involved than as passive and disconnected. The audience chooses its media and does so for a variety of reasons. As Klapper (1963) indicated, UGT reverses the focus of media effects theorizing: The question is not what the media *does* to people, but what people *do with* the media. In other words, UGT explains why people choose, use, and receive benefits from attuning to the media.[7]

Rubin (1993), from a review of the UGT literature, concluded that it possesses five primary assumptions: (1) media use is typically goal-directed and motivated; (2) people select media sources and media messages to satisfy felt needs and desires; (3) media sources compete among themselves and with interpersonal communication for selection, attention, and use; (4) interpersonal communication is generally more influential than media communication; and (5) demo-psycho-sociographics affect an audience member's selection of media. From these assumptions, you can see readily why UGT is sometimes called a limited effects theory of mass communication.

Herzog (1944) conducted the initial landmark study of radio daytime serials (soap operas) that initially grounded UGT. Lowery and DeFleur (1995) reported that they surveyed the radio listening habits of 5,320 Iowa women, 4,991 nonfarm women nationwide, 1,500 women in Erie County, Ohio, and conducted qualitative interviews in Syracuse, New York, Memphis, Tennessee, and Minneapolis, Minnesota. They found that the listening audience was large and enthusiastic, not socially isolated, voted less, possessed a lower level of formal education, and preferred less sophisticated reading material. She also found that the gratifications provided by regular listening to these serials included emotional release, wishful thinking, and valuable advice. This was the first study to view audiences as active listeners who choose the medium (radio) and the program content (soap operas) to gain satisfaction.

UGT's basic concept is audience activity, or as Rubin (1993) said: "Audience activity is U&G's core concept" (p. 99). This activity includes seeking out media to provide information, entertainment, and social orientation. Information, entertainment, and social orientation would provide the broad categories under which all gratifications would be classified (Blumler, 1979; Blumler & Katz, 1974; Palmgreen, Wenner, & Rayburn, 1980). UGT's message structure concepts are best understood in view of McLuhan's notion that the medium is the message. Each medium formats the same information differently and people select one medium over another because of the structural characteristics of that format. Some people would rather read about Easy Rawlins in Walter Mosley's (1990) *Devil in a Blue Dress* while others would prefer the movie version with Denzel Washington. You may have already abandoned your media dependency regarding reading the daily paper at the kitchen table in favor of reading the paper on the Internet. Similarly, you may have abandoned the passive watching of cartoons on television and now prefer an interactive game at your computer where you affect the plot line of the adventure. Our point is that the message structure concepts of this theory are literally the inherent message formats of the different media—print, radio, TV, computer, magazine, newspaper, periodical, interpersonal. The medium may not be the message, literally, but its structure affects your selectivity and attention to and ultimately the gratification you receive from the message.

UGT's communication dynamic concerns the tension between an active (instrumental), passive (ritualized), avoiding (avoidance) audience before, during, and after media engagement (Rubin, 1984, 1993; Rubin & Rubin, 1985; Perse & Rubin, 1990). You can comprehend this dynamic by looking at your own media habits. You may have told a friend: "The local news is depressing; I don't watch it anymore." Such a statement indicates avoidance. Akin to this, you might have told another friend: "Gee, is that Internet addictive; I used it and found myself surfing for eight hours for information for my term paper; I've got enough stuff to write a book chapter." Such a statement indicates active, instrumental usage. Conversely, you might have told your roommate: "It's Friday night. I rented some old horror movies; I'm going to just veg out." Such a statement indicates a passive, ritualistic usage.

Of real interest with this theory is UGT's communicator structure. It's an *intra*personal interaction in which the audience is talking to itself by way of and about a mediated stimulus. As humans, we're all a little embarrassed to admit that we do this, that is, that we talk to ourselves. We talk back to movies, yell at the TV, and cry as we read a romantic novel. Indeed, Christ and Biggers (1984) offered emotional response as a predictor of media preference. UGT's medium$_2$ substance in which it propagates and grows is a world of ever-increasing media choices. Newspapers, magazines, books, comics, radio niche programming, 300 TV channels, tape players, cassette players, CD players, videos, computers, VCRs, and CD-ROMs are producing what McLuhan envisioned as the retribalization of people into small, fragmented, mediated worlds. Indeed, UGT dismisses the view of a mass audience listening to mass media as an obsolete twentieth century concept.

UGT's evaluative concepts are the *ratio of gratifications* sought or expected versus those obtained, and *media satisfaction* in terms of information received, entertainment derived, and social orientation confirmed. In short, you would use this theory by asking yourself: "Did I get the gratification I sought from the medium and was it worth my effort?" We've been hauling you over hill and through valley acting as trail guides and arguing all the way that you would learn the discipline's general theories, contextual theories, and microtheories, and that the trip would be worth it. UGT puts us to the test. Did you receive satisfaction from reading this book (your media selection), and did the gratifications you obtained exceed, equal, or fall short of your expectations (did you receive the value you expected?)?

Unifying the General and Contextual Mass Communication Theories

Let's slow our pace a bit and take a rest stop. Let's think about how far we've come. We now know that the six general communication theories explored in Chapters 2–7 and the four contextual theories just discussed provide a unified understanding of the mass communication context. For example, Information Systems Theory tells us that in machine-to-machine, machine-to-human, and mixed communication systems information is shared at both the semantic and pragmatic level actively, interactively, and transactionally. It provides the mathematical explanation of how messages are optimized within those systems. IST drives our modern radio, telephone, television, computer, and Internet systems. IST advises the mass media consumer to develop selection strategies for optimizing the information available on mass media channels lest he or she suffer information overload. In writing this book, we worked hard to bring order out of chaos by optimizing and sequencing the amount of information we felt you needed to know about the forty-plus communication theories. As well, this summary and the "Nutshells" are examples of using redundancy to help you retain the massive amounts of information provided in this book. As well, we know that Rational Argumentation Theory helps journalists analyze competing arguments on controversial issues. RAT also allows the consumer of mass media to assess the validity of competing cases on such important mediated issues as employment, health care, and foreign policy. Additionally, we know that Symbolic Convergence Theory helps explain how newspaper, television, and radio programs create fantasy themes and fantasy types that can be used by politicians and advertisers as they try to persuade. For example, President Clinton frequently used the fantasy type "seize the day" popularized by the movie the *Dead Poet's Society*. Also, the recycling advocates used the fantasy type of "Do the Right Thing" (recently repopularized by Spike Lee's movie of the same name) on their recycling containers. Similarly, we know that Uncertainty Reduction Theory points to how individuals form a relationship with fictitious characters in soap operas and television programs. URT also explains that personal disclosures by talk show hosts build trust and liking within the mass audience. Then, too, we know that Narrative Paradigm Theory explains how the mythic stories aired via the media provide idealistic/moralistic and materialistic values for society. It explains how such movies as *Dancing with Wolves* or a book like *Bury My Heart at Wounded Knee* (Brown, 1970) convey a new sympathy and empathy for Native American cultures. Finally, we know that Diffusion of Innovations Theory explains the role of the mass media in creating awareness for the spread of new innovations and how infomercials create the interpersonal dynamic necessary for diffusion to occur. DIT also explains the necessary interaction between mass media channels and face-to-face interpersonal channels for the diffusion of ideas and products. It tells us that without such interfaces, critical mass will not be reached and the idea or product will not diffuse.

Then, when we add the four contextual theories, our explanation of the phenomena of mass communication becomes even more complete. For example, the Spiral of Silence Theory explains how the mass media can work in conjunction with majority opinion and authoritative rule to silence minority beliefs and engender conformity. Additionally, Agenda-Setting Theory explains the effect of the mass media in shaping what issues people think about. Cultivation Effects Theory explains that heavy exposure to television distorts our view of reality and makes us more fearful and distrustful of others. This theory tells you that if you want to feel safe, don't pay attention to the mass media. Finally, Uses and Gratifications Theory maintains that the mass media exhibit only minor effects on audiences because the individual audience member exerts control over media selection and information processing. As a whole, the six general communication theories and four contextual theories provide you with a unified understanding of the mass communication context. They enable you to describe, explain, and predict human action as it is affected by the media. **Figure 10-1** portrays Corey, our communication graduate on-the-job, using a mass communication contextual theory to good advantage.

"Because our corporation doesn't want to foster a false image of a violent, depraved America, as predicted by Cultivation Effects Theory, I recommend that we place our ads on TV programs that foster family values."

FIGURE 10-1.   Communication Graduate On-the-Job

Intercultural Communication Context Theories

Chen and Starosta (1996) concluded that "as we encounter ever greater cultural and cocultural diversity, the careful study of intercultural communication competence becomes increasingly important" (p. 373). Kim and Paulk (1994) reported that more than a half-million people work for Japanese-owned and -operated companies in the United States. Lustig and Koester (1996) pointed out that four out of five new jobs generated in the United States are the direct result of foreign trade. Here, it is time for a rest stop on our trail to understanding communication theories to share with you how we emphasize the importance of intercultural communication to our communication theory students. We ask them to think of the world as an apartment building with one hundred people in it representing the various national cultures. The building would have fifty-nine Asians, twelve Africans, ten Europeans, eight Latin Americans, six former members of the Soviet Union, and five North Americans (residents of the Canadian Commonwealth, the United States of America, and the United States of Mexico). In addition, the U.S. is a multicultural society in which half of us regard ourselves as hyphenated Americans, that is, African-Americans, Asian-Americans, Italian-Americans, Irish-Americans, Mexican-Americans, and so forth. Nonetheless, U.S. Americans are notoriously delinquent in our acquisition of second languages. A popular joke that the French tell about us goes like this: What do you call a person who speaks three languages? Answer: Trilingual. What do you call a person who speaks two languages? Answer: Bilingual. What do you call a person who speaks one language? Answer: American.

There is little doubt that both our geographic and historically political separation from the rest of the world contributed to the monolingual characteristic. Similarly, there is little doubt that the experience of World War II taught our nation that we must not isolate ourselves from the world community; we must play an active role on the international economic and political stage. With that role, the nation quickly discovered that they needed to increase their individual intercultural communication competence. Thus, you should not find it surprising that the roots of the intercultural communication context emerged from the Foreign Service Institute, which was part of the Department of State from 1946–1956 (Leeds–Hurwitz, 1990).

Edward Hall, a U.S. anthropologist, worked with the Foreign Service Institute training soldiers and U.S. diplomats in culture. Hall's lessons, developed for the foreign service, soon led to his teaching intercultural communication. Hall (1959, 1966, 1976, 1984) believed that culture is communication—a process that is patterned, learned, and identifiable. Hall's *The Silent Language* (1959) became an important book for the fledgling interest in the intercultural communication context. The book also served as the springboard for studies of nonverbal communication. The reason that Hall's writings interested scholars studying both intercultural and nonverbal communication is that his strategy for teaching intercultural communication competence at the Foreign Service Institute (Leeds–Hurwitz, 1990), presented initially in Hall and Trager (1953), used a metatheory for comparing two cultures that included such linguistic metaconcepts as *proxemics, time, paralanguage,* and *kinesics.* In other words, Hall and Trager taught that cultures varied on the dimension of preferred personal space (proxemics), on the importance of punctuality and immediate decision-making (time), on the use and place of grunts, belches, and laughter (paralanguage), and on the use of gestures, eye contact, and body movements (kinesics).

In Chapter 5, we briefly discussed three cross-cultural studies (Hammer & Martin, 1992; Kramer, 1993; Olaniran & Williams, 1995). Each one pointed to the need for training in intercultural communication competence as they grounded URT in the intercultural context. These studies reflected the discipline's ongoing interest in training people to be interculturally competent. As a consequence of that interest, several theories of interpersonal and intercultural communication competency exist (Spitzberg, 1988). Spitzberg and Cupach (1984) developed a Theory of Interpersonal Communication competence that has been adapted for use in intercultural communication training (Lustig & Koester, 1996). Spitzberg and Cupach (1994) defined communication competence as the "ability to adapt messages appropriately to the interaction context" (p. 63). In the case of intercultural communication, for example, if you were living with a roommate from another country, would you feel competent to engage in appropriate and effective communication behaviors? Does your competence allow you to avoid insulting your roommate with inappropriate communication? Can you achieve your communication goals effectively when talking to that roommate? To achieve the cross-cultural competency objectives, Spitzberg and Cupach (1994) argued that you need three qualities: (1) knowledge about your roommate and his or her culture; (2) suitable motivation for communicative interaction; and (3) the requisite communication skills.

Koester and Olebe (1988) and Olebe and Koester (1989) identified eight requisite skills that demonstrate intercultural communication competency: (1) display respect; (2) correctly orient knowledge (differentiate between opinion and fact); (3) convey empathy (feel as they feel); (4) choose appropriate task–role behavior (work well in cross-cultural groups); (5) appropriately manage interaction (greeting and leaving skills, turn-taking skills); (6) display relational role behavior (building and maintaining harmonious interpersonal relations skills); (7) show tolerance for ambiguity (don't panic at new and uncomfortable situations); and (8) accept an appropriate interaction posture (nonjudgmental).

Edward Hall (1976), while at the Foreign Service Institute, identified variances in two cultures' placement on a *high-context* versus *low-context continuum* as the most likely place where people would be different enough that their respective communication competencies would be threatened. For example, the competent intercultural communicator needs to know that members of high-context cultures rely more on environmental cues and nonverbal codes than members of low-context cultures, who prefer to state the message explicitly. The Japanese, African American, and Mexican American cultures tend to be high-context cultures that internalize the meaning of messages conveyed by contexts and use more nonverbal coding, whereas the English, European-American, German, and Israeli cultures tend to be more low-context, ignore environment messages, speak directly, and use less nonverbal coding.

Gert Hofstede (1980, 1983) reported on four additional places or continua that at the macro level impinge on intercultural communication competency: power distance versus social equals, uncertainty avoidance versus uncertainty tolerance, masculinity versus femininity, and individualist versus collectivist continua. The *power distance* versus *social equals* continuum is concerned with human equality and inequality that may derive from social hierarchies based on such antecedents as wealth, age, physical strength, occupation, education, and birth order. For example, countries such as Sweden and Canada display more social equality than power distance cultures such as Japan or Portugal. *Uncertainty avoidance* versus *uncertainty tolerance* is the tendency for a culture not to tolerate or to tolerate ambiguity and change. Cultures with a low tolerance for uncertainty build institutions and rules to create stability, whereas cultures with a high tolerance for uncertainty allow for more differences in individuals. The United States and Denmark exhibit a high tolerance for uncertainty, whereas the Japanese and Greek cultures use more rituals to enculturate within a narrow range of accepted activities. The *masculinity* versus *femininity* continuum reflects a culture's placement on such issues as achievement versus nurturing, patriarchal versus matriarchal, and gender inequality or equality. Japan and Austria typify high masculinity cultures and Sweden and Norway typify low masculinity cultures. The final continuum regards a culture's placement on the *individualist* versus *collectivist* range. Individualist cultures put a high value on individual initiative; collectivist cultures place a high value on the family, the group, the organization, and the society. Austria, Great Britain, and the United States exemplify high individualist cultures; Peru, South Korea, and Venezuela exemplify high collectivist cultures. Hofstede's typology is based on a worldwide study of 100,000 IBM employees from 50 countries.

Anxiety/Uncertainty Management Theory (AUMT)

William Gudykunst (1988, 1993, 1995) introduced Anxiety/Uncertainty Management Theory (AUMT). AUMT explains effective communication in the intercultural context. The theory is a derivative of Information Systems Theory that we presented in Chapter 2 and a direct analogue of Uncertainty Reduction Theory presented in Chapter 5 (Asante & Gudykunst, 1989). After working with Charles Berger for several years to ground Uncertainty Reduction Theory in the intercultural communication context, Gudykunst set out in 1988 to develop a free-standing theory—AUMT—that would be bound to the intercultural communication context.[8] AUMT seeks to minimize communication errors that might occur when a stranger approaches a person or group of persons from another culture. As Gudykunst (1995) put it: "Communication is effective to the extent that we are able to minimize misunderstandings" (p. 15). AUMT helps to minimize misunderstandings by optimizing uncertainty reduction and anxiety reduction.

Gudykunst (1988, 1995) specified AUMT's assumptions: (1) the management of anxiety and uncertainty is the basic cause influencing effective communication; (2) social information needs to be optimized so that anxiety and uncertainty reach neither their maximum nor minimum thresholds; (3) at least one participant in an intergroup or intercultural encounter is a stranger; (4) social information is both interpersonal and intercultural; (5) in same-culture contacts we are not usually aware of our communication process, but we are in new intercultural contacts; (6) strangers overestimate their communication effectiveness; and (7) if we are mindful of the communication process, we can communicate effectively with strangers.

AUMT's basic concept, like URT's, is social information-sharing; however, with AUMT the information shared will be about both the respective individuals and the respective cultures. As Gudykunst (1995) stated: "The amount of anxiety we experience when we interact with strangers affects the quality of the [personal and cultural] information we gather" (p. 40). Dr. Cragan's youngest daughter's wedding was in Platsa, Greece. In this little Greek village the custom was for the bride's family to walk to the church and meet the groom at the door. At this point, custom dictated that the groom would show deference (power distance) to the father of the bride by kissing his hand. Fortunately, Professor Cragan's daughter informed him of this custom so that he would be mindful and would not commit a social faux pas. It is this type of social information-sharing that makes

Gudykunst's AUMT a truly contextual theory of intercultural communication and not just a heuristic application of the general communication theory called Uncertainty Reduction.

AUMT's message structure concepts include scripts, the cognitive structures that help us understand the situation and call forth the required communication (message organization packets). However, many scripts from the native culture will cause confusion, and we need actively to seek out the information that will tell us the scripts of the new culture.

AUMT's communication dynamic is not specifically outlined in works written to this date. Nonetheless, Gudykunst's concept of *mindfulness*—being open to new information, being aware of more than one perspective, and focusing on the communication process—indicates that the benign dynamic of URT has been carried over to the new theory. Gudykunst has yet to ground the effects of URT's strategic dynamic on AUMT. Recall, however, that Hall began his intercultural training with full knowledge of the State Department's concern about strategic communication at the height of the Cold War. Today, we still use strategic communication to help meet our national economic and political goals. Likewise, a U.S. stranger may approach a Japanese or Mexican group for the purposes of selling a product; or you may participate in a Japanese American work team in which the members are highly competitive. The effects of carrying over URT's strategic dynamic have yet to be studied because, to date, AUMT assumes only a benign, cooperative, intercultural experience.

AUMT uses an axiomatic format to establish the relationship among its theoretical concepts. As of 1995, AUMT contained ninety-four axioms with the promise of more to come. Although this axiomatic format makes for cumbersome reading, it is easily understood in terms of The Communication Metatheory (Chapter 1) when one recognizes that most of its axioms concern communicator attributes and medium$_2$ cultural–contextual complexities of a stranger meeting another cultural group.

The communicators in AUMT include a *stranger* and the *new cultural group* with which he or she is in contact. Everyone is a potential stranger who may contact a new intercultural group and everyone we meet is a potential stranger. Again, the role of being a stranger causes anxiety and uncertainty and we seek and give information to reduce this anxiety and uncertainty. Following the lead of interpersonal communication competency theorists discussed in the introduction to this section, Gudykunst discusses more than a dozen communicator attributes classified under the interpersonal competency theory's concepts of motivation, knowledge, and skills. These attributes constitute AUMT's initial thirty-seven axioms. Motivation attributes include the needs for inclusion, conformity, and confidence. Knowledge attributes include mindfulness, self-monitoring, and adaptability. Skills attributes include information-gathering, information-processing, and information-giving.

The medium$_2$ substances in which AUMT propagates and grows consist of the potential divergent placements of a stranger and a new culture on any of the five cultural continua stipulated in the introduction to this contextual area: high-context versus low context, power distance versus social equals, uncertainty avoidance versus uncertainty tolerance, masculinity versus femininity, and individualist versus collectivist. From these continua Gudykunst (1995) generated more than forty axioms concerning such situations as a low-context, individualistic, U.S. citizen meeting a high-context, collectivist Japanese group. For example, Axiom 54 states that "an increase in collectivism will be associated with an increase in the need for a sense of group inclusion when meeting with strangers" (p. 47).

Then, Axiom 85 states that "an increase in collectivism will be associated with an increase in the ability to gather appropriate information about strangers" (p. 53).

AUMT's evaluative concepts are optimized anxiety and optimized uncertainty. *Anxiety* is the affective (emotional) equivalent of uncertainty; it is anticipatory fear. *Uncertainty* concerns both one's knowledge of the stranger's attitudes, feelings, and beliefs (cognitive uncertainty) and one's ability to predict her or his behavior (behavioral uncertainty). Much like its kissin' cousin Information Systems Theory (presented in Chapter 2), Gudykunst's (1995, p. 13) AUMT recognizes that both too little information and too much information are bad. In terms of anxiety, if our fear levels are too high we will be catatonic, but on the other hand, if we become too complacent we will not pay attention to what is happening and miscues and misunderstandings will occur. Similarly, if our uncertainty levels are too high we don't know anything and can't predict the stranger's behavior, and can't talk with them. On the other hand, if uncertainty is too low, the conversation loses its novelty and we will become bored.

Face Negotiation Theory (FNT)

Face Negotiation Theory (FNT), developed by Stella Ting–Toomey (1985, 1988a), grew out of her intercultural application of her work on cultural rhetorical sensitivity, decision-making style in intercultural organizations, and communication in relationships.[9] FNT will be easy for you to understand given what you have learned so far in this textbook. FNT is a stitched-together theory that combines elements of Face Management Theory (presented in Chapter 8), two of the five continua of cultural variability (individualist versus collectivist cultures and high-context versus low-context cultures) introduced in the initial discussion of the intercultural context, and a typology of negotiation styles (controlling/confronting and obligating/avoiding) to explain conflicts in East–West intercultural negotiation, particularly conflicts arising between representatives of the U.S. and Japanese cultures. Morisaki and Gudykunst (1994) described FNT as "a theory designed to explain how people in individualistic and collectivistic cultures negotiate face and deal with conflict" (p. 52).

According to Ting–Toomey and Cocroft (1994), FNT exhibits five assumptions: (1) people in all cultures try to maintain and negotiate face in all communication situations; (2) face is only problematic when situated identities are questioned; (3) communication conflict situations demand active facework management by both conflict parties; (4) conflict parties will engage in four types of facework management—self-face concern and other-face concern, and autonomy-face and approval-face maintenance; and (5) the cultural variability continua influence the communicators' selection of facework strategies and conflict or negotiation styles.

Gudykunst and Ting–Toomey with Elizabeth Chua (1988), Morisaki and Gudykunst (1994), and Ting–Toomey (1988a, 1988b) contributed to the development of FNT. Ting–Toomey (1988) presented FNT's axiomatic propositions. FNT assumes that (1) members of all cultures negotiate over the concept of face; (2) face is problematic in uncertain situations; (3) face-negotiation entails multiple goal orientations; (4) all negotiators are concerned about self-face in uncertain situations; (5) negotiators are concerned about positive and negative face in uncertain situations; (6) relational variables affect the concern for face; (7) situational variables affect the concern for face; (8) and cultural variables affect the face strategies selected (Ting–Toomey, 1988, pp. 219–220).

Ting–Toomey envisioned a kind of "Americans are from Mars and Japanese are from Venus" type of conflict. This bipolar conflict of individualist, low-context, cultures and collectivist, high-context, cultures serves as the communication dynamic of the theory. For example, people from the United States operate from the "I" identity system while the Japanese operate from the "we" identity system. The U.S. individuals use a Western conceptualization of face that includes self-protection, while the Japanese operate from an Eastern definition of face that centers on the protection of mutual-face and other-face. FNT's communication dynamic produces a dichotomous, nonisomorphic negotiation style in all communication aspects. The stereotype is that the individualistic, low-context, U.S. culture has negotiators who are concerned with self-face preservation and autonomy, use a direct, problem-solving style of negotiation, and use direct speech and direct emotional expressions. On the other hand, this same communication dynamic characterizes the collectivist, high-context Japanese negotiators as concerned with the other person's face and mutual face, who use an obligating or avoidance style of negotiation, and who use indirect speech and indirect emotional expressions.

FNT strikes a certain believable chord when we look at the continuing failure of the United States and Japan to resolve their trade policy conflicts. In the last quarter of the twentieth century, each U.S. administration has claimed it has solved the trade deficit problems with Japan while at the same time each Japanese Prime Minister has reaffirmed to the Japanese that their international dignity has been maintained by standing up to the United States.

The medium$_2$ in which FNT propagates and prospers is situated conflict within intercultural or cross-cultural situations. FNT exhibits an implied evaluative concept of *intercultural communication competency*. Implicitly, FNT says that without cross-cultural training, negotiators from both individualist and collectivist cultures will fail when confronting each other. At present, the major grounding studies for this theory are Stewart, et al. (1986), Ting–Toomey (1988b), and Ting–Toomey, et al. (1991). However, the 1991 study did not confirm the predicted stereotypic behavior of the "I" and "we" cultures. In fact, the data seemed to support the opposite conclusion. For example, Morisaki and Gudykunst (1994) argued that the data indicated that "the Japanese respondents were more concerned with self-face than the respondents from the United States" (p. 55). However, Morisaki and Gudykunst attributed these unusual findings to an error in the measuring instrument. The instrument did not assess mutual face. As a result, FNT awaits grounding research that resolves this anomaly.

will understand
this better once
research course
is done!

Cross-Cultural Adaptation Theory (CCAT)

Young Yun Kim's (1995) Cross-Cultural Adaptation Theory (CCAT) explains the diffusion of a new host culture through a population of immigrants.[10] It's a systems network theory that envisions a two-step flow of mass and interpersonal communication information to help assist an immigrant population in adapting to a host culture. CCAT's roots reside in the general theory, Diffusion of Innovations, presented in Chapter 7. Indeed, if you can envision the diffusion of the elements of a new culture occurring inside an individual's head, as well as to a population of immigrants, you understand this theory in a nutshell. Kim's longitudinal study of Korean immigrants indicated that it took about seven years for a Korean to acculturate to the U.S. culture. Through a series of research reports presented over a twenty-year period, Kim developed and refined her intercultural communication theory of acculturation.

Kim (1995) stated that for CCAT to hold true, three assumptions are required: (1) the strangers must have had a primary socialization in one culture (or subculture) and have moved into a different and unfamiliar culture (or subculture); (2) the strangers are at least minimally dependent on the host environment for meeting their personal and social needs; and (3) the strangers are engaged in continuous, firsthand communication experiences with that environment.

CCAT's basic concept is *host culture information*, which may include subtleties of the language, customs, mores, values, habits, day-to-day living patterns of the host culture, and so forth. This host culture information is received interpersonally and through mass media channels and is processed by the immigrant as personal and public communication through both the host and ethnic mass media and host and ethnic interpersonal communication. Put simply, a new Korean immigrant to Chicago is going to read Korean language newspapers and U.S. newspapers and she's going to talk to people who speak English in English and to Korean Americans in both English and Korean. Kim found this multilayered communication network to be necessary for the new immigrant to acculturate successfully. In other words, Kim found that new Korean immigrants needed to keep one foot in both cultures for a period of time as they learn their new culture.

Kim (1995) explained the *intra*personal communication dynamic that occurs within the head of the new immigrant as the "*stress–adaptation–growth* dynamic" (p. 176). Stress occurs by confronting a new and unfamiliar culture, adaptation means acquiring the new culture's customs, and growth springs from the learning of a new idea. However, Kim's research showed that the stress–adaptation–growth dynamic is not a linear process. The immigrant is engaged in a dialectic with the new culture and must periodically draw back into the old culture for emotional release and comfort. This is where the ethnic mass media and ethnic interpersonal communication becomes so necessary.

You may have traveled in another country testing your newly acquired foreign language skills and found that after just a couple of days of speaking the foreign language, getting directions in the foreign language, ordering food in the foreign language, and talking with foreigners, you were relieved to find a U.S. newspaper, an English newscast, a fellow U.S. citizen, and even a McDonald's. Kim described this dynamic as a "draw-back-to-leap" forward pattern that actually assists and serves as a necessary part of the acculturation process. One litmus test of when you have successfully acculturated is when you can have dreams in the new culture's language.

CCAT's communicator terms are *stranger(s)* and *host society*. Kim (1995) explained that strangers include such people as immigrants, resettlers, vacationers, sojourners, refugees, exchange students, and business employees who begin the cultural adaptation process as outsiders. One of the key characteristics for the stranger to succeed in adapting is motivation to learn the culture. The host society cocommunicator also exhibits several communicator attributes. These include receptivity, conformity pressure, and ethnic group strength.

CCAT's medium$_2$ concept that allows propagation and growth is the host culture, explained above. The theory's sole evaluative concept is host culture communication competency. *Host culture communication competency* includes cognitive competency (knowledge of the host culture and language including history, worldviews, beliefs, and mores), cognitive complexity (the ability to think and process information in complex ways), and affective competency (the ability to acquire the new culture's aesthetic and emotional sensibilities). These three elements go together to help the stranger function verbally and nonverbally in the new culture's social settings.

Unifying the General and Contextual Intercultural Theories

Let's slow our pace a bit and take a rest stop. Let's think about how far we've come. We now know that the six general communication theories explored in Chapters 2–7 and the three contextual theories just discussed provide a unified understanding of the intercultural communication context. For example, Information Systems Theory explains that the clashing of two cultures produces a lot of noise in the communication system and that the difficulty of translating diverse coding systems creates large amounts of ambiguity. IST cautions that redundancy must be increased and speaking rate slowed in intercultural communication episodes. Similarly, the use of nonverbal gestures are fraught with danger when used interculturally. The U.S. OK sign is not universally decoded in the same way by everyone. As well, we know that Rational Argumentation Theory presents a common base, known as the rational decision-making process, used in all civilized cultures. However, RAT also tells us that some arguments are field (culturally) dependent. Additionally, we know that the fantasy-chaining process analyzed by Symbolic Convergence Theory occurs in all cultures. However, we also know that a fruitful U.S. fantasy type does not necessarily work well in Japan or Saudi Arabia. Similarly, with Uncertainty Reduction Theory, we know that social information-sharing reduces uncertainty across cultures, although the type of information shared and the sequence of sharing is culturally variant. With Narrative Paradigm Theory, we know that all cultures exhibit archetypal myths that drive their value systems, but as yet we do not yet know how closely those values fit the idealistic/moralistic and materialistic strains of the American Dream. Finally, we know that scores of studies demonstrate that the Diffusion of Innovations Theory needs to be applied differently in other cultures. The way in which diffusion talk works varies by whether a given culture is an individualistic, collectivist, or authoritarian social system.

Then, when we add the three contextual theories, our explanation of the intercultural context becomes even more complete. For example, Anxiety/Uncertainty Management Theory explains how communication error can be reduced when strangers approach a new group or culture. This is especially true when the individual is coming from an individualistic or collectivist culture, or vice versa. Face Negotiation Theory explains how people in individualist and collectivist cultures adjust their respective negotiation and communication styles to maintain interpersonal face. Cross-Cultural Adaptation Theory explains the seven-year assimilation process of an immigrant to a new culture. That process requires a movement back and forth between the original culture and the new culture for successful assimilation. As a whole, the six general communication theories and the three contextual theories provide you with a unified understanding of the intercultural communication context. They enable you to describe, explain, predict, and control human action within cross-cultural encounters. **Figure 10-2** provides a view of Corey, our communication graduate on-the-job, using an intercultural communication theory to good advantage.

"With the implementation of our new overseas division, it is imperative that we reduce the uncertainty of our employees by providing training in AUMT. Also, our sales representatives need special training following the advice of Face Negotiation Theory. We don't want to hinder sales by committing intercultural social blunders."

FIGURE 10-2.   Communication Graduate On-the-Job

Summary

This chapter introduced you to the communication theories endemic to the mass and intercultural communication contexts. The chapter indicated how the general and contextual theories together explain communication within the mass and intercultural communication contexts. In the first half of the chapter, we introduced you to four mass communication context theories, Spiral of Silence, Agenda-Setting, Cultivation Effects, and Uses and Gratifications Theory. In the second half of the chapter, we introduced you to three intercultural communication context theories, Anxiety/Uncertainty Management, Face Negotiation, and

Cross-Cultural Adaptation Theory. **Box 10-1**, entitled "Understanding Mass and Intercultural Communication Context Theories in a Nutshell," presents a synthesized look at the theories.

BOX 10-1   Understanding Mass and Intercultural Communication Context Theories in a Nutshell

Mass Communication Context. This chapter introduced four contextual mass communication theories: Spiral of Silence Theory, Agenda-Setting Theory, Cultivation Effects Theory, and Uses and Gratifications Theory. Of course, in Chapter 7, we presented a general communication theory, Diffusion of Innovations Theory, that is widely discussed in mass communication texts. Also, in Chapter 11, we present Marshall McLuhan's Media Law Theory, a communication microtheory with application to the mass communication context. As well, we would remind you that the other general communication theories—Information Systems Theory, Rational Argumentation Theory, Symbolic Convergence Theory, Uncertainty Reduction Theory, and Narrative Paradigm Theory—by definition work to explain communication in the mass communication context.

Spiral of Silence Theory (SST). SST explains the long-term effect of the mass media on public opinion and human action and inaction. SST explains how the mass media work in conjunction with majority opinion to silence minority beliefs on political issues and engender conformity.

Agenda-Setting Theory (AT). AT explains the effect of the mass media in shaping what issues people think about. AT argues that people's beliefs about the importance of an issue correlates with the amount of attention that the mass media gives to that issue.

Cultivation Effects Theory (CET). CET posits that heavy exposure to television's images and messages leads viewers to see the real world as consistent with those mediated portrayals. CET reports that heavy viewers of television are more fearful and distrustful of others than they would otherwise be.

Uses and Gratifications Theory (UGT). UGT explains why people choose, use, and receive benefits from attending to the mass media. UGT argues that

the media actually have limited effects on audiences because the individual audience member exerts control over media selection and information processing.

Intercultural Communication Context. This chapter also introduced three contextual intercultural communication theories: Anxiety/Uncertainty Management Theory, Face Negotiation Theory, and Cross-Cultural Adaptation Theory. Also, in Chapter 11, we present a number of communication microtheories that help explain intercultural communication; Speech/Communication Accommodation Theory is especially useful. Likewise, the six general communication theories explain the intercultural communication context. For example, Uncertainty Reduction Theory has been grounded extensively in the intercultural context and Symbolic Convergence Theory is often used to explain the visions that provide meaning, emotion, and motive for action for the participants in various cultures.

Anxiety/Uncertainty Management Theory (AUMT). AUMT explains effective communication in intercultural contexts. AUMT seeks to minimize communication error that might occur when a stranger approaches a person or group from another culture by optimizing the social information that is provided.

Face Negotiation Theory (FNT). FNT explains how people in individualistic and collectivist cultures negotiate face and deal with conflict. FNT stitches together elements of Face Management Theory (Chapter 8) to explain how two or more people from different cultures adjust their negotiation styles to maintain face.

Cross-Cultural Adaptation Theory (CCAT). CCAT explains how an immigrant or sojourner adapts and assimilates to a new culture. CCAT posits that the person new to a culture moves back and forth between the original culture and the new culture to achieve successful acculturation.

Chapter 11

Communication Microtheories

Communication scholars theorize about narrow but important bands of communicative interaction.

Chapter Outline

Communication microtheories are powerful, thin-banded theories that illuminate some critical aspect of communicators communicating in a medium. Like general communication theories, communication microtheories are not context-bound. Microtheories may of course be anatomically correct in that they exhibit basic, structural, and evaluative technical concepts; nevertheless, the breadth of their explanation is limited to a narrow band of communication. In other words, communication microtheories are like a laser beam, focusing on only one part of communicators communicating in a medium. As such, communication microtheories tend to feature one of the six metatheoretical technical concepts of The Communication Metatheory (TCM) used throughout this book. In this chapter, we will present a dozen microtheories whose narrow band of communication rests or resides primarily within one of the six VENN circles. In short, the communication microtheories presented in this chapter reflect and emphasize either a basic, message, dynamic, communicator, medium, or evaluative metatheoretical anatomical metaconcept as they explain a narrow, yet important, band of communication.

Basic Concept Microtheories

Let's take a brief rest stop and look at where we are going. Recall that, in Chapter 1, we explained that a basic technical concept is the unit of analysis that a theory primarily observes in communication interaction. A basic technical concept is often isomorphic to a communicative force as we saw in Chapters 2–7. There, we looked at the force of social information-sharing, the force of diffusing innovative talk, the force of fantasy-chaining, and so forth. In this section, we focus on three communication theories, two of which explain the force of lying, called deceptive communication, and one that explains the force of interpersonal requests on communicative interaction, called compliance-gaining.

Knapp and Comadena (1979) sketched out and defined deceptive communication as a topic for theory-building. They stated that deception is "the conscious alteration of information a person believes to be true in order to change significantly another's perceptions from what the deceiver thought they would be without the alteration" (p. 271). O'Hair and Cody (1994) portrayed deceptive or lying communication "as the dark side of communication" (p. 183). Ekman (1985) identified two categories of deception: concealment and falsification. Hopper and Bell (1984) presented a six category system: fictions (white lies), playing (tricks), lies (untruths), crimes (disguise), masked (two-faced), and *un*lies (distortions). However, by the 1990s, two lines of research had developed that moved scholarship beyond the presentations of mere taxonomies of lies to theorizing about deceptive communication as a whole and peoples' responses to it (e.g., Levine & McCornack, 1996; Buller, Stiff, & Burgoon, 1996).

Information Manipulation Theory (IMT)

IMT provides "a framework for describing the different ways that information can be manipulated to accomplish deceit" (McCornack, 1992, p. 17). McCornack (1992) defined deceptive messages as ones that "mislead listeners by covertly violating the principles that underlie and guide conversational understanding" (p. 2). IMT draws together within one theory research on four ways of deceiving or manipulating information: fabrication, con-cealment, distortion, and equivocation (Jacobs, Dawson, & Brashers, 1996). McCornack developed IMT from the conversational maxims of H. Paul Grice's (1975, 1989) Linguis-tic Theory of Conversational Implicature. Grice's maxims reflect the principle of coopera-tion, that is, communicators will (1) optimize the information presented; (2) provide truthful, supported, quality information; (3) offer information relevant to the context; and (4) present the information in an appropriate manner that is not obscure or ambiguous. In other words, the cooperative principle indicates a deep structure of human conversation that says humans strive to be informative, truthful, relevant, and clear.

IMT clicks in when a communicator violates one of the maxims and thereby deviates from a spirit of cooperative conversational behavior. IMT explains that the listener or receiver will perceive the deception—regardless of the infinite variety of deceptive messages—as vi-olating one of the four maxims of the cooperative principle (McCornack, 1992). Moreover, such violations will result in an increase in emotional intensity on the part of the listener or receiver and create a crisis in the relationship.

McCornack and his colleagues tested IMT by developing scenarios of typical sensitive dating situations that many college students have experienced. They then had students de-velop five responses that reflected a completely truthful response plus a violation of each one of the four maxims. To understand a typical scenario, imagine that you were confronted with a situation in which you had made a date for Friday night with one person and another person that you had just started dating arrives unexpectedly hoping to spend the evening with you. How would you react to that situation. The completely truthful response might be: *"I wish you would have called. I'm sorry, but I already have a date for tonight. I hope you'll understand, because I don't want to lose your company in the future."* A deceitful re-sponse that violates the quantity maxim might be: *"Thanks for stopping by. I really want to see you, but not tonight. Sorry!"* A deceitful violation of the truthfulness maxim might be: *"I can't see you tonight. I really don't feel very well. I'm staying home by myself. I'll call you tomorrow."* A violation of the relevance maxim might be: *"God I'm glad you showed up. I forgot when I saw you last that I'd thought about a late study date. I'll meet you in the Library at 11:30. I always enjoy studying with you."* An ambiguous violation might be: *"Sorry, I can't talk now. I'm just frazzled with all the things I have to do. See you!"* Mc-Cornack, et al. (1992) asked over 1,000 college students to rate responses like these in terms of their honesty and competency. They found that college students rated the quality viola-tion (actual lying) as the most deceitful violation, but the students also viewed the quantity, clarity, and relevance violations as significantly deceitful. They rated the truthful answer as the most competent response. Interestingly, the IMT researchers also found that a minimal level of suspicion is fundamental to the process of detecting deception, that relational part-ners adopt a "truth bias" toward judging all of a partner's messages as truthful, that partners abandon their "truth bias" at the first sign of potential deception, and that partners then be-come "fairly accurate at detecting attempts at deception on the parts of their relational part-ners" (McCornack & Levine, 1990a, 1990b, p. 229; McCornack & Parks, 1986, 1990).

IMT provides a conceptual framework for systematically identifying and classifying deception into four types regardless of the myriad ways in which people can individually express deception. To date, there have been a half-dozen grounding studies for the theory and one replication. Although Jacobs, Dawson, and Brashers (1996) claimed that their replication failed to corroborate the earlier findings, their purpose was to test the presence of receivers dismissing the discovered manipulations of information, a possibility that Mc-Cornack (1992) noted. At the same time, he stipulated such concerns were beyond the scope of his theory (p. 14). Here, we begin to see the clash of the active, interactive, trans-active communication dynamic of spin-off theories of Information Systems Theory. Mc-Cornack is theorizing assuming the interplay of an active and interactive dynamic and Jacobs, Dawson, and Brashers are criticizing assuming a transactional dynamic.

Interpersonal Deception Theory (IDT)

IDT is a communication microtheory developed at the University of Arizona under the direction of David Buller and Judee Burgoon. In 1996, Donald Ellis, the editor of *Communication Theory,* devoted an entire journal issue to this theory and two of its grounding studies and included two extensive criticisms of IDT along with a final rejoinder by Buller and Burgoon (1996) which indicated that they developed IDT from the belief that "a complete understanding of deception requires approaching it as a dynamic, iterative, process of mutual influence between senders who manipulate information to depart from the truth and receivers who attempt to establish the validity of those messages" (p. 235). Specifically, IDT posits the receiver as fulfilling the "starring role" in this theory, that is, the receiver is trying to detect deception (Burgoon, et al., 1996a). Buller and Burgoon (1996a) indicated that deceptive messages have three aspects: (1) the central deceptive message (usually verbal); (2) ancillary messages (both verbal and nonverbal) bolstering the "truthfulness" of a deceptive message; and (3) inadvertent behaviors (mostly nonverbal) that provide leakage pointing to the deceptive intent of the sender.

IDT is an axiomatic microtheory that contains to date eighteen general propositions that express the complex relationship between lying senders and interactive receivers who are aware of the global nature of the context and the relationship (Buller & Burgoon, 1996). The locus of their theoretical explanation of deception centers in the relevant features of the specific arena of face-to-face interpersonal communication. Burgoon and Buller (1996) stressed that IDT concerns "how senders attempt to produce credible messages; how receivers process and judge such messages; and how structural and functional features of communication itself, including the coordination of interaction between sender and receiver, influence this process" (p. 312).

The real-world benefit of IDT and its attendant research is that it calls into question the validity of a long-held belief that people can be trained to identify certain "nonverbal leakage cues" that indicate that a communicator is being deceitful or lying. The assumption suggested by Ekman and Friesen (1969) that nonverbal behavior is more telltale than verbal behavior as cues indicating the presence of deceptive messages is called seriously into question by IDT. Burgoon and Buller caution that as communication scholars "we need to alert consumers and colleagues that nonverbal cues are not surefire indicators of deceit" (p. 316). So far, the empirical findings indicate that, under many circumstances, deceivers dramatically change their verbal and nonverbal cues under interactive conditions with a suspicious receiver (Burgoon and Buller, 1994).

However, even when deception is viewed interactively through the lens of IDT, there still appears to be some consistency in the verbal and nonverbal cues emanating from deceitful communicators.[1] Buller, et al. (1996) indicated that both senders and receivers engage in strategic verbal behavior and nonstrategic nonverbal behavior. Nonetheless, "deceivers manage behavior through submissive, formal, and nonimmediate actions; they project a positive image with more pleasantness and relaxation; and they manage information through hesitant and brief messages" (p. 268). Moreover, deceivers "leak nervousness, arousal, and negative affect and suffer impaired performances that create disfluencies and poor impressions" (p. 268). DeTurck and Miller (1990) and deTurck, et al. (1990) reported success in training people to detect deception.

Compliance-Gaining/Resisting Theory (CGRT)

As communication scholars, we feel that we ought to be able to explain, that is, make a theory about, simple, verbal compliance-gaining requests. We seek to be able to explain the kinds of requests that fit certain situations, and the types of requests that will work. Professor Cragan is especially interested in this area of communication research because of his ineptitude at it. He can't even get his dog to lie down, much less gain the compliance of his grandsons. He's tried promises, he's tried threats, he's tried rational explanations, he's tried begging. All seem to fall on deaf ears as in: "I didn't hear you; I didn't think you meant for me to do it right now; or I thought you meant something else." Yes, Professor Cragan is truly the Rodney Dangerfield of effective compliance-gaining communication.

Despite the combined efforts of a score of researchers, the passage of more than twenty years of concerted effort, and the production of one hundred-plus published studies, the communication discipline remains without a unified theoretical explanation of compliance-gaining and -resisting. Frank Boster (1995), a co-winner of a national research award for scholarship of exceptional quality and influence for the initial study of compliance-gaining in the discipline (Miller, et al., 1977), evaluated the research program and concluded that the number one problem with it was the inability to find one unifying theory to explain all the data. As Boster (1995) noted: "Put simply, there is no theory, or set of competing theories, to explain the existing data adequately" (p. 92). In reviewing the compliance-gaining/resisting research, Berger (1994) came to a similar conclusion, that the number one problem with it was a "lack of firm theoretical grounding" (p. 492).

The research program's two primary weaknesses centered on the fact that the researchers studied self-reports of communication strategies rather than actual compliance-gaining/resisting communication and that they concentrated solely on verbal behavior and denied any role for nonverbal behavior in relationships. Berger (1994) argued that the "failure to take into account nonverbal behavior in the study of communication and power relationships is to doom oneself to study the tip of a very large iceberg" (p. 243).

However, there is research that reports actual communication interaction in compliance-gaining situations rather than using recall data or reactions to hypothetical scenarios and lists of strategies. Shields (1993) pointed out that the primary problem in theory-building is that there are two distinct compliance-gaining theories. One comes from work done in psychology and sociology (Marwell & Schmidt, 1967; and McGuire, 1964) that focuses on power, pressure, and dominance and other coercive strategies as explanations for compliance.[2] The other, CGRT, draws from work completed within the communication discipline that concentrates on actual compliance messages (Reardon, 1981, 1987) with a focus on noncoercive persuasive strategies such as appeals to appropriateness, consistency, the receiver's identity and values, and the effectiveness of the outcomes.[3] For example, Burke (1989) tested face, convergent, and criterion-related procedures for eliciting compliance strategies. She reported superiority for the actual message construction procedure over a checklist of pre-picked strategies that related to the Marwell and Schmidt (1967) coercive strategies. Reardon labeled the emphasis on actual communicative appeals the ACE model of compliance-reasoning.

Reardon and colleagues demonstrated that the message-centered compliance-gaining theory will hunt. For example, Reardon, et al. (1989) reported a compliance-resisting strategy study of 268 seventh-graders. They found that the seventh-graders employed three reasoning strategies (simple rejection, statement of typical behavior, expression of attitude/belief) and two antisocial strategies (rejection of person and walk away) to resist the offer of a cigarette. The antisocial strategies came into play when the seventh-graders had been pressured a second time. The "Just say no!" strategy emerged with acquaintances rather than friends and when the seventh-graders were in a group rather than a dyadic situation. Overall, compliance-resistance statements expressed personal beliefs, rules, and attitudes followed by statements of the negative consequences of smoking. Similarly, Alberts, Miller–Rassulo, and Hecht (1991) generated a set of drug (alcohol and marijuana) resistance strategies from narratives of thirty adolescents that complemented the Reardon, et al. (1989) resistance strategies for cigarette-smoking and provided evidence of their applicability to alcohol and marijuana resistance. Finally, Grant, King, and Behnke (1994) reported that such persuasive message strategies as explaining, promising, and ingratiating were significantly more effective than threats and warnings. Ifert and Roloff (1996) reported that males and females enact similar persistence behaviors (request for explanation, reason for rejection, and acknowledgment of legitimacy of the refusal) after receiving refusals based on unwillingness, inability, or imposition.

Message Structure Microtheories

Again, recall from Chapter 1 that the structural concepts of a communication theory provide a blueprint, design, or form to help frame basic concepts. Message concepts dress up and flesh out a theory. Some communication microtheories emphasize message structure as they provide a rich explanation of a narrow band of communication phenomena. In this section, we present three communication microtheories that emphasize the message structure theoretical metaconcept of The Communication Metatheory first presented in Chapter 1. Each exhibits high utility in terms of real-world application.

Action Assembly Theory (AAT)

In Chapter 5, we presented Uncertainty Reduction Theory's message structure concept of memory organization packets (MOPs), what are sometimes called scripts, that we as communicators develop and store to guide us in our daily interpersonal conversations. John Greene (1984, 1989, 1995), in a research program begun at the University of Wisconsin and Cleveland State University and continued at Purdue University, developed a communication microtheory called Action Assembly Theory. AAT is designed to explain the generative mechanisms of action involved in the creation of MOPs. Greene (1995) emphasized that "the theory posits a long-term memory store of modular elements" (p. 59) that link content and procedural knowledge into message production.

You can ground the validity of Greene's theory by simply telling out loud a story you have told many times. You will discover that you tell the story at about the same rate, using the same words, and the story follows a routine sequence. You even use the same gestures at the same time. Recall also that children will expect the story to be told the same way; they take pleasure in the redundancy. You learned by storytelling that practice makes perfect.

Greene and Lindsey (1989), Greene, Lindsey, and Hawn (1990), and Lindsey, et al. (1995) demonstrated that multiple goal messages are characterized by greater hesitancy at the onset and a greater number of nonverbal pauses and verbal fillers, that is, "ahs," "hmm's," "you knows," than single goal social messages. Such messages take more practice before you get them right. The need for more practice is especially true when the multiple goals are incompatible (Greene, et al., 1993).

You may have been using Greene's theory and not have known it when you last prepared a public speech, presented an oral report, asked a new friend out on a date, or asked your boss for a raise. Greene (1995) reported that the AAT research demonstrated that the actual practice of talk will make you more fluent because it allows you to coordinate your thought process with your verbal and nonverbal skills.[4] Moreover, the more complex the messages conveyed in talk, the more practice that is needed (Greene & Ravizza, 1995). So, if you want to be sure of what you are going to say (competence) and you want to say it right (performance), be sure and practice it ahead of time.

Speech/Communication Accommodation Theory (SCAT)

SCAT explains why Professor Cragan speaks English with a French accent as he orders dinner in Paris. It explains why Professor Shields talks like a seven-year-old when discussing cartoons with his nephew Philly. It explains why you might mimic the speech patterns of an employer during an employment interview. SCAT explains the tendency for communicators to experience *convergence* (a linguistic strategy whereby individuals accommodate vocal differences between themselves and others) of their speech styles. It's akin to talking baby talk to a baby. However, such convergence is not silly. It helps communicators achieve increased efficiency, gain approval, and maintain a positive social identity (Giles, et al., 1987). SCAT also explains that sometimes people choose not to accommodate vocal differences, but, instead, select the strategy of *divergence* to maintain or underscore social differences between speakers. For example, Giles and Powesland (1975) reported that a Welshman might emphasize his different dialect in the presence of an Englishman to assert his Welsh identity. In the eyes of the Englishman, the Welshman might appear less attractive for doing so, but the Welshman will have achieved his purpose of asserting his identity.

Buller and Aune (1988) found that if a speaker who is seeking compliance to a request for help will converge his or her speech rate to that of the listener's speech rate, compliance will increase. Such research may provide some hope for Professor Cragan. It indicates that if he will adapt his speech rate, sound, and vocabulary to that of his young grandsons, they might start complying with his behavior. You may have noted that at campus you adopt the patterns of the professors and students around you. Conversely, on your part-time or summer job you accommodate the speech style of others on the job. University educated African Americans often speak the language of the university in some settings and the language of their nonacademic brothers and sisters in others (Johnson & Buttny, 1982). Similar patterns occur among women in general. Hogg (1985) found that female speech patterns became more masculine in mixed-sex groups and more feminine in all-female groups.

Recently, Williams and Giles (1992) and others have been working on grounding SCAT to accommodate a number of subpopulations. Williams and Giles (1996) report less sweeping accommodation between subpopulations as the theory grows beyond speech accommodation to include message structures. They call this new line of research Communication Accommodation Theory.[5] Interestingly, Buzzanell, et al. (1996) grounded SCAT to the recorded and live messages left on telephone answering machines. They found that callers conform to the recorded messages. So, if you want brief responses, use brief machine messages. On the other hand, if you want lengthy responses, use long messages. Likewise, serious messages beget serious responses, humorous messages beget humorous responses, and deliberate messages beget deliberate responses.

Expectancy Violation Theory (EVT)

Another communication microtheory spawned in the research laboratories of the University of Arizona is EVT. It seeks to explain the effects of a narrow band of communicative interaction know as expectancy violation. To date, grounding has occurred primarily in the arena of nonverbal communication.[6] Burgoon and Hale (1988) stated that the "communication literature is rife with the assumption, and often the explicit dictum, that the road to success lies in conformity to social norms. One perspective that challenges that notion is nonverbal expectancy violation theory" (p. 58). They then noted that there are "circumstances under which violations of social norms and expectations may be a superior strategy to conformity" (p. 58).

Expectancy violation occurs whenever norms are violated, but such a violation is most meaningful when someone regards the violator as good or bad. For example, if you are similar to most people in the United States, you maintain a proxemic distance of about eighteen to forty-cight inches when talking to someone else. It's called *personal space.* Personal space is the bubble we have around us. Of course, Edward Hall (1959), in *The Silent Language,* sensitized us to this proxemics issue. He also indicated that such a normative distance differs cross-culturally. In the United States, you violate the distance expectancy by moving within zero to eighteen inches. The violation may be potentially good if the other person is attracted to you or potentially bad if the person is your academic advisor and is skeptical about your academic sincerity.

Judee Burgoon (1995) explained that EVT "postulates that if (a) an act is unexpected, (b) it is assigned favorable interpretations, and (c) it is evaluated positively, it will produce more favorable outcomes than an expected act with the same interpretations and evaluations" (p. 207). Burgoon and Jones (1976) grounded the idea that others perceive positively valenced communicators as more credible and attractive at proxemic violation distances while they rate negatively-valenced communicators most favorably at the expected normative distance. Thus, EVT tells us that communicators who can assume that they are well evaluated by another, others, or an audience can engage in expectancy violation and profit from it. Communicators who cannot predict that they are well liked are better off not violating expectations in most situations.

The predictive communication expectancies of the favorable evaluation are shaped by *communicator* (demo-psycho-socio-graphics), *relationship* (degree of familiarity, liking, attraction, social status), and *contextual* (formal, informal, task requirements) *characteristics.* These characteristics intermesh to form a *valence* that runs from highly positive (+1) through zero (0) to highly negative (–1). Such a *predictive communication valence* is triggered when an expectancy violation occurs. On seeing or hearing a violation of normative behavior, you immediately become aroused and try to evaluate the communicator. If it's someone you like, and they have violated their normative behavior by paying special attention to you, you may be pleased and more satisfied than you usually are with this person. On the other hand, if it is a person you do not care for or whom you suspect is manipulative, you may reject—even with hostility—prolonged eye contact, smiling, close proxemics, and so forth.

Dynamic Structure Microtheories

Again, it's time for a brief rest stop. TCM (Chapter 1) posited that one of the anatomical metatheoretical concepts of communication theories centers on a theory's communication dynamic. Recall that a theory's *communication dynamic structure* concerns a deep structure tension as to how the message should be formed, molded, or cast. The theories we present in this section focus on the communication dynamic structure concept of TCM. They are Relational Control Theory and Marital Communication Theory.

Relational Control Theory (RCT)

RCT's origin and roots rest in what has loosely been called "The Palo Alto Group." The group included a number of academics associated with The Mental Research Institute in Palo Alto, CA (near Stanford University). The anthropologist, Gregory Bateson, founded the institute in the 1950s. He initiated the development of a relational communication theory in conjunction with Paul Watzlavik, a psychologist who joined the group in the early 1960s. From 1959 to 1979, the Palo Alto Group published over one hundered articles and twenty books on relational communication. Wilder (1979) indicated that their most famous was Watzlavik, Beavin, and Jackson's (1967) *The Pragmatics of Human Communication.* Bateson (1957) indicated that the relational approach to communication owed a deep debt to information systems theorists' such as Norbert Wiener and Claude Shannon (see Chapter 2). Also, recall that we praised the relational control work of Rogers and Farace (1975) for developing a coding system for the pragmatic dimension of language when we presented Information Systems Theory in Chapter 2.[7]

The Palo Alto Group built their relational interactional approach to the study of communication and family therapy on five now famous communication axioms. Watzlavik, Beavin, and Jackson (1967) first reported these axioms. They have appeared in nearly every communication theory book written since that time. The first axiom is that "one cannot not communicate" (pp. 48–51). The axiom means that, from the relational perspective, you are always communicating even if you are acting like you don't want to communicate. The second axiom is that "messages contain content and relational dimensions" (pp. 51–54). The relational dimension classifies the content dimension and is therefore an ever-present meta-communication. The axiom means that if you say to your significant other, "Kiss me!" (a content message) any vocal quality of submissiveness, domineeringness, or sarcasm will serve as a metacommunication to help her or him peg the meaning of the statement. The third axiom is "the punctuation of the sequence of events" (pp. 54–59). This axiom means that communication is interactive over a series of exchanges, and the communicators may put a different punctuation on them. In other words, one person may think his or her spouse has a drinking problem, no matter what the exchange, and the second person may think the first spouse has a nagging problem, no matter what the exchange. In other words, communication in ongoing relationships is punctuated with the emotional interpretations of what has come before. The fourth axiom is "digital and analogic communication" (pp. 60–67) is present in all communication. Digital communication involves words and their referents. Words are an on–off switch—you either say them or you don't. Digital sound recording allows a specific start of the tone, a duration of the tone, and an end point for the tone. Analogic communication includes nonverbal signs and the referents they stand for. Such analogic elements of communication can be ongoing—they are not easily ended. For example, the analogic meaning of your raising your voice to your mother can affect not only the discussion at hand, but the next one, or two or three discussions after that. Just like analog recorded music, one sound blends into the next. The fifth axiom is that "all communicational interchanges are either symmetrical or complementary depending on whether they are based on equality or difference" (p. 70). Carol Wilder's (1979) review of the Palo Alto research program characterized it as "theoretically and epistemologically in progress" (p. 177). However, the concepts contained in the fifth axiom soon formed the central concepts in a theory of relational control.

Frank Millar and Edna Rogers (1976, 1987) developed the Theory of Relational Control as the output of a number of operational and grounding studies.[8] Their communication microtheory centered on the question, "Who controls a relationship?" They explained that the answer to the question is codefined by the communicators through redundant patterns of communication that are played over and over. They indicated that control may vary from topic to topic among partners, that is, one partner may control the budget and the other vacations. Zeitlow and VanLear (1991) reconfirmed the notion that couples negotiate issues of dominance and submission continually.

Relational Control Theory takes as its starting point the identification of two dynamic levels in communication. The first is the dynamic between the content and relationship dimensions of messages. The second is the tension or dynamic between one-up, one-down, and one-across potential states of any interactive message exchange.

Millar and Rogers (1976, 1987) posited *relational control* as the most important concept in explaining relational satisfaction. The RCT researchers further stipulated that there is a difference between dominance, domineering, and parallel control. *Dominance* means that one partner willingly yields control to the other ("You're the boss!"). On the other hand, when neither relationship partner wants to yield and both want to control *domineering* occurs ("That's my job!" "No it isn't!" "You'd better let me do it!"). When domineering is present, neither partner is pleased with the relationship.[9] *Parallel* means that power is distributed with each partner taking primary authority or control in certain realms ("You keep the checkbook; I'll take care of the yard!"). Wood (1995b) observed that the parallel distribution of power results in equality over all.

RCT exhibits real-world utility in the study of troubled relationships. Teresa Sabourin's (1995) study of spousal abuse is a good case in point. She found that, compared to nonabusive couples, spouses in abusive relationships tended to escalate their verbal exchanges by constantly responding with one-up moves to each other's comments. She concluded that this domineering message pattern, in which neither spouse will give in, may be the result of skill deficiency in arguing constructively. She emphasized, however, that training of both spouses may be necessary in order to reduce abuse. Recall that one of the real-world benefits of training in Rational Argumentation Theory concerned the reduction of verbal hostilities and direct aggression between adversaries.

Marital Communication Theory (MCT)

Mary Anne Fitzpatrick of the University of Wisconsin–Madison is primarily responsible for the development of MCT.[10] In the 1970s, she developed a marital couple typology (classification system) that captured distinct marital schemata. Fitzpatrick (1991) defined a *marital schemata* as "knowledge structures that represent the external world of marriage and provide guidelines about how to interpret incoming data" (p. 79). Fitzpatrick then developed a classification of marriage types based on responses to a seventy-seven-item questionnaire called the Relational Dimension Inventory (Fitzpatrick, 1977, 1988). Fitzpatrick and Ritchie (1994) reported that this inventory captured the responses of each member of a marital dyad on the dimensions of interdependency (sharing versus autonomy), ideology (traditionalism versus change), and communication (discussion versus conflict avoidance). Through a series of grounding studies, Fitzpatrick identified three pure communication dynamics. She named these patterns *traditional, independent,* and *separate.* She also found mixed patterns such as male-separate and female-traditional, and female-separate and male-traditional. About two-thirds of all couples classified as one of the three pure types with traditionals being the largest category and separatists being the smallest category (Fitzpatrick and Ritchie, 1994; Segrin and Fitzpatrick, 1992). The remaining third of the couples were mixed.

This theory richly describes the communication dynamic differences of these marital types (Fitzpatrick, 1977, 1988, 1991; Fitzpatrick & Ritchie, 1994; Segrin & Fitzpatrick, 1992). Traditionalists, which represent more than 30 percent of couples, is a pure type. Both the male and female tend to be cooperative and conciliatory. They hold traditional values of parenting and spending time together such as regular mealtimes. They value mutual interdependency over individual autonomy. They exhibit traditional sex-role divisions, with the woman taking the man's name in marriage and the man engaging in self-disclosure to the woman. They are high on sharing and low on conflict avoidance. However, they tend to argue about content as opposed to relational issues.

Independents, which represent about 20 percent of couples, is a pure type. Both the female and the male constantly renegotiate their relational roles. These partners value their careers, coworkers, and friends outside the relationship. They need more physical space autonomy and emotional autonomy than the traditionalist couples. Independents engage in a lot of conflict communication and the arguments are often about the nature of their relationship.

Separates, which represent about 10 percent of couples, is the final pure type. Both the female and the male seek to maintain psychological and social distance from their spouses. They avoid open expressions of feelings and opinions. As well, they avoid communication conflict. When conflict does occur, they are rarely able to resolve it effectively. Yet, they regard themselves as fulfilling traditional sex-based, marital roles.

MCT is an important microtheory because it identifies enduring communication interaction patterns or schemas that predict certain functional and dysfunctional marital couple and family communication behaviors. In one study, the researchers demonstrated that verbal aggressiveness and depression associated closely with the separatist marital schemata (Segrin & Fitzpatrick, 1992). In this study, Segrin and Fitzpatrick offered some concrete advice for family therapists. They argued that "a fruitful avenue for treating clinical couples may therefore lie in training partners, especially wives, to express their negative affect without directly attacking their partner, while simultaneously encouraging husbands to express their dysphoria to their wives rather than withdrawing" (p. 89).

The research of Fitzpatrick and Ritchie (1994) expanded the application of MCT beyond the marital dyad to family group communication. In this research, they reported the use of a newly created scaling procedure called Family Communication Environment. The scale allows them to describe and analyze family communication. In general, they reported that traditional couples tended to develop consensual family communication interaction patterns with their children that mirrored their own dyadic communication interaction. The other family communication schemata also dovetailed with the marital pure types of independent and separate. It appears that Fitzpatrick and her colleagues have discovered a deep structure dynamic interaction pattern that individuals may bring to their communicative interaction in long-term small groups in organizational communication, and in long-term dyadic and small group intercultural communication. As such, MCT becomes more than an interpersonal context theory, it becomes a communication microtheory.

VanLear and Zeitlow (1990) conducted a study to unify the dynamics of Relational Control Theory and Marital Communication Theory. They found that relational equivalence behavior explained satisfaction by couple type. In other words, no matter the characteristics of the couple types (independents, separatists, traditionalists) in the relationships people enter, if they use equivalent communication behaviors, they will be more satisfied.

Communicator and Medium Structure Microtheories

This is a good spot for another brief rest stop. Recall that TCM presented in Chapter 1 posited two metaconcepts, communicator structure and medium structure. *Communicator structure* concepts identify the people (communicators) who communicate over time in a medium. Each communication theory, as you have seen throughout this book, uniquely names the communicators and ascribes certain attributes to them. However, there are some communicator attribute concepts that are common to communicators in all settings. We present the most important one, communication apprehension, in this section. Finally, as we explained in Chapter 1, the *medium structure* concepts of theories depict the substance(s) in which theories function, propagate, and travel. We present one theory in this section, McLuhan's Media Law Theory, that focuses on the medium$_2$ substance within which the theory propagates.

Communication Apprehension Theory (CAT)

Throughout the book, we have identified the specific communicator concepts and attributes associated with each particular communication theory. We've also discussed certain communicator attributes that often cross communication theories. Communicator competence, communicator style, and rhetorical sensitivity come to mind. Here, we'd like to present one more communicator attribute that may be present no matter what the communication theory discussed. That communicator attribute is communication apprehension.

Communication apprehension is the most widely studied communicator attribute in the discipline. It belongs with a class of social anxieties first mentioned in the social sciences by Darwin (1872/1955). Robinson (1915) made the first mention of stage fright in public speaking, although the concept had been used in theater since classical times. In contemporary times, McCroskey (1970) offered *communication anxiety* as a communicator *trait* (as in a personality trait) and distinguished it from a situational *state* of anxiety such as stage fright in a particular context. Others, such as Wheeless (1975) and Ayres, Wilcox, and Ayres (1995) added receiver apprehension. Wheeless (1975) defined *receiver apprehension* as "the fear of misinterpreting, inadequately processing, and/or not being able to adjust psychologically to messages sent by others" (p. 263). Today, we now study communication anxiety, reticence, shyness, and stage fright under the rubric of communication apprehension (McCroskey, 1993). McCroskey (1977b) defined *communication apprehension* as "an individuals' level of fear or anxiety associated with either real or anticipated communication with another person or persons" (p. 78). Whether you specify communication apprehension as a trait, state, contextual, or receiver phenomenon, or even as a *continuum of anxiety,* the research program supports the conclusion that its presence harms communication effectiveness.[11]

This would be another good time to pause along our trail to understanding communication theories to consider an important point. Although communication apprehension (CA) is not a why explanation of the phenomenon of apprehension, the construct is robust. The research contributors have grounded its presence in a number of contexts from public speaking to intercultural communication and even communication among the signing deaf (Booth–Butterfield & Booth–Butterfield, 1994). For example, Daly, Vangelisti, and Weber (1995) reported that speech anxiety even affects how people prepare speeches. Richmond (1984) demonstrated that high levels of CA devastate communicative interaction in organizational settings and contribute to low job satisfaction. Daly and Stafford (1984) found that people with high CA exhibit reduced amounts of interpersonal involvement in terms of both quality and quantity. Comadena (1984) reported that people suffering from CA exhibit less brainstorming effectiveness than people with low CA. Aida (1993) reported that highly apprehensive people had more difficulty in marital communication. It appears that everyone can identify at least one situation in which they were highly communicatively apprehensive. Professor Cragan, who exhibits little communication apprehension and regards himself as a regular and good public speaker, found himself speechless at his daughter Katie's wedding dinner. After several seconds of nothing coming out of his dry mouth, the wedding guests applauded for a speech that was not given and he sat down.

Four context-based situations—interpersonal dyadic interaction, small group discussion, talking at a meeting, and public speaking—predominate as locations for apprehension. If you regularly feel apprehensive—more than just nervous—in one or more of these contexts, then you may suffer from CA. However, McCroskey (1993) believes there is much you can do to reduce your anxiety and increase your communicative effectiveness. He states: "The key term is complete preparation. The more fully and carefully prepared you are, the less likely any situational factor will be [able] to get to you" (p. 52). Skills courses in public speaking, interpersonal communication, small group communication, and radio and television broadcasting normally significantly reduce a student's CA. As well, participation on the debate team, or speech team, or announcing on the student radio and television stations provide excellent ways to eliminate high CA.

Regarding CAT's real-world benefit, Booth–Butterfield and Thomas (1995) reported a study of CA among secretarial students. Training reduced their anxiety. Similarly, Kondo (1994) developed a training program for reducing public speaking anxiety in Japan. As well, Neer (1987, 1990) and Neer and Kircher (1989) reported that such classroom intervention strategies as notification of discussion topics and fewer challenges to students to defend their answers reduced student apprehension. Olaniran and Stewart (1996) validated such classroom strategies cross-culturally; as well they determined that culture affected whether or not an international student displayed apprehension when confronted.

McLuhan's Media Law Theory (MLT)

Let's pause once again by the trail. Recall that TCM posited that every theory offers a medium structure concept. Here we present a communication microtheory that emphasizes the medium metaconcept (McLuhan, 1962, 1964; McLuhan & Fiore, 1967). It is Marshall McLuhan's Media Law Theory (MLT).

McLuhan began his career as a Canadian literary critic. He became very popular in the 1960s for his belief that communication technological innovations influenced and shaped sociological change. A popular work of this period was *Understanding Media* (1964). McLuhan shaped MLT through the influence of Harold Innis. Innis, a Canadian, neo-Marxist economist published two books: *The Empire and Communications* (1950) and *The Bias of Communication* (1951). In them, Innis argued that political elites in ancient times controlled their populace by controlling the written word. In turn, this information control allowed them to expand their empires continuously over long periods of time. McLuhan took Innis's thesis that the media influenced communication as a presupposition of MLT. Because of this presupposition and McLuhan's association with Innis, MLT is sometimes called "technological determinism," but it's a phrase McLuhan never used to characterize his theory (McLuhan, 1975, 1977).

MLT has three important assumptions: (1) media are an extension of humans' senses (eyes, ears, touch, smell, taste); (2) the medium is the message and the media users are the content; and (3) media innovation relentlessly drives social change over space and time. MLT's basic concept is, of course, media. Its associative basic concepts refer to the various types of media innovation, such as the phonetic alphabet, the printing press, the telegraph, radio, television, computers, and the Internet. McLuhan's theory is Darwinian in form in that he divides all human history into epochs, or long periods of time, punctuated by technological innovations in media (McLuhan, 1962, 1964; McLuhan & Fiore, 1967). The first epoch was the tribal age, dominated by the ear and face-to-face storytelling. The second epoch was the literate age, dominated by the phonetic alphabet and the arrival of empires. The third epoch was the print age, also dominated by the eye, that came into being with the creation of the printing press which led to the creation of nation–states. The fourth epoch is the electronic age in which we now live. This latest epoch is dominated by a series of technological inventions such as the telegraph, radio, television, computer, modem, and the Internet (McLuhan, 1974).

McLuhan and Powers (1981, 1989) foreshadowed the effects of information traveling at instantaneous speeds when people could cover great distances in real time electronically. They viewed the electronic age as exhibiting the capacity to create the global village where everybody is aware of everybody else (McLuhan & Fiori, 1967). McLuhan (1974) noted that "at instant speeds the public begins to participate directly in actions which it had previously heard about at a distance in place or time" (p. 54). Professor Shields, in teaching "Introduction to Communication Technology," has viewed his students as they travel at the speed of light on the Internet in wide-eyed wonder retrieving political speeches (sometimes even before they are given), viewing Monet's paintings in the Louvre in Paris, chatting in real-time via print–voice–visual with persons thousands of miles away, and reading the major metropolitan newspapers from their computer screens. McLuhan has proven to be a true visionary of the coming of the Internet global village.

Baran and Davis (1995) explained what McLuhan meant by his famous phrases "the medium is the message" and "the medium is the massage." They indicated that "new forms of media transform (message) our experience of ourselves and our society, and this influence is ultimately more important than the content that is transmitted in its specific messages" (pp. 326–327).

Because the medium is the message, MLT's basic and message structure concepts are synonymous. They include hot media and cold media. A *hot medium* "is one that extends one single sense in high definition" (1964, p. 36). Therefore, a book or the radio is hot. Hot media lessen receiver participation because he or she needs only to attend with one of the five senses. A *cool medium* is one that is "high in participation or completion by the audience" (1964, p. 36). Therefore, television and cartoons are cool media because you have to fill in the dots with your eyes and you have to both watch and listen. A lecture is hot because you can't participate very much; you need only listen. A graduate seminar is cool because you can engage in dialogue with the Professor (McLuhan, 1974, p. 37). McLuhan believed that the cool media would prevail (survival of the fittest). As a result, television, CD-ROMs, and the Internet would grow while newspapers and books would shrink.

MLT's communication dynamic concepts involve McLuhan's four laws that govern the effects on society of media technological innovation. These laws are (1) the law of acceleration; (2) the law of obsolescence; (3) the law of synthesis; and (4) the law of retrieval (McLuhan & McLuhan, 1988; Miles, 1996). The availability of the World Wide Web of the Internet is the sort of technological innovation that McLuhan would point to in explaining the kinds of social change created by new media. With the Internet, viewed in terms of the *law of acceleration,* we clearly see an accelerated increase in interactive communication that instantly shrinks time and space in the form of e-mail, visual and audio conversations, and group interactive discussion in electronic chat rooms and through video conferencing.

The retrieval of information is also speeded up in terms of database searches in libraries, newspaper morgues, and various private and public computer banks. New software allows Internet users to browse for the answer to some question and download it for use.

The *law of obsolescence* is also obvious. In the presence of e-mail and electronic banking why would you mail a letter and have a postal delivery? Why go out in the rain or snow and pick up a newspaper when you can scan it on the Internet hours before it will have arrived in the puddle or snowbank in your front yard. Indeed, books like the one you are reading are rapidly becoming obsolete. This book could be stored on CD-ROM and retrieved on demand through the Internet for scanning or printing by electronic computer.

The *law of synthesis* is also evident. With the Internet and CD-ROMs you have the fusion of the computer, phones, satellites, video, and so forth into a synthesized form of communication. Indeed, the form is so new that we as a discipline have yet to label it. Certainly CD-ROM interactive stories and games are one form of such synthesis.

The *law of retrieval* means the rediscovery of the village—in this case a global village. With its rediscovery, we are returning to instantaneous oral communication, talking in real time, face-to-face, by way of technology.

MLT's communicator concept concerns the *media users* who are influenced and transformed by the types of media they use. So, depending on the technology, the users exhibit different attributes. For example, the major effect of the telephone before caller ID was to remove the identity of the caller (McLuhan & Powers, 1981). Chesebro (1995) developed a typology from oral speech through writing, television, and computer-based telecommunication technologies that links cognitive requirements and abilities to each mode of communication. MLT's evaluative concepts concern whether or not the new media technology brings about *social change* and the *consequences* of that change. In this respect, it is akin to Diffusion of Innovations Theory (presented in Chapter 7).

McLuhan (1975), predicting that his dog could hunt, asked his readers to write him in response to the question: "Does the history of technology 'prove' or 'disprove' my postulates [laws]" (p. 75). Bledstein (1976) found that the print media helped create professions like the Speech Communication Association by allowing regular and rapid contact. Hiltz and Turoff (1978) demonstrated that electronic communication increased a sense of community and decreased isolation. Mills (1996) argued that the CD-ROM novel, *Myst*, grounds McLuhan's fourth law of the media (retrieval). It is a continually reconstructed text that leaves different traces on each reader. Thus, Mills insists, this interactive novel "tends to subvert the ideological and epistemological paradigms, namely deconstruction, post-structuralism, or post-modernism, that currently reign on our campuses" (p. 17).

Evaluative Microtheories

Let's take a final rest stop before completing our discussion of the communication microtheory landmark on the trail to understanding communication theories. Recall that TCM (Chapter 1) posited that the evaluative concepts of communication theories allow you to ascertain and make assessments and judgments regarding the competency, quality, and outcomes of communicators communicating in a medium. All communication theories—general, contextual, and micro—have implicit or explicit evaluative concepts. However, some communication microtheories focus directly and entirely on the evaluative function of communicators communicating in a medium. Thus, the theories presented in this part of the chapter represent communication microtheories whose important, but narrow-banded, focus concerns the evaluation of existing forms of communication.

Also, recall that TCM posited a continuum of law-based through rule-based to principle-based theories to depict the types of relationship statements established between the concepts of communication theories. Here, it is important to point out that the communication microtheories presented in this section of the chapter reflect a principle-based relationship among their concepts.

The communication discipline exhibits two strains of feminist research and several strains of Marxist and cultural critical theorizing. One of the two strains of feminist research reflects a desire on the part of the researchers to contribute to the building of an interdisciplinary, unified, feminist theory that could then be used by all disciplines. The other strain of feminist research reflects a desire on the part of the researchers to develop discipline-based, feminist communication theories (Dow, 1995). We present the products of the second strain of feminist theory-building in keeping with the disciplinary focus of this book. We present Muted Group Theory and Feminist Genre Theory as representative evaluative communication microtheories. Finally, we end this section with the most famous of the Continental Marxist critics, Jurgen Habermas, and his Critical Theory.

Foss, Foss, and Trapp (1991) defined feminism as "the belief that women and men should have equal opportunities for self-expression" (p. 275). They also argued that all feminist theories embrace three assumptions: (1) gender has been constructed in such a way that women's experiences are subordinated to those of men; (2) women's shared experience of oppression germinated values such as interdependence, self-questioning, and the egalitarian use of power that are very different from men's experiences and men's values; and (3) feminist theorizing and research is conducted for the purposes of improving women's lives by empowering women. Hence, Feminist Communication Theories, either implicitly or explicitly, seek social change through their evaluation of communicators communicating in a medium.

Muted Group Theory (MGT)

MGT springs from every woman's experience with male-gendered sexist and exclusionary language. This communication problem is not something that we discovered in the 1970s, solved, and then moved on to other things. The matter-of-fact reliance on sexist and exclusionary language is something every female, worldwide, has experienced. It is something that both males and females continue to use. Professor Cragan's youngest daughter is a twice-degreed mechanical engineer with an androgynous first name. As an undergraduate student in the 1990s at the University of Iowa, she attended an engineering awards banquet to receive one of six academic achievement awards. The male engineering professor who was presenting the awards became nervous, turned to the five male recipients, and asked: "I wonder where the sixth guy is?" Keary responded, "I'm the sixth 'guy' you're waiting for!" Keary found that she had been excluded by the language, by the professor, and by the sound of her androgynous name. She returned to her room, made a few phone calls, and founded the local student chapter of "Women in Engineering."

The origin and roots of this theory, and for that matter feminist theorizing in our discipline, can be found in a special issue of a student-run, nationally distributed, professional journal called, *Moments in Contemporary Rhetoric and Communication.* In 1971, the year that Keary Cragan was born, Professor Cragan and Professor James Chesebro, a recent past-President of the National Communication Association, as editors, devoted a special issue of *Moments* to studies of the rhetoric of women's liberation (Chesebro & Cragan, 1971). Professor Shields provided a critical response to those studies (1971). The issue included five studies. Professor Virginia Kidd (1971) entitled one contribution, "A Study of the Images Produced through the Use of the Male Pronoun as the Generic." Through this empirical study, Kidd demonstrated that women had been muted and marginalized by the use of the male pronoun as the generic. She concluded her report by observing that

> *It is altogether possible that pronouns serve as a completely unconscious form of concept shaping, that children, exposed continually to a language describing all accomplishments in masculine terminology grow to conceive of accomplishment in masculine images and to identify accordingly. It is also possible, of course, that pronouns are merely a concept reflection; that this society forges a strong image of the male as the active member of society, and pronouns in reflecting the image have little additional impact. In any case, the masculine pronoun, if not forming the image, certainly does nothing to contradict it and very likely reinforces it on an 'out of awareness' level (p. 28).*

In 1974, Cheris Kramarae (then Kramer), mirrored Kidd's themes with her article in *The Quarterly Journal of Speech,* entitled, "Women's Speech: Separate but Unequal?" By 1981, Kramarae had formally articulated MGT in her book, *Women and Men Speaking.*

MGT explains how women are marginalized, muted, and oppressed by language itself. The theory posits that language manifests an inherent male bias because men created our public language. The result is that our public language reflects men's perceptions of things. As a corollary, the theory posits that women's private language, which reflects different values than exhibited in the public language, is muted, kept in the closet, devalued (treated as "chit-chat" or "women's talk").

MGT calls for women to eliminate sexist and exclusionary language, and go forth into the public arena with their private, feminist value-embedded, women's language. To this end, Kramarae and Treichler (1992) published *A Feminist Dictionary,* now in its second edition. As well, Foss and Foss (1991) celebrated the value of women's eloquence. Similarly, most of us have worked diligently to stomp out the use of sexist language, as illustrated by the use of Ms. instead of Mrs. and Miss. We have also learned to use alternating female/male pronouns in professional writing. In addition, we have changed our language to reflect neutrality through the use of such words as *chair* or *chairperson* for *chairman* and *utility hole* for *manhole.* Patrice Buzzanell (1994, 1995) of Northern Illinois University challenges us to go further. For example, in regard to organizational communication she urges us to "create awareness of and promote community as an ongoing dialectic process . . . by revaluing women's contributions and offering models" (p. 343) that would allow us to alter organizational life through feminist standpoint theories. Ashcraft and Pacanowsky (1996) studied "an organization founded by and largely comprised of women" (p. 217). They found that women still have far to go. Although the women in this organization displayed "a narrative of collective self-awareness as a distinctly 'female' community," the members told a "tale of a divisiveness—a 'cattiness'—that they perceive as a uniquely 'female' practice" (p. 217). Ashcroft and Pacanowsky concurred with Wood's (1993, 1995a) feminist view that material, social, and symbolic conditions continue to shape women's thinking and help make women "their own enemies" (p. 232). As one member of the organization expressed it, "a woman's worst enemy is another woman" (p. 234). The result is a "female battle," or as Ashcraft and Pacanowsky put it, "it is the reversal of the age-old social maxim: 'Boys will be boys' " (p. 234). Over time, MGT offers the potential for the self-awareness necessary to the reduction of this irony. For example, on hearing Ashcraft and Pacanowsky's report, "several participants expressed hope that recognition of their own voice in the narrative would point toward the potential for transforming the divisive themes" (p. 235).

Feminist Genre Theory (FGT)

FGT starts from the same premises as Muted Group Theory, but looks to give *voice* to women by viewing gender as *genre*. "Genres frame symbolic behavior in ways that enable audiences to understand its meaning and to know what kinds of action are expected and what sorts of responses are appropriate" (Campbell, 1995, p. 479). FGT seeks to rediscover feminist speakers and reframe their speaking as models for feminist liberation. In such a way, women come to know and appreciate that they possess a distinct voice of their own. Professor Karlyn Kohrs Campbell, of the University of Minnesota, is the main creator of and a twenty-five-year contributor to this theory. She seeks to empower students, to give them a voice in her public speaking classes, and especially she wants to give female students a voice of their own (Campbell, 1991).

FGT's origin resides in the article, "The Rhetoric of Women's Liberation: An Oxymoron" (1973). In it, Campbell argued that the women's movement could not be judged by male-gendered, rhetorical standards because women's rhetoric reflected the unique experience of women. Campbell (1989a) indicated that women are "unique in rhetorical history because a central element in women's oppression was denial of their right to speak" (p. 9). She also argued that all previous speaking genres were gendered masculine; thus, when women began to speak in public they faced significant obstacles including the fact that speaking in public *per se* was violating a social norm. For Campbell, women public speakers faced the double bind of having both to reaffirm femininity and use male-engendered styles of speaking that resulted in the criticism that they were speaking "like a man." For Campbell (1989a, 1989b, 1994, 1995), this double bind caused a unique, female genre of speaking to emerge. This genre was marked in later years by a female speaking style developed out of consciousness-raising.

Spitzack and Carter (1987) observed that most accounts of human communication simply leave women out. They call this "womanless communication research" (p. 402). Campbell (1986, 1989a/b, 1991, 1994, 1995), Dow and Tonn (1993), and Vonnegut (1992) have set out to correct these oversights regarding the history of American public address. They have researched and rediscovered important U.S. women speakers from Colonial days to the present, analyzed their speaking, and fitted them into a gendered genre.

Foss and Griffin (1992, 1995) have outlined the rudiments of a complete women's rhetorical theory called an *invitational rhetoric*. They, like the contributors to MGT and FGT, reject the patriarchal speaking standards of traditional rhetorical theories. As well, they would break away from the mere modeling of a feminist genre to create a whole new theory based on the feminist principles of equality, immanent value, and self-determination that could be used by both men and women. As they stated, their invitational rhetoric of *resourcement* (women power) and *offering* perspective to expression without intent to persuade "engenders appreciation, value, and a sense of equality" (1995, p. 5).

The underrepresentation of women in public life has put our society at a decided disadvantage in terms of positive female role models that both men and women can emulate. As we see it, the dearth of public speaking role models is only part of the problem. The field of communication in all its various contexts has been late to provide appropriate role models for women in classrooms, in print and electronic news rooms, and in research labs. Foss and Foss (1983) and Steeves (1987) meticulously documented these omissions. FGT points up the importance of presenting models of communicative behavior that students can examine and emulate if they wish.

Habermas's Critical Theory (HCT)

Although we call this microtheory HCT, in truth it is really hard to name. Habermas (1990) evolved the theory over three decades.[12] Habermas (1970a, 1970b, 1984) called it respectively a theory of communicative competence and a theory of communicative action. Baynes (1994) labeled it a theory of communicative ethics. Burleson and Kline called it a "comprehensive theory of communicative competency" (1979, p. 412). Hardt (1992) labeled it a theory of communicative action. Foss, Foss, & Trapp (1991) labeled it a theory of speech acts and universal pragmatics. Nonetheless, a rose by any other name is still a rose.

What Habermas offers is an ideal, moral, competency-based communication theory that promotes understanding and human action. Habermas (1976a) considered "the type of action aimed at reaching understanding to be fundamental" (p. 1). In turn, understanding meant to achieve mutuality of agreement both interpersonally and intersubjectively through "shared knowledge, mutual trust, and accord with each other" (p. 3). Habermas envisioned an *ideal speech situation* that emancipates the communicators from the forces of ideologies and private interests so that "discourse would be determined by the force of better argument alone" (Thompson, 1981, p. 93). Habermas describes himself as a critical theorist, or as one who is concerned with penetrating "the veil of ideology" and elucidating "the mechanisms of repression which characterize a particular social formation" (Thompson, 1981, p. 95). Then, the goal is to take action and overcome the repression of that veil.

In the tradition of the neo-Marxists, Habermas sees two evil forces impinging on human action. The first is that technological talk about doing our jobs in modern society is overwhelming our social domain. The other is that the hierarchical power structure of society is suppressing dialogue in the public sphere. These combined phenomena serve to squeeze out and displace public dialogue about our social contract of how we can live together in a just society. For example, you may feel powerless during our national election cycles because the special interests—such as the American Rifle Association, the American Medical Association, the Tobacco Industry, and the Lumber Industry—are unduly influencing political candidates with lobbying and money. Also, you may feel that even if you had the power, you have little time—given the demands of work and/or school—to engage in public discussion of such issues as health care, gun control, and euthanasia.

In addition to its embedded Marxist assumptions discussed above, HCT, as a theory of communicative action, assumes that (1) communicators as social agents are not simply the bearers of preferences; (2) communicators can achieve a degree of reflexive distance toward those preferences; and (3) with reflexive distance, communicators can revise their conceptions of the world, assess various courses of action, and attain some form of dialectical unity with their life plans (life-world) and those courses of action. As Hardt (1992) put it: "Culture, society, and the individual are structural components of the 'life-world' in which communicative action serves to reproduce cultural knowledge, to integrate individuals, and to shape personalities" (p. 164).

HCT's basic concept is the speech act. A *speech act* is a basic unit of language for expressing intention; it takes the form of a communicative statement that contains prepositional content and illocutionary force. Speech acts are of three types: constatives, regulatives, and avowals. A *constative speech act* occurs when a person asserts a truth claim. For example: "The university's parking system is in chaos" is a truth claim. A *regulative speech act* governs or regulates behaviors and occurs when a person utters a command or request. For example: "Pass the salt!" The illocutionary element of this kind of speech act is its appropriateness. The statement would be more appropriate if it were worded, "Pass the salt, please." Hence, regulatives emphasize the relationship dimension of language. An *avowal speech act* occurs when you disclose your feelings, wishes, and intentions. For example, "I wish I were a more sensitive person." Borrowing from Rational Argumentation Theory (Chapter 3), Habermas would support these speech acts using data, warrants, and claims.

HCT depicts an idealized message structure that is textured through various levels of discourse. This discourse occurs at five levels: sincerity discourse (dialogue about true intentions), theoretic discourse (dialogue about factual truth), practical discourse (dialogue that questions norms), metatheoretical discourse (dialogue negotiating appropriate norms or criteria), and metaethical discourse (dialogue about the nature of knowledge itself). All of these claims and levels of dialogue are governed by rules that Habermas believes competent communicators can intuit or learn through training. The rules spell out the structuring of the three kinds of speech acts and the procedures necessary for working through the levels for establishing the validity of the truthfulness, correctness, and sincerity of the speech acts.

HCT's communication dynamic centers on the dialectical tension of private interests impinging on the *public sphere* and the dialectical tension between our own private need to do work and our commitment to do public good as part of our life plans. The conflict is between an emancipated discourse on the one hand and a corrupted, stifling discourse on the other in which all the communicators are not equal. HCT is an action-oriented theory, and there is the expectation that people will be taking corrective action, and that as a result the independent print and electronic media and concerned citizens groups like Common Cause, the League of Women Voters, and the American Civil Liberties Union will form a *public sphere* to assist in that corrective action. HCT critiques society in a way that commits those who adhere to the theory to commit to a specific social action of emancipating themselves from the ravages of the twin dialectical tensions.

HCT envisions competent communicators who have acquired their various competencies through a process of socialization (child-rearing, schooling, training) that gives them autonomy competencies (Baynes, 1994, p. 319). These competent communicators communicate ideally on a level plane or playing field relying on reciprocal, truthful, appropriate, and sincere speech acts. Other communicator attributes include the ability to take another's perspective, be self-reflexive, and exhibit moral autonomy (Baynes, 1994, p. 319). As Habermas stated: "The universal validity claims (truth, correctness, sincerity), which the parties concerned must at least implicitly maintain and reciprocally acknowledge, makes possible the consensus which carries the collective action" of discourse (cited in Thompson, 1981, p. 104).

HCT's medium$_2$ concepts include the semantic field of symbolic contents, the social space of one's life-world, and historical time (Habermas, 1984). Out of the interplay of these blossoms *the idealized speech situation* within the individual, the group, and the public sphere in which general symmetry exists. Achieving an idealized speech situation requires meeting several principles: (1) unrestricted free speech; (2) equal opportunity to speak; (3) legitimization of differing perspectives; and (4) power parity with no undue advantage to communicate due to money and status. This criterion of an idealized medium could be applied to your university. For example, as a student are you free to speak up about university governance? Do you possess the same access to the campus media? Are your views on governance accepted as legitimate? Are your inputs on governance reflected equally with those of the deans, chairs, and professors on your campus? If not, this theory would suggest that you engage in self-reflexive and interactive discourse with other students to achieve emancipation.

HCT's evaluative concept is emancipatory communication. *Emancipatory communication* occurs when the idealized speech situation is met through either self-reflective conversations or discourse with others. The society as a whole is emancipated—made aware of its weaknesses and reformed—when the society is liberated from unnecessary forms of control. In these two senses, self-reflection and reform of society, we are all critical theorists. Many speech organizations and professional communication societies have committed themselves to a Habermas-like ideal. For example, the Speech Communication Association has its "Credo for Free and Responsible Communication in a Democratic Society." That Credo states in part: "We believe that freedom of speech and assembly must hold a central position among American Constitutional principles . . . We encourage our students to accept the role of well-informed and articulate citizens, to defend the communication rights of those with whom they may disagree, and to expose abuses of the communication process" (Speech Communication Association, 1975). Similarly, the Code of Ethics of Associated Press Managing Editors reads: "Editorially, the newspaper should advocate needed reform in the public interest. It should vigorously expose wrongdoing or misuse of power, public or private" (Fink, 1988, p. 297).

In America, HCT has been used in the quest for an idealized speech situation. In 1992, the *Star Tribune,* a Minneapolis, Minnesota newspaper, helped create more than one hundred groups of concerned citizens who engaged in weekly dialogues on issues of public policy. The *Star Tribune* aided the group by providing literature and other materials and reporting their discussions in the newspaper (Allen, 1995). Recently, *The St. Louis Post Dispatch,* as part of that newspaper's offerings on the Internet, created "chat rooms" in an effort to involve citizens of the public sphere in civic consensus-building. Gonzalez (1989) used HCT's concepts of the "norms of the ideal speech situation" (p. 308) and "the public sphere" as the "framework for investigating how equality, participation, and symmetry" (p. 309) would work to uncover instances of the unequal diffusion of innovations. We reported this study in Chapter 7. Our point here is that this dog will hunt. **Figure 11-1** provides a snapshot of

"In the communicative attitude it is possible to reach understanding oriented to validity claims; in the strategic attitude, by contrast, only an indirect understanding via determinative indicators is possible." Habermas, 1976, 209)

"McLuhan's Media Law Theory made it possible for us to predict the synthesis of machine and human communication. That's why our software interactive packages are doing so well in the marketplace. They prove that the medium is the message."

FIGURE 11-1. Communication Graduate On-the-Job

Corey, our communication graduate on-the-job, using a communication microtheory to good advantage.

Summary

This chapter used the six metaconcepts of The Communication Metatheory to organize the communication microtheories of our discipline. As you recall, communication microtheories are powerful, thin-banded theories that illuminate some important aspect of communicators communicating in a medium. In this chapter we presented a baker's dozen of microtheories.

Three microtheories focused on basic concepts: Information Manipulation Theory, Interpersonal Deception Theory, and Compliance-Gaining/Resisting Theory. We also presented three microtheories that focus predominantly on message structure concepts: Action Assembly Theory, Speech/Communication Accommodation Theory, and Expectancy Violation Theory. Two theories focused on dynamic structure concepts. They are Relational Control Theory and Marital Communication Theory. Communication Apprehension Theory illustrates the metaconcept of communicator attributes. McLuhan's Media Law Theory highlights the metaconcept of medium. Finally, we presented three evaluative microtheories: Muted Group Theory, Feminist Genre Theory, and Habermas's Critical Theory. **Box 11-1** synthesizes these microtheories "in a nutshell."

BOX 11-1   Understanding Communication Microtheories in a Nutshell

Communication Microtheories. Communication microtheories are powerful, thin-banded theories that illuminate some important aspect of communicators communicating in a medium. Microtheories explain this thin band of communication across the various communication contexts. Communication microtheories, although anatomically correct, tend to feature one of the six metatheoretical metaconcepts of The Communication Metatheory (TCM) used throughout this book. This chapter introduced from one to three microtheories for each TCM metaconcept: basic, message structure, communication dynamic structure, communicator structure, medium structure, and evaluative.

Information Manipulation Theory (IMT). IMT concentrates on explaining a basic concept of communication as it illustrates four ways of deceiving and manipulating information: fabrication, concealment, distortion, and equivocation. IMT explains how listeners are covertly mislead. IMT microtheory features the basic concept of information manipulation.

Interpersonal Deception Theory (IDT). IDT also concentrates on a basic concept of communication as it views the receiver as the active communicator who attempts to detect deception. IDT posits that deceptive messages encompass three basic concepts: the central deceptive message (verbal), the bolstering ancillary message (verbal and nonverbal), and inadvertent leakage behaviors (mostly nonverbal) that point up deception.

Compliance-Gaining/Resisting Theory (CGT). CGT concentrates on the basic concept of communication known as compliance-gaining and -resisting. It possesses two theoretical research strains, one coercive and one noncoercive. The noncoercive compliance-gaining/resisting research shows the most promise as a communication theory with practical, persuasive applications. CGT explains the effect of several types of reasoned-based requests and reasoned-based denials.

Action Assembly Theory (AAT). AAT centers on the message structure of communication. It explains the generative mechanisms of action involved in creating coordinated speech. AAT explains how we develop and store memory organization packets or scripts that can be recalled and used in the same manner again and again. AAT argues that speech practice is the only successful way to store and recall communicative scripts.

Speech/Communication Accommodation Theory (SCAT). SCAT also centers on the message aspect of communication. SCAT explains the tendency for communicators to experience convergence (a linguistic strategy whereby individuals accommodate vocal differences between themselves and others) of their speech and communication styles. SCAT argues that communicators engage in convergence to increase efficiency, gain approval, and maintain a positive social identity.

Expectancy Violation Theory (EVT). EVT explores the message structure of nonverbal messages. It explains a narrow band of communicative interaction

Continued

BOX 11-1   *Continued*

grounded primarily in the arena of nonverbal communication messages. EVT predicts that when communicative norms are violated nonverbally or verbally, the violation may be regarded by receivers as excusable or inexcusable depending on the esteem they accord the violator.

Relational Control Theory (RCT). RCT explores the realm of the communication dynamic of communicative interaction. It argues that relational control, a communication dynamic concept, is the most important concept in explaining relational satisfaction. RCT argues that couples continually negotiate their dominant–submissive relationship to one another across a host of issues, with *domineering* (both competing for and not resolving dominance) as a major source of relationship dissatisfaction.

Marital Communication Theory (MCT). MCT also explores the realm of the communication dynamic of communicative interaction. It explains the warring marital communication schema known as: traditional, independent, separate, and mixed. Marital participation in specific schema predicts both functional and dysfunctional communicative behaviors both in dyads and the family group.

Communication Apprehension Theory (CAT). CAT is a communication construct that explains a most important communicator attribute across all contexts. CAT is both a communicator trait and a situational state of anxiety. People that exhibit *high* communication apprehension appear to be communicatively incompetent across one or more of the communication contexts.

McLuhan's Media Law Theory (MLT). MLT is a medium metaconcept theory. MLT argues that the medium is the message, that is, that new forms of mass media transform the message so that ultimately the medium is more important than its specific content. MLT argues that four laws govern the media's impact on society. They are the laws of acceleration, obsolescence, synthesis, and retrieval.

Muted Group Theory (MGT). MGT focuses on an evaluative metaconcept of The Communication Metatheory. MGT posits that women are marginalized, muted, and oppressed by male-gendered, sexist language. MGT explains that traditional language possesses an inherent male bias because men, almost exclusively, created our public language.

Feminist Genre Theory (FGT). FGT evaluates communication by identifying feminist speakers and reframing their speaking qualities as models for women's liberation. FGT seeks to eliminate the ideology of male dominant rhetoric. It seeks to replace it with feminist principles of safety, values, and freedom that are available for both men and women.

Habermas's Critical Theory (HCT). HCT is an ideal, moral, competency-based, communication theory for human action. HCT creates this ideal through shared knowledge, mutual trust, and accord with each other represented by an idealized speech situation. HCT is an evaluative communication microtheory because it seeks to throw off and replace repressive ideologies so that communicators may engage in emancipated communication in the public sphere. The idealized speech situation in the public sphere assumes unrestricted free speech, equal opportunity to speak, the legitimization of competing perspectives, and power parity with respect to money and status.

C h a p t e r 12

Capstone

Communication theories constitute the field of communication.

Chapter Outline

For a mason, the capstone is the final or crowning stone placed at the top of a structure or wall. As such, the capstone defines the limits of the structure. Placing the capstone is emotionally pleasing to the mason because it provides a sense of finality and completion. So, we're happy! This is the last chapter of the book. However, this capstone should not "cap" your study of communication. Hopefully, we have given you the necessary tools (theories) to help you in your everyday living and in your future studies and chosen career.

This chapter will function much like the "Nutshells" of the preceding chapters. Here, we're going to sum up what we've taught in this book. However, we're going to present our summary in a novel way (as you may have noticed from the chapter's outline). In Chapter 1, we introduced the Communication Tree of Knowledge and in each succeeding chapter we cracked one or more theory nuts and showed you the anatomical parts of each theory. Now, however, we're going to switch metaphors because we've reached the end of the trail to understanding communication theories. We are switching in part for reasons of novelty and aesthetics and in part to provide another means of helping you indelibly remember what you have learned.

Finding the Communication Rosetta Stone

As we said, we've now reached the end of our trail. As U.S. citizens, we know that we are now in Oregon. The long journey is over. We can recall a lot of backtracking and even a few boxed canyons, but we know that we've been moving steadily west all the time. With the completion of our journey, we want to take a final rest stop and point out one last historical marker before we introduce our communication theory field of flowers.

A stone or rock has always meant permanency to us as humans. We're used to statements such as "Upon this rock I will build my church," "Let's etch this idea in stone," or "We're going to set this idea in concrete." Anthropologists long ago discovered that human civilizations literally etch important ideas in stone in the hopes that they will not be forgotten. Probably the most famous stone with etchings on it is the Rosetta Stone. You may recall from your history classes that the Rosetta Stone provided the key to unlocking the meaning of ancient Egyptian hieroglyphics. In 1799, at the Rosetta mouth of the Nile River, an officer of Napoleon's engineering corps found a 2' × 3' × 1' basaltic stone on which Egyptian priests had recorded some important ideas regarding the Egyptian King, Ptolemy Epiphanes, in three different languages: Ancient Egyptian hieroglyphics, the vernacular Egyptian language of 200 BC, and Greek. Jean Franquois Champollion, in the early 1800s, used the writings on the stone to unravel the meaning of the symbols used in the ancient Egyptian hieroglyphics language. Metaphorically, we want you to remember the three levels of communication introduced in Chapter 1 as being etched on our Communication Rosetta Stone. See **Figure 12-1.**

You should recall from Chapter 1, **Table 1-1,** that Level 1 communication is the ordinary, everyday talk about which we theorize as communication scholars. Level 2 communication comprises the communication theories we've developed to describe, explain, and evaluate Level 1 communication. In this book we have presented forty-plus communication theories that order and explain human communication. Level 3 communication is The Communication Metatheory (TCM) that allowed us to describe, classify, analyze, and evaluate the Level 2 communication theories. When we initially introduced TCM in Chapter 1, it might have seemed like Greek to you. Nonetheless, we promised that TCM would be the key to understanding the similarities and differences in communication theories that in turn allow you to understand communication or actual talk.

You now know that there are five categories of communication theories: general, contextual, micro, special, and symbiotic. As well, you know that in this book we only highlighted general communication theories, contextual communication theories, and communication microtheories. Recall also that TCM contained several metatheoretical anatomical concepts that are relevant to each communication theory. These included the communicative force explained by the theory, the origin and roots of the theory, the three types of assumptions exhibited by the theory, the paradigm reflected by the theory, the theory's technical concepts (basic, message structure, communication dynamic structure, communicator structure,

**FIGURE 12-1. The Communication
Rosetta Stone**

medium structure, and evaluative), and the theory–method complex for each theory, including its qualitative method and real-world benefits.

As well, TCM provided us with a Level 3 metavocabulary for evaluating all communication theories. We trust it has by now become rather ordinary and routine for you to choose from among the nine criteria of power, scope, validity, heuristic, isomorphic, parsimony, elegance, utility, and withstanding the critics to assess the theories presented in this book. For Champollion, the Greek language on the Rosetta Stone provided the key that unlocked the meaning of vernacular Egyptian and in turn Egyptian Hieroglyphics. For us, TCM is the key that provides the wherewithal to unlock, describe, and evaluate the forty-plus communication theories that in turn describe, explain, control, and predict ordinary communication. We hope that you remember TCM as our Communication Rosetta Stone. We believe that on this stone you can build a career.

Growing Communication Daisies and Other Flowers

Now that our trail-guiding days are over, we're going to take off our ranger hats and put on our horticulture caps. Here, we are sodbusters at heart. We prefer to grow scholarship rather than talk about it. For the past thirty years, we've been part-time trail guides and full-time horticulturists building communication theory. Nonetheless, don't misunderstand us. As we stand here atop our Rosetta Stone we are proud to look out over the wide valleys of Oregon and show you our communication field and the crops that grow in it.

Figure 12-2 displays the General Communication Theory Daisy. Of course, the daisy is our prizewinning flower. The daisy is our most important flower because it represents our

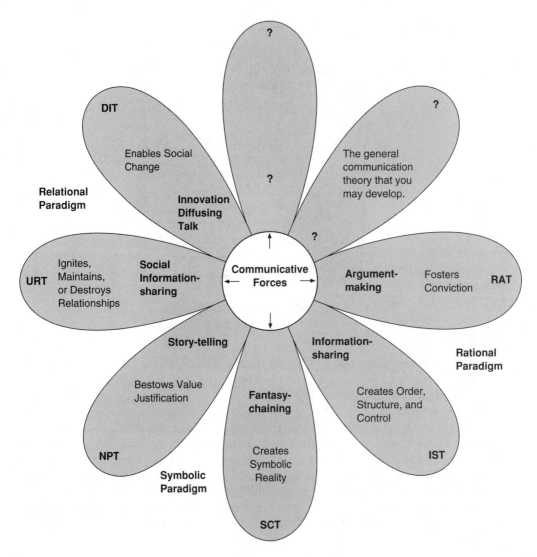

FIGURE 12-2.   General Communication Theory Daisy

general communication theories that grow in all sections (contextual areas) of the field. The daisy in **Figure 12-2** is a floral representation of nearly all that you learned from Chapters 1–7. At the center of the daisy are the communicative forces that affect human action. Each petal represents a general communication theory that explains a particular force. Thus, the force of information-sharing creates order, structure, and control. Similarly, the force of argument creates rational decision-making. Also, the force of fantasy-chaining creates symbolic reality. Likewise, the force of storytelling bestows value justification. As well, the force of social information-sharing ignites, maintains, or destroys personal relationships.

Finally, the force of diffusing innovation talk initiates adoption of new innovations and ideas and enables social change. You'll recall that we devoted an entire chapter to each petal on this daisy. Of course, communication general theories are not static. The petal at the top with the question marks is awaiting the grounding of a new general communication theory. Also, the petal to its immediate right represents the potential communication theory that explains a new communicative force that you may develop.

If we had a microscope and examined each petal closely we would also see the anatomical parts of each theory. For example, we would see SCT's basic terms of fantasy, fantasy type, symbolic cue, and saga. Or, we would see NPT's dynamic structure of the competing idealistic/moralistic and materialistic thrusts of the American Dream. You recall, of course, the anatomical parts of the other general communication theories. If you do not, you may want to refresh your memory by reexamining Chapters 2–7.

The field has been carefully tilled, planted, cultivated, fertilized, watered, weeded, and harvested for nearly one hundred years, not only by us, but by the hundreds of pioneering scholars who have invented the plants and hybrids that grow in the field. Recall that in Chapter 1 we asked you to suspend your judgment about which theory or theories you preferred. Now, we invite you to be selective. You can't cultivate all of the theories at the same time, nor can you harvest all the theories at once to apply them to the solution of a real-world problem. We emphasize this need for judgment by the caption at the bottom of **Figure 12-2**: "I love SCT . . . I love it not!" Here, also, we offer the opportunity for you to use a certain amount of aesthetic judgment in your selection of your favorite theories. To spend the next thirty years growing and pruning flowers and taking them to market to solve real-world problems means that you have to like them. If you don't like any of these forty flowers, we'd suggest you leave the communication flower garden and go find an academic field more to your liking. Perhaps you would like the flowers in the field of psychology, sociology, or political science better. On the other hand, if you choose to stay and help us tend the field of communication flowers, there are still aesthetic judgments to be made. You may like the study of decision-making and role-formation in small groups, maybe not. You might like studying the use of diffusing communication to effect social change, or you might like studying political arguments, or you might like studying the communication of close personal relationships best. Whatever section of the field you select as your area of specialty, we hope you select it because you enjoy doing it. In other words, it's not that you can't study small group communication, it's that you prefer studying mass communication. The choice is a matter of taste, a matter of what pleases you, a matter of the types of flowers you want to cultivate and grow.

Viewing the Communication Field of Flowers

Notice as we stand looking down on our communication field that it is cordoned off into six sections: interpersonal, small group, public speaking, organizational, mass, and intercultural communication. See **Figure 12-3.** For each section there are unique flowers that represent each context. Of course, the daisies represent our general communication theories that explain communication across the contexts. Because they are general communication theories the daisies grow in each section of the field.

In the interpersonal context section of the field there are daisies and wild roses. Again, the daisies represent our general communication theories that explain communication

Key: Daisies (General Theories); Wild Roses (Interpersonal Theories); Marigolds (Public Speaking Theories); Irises (Mass Communication Theories); Poppies (Small Group Communication Theories); Bluebells (Organizational Communication Theories); Indian Paintbrushes (Intercultural Communication Theories); Ladybugs (Communication Microtheories); Butterflies (Evaluative Microtheories).

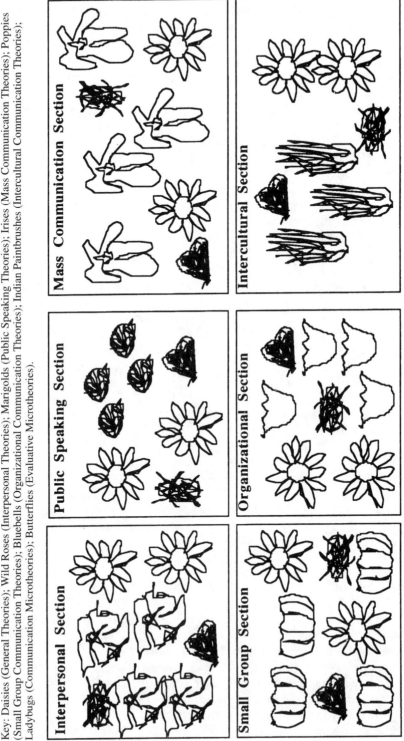

FIGURE 12-3. Viewing the Communication Theory Field of Flowers

across contexts. The wild roses represent the four interpersonal contextual theories that we discussed in Chapter 8: Constructivist Theory, Coordinated Management of Meaning Theory, Dialectical Relationship Theory, and Face Management Theory.

In the small group section of the field are daisies and poppies. Again, the daisies represent our general communication theories that explain communication across contexts. The poppies represent the four small group contextual theories: Decision-Emergence Theory, Role Emergence Theory, Functional Decision-Making Theory, and Adaptive Structuration Theory.

In the public speaking context section there are both daisies and marigolds. Again, the daisies represent our general communication theories that explain communication across contexts. The marigolds represent the four public speaking context theories presented in Chapter 9: Neo-Aristotelian Theory, Burke's Dramatism Theory, Vid-Oral Theory, and Image Restoration Theory.

In the organizational communication section of the field there are general communication theory daisies and bluebells. Again, the daisies represent our general communication theories that explain communication across contexts. The bluebells represent the four organizational contextual theories: Weick's Organizing Theory, Unobtrusive Control Theory, Artistic Ethnography Theory, and Organizational Assimilation Theory.

In the mass communication section of the field are daisies and irises. Again, the daisies represent our general communication theories that explain communication across contexts. The irises represent the four mass communication context theories presented in Chapter 10: Spiral of Silence Theory, Uses and Gratifications Theory, Agenda-Setting Theory, and Cultivation Effects Theory.

In the intercultural communication section of the field are daisies and Indian Paintbrushes. Again, the daisies represent our general communication theories that explain communication across contexts. The Indian Paintbrushes represent the three intercultural communication contextual theories: Anxiety/Uncertainty Management Theory, Face Negotiation Theory, and Cross-Cultural Adaptation Theory.

By looking again at **Figure 12-3** you should also notice some ladybugs and butterflies. The ladybugs represent the microtheories that illustrate one of the metastructural components (basic concepts, message concepts, dynamic concepts, communicator concepts, and medium concepts) of The Communication Metatheory. For example, we illustrated communication microtheories that concentrate on basic communication concepts when we discussed Information Manipulation Theory, Interpersonal Deception Theory, and Compliance Gaining/Resisting Theory. Also, we illustrated communication microtheories that concentrate on message structure concepts when we discussed Action Assembly Theory, Speech/Communication Accommodation Theory, and Expectancy Violation Theory. Then, too, we illustrated communication microtheories that concentrate on dynamic structure concepts when we discussed Relational Control Theory and Marital Communication Theory. In addition, we illustrated communication microtheories that concentrate on communicator structure concepts when we presented Communication Apprehension Theory. Finally, we illustrated communication microtheories that concentrate on medium structure concepts when we presented Media Law Theory.

The butterflies represent the evaluative communication microtheories. Recall that we presented two feminist theories (Muted Group Theory and Feminist Genre Theory) and one critical theory (Habermas's Critical Theory) that illustrate evaluative microtheories. The ladybugs and butterflies do their work throughout the field just as the daisies grow throughout the field. However, you should recall that the communication microtheories explain a narrow band of communication across all of the contextual areas of communication whereas the general theories explain a broad band of communication.

We need to make one last point about viewing communication as a field of flowers. Please understand that regardless of your chosen academic specialty—interpersonal, small group, public speaking, organizational, mass, or intercultural communication—you have upwards of a dozen theories that you can pull from your communication theory toolbox to help you solve communication problems. Let's take the small group communication context area and show you what we mean. Over the years, we've been asked by a number of organizations to come and train their employees in small group decision-making. Usually, we use Symbolic Convergence Theory to explain how a group creates its own unique identity. We encourage the group members to name the group, develop a logo, and create a group slogan knowing that this activity will cause fantasies to chain out regarding their group identity and that the activity will build cohesion and commitment. We use Information Systems Theory to emphasize ways to sequence information in the group. We use Uncertainty Reduction Theory to point out to the group the importance of certain personal disclosures that build trust among the members. We use Rational Argumentation Theory, particularly its dialectical dynamic, to teach them how to make better, more reasoned decisions. We use Narrative Paradigm Theory to point out the importance of creating group stories that hang together and ring true and convey the value justification for action. We use Diffusion of Innovations Theory to illustrate how the group can disseminate their solutions throughout the organization. Then, we turn to the contextual group communication theories. For example, we use Role-Emergence Theory to teach them about the importance of such roles as task leader, social-emotional leader, information provider, tension-releaser, and central negative (critic). We use Decision Emergence Theory to show them how the stages of the task process parallel the role-formation process. We use Functional Decision-Making Theory to point out important communication episodes that need to be performed to improve the quality of decision-making. We use a symbiotic theory called Groupthink, developed by the psychologist Irving Janis, to point out the dangers of premature group consensus and the need for heavy doses of ideational conflict. We then teach the special communication theories of brainstorming and nominal group technique that improve the quantity and quality of the ideas generated by the group. Finally, we provide a feminist critique of the group process using the communication microtheory called Muted Group Theory to encourage androgynous communication and avoid the sex-stereotyping of group roles. We could go on, but we think you now see our point. All five classes of theories—general, contextual, micro, special, and symbiotic—can be focused on any contextual area. We call this flower power! Having armed you with a wheelbarrow full of useful communication theories, you're now prepared to make a professional contribution to society.

Peddling Our Communication Flowers

Communication scholars often come in two types: basic researchers and applied researchers. The basic researchers are horticulturists who like to stay in the field tending the flowers. Applied researchers are horticulturists who are concerned with the question: "Will the dog hunt?" They want to load up their flowers at harvest time and check out their use in solving real-world problems. Although we have done quite a bit of basic research, we enjoy being called applied communication researchers. We regularly take our communication theories hunting to check their use in solving real-world problems. You may have recognized our bias when, at the end of the discussion of each theory, we examined its real-world benefit. **Figure 12-4** displays a basic and an applied researcher working with the field of flowers.

Career Opportunities

In the job interview process it will be important for you to distinguish yourself from other college graduates with different majors. A job interviewer may ask you to explain what you as a communication graduate can do for his or her company. You can say, I have "flower power," but of course you have to explain it more fully. As you see in **Figure 12-4,** you'll be one of the flower peddlers leaving the communication flower field and applying communication theories to the solution of a number of real-world problems in such applied contexts as legal, health, family, public relations, marketing, political, and advertising communication. At both our respective campuses there are more than 400 communication majors and the majority of them complete internships at various public and private organizations. In such internship situations the first communication theories you get to use are special communication theories that help you write press releases, put together a newsletter, or develop ad copy.

It's always helpful to do some apprentice work peddling flowers. If you are not in a formal internship program, you can sometimes team up with one of your professors and work on some consulting project with her or him. Of course, you can also team up with other communication students and do volunteer work for some nonprofit organization. For example, you might help your local heart association develop its communication-based fundraising campaign, or your lung association might allow you to conduct a market research study. Similarly, other agencies may allow you to develop public service announcements for radio and TV. Finally, your favorite local politician would be more than happy to allow you to practice your craft in getting him or her elected. Our point is, you need some apprentice experience to help you refine your flower peddling skills. With a Master's or Ph.D. degree in communication, other career opportunities open up for you. The most obvious one is that you too can become a communication horticulturist and trail guide, that is, you can teach and train others about communication theories. Another opportunity is that you can work in the communication department of major organizations such as Bank One, State Farm, or Monsanto. Another opportunity is to start your own business. Here, you own your own flower wagon. Many of our graduates now have their own advertising, marketing, communication training, public relations, and video production companies. If you choose to start your own business it is probably helpful to take the research methods and applied communication research classes and work up a graduate level internship with an existing consulting company. Finally, remember that if someone asks you to name your five favorite communication theories and indicate their use, you can say, "That's too few; depending on the problem, I might use a dozen theories." The real key to this answer is that the class projects, internships, and volunteer projects that you have completed have provided you with your own personal examples of real-world problems that you've solved using communication theories.

Key: Daisies (General Theories); Wild Roses (Interpersonal Theories); Marigolds (Public Speaking Theories); Irises (Mass Communication Theories); Poppies (Small Group Communication Theories); Bluebells (Organizational Communication Theories); Indian Paintbrushes (Intercultural Communication Theories); Ladybugs (Communication Microtheories); Butterflies (Evaluative Microtheories).

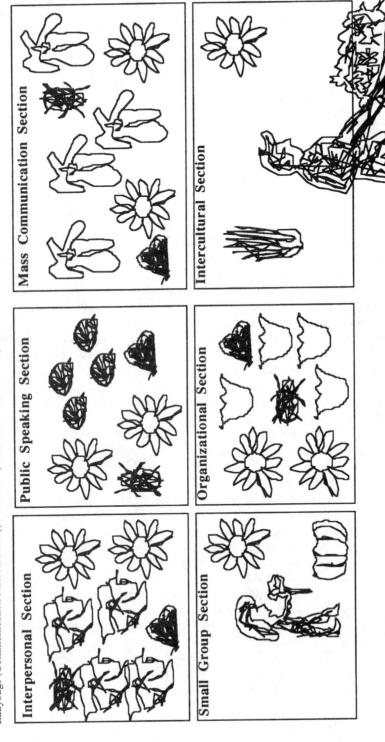

FIGURE 12-4. Communication Theory Flower Peddlers

Professional Ethics

By now, your personal ethical code is developed and you can readily articulate it if people ask you about it. You may well describe yourself as an honest, loyal, fair-playing, rational individual. You also have developed your ethical stand on such issues as capital punishment, abortion, and euthanasia. However, you are less likely to have spent much time considering your professional ethical code. Most professional societies go so far as to formalize their ethical codes as we saw in the discussion of Habermas's Critical Theory in Chapter 11. We would like to go beyond a formal code and discuss with you three practical ethical issues to which you must develop your own professional ethical response: (1) the misuse of theories; (2) the misuse of human subjects; and (3) the misuse of privileged information.

At the core of professional ethics is the competent use of expert knowledge (communication theories). If an attorney does not know the law we think of her or him as not only incompetent but unethical in trying to practice without sufficient expert knowledge. The same is true of a plumber, auto mechanic, electrician, dentist, or physician. As a communication professional, people will expect you to have a working knowledge of the communication field (communication theories). Knowing communication theories is not only a matter of competency, but it is also a matter of professional ethics. It would be unethical of you to offer your services as a communication specialist without knowing communication theories and how to apply them. Our respective universities hired us as communication professors with the clear expectation that we would teach communication theories in our communication courses. If it turned out that we walked into our communication courses and didn't teach communication theories such as the forty-plus presented in this book, but instead taught a third, or half, or more of the course using psychological, sociological, and linguistic theories, the university could rightfully question our professional ethics. As well, our colleagues in psychology, sociology, and linguistics would soon be accusing us of practicing *their* craft without a license. Again, don't misunderstand us. There are useful symbiotic theories, and we all must teach some of them to provide a grounded, theoretical explanation of communicators communicating in a medium. It's just that the symbiotic theories should not dominate our courses in communication theory.

Because we study humans engaging in communicative interaction we must necessarily show concern for their ethical treatment. Research universities and colleges have a formal ethical code that sets the parameters of the ethical treatment of human subjects. For example, if deception is used in a study, the subjects must be debriefed after the experiment is completed. Indeed, universities and colleges possess standing committees that review research designs with an eye for ethical breaches in the treatment of human subjects. If you choose to practice your communication specialty in a college or university these standing ethical codes will help guide you. However, if you form your own communication company or work in the communication department of some organization, you may well have to make the treatment of human subjects judgments by yourself. For example, Professor Cragan was asked to finish the small group training of a corporation's managers because the corporation had fired a previous trainer for the unethical use of human subjects. The former trainer had used experiential exercises that required the managers to sit in each other's laps and pass an orange from under the chin of one person to under the chin of another. Several managers complained that they were forced to engage in inappropriate touching of their colleagues and felt humiliated by the experience.

Information is power and as such is open to unethical use. As a communication consultant from within or outside an organization, one becomes aware of corporate secrets and gains an intimate knowledge of the company's employees. Professor Shields, over the course of five years, trained Worldwide Monsanto's R&D managers in how to present their research proposals in a concise and clear way. As a consequence, he became aware of nearly all of the company's corporate secrets in terms of their research plans. However, for him to divulge such corporate secrets would be highly unethical. If you choose to become a communication consultant, you must ethically keep insider information secret.

The Last Bouquet

It's time for us to say, "Good-bye!" As they say in the restaurant business, "Put a fork in us; we're done!" We trust this book "hunts" for you. We enjoyed writing it and we hope you enjoyed reading it. Writing it has increased our understanding of communication theories. We trust that reading it has increased your understanding, too. We tried to put at least one good laugh in each chapter, because a sense of humor helps us get through life and we wanted you to see that work should be play. We take our work seriously, but we try not to take ourselves seriously. If you choose to stay in the communication field, we'll probably see you at one of our communication association conventions. We'll be easy to spot. We'll be walking a mangy hound and wearing a Rosetta Stone tie tack. Our blazers' insignia will be a reproduction of The Communication Metatheory's VENN diagram. We'll have flowers in our lapels and a pocket full of nutshells. Also, the potted plant in the wagon we're pulling will be the communication tree of knowledge fighting for space in the academy for our daisies, bluebells, Indian Paintbrushes, irises, marigolds, poppies, and wild roses. We leave you with three final thoughts: remember that power is in the flower; your communication theories will make you strong; and may the communicative forces be with you.

Endnotes

Chapter 1   Introduction to Communication Theory

1. Here we are saying that communication exists. *Understanding Communication Theory* presents explanations of communication phenomena. It is not concerned with explanations of how communication came about. We presuppose that in its broadest sense, communication's constituent parts include the phenomena of language, speech, writing, and signing systems. We take such systems as given. However, we believe that theorizing about such systems, called *semiotics,* is the proper concern of linguistics, an allied or symbiotic discipline.

2. In Chapter 2, we present Information Systems Theory, a theory that explains in part how the transfer of information from a source (the originator of a communication episode) to a receiver (the recipient of a piece of communication) may be optimized for flow within an electronic communication channel (the substance within which a piece of communication travels). With Information Systems Theory, communication is depicted as the transfer of messages, messages are bits of information carried optimally by a channel, and the communicators are senders and receivers, all monitored by a self-correcting feedback device. In Chapter 3, we explain Rational Argumentation Theory. With Rational Argumentation Theory, messages are arguments (points of contention) that occur in a medium (substance) called an *argumentation field,* and the communicators are the *arguers,* along with a real or implied *critic.* With Symbolic Convergence Theory, introduced in Chapter

4, the communicators are *fantasizers* (artistic dramatizers) and the messages are *chaining fantasy themes* (dramatizations) that swirl together in composite fashion to form a vision of reality (called a *rhetorical vision*) that provides meaning, emotion, and motive for action for those who adhere to the vision. With Uncertainty Reduction Theory, explained in Chapter 5, the communicators are *social information seekers* and *givers* and their messages are the question-asking and disclosing techniques that reduce uncertainty (what is not known). With Narrative Paradigm Theory, presented in Chapter 6, storytellers offer narrations filled with *value-laden reasons* (for example, the moral of the story) that produce action because they are coherent and ring true to an idealized or actual *audience.* With Diffusion of Innovations Theory, introduced in Chapter 7, *adopters, rejecters, opinion leaders, change agents,* and *laggards* are the typical communicators, and the message is a novel idea diffusing by way of *awareness-, opinion-, practice-,* and *advocacy*-talk in the mass and interpersonal communication channels.

3. The Communication Metatheory (TMC), although not new in its particular parts, is new in its totality. We derived it through the careful observation of the workings of the various communication theories. We chose it because it works nicely for us, it fits nicely with our definition of communication theory, and it accurately represents the nature of communication theories. TCM contains about thirty-five metaconcepts.

Every one is needed, although not all at once. Although that may appear to be a lot of technical terms, it's only about a third of the terms that you need to appreciate the game of baseball. You may already know many of TCM's metaconcepts such as *assumptions* (in baseball teams compete to win), *model* (in baseball the playing field from home plate to the outfield is modeled as a diamond), *theoretical concepts* (baseball has its share, such as squeeze play, double steal, triple play, sacrifice, infield fly rule, and so forth), *technical definitions* (in baseball the *catcher* is the fielder who positions himself immediately behind the batter and home plate in foul territory and catches the ball thrown by the pitcher that the batter does not hit; the catcher is the player who is heavily protected with face, leg, and chest protectors), *relationship statements* (baseball has them, such as, if a batter receives four pitches outside the strike zone without swinging at them she or he is entitled to occupy first base), and *utility* (with baseball, its collected rules allow you to play the game correctly).

4. Among the participants were: Ray Birdwhistell, Ph.D. (1967), an anthropologist and theorist on the evolutionary aspects of nonverbal communication processes, especially kinesics; Kenneth Burke, a literary critic for *The Dial* and *The Nation* and periodically a lecturer on Dramatism at a number of American universities; Colin Cherry, Ph.D., Professor, Cambridge, England, and author of *On Human Communication* (1957); Malcolm S. MacLean, Jr., Ph.D., Professor of Mass Communication, University of Iowa and co-author with B. H. Westley (1957) of "A conceptual model for communication research"; and William Stephenson, Ph.D., Professor of Journalism at the Universities of Chicago and Missouri, who created Q-technique (1953) and the Play Theory of Mass Communication (1967) and whose research named the Ford Thunderbird.

5. Some early communication theorists liberally borrowed theories from other disciplines, and they adapted them to the purpose of explaining communicators communicating in a medium. Just as the United States benefited from immigration, so has the communication discipline benefited from our interdisciplinary roots. However, a word of caution is in order. Pluralism at the theory level is good for our discipline, but at the *meta*metatheory level it can be destructive to describe, explain, and classify our indigenous and adapted theories on the basis of an interdisciplinary framework. Just as Americans must emphasize the ties that bind us together (common language, republican form of govern-

ment, personal freedoms, attitude) and deemphasize our differences (historical nationalities, racial stock, religious affiliations) so too must our discipline emphasize what we all hold in common. What we hold in common as a discipline is our tool box of core communication theories.

6. One popular way to metametatheorize is to classify communication theories by using interdisciplinary frames. For example, if one were to use a biological, organic system frame, one might classify communication theories using the biologist's taxonomic classification categories of kingdom, phylum, subphylum, superclass, class, order, family, genus, species, and subspecies. Of course, such a frame uses a biologist's metaconcepts as the metatheory's *meta*metaconcepts. If such a usage appears far-fetched, we refer you to a special issue of *Journal of Communication,* edited by Joseph Capella (1996), entitled "Biology and Communication." Other communication theorists have classified theories as organic or nonorganic, systemic or nonsystemic, and as human and nonhuman (Littlejohn, 1996). Similarly, Hewes (1995) linked Constructivist Theory (Delia, 1974), Action Assembly Theory (Greene, 1984), and Uncertainty Reduction Theory (Berger & Calabrese, 1975) to the interdisciplinary *meta*metavocabulary of cognitive psychology and labeled them all cognitive theories. Similarly, Littlejohn (1996) tied Symbolic Convergence Theory (Bormann, 1980, 1985a, 1985b), Narrative Paradigm Theory (Fisher, 1987), and Burke's Dramatism Theory (Burke, 1968) to the interdisciplinary *meta*metavocabulary of the Symbolic Interactionist School of Sociology that originated early in the twentieth century with the thinking of Charles Horton Cooley and George Herbert Mead at the University of Chicago (Stone & Farberman, 1970). Others, such as Poole (1994), have called for the formation of an interdisciplinary team to build *meta*metatheories to explain small group behavior.

Although we recognize that such attempts at Level 4 *meta*metatheorizing are well intended, we believe that tying explanations of our disciplinary theories to such interdisciplinary *meta*metatheorizing creates unnecessary problems. The first problem regards the stature of the communication discipline within the academy. The second problem regards unnecessarily cluttering your ability to learn and differentiate communication theories. Regarding communication's stature within the academy, the interdisciplinary labels marginalize at best and obscure at worst the core theories of our communication discipline. We still agree with Cragan and Shields (1995),

Cragan, Shields, and Wright (1994), and Shields and Cragan (1975) that if we abandon our central theories in the name of interdisciplinary *meta*metatheorizing, we will lose our ability to distinguish ourselves from psychologists, sociologists, economists, and social psychologists. What is our unique contribution that justifies a department of communication at an institution of higher learning? We find it difficult to justify our seat at the academic table by saying that we are interdisciplinary *meta*metatheorists. No other discipline justifies its seat at the academic table by using another discipline's labels to name and compare its theories. As well, no other discipline calls its scholars interdisciplinary theorists. Indeed, psychologists offer theories of the individual, sociologists offer theories of society, economists offer theories of the economy, and physicists offer theories of the physical world. We believe communication scholars must offer discipline-based theories of communication. As well, we believe that communication scholars must use sensible, communication-based metatheories to describe, explain, and compare them.

Oh! You caught us. Would it help if we said we just forgot our promise not to preach? Well, we did forget. Nonetheless, it seems only natural to us that a book named *communication theory* would present communication theories and use a communication-based metatheory. Conversely, a book organized from the lens of an interdisciplinary *meta*metatheory will inherently offer theoretical explanations of communication drawn from economics, psychology, sociology, and social psychology and in so doing marginalize communication theories. We believe that the communication discipline competes quite favorably by comparison with any *one* other discipline. Our discipline exhibits six general communication theories, twenty-two contextual theories, and twelve microtheories. However, a false impression is created when say our six general theories are compared at the interdisciplinary level to all the theories of the other disciplines. After all, communication is only one discipline among many. In the 1990s, Berger (1991, 1992), Levy (1993), and Nass and Reeves (1991) published commentaries disparaging the fragmentation of the field first noted by Gerbner (1983). We have concluded that the fact that the lineage of the adopted interdisciplinary theories tracks so easily to their original discipline produced the apparent fragmentation about which so many rightfully worried.

Another popular *meta*metatheoretical approach to classifying communication theories occurs when textbook writers turn to the philosophers of science in the hope of making order out of chaos. Here, the fragmentation problem is avoided, but the lack of clarity and difficulty of understanding problems are intensified. Typically, such writers have turned to some philosophy of science continuum like "Science—Social Science—Humanities," "laws—rules—principles," or "causal—logical—practical necessity" and attempted to pigeonhole communication theories into one or another of such three-part divisions. The disadvantages of this approach are that such placement is often artificial and the placement highlights only one aspect of what makes a theory unique. Once that aspect is understood, the resultant sort system appears rather flat and mundane. As well, such a classification highlights simplistic *meta*metatheoretical differences in communication theories. For example, to say that this theory is law-based and that one is rule-based ignores the key ingredient that holds our core theories together. Each and every communication theory describes and explains and predicts communication events. It's like creating an uproar between teammates and encouraging them to fight over nothing while you watch grinning from the sidelines. The fighting distracts the team from its core goal.

7. For example, Symbolic Convergence Theory (presented in Chapter 4) began in the small group and public communication contexts. Uncertainty Reduction Theory (presented in Chapter 5) began in the interpersonal communication context. Currently, Burke's Dramatism Theory (presented in Chapter 9) is showing signs of breaking out of the public context. Burke's Dramatism Theory has already provided explanations for both organizational and mass communication phenomena (Cragan & Shields, 1995). As well, Burke's Dramatism deals with the communicative force of motive-embedded symbols on human action. As Dramatism is grounded in new contexts, it will gain a place as a general communication theory. We anticipate that other theories will break out of their contexts to become good candidates for future placement as general communication theories.

8. We've picked Alan Monroe's (1962) motivated sequence to illustrate what's involved in a special theory. Monroe offered a pattern for organizing a talk or speech. His steps include *attention* (gain the audience's interest), *need* (describe the problem as you see it), *satisfaction* (tell how you will solve the problem), *visualization* (show what the world will look like once the problem is solved), and *action* (suggest how the audience can help

to implement the solution). The attention step is the central concern of the introduction. The need, satisfaction, and visualization steps are the central concern of the body of the speech. The action step is the central concern of the conclusion.

9. Paradigms possess assumptions just as theories do. We use the word *presupposition* to refer to the assumptions of a paradigm. Elsewhere (Cragan & Shields, 1995), we noted that "all communication theories focus on the discovery of one or more of the three types of social science facts: material, social, or symbolic" (p. 18). In the earliest accounts of theory-building, people agreed that only material facts existed. People used the five bodily senses of hearing, seeing, smelling, tasting, or touching to confirm material facts. If you could not hear, see, smell, taste, or touch something then it did not exist. Early theory-builders believed that without verification by way of the senses a phenomenon lacked meaning or sense. In other words, the phenomenon had no essence. Today's material communication facts include such things as volume, words, scripts, talks, and so forth. *doesn't this slip into symbol/ connotative power?*

Emile Durkheim (1898/1938), who founded the discipline of sociology, gave the social sciences the concept of *social facts.* He argued forcefully that facts created and constituted by society—such as *anomie* or cultural malaise, *suicide,* and *roles*—exist in addition to material facts. He noted the difficulty of confirming social facts directly by the senses. Confirmation, he argued, would come through the use of technical definitions, scientific testing methods, reliable instruments, and valid procedures. Today, communication social facts include such entities as communication networks, group roles, family roles, superior–subordinate relationships, organizational hierarchies, and so forth.

During the twentieth century, theorists began concluding that symbolic facts exist just like material and social facts. George Herbert Mead (1938) left us with the notion of communication as symbolic interaction. Flew (1985), by including the symbolic realm, extended Berger and Luckman's (1966) notion about the social construction of reality. Bormann abandoned the social construction of reality and introduced the notion of the symbolic construction of reality (1980, 1985b). These and other theorists contributed procedures to ascertain the presence of symbolic facts. *Symbolic facts* are language representations that provide interpretations of the way things are. They may or may not possess a referent in social or material reality. Today, symbolic facts in-

clude such entities as worldviews, ideologies, myths, interpretive frames, ideographs, perspectives, speech codes, and rhetorical visions.

10. Euclid, who lived in the third century, B.C., authored the *Elements,* in which he presented the earliest systematic treatment of geometry developed from the essentially undefined concepts of point, line, and plane.

11. In the study of communication, we do not have as many, nor as many well-known, mathematically expressed relationship statements. However, we do have some. In Chapter 2, we will introduce you to Claude Shannon's Mathematical Theory of Communication from which scholars developed Information Systems Theory. Then, in Chapter 7 we introduce you to the normal and exponential (logistic) diffusion curves of Diffusion of Innovation Theory.

12. To illustrate what an axiom and its resultant theorems would look like, we offer the following from Berger and Calabrese (1975) regarding Uncertainty Reduction Theory: "Axiom 5: High levels of uncertainty produce high rates of reciprocity. Low levels of uncertainty produce low reciprocity rates" (p. 105). From this axiom and several others, Berger and Calabrese derived the following theorems stipulating the logical relationship between reciprocity and other concepts: "Theorem 4: Amount of communication and reciprocity rate are inversely related" (p. 107); "Theorem 13: Intimacy level of communication content and reciprocity rate are inversely related" (p. 109); "Theorem 16: Information seeking and reciprocity rate are positively related" (p. 109); "Theorem 19: Reciprocity rate and liking are negatively related" (p. 109); and "Theorem 20: Reciprocity rate and similarity are negatively related" (p. 109). As you can see, the axiomatic form of theory-building is meticulous and rigorous.

Of the theories discussed in this book, all but a few use ordinary language to state the relationship among theoretical concepts and to formulate theoretical relationship statements. In Chapter 4, we present Symbolic Convergence Theory. One of the theoretical relationship statements of that theory was developed from our own field research (Cragan & Shields, 1992). An illustrative theoretical statement using ordinary language is that rhetorical visions—the composite dramas that catch up large groups of people in a common symbolic reality—"exist on a continuum from pure to mixed with the result that the more pure the vision the fewer the participants and the more mixed the vision the greater the number of adherents" (p. 214).

13. There are several reason why such distinctions become problematic in the world of theory-building. One reason is that all theories use a qualitative method (often associated with humanists) to identify their basic concepts; at the same time, however, they must use a quantitative procedure (often associated with scientists) to capture it, count it, and measure it. As well, some communication theories started in scientific thinking (such as Information Systems Theory), but are now applied to answer social scientific and humanistic problems. Conversely, some communication theories started in humanistic artistic thinking (such as Symbolic Convergence Theory), but are now applied to answer social scientific research questions. We could go on, but you should get our point.

14. We concur with Bostrom and Donohew (1992) and Speyer (1994) that, in both contemporary quantum physics and contemporary communication theorizing, laws are not viewed as absolute, causal, functional—$f(x)$—relationships, but are expressed in terms of statistical probability. Such a view led us to the realization that if a law is only "probably" true, then it is not a law in the Newtonian sense of the word. Then, we realized that even Newton's laws of motion are time-bound, due to the eventual heat death of the universe because of entropy. Most of the relationship statements, of most of the theories, in most of the academic disciplines state observed regularities in terms of rules or principles more often than laws. With most theories, either the underlying "law" is an overconfidently stated rule, or the manifest "rule" is an understated law. Moreover, all theories, as they become applied to the solution of real-world problems, exhibit principles.

15. Let's take a rest stop and illustrate this point. Bormann (1990) reported that the Minnesota Studies on small group communication found that "most of the time" a leader emerged within a zero-history, initially leaderless, problem-solving group. From that statement, we would extrapolate the "rule" that most of the time leaders emerge from zero-history, problem-solving groups, but not necessarily. Similarly, Shields (1993) reported that the Yale Communication Studies

discovered a principle guiding the arrangement of persuasive arguments: "Place the strongest argument first, the second strongest argument last, and the weakest argument in the middle of your message" (p. 54). Thus, we extrapolate the probability-based principle that persuaders ought to arrange their arguments this way to increase their chances of success. Most of the theoretical relationship statements that comprise special contextual communication theories and special applied communication theories are principle-based. These theories, and hence the statements, are highly time-bound (short-lived) and tend to exhibit low-level probability expressions when tested empirically. Of course, space limitations preclude the inclusion of the many special communication theories in this book. Nonetheless, we do point to some contextual theories and microtheories that reflect the fleeting, ephemeral nature of principle-based theorizing in Chapters 10 and 11.

16. For example, with Symbolic Convergence Theory, presented in Chapter 4, the basic concept is a *fantasy theme*. The attendant qualitative method needed to flush out fantasy themes in communicative interaction is called Fantasy Theme Analysis. Fantasy Theme Analysis provides a set of procedures to help you find, depict, and classify fantasy themes as representing the various structural concepts of Symbolic Convergence Theory. Similarly, with Information Systems Theory, presented in Chapter 2, the basic concept is *information*. The attendant qualitative method needed to flush out information in communicative interaction is Information Flow Analysis. Information Flow Analysis provides the necessary qualitative tools to code, track, and model information flowing in an information system. Of course, the other general communication theories possess their own unique theory–method complex.

17. For an example of such a debate, see the interchange among Andersen (1991), Bavelas (1990), Beach (1990), and Motley (1990a, 1990b, 1991) regarding whether or not one cannot not communicate.

18. See the discussion of compliance-gaining research in Chapter 11.

Chapter 2   Information Systems Theory

1. For *Cybernetics,* see Wiener (1948); for the mathematical theory of communication, see Shannon (1948a, 1948b) and Shannon and Weaver (1949).

2. Professor Cragan's information systems tend toward chaos. It's nearly impossible to communicate with him. His mailbox overflows with memos and letters. His

voice-mail is full and the computer instructs the caller that no more messages can be added. His e-mail goes unread. His problem is not the exception.

3. See, for example, Cherry (1966), Fulton (1963), Hyvarinen (1968), Jumarie (1990), Morris (1938), Shannon (1948a, 1948b), Watzlawick, Beavin, and Jackson (1967), and Wilder (1977).

4. See, for example, Cummings, Long, and Lewis (1987), Farace, Monge, and Russell (1977), Goldhaber (1993), and Weick (1979).

5. See, for example, Kapp and Barnett (1983), Kogler–Hill, Bahniuk, and Dobos (1989), Spiker and Daniels (1981).

6. Contributors to the perceived understanding research program included: Cahn (1983, 1984, 1986,

1987, 1990), Cahn and Frey (1990), Cahn and Hanford (1984), Cahn and Shulman (1984).

7. For scholarly reports of this research, see Miller and Fonts (1979); Miller and Sunnafrank (1984); and Miller, et al. (1983).

8. See, for example, Conant (1979), Dean, Allen, and Aloimonos (1995), Hyvarinen (1968), Jumarie (1990).

9. They also erroneously attribute the model to Shannon and Warren Weaver, as in the phrase, "Shannon and Weaver's model of communication" (Littlejohn, 1995, p. 54). Weaver (1949) merely pointed to the importance of Shannon's theory; he did not model it or develop it.

Chapter 3   Rational Argumentation Theory

1. For a sampling of the contributions of the Illinois scholars to RAT, see Brockriede (1972, 1974, 1975, 1977), Delia (1970), O'Keefe (1977), Scott (1960, 1967, 1976, 1990), Wenzel (1977, 1979, 1980, 1987, 1990), and Willard (1983, 1989, 1990).

2. Compare with McKerrow (1980), Trapp (1981), and Zarefsky (1980).

3. Dr. Kevorkian, between 1990 and 1996, assisted the suicide deaths of more than forty terminally ill persons. During that time three different Michigan juries acquitted Dr. Kevorkian, seeing his actions as merciful (The Associated Press, 1997).

4. See, for example, Vancil (1993), Warnick and Inch (1994), and Ziegelmueller, Kay, and Dause (1990).

Chapter 4   Symbolic Convergence Theory

1. See, for example: Bormann (1982c, 1983a, 1985b, 1990), Bormann, Cragan, and Shields (1994, 1996), Cragan and Shields (1981a, 1992, 1995a).

2. For samples of mediated symbolic facts chaining in the print media, see, for example: Doyle (1985), Haskins (1981), Hubbard (1985), Kidd (1975), and Turner (1977). For examples of mediated symbolic facts chaining in the electronic media, see, for example: Bantz (1975), Bormann (1973), Nimmo and Combs (1982), and Sharf (1986).

3. See, for example, Brown (1976), Cragan and Shields (1977), Foss and Littlejohn (1986), Rarick, et al. (1977), Rosenfeld and Schrag (1985), and Schrag, Hudson, and Bernado (1981).

4. See Bormann (1972, 1980, 1985a), Bormann, Cragan, and Shields (1994, 1996), and Cragan and Shields (1981a, 1992, 1995a).

5. Attila was a fifth century King of the Huns. He was called "the Scourge of God."

6. Elsewhere (Cragan & Shields, 1995a), we tell a joke about the movie attendee who, on leaving Spike Lee's movie, *Malcolm X,* commented: "I loved that movie *Malcolm X.* I think I'll go rent the other nine." The joke portrays a movie-goer who did not chain-out the "X" symbolic cue in the same way as the participants in the rhetorical vision celebrating the life of Malcolm X.

7. *Style* also has a much narrower definition as it specifies a communication construct that relates to an attribute of an individual communicator possessing a strikingly different mode of expression (Norton, 1978, 1983).

8. See Bormann, Koester, and Bennett (1978), Bormann, Kroll, Watters, and McFarland(1984), Cragan and Shields (1977, 1992), Cragan, Shields, and Nichols (1981), Cragan, Shields, Pairitz, and Jackson (1978, 1981), Endres (1989, 1994), Faules (1982), Foss and Littlejohn (1986), McFarland (1985), Rarick, et al. (1977), Rosenfeld and Schrag (1985), and Shields (1974, 1981f).

9. For studies of shared and unshared group consciousness, see: Aden (1986), Ball (1992), Bormann (1983b, 1983c), Bormann, Pratt, and Putnam (1978), Campbell (1982), Cragan, 1975, Glaser and Frank (1982), Heisey and Trebing (1983), Kiewe and Houck (1989), Kroll (1983), Mayerle (1987), Shields (1981c, 1981d, 1981e, 1981f), and Solomon (1980).

10. For more complete explanations of fantasy theme analysis than space permits here, see: Bormann (1972, 1982c, 1985a, 1985b, 1986, 1989, 1990), Bormann, Bormann, and Harty (1995), Bormann, Cragan, and Shields (1994, 1996), Cragan and Shields (1981a, 1995a, 1995b), Shields (1981a, 1988), and Shields and Preston (1985).

11. To find detailed explanations of these procedures, see: Cragan and Shields (1992, 1995a, 1995b), Shields and Preston (1985), and Shields (1981b, 1988).

12. See, for example, Bormann, Pratt, and Putnam (1978), Chesebro, Cragan, and McCullough (1973), Porter (1976), and Shields (1974).

13. See, for example, Bormann (1973), Bormann, et al. (1984), Brown (1976), Chesebro (1980), Cragan and Shields (1977), Kroll (1983), Nimmo and Combs (1982), Rarick, et al. (1977), Rosenfeld and Schrag (1985), and Schrag, Hudson, and Bernado (1981).

14. See, for example, Bantz (1975), Bormann (1972, 1985b), Bormann, Cragan, and Shields (1996), Callahan (1992), Cragan (1975, 1981), Daniel (1995), Duffy (1997), Endres (1994), Foss and Littlejohn (1986), Ford (1989), Hensley (1975), Ilka (1977), Kidd (1975), Koester (1982), Lee and Hoon (1993).

15. See, for example, Bormann, Cragan, and Shields (1996), Cragan and Shields (1977, 1978), Rarick, et al. (1977), and Shields (1974, 1981f).

16. See, for example, Cragan and Shields (1981c), Endres (1989, 1994), McFarland (1985).

17. See, for example, Cragan and Shields (1978), Cragan, Shields, and Nichols (1981), Cragan, et al. (1978, 1981), Rarick, et al. (1977).

18. See, for example, Bormann (1985b), Cragan (1975), Cragan and Cutbirth (1984), and Cragan, Semlak, and Cuffe (1984).

19. Among the critics espousing such views were: Black (1980), Brummett (1984), Farrell (1982), Gronbeck (1980), Hart (1986), Ivie (1987), Mohrmann (1980, 1982a, 1982b), Osborn (1986), and Vatz and Weinberg (1987).

20. See, especially, Bormann, Cragan, and Shields (1996), Cragan (1975), Kroll (1983), Mayerle (1987), and Shields (1981f).

Chapter 5   Uncertainty Reduction Theory

1. URT would predict that just as you were getting to know and could predict the kinds of student-relevant examples we might use, we engaged in deviant communication behavior by offering this opera example, thereby raising your level of uncertainty about us.

2. See, for example, Berger (1975, 1979, 1985, 1988, 1994, 1995a, 1995b), Berger and Bell (1988), Berger and Bradac (1982), Berger and diBattista (1992, 1993), Berger and Douglas (1981), Berger, et al. (1976a), Berger and Gudykunst (1991), Berger and Jordan (1992), Berger and Kellermann (1983, 1989), Berger and Roloff (1982), Clatterbuck (1979), Douglas (1983, 1984, 1985, 1990, 1991, 1994), Gudykunst (1983, 1985a, 1985b, 1988), Gudykunst and Hammer (1987, 1988), Gudykunst and Nishida (1984, 1986), Gudykunst, Nishida, and Schmidt (1989), Gudykunst, Soldetani, and Sonoda (1987), Kellermann (1984, 1986, 1991), Kellermann and Berger (1984), Kellermann and Reynolds (1990), Parks and Adelman (1983), Planalp and Honeycutt (1985), Prisbell and Andersen (1980), Rubin (1977), Sheer and Cline (1995), and Waldron (1990).

3. Compare URT research such as Ayres (1979), Booth–Butterfield and Trotta (1994) and Hecht (1978) with Altman and Taylor (1973), Heider (1958), Kelley (1967, 1973), and Kelly (1955).

4. For compliance-gaining research related to influence-gaining, see Boster (1995), Cody and McLaughlin (1980), and Miller, et al. (1977); for related affinity-seeking research, see Bell and Daly (1984); for related relationship termination research, see Baxter (1982).

5. See, for example, Berger (1979, 1986), Berger and Bradac (1982), Berger, et al. (1976a), and Berger and Perkins (1978).

6. See, for example, Comer (1991), Kim and Sharkey (1995), Lester (1987), Mignerey, Rubin, and Gordon (1995), Miller and Jablin (1991), Putnam and Sorenson (1982), Spiker and Daniels (1981), and Teboul (1994).

Chapter 6   Narrative Paradigm Theory

1. See, for example, Bass (1985); Brown and McMillan (1991); Collins and Clark (1992); Cragan and Shields (1995); Deming (1985); Dobkin (1992); Downs, Javidi, and Nussbaum (1988); Fisher (1978, 1980, 1984, 1985a, 1985b, 1987a, 1987b, 1988, 1989, 1992, 1995); Gronbeck (1992); Hollihan, Baaske, and Riley (1985, 1987); Hollihan and Riley (1987a); Langellier (1989); Mechling and Mechling (1983); Moore (1992); Mumby (1987); Payne (1992); Schuetz (1988); Stuckey (1992); and Whittenberger–Keith (1992).

2. See, Cali (1993); Condit (1987); Gass (1988); Gronbeck (1987); Kirkwood (1992); Lucaites and Condit (1985); Megill (1987); Rowland (1987, 1988, 1989); and Warnick (1987).

3. For a more extended defense of NPT, see Cragan and Shields (1995) and Fisher (1988).

Chapter 7   Diffusion of Innovations Theory

1. For a sampling of news diffusion studies, see Allen and Colfax (1968); Bantz, Petronio, and Rarick (1983); Gantz (1983); Greenberg (1964a, 1964b); Hanneman and Greenberg (1973); Kubey and Peluso (1990); Levy (1969); Steinfatt, et al. (1973); Weaver–Lariscy, Sweeney, and Steinfatt (1984).

2. Rogers and Kinkaid (1981), following Cherry (1978, p. 27), stressed that *communico*—the Latin root of *communication*—means 'share.'

3. See, for example, Bardini and Horvath (1995), and Rice and Rogers (1980).

4. See, for example, Beltran (1976); Bordenave (1976); Chaffee, Gomez–Palacio, and Rogers (1990); Donohue, Tichenor, and Olien (1975); Fredin, Monnett, and Kosicki (1994); Rogers (1976a, 1976b); Rogers, Burdge, Korsching, and Donnermeyer (1988); and Roling, Ashcroft, and Chege (1976).

5. On retirement, Professor Cragan plans to become a fashion innovation toad. In other words, he plans to become an active resister to fashion change. The day he retires, he plans to store a black suit, a white shirt, a red tie, one pair of boxer shorts, and a pair of black socks in a plastic suit bag. Then, he hopes only to use the bag's contents for weddings, anniversaries, and funerals. Similarly, Professor Shields is unadopting things he has previously adopted. Gone are the fax machine, conference calling, and the modem. He apparently can no longer stand up for his principles. Indeed, he says that after fifty it's hard enough to stand up in the shower.

6. McLaurin (1995) reported on the adverse effects of public health campaigns targeted at African American at-risk youth when homogeneity is absent from the message, the communication style, and the change agent messengers.

7. It is often standard practice for change agents to offer trial adoptions with money-back guarantees. For example, America On-Line in 1996 distributed free software to "Hook Up, Hang Out, Have Fun." As well, they offered fifty free hours to try the Internet. Similarly, seed dealers offer samples of seed for farmers to try in test plots, and car dealers encourage the prospective buyer to test-drive before purchasing. Of course, some people try an innovation and then actively reject it. Others passively reject an innovation without ever trying it.

8. Indeed, Barnett, Fink, and Sebus (1989) found that even new academic theories become fashionable as they follow the S-curve of cumulative citation frequency.

9. Studies by O'Keefe (1985), Rogers (1973, 1977), Schramm (1971), and Witte, et al. (1993) are typical of the explications of using DIT in communication campaigns.

10. See, for example, Damonpour (1988); Dearing and Meyer (1994); Dearing, Meyer, and Kazmierczak (1994).

11. See, for example, Danko and MacLachlan (1983); Gantz, Fitzmaurice, and Yoo (1990); Gonzalez (1989); Hyman and Sheatsley (1947); Kopfman and Smith (1996).

12. See, for example, McNelly, Rush, and Bishop (1968); Richmond (1977, 1980); Rogers (1958, 1995).

13. See, for example, Deering and Rogers (1996); Rogers and Deering (1988); Rogers, Deering, and Chang (1991).

14. See, for example, Shoemaker, Wanta, and Leggett (1989) and Singer, Rogers, and Glassman (1991).

15. See, for example, Hyman and Sheatsley (1947); Mendelsohn (1973); Rogers (1995).

16. See, for example, Gonzalez (1989); Menzel and Katz (1955–1956); Valente (1995).

17. See, for example, Miller and Monge (1985); Miller, Johnson, and Grau (1994); Papa (1990); Papa and Tracy (1988); Rogers (1995).

18. For example, Beyer and Trice (1978); Hoffman and Roman (1984); Leonard–Barton (1988); Manross and Rice (1986).

19. For studies of individualist social systems, see Bardini and Horvath (1995); Barnett and Seigel (1988); Carrocci (1985); Danko and MacLachlan (1983); LaRose and Mettler (1989); O'Keefe (1969).

20. See, for example, Katz (1957, 1960, 1962, 1968); Katz and Lazarsfeld (1955); Rogers (1995).

21. See, for example, Lazarsfeld, Berelson, and Gaudet (1944); Gross (1942); Ryan and Gross (1943).

22. For examples of the line of research representing the knowledge gap, see Donohue, Tichenor, and Olien (1973, 1975); Ettema and Kline (1977); Fredin, Monnett, and Kosicki (1994); Gaziano (1983); Genova and Greenberg (1979); Hagins (1996); Seeman (1966); Tichenor, Donohue, and Olien (1970); Tichenor, Olien, and Donohue (1973); Wade and Schramm (1969).

23. For studies viewing the knowledge gap as an effects gap, see Dutton, Rogers, and Jun (1987); Galloway (1977); Hall (1991); Roling, Ashcroft, and Chege (1976); Shingi and Mody (1976); Stauffer, Frost, and Rybolt (1978); Suominen (1976); Werner (1975); Williams and Lindsay (1971).

24. See, for example, Pinelli, et al. (1991a, 1991b, 1992, 1994); Pinelli, Barclay, and Kennedy (1993); Pinelli, Kennedy, and Barclay (1991, 1993).

25. Studies by Coleman, Katz, and Menzel (1957, 1966), Dutton, Rogers, and Jun (1987), Ostland (1973), Troldahl and Van Dam (1965), and Valenti (1995) are typical.

26. See, for example, Danko and MacLachlan (1983); Gantz, Fitzmaurice, and Yoo (1990); and Star and Hughes (1950).

27. See, for example, Antonelli (1986); Bolton (1983); Cheney, Block, and Gordon (1986); Katzman (1974).

28. See, for example, Albrecht and Ropp (1984); Cheney, Block, and Gordon (1986); Hurt and Tiegen (1977); Kanter (1988); Miller and Monge (1985); Miller, Johnson, and Grau (1994); Rice and Aydin (1991); Sparkes and Kang (1986).

29. See, for example, Fairhurst (1993); Fairhurst and Wendt (1993); Hayes and Clark (1986); Lewis and Siebold (1983, 1996); Rice and Manross (1986); Rubinyi (1989); Wildemuth (1992).

30. See, for example, Melkote (1984) and Walton (1987).

31. See, for example, Antola and Rogers (1984); Markus (1987); Rogers (1976a); Rogers and Antola (1985); Singhal and Rogers (1988, 1989); Wade and Schramm (1969).

32. See, for example, Adams, Mullen, and Wilson (1969); Budd, MacLean, and Barnes (1966); DeFleur (1987a, 1987b); Fathi (1973); Fine (1975); Gantz, Krendal, and Robertson (1986); Gantz, Fitzmaurice, and Fink (1991); Gantz, Trenholm, and Pittman (1976); Haroldsen, et al. (1987); Hill and Bonjean (1964); Jeffres and Quarles (1984); Kepplinger, et al. (1987); Larson and Hill (1954); Levy (1969); Mayer, et al. (1990); Mendelsohn (1964); Quarles, et al. (1983); Riffe and Stovall (1987); Rosengren (1987a, 1987b); Sheatsley and Feldman (1965); Smith (1987); Spitzer and Spitzer (1965).

33. For studies of news as innovation diffusion, see Antola and Rogers (1984); Contractor, Singhal, and Rogers (1988); Heine–Geldern (1968); Kobrin (1985); Rosengren (1987b); Schmitz, et al. (1995); Weibull, Lindahl, and Rosengren (1987). For studies of the diffusion of American television programming, see, for example, Cook, et al. (1975); Contractor, Singhal, and Rogers (1988); Mayo, et al. (1984). For studies of the intercultural diffusion of technology, see, for example, Deutchmann (1963) and Hornik (1975, 1980).

34. For studies of the effects of third world development campaigns, see Bogart (1957–1958); Deutchmann (1963); Freedman (1964); Hagerstrand (1968); Hornik (1975, 1980); Mayo, et al. (1984); McPhail (1987); Pelto (1973); Shingi and Mody (1976); Tichenor, Donahue, and Olien (1970); Tichenor, Olien, and Donahue (1973); Werner (1975); Williams and Lindsay (1971).

35. DIT knowledge gap studies include Donohue, Tichenor, and Olien (1973, 1975); Ettema & Kline (1977); Fredin, et al., (1994); Galloway (1977); Gaziano (1983); Hall (1991); Roling, Ashcroft, and Chege (1976); Stauffer, Frost, and Rybolt (1978); Suominen (1976); Tichenor, Donohue, and Olien (1970); Tichenor, Olien, and Donohue (1973); Werner (1975); Williams and Lindsey (1971).

Chapter 8   *Interpersonal and Small Group Communication Context Theories*

1. Their respective insights may be found in: Buber (1958, 1963, 1965); Fromm (1956); Jourard (1967); Maslow (1962, 1970); May (1967); Powell (1969); Rogers (1961, 1965).

2. For example, Poulakos (1974) discussed the elements of dialogue, Wise (1972) characterized the antecedents of interpersonal communication, and Zima (1971) introduced an inventory for analyzing the self.

3. From 1970 to 1973 texts such as Keltner's (1970) *Interpersonal speech-communication,* Giffin and Patton's (1971a, 1971b) *Basic readings in interpersonal communication* and *Fundamentals of interpersonal communication,* McCroskey, Larson, and Knapp's (1971) *Introduction to interpersonal communication,* Bormann and Bormann's (1972b) *Speech communication: An interpersonal approach,* Stewart's (1972) *An interpersonal approach to the basic course,* and Stewart's (1973) *Bridges not walls: A book about interpersonal communication* focused on the role of the individual in the communication process.

4. Contributors helping to ground the constructivist research program included Clark and Delia (1976, 1977), Delia (1977), Delia and Clark (1977), Hale and Delia (1976), O'Keefe (1984, 1988), O'Keefe and Delia (1982).

5. See, for example, Delia, Clark, and Switzer (1979); Hale & Delia (1976); Kline & Ceropski (1984); O'Keefe (1988); and O'Keefe and Delia (1982).

6. Among the scholars contributing to the research program grounding CMM were Cronen, Pearce and Harris (1979, 1982), Pearce and Conklin (1979), Pearce and Cronen (1980), Pearce (1989), and Stamm and Pearce (1971, 1974).

7. See, especially, Cronen, Chen, and Pearce (1988); Pearce, Littlejohn, and Alexander (1987); Wolfson and Pearce (1983).

8. See, for example, Baxter, 1988, 1990; Canary & Stafford, 1994; Dindia & Baxter, 1987; Goldsmith & Baxter, 1996.

9. For example, Rawlins (1989) found these additional dialectics: Ideal–Real (Prince Charming versus Joe, my boyfriend), Affection–Instrumentality (liking/loving versus using), Judgment–Acceptance (judgmental versus accepting).

10. Petronio, et al. (1996) refashioned the microtheory's name as The Communication Management of Privacy Theory and used it to examine child and adolescent disclosures of sexual abuse.

11. Among the works of the theory's contributing communication scholars are Baxter (e.g., 1988, 1990, 1992a), Baxter and Dindia (1987, 1990), Baxter and Montgomery (1996), Baxter and Simon (1993), Baxter and Wilmot (1984), Canary and Stafford (1994), Dindia & Baxter (1987), Goldsmith and Baxter (1996), Montgomery (1992), Rawlins (1983a, 1983b, 1992), Simon and Baxter (1993), Stafford and Canary (1991), VanLear (1991), VanLear and Zeitlow (1990), Werner and Baxter (1994), Wood (1995), Wood, et al. (1994), and Zorn (1995).

12. Emmers and Hart (1996) reported the coping strategies (rituals) used by individuals disengaging from romantic relationships. They indicated that both "leavers" and "lefts" turn to their communication network of friends. As well, leavers typically avoid the left partner.

13. The FMT researchers have grounded a number of face-saving communication strategies in a variety of interpersonal situations. The theorists contributing to the research program included Carbaugh (1994); Cupach (1994); Cupach and Imahori (1993a, 1993b); Cupach and Metts (1990, 1993, 1994); Cupach, Metts, and Hazelton (1986); Fairhurst, Green, & Snavely (1984); Knapp, Stafford, and Daly (1986); Lim (1990); Lim & Bowers (1991); McLaughlin, Cody, and O'Hair (1983); Metts (1992), Metts and Cupach (1989a, 1989b); Petronio (1984); Petronio, Olson, & Dollar (1988); Shimanoff (1988); Ting–Toomey (1988, 1993, 1994); Tracy (1990); Tracy and Baratz (1994).

14. For research confirming these kinds of facework, see Cupach and Metts (1990, 1994); Goffman (1967); Hewitt and Stokes (1975).

15. For example, see Cupach and Metts (1990, 1992); Cupach, Metts, and Hazelton (1986); and Metts and Cupach (1989b).

16. For a sample of communication scholars studying brainstorming, see Comadena (1984); Jablin (1981); Jablin, Seibold, & Sorenson (1977); Jablin, Sorenson, & Seibold (1978).

17. For a sample of such calls for research, see Bormann (1970a, 1970b); Fisher (1971); Fisher & Hawes (1971); Gouran (1970a, 1970b, 1973); and Mortensen (1970).

18. For a recent history of theory and research in small group communication, see Frey (1996).

19. They did so by stitching together Symbolic Convergence Theory's explanation of how groups create an identity, Uncertainty Reduction Theory's explanation of how group members develop interpersonal trust, Role Emergence Theory's explanation of the fulfillment of five key group roles, and Decision-Emergence Theory's explanation of the stages or phases of the decision-making process that lead groups toward consensus decisions. Then they used the unified theory to explain how the communicative interactions of problem-solving talk, role talk, trust-building talk, and team-building talk effect the major group outcomes of productivity, quality of work, consensus, and membership satisfaction.

20. As well, Bormann, Bormann, and Harty (1995), Cragan and Shields (1995) and Shields (1981a, 1981b, 1981c, 1981d, 1988) used SCT to undergird and facilitate information retrieval using focus group interviews.

21. The Spiral of Silence Theory presented in Chapter 10 provides a viable explanation of why this form of communicative interaction occurs in this stage of the group process; the explanation concerns the majority opinion muting the minority opinion.

22. In a parallel line of research on decision-making, Beatty (1987, 1988) found that decision-making could be enhanced through training in a special communication theory emphasizing choice-making and decision rule use.

23. Of interest is the ability of Symbolic Convergence Theory, a general communication theory presented in Chapter 4, to explain the dynamics of the communication in Lewin's *lifespace* that leads to interdependence and cohesion. SCT, for example, explains the force of fantasy-sharing on group identity and team-building.

24. Berg (1967a, 1967b); Bormann (1969, 1975, 1980b, 1990); Bormann and Bormann (1972a, 1988); Bormann, Pratt, & Putnam (1978); Chesebro, Cragan, and McCullough (1973); Fisher (1970a, 1970b, 1971); Fisher and Hawes (1971); Forston (1968); Geier (1963, 1967); Larson, C. U. (1971); Mortensen (1966); Putnam (1979); Shields and Kidd (1973).

25. Shields and Kidd (1973), in a study of *The Poseidon Adventure,* demonstrated that popular movies often allow the observance of role emergence in complex task groups. Other movies illustrating role formation during group decision-making include *Twelve*

Angry Men, The Dirty Dozen, The Magnificent Seven, The Breakfast Club, and *First Wives.*

26. See, for example, Gouran and Hirokawa (1986); Hirokawa (1985, 1987, 1988, 1990); Hirokawa, Gouran, and Martz (1988); Hirokawa, Ice, and Cook (1988); Hirokawa and Pace (1983); Hirokawa and Scheerhorn (1986); Propp and Julian (1994); Salazar, et al. (1994).

27. Cline (1994) examined the Watergate transcripts and concurrently validated the presence of the illusion of unanimity, avoidance of disagreement, and forcing group conformity. On the other hand, Ball (1994) explained the escalation of the Vietnam War using the explanatory power of the force of fantasy from Symbolic Convergence Theory, a general communication theory.

28. On the other hand, Cragan and Wright's (1993) replicative research suggested that the four functions may vary as to their importance in solving a particular problem. Putnam and Stohl (1990) and Billingsley (1993) cautioned that FDT has yet to be grounded with naturalistic groups in real-world settings.

29. For more than sixty years, communication specialists in group decision-making have reiterated the importance of sequentially following a normative agenda system. The system could be McBurney and Hance's (1939) adaptation of the five steps in John Dewey's reflective thinking process, or Ross's (1974) four step agenda system, or the Phillips (1966) standard agenda system for problem-solving. The hypothesis was that by following the order of the system, the group would reach a quality decision.

30. See, for example, Billingsley (1993); Contractor and Seibold (1993); Poole and DiSanctis (1990); Poole, Seibold, and McPhee (1985, 1986).

31. For example, Poole, McPhee, and Seibold (1982) and McPhee, Poole, and Seibold (1982).

32. For example, Canary, Brossman, and Seibold (1987) and Seibold and Meyers (1986).

33. For example, Poole (1981, 1983a, 1983b) and Poole and Roth (1989a, 1989b).

34. For example, Contractor and Seibold (1993); Poole and DiSanctis (1990, 1992); Poole, Holmes, and DiSanctis (1991); Poole and Jackson (1993).

35. Dennis, Nunamaker, and Vogle (1990–1991), Kasch (1996), and Kraemer and Pinsonneault (1990) reviewed the studies of GDSS laboratory and field research. They concluded that the research demonstrated the viability of GDSS groups in terms of improving member satisfaction, group productivity, and work efficiency.

Chapter 9   *Public Speaking and Organizational Communication Context Theories*

1. Recall that these grew into Bormann's (1982, 1985) Symbolic Convergence Theory and Fisher's (1984, 1987) Narrative Paradigm theory.

2. Also see, Hart, Carlson, and Eadie (1980).

3. See, for example, Hewgill and Miller (1965); Kraus, El-Assal, and DeFleur (1966); Miller (1963); Powell (1965); Smith (1977); Sussman (1973); Witte (1992, 1993, 1994); Witte and Morrison (1995).

4. For example, Clark (1974) and Rosnow (1966) examined the importance of argument placement in a message. Luchok and McCroskey (1978) researched the effect of the inclusion of quality evidence on persuasion. Allen, et al. (1990) and McCroskey, Young, and Scott (1972) examined the effects on persuasion of presenting only one side of an argument versus two sides. Still others researched the effects of logical versus emotional arguments on persuasion (Matthews, 1947), and whether evidence (Harte, 1976), such as facts or authority-based assertion (Whitehead, 1971), or opinion-based assertion (Miller & Basehart, 1969) affected persuasion. Still others studied the effect of evidence that seemed consistent or inconsistent with itself or with the views of an audience (Schunk, 1969) when evidence was given reluctantly (Arnold & McCroskey, 1967) or presented equivocally (Goss & Williams, 1973). Atwood (1966) studied the effects on persuasion of incongruity between message and source credibility.

Many social science researchers studied the effects of arrangement on persuasion. Some examined the effect of sentence structure on the recall of messages (A. C. Nichols, 1965). Others examined the effect of disorganized versus organized messages (R. G. Smith, 1951). Others studied the effect of brevity on persuasiveness (Ragsdale, 1968). Still others researched the use of climax versus anti-climax order (Sponberg, 1946), and the order of presentation of arguments and messages (Bryant & Comisky, 1978; Cromwell, 1950, 1954; Gilkinson, Paulson, & Sikkink, 1954; and Clark, 1974) on attitude change and learning (Daniels & Whitman, 1981). A number of communication researchers studied ways to stylize message content and their effect on persuasion. For example, Matthews (1947) studied the effect of loaded language, Bostrom, Basehart, and Rossiter (1973) and Mulac (1976) studied the effect of obscene language, and Wheeless (1973) studied the effect of credible language choice on persuasion. Schunk (1969) reported the effects of self-contradiction in a persuasive communication. Others examined the per-

suasive effect of stylistic devices like using figurativeness, metaphors, similes, and analogies (Bowers & Osborn, 1966; Jordan & McLaughlin, 1976; McCroskey & Combs, 1969; Reinsch, 1971; and Siltanen, 1981). Seiler (1971) researched the effects of visual materials on attitudes, retention, and credibility. Gruner (1967) and Taylor (1973) researched the effect of humor and Pokorny and Gruner (1969) researched the effect of satire on persuasion.

5. Of course, in addition to the one-to-many context of public speaking, Blankenship and Robson (1995), Carcillo, Ray, and Pettey (1995), Garko (1993), Hawes (1972), Norton and Miller (1975), Ralston (1993), and Talley and Richmond (1980) applied the communicator style concept to one-to-one interviews in various settings.

6. For example, Addington (1968), McCroskey and Mehrley (1969), and Sereno and Hawkins (1967) looked at the effect of fluency. Bowers (1963), Bradac, Bowers, and Courtright (1979), and McEwen and Greenberg (1970) examined the effect of language intensity. Addington (1965) and Kibler and Barker (1968) examined the effect of mispronunciation. Buck (1968), Giles (1978), and Bock and Pitts (1975) studied the effect of dialectical variation, and Bradac, Konsky, and Davies (1976) reported on the effect of linguistic diversity on persuasion. Researchers also studied such nonverbal communicator elements as the effect of vocal and paralinguistic cues (Pearce, 1971; Beatty & Behnke, 1980), attractiveness by physical characteristics, attire, and sex of source (Bassett, Stanton–Spicer, & Whitehead, 1979; Bostrom & Kemp, 1969; Montgomery & Burgoon, 1977; Rosenfeld & Christie, 1974; Widgery, 1974), and even tardiness (Wheeless, Jones, & King, 1974) on persuasion.

7. Other studies examined the quality of motivation present in rhetoric stemming from such linguistic vantage points as orientation, perspective by incongruity, and dialectic. Gibson (1970) explored the motivational strategies involved in Eugene Talmadge's 1934 campaign for the United States Senate. Ivie (1974) examined the quality of motivation present in presidential explanations of going to war. Klumpp and Lukehart (1978) found that poor choices in motivational strategy accounted for the failure of Gerald Ford's speech pardoning Richard Nixon of any wrongdoing in the 1970s Watergate Affair. In a broader sense, Jameson (1978) explored the motivational strategies of political ideology. Preston (1984) ex-

plained how President Reagan's motive-embedded symbols differed substantially from those of President Franklin Roosevelt, and argued that the comparisons offered at the time were premature and ideologically inappropriate. Peterson (1986) looked at the degree to which the dust bowl farmer identified with the motive-embedded symbols regarding conservation of land. To Rushing (1986), the quality of motivation contained in his motive-embedded symbols explained the success of Reagan's Star Wars rhetoric. In a similar vein, Schiappa (1989) explored the motivational impact of "nuke-speak."

8. Other studies employed the elements of BDT's hexad. Here, the researchers engaged in ratio analysis as they assessed the quality of motivation in political rhetoric. For example, Ling (1970) found that by stressing the scene in a speech about the Chappaquiddick car drowning of a female passenger, Senator Edward Kennedy (D–MA) rescued his political career. Blankenship, Fine, and Davis (1983) discovered an agent presence so dominating during the 1980 GOP New Hampshire primary that Reagan created a springboard to his ultimate nomination as the standard-bearer of the Republican Party. Birdsell (1987) used the hexadic elements to explain President Reagan's inconsistent foreign policy reactions to Lebanon and Grenada. Kelly (1987) discovered that the hexad allowed for structuring an explanation of local campaigns in his study of Representative George Hansen's 1984 campaign. Olsen (1989) explained Reagan's discourse concerning a controversial visit to a war cemetery in Bitburg, Germany, as that of redefining the scene. Mullican (1971) found that a comic attitude enabled scholars to better conduct their analyses of political propaganda. Bostdorff (1987) found that a similar attitude explained the impact of political cartoons concerning former Secretary of the Interior James Watt, who often acted with seemingly little commitment to the stewardship of national lands.

9. For studies applying the Ware and Linkugel elements of apologia to organizational communication, see Benoit and Lindsey (1987), Dionisopoulos and Vibbert (1988), and Violanti (1996).

10. See, for example, Daniels, Spiker, and Papa (1997); Eisenberg and Goodall (1993); Goldhaber (1993); Kreps (1990); Schockley–Zalabak (1995).

11. See Bantz, McCorkle, and Baade (1980); Bantz and Smith (1977); Kreps (1980); Putnam and Sorenson (1982).

12. Tompkins, et al. (1975) argued that as early as 1951 Burke was "cognizant of the implications of his notions for the study of human organizations. For example, the appendix to *Permanence and Change* [entitled] ('On Human Behavior Considered "Dramatistically" ') is, in Burke's words, 'the somewhat reworked version of a paper that was originally presented in a symposium on "Organizational Behavior" held at Princeton in 1951' " (p. 136).

13. See, for example, Barker and Cheney (1994); Bullis and Bach (1989); Bullis and Tompkins (1989); Cheney (1983a, 1983b, 1991); Cheney and Tompkins (1987); Sass and Canary (1991); Tompkins and Cheney (1983, 1985); Tompkins, et al. (1975).

14. See, for example, Bormann (1983); Bormann, Howell, Nichols, and Shapiro (1969); Cragan and Shields (1992); Schockley–Zalabak and Morley (1994).

15. For example, a scholar might use a feminist critical theory to evaluate the National Football League and judge it to be macho and sexist. Or, a scholar might use an ethical critical theory to look at Wall Street and judge it to be base and corrupt. As well, a scholar might apply a cultural critical theory in the analysis of a fast-food chain culture such as Denny's and conclude that it has been discriminatory toward non-Caucasian groups. Finally, a scholar might use a Marxist critical theory to look at a company and judge it as oppressing its workers.

16. See, for example, Pacanowsky (1983) and Pacanowsky and O'Donnell–Trujillo (1982, 1983).

17. See, for example, Bach (1990); Brown (1985); Jablin (1982, 1984, 1985, 1987); Jablin and Krone (1987); and Jablin and McComb (1984).

18. Compare with DiSanza (1993).

Chapter 10   Mass and Intercultural Communication Context Theories

1. Of course, Fortner (1995) has argued that not everyone will participate in the global village due to the knowledge gap preventing universal use of technology. Nonetheless, the village is here, even as some predict that not all will have the means to visit it.

2. For reviews and research on the Spiral of Silence Theory, see Noelle–Neumann (1973, 1974, 1977, 1979, 1980, 1983, 1984, 1985, 1991); Noelle–Neumann and Mathes (1987); Simpson (1996); and Kielwasser and Wolf (1992).

3. For a sampling of agenda-setting research, see Berkowitz (1990); Demers, et al. (1989); Edelstein (1993); Iyengar and Simon (1993); Kosicki (1993); Lasorrsa and Wanta (1990); Shaw and Martin (1992); Wanta and Foote (1994); Wanta, et al. (1989); Watt, Mazza, and Snyder (1993); Zhu, et al. (1993). For a review of agenda-setting research, see McCombs and Shaw (1993).

4. Brosius and colleagues have studied the effects of agenda-setting widely in Germany. See, for example, Fan, Brosius, and Kepplinger (1994), Brosius and Kepplinger (1990, 1992a, 1992b), and Brosius and Weimann (1996).

5. For a sampling of the cultivation effects research, see Gerbner (1980, 1990); Gerbner and Gross (1979); Gerbner, et al. (1977a; 1977b, 1978, 1979a, 1979b, 1980a, 1980b, 1981, 1982, 1986); Hansen and Hansen (1991); Hawkins and Pingree (1980, 1981a, 1981b); Hirsch (1980, 1981); Morgan (1980, 1983, 1984, 1986); Morgan and Signorielli (1990); Oliver (1996); Perse (1986); Pfau, Mullen, and Garrow (1995); Potter (1986, 1988), Potter and Chang (1990); Shapiro and Lang (1991); Shrum and O'Guinn (1993); Signorielli (1989); Signorielli and Morgan (1990); Sparks and Ogles (1990); Vande Berg and Streckfuss (1992); Weaver and Wakshlag (1986); Wober (1978).

6. For a sampling of studies from the perspective of the uses and gratifications limited effects theory, see Austin (1993); Austin and Meili (1994); Austin and Nelson (1993); Barrow (1989); Canary and Spitzberg (1993); Herzog (1944); Hoffner and Haefner (1994); Jacobs (1995); Katz (1957, 1959); Krugman and John-

son (1991); Massey (1995); McLeod (1995); Schmitz and Fulk (1991); Rafaeli and LaRose (1993); Sullivan (1991); Trevino and Webster (1992); Zillmann, et al. (1994).

7. For a sampling of uses and gratifications studies, see Austin (1986); Barrow and Swanson (1988); Blumler (1979); Palmgreen and Rayburn (1985); Rubin (1993); Rubin and Windahl (1986); Swanson (1977). For a Burkean-based uses and gratifications study, see the discussion of Chesebro's longitudinal study of TV viewing in Chapter 8.

8. For reviews and research on the AUMT, see Gudykunst (1985, 1988, 1993, 1995); Gudykunst and Hammer (1988); Gudykunst, Hammer, and Wiseman (1977); Gudykunst and Nishida (1986, 1989); Gudykunst, Ting–Toomey, and Wiseman (1991); Hammer and Martin (1992); Witte (1993). Also see Gudykunst references for Chapter 5, the intercultural grounding of Uncertainty Reduction Theory.

9. See Stewart, et al. (1986) and Ting–Toomey (1983a, 1983b, 1988b). For reviews and studies of the research program for FNT, see Cocroft and Ting–Toomey (1994), Ting–Toomey (1985, 1988a, 1988b, 1990, 1993, 1994), Ting–Toomey and Cocroft (1994), and Ting–Toomey, et al. (1991).

10. For reviews and studies of the research program for CCAT, see Kim (1977a, 1977b, 1978, 1979, 1984, 1986a, 1986b, 1987, 1988a, 1988b, 1989, 1990, 1991, 1994a, 1994b, 1994c, 1994d, 1995, 1996); Kim and Gudykunst (1988); Kim and Paulk (1994); Kim and Ruben (1988).

Chapter 11   Communication Microtheories

1. Buller and Aune (1987); Buller and Burgoon (1994); Buller, et al. (1989); Buller, et al. (1994); Buller, Strzyzewski, and Comstock (1991); Burgoon and Buller (1994); Burgoon, et al. (1995); Burgoon, et al. (1996a); Burgoon, et al. (1996b).

2. See, for example, Bell, et al. (1994); Bowers (1974); Cody and McLaughlin (1980); Dillard and Burgoon (1985); Schenck–Hamlin, Wiseman, and Georgacarakos (1982); Wiseman and Schenck–Hamlin (1981); Witteman and Fitzpatrick (1986).

3. See, for example, Baxter (1984); Craig, Tracy, and Spisak (1986); Metts, Cupach, and Imahori (1992); Newton and Burgoon (1990); Shimanoff (1987).

4. For a review of recent grounding studies for Action Assembly Theory, see Greene and Geddes (1988, 1993) and Greene, et al. (1993).

5. See, for example Coupland, et al. (1988); Coupland, et al. (1990); Ferara (1991); Fox and Giles (1993); Gallois, et al. (1988); Giles, Coupland, and Coupland (1991); Giles and Williams (1994); Linell (1991); Street, Brady, and Lee (1984).

6. See, for example, Burgoon (1978, 1992, 1993, 1995); Burgoon and Aho (1982); Burgoon and Hale (1988); Burgoon and Jones (1976); Burgoon and Le Poire (1993); Burgoon, et al., (1989); Burgoon & Walther (1990).

7. Mark (1971) offered an early approach to coding relational communication.

8. For reviews and studies grounding RCT, see Courtright, Millar, and Rogers–Millar (1979); Courtright, et al. (1990); Ellis (1978, 1979); Ellis and McCallister (1980); Engler–Parrish and Millar (1989); Mark (1971); Rogers and Bagarozzi (1983); Rogers, Courtright, and Millar (1980); Rogers and Farace (1975); Zeitlow and VanLear (1991). The Ellis citations ground the RCT coding system to communication in small groups.

9. For studies of domineering and dominance, see Courtright, Millar, and Rogers–Millar (1979); Millar, Rogers–Millar, and Courtright (1979); Rogers–Millar and Millar (1979).

10. See, for example, Fitzpatrick (1977, 1981, 1983, 1984, 1988, 1991); Fitzpatrick and Badzinski (1986); Fitzpatrick and Best (1979); Fitzpatrick and Indvik (1982); Fitzpatrick and Ritchie (1994); and Segrin and Fitzpatrick (1992).

11. See, for example, McCroskey (1971, 1977a, 1977b, 1978, 1984); McCroskey, Ralph, and Barrick (1970); Richmond (1984); Richmond and McCroskey (1992).

12. See, for example, Habermas (1964, 1970a, 1970b, 1976a, 1976b, 1984, 1989, 1990, 1993).

References

Chapter 1   Introduction to Communication Theory

Andersen, P. A. (1991). When one cannot not communicate: A challenge to Motley's traditional communication postulates. *Communication Studies, 42,* 309–325.

Babrow, A. S. (1992). Communication and problematic integration: Understanding diverging probability and value, ambiguity, ambivalence, and impossibility. *Communication Theory, 2,* 95–130.

Bavelas, J. B. (1990). Behaving and communicating: A reply to Motley. *Western Journal of Speech Communication, 54,* 593–602.

Beach, W. A. (1990). On (not) observing behavior interactionally. *Western Journal of Speech Communication, 54,* 603–612.

Berger, C. R. (1977). The covering law perspective as a theoretical basis for the study of human communication. *Communication Quarterly, 25,* 7–18.

Berger, C. R. (1991). Communication theories and other curios. *Communication Monographs, 58,* 101–113.

Berger, C. R. (1992). Curiouser and curiouser curios. *Communication Monographs, 59,* 101–107.

Berger, C. R., & Calabrese, R. J. (1975). Some explorations in initial interaction. *Human Communication Research, 1,* 99–112.

Berger, P. L., & Luckman, T. (1966). *The social construction of reality: A treatise in the sociology of knowledge.* Garden City, NY: Anchor Books, Doubleday.

Birdwhistell, R. L. (1967). Some body motion elements accompanying spoken American English. In L. Thayer (Ed.), *Communication: Concepts and Perspectives* (pp. 53–76). Washington, DC: Spartan Books.

Bormann, E. G. (1980). *Communication theory.* New York: Holt, Rinehart, & Winston.

Bormann, E. G. (1985a). Symbolic convergence theory: A communication formulation. *Journal of Communication, 35,* 128–138.

Bormann, E. G. (1985b). *The force of fantasy: Restoring the American dream.* Carbondale, IL: Southern Illinois University Press.

Bormann, E. G. (1990). *Small group communication: Theory and practice* (3rd ed.). New York: HarperCollins.

Bormann, E. G., Cragan, J. F., & Shields, D. C. (1996). An expansion of the rhetorical vision component of the symbolic convergence theory: The cold war paradigm case. *Communication Monographs, 63,* 1–28.

Bostrom, R. & Donohew, L. (1992). The case for empiricism: Clarifying fundamental issues in communication theory. *Communication Monographs, 59,* 109–129.

Burgoon, J. K., & Hale, J. L. (1988). Nonverbal expectancy violations: Model elaboration and application. *Communication Monographs, 55,* 58–79.

Burke, K. (1966). *Language as symbolic action: Essays on life, literature, and method.* Berkeley: University of California Press.

Burke, K. (1968). Dramatism. *International encyclopedia of the social sciences, 7* (pp. 445–452). New York: Macmillan and Free Press.

Cameron, G. T., Schleuder, J., & Thorson, E. (1991). The role of news teasers in processing TV news and commercials. *Communication Research, 18,* 667–684.

Capella, J. N. (1996). Symposium: Biology and Communication. *Journal of Communication* (Special Issue), 46:3, 4–84.

Chaffee, S. H., & Berger, C. R. (1987). What communication scientists do. In C. R. Berger & S. H. Chaffee (Eds.), *Handbook of communication science* (pp. 99–122). Newbury Park, CA: Sage.

Cherry, C. (1957). *On human communication.* Cambridge, MA: MIT Press.

Cragan, J. F., & Shields, D. C. (1992). The use of symbolic convergence theory in corporate strategic planning: A case study. *Journal of Applied Communication Research, 20,* 199–218.

Cragan, J. F., & Shields, D. C. (1995). *Symbolic theories in applied communication research: Bormann, Burke, and Fisher.* Cresskill, NJ: Hampton Press and the Speech Communication Association.

Cragan, J. F., Shields, D. C., & Wright, D. L. (1994). Revitalizing the study of small group communication: A thematic critique. *Communication Studies, 45,* 92–96.

Cragan, J. F., Shields, D. C., & Wright, D. L. (1996). A unified theory of small group communication. In J. F. Cragan & D. W. Wright (Eds.), *Theory and research in small group communication* (pp. 69–91). Edina, MN: Burgess.

Cushman, D. P. (1977). The rules perspective as a theoretical basis for the study of human communication. *Communication Quarterly, 25,* 30–45.

Delia, J. G. (1974). Attitudes toward the disclosure of self-attributions and the complexity of interpersonal constructs. *Speech Monographs, 46,* 274–281.

Durkheim, E. (1938). *The rules of sociological method* (8th ed., S. A. Soloway & J. H. Mueller, trans., G. E. Catlin, Ed.). Chicago: University of Chicago Press.

Ewing, R. P. (1979, Winter). The uses of futurist techniques in issues management. *Public Relations Quarterly, 24,* 15–18.

Farrell, T. B. (1987). Beyond science: Humanities contributions to communication theory. In C. R. Berger & S. H. Chaffee (Eds.), *Handbook of communication science* (pp. 123–139). Newbury Park, CA: Sage.

Fisher, W. R. (1987). *Human communication as narration: Toward a philosophy of reason, value, and action.* Columbia: University of South Carolina Press.

Flew, A. (1985). *Thinking about social thinking: The philosophy of the social sciences.* New York: Basil Blackwell.

Ford, L. A., Babrow, A. S., & Stohl, C. (1996). Social support messages and the management of uncertainty in the experience of breast cancer: An application of problematic integration theory. *Communication Monographs, 63,* 189–207.

Gerbner, G. (Ed.). (1983, Summer). Ferment in the field (special issue). *Journal of Communication, 43.*

Greene, J. O. (1984). A cognitive approach to human communication: An action assembly theory. *Communication Monographs, 51,* 289–306.

Hawes, L. C. (1975). *Pragmatics of analoguing: Theory and model construction in communication.* Reading, MA: Addison-Wesley.

Hewes, D. (Ed.). (1995). *The cognitive bases of interpersonal communication.* Hillsdale, NJ: Erlbaum.

Isaacs, A. (Ed.). (1990). *A concise dictionary of physics.* Oxford, England: Oxford University Press.

Kraft, R. N., Canto, P., & Gottdiener, C. (1991). The coherence of visual narratives. *Communication Research, 18,* 601–616.

Kuhn, T. S. (1970). *The structure of scientific revolutions* (2nd ed.). Chicago: University of Chicago Press.

Levy, M. R. (Ed.). (1993, Summer). The future of the field (special issue). *Journal of Communication, 53.*

Liska, J., & Cronkhite, G. (1995). *An ecological perspective on human communication theory.* Fort Worth, TX: Harcourt Brace.

Littlejohn, S. W. (1996). *Theories of human communication* (5th ed.). New York: Wadsworth.

McLuhan, M. (1964). *Understanding media.* New York: McGraw–Hill.

Mead, G. H. (1938). *The philosophy of the act.* Chicago: University of Chicago Press.

Monroe, A. H. (1962). *Principles and types of speech* (5th ed.). Glenview, IL: Scott, Foresman.

Motley, M. T. (1990a). Communication as interaction: A reply to Beach and Bavelas. *Western Journal of Speech Communication, 54,* 613–623.

Motley, M. T. (1990b). On whether one can(not) communicate: An examination via traditional communication postulates. *Western Journal of Speech Communication, 54,* 1–20.

Motley, M. T. (1991). How one may not communicate: A reply to Andersen. *Communication Studies, 42,* 326–339.

Nass, C. I., & Reeves, B. (1991). Combining, distinguishing, and generating theories in communication: A domain of analysis framework. *Communication Research, 18,* 240–261.

Newton, I. (1687/1934). *The mathematical principles of natural philosophy.* Trans. A. Motte. Berkeley, CA: University of California Press.

Pearce, W. B., Cronen, V. E., & Harris, L. M. (1982). Methodological considerations in building human communication theory. In F. E. X. Dance (Ed.), *Human communication theory* (pp. 1–41). New York: Harper & Row.

Poole, M. S. (1990). Do we have any theories of group communication? *Communication Studies, 41,* 237–247.

Poole, M. S. (1994). Breaking the isolation of small group communication studies. *Communication Studies, 45,* 20–28.

Poole, M. S., Seibold, D. R., & McPhee, R. D. (1985). Group decision-making as a structurational process. *Quarterly Journal of Speech, 71,* 74–102.

Schleuder, J. D., White, A. V., & Cameron, G. T. (1993). *Journal of Broadcasting & Electronic Media, 37,* 437–452.

Shannon, C. E. (1948a). A mathematical theory of communication. *Bell System Technical Journal, 27,* 379–423.

Shannon, C. E. (1948b). A mathematical theory of communication. *Bell System Technical Journal, 27,* 623–656.

Shields, D. C. (1981). A dramatistic approach to applied communication research: Theory, methods, and applications. In J. F. Cragan & D. C. Shields (Eds.), *Applied communication research: A dramatistic approach* (pp. 5–13). Prospect Heights, IL: Waveland Press.

Shields, D. C. (1993). Drug education and the communication curricula. In S. H. Decker, R. B. Rosenfeld, & R. Wright (Eds.), *Drug and alcohol education across the curriculum* (pp. 43–90). Saratoga Springs, CA: R&E Publishers.

Shields, D. C., & Cragan, J. F. (1975). Miller's humanistic/scientific dichotomy of speech communication inquiry: A help or hindrance? *Western Speech Journal, 40,* 278–283.

Shields, D. C., & Cragan, J. F. (1981). A communication-based political campaign: A theoretical and methodological perspective. In J. F. Cragan & D. C. Shields (Eds.), *Applied communication research: A dramatistic approach* (pp. 177–196). Prospect Heights, IL: Waveland.

Shields, D. C., & Preston, C. T., Jr. (1985). Fantasy theme analysis in competitive rhetorical criticism. *National Forensic Journal, 3,* 102–115.

Speyer, E. (1994). *Six roads from Newton: Great discoveries in physics.* New York: John Wiley & Sons.

Stephenson, W. (1953). *The study of behavior: Q-technique and its methodology.* Chicago: University of Chicago Press.

Stephenson, W. (1967). *The play theory of mass communication.* Chicago: University of Chicago Press.

Stewart, C. J., & Cash, W. B., Jr. (1988). *Interviewing: Principles and practices* (5th ed.). Dubuque, IA: Brown.

Stone, G. P., & Farberman, H. A. (Eds.). (1970). *Social psychology through symbolic interaction.* Waltham, MA: Ginn-Blaisdell.

Thayer, L. (Ed.). (1965). *Communication: Theory and research; Proceedings of the first international symposium.* Springfield, IL: Charles C. Thomas.

Thayer, L. (Ed.). (1967). *Communication: Concepts and perspectives.* Washington, DC: Spartan Books.

Verderber, R. F. (1978). *Communicate!* Belmont, CA: Wadsworth.

von Bertalanffy, L. (1968). *General systems theory: Foundations, development, applications.* New York: Braziller.

Watzlawick, P., Beavin, J. H., & Jackson, D. D. (1967). *Pragmatics of human communication: A study of interaction patterns, pathologies, and paradoxes.* New York: W. W. Norton.

Westley, B. H., & MacLean, M. S., Jr. (1965). A conceptual model for communication research. In J. H. Campbell & H. W. Hepler (Eds.), *Dimensions in communication* (pp. 55–65). Belmont, CA: Wadsworth.

Chapter 2 Information Systems Theory

Atkinson, J. M., & Heritage, J. (1984). *Structures of social action: Studies in conversation analysis.*

Ayres, H. J., Brand, V. R., & Faules, D. F. (1973). An assessment of the flow of communication in nursing teams. *Journal of Applied Communication Research, 1,* 75–90.

Bales, R. F. (1950). *Interaction process analysis: A method for the study of small groups.* Cambridge, MA: Addison-Wesley.

Bahniuk, M. H., Kogler Hill, S. E., Darus, H. (1996). The relationship of power-gaining communication strategies to career success. *Western Journal of Communication, 60,* 358–378.

Basil, M. D. (1994). Multiple resource theory I: Application to television viewing. *Communication Research, 21,* 177–207.

Beach, W. A. (1989). Foreword: Sequential organization of conversational activities. *Western Journal of Speech Communication, 53,* 85–90.

Berger, C. R., & Calabrese, R. J. (1975). Some explorations in initial interaction and beyond: Toward a developmental theory of interpersonal communication. *Human Communication Research, 1,* 99–112.

Berlo, D. K. (1960). *The process of communication: An introduction to theory and practice.* San Francisco: Rinehart Press.

Bormann, E. G. (1980). *Communication theory.* New York: Holt, Rinehart and Winston.

Bormann, E. G., Howell, W. S., Nichols, R. G., & Shapiro, G. L. (1969). *Interpersonal communication in the modern organization.* Englewood Cliffs, NJ: Prentice-Hall.

Brissey, F. L. (1961). The factor of relevance in the serial reproduction of information. *Journal of Communication, 11,* 211–219.

Broadhurst, A. R., & Darnell, D. K. (1965). Introduction to cybernetics and information theory. *Quarterly Journal of Speech, 51,* 442–453.

Brooks, K., Callicoat, J., & Siegerdt, G. (1979). The ICA communication audit and perceived communication effectiveness changes in 16 audited organizations. *Human Communication Research, 5,* 130–137.

Cahn, D. D. (1983). Relative importance of perceived understanding in initial interaction and development of interpersonal relationships. *Psychological Reports, 52,* 923–29.

Cahn, D. D. (1984). Teacher-student relationships: Perceived understanding. *Communication Research Reports, 1,* 65–67.

Cahn, D. D. (1986). Perceived understanding, superior-subordinate communication, and organizational effectiveness. *Central States Speech Journal, 37,* 19–28.

Cahn, D. D. (1987). *Letting go: A practical theory of relationship disengagement and reengagement.* Albany, NY: SUNY Press.

Cahn, D. D. (1990). Perceived understanding and interpersonal relationships. *Journal of Social and Professional Relationships, 7,* 231–44.

Cahn, D., & Frey, L. (1990). Behavioral impressions associated with perceived understanding. *Perceptual and Motor Skills, 69,* 1299–1302.

Cahn, D. D. & Hanford, J. T. (1984). Perspectives on human communication research: Behaviorism, phenomenology, and an integrated view. *Western Journal of Speech Communication, 48,* 277–92.

Cahn, D. D., & Shulman, G. M. (1984). The perceived understanding instrument. *Communication Research Reports, 1,* 122–25.

Cherry, C. (1966). *On human communication: A review, a survey, and a criticism.* Cambridge, MA: MIT Press.

Chomsky, N. (1957). *Syntactic structures.* The Hague: Mouton.

Cody, M. J., & McLaughlin, M. L. (1985). Models for the sequential construction of accounting episodes: Situational and interactional constraints on message selection and evaluation. In R. L. Street, Jr., & J. N. Cappella (Eds.), *Sequence and pattern in communicative behavior* (pp. 50–69). Baltimore, MD: Edward Arnold.

Conant, R. C. (1979). A vector theory of information. In Dan Nimmo (Ed.), *Communication Yearbook 3* (pp. 177–194). New Brunswick, NJ: International Communication Association and Transaction Books.

Cummings, H. W., Long, L. W., & Lewis, M. L. (1987). *Managing communication in organizations: An introduction.* Dubuque, IA: Gorush Scarisbrick Publisher.

Daniels, T. D., & Spiker, B. K. (1983). Social exchange and the relationship between information adequacy and relational satisfaction. *Western Journal of Speech Communication, 47,* 118–137.

Davis, W. L., & O'Connor, J. R. (1977). Serial transmission of information: A study of the grapevine. *Journal of Applied Communication Research, 5,* 61–72.

Dean, T., Allen, J., Aloimonos, Y. (1995). *Artificial intelligence: Theory and practice.* Redwood City, CA: Benjamin/Cummings.

DeFleur, M. L., & Ball–Rokeach, S. (1989). *Theories of mass communication.* White Plains, NY: Longman.

Drum, D. D. (1956). What is information? *Communication Education, 4,* 174–178.

Farace, R., Monge, P., & Russell, H. (1977). *Communicating and organizing.* Reading, MA: Addison-Wesley.

Finn, S., & Roberts, D. F. (1984). Source, destination, and entropy: Reassessing the role of information theory in communication research. *Communication Research, 11,* 453–476.

Fisher, B. A. (1974). *Small group decision-making: Communication and the group process.* New York: McGraw–Hill.

Fisher, B. A. (1978). *Perspectives on human communication.* New York: Macmillan.

Fisher, B. A., & Ellis, D. G. (1990). *Small group decision-making: Communication and the group process.* New York: McGraw–Hill.

Fisher, B. A., Drecksel, G. L., & Werbel, W. S. (1978). Social information processing analysis (SIPA): Coding ongoing human communication. *Small Group Behavior, 10,* 3–19.

Fisher, B. A., & Hawes, L. C. (1971). An interact system model: Generating a grounded theory of small group decision-making. *Quarterly Journal of Speech, 58,* 444–453.

Flanagan, J. (1954). The critical incident technique. *Psychological Bulletin, 51,* 327–357.

Frandsen, K. D., & Millis, M. A. (1993). On conceptual, theoretical and empirical treatments of feedback in human communication: Fifteen years later. *Communication Reports, 6,* 79–91.

Frankel, R. M. (1989). "I wz wondering—uhm could *Raid* uhm effect the brain permanently d'y know?": Some observations on the intersection of speaking and writing in calls to a poison control center. *Western Journal of Speech Communication, 53,* 195–226.

Frey, L. R. (1995). Introduction: Applied communication research on group facilitation in natural settings. In L. R. Frey (Ed.), *Innovations in group facilitation: Applications in natural settings* (1–24). Cresskill, NJ: Speech Communication Association and Hampton Press.

Fulton, R. B. (1963). Information theory and linguistic structuring. *Communication Studies, 14,* 247–257.

Goetzinger, C., & Valentine, M. (1962). Communication channels, media, directional flow and attitudes in an academic community. *Journal of Communication, 12,* 23–26.

Goldhaber, G. M. (1993). *Organizational communication.* Madison, WI: Brown & Benchmark.

Goldhaber, G. M., & Krivonos, P. (1977). The ICA communication audit: Process, status and critique. *Journal of Business Communication, 15,* 41–64.

Goldhaber, G. M., & Rogers, D. P. (1979). *Auditing organizational communication systems: The ICA communication audit.* Dubuque, IA: Kendall/Hunt.

Griffin, E. (1994). *A first look at communication theory* (2nd ed.). New York: McGraw–Hill.

Griffin, E. (1996). *A first look at communication theory* (3rd ed.). New York: McGraw–Hill.

Griffith, B. C. (1989). Understanding science: Studies of communication and information. *Communication Research, 16,* 600–614.

Gudykunst, W. B. (1985). The influence of cultural similarity, type of relationship, and monitoring on uncertainty reduction processes. *Communication Monographs, 52,* 203–217.

Gudykunst, W. B. (1988). Uncertainty and anxiety. In Y. Y. Kim and W. B. Gudykunst (Eds.), *Theories in intercultural communication* (pp. 123–156). Newbury Park, CA: Sage.

Hansen, C. R., & Hansen, R. D. (1991). Schematic information processing of heavy metal lyrics. *Communication Research, 18,* 373–411.

Hyvarinen, L. P. (1968). *Information theory for systems engineers.* Berlin: Springer–Verlag.

Jefferson, G. (1978). Sequential aspects of storytelling in conversation. In J. Schenkein (Ed.), *Studies in the organization of conversational interaction* (pp. 219–248). New York: Academic Press.

Jefferson. G. (1991). List construction as a task and interactional resource. In G. Psathas (Ed.), *In-*

teractional competence (pp. 63–92). New York: Irvington.

Jefferson, G. (1996). On the poetics of ordinary talk. *Text and Performance Quarterly, 16,* 1–61.

Jumarie, G. (1990). *Relative information: Theories and applications.* Berlin: Springer–Verlag.

Kapp, J. E., & Barnett, G. A. (1983). Predicting organizational effectiveness from communication activities: A multiple indicator model. *Human Communication Research, 9,* 239–254.

Kogler–Hill, S. E., Bahniuk, M. H., & Dobos, J. (1989). The impact of mentoring and collegial support of faculty success: An analysis of support behavior, information adequacy, and communication apprehension. *Communication Education, 38,* 15–33.

Krippendorff, K. (1986). *Information theory: Structural models for qualitative data.* Newbury Park, CA: Sage.

Kurke, L. B., Weick, K. E., & Ravlin, E. C. (1989). Can information loss be reversed? Evidence for serial reconstruction. *Communication Research, 16,* 3–24.

Littlejohn, S. W. (1996). *Theories of human communication.* Belmont, CA: Wadsworth.

McLaughlin, M. L., Cody, M. J., & Rosenstein, N. E. (1983). Account sequences in conversations between strangers. *Communication Mongraphs, 50,* 102–125.

Millar, F. E., & Rogers, L. E. (1976). A relational approach to interpersonal communication. In G. R. Miller (Ed.), *Explorations in interpersonal communication* (pp. 87–103). Beverly Hills, CA: Sage.

Millar, F. E., & Rogers, L. E. (1987). Relational dimensions in interpersonal dynamics. In M. E. Roloff and G. R. Miller (Eds.), *Interpersonal processes: New directions in communication research* (pp. 117–139). Newbury Park, CA: Sage.

Miller, G. R., & Fonts, N. E. (1979). *Videotape on trial: A view from the jury box.* Beverly Hills, CA: Sage.

Miller, G. R., Fonts, N. E., Boster, F. J., & Sunnafrank, M. J. (1983). Methodological issues in legal communication research: What can trial simulations tell us? *Communication Monographs, 50,* 33–46.

Miller, G. R., & Sunnafrank, M. J. (1984). Theoretical dimensions of applied communication research. *Quarterly Journal of Speech, 70,* 255–263.

Monkhouse, C. (1873). Limerick: The lady from Niger. In R. Baker & K. L. Baker (1984, Eds.), *Book of light verse* (p. 160). New York: Norton.

Morris, C. W. (1938). *Foundations of the theory of signs.* Chicago: University of Chicago Press.

Mortensen, C. D. (1972). *Communication: The study of human interaction.* New York: McGraw–Hill.

O'Reilly, C. A., & Anderson, J. C. (1980). Trust and the communication of performance appraisal information: The effect of feedback on performance and job satisfaction. *Human Communication Research, 6,* 290–298.

Poole, M. S. (1983). Decision development in small groups III: A multiple sequence model of group decision development. *Communication Monographs, 50,* 206–232.

Poole, M. S., & DeSanctis, G. (1992). Microlevel structuration in computer-supported group decision-making. *Human Communication Research, 19,* 5–49.

Poole, M. S., & Jackson, M. H. (1993). Communication theory and group support systems. In L. M. Jessup and J. S. Valacich (Eds.), *Group support systems* (pp. 281–293). New York: Macmillan.

Ritchie, D. (1986). Shannon and Weaver: Unraveling the paradox of information. *Communication Research, 13,* 278–298.

Ritchie, L. D. (1991). *Information.* Newbury Park, CA: Sage.

Rogers, E. M. (1994). *A history of communication study: A biographical approach.* New York: Free Press.

Rogers, L. E., & Farace, R. V. (1975). Analysis of relational communication in dyads: New measurement procedures. *Human Communication Research, 1,* 222–239.

Ruesch, J., & Bateson, G. (1951). *Communication, the social matrix of psychiatry.* New York: Norton.

Salem, P., & Williams, M. L. (1984). Uncertainty and satisfaction: The importance of information in hospital communication. *Journal of Applied Communication Research, 12,* 75–89.

Schramm, W. (1954). How communication works. In W. Schramm (Ed.), *The process and effects of mass communication* (pp. 3–26). Urbana, IL: University of Illinois Press.

Shannon, C. E. (1948a). A mathematical theory of communication. *Bell System Technical Journal, 27,* 379–423.

Shannon, C. E. (1948b). A mathematical theory of communication. *Bell System Technical Journal, 27,* 623–656.

Shannon, C. E., & Weaver, W. (1949). *The mathematical theory of communication.* Urbana, IL: University of Illinois Press.

Sheer, V. C., & Cline, R. J. (1995). Testing a model of perceived information adequacy and uncertainty reduction in physician–patient interactions. *Journal of Applied Communication Research, 23,* 44–59.

Spielberg, N., & Anderson, B. D. (1987). *Seven ideas that shook the universe.* New York: John Wiley & Sons.

Spiker, B. K., & Daniels, T. D. (1981). Information adequacy and communication relationships: An empirical examination of 18 organizations. *Western Journal of Speech Communication, 45,* 342–354.

Timmis III, J. H. (1985). Textual and information-theoretic indexes of style as discriminators between message sources. *Communication Monographs, 52,* 136–155.

Trenholm, S. (1991). *Human communication theory.* Englewood Cliffs, NJ: Prentice–Hall.

von Bertalanffy, L. (1968). *General systems theory.* New York: Braziller.

Watt, J. H., Jr., & Krull, R. (1974). An information theory measure for television programming. *Communication Research, 1,* 44–68.

Watzlawick, P., Beavin, J. H., & Jackson, D. D. (1967). *Pragmatics of human communication: A study of interactional patterns, pathologies, and paradoxes.* New York: W. W. Norton.

Weaver, W. (1949, July). The mathematics of communication. *Scientific American, 181:1,* 11–15.

Weick, K. (1979). *The social psychology of organizing.* Reading, MA: Addison-Wesley.

Wiener, N. (1948). *Cybernetics: Or control and communication in the animal and the machine.* Cambridge, MA: MIT Press.

Wilder, C. (1977). A conversation with Colin Cherry. *Human Communication Research, 3,* 354–362.

Chapter 3   Rational Argumentation Theory

Allen, M., & Burrell, N. (1992). Evaluating the believability of sequential arguments. *Argumentation and Advocacy, 28,* 135–144.

Anderson, J., Schultz, B., & Courtney, C. (1987). Training in argumentativeness: New hope for nonassertive women. *Women's Studies in Communication, 10,* 58–66.

Aristotle (1960). *Rhetoric* (L. Cooper, trans.). New York: Appleton-Century-Crofts.

Baker, G. P. (1895). *The principles of argumentation.* Boston, MA: Ginn.

Balthrop, B. (1980). Argument as linguistic opportunity: A search for form and function. In J. Rhodes & S. Newell (Eds.), *Proceedings of the summer conference on argumentation* (pp. 25–31). Annandale, VA: Speech Communication Association.

Bantz, C. R. (1981). Public arguing in the regulation of health and safety. *Western Journal of Speech Communication, 45,* 71–87.

Beardsley, M. C. (1950). *Practical logic.* New York: Prentice-Hall.

Benoit, W. L. (1991). Argumentation in *Miranda v. Arizona. Communication Studies, 42,* 129–140.

Benoit, W. L., & Lindsey, J. J. (1986). Argument fields and forms of argument in natural language. In F. H. van Eemeren, R. Grootendorst, J. A. Blair, & C. A.

Willard (Eds.), *Argumentation: Perspectives and approaches* (pp. 215–224). Dordrecht, Holland: Foris.

Black, E. (1994). Gettysburg and silence. *Quarterly Journal of Speech, 80,* 21–36.

Brembeck, W. L. (1949). The effects of a course in argumentation on critical thinking ability. *Speech Monographs, 16,* 177–189.

Brock, B. L., Chesebro, J. W., Cragan, J. F., & Klumpp, J. F. (1973). *Public policy decision-making: Systems analysis and comparative advantage debate.* New York: Harper and Row.

Brockriede, W. (1972). Arguers as lovers. *Philosophy and Rhetoric, 5,* 1–11.

Brockriede, W. (1974). Rhetorical criticism as argument. *Quarterly Journal of Speech, 40,* 165–174.

Brockriede, W. (1975). Where is argument? *Journal of the American Forensic Association, 11,* 179–182.

Brockriede, W. (1977). Characteristics of arguments and arguing. *Journal of the American Forensic Association, 13,* 129–132.

Brockriede, W., & Ehninger, D. (1960). Toulmin on argument: Interpretation and application. *Quarterly Journal of Speech, 46,* 44–53.

Canary, D. J., Brossmann, J. E., Brossmann, B. G., & Weger, Jr., H. (1995). Toward a theory of minimally rational argument: Analysis of episode-specific effects of argument structures. *Communication Monographs, 62,* 183–212.

Chaffee, S. H. (1978). Presidential debates—are they helpful to voters? *Communication Monographs, 45,* 330–346.

Chesebro, J. W. (1968). The comparative advantage case. *Journal of the American Forensic Association, 5,* 57–63.

Comeaux, P. (1993). *Workbook for public speaking.* Madison, WI: Brown and Benchmark.

Condit, C. M. (1987). Democracy and civil rights: The universalizing influence of public argumentation. *Communication Monographs, 54,* 1–18.

Cox, J. R., & Willard, C. A. (1982). Introduction: The field of argumentation. In J. R. Cox & C. A. Willard (Eds.), *Advances in argmentation theory and research* (pp. xiii–xlvii). Carbondale, IL: Southern Illinois University Press.

Cragan, J. F., & Shields, D. C. (1970). The comparative advantage negative. *Journal of the American Forensic Association, 7,* 85–91.

Cragan, J. F., & Shields, D. C. (1972). *Nationalized medical care: Issues and answers.* Minneapolis, MN: Campus Press.

Cragan, J. F., & Wright, D. W. (1995). *Communication in small groups: Theory, process, skills* (5th ed.). St. Paul, MN: West Publishing.

Darnell, D., & Brockriede, W. (1975). *Persons communicating.* Englewood Cliffs, NJ: Prentice-Hall.

Delia, J. G. (1970). The logic fallacy, cognitive theory, and the enthymeme: A search for the foundations of reasoned discourse. *Quarterly Journal of Speech, 56,* 140–148.

Dewey, J. (1910). *How we think.* New York: Heath.

Drew, D., & Weaver, D. (1991). Voter learning in the 1988 presidential election: Did the debates and the media matter? *Journalism Quarterly, 68,* 27–37.

Dunbar, N. R. (1986). Laetrile: A case study of a public controversy. *Journal of the American Forensic Association, 22,* 196–211.

Ehninger, D., & Brockriede, W. (1963). *Decision by debate.* New York: Dodd, Mead & Company.

Ehninger, D., Gronbeck, B. E., McKerrow, R. E., & Monroe, A. H. (1986). *Principles and types of speech communication.* Glenview, IL: Scott, Foresman.

Feyerabend, P. K. (1975). *Against method: Outline of an anarchistic theory of knowledge.* London: Humanities Press.

Freeley, A. J. (1961). *Argumentation and debate.* San Francisco, CA: Wadsworth.

Gan, X. (1994). Debates contribute to the development of the journalistic science. *Journal of Communication, 44*(3), 38–51.

Garlick, R. (1993). Single, double, triple minorities and the evaluation of persuasive arguments. *Communication Studies, 44,* 273–284.

Hample, D. (1980). A cognitive view of argument. *Journal of the American Forensic Association, 16,* 151–158.

Hample, D. (1988). Argument: Public and private, social and cognitive. *Journal of the American Forensic Association, 25,* 13–19.

Hazen, M. D. (1989). The role of argument, reasoning and logic in tacit, incomplete, and indirect communication: The case of Japan. In B. E. Gronbeck (Ed.), *Spheres of argument: Proceedings of the sixth SCA/AFA conference on argumentation* (pp. 497–504). Annandale, VA: Speech Communication Association.

Heath, R. L. (1988). The rhetoric of issue advertising: A rationale, a case study, a critical perspective—and more. *Central States Speech Journal, 39,* 99–109.

Hirokawa, R. Y. (1985). Discussion procedures and decision-making performance: A test of the functional perspective. *Human Communication Research, 12,* 203–224.

Hollihan, T. A., Riley, P., & Freadhoff, K. (1986). Arguing for justice: An analysis of arguing in small claims court. *Journal of the American Forensic Association, 22,* 187–195.

Hultzen, L. S. (1958). Status in deliberative analysis. In D. C. Bryant (Ed.), *The rhetorical idiom* (pp. 97–123). Ithaca, NY: Cornell University Press.

Infante, D. A. (1982). The argumentative student in the speech communication classroom: An investigation and implications. *Communication Education, 31,* 141–148.

Infante, D. A., Chandler, T. A., & Rudd, J. E. (1989). Test of an argumentative skill deficiency model of interspousal violence. *Communication Monographs, 56,* 163–177.

Infante, D. A., & Gordon, W. I. (1987). Superior and subordinate communication profiles: Implications for independent-mindedness and upward effectiveness. *Central States Speech Journal, 38,* 73–80.

Infante, D. A., Myers, S. A., and Buerkel, R. A. (1994). Argument and verbal aggression in constructive and destructive family and organizational disagreements. *Western Journal of Communication, 58,* 73–84.

Infante, D. A., Trebing, J. D., Shepherd, P. E., & Seeds, D. E. (1984). The relationship of argumentativeness to verbal aggression. *Southern Speech Journal, 50,* 67–77.

Jacobs, S., & Jackson, S. (1982). Conversational argument: A discourse analytic approach. In J. R. Cox & C. A. Willard (Eds.), *Advances in argumentation research* (pp. 205–237). Carbondale, IL: Southern Illinois University Press.

Jensen, J. V. (1992). Values and practices in Asian argumentation. *Argumentation and advocacy, 28,* 153–166.

Johnson, D., & Sellnow, T. (1995). Deliberative rhetoric as a step in organizational crisis management: Exxon as a case study. *Communication reports, 8,* 54–60.

Krumboltz, J. D. (1957, January). The relation of extracurricular participation to leadership criteria. *Personnel and Guidance Journal, 35,* 307–314.

Kuhn, T. S. (1970). *The structure of scientific revolutions* (2nd ed.). Chicago: University of Chicago Press.

Larson, C. U. (1986). *Persuasion: Reception and responsibility.* Belmont, CA: Wadsworth.

Lemert, J. B. (1993). Do televised presidential debates help inform voters? *Journal of Broadcasting and Electronic Media, 37,* 83–94.

McBath, J. H. (1963). *Argumentation and debate: Principles and practices.* New York: Holt, Rinehart and Winston.

McBurney, J. (1936). The place of the enthymeme in rhetorical theory. *Speech Monographs, 3,* 49–74.

McKerrow, R. E. (1980). Argument communities: A quest for distinctions. In J. Rhodes & S. Newell (Eds.), *Proceedings of the summer conference on argumentation* (pp. 214–227). Annandale, VA: Speech Communication Association.

Monroe, A. (1935). *Principles and types of speech.* Chicago, IL: Scott, Foresman.

Morello, J. T. (1988). Argument and visual structuring in the 1984 Mondale–Reagan debates: The medium's influence on the perception of clash. *Western Journal of Speech Communication, 52,* 277–290.

Neer, M. R. (1994). Argumentative flexibility as a factor influencing message response style to argumentative and aggressive arguers. *Argumentation and Advocacy, 31,* 17–33.

Ochs, D. J. (1969). Aristotle's concept of formal topics. *Speech Monographs, 36,* 419–425.

O'Keefe, D. J. (1977). Two concepts of argument. *Journal of the American Forensic Association, 13,* 121–128.

O'Rourke, S. P., & Manuto, R. (1994). Perceptions of rhetoric from the federal judiciary. *Communication Reports, 7,* 76–87.

Perelman, C., & Olbrechts–Tyteca, L. (1969). *The new rhetoric: A treatise on argumentation.* Notre Dame, IN: University of Notre Dame Press.

Pfau, M., & Burgoon, M. (1989). The efficacy of issue and character attack message strategies in political campaign communication. *Communication Reports, 2,* 54–61.

Putnam, L. L., & Geist, P. (1985). Argument in bargaining: An analysis of the reasoning process. *Southern Speech Communication Journal, 50,* 225–245.

Rasmussen, K. (1974). *Implications of argumentation for aesthetic experience: A transactional perspective.* Unpublished Ph.D. dissertation, University of Colorado at Boulder.

Ryan, H. R. (1982). *Kategoria* and *apologia:* On their rhetorical criticism as a speech set. *Quarterly Journal of Speech, 68,* 254–261.

Ryan, H. R. (1984). Baldwin vs. Edward VIII: A case study in *kategoria* and *apologia. Southern Speech Communication Journal, 49,* 125–134.

Ryan, H. R. (Ed.). (1988). *Oratorical encounters: Selected studies and sources of Twentieth Century political accusations and apologies.* Westport, CT: Greenwood Press.

Sanders, J. A., Gass, R. H., Wiseman, R. L., & Bruschke, J. C. (1992). An analysis and ethnic comparison of argumentativeness, verbal aggressiveness, and need for cognition. *Communication Reports, 5,* 50–56.

Sanders, J. A., Wiseman, R. L., & Gass, R. H. (1994). Does teaching argumentation facilitate critical thinking? *Communication Reports, 7,* 27–35.

Scott, R. L. (1960). On the meaning of the term *prima facie* in argumentation. *Central States Speech Journal, 12,* 33–37.

Scott, R. L. (1967). On viewing rhetoric as epistemic. *Central States Speech Journal, 18,* 9–17.

Scott, R. L. (1976). On viewing rhetoric as epistemic: Ten years later. *Central States Speech Journal, 27,* 258–266.

Scott, R. L. (1990). Eisenhower's farewell: The epistemic function of argument. In R. Trapp & J.

Schuetz (Eds.), *Perspectives on argumentation: Essays in honor of Wayne Brockriede* (pp. 151–161). Prospect Heights, IL: Waveland Press.

Semlak, W. D., & Shields, D. C. (1977). The effect of debate training on students participating in the bicentennial youth debates. *Journal of the American Forensic Association, 13,* 192–196.

Stehle, P. (1994). *Order, chaos, order: The transition form classical to quantum physics.* New York: Oxford University Press.

The Associated Press (1997, January 5). *Kansas City Star,* p. A-13.

Toulmin, S. E. (1958). *The uses of argument.* London: Cambridge University Press.

Trapp, R. (1981). Special report on argumentation: Introduction. *Western Journal of Speech Communication, 45,* 111–117.

Trapp, R., & Schuetz, J., Eds. (1990). *Perspectives on argumentation: Essays in honor of Wayne Brockriede.* Prospect Heights, IL: Waveland Press.

Vancil, D. L. (1993). *Rhetoric and argumentation.* Boston, MA: Allyn & Bacon.

van Eemereen, F. H., & Grootendorst, R. (1990). Analyzing argumentative discourse. In R. Trapp & J Schuetz (Eds.), *Perspectives on argumentation: Essays in honor of Wayne Brockriede* (pp. 86–106). Prospect Heights, IL: Waveland Press.

van Eemeren, F. H., de Glopper, K., Grootendorst, R., & Oostdam, R. (1995). Identification of unexpressed premises and argumentation schemes by students in secondary school. *Argumentation and Advocacy, 31,* 151–162.

Warnick, B., & Inch, E. S. (1994). *Critical thinking and communication: The use of reason in argument.* New York: Macmillan.

Wenzel, J. W. (1977). Toward a rationale for value-centered argument. *Journal of the American Forensic Association, 16,* 83–94.

Wenzel, J. W. (1979). Jurgen Habermas and the dialectical perspective on argumentation. *Journal of the American Forensic Association, 16,* 83–94.

Wenzel, J. W. (1980). Perspectives on argument. In J. Rhodes & S. Newell (Eds.), *Proceedings of the summer conference on argumentation* (pp. 112–133). Annandale, VA: Speech Communication Association.

Wenzel, J. W. (1987). The rhetorical perspective on argument. In F. H. van Eemeren, R. Grootendorst, J. A. Blair, & C. A. Willard (Eds.), *Argumentation: Across the lines of discipline* (pp. 101–109). Dordrecht, Holland: Foris.

Wenzel, J. W. (1990). Three perspectives on argument: Rhetoric, dialectic, logic. In R. Trapp & J. Schuetz (Eds.), *Perspectives on argumentation: Essays in honor of Wayne Brockriede* (pp. 9–26). Prospect Heights, IL: Waveland Press.

Whaley, B. B., & Babrow, A. S. (1993). Analogy in persuasion: Translator's dictionary or art? *Communication Studies, 44,* 239–253.

Wiethoff, W. E. (1981). *Topoi* of religious controversy in the American catholic debate of vernacular reform. *Western Journal of Speech Communication, 45,* 172–181.

Willard, C. A. (1983). *Argumentation and the social grounds of knowledge.* Tuscaloosa, AL: University of Alabama Press.

Willard, C. A. (1989). *A theory of argumentation.* Tuscaloosa, AL: University of Alabama Press.

Willard, C. A. (1990). Argumentation and postmodern critique. In R. Trapp & J. Schuetz (Eds.), *Perspectives on argumentation: Essays in honor of Wayne Brockriede* (pp. 221–231). Prospect Heights, IL: Waveland Press.

Zarefsky, D. (1980). Product, process, or point of view? In J. Rhodes & S. Newell (Eds.), *Proceedings of the summer conference on argumentation* (pp. 228–238). Annandale, VA: Speech Communication Association.

Ziegelmueller, G. W., Kay, J., & Dause, C. A. (1990). *Argumentation: Inquiry and advocacy.* Englewood Cliffs, NJ: Prentice–Hall.

Chapter 4   Symbolic Convergence Theory

Aden, R. C. (1986). Fantasy themes and rhetorical visions in the 1984 presidential campaign: Explaining the Reagan mandate. *Speaker and Gavel, 23*(3), 87–94.

Bales, R. F. (1970). *Personality and interpersonal behavior.* New York: Holt, Rinehart and Winston.

Ball, M. A. (1992). *Vietnam-on-the-Potomac.* New York: Praeger.

Bantz, C. R. (1975). Television news: Reality and research. *Western Speech, 39,* 123–130.

Barton, S. N., & O'Leary, J. B. (1974). The rhetoric of rural physicians procurement campaigns: An application of Tavistock. *Quarterly Journal of Speech, 60,* 144–154.

Black, E. (1980). A note on theory and practice in rhetorical criticism. *Western Journal of Speech Communication, 44,* 331–336.

Blum, J. M., Catton, B., Morgan, E. S., Schlesinger, Jr., A. M., Stampp, K. M., & Woodward, C. V. (1963). *The national experience: A history of the United States.* New York: Harcourt, Brace & World.

Bormann, E. G. (1972). Fantasy and rhetorical vision: The rhetorical criticism of social reality. *Quarterly Journal of Speech, 58,* 396–407.

Bormann, E. G. (1973). The Eagleton affair: A fantasy theme analysis. *Quarterly Journal of Speech, 59,* 143–159.

Bormann, E. G. (1977). Fetching good out of evil: A rhetorical use of calamity. *Quarterly Journal of Speech, 63,* 130–139.

Bormann, E. G. (1980). *Communication theory.* New York: Holt, Rinehart and Winston.

Bormann, E. G. (1982a). A fantasy theme analysis of the television coverage of the hostage release and the Reagan inaugural. *Quarterly Journal of Speech, 68,* 133–144.

Bormann, E. G. (1982b). Fantasy and rhetorical vision: Ten years later. *Quarterly Journal of Speech, 68,* 288–305.

Bormann, E. G. (1982c). The symbolic convergence theory of communication: Applications and implications for teachers and consultants. *Journal of Applied Communication Research, 10,* 50–61.

Bormann, E. G. (1983a). Rhetoric as a way of knowing: Ernest Bormann and fantasy theme analysis. In J. L. Golden, G. F. Berquist, & W. E. Coleman (Eds.), *Rhetoric of Western thought* (3rd ed., pp. 431–449). Dubuque, IA: Kendall/Hunt.

Bormann, E. G. (1983b). Symbolic convergence: Organizational communication and culture. In L. Putnam & M. E. Pecanowsky (Eds.), *Communication and organizations: An interpretive approach* (pp. 99–122). Beverly Hills, CA: Sage.

Bormann, E. G. (1983c). The symbolic convergence theory of communication and the creation, raising, and sustaining of public consciousness. In J. I. Sisco (Ed.), *The Jensen lectures: Contemporary communication studies* (pp. 71–90). Tampa, FL: Department of Communication, University of South Florida.

Bormann, E. G. (1985a). Symbolic convergence theory: A communication formulation. *Journal of Communication, 35,* 128–138.

Bormann, E. G. (1985b). *The force of fantasy: Restoring the American dream.* Carbondale, IL: Southern Illinois University Press.

Bormann, E. G. (1986). Symbolic convergence theory and communication in group decision-making. In R. Y. Hirokawa & M. S. Poole (Eds.), *Communication and group decision-making* (pp. 219–236). Beverly Hills, CA: Sage.

Bormann, E. G. (1989). The "empowering organization" as a heuristic concept in organizational communication. In J. A. Anderson (Ed.), *Communication yearbook 11* (pp. 391–404). Beverly Hills, CA: Sage.

Bormann, E. G. (1990). *Small group communication: Theory and practice* (3rd ed.). New York: Harper-Collins.

Bormann, E. G., Bormann, E., & Harty, K. C. (1995). Using symbolic convergence theory and focus group interviews to develop communication designed to stop teenage use of tobacco. In L. R. Frey (Ed.), *Innovations in group facilitation: Applications in natural settings* (pp. 200–232). Cresskill, NJ: Hampton Press and the Speech Communication Association.

Bormann, E. G., Cragan, J. F., & Shields, D. C. (1994). In defense of symbolic convergence theory: A look at the theory and its criticisms after two decades. *Communication Theory, 4,* 259–294.

Bormann, E. G., Cragan, J. F., & Shields, D. C. (1996). An expansion of the rhetorical vision concept of symbolic convergence theory: The cold war paradigm case. *Communication Monographs, 63,* 1–28.

Bormann, E. G., Koester, J., & Bennett, J. (1978). Political cartoons and salient rhetorical fantasies: An empirical analysis of the '76 presidential campaign. *Communication Monographs, 45,* 312–329.

Bormann, E. G., Kroll, B. S., Watters, K., & McFarland, D. (1984). Rhetorical visions of committed voters in the 1980 presidential campaign: Fantasy theme analysis of a large sample survey. *Critical Studies in Mass Communication, 1,* 287–310.

Bormann, E. G., Pratt, J., & Putman, L. (1978). Power, authority and sex: Male response to female leadership. *Communication Monographs, 45,* 119–155.

Brown, W. R. (1976). The prime-time television environment and emerging rhetorical visions. *Quarterly Journal of Speech, 62,* 389–399.

Brummett, B. A. (1984). Rhetorical theory as heuristic and moral: A pedagogical justification. *Communication Education, 33,* 97–107.

Bush, R. R. (1981). Applied Q-methodology: An industry perspective. In J. F. Cragan & D. C. Shields (Eds.), *Applied communication researcher: A dramatistic approach* (pp. 367–371). Prospect Heights, IL: Waveland Press.

Callahan, L. F. (1992). Corporations, the news media and other villains within Jesse Jackson's rhetorical vision. *Western Journal of Black Studies, 16,* 190–198.

Campbell, J. L. (1982). In search of the New South. *Southern Speech Communication Journal, 47,* 361–388.

Chesebro, J. W. (1980). Paradoxical views of 'homosexuality' in the rhetoric of social scientists: A fantasy theme analysis. *Quarterly Journal of Speech, 66,* 127–139.

Chesebro, J. W., Cragan, J. F., & McCullough, P. W. (1973). The small group technique of the radical revolutionary: A synthetic study of consciousness-raising. *Communication Monographs, 40,* 136–146.

Cragan, J. F. (1975). Rhetorical strategy: A dramatistic interpretation and application. *Central States Speech Journal, 26,* 4–11.

Cragan, J. F. (1981). The origins and nature of the cold war rhetorical vision, 1946–1972: A partial history. In J. F. Cragan & D. C. Shields (Eds.), *Applied communication research: A dramatistic approach* (pp. 47–66). Prospect Heights, IL: Waveland Press.

Cragan, J. F., & Cutbirth, C. W. (1984). A revisionist perspective on political *ad hominem* argument. *Central States Speech Journal, 26,* 4–11.

Cragan, J. F., Semlak, W. D., & Cuffe, M. (1984). Measuring chairperson/faculty satisfaction in various academic leadership sub-cultures. *Proceedings of academic chairpersons: Administrative responsibilities* (vol. 13, 106–117). Manhattan, KS: Kansas State University.

Cragan, J. F., & Shields, D. C. (1977). Foreign policy communication dramas: How mediated rhetoric

played in Peoria in campaign '76. *Quarterly Journal of Speech, 63,* 274–289.

Cragan, J. F., & Shields, D. C. (1978). Communication in American politics: Symbols without substance. *USA Today, 108,* 60–62.

Cragan, J. F., & Shields, D. C. (Eds.). (1981a). *Applied communication research: A dramatistic approach.* Prospect Heights, IL: Waveland Press.

Cragan, J. F., & Shields, D. C. (1981b). Communication-based market segmentation study: Illustrative excerpts. In J. F. Cragan & D. C. Shields (Eds.), *Applied communication research: A dramatistic approach* (pp. 357–365). Prospect Heights, IL: Waveland Press.

Cragan, J. F., & Shields, D. C. (1981c). Uses of Bormann's rhetorical theory in applied communication research. In J. F. Cragan & D. C. Shields (Eds.), *Applied communication research: A dramatistic approach* (pp. 31–42). Prospect Heights, IL: Waveland Press.

Cragan, J. F., & Shields, D. C. (1992). The use of symbolic convergence theory in corporate strategic planning: A case study. *Journal of Applied Communication Research, 20,* 199–218.

Cragan, J. F., & Shields, D. C. (1995a). *Symbolic theories in applied communication research: Bormann, Burke, and Fisher.* Cresskill, NJ: Hampton Press and the Speech Communication Association.

Cragan, J. F., & Shields, D. C. (1995b). Using SCT-based focus group interviews to do applied communication research. In L. Frey (Ed.), *Innovations in group facilitation: Applications in natural settings* (pp. 233–256). Cresskill, NJ: Hampton Press and the Speech Communication Association.

Cragan, J. F., Shields, D. C., & Nichols, N. E. (1981). Marketing farm management services: An internal study. In J. F. Cragan & D. C. Shields (Eds.), *Applied communication research: A dramatistic approach* (pp. 271–307). Prospect Heights, IL: Waveland Press.

Cragan, J. F., Shields, D. C., Pairitz, L. A., & Jackson, L. H. (1978, October). The identifying characteristics of public fire safety educators. *Fire Chief Magazine,* 44–50.

Cragan, J. F., Shields, D. C., Pairitz, L. A., & Jackson, L. H. (1981). The identifying characteristics of public fire safety educators: An empirical analysis. In J. F. Cragan & D. C. Shields (Eds.), *Applied communication research: A dramatistic approach* (pp. 219–234). Prospect Heights, IL: Waveland Press.

Daniel, A-M. A. (1995), U.S. media coverage of the Intifada and American public opinion. In Y. R. Kamalipour (Ed.), *The U.S. media and the Middle East: Image and perception* (pp. 62–72). Westport, CT: Greenwood Press.

Doyle, M. V. (1985). The rhetoric of romance: A fantasy theme analysis of Barbara Cartland novels. *Southern Speech Communication Journal, 51,* 24–48.

Duffy, M. (1997). High Stakes: A fantasy theme analysis of the selling of riverboat gambling in Iowa. *Southern Communication Journal, 62,* 117–132.

Endres, T. G. (1989). Rhetorical visions of unmarried mothers. *Communication Quarterly, 37,* 134–150.

Endres, T. G. (1994). Co-existing master analogues in symbolic convergence theory: The Knights of Columbus quincentennial campaign. *Communication Studies, 45,* 294–308.

Farrell, T. B. (1982). [Review of *Applied communication research: A dramatistic approach*]. *Quarterly Journal of Speech, 68,* 96–97.

Faules, D. (1982). The use of multi-methods in the organizational setting. *Western Journal of Speech Communication, 46,* 150–161.

Ford, L. A. (1989). Fetching good out of evil in AA: A Borrmannean fantasy theme analysis of *The Big Book* of Alcoholics Anonymous. *Communication Quarterly, 37,* 1–15.

Foss, K. A., & Littlejohn, S. W. (1986). 'The day after': Rhetorical vision in an ironic frame. *Critical Studies in Mass Communication, 3,* 317–336.

Glaser, S. R., & Frank, D. A. (1982). Rhetorical criticism of interpersonal discourse: An exploratory study. *Communication Quarterly, 30,* 353–358.

Goodnight, G. T., & Poulakos, J. (1981). Conspiracy rhetoric: From pragmatism to fantasy in public discourse. *Western Journal of Speech Communication, 45,* 299–316.

Gronbeck, B. E. (1980). Dramaturgical theory and criticism: The state of the art (or science?). *Western Journal of Speech Communication, 44,* 315–330.

Hart, R. P. (1986). Contemporary scholarship in public address: A research editorial. *Western Journal of Speech Communication, 50,* 75–95.

Haskins, W. A. (1981). Rhetorical vision of equality: Analysis of the rhetoric of the southern black press during reconstruction. *Communication Quarterly, 29,* 116–122.

Heisey, D. R., & Trebing, J. D. (1983). A comparison of the rhetorical visions and strategies of the Shah's White Revolution and Ayatollah's Islamic Revolution. *Communication Monographs, 50,* 158–174.

Hensley, C. W. (1975). Rhetorical vision and the persuasion of a historical movement: The disciples of Christ in Nineteenth Century American culture. *Quarterly Journal of Speech, 61,* 250–264.

Hubbard, R. C. (1985). Relationship styles in popular romance novels, 1950 to 1983. *Communication Quarterly, 33,* 113–125.

Huxman, S. S. (1996). Mary Wollstonecraft, Margaret Fuller, and Angelina Grimké: Symbolic convergence and a nascent rhetorical vision. *Communication Quarterly, 44,* 16–28.

Hyde, M. J. (1980). [Jacques Lacan's psychoanalytic theory of speech and language. Review of *Ecrits, a selection* and *The four fundamental concepts of psychoanalysis*]. *Quarterly Journal of Speech, 66,* 96–108.

Ilka, R. J. (1977). Rhetorical dramatization in the development of American communism. *Quarterly Journal of Speech, 63,* 413–427.

Ivie, R. L. (1987). The complete criticism of political rhetoric. *Quarterly Journal of Speech, 73,* 98–107.

Kidd, V. V. (1975). Happily ever after and other relationship styles: Advice on interpersonal relations in popular magazines. *Quarterly Journal of Speech, 61,* 31–39.

Kiewe, A., & Houck, D. W. (1989). The rhetoric of Reaganomics: A redemptive vision. *Communication Studies, 40,* 97–108.

Koester, J. (1982). The Machiavellian princess: Rhetorical dramas for women managers. *Communication Quarterly, 30,* 165–172.

Kroll, B. S. (1983). From small group to public view: Mainstreaming the women's movement. *Communication Quarterly, 31,* 139–147.

Lee, S. K. J., & Hoon, T. H. (1993). Rhetorical vision of men and women managers in Singapore. *Human Relations, 46,* 527–542.

Mayerle, J. (1987). A dream deferred: The failed fantasy to Norman Lear's *A. k. a. Pablo. Central States Speech Journal, 38,* 223–239.

McFarland, D. D. (1985). Self-images of law professors: Rethinking the schism in legal education. *Journal of Legal Education, 35,* 232–260.

McLuhan, M. (1964). *Understanding media.* New York: McGraw–Hill.

Mohrmann, G. P. (1980). Elegy in a critical graveyard. *Western Journal of Speech Communication, 44,* 265–274.

Mohrmann, G. P. (1982a). An essay on fantasy theme criticism. *Quarterly Journal of Speech, 68,* 109–132.

Mohrmann, G. P. (1982b). Fantasy theme criticism: A peroration. *Quarterly Journal of Speech, 68,* 306–313.

Nimmo, D., & Combs, J. E. (1982). Fantasies and melodrama in television network news: The case of Three Mile Island. *Western Journal of Speech Communication, 46,* 45–55.

Osborn, M. (1986). Review of *Force of Fantasy. Communication Education, 35,* 204–205.

Nichols, M. H. (1952). Kenneth Burke and the 'new rhetoric'. *Quarterly Journal of Speech, 38,* 133–141.

Norton, R. (1978). Foundation of a communicator style construct. *Human Communication Research, 4,* 99–112.

Norton, R. (1983). *Communicator style: Theory, applications, and measures.* Newbury Park, CA: Sage.

Norton, R., & Miller, L. D. (1975). Dyadic perception of communication style. *Communication Research, 2,* 50–67.

Porter, L. W. (1976). The White House transcripts: Group fantasy events concerning the mass media. *Central States Speech Journal, 27,* 272–279.

Putnam, L. L., Van-Hoeven, S. A., & Bullis, C. A. (1991). The role of rituals and fantasy themes in teachers' bargaining. *Western Journal of Speech Communication, 55,* 85–103.

Rarick, D. L., Duncan, M. B., Lee, D. G., & Porter, L. W. (1977). The Carter persona: An empirical analysis of the rhetorical visions of campaign '76. *Quarterly Journal of Speech, 63,* 258–273.

Rosenfeld, L. B., & Schrag, R. L. (1985). Empirical validation for the critical construct "humane collectivity." *Central States Speech Journal, 36,* 193–200.

Schrag, R. L., Hudson, R. A., & Bernado, L. M. (1981). Television's new humane collectivity. *Western Journal of Speech Communication, 45,* 1–12.

Sharf, B. F. (1986). Send in the clowns: The image of psychiatry during the Hinckley trial. *Journal of Communication, 36,* 80–93.

Shields, D. C. (1974). Firefighters' self-image, projected-image, and public-image. *Fire Command, 41,* 26–28.

Shields, D. C. (1981a). A dramatistic approach to applied communication research: Theory, methods and applications. In J. F. Cragan & D. C. Shields (Eds.), *Applied communication research: A dramatistic approach* (pp. 5–13). Prospect Heights, IL: Waveland Press.

Shields, D. C. (1981b). Dramatistic communication based focus group interviews. In J. F. Cragan & D. C. Shields, (Eds.), *Applied communication research: A dramatistic approach* (pp. 313–319). Prospect Heights, IL: Waveland Press.

Shields, D. C. (1981c). Feed dealer focus group interview on Shell's gestation litter conditioner. In J. F. Cragan & D. C. Shields (Eds.), *Applied communication research: A dramatistic approach* (pp. 335–349). Prospect Heights, IL: Waveland Press.

Shields, D. C. (1981d). Hog producer focus group interviews on Shell's gestation litter conditioner. In J. F. Cragan & D. C. Shields (Eds.), *Applied communication research: A dramatistic approach* (pp. 321–334). Prospect Heights, IL: Waveland Press.

Shields, D. C. (1981e). Malcolm X's black unity addresses: Espousing middle-class fantasy themes as American as apple-pie. In J. F. Cragan & D. C. Shields (Eds.), *Applied communication research: A dramatistic approach* (pp. 79–91). Prospect Heights, IL: Waveland Press.

Shields, D. C. (1981f). The St. Paul firefighters' *dramatis personae:* Concurrent and construct validity for the theory of rhetorical vision. In J. F. Cragan & D. C. Shields (Eds.), *Applied communication research: A dramatistic approach* (pp. 235–270). Prospect Heights, IL: Waveland Press.

Shields, D. C. (1988). *Communication-based focus group interviews: A Speech Communication Association short-course manual.* Manual presented at the annual meeting of the Speech Communication Association. Chicago, IL. (Available from D. C. Shields, Department of Communication, University of Missouri–St. Louis 63121.)

Shields, D. C., & Preston, C. T., Jr. (1985). Fantasy theme analysis in competitive rhetorical criticism. *National Forensic Journal, 3,* 102–115.

Solomon, M. (1980). Redemptive rhetoric: The continuity motif in the rhetoric of right to life. *Central States Speech Journal, 31,* 52–62.

Tiegen, J. (1973). *The Minneapolis Tribune* (p. 8A).

Turner, K. J. (1977). Comic strips: A rhetorical perspective. *Central States Speech Journal, 28,* 24–35.

Vasquez, G. (1994). A *homo narrans* paradigm for public relations: Combining Bormann's symbolic convergence theory and Grunig's situational theory of publics. *Journal of Public Relations, 5,* 201–216.

Vatz, R. E., & Weinberg, L. S. (1987). The critic as rhetor: Psychiatry and fantasy theme analysis. *Journal of Communication, 37,* 163–169.

Watzlawick, P., Beavin, J. H., & Jackson, D. D. (1967). *Pragmatics of human communication: A study of interactional patterns, pathologies, and paradoxes.* New York: Norton.

Chapter 5   Uncertainty Reduction Theory

Afifi, W. A., & Reichert, T. (1996). Understanding the role of uncertainty in jealousy experience and expression. *Communication Reports, 9,* 93–103.

Alperstein, N. M. (1991). Imaginary social relationships with celebrities appearing in television commercials. *Journal of Broadcasting & Electronic Media, 35,* 43–58.

Altman, I., & Taylor, D. A. (1973). *Social penetration: The development of interpersonal relationships.* New York: Holt, Rinehart and Winston.

Ayres, J. (1979). Uncertainty and social penetration theory expectations about relationship communication: A comparative test. *Western Journal of Speech Communication, 43,* 192–200.

Baxter, L. A. (1982). Strategies for ending relationships: Two studies. *Western Journal of Speech Communication, 46,* 223–241.

Baxter, L. A., & Wilmot, W. W. (1984). "Secret tests": Social strategies for acquiring information about the state of the relationship. *Human Communication Research, 11,* 171–201.

Bell, R. A., & Daly, J. A. (1984). The affinity-seeking function of communication. *Communication Monographs, 51,* 91–115.

Berger, C. R. (1975). Proactive and retroactive attribution processes in interpersonal communications. *Human Communication Research, 2,* 33–50.

Berger, C. R. (1979). Beyond initial interactions: Uncertainty, understanding and the development of interpersonal relationships. In H. Giles & R. Sinclair (Eds.), *Language and social psychology* (pp. 122–144). Oxford, England: Basil Blackwell.

X Berger, C. R. (1985). Social power and interpersonal communication. In M. L. Knapp & G. R. Miller (Eds.), *Handbook of interpersonal communication* (pp. 439–499). Newbury Park, CA: Sage.

⋎ Berger, C. R. (1986). Response. Uncertain outcome values in predicted relationships: Uncertainty reduc-tion theory then and now. *Human Communication Research, 13,* 34–38.

Berger, C. R. (1987). Communicating under uncertainty. In M. E. Roloff & G. R. Miller (Eds.), *Interpersonal processes: New directions in communication research* (pp. 39–62). Newbury Park, CA: Sage.

Berger, C. R. (1988). Uncertainty and information exchange in developing relationships. In S. W. Duck (Ed.), *Handbook of personal relationships* (pp. 239–255). Chichester, England: John Wiley & Sons.

Berger, C. R. (1994). Power, dominance, and social interaction. In M. L. Knapp & G. R. Miller (Eds.), *Handbook of interpersonal communication* (pp. 450–507). Newbury Park, CA: Sage.

Berger, C. R. (1995a). A plan-based approach to strategic communication. In D. E. Hewes (Ed.), *The cognitive bases of interpersonal communication* (pp. 141–179). Hillsdale, NJ: Erlbaum.

Berger, C. R. (1995b). Inscrutable goals, uncertain plans, and the production of communicative action. In C. R. Berger & M. Burgoon (Eds.), *Communication and social influence processes* (pp. 1–28). East Lansing, MI: Michigan State University Press.

Berger, C. R., & Bell, R. A. (1988). Plans and the initiation of social relationships. *Human Communication Research, 15,* 217–235.

Berger, C. R., & Bradac, J. J. (1982). *Language and social knowledge: Uncertainty in interpersonal relations.* London: Edward Arnold.

Berger, C. R., & Calabrese, R. J. (1975). Some explorations in initial interaction and beyond: Toward a developmental theory of interpersonal communication. *Human Communication Research, 1,* 99–112.

Berger, C. R., & diBattista, P. (1992). Information seeking and plan elaboration: What do you need to know to know what to do? *Communication Monographs, 59,* 368–387.

Berger, C. R., & diBattista, P. (1993). Communication failure and plan adaptation: If at first you don't succeed, say it louder and slower. *Communication Monographs, 60,* 220–238.

Berger, C. R., & Douglas, W. (1981). Studies in interpersonal epistemology III: Anticipated interaction, self-monitoring, and observational context selection. *Communication Monographs, 48,* 183–196.

Berger, C. R., Douglas, W., & Rodgers, M. J. (1980, May). Communication and uncertainty in long and short term relationships. Paper presented at the annual meeting of the International Communication Association, Acapulco, Mexico.

Berger, C. R., Gardner, R. R., Clatterbuck, G. W., & Schulman, L. S. (1976a). Perceptions of information sequencing in relationship development. *Human Communication Research, 3,* 29–46.

Berger, C. R., Gardner, R. R., Parks, M. R., Schulman, L., & Miller, G. R. (1976b). Interpersonal epistemology and interpersonal communication. In G. R. Miller (Ed.), *Explorations in interpersonal communication: Sage annual reviews of communication research, vol. V* (pp. 149–171). Beverly Hills, CA: Sage.

Berger, C. R., & Gudykunst, W. B. (1991). Uncertainty and communication. In B. Dervin & M. J. Voigt (Eds.), *Progress in communication sciences, vol. X* (pp. 21–66). Norwood, NJ: Ablex.

Berger, C. R., & Jordan, J. M. (1992). Planning sources, planning difficulty, and verbal fluency. *Communication Monographs, 59,* 130–149.

Berger, C. R., Karol, S. H., & Jordan, J. M. (1989). When a lot of knowledge is a dangerous thing: The debilitating effects of plan complexity on verbal fluency. *Human Communication Research, 16,* 91–119.

Berger, C. R., & Kellermann, K. A. (1983). To ask or not to ask: Is that a question? In R. N. Bostrom (Ed.), *Communication Yearbook 7* (pp. 342–368). Newbury Park, CA: Sage.

Berger, C. R., & Kellermann, K. (1989). Personal opacity and social information gathering: Explorations in strategic communication. *Communication Research, 16,* 314–351.

Berger, C. R., & Kellermann, K. (1994). Acquiring social information. In J. A. Daly & J. M. Wiemann (Eds.), *Communicating strategically* (pp. 1–31). Hillsdale, NJ: Erlbaum.

Berger, C. R., Knowlton, S. W., & Abrahams, M. F. (1996). The hierarchy principle in strategic communication. *Communication Theory, 6,* 111–142.

Berger, C. R., & Perkins, J. W. (1978). Studies in interpersonal epistemology I: Situational attributes in observational context selection. In B. D. Ruben (Ed.), *Communication yearbook 2* (pp. 171–184). New Brunswick, NJ: Transaction Press.

Berger, C. R., & Roloff, M. (1982). Thinking about friends and lovers: Social cognition and relational trajectories. In M. Roloff & C. R. Berger (Eds.), *Social cognition and communication* (pp. 151–192). Beverly Hills, CA: Sage.

Bochner, A. (1978). On taking ourselves seriously: An analysis of some persistent problems and promising directions in interpersonal research. *Human Communication Research, 6,* 179–191.

Booth–Butterfield, M., & Trotta, M. R. (1994). Attributional patterns for expressions of love. *Communication Reports, 7,* 119–129.

Booth–Butterfield, M., Booth-Butterfield, S., Koester, J. (1988). The function of uncertainty reduction in alleviating primary tension in small groups. *Communication Research Reports, 5,* 146–153.

Boster, F. J. (1995). Commentary on compliance-gaining message behavior research. In C. R. Berger & M. Burgoon (Eds.), *Communication and social influences processes* (pp. 91–113). East Lansing, MI: Michigan State University Press.

Clatterbuck, G. W. (1979). Attributional confidence and uncertainty in initial interaction. *Human Communication Research, 5,* 147–157.

Cody, M. J., & McLaughlin, M. L. (1980). Perceptions of compliance-gaining situations: A dimensional analysis. *Communication Monographs, 47,* 132–148.

Comer, D. (1991). Organizational newcomers' acquisition of information from peers. *Management Communication Quarterly, 5,* 64–89.

Conville, R. L. (1983). Second-order development in interpersonal communication. *Human Communication Research, 9,* 195–207.

Cupach, W. R., & Metts, S. (1994). *Facework.* Thousand Oaks, CA: Sage.

Dimmick, J. W., Sikand, J., & Patterson, S. J. (1994). The gratifications of the household telephone: Sociability, instrumentality, and reassurance. *Communication Research, 21,* 643–663.

Douglas, W. (1983). Scripts and self-monitoring: When does being a high self-monitor really make a difference? *Human Communication Research, 10,* 81–96.

Douglas, W. (1984). Initial interaction scripts: When knowing is behaving. *Human Communication Research, 11,* 203–219.

Douglas, W. (1985). Anticipated interaction and information-seeking. *Human Communication Research, 12,* 243–258.

Douglas, W. (1990). Uncertainty, information-seeking, and liking during initial interaction. *Western Journal of Speech Communication, 54,* 66–81.

Douglas, W. (1991). Expectations about initial interaction: An examination of the effects of global uncertainty. *Human Communication Research, 17,* 355–384.

Douglas, W. (1994). The acquaintanceship process: An examination of uncertainty, information-seeking, and social attraction during initial conversation. *Communication Research, 21,* 154–176.

Friedrich, G. W., & Cooper, P. J. (1990). The first day. In J. Daly, G. W. Friedrich, & A. L. Vangelisti (Eds.), *Teaching communication: Theory, research, and methods* (pp. 23–52). Hillsdale, NJ: Erlbaum.

Goffman, E. (1959). *The presentation of self in everyday life.* New York: Overlook.

Gudykunst, W. B. (1983). Uncertainty reduction and predictability of behavior in low- and high-context cultures: An exploratory study. *Communication Quarterly, 31(1),* 49–55.

Gudykunst, W. B. (1985a). The influence of cultural similarity, type of relationship, and monitoring on uncertainty reduction processes. *Communication Monographs, 52,* 203–217.

Gudykunst, W. B. (1985b). An exploratory comparison of close intracultural and intercultural friendships. *Communication Quarterly, 33,* 270–283.

Gudykunst, W. B. (1985c). A model of uncertainty reduction in intercultural encounters. *Journal of Language and Social Psychology, 4,* 79–98.

Gudykunst, W. B. (1988). Uncertainty and anxiety. In Y. Y. Kim & W. B. Gudykunst (Eds.), *Theories in intercultural communication* (pp. 123–156). Newbury Park, CA: Sage.

Gudykunst, W. B., Chua, E., & Gray, A. J. (1987). Cultural dissimilarities and uncertainty reduction processes. In M. L. McLaughlin (Ed.), *Communication Yearbook 10* (pp. 456–469). Newbury Park, CA: Sage.

Gudykunst, W. B., & Hammer, M. R. (1987). Strangers and hosts: An uncertainty reduction based theory of intercultural adaptation. In Y. Y. Kim & W. B. Gudykunst (Eds.), *Cross-cultural adaptation: Current approaches* (pp. 106–139). Newbury Park, CA: Sage.

Gudykunst, W. B., & Hammer, M. R. (1988). The influence of social identity and intimacy of inter-ethnic relationships on uncertainty reduction process. *Human Communication Research, 14,* 569–601.

Gudykunst, W. B., & Nishida, T. (1984). Individual and cultural influences on uncertainty reduction. *Communication Monographs, 51,* 23–36.

Gudykunst, W. B., & Nishida, T. (1986). Attributional confidence in low- and high-context cultures. *Human Communication Research, 12,* 525–549.

Gudykunst, W. B., Nishida, T., and Chua, E. (1986). Uncertainty reduction processes in Japanese–North American dyads. *Communication Research Reports, 3,* 39–46.

Gudykunst, W. B., Nishida, T., & Schmidt, K. L. (1989). The influence of cultural, relational, and personality factors on uncertainty reduction processes. *Western Journal of Speech Communication, 53,* 13–29.

Gudykunst, W. B., Sodetani, L. L., & Sonoda, K. T. (1987). Uncertainty reduction in Japanese-American/Caucasian relationships in Hawaii. *Western Journal of Speech Communication, 51,* 256–278.

Gudykunst, W. B., Yang, S. M., & Nishida, T. (1985). A cross-cultural test of uncertainty reduction theory: Comparisons of acquaintances, friends, and dating relationships in Japan, Korea, and the United States. *Human Communication Research, 11,* 407–454.

Hammer, M. R., & Martin, J. N. (1992). The effects of cross-cultural training on American managers in a Japanese-American joint venture. *Journal of Applied Communication Research, 20,* 161–182.

Haleta, L. L. (1996). Student perceptions of teachers' use of language: The effects of powerful and powerless language on impression formation and uncertainty. *Communication Education, 45,* 16–28.

Hecht, M. (1978). Measures of communication satisfaction. *Human Communication Research, 4,* 351–368.

Heider, F. (1958). *The psychology of interpersonal relations.* New York: John Wiley.

Hewes, D. E., Graham, M. K., Doegler, J. A., & Pavitt, C. (1985). "Second-guessing": Message interpretations in social networks. *Human Communication Research, 11,* 299–334.

Kellermann, K. (1984). The negativity effect and its implication for initial interaction. *Communication Monographs, 51,* 37–55.

Kellermann, K. (1986). Anticipation of future interaction and information exchange in initial interaction. *Human Communication Research, 13,* 41–75.

Kellermann, K. (1991). The conversation MOP II: Progression through scenes in discourse. *Human Communication Research, 17,* 385–414.

Kellermann, K., & Berger, C. R. (1984). Affect and social information acquisition: Sit back, relax, and tell me about yourself. In R. N. Bostrom (Ed.), *Communication Yearbook 8* (pp. 412–445). Beverly Hills, CA: Sage.

Kellermann, K., Broetzmann, S., Lim, T. S., & Kitao, K. (1989). The conversation MOP: Scenes in the stream of discourse. *Discourse Processes, 12,* 27–61.

Kellermann, K., & Reynolds, R. (1990). When ignorance is bliss: The role of motivation to reduce uncertainty in uncertainty reduction theory. *Human Communication Research, 17,* 5–75.

Kelley, H. H. (1967). Attribution theory in social psychology. In D. Levine (Ed.), *Nebraska symposium on motivation* (pp. 192–237). Lincoln: University of Nebraska Press.

Kelley, H. H. (1973). The processes of causal attribution. *American Psychologist, 28,* 107–128.

Kelly, G. (1955). *The psychology of personal constructs.* New York: Norton.

Kim, M. S., & Sharkey, W. F. (1995). Independent and interdependent construals of self: Explaining cultural patterns of interpersonal communication in multi-cultural organizational settings. *Communication Quarterly, 43,* 20–38.

Knapp, M. L., & Vangelisti, A. (1992). *Interpersonal communication and human relationships.* Boston: Allyn & Bacon.

Kramer, M. W. (1993). Communication and uncertainty reduction during job transfers: Leaving and joining processes. *Communication Monographs, 60,* 178–198.

Lester, R. E. (1987). Organizational culture, uncertainty reduction, and the socialization of two organizational members. In S. Thomas (Ed.), *Communication—methodology, behavior, artifacts and institutions* (pp. 105–113). Norwood, NJ: Ablex.

McCroskey, J. C., Richmond, V. P., Daly, J. A., & Cox, B. G. (1975). The effects of communication apprehension on interpersonal attraction. *Human Communication Research, 1,* 51–65.

Mignerey, J. T., Rubin, R. B., & Gordon, W. I. (1995). Organizational entry: An investigation of newcomer communication behavior and uncertainty. *Communication Research, 22,* 54–85.

Miller, G. R., Boster, F. J., Roloff, M. E., & Seibold, D. R. (1977). Compliance-gaining message strategies: A typology and some findings concerning effects of situational difference. *Communication Monographs, 44,* 37–51.

Miller, V., & Jablin, F. (1991). Information-seeking during organizational entry: Influences, tactics, and a model of the process. *Academy of Management Review, 16,* 92–120.

Ng, K. H., & Bradac, J. J. (1993). *Power in language: Verbal communication and social influence.* Newbury Park, CA: Sage.

Okabe, R. (1983). Cultural assumptions of East and West: Japan and the United States. In W. Gudykunst (Ed.), *Intercultural communication theory: Current perspectives* (pp. 21–44). Beverly Hills, CA: Sage.

Olaniran, B. A., & Williams, D. E. (1995). Communication distortion: An intercultural lesson from the visa application process. *Communication Quarterly, 43,* 225–240.

Parks, M. R., & Adelman, M. B. (1983). Communication networks and the development of romantic relationships: An expansion of uncertainty reduction theory. *Human Communication Research, 10,* 55–79.

Planalp, S., & Honeycutt, J. M. (1985). Events that increase uncertainty in personal relationships. *Human Communication Research, 11,* 593–604.

Planalp, S., Rutherford, D. K., & Honeycutt, J. M. (1988). Events that increase uncertainty in personal relationships II: Replication and extension. *Human Communication Research, 14,* 516–547.

Prisbell, M., & Andersen, J. F. (1980). The importance of perceived homophily, level of uncertainty, feeling good, safety, and self-disclosure in interpersonal relationships. *Communication Quarterly, 28 (3),* 22–33.

Putnam, L. L., & Sorenson, R. (1982). Equivocal messages in organizations. *Human Communication Research, 8,* 114–132.

Rubin, R. B. (1977). The role of context in information seeking and impression formation. *Communication Monographs, 44,* 81–90.

Schank, R. C. (1982). *Dynamic memory.* Cambridge, England: Cambridge University Press.

Shannon, C. E. (1948a). A mathematical theory of communication. *Bell System Technical Journal, 27,* 379–423.

Shannon, C. E. (1948b). A mathematical theory of communication. *Bell System Technical Journal, 27,* 623–656.

Sheer, V. C., & Cline, R. J. (1995). Testing a model of perceived information adequacy and uncertainty reduction in physician–patient interactions. *Journal of Applied Communication Research, 23,* 44–59.

Spiker, B., & Daniels, T. (1981). Information adequacy and communication relationships: An empirical investigation of 18 organizations. *Western Journal of Speech Communication, 45,* 342–354.

Spitzberg, B. H. (1994). The dark side of (in)competence. In W. R. Cupach & B. H. Spitzberg (Eds.), *The dark side of interpersonal communication* (pp. 25–49). Hillsdale, NJ: Erlbaum.

Stacks, D., Hickson, III, M., & Hill, Jr., S. R. (1991). *An introduction to communication theory.* Fort Worth, TX: Holt, Rinehart and Winston.

Sunnafrank, M. (1986a). Predicted outcome value during initial interactions: A reformulation of uncertainty reduction theory. *Human Communication Research, 13,* 3–33.

Sunnafrank, M. (1986b). Rejoinder: Predicted outcome values: Just now and then? *Human Communication Research, 13,* 39–40.

Sunnafrank, M. (1990). Predicted outcome value and uncertainty reduction theories: A test of competing perspectives. *Human Communication Research, 17,* 76–103.

Teboul, J.–C. B. (1994). Facing and coping with uncertainty during organizational encounters. *Management Communication Quarterly, 8,* 190–224.

Ting–Toomey, S. (1981). Ethnic identity and close friendship in Chinese–American college students. *International Journal of Intercultural Relations, 5,* 383–406.

Trenholm, S. (1991). *Human communication theory* (2nd ed.). Englewood Cliffs, NJ: Prentice-Hall.

VanLear, C. A., & Trujillo, N. (1986). On becoming acquainted: A longitudinal study. *Journal of Personal and Social Relationships, 3,* 375–392.

Waldron, V. R. (1990). Constrained rationality: Situational influences on information acquisition plans and tactics. *Communication Monographs, 57,* 184–201.

Walther, J. B. (1994). Anticipated ongoing interaction versus channel effects on relational communication in computer-mediated interaction. *Human Communication Research, 20,* 473–501.

Walther, J. B., & Burgoon, J. K. (1992). Relational communication in computer-mediated interaction. *Human Communication Research, 19,* 50–88.

Chapter 6   Narrative Paradigm Theory

Aden, R. C. (1994). Back to the garden: Therapeutic place metaphor in *Field of Dreams. Southern Communication Journal, 59,* 307–317.

Alberts, J. K., Miller–Rassulo, M. A., & Hecht, M. L. (1991). A typology of drug resistance strategies. *Journal of Applied Communication Research, 19,* 129–151.

Aristotle (1954). *Rhetoric* (W. R. Roberts, tran.). New York: Random House.

Baesler, E. J. (1995). Construction and test of an empirical measure for narrative coherence and fidelity. *Communication Reports, 8,* 97–109.

Baker, G. P. (1898). *The principles of argumentation.* Boston: Ginn & Company.

Bass, J. D. (1985). The appeal to efficiency as narrative closure: Lyndon Johnson and the Dominican crisis, 1965. *Southern Speech Communication Journal, 50,* 103–120.

Brown, D. (1970). *Bury my heart at wounded knee: An Indian history of the American West.* New York: Bantam Books.

Brown, M. H., & McMillan, J. J. (1991). Culture as text: The development of an organizational narrative, *Southern Communication Journal, 57,* 49–60.

Cali, D. D. (1993). Chiara Lubich's 1977 Templeton Prize acceptance speech: Case study in the mystical narrative. *Communication Studies, 44,* 132–143.

Carpenter, R. H. (1986). Admiral Mahan, "narrative fidelity," and the Japanese attack on Pearl Harbor. *Quarterly Journal of Speech, 72,* 290–305.

Clair, R. P., Chapman, P. A., & Kunkel, A. W. (1996). Narrative approaches to raising consciousness about sexual harassment: From research to pedagogy and back again. *Journal of Applied Communication Research, 24,* 241–259.

Collins, C. A., & Clark, J. E. (1992). A structural narrative analysis of *Nightline's* "this week in the Holy Land." *Critical Studies in Mass Communication, 9,* 25–43.

Condit, C. (1987). Crafting virtue: The rhetorical construction of public morality. *Quarterly Journal of Speech, 73,* 79–97.

Cragan, J. F., & Shields, D. C. (1990, July). *The uses of narrative in market research and advertising.* Paper presented at the Narrative of the Human Sciences Conference, University of Iowa, Iowa City, IA. (Available on request from J. F. Cragan, Department of Communication, Illinois State University, Normal, IL 61701.)

Cragan, J. F., & Shields, D. C. (1995). *Symbolic theories in applied communication research: Bormann, Burke, and Fisher.* Cresskill, NJ: Hampton Press and Speech Communication Association.

Darwin, C. [1871] (1964). *On the origin of species.* Cambridge, MA: Harvard University Press.

Deming, C. J. (1985). *Hill Street Blues* as narrative. *Critical Studies in Mass Communication, 2,* 1–22.

Dobkin, B. A. (1992). Paper tigers and video postcards: The rhetorical dimensions of narrative form in ABC news coverage of terrorism. *Western Journal of Communication, 56,* 143–160.

Downs, V. C., Javidi, M., & Nussbaum, J. F. (1988). An examination of teachers' verbal communication within the college classroom: Use of humor, self-disclosure, and narratives. *Communication Education, 37,* 127–141.

Fisher, W. R. (1973). Reaffirmation and subversion of the American dream. *Quarterly Journal of Speech, 59,* 160–167.

Fisher, W. R. (1978). Toward a logic of good reasons. *Quarterly Journal of Speech, 64,* 367–384.

Fisher, W. R. (1980). Rationality and the logic of good reasons. *Philosophy and Rhetoric, 13,* 121–130.

Fisher, W. R. (1982). Romantic democracy, Ronald Reagan, and presidential heroes. *Western Journal of Speech Communication, 46,* 299–310.

Fisher, W. R. (1984). Narration as a human communication paradigm: The case of public moral argument. *Communication Monographs, 51,* 1–22.

Fisher, W. R. (1985a). The narrative paradigm: An elaboration. *Communication Monographs, 52,* 347–367.

Fisher, W. R. (1985b). The narrative paradigm: In the beginning. *Journal of Communication, 35,* 74–89.

Fisher, W. R. (1987a). *Human communication as narration: Toward a philosophy of reason, value, and action.* Columbia, SC: University of South Carolina Press.

Fisher, W. R. (1987b). Technical logic, rhetorical logic, and narrative rationality. *Argumentation, 1,* 3–22.

Fisher, W. R. (1988). The narrative paradigm and the interpretation and assessment of historical texts. *Argumentation and Advocacy, 25,* 49–53.

Fisher, W. R. (1989). Clarifying the narrative paradigm. *Communication Monographs, 56,* 55–58.

Fisher, W. R. (1992). Narration, reason, and community. In R. H. Brown (Ed.), *Writing the social text: Poetics and politics in social science discourse* (pp. 199–217). New York: Aldine De Gruyter.

Fisher, W. R. (1995). Narration, knowledge, and the possibility of wisdom. In R. Goodman & W. Fisher (Eds.), *Rethinking knowledge: Reflections across the disciplines* (pp. 169–192). Albany, NY: SUNY Press.

Fisher, W. R., & Filloy, R. A. (1982). Argument in drama and literature: An exploration. In J. R. Cox & C. A. Willard (Eds.), *Advances in argumentation theory and research* (pp. 343–362). Carbondale, IL: American Forensic Association and Southern Illinois University Press.

Fitzgerald, F. S. (1925). *The great Gatsby.* New York: Scribner's Sons.

Flanagan, J. (1954). The critical incident technique. *Psychological Bulletin, 51,* 327–357.

Glass, R. H. (1988). The narrative perspective in academic debate: A critique. *Argumentation and Advocacy, 25,* 78–92.

Gronbeck, B. E. (1987). The argumentative structures of selected Eighteenth-Century British political historians. In J. W. Wenzel (Ed.), *Argument and critical practices: Proceedings of the fifth SCA/AFA conference on argumentation* (pp. 569–577). Annandale, VA: Speech Communication Association.

Gronbeck, B. E. (1992). Negative narratives in 1988 presidential campaign ads. *Quarterly Journal of Speech, 78,* 333–346.

Hitler, A. (1943), *Mein Kampf* (R. Manheim, tran.). Boston, MA: Houghton Mifflin. (Original work published 1923).

Hollihan, T. A., Baaske, K. T., & Riley, P. (1985). The art of storytelling: An argument for a narrative perspective in academic debate. In J. R. Cox, M. O. Sillars, & G. B. Walker (Eds.), *Argument and social practice: Proceedings of the fourth SCA/AFA conference on argumentation* (pp. 807–826). Annandale, VA: Speech Communication Association.

Hollihan, T. A., Baaske, K. T., & Riley, P. (1987). Debaters as storytellers: The narrative perspective in academic debate. *Journal of the American Forensic Association, 23,* 184–193.

Hollihan, T. A., & Riley, P. (1987a). Academic debate and democracy: A clash of ideologies. In J. W. Wenzel (Ed.), *Argumentation and critical practice: Proceedings of the fifth SCA/AFA conference on argumentation* (pp. 399–404). Annandale, VA: Speech Communication Association.

Hollihan, T. A., & Riley, P. (1987b). The rhetorical power of a compelling story: A critique of a "tough love" parental support group. *Communication Quarterly, 35,* 13–25.

Katriel, T., & Shenhar, A. (1990). Tower and stockade: Dialogic narration in Israeli settlement ethos. *Quarterly Journal of Speech, 76,* 359–380.

King, M. L. (1969). "I have a dream." In W. A. Linkugel, R. R. Allen, & R. L. Johannesen, *Contemporary American Speeches: A Sourcebook of Speech Forms and Principles* (2nd ed., pp. 290–294). Belmont, CA: Wadsworth.

Kirkwood, W. G. (1992). Narrative and the rhetoric of possibility. *Communication Monographs, 59,* 30–47.

Lang, A., Sias, P. M., Chantrill, P., & Burek, J. A. (1995). Tell me a story: Narrative elaboration and memory for television. *Communication Reports, 8,* 102–110.

Langellier, K. M. (1989). Personal narratives: Perspectives on theory and research. *Text and Performance Quarterly, 9,* 243–276.

Lucaites, J. L., & Condit, C. M. (1985). Re-constructing narrative theory: A functional perspective. *Journal of Communication, 35,* 90–108.

Mackey–Kallis, S. (1991). Spectator desire and narrative closure: The Reagan 18-minute political film. *Southern Communication Journal, 56,* 308–314.

Mechling, E. W., & Mechling, J. (1983). Sweet talk: The moral rhetoric against sugar. *Central States Speech Journal, 34,* 19–32.

Megill, A. (1987). Disciplinary history and other kinds. In J. W. Wenzel (Ed.), Argument and critical practices: Proceedings of the 5th SCA/AFA conference on argumentation (pp. 557–563). Annandale, VA: Speech Communication Association.

Meyer, J. C. (1995). Tell me a story: Eliciting organizational values from narratives. *Communication Quarterly, 43,* 210–224.

Miller, A. (1955). Death of a salesman. In B. Atkinson (Ed.), New voices in the American theatre (pp. 111–226). New York: Random House.

Moore, M. P. (1992). The Quayle quagmire: Political campaigns in the poetic form of burlesque. *Western Journal of Communication, 56,* 108–124.

Mumby, D. K. (1987). The political function of narrative in organizations. *Communication Monographs, 54,* 113–127.

Payne, D. (1992). Political vertigo in *Dead Poets Society. Southern Communication Journal, 58,* 13–21.

Perelman, C. (1979). *The new rhetoric and the humanities: Essays on rhetoric and its application.* Dordrecht, Holland: D. Reidel.

Perelman, C. (1982). *The realm of rhetoric* (W. Kluback, trans.). Notre Dame, IN: University of Notre Dame Press.

Plato. (1951a). *The dialogues of Plato* (B. Jowett, trans.). Chicago, IL: William Benton.

Plato. (1952b). *The Gorgias.* In B. Jowell (Trans.), *The dialogues of Plato* (pp. 252–294). Chicago, IL: William Benton.

Rosteck, T. (1992). Narrative in Martin Luther King's *I've been to the mountain top. Southern Communication Journal, 58,* 22–32.

Rowland, R. C. (1987). Narrative: Mode of discourse or paradigm? *Communication Monographs, 54,* 264–275.

Rowland, R. C. (1988). The value of the rational world and narrative paradigms. *Central States Speech Journal, 39,* 204–217.

Rowland, R. C. (1989). On limiting the narrative paradigm. *Communication Monographs, 56,* 39–54.

Schuetz, J. (1988). Narrative *montage:* Press coverage of the Jean Harris trial. *Argumentation and Advocacy, 25,* 65–77.

Sharf, B. F. (1990). Physician–patient communication as interpersonal rhetoric: A narrative approach. *Health Communication, 2,* 217–231.

Sharf, B., & Poirier, S. (1988). Exploring (UN) common ground: Communication and literature in a health care setting. *Communication Education, 37,* 224–236.

Smith, L. D. (1989). A narrative analysis of the party platforms: The Democrats and Republicans of 1984. *Communication Quarterly, 37,* 91–99.

Solomon, M. (1991). Autobiographies as rhetorical narratives: Elizabeth Cady Stanton and Anna Howard Shaw as "new women" [special section]. *Communication Studies, 42,* 354–370.

Solomon, M., & McMullen, W. J. (1991). Places in the Heart: The rhetorical force of an open test. *Western Journal of Speech Communication, 55,* 339–353.

Strine, M. S., & Pacanowsky, M. E. (1985). How to read interpretative accounts of organizational life: Narrative bases of textual authority. *Southern Speech Communication Journal, 50,* 283–297.

Stuckey, M. E. (1992). Anecdotes and conversations: The narrational and dialogic styles of modern presidential communication. *Communication Quarterly, 40,* 45–55.

Vanderford, M. L., Smith, D. H., & Harris, W. S. (1992). Value identification in narrative discourse: Evaluation of an HIV education demonstration project. *Journal of Applied Communication Research, 20,* 123–160.

Warnick, B. (1987). The narrative paradigm: Another story. *Quarterly Journal of Speech, 73,* 172–182.

Watson, J. D., & Crick, F. H. (1953). A structure for deoxyribose nucleic acid. *Nature, 71,* 737–740.

Whittenberger-Keith, K. (1992). The good person behaving well: Rethinking the rhetoric of virtue. *Southern Communication Journal, 58,* 33–43.

Chapter 7   Diffusion of Innovations Theory

Adams, J. B., Mullen, J. J., & Wilson, H. M. (1969). Diffusion of a 'minor' foreign affairs news event. *Journalism Quarterly, 46,* 545–551.

Albrecht, T. L., & Hall, B. (1991). Facilitating talk about new ideas: The role of personal relationships in organizational innovation. *Communication Monographs, 58,* 273–288.

Albrecht, T. L., & Ropp, V. A. (1984). Communicating about innovation in networks of three U.S. organizations. *Journal of Communication, 34,* 78–91.

Allen, I. L., & Colfax, J. D. (1968). The diffusion of news of LBJ's March 31 decision. *Journalism Quarterly, 45,* 321–324.

Antola, L., & Rogers, E. M. (1984). Television flows in Latin America. *Communication Research, 11,* 183–202.

Antonelli, C. (1986). The diffusion of information technology and the demand for telecommunication services. *Telecommunication Policy, 9,* 255–264.

Bach, B. W. (1989). The effect of multiplex relationships upon innovation adoption: A reconsideration of Rogers's model. *Communication Monographs, 56,* 133–149.

Bantz, C. R., Petronio, S. G., & Rarick, D. L. (1983). News diffusion after the Reagan shooting. *Quarterly Journal of Speech, 69,* 317–327.

Barclay, R. O., Pinelli, T. E., Tan, A. S. T., & Kennedy, J. M. (1993). Technical communications practices and the use of information technologies as reported by Dutch and U.S. aerospace engineers. In Section 17: International data collection and reporting, *Proceedings of the International Professional Communication Conference, October 5–8, 1993* (pp. 221–226). Amsterdam, The Netherlands: International Professional Communication Association.

Bardini, T., & Horvath, A. T. (1995). The social construction of the personal computer user. *Journal of Communication, 45*(3), 40–65.

Barker, J. R., Melville, C. W., & Pacanowsky, M. (1993). Self-directed teams at XEL: Changes in communication during a program of cultural transformation. *Journal of Applied Communication Research, 21,* 297–312.

Barnett, G. A., Fink, E. L., & Sebus, M. B. (1989). A mathematical model of academic citation age. *Communication Research, 16,* 510–531.

Barnett, G. A., & Seigel, G. (1988). The diffusion of computer-assisted legal research systems. *Journal* of the American Society for Information Sciences, *39*, 224–234.

Basil, M. D., & Brown, W. J. (1994). Interpersonal communication in news diffusion: A study of "Magic" Johnson's Announcement. *Journalism Quarterly, 71*, 305–320.

Bass, F. M. (1969). A new product growth model for consumer durables. *Management Science, 15*(5), 215–227.

Bass, F. N. (1980). The relationship between diffusion rates, experience curves, and demand elasticities for consumer durable technological innovations. *Journal of Business, 53*, 51–67.

Bass, F. N. (1986, Oct.). Diffusion systems for education and learning about health. *Family Community Health*, p. 1–26.

Beltran, L. R. (1976). Alien premises, objects, and methods in Latin American communication research. *Communication Research, 3*, 107–134.

Benton, M., & Frazier, P. J. (1976). The agenda setting function of the mass media at three levels of 'information holding'. *Communication Research, 3*, 261–274.

Beyer, J. M., & Trice, H. M. (1978). *Implementing change: Alcoholism policies in work organizations*. New York: Macmillan.

Bogart, L. (1957/1958). Measuring the effectiveness of an overseas information campaign: A case history. *Public Opinion Quarterly, 21*, 475–498.

Bolton, W. T. (1983). Perceptual factors that influence the adoption of videotex technology: Results of Channel 2000 field test. *Journal of Broadcasting, 27*, 141–153.

Bordenave, J. D. (1976). Communication of agricultural innovations in Latin America: The need for new models. *Communication Research, 3*, 135–154.

Bormann, E. G. (1980). *Communication Theory*. New York: Harper & Row.

Budd, R. W., MacLean, M. S., & Barnes, A. M. (1966). Regularities in the diffusion of two major news events. *Journalism Quarterly, 43*, 221–230.

Bush, R. R. (1981). Applied q-methodology: An industry perspective. In J. F. Cragan & D. C. Shields (Eds.), *Applied communication research: A dramatistic approach* (pp. 367–371). Prospect Heights, IL: Waveland Press.

Caplan, N., & Nelson, J. (1973). On being useful: The nature and consequences of psychological research on social problems. *American Psychologist, 28*, 199–211.

Carey, J., & Moss, M. L. (1985). The diffusion of new telecommunication technologies. *Telecommunication Policy, 6*, 145–158.

Carrocci, N. M. (1985). Diffusion of information about cyanide-laced Tylenol. *Journalism Quarterly, 62*, 630–633.

Chaffee, S. H., Gomez–Palacio, C., & Rogers, E. M. (1990). Mass communication research in Latin America: Views from here and there. *Journalism Quarterly, 67*, 1015–1024.

Chan, J. M. (1994). Media internationalization in China: Processes and tensions. *Journal of Communication, 44*(3), 70–88.

Cheney, G., Block, B. L., & Gordon, B. S. (1986). Perceptions of innovativeness and communication about innovations: A study of three types of service organizations. *Communication Quarterly, 34*, 213–230.

Cherry, C. (1978). *World communication: Threat or promise*. New York: Wiley–Interscience.

Coleman, J. S., Katz, E., & Menzel, H. (1957). The diffusion of innovation among physicians. *Sociometry, 20*, 253–270.

Coleman, J. S., Katz, E., & Menzel, H. (1966). *Medical innovation: A diffusion study*. New York: Bobbs–Merrill.

Contractor, N. S., Singhal, A., & Rogers, E. M. (1988). Metatheoretical perspectives on satellite television and development in India. *Journal of Broadcasting and Electronic Media, 32*, 129–148.

Cook, T. D., Appleton, H., Conner, R. F., Shaffer, A., Tamkin, G. A., & Weber, S. J. (1975). *Sesame Street revisited*. New York: Russell Sage.

Coughenour, C. M. (1955). The problem of reliability of adoption data in survey research. *Rural Sociology, 30*, 184–203.

Damonpour, F. (1988). Innovation type, radicalness, and the adoption process. *Communication Research, 15*, 545–567.

Danko, W. D., & MacLachlan, J. M. (1983). Research to accelerate the diffusion of a new innovation: The case of personal computers. *Journal of Advertising Research, 23*(3), 39–43.

Dearing, J. W., & Meyer, G. (1994). An exploratory tool for predicting adoption decisions. *Science Communication, 16*(1), 43–57.

Dearing, J. W., Meyer, G., & Kazmierczak, J. (1994). Portraying the new: Communication between university innovators and potential users. *Science Communication, 16*(1), 11–42.

Dearing, J. W., & Rogers, E. M. (1992). AIDS and the media agenda. In T. Edgar, M. A. Fitzpatrick, & V. S. Freimuth (Eds.), *AIDS: A communication perspective* (pp. 173–194). Hillsdale, NJ: Erlbaum.

Dearing, J. W., & Rogers, E. M. (1996). *Agenda-setting.* Newbury Park, CA: Sage. DeFleur, M. (1987a). The growth and decline of research on the diffusion of news, 1945–1985. *Communication Research, 14,* 109–130.

DeFleur, M. (1987b). Diffusing information. *Society, 25,* 72–81.

Deutchmann, P. J. (1963). The mass media in an underdeveloped village. *Journalism Quarterly, 40,* 27–35.

Deutchmann, P. J., & Danielson, W. A. (1960). Diffusion of knowledge of the major news story. *Journalism Quarterly, 37,* 345–355.

Dodd, S. C. (1955). Diffusion is predictable: Testing probability models for laws of interaction. *American Sociological Review, 2,* 392–401.

Donohue, G. A., Tichenor, P. J., & Olien, C. N. (1973). Mass media functions, knowledge, and social control. *Journalism Quarterly, 50,* 652–659.

Donohue, G. A., Tichenor, P. J., & Olien, C. N. (1975). Mass media and the knowledge gap: A hypothesis reconsidered. *Communication Research, 2,* 2–23.

Downs, G. W., & Mohr, L. B. (1976). Conceptual issues in the study of innovations. *Administrative Science Quarterly, 21,* 700–714.

Dutton, W. H., Rogers, E. M., & Jun, S. H. (1987). Diffusion and social impacts of personal computers. *Communication Research, 14,* 219–250.

Edmonson, M. S. (1961). Neolithic diffusion rates. *Current Anthropology: A World Journal of the Sciences of Man, 2*(2), 71–102.

Ettema, J. S., & Kline, F. G. (1977). Deficits, differences, and ceilings: Contingent conditions for understanding the knowledge gap. *Communication Research, 4* 179–202.

Fairhurst, G. T. (1993). Echoes of the union: When the rest of the organization talks total quality. *Management Communication Quarterly, 6,* 331–371.

Fairhurst, G. T., & Wendt, R. F. (1993). The gap in total quality: A commentary. *Management Communication Quarterly, 6,* 441–451.

Fan, D. P. (1985). Ideodynamics: The kinetics of the evolution of ideas. *Journal of Mathematical Sociology, 11,* 1–24.

Fan, D. P., & McAvoy, G. (1989). Predictions of public opinion on the spread of AIDS: Introduction of new computer technologies. *Journal of Sex Research, 26,* 159–187.

Fathi, A. (1973). Diffusion of a 'happy' news event. *Journalism Quarterly, 50,* 271–277.

Fine, G. A. (1975). Recall of information about diffusion of a major news event. *Journalism Quarterly, 52,* 751–755.

Fredin, E. S., Monnett, T. H., & Kosicki, G. M. (1994). Knowledge gaps, social locators, and media schemata: Gaps, reverse gaps, and gaps of disaffection. *Journalism Quarterly, 71,* 176–190.

Freedman, R. (1964). Sample surveys for family planning research in Taiwan. *Public Opinion Quarterly, 28,* 374–382.

Galloway, J. J. (1977). The analysis and significance of communication effects gaps. *Communication Research, 4,* 363–386.

Gantz, W. (1983). The diffusion of news about the attempted Reagan assassination. *Journal of Communication, 33*(1), 56–66.

Gantz, W., Fitzmaurice, M., & Fink, E. (1991). Assessing the active component of information-seeking. *Journalism Quarterly, 63,* 630–637.

Gantz, W., Fitzmaurice, M., & Yoo, E. (1990). Seat belt campaigns and buckling up: Do the media make a difference? *Health Communication, 2*(1), 1–12.

Gantz, W., Krendal, K. A., & Robertson, S. R. (1986). Diffusion of a proximate news event. *Journalism Quarterly, 63,* 282–287.

Gantz, W., Trenholm, S., & Pittman, M. (1976). The impact of salience and altruism on the diffusion of news. *Journalism Quarterly, 53,* 727–732.

Gaziano, C. (1983). The knowledge gap: An analytical review of media effects. *Communication Research, 10,* 447–486.

Genova, B. K. L., & Greenberg, B. S. (1979). Interests in news and the knowledge gap. *Public Opinion Quarterly, 43,* 79–91.

Gonzalez, H. (1989). Interactivity and feedback in third world development campaigns. *Critical Studies in Mass Communication, 6,* 295–314.

Greenberg, B. S. (1964a). Diffusion of news of the Kennedy assassination. *Public Opinion Quarterly, 28,* 225–232.

Greenberg, B. S. (1964b). Person to person communication in the diffusion of news events. *Journalism Quarterly, 41,* 336–342.

Gross, N. C. (1942). *The diffusion of a culture trait in two Iowa townships.* Unpublished M. A. Thesis, Department of Rural Sociology, Iowa State University.

Hagerstrand, T. (1968). The diffusion of innovations. In D. L. Sills (Ed.), *International encyclopedia of the social sciences, vol. 4* (pp. 174–178). New York: Macmillan & Free Press.

Hagins, J. (1996). The inconvenient public interest: Policy challenges in the age of information. *Journal of Applied Communication Research, 24,* 83–92.

Hall, B. (1991). Relational and content differences between elites and outsiders in innovation networks. *Human Communication Research, 17,* 536–561.

Hanneman, G. J., & Greenberg, B. S. (1973). Relevance and diffusion of news of major and minor events. *Journalism Quarterly, 50,* 433–437.

Haroldsen, G., Broddason, T., Hedinsson, E., Kalkkinen, M. L., & Svendsen, N. (1987). News diffusion of the assassination of a neighbor. *European Journal of Communication, 2,* 171–184.

Hayes, R. H., & Clark, K. B. (1986). Why some factories are more productive. *Harvard Business Review, 64,* 66–73.

Heine–Geldern, R. (1968). Cultural diffusion. In D. L. Sills (Ed.), *International encyclopedia of the social sciences, vol. 4* (pp. 169–173). New York: Macmillan & Free Press.

Hertog, J. K., & Fan, D. P. (1995). The impact of press coverage on social beliefs: The case of HIV transmission. *Communication Research, 22,* 545–574.

Hill, R. J., & Bonjean, C. M. (1964). News diffusion: A test of the regularity hypothesis. *Journalism Quarterly, 41,* 336–342.

Hoffman, E., & Roman, P. M. (1984). Information diffusion in the implementation of innovation process. *Communication Research, 11,* 117–140.

Holland, M. P., Pinelli, T. E., Barclay, R. O., & Kennedy, J. M. (1991). Engineers as information processors: A survey of US aerospace engineering faculty and students. *European Journal of Engineering Education, 16,* 317–336.

Holmov, P. G., & Warneryd, K. (1990). Adoption and use of fax in Sweden. In M. Carnevale, M. M. Lucertini, & S. Nicosia (Eds.), *Modeling the innovation: Communications, automation and information systems* (pp. 95–108). Amsterdam: Elsevier Science Publishers.

Hornik, R. C. (1975). Television, background characteristics, and learning in El Salvador's educational reform. *Instructional Science, 4,* 293–302.

Hornik, R. C. (1980). Communication as complement in development. *Journal of Communication, 30*(1), 10–24.

Hurt, H. T., & Tiegen, C. W. (1977). The development of a measure of perceived organizational innovativeness. In B. D. Ruben (Ed.), *Communication yearbook 1* (pp. 377–385). New Brunswick, NJ: Transaction Books.

Hyman, H. H., & Sheatsley, P. B. (1947). Some reasons why information campaigns fail. *Public Opinion Quarterly, 11,* 412–423.

Jeffres, L. W., & Quarles, R. (1984). A panel study of news diffusion. *Journalism Quarterly, 60,* 722–724.

Kanter, R. M. (1988). Three tiers for innovation research. *Communication Research, 15,* 509–523.

Katz, E. (1957). The two-step flow of communication: An up-to-date report on an hypothesis. *Public Opinion Quarterly, 21,* 61–78.

Katz, E. (1960). Communication research and the image of society: Convergence of two traditions. *American Journal of Sociology, 65,* 435–440.

Katz, E. (1962). The social itinerary of social change: Two studies on the diffusion of innovation. *Human Organization, 20,* 70–82.

Katz, E. (1968). Diffusion: Interpersonal influence. In D. L. Dills (Ed.), *International encyclopedia of the social sciences, vol. 4* (pp. 178–185). New York: Macmillan & Free Press.

Katz, E., Lazarsfeld, P. F. (1955). *Personal influence: The part played by people in the flow of mass communications.* New York: Free Press.

Katzman, N. (1974). The impact of communication technology: Promises and prospects. *Journal of Communication, 24*(1), 47–58.

Kendall, R. (1996). *Public relations campaign strategies: Planning for implementation* (2nd ed.). New York: HarperCollins College Publishers.

Kepplinger, H. M., Levendel, A., Livolsi, M., & Wober, M. (1987). More than learning: The diffusion of the news on the assassination of Olof Palme in England, Germany, Italy, and Hungary. *European Journal of Communication, 2,* 185–195.

Kobrin, S. J. (1985). Diffusion as an explanation of oil nationalization or the domino effect rides again. *Journal of Conflict Resolution, 29*(3), 3–32.

Kopfman, J. E., & Smith, S. W. (1996). Understanding the audiences of a health communication campaign: A discriminant analysis of potential organ donors based on intent to donate. *Journal of Applied Communication Research, 24,* 33–49.

Krendal, K. A., Olson, B., & Burke, R. (1992). Preparing for the environmental decade: A field experiment on recycling behavior. *Journal of Applied Communication Research, 20,* 19–36.

Kubey, R. W., & Peluso, T. (1990). Emotional response as a cause of interpersonal news diffusion: The case of the space shuttle tragedy. *Journal of Broadcasting and Electronic Media, 34,* 69–76.

LaRose, R., & Mettler, J. (1989). Who uses information technologies in rural America? *Journal of Communication, 39*(3), 48–60.

Larson, O. N., & Hill, R. J. (1954). Mass media and interpersonal communication in the diffusion of a news event. *American Sociological Review, 19,* 426–433.

Lazarsfeld, P. F., Berelson, B., & Gaudet, H. (1944). *The people's choice: How the voter makes up his mind in a presidential election.* New York: Duell, Sloan, and Pearce; reprinted 1948, 1968, New York: Columbia University Press.

Leonard–Barton, D. (1988). Implementation characteristics of organizational innovations: Limits and opportunities for management strategies. *Communication Research, 15,* 603–631.

Levy, S. S. (1969). How population subgroups differed in knowledge of six assassinations. *Journalism Quarterly, 46,* 685–698.

Lewis, L. K., & Siebold, D. R. (1983). Innovation modification during intraorganizational adoption. *Academy of Management Review, 18,* 322–354.

Lewis, L. K., & Siebold, D. R. (1996). Communication during intraorganizational innovation adoption: Predicting users' behavioral coping responses to innovations in organizations. *Communication Monographs, 63,* 131–157.

Mahajan, V., Muller, E., & Bass, F. M. (1990). New product diffusion models in marketing: A review and directions for research. *Journal of Marketing, 54,* 1–26.

Manross, G. G., & Rice, R. E. (1986). Don't hang up! Organizational diffusion of the intelligent telephone. *Information and Management, 10*(3), 161–175.

Markus, M. L. (1987). Toward a 'critical mass' theory of interactive media: Universal access, interdependency, and diffusion. *Communication Research, 14,* 491–511.

Mayer, M. E., Gudykunst, W. B., Perrill, N. K., & Merrill, B. D. (1990). A comparison of competing models of the news diffusion process. *Western Journal of Communication, 54,* 113–123.

Mayo, J. K., Araujo E Oliveira, J. B., Rogers, E. M., Pinto Guimaraes, S. D., & Morett, F. (1984). The transfer of *Sesame Street* to Latin America. *Communication Research, 11,* 259–280.

McAnany, E. G. (1984). The diffusion of innovation: Why does it endure? *Critical Studies in Mass Communication, 1,* 439–442.

McLaurin, P. (1995). An examination of the effect of culture on pro-social messages directed at African-American at-risk youth. *Communication Monographs, 62,* 301–326.

McNelly, J. T., Rush, R. R., & Bishop, M. E. (1968). Cosmopolitan media usage in the diffusion of international affairs news. *Journalism Quarterly, 45,* 329–332.

McPhail, T. L. (1987). *Electrical colonialism: The future of international broadcasting and communication.* Newbury Park, CA: Sage.

Melkote, S. R. (1984). Communication constraints to adoption of agricultural innovations: An investigation of message biases. *Journal of Communication Inquiry, 8*(1), 59–70.

Mendelsohn, H. (1964). Broadcast vs. personal sources of information in emergent public crises: The presidential assassination. *Journal of Broadcasting, 8,* 147–156.

Mendelsohn, H. (1973). Some reasons why information campaigns can succeed. *Public Opinion Quarterly, 39,* 50–61.

Menzel, H. (1957). Public and private conformity under different conditions of acceptance in the group. *Journal of Abnormal and Social Psychology, 55,* 398–402.

Menzel, H., & Katz, E. (1955/1956). Social relations and innovation in the medical profession: The epidemiology of a new drug. *Public Opinion Quarterly, 19,* 338–352.

Miller, D. C. (1945). A research note on mass communication: How our community heard about the death of President Roosevelt. *American Sociological Review, 10,* 691–694.

Miller, K. I., & Monge, P. R. (1985). Social information and employee anxiety about organizational change. *Human Communication Research, 11,* 365–386.

Miller, V. D., Johnson, J. R., & Grau, J. (1994). Antecedents to willingness to participate in a planned organizational change. *Journal of Applied Communication Research, 22,* 59–80.

O'Keefe, G. J. (1985). "Taking a bite out of crime": The impact of a public information campaign. *Communication Research, 12,* 147–178.

O'Keefe, M. T. (1969). The first human heart transplant: A study of diffusion among doctors. *Journalism Quarterly, 46,* 237–242.

O'Keefe, R. D., Kernaghan, J. A., & Rubenstein, A. H. (1975). Group cohesiveness: A factor in the adoption of innovations among scientific work groups. *Small Group Behavior, 6,* 282–292.

Ostland, L. E. (1973). Interpersonal communication following McGovern's Eagleton Decision. *Public Opinion Quarterly, 37,* 751–755.

O'Sullivan, P. B. (1995). Computer networks and political participation: Santa Monica's teledemocracy project. *Journal of Applied Communication Research, 23,* 93–107.

Papa, M. J. (1990). Communication network patterns and employee performance with new technology. *Communication Research, 17,* 344–368.

Papa, M. J., & Tracy, K. (1988). Communicative indices of employee performance with new technologies. *Communication Research, 15,* 524–544.

Pelto, P. J. (1973). *The snowmobile revolution: Technology and social change in the Arctic.* Menlo Park, CA: Cummings.

Pemberton, H. E. (1936). The curve of culture diffusion rate. *American Sociological Review, 1,* 547–556.

Pemberton, H. E. (1937). The effect of a social crisis on the curve of diffusion. *American Sociological Review, 2,* 55–61.

Perlof, R. M. (1991). Effects of an AIDS communication campaign. *Journalism Quarterly, 68,* 638–643.

Peterson, T. R., Witte, K., Enkerlin–Hoeflich, E., Espericueta, L., Flora, J. T., Florey, N., Loughran, T., & Stuart, R. (1994). Using informant directed interviews to discover risk orientation: How formative evaluations based in interpretive analysis can improve persuasive safety campaigns. *Journal of Applied Communication Research, 22,* 199–215.

Pinelli, T. E., Barclay, R. O., Holland, M. P., Keene, M. L., & Kennedy, J. M. (1991a). Technological innovation and technical communications: Their place in aerospace engineering curricula. A survey of European, Japanese and US aerospace engineers and scientists. *European Journal of Engineering Education, 16,* 337–351.

Pinelli, T. E., Barclay, R. O., & Kennedy, J. M. (1993). The U.S. government technical report and the transfer of federally funded aerospace R&D. *Government Publications Review, 20,* 393–411.

Pinelli, T. E., Bishop, A. P., Barclay, R. O., & Kennedy, J. M. (1992). The electronic transfer of information and aerospace knowledge diffusion. *International Forum on Information and Documentation, 17*(4), 8–16.

Pinelli, T. E., Bishop, A. P., Barclay, R. O., & Kennedy, J. M. (1993). The information-seeking behavior of engineers. *Encyclopedia of library and information science, 52*(15), 167–201.

Pinelli, T. E., Glassman, N. A., Affelder, L. O., Hecht, L. M., Kennedy, J. M., & Barclay, R. O. (1994). Technical uncertainty as a correlate of information use by U.S. industry-affiliated aerospace engineers and scientists. Paper 36, NASA/DOD Aerospace Knowledge Diffusion Research Project, presented January 11 at the 32nd Aerospace Sciences meeting and exhibit of the American Institute of Aeronautics and Astronautics, Reno, NV.

Pinelli, T. E., Kennedy, J. M., & Barclay, R. O. (1991). The NASA/DOD aerospace knowledge diffusion research project. *Government Information Quarterly, 8*(2), 219–233.

Pinelli, T. E., Kennedy, J. M., & Barclay, R. O. (1993). The role of the information intermediary in the diffusion of aerospace knowledge. *Science and Technology Libraries, 11*(2), 59–76.

Pinelli, T. E., Kennedy, J. M., Barclay, R. O., & White, T. F. (1991b). Aerospace knowledge diffusion research. In R. Jones (Ed.), *World aerospace technology '91* (pp. 31–34). London: Sterling Publications International.

Quarles, R., Jeffres, L. W., Sanchez, C. I., & Neuwirth, K. (1983). News diffusion of assassination attempts on President Reagan and Pope John Paul II. *Journal of Broadcasting, 27,* 387–394.

Rice, R. E. (1993). Using network concepts to clarify sources and mechanisms of social influence. In W. D. Richards & G. A. Barnett (Eds.), *Progress in the communication sciences XII* (pp. 44–62). Norwood, NJ: Ablex.

Rice, R. E., & Aydin, C. (1991). Attitudes toward new organizational technology: Network proximity as a mechanism for social information processing. *Administrative Science Quarterly, 36,* 219–244.

Rice, R. E., & Manross, G. (1986). The case of the intelligent telephone: The role of job category to the adoption of an organizational communication technology. In M. McLaughlin (Ed.), *Communication Yearbook 10* (pp. 727–742). Newbury Park, CA: Sage.

Rice, R. E., & Rogers, E. M. (1980). Re-invention in the innovation process. *Knowledge, 1,* 449–514.

Richmond, V. P. (1977). The relationship between opinion leadership and information acquisition. *Human Communication Research, 4,* 38–43.

Richmond, V. P. (1980). Monomorphic and polymorphic opinion leadership within a relatively closed communication system. *Human Communication Research, 6,* 111–116.

Riffe, D., & Stovall, J. G. (1987). Diffusion of news of the shuttle disaster: What role for emotional response? *Journalism Quarterly, 64,* 551–556.

Rogers, E. M. (1958). Categorizing the adopters of agricultural practices. *Rural Sociology, 23,* 345–354.

Rogers, E. M. (1962). *Diffusion of innovations.* New York: The Free Press.

Rogers, E. M. (1965/1966). Mass media exposure and modernization among Colombian peasants. *Public Opinion Quarterly, 29,* 614–625.

Rogers, E. M. (1971). *Communication of innovations: A cross-cultural approach* (2nd ed.). New York: Free Press.

Rogers, E. M. (1973). *Communication strategies for family planning.* New York. Free Press.

Rogers, E. M. (1976a). Communication and development: The passing of the dominant paradigm. *Communication Research, 3,* 121–148.

Rogers, E. M. (1976b). Where are we in understanding the diffusion of innovations? In W. Schramm & D. Lerner (Eds.), *Communication and change: The last ten years—and the next.* Honolulu: University Press of Hawaii.

Rogers, E. M. (1977). Network analysis of the diffusion of innovations: Family planning in Korean villages. In D. Lerner & L. M. Nelson (Eds.), *Communication research: A half-century appraisal* (pp. 117–147). Honolulu: University Press of Hawaii.

Rogers, E. M. (1983). *Diffusion of innovations* (3rd ed.). New York: Free Press.

Rogers, E. M. (1985). The diffusion of home computers among households in Silicon Valley. *Marriage and Family Review, 8,* 89–101.

Rogers, E. M. (1994). *A history of communication study: A biographical approach.* New York: Free Press.

Rogers, E. M. (1995). *Diffusion of innovations* (4th ed.). New York: Free Press.

Rogers, E. M., & Antola, L. (1985). *Telenovelas:* A Latin American success story. *Journal of Communication, 35*(4), 24–35.

Rogers, E. M., Ashcroft, J. R., & Roling, N. G. (1970). *Diffusion of innovations in Brazil, Nigeria, and India: Department of Communication Research Report No. 24.* East Lansing, MI: Department of Communication.

Rogers, E., Burdge, R., Korsching, P., & Donnermeyer, J. (1988). *Social change in rural societies.* Englewood Cliffs, NJ: Prentice-Hall.

Rogers, E. M., & Dearing, J. W. (1988). Agenda-setting research: Where has it been, where is it going? In J. Anderson (Ed.), *Communication Yearbook 11* (pp. 555–593). Newbury Park, CA: Sage.

Rogers, E. M., Dearing, J. W., & Chang, S. (1991). *AIDS in the 1980s: The agenda-setting process for a public issue. Journalism Monographs 126.* Columbia, SC: Association for Education in Journalism and Mass Communication.

Rogers, E. M., Dearing, J. W., Rao, N., Campo, S., Meyer, G., Betts, G. J. F., Casey, M. K. (1995). Communication and community in a city under siege: The AIDS epidemic in San Francisco. *Communication Research, 22,* 664–678.

Rogers, E. M., & Kincaid, D. L. (1981). *Communication networks: Toward a new paradigm for research.* New York: Free Press.

Rogers, E. M., with Shoemaker, F. F. (1971). *Communication of innovations: A cross-cultural approach* (2nd ed.). New York: Free Press.

Rogers, E. M., & Storey, J. D. (1987). Communication campaigns. In C. R. Berger & S. H. Chaffee (Eds.), *Handbook of communication science* (pp. 817–846). Newbury Park, CA: Sage.

Roling, N. G., Ashcroft, J., & Chege, F. W. (1976). The diffusion of innovations and the issue of equity in rural development. *Communication Research, 3,* 155–170.

Rosengren, K. E. (1987a). Introduction to a special issue on news diffusion. *European Journal of Communication, 2,* 135–142.

Rosengren, K. E. (1987b). The comparative study of news diffusion. *European Journal of Communication, 2,* 227–255.

Rubinyi, R. M. (1989). Computers and community: The organizational impact. *Journal of Communication, 39*(3), 110–123.

Ryan, B., & Gross, N. C. (1943). The diffusion of hybrid seed corn in two Iowa communities. *Rural Sociology, 8,* 15–24.

Schmitz, J., Rogers, E. M., Phillips, K., & Paschal, D. (1995). The public electronic network (PEN) and the homeless in Santa Monica. *Journal of Applied Communication Research, 23,* 26–43.

Schooler, C., Flora, J. A., & Farquhar, J. W. (1993). Moving toward synergy: Media supplementation in the Stanford five-city project. *Communication Research, 20,* 587–610.

Schramm, W. (1971, April). Communication in family planning. *Reports on Population/Family Planning (A Publication of the Population Council), 7,* 1–43.

Seeman, M. (1966). Alienation, membership and political knowledge: A comparative study. *Public Opinion Quarterly, 30,* 352–367.

Sheatsley, P. B., & Feldman, J. J. (1964). The assassination of President Kennedy: A preliminary report on public reactions and behavior. *Public Opinion Quarterly, 28,* 189–215.

Sheatsley, P. B., & Feldman, J. J. (1965). A national survey of public reactions and behavior. In B. S. Greenberg & E. B. Parker (Eds.), *The Kennedy assassination and the American public* (pp. 149–177). Stanford, CA: Stanford University Press.

Shingi, P. M., & Mody, B. (1976). The communication effects gap: A field experiment on television and agricultural ignorance in India. *Communication Research, 3,* 171–190.

Shoemaker, P. J., Wanta, W., & Leggett, D. (1989). Drug coverage and public opinion, 1972–1986. In P. J. Shoemaker (Ed.), *Communication campaigns about drugs* (pp. 67–80). Hillsdale, NJ: Erlbaum.

Singer, E., Rogers, T. F., & Glassman, M. B. (1991). Public opinion about AIDS before and after the 1988 U.S. government public information campaign. *Public Opinion Quarterly, 55,* 161–179.

Singhal, A., & Rogers, E. M. (1988). Television soap operas for development in India. *Gazette, 41,* 109–126.

Singhal, A., & Rogers, E. M. (1989). Pre-social television for development in India. In E. Rice & C. Atkin (Eds.), *Public communication campaigns* (2nd ed., pp. 331–350). Newbury Park, CA: Sage.

Smith, K. A. (1987). Newspaper coverage and public concern about community issues: A time-series analysis. *Journalism Monographs, 101,* 1–32.

Snyder, L. B. (1990). Channel effectiveness over time and knowledge and behavior gaps. *Journalism Quarterly, 67,* 875–886.

Sparkes, V. M., & Kang, N. J. (1986). Public reactions to cable television: Time in the diffusion process. *Journal of Broadcasting and Electronic Media, 30,* 213–299.

Spitzer, S. P., & Spitzer, N. S. (1965). Diffusion of news of the Kennedy and Oswald deaths. In B. S. Greenberg & E. B. Parker (Eds.), *The Kennedy assassination and the American public* (pp. 99–111). Stanford, CA: Stanford University Press.

Star, S. A., & Hughes, H. G. (1950). Report on an education campaign: The Cincinnati plan for the United Nations. *American Journal of Sociology, 55,* 389–400.

Starosta, W. J. (1976). The village worker as rhetorician: An adaptation of diffusion theory. *Central States Speech Journal, 27,* 144–150.

Stauffer, J., Frost, R., & Rybolt, W. (1978). Literacy, illiteracy, and learning from television news. *Communication Research, 5,* 221–232.

Steinfatt, T. M., Gantz, W., Seibold, D. R., & Miller, L. D. (1973). News diffusion of the George Wallace shooting: The apparent lack of interpersonal communication as an artifact of delayed measurement. *Quarterly Journal of Speech, 59,* 401–412.

Sultan, F., Farley, J. U., & Lehmann, D. R. (1990). A meta-analysis of diffusion models. *Journal of Marketing Research, 37,* 70–77.

Suominen, E. (1976). Who needs information and why. *Journal of Communication, 26*(4), 115–119.

Tarde, G. (1903). *The laws of imitation.* (E. C. Parsons, Trans.). New York: Holt.

Troldahl, V. C., & Van Dam, R. (1965). Face-to-face communication about major topics in the news. *Public Opinion Quarterly, 29,* 626–634.

Tichenor, P. J., Donohue, G. A., & Olien, C. N. (1970). Mass media flow and differential growth in knowledge. *Public Opinion Quarterly, 34,* 159–170.

Tichenor, P. J., Olien, C. N., Donahue, G. A. (1973). Mass media communication research: Evolution of a model. *Journalism Quarterly, 50,* 419–425.

Tjosvold, D., & McNeely, L. T. (1988). Innovation through communication in an educational bureaucracy. *Communication Research, 15,* 568–581.

Valente, T. W. (1993). Diffusion of innovations and policy decision-making. *Journal of Communication, 43*(1), 30–45.

Valente, T. W. (1995). *Network models of the diffusion of innovations.* Cresskill, NJ: Hampton Press.

Valente, T. W., Kim, Y. A., Lettenmaier, C., Glass, W., & Dibba, Y. (1994). Radio and the promotion of family planning in The Gambia. *International Family Perspectives Planning, 20*(3), 96–100.

Van de Ven, A. H., & Rogers, E. M. (1988). Innovations and organizations: Critical perspectives. *Communication Research, 15,* 632–651.

Wade, S., & Schramm, W. (1969). The mass media as sources of public affairs, science, and health knowledge. *Public Opinion Quarterly, 33,* 197–209.

Wall, V. D., & McCain, T. A. (1975). River Ridge I: Structural elements in a school district's collective innovation–decision. *Human Communication Research, 1,* 345–352.

Walton, R. (1987). *Innovating to compete.* San Francisco: Jossey–Bass.

Weaver–Lariscy, R. A., Sweeney, B., & Steinfatt, T. (1984). Communication during assassination attempts: Diffusion of information in attacks on President Reagan and the Pope. *Southern Speech Communication Journal, 49,* 258–276.

Weibull, L., Lindahl, R., Rosengren, K. E. (1987). News diffusion in Sweden: The role of the media. *European Journal of Communication, 2,* 143–170.

Wellin, E. (1955). Water boiling in a Peruvian town. In B. D. Paul (Ed.), *Health, culture, and community* (pp. 127–157). New York: Russell Sage Foundation.

Werner, A. (1975). A case of sex and class socialization. *Journal of Communication, 25*(4), 45–50.

Wildemuth, B. M. (1992). An empirically grounded model of the adoption of intellectual technologies. *Journal of the American Society for Information Science, 43,* 210–224.

Williams, F., & Lindsay, H. (1971). Ethnic and social class differences in communication habits and attitudes. *Journalism Quarterly, 48,* 672–678.

Witte, K., Stokols, D., Ituarte, P., & Schneider, M. (1993). Testing the health belief model in a field study to promote bicycle safety helmets. *Communication Research, 20,* 564–586.

Woods, G. B. (1993). Merchandising Malcolm X: Melding man and myths for money. *Western Journal of Black Studies, 17*(1), 44–51.

Zelizer, B. (1995). Journalism's "last" stand: Wirephoto and the discourse of resistance. *Journal of Communication, 45*(2), 78–92.

Zhu, J. H., Watt, J. H., Snyder, L. B., Yan, J., & Jiang, Y. (1993). Public issue priority formation: Media agenda-setting and social interaction. *Journal of Communication, 43*(1), 8–29.

Chapter 8   Interpersonal and Small Group Communication Context Theories

Alberts, J. K., Kellar–Guenther, Y., and Corman, S. R. (1996). That's not funny: Understanding recipients' responses to teasing. *Western Journal of Communication, 60,* 337–357.

Arnett, R. C. (1981). Toward a phenomenological dialogue. *Western Journal of Speech Communication, 45,* 201–212.

Bales, R. F. (1950). *Interaction process analysis: A method for the study of small groups.* Cambridge, MA: Addison-Wesley.

Bales, R. F. (1970). *Personality and interpersonal behavior.* New York: Holt, Rinehart and Winston.

Bales, R. F., & Slater, P. E. (1955). Role differentiation in small decision-making groups. In T. Parsons, et al. (Eds.), *The family, socialization, and interaction process* (pp. 259–306). Glencoe, IL: Free Press.

Bales, R. F., & Strodtbeck, F. L. (1951). Phases in group problem-solving. *Journal of Abnormal Psychology, 46,* 485–495.

Ball, M. A. (1994). Vacillating about Vietnam: Secrecy, duplicity, and confusion in the communication of President Kennedy and his advisors. In L. R. Frey (Ed.), *Group communication in context: Studies in natural groups* (pp. 181–198). Hillsdale, NJ: Erlbaum.

Barnland, D. C. (1962). Toward a meaning-centered philosophy of communication. *Journal of Communication, 11,* 197–211.

Baxter, L. A. (1988). A dialectic perspective on communication strategies in relationship development. In S. W. Duck, D. F. Hay, S. E. Hobfoll, W. Iches, & B. Montgomery (Eds.), *Handbook of personal relationships: Theory, research and interventions* (pp. 257–288). Chichester, UK: Wiley.

Baxter, L. A. (1990). Dialectical contradictions in relationship development. *Journal of Social and Personal Relationships, 7,* 69–88.

Baxter, L. A. (1992a). Forms and functions of intimate play in personal relationships. *Human Communication Research, 18,* 336–363.

Baxter, L. A. (1992b). Interpersonal communication as dialogue: A response to the 'social approaches' forum. *Communication Theory, 2,* 330–337.

Baxter, L. A. (1993). A dialectical perspective on communication strategies in relationship development. In S. Duck (Ed.), *A handbook of personal relationships* (pp. 257–273). New York: Wiley.

Baxter, L. A., & Dindia, K. (1987). Strategies for maintaining and repairing marital relationships. *Journal of Social and Personal Relationships, 4,* 143–158.

Baxter, L. A., & Dindia, K. (1990). Marital partners' perceptions of marital maintenance strategies. *Journal of Social and Personal Relationships, 7,* 187–208.

Baxter, L. A., & Montgomery, B. M. (1996). *Relating: Dialogues and dialectics.* New York: Guilford.

Baxter, L. A., & Philpott, J. (1982). Attribution-based strategies for initiating and terminating friendships. *Communication Quarterly, 30,* 217–224.

Baxter, L. A., & Simon, E. P. (1993). Relationship maintenance strategies and dialectical contradictions in personal relationships. *Journal of Social and Personal Relationships, 10,* 225–242.

Baxter, L. A., & Wilmot, W. (1984). Secret tests: Social strategies for acquiring information about the state of the relationship. *Human Communication Research, 11,* 171–201.

Beatty, M. J. (1987). Cognitive backlog and decision rule use. *Communication Research Reports, 4,* 79–81.

Beatty, M. J. (1988). Increasing students' choice-making consistency: The effect of decision rule-use training. *Communication Education, 37,* 95–105.

Benne, K. D., & Sheats, P. (1948). Functional roles of group members. *Journal of Social Issues, 4,* 41–49.

Berg, D. M. (1967a). A descriptive analysis of the distribution and duration of themes discussed by task-oriented small groups. *Speech Monographs, 34,* 172–175.

Berg, D. M. (1967b). A thematic approach to the analysis of the task-oriented small group. *Central States Speech Journal, 18,* 285–291.

Billingsley, J. (1993). An evolution of the functional perspective in small group communication. In S. A. Deetz (Ed.), *Communication Yearbook 16* (pp. 615–622). Newbury Park, CA: Sage.

Bormann, E. G. (1969). *Discussion and group methods.* New York: Harper & Row.

Bormann, E. G. (1970a). Pedagogic space: A strategy for teaching discussion. *Speech Teacher, 19,* 272–277.

Bormann, E. G. (1970b). The paradox and promise of small group research. *Speech Monographs, 37,* 211–217.

Bormann, E. G. (1975). *Discussion and group methods: Theory and practice* (2nd ed.). New York: Harper & Row.

Bormann, E. G. (1980a). *Communication theory.* New York: Holt, Rinehart and Winston.

Bormann, E. G. (1980b). The paradox and promise of small group communication revisited. *Central States Speech Journal, 31,* 214–220.

Bormann, E. G. (1990). *Small group communication: Theory and practice* (3rd ed.). New York: Harper-Collins.

Bormann, E. G., & Bormann, N. C. (1972a). *Effective small group communication.* Minneapolis: Burgess.

Bormann, E. G., & Bormann, N. C. (1972b). *Speech communication: An interpersonal approach.* New York: Harper & Row.

Bormann, E. G., & Bormann, N. C. (1988). *Effective small group communication* (4th ed.). Minneapolis: Burgess.

Bormann, E. G., Bormann, E., & Harty, K. C. (1995). Using symbolic convergence theory and focus group interviews to develop communication designed to stop teenage usage of tobacco. In L. R. Frey (Ed.), *Innovations in group facilitation* (pp. 200–232). Cresskill, NJ: Hampton Press and the Speech Communication Association.

Bormann, E. G., Pratt, J., & Putnam, L. L. (1978). Power, authority, and sex: Male response to female leadership. *Communication Monographs, 45,* 119–155.

Braithwaite, D. O., & Baxter, L. A. (1995). 'I do' again: The relational dialectics of renewing marriage vows. *Journal of Social and Personal Relationships, 12,* 177–198.

Branham, R. J., & Pearce, W. B. (1985). Between test and context: Toward a rhetoric of contextual reconstruction. *Quarterly Journal of Speech, 71,* 19–36.

Brown, P. (1990). Politeness theory: Exemplar and exemplary. In I. Rock (Ed.), *The legacy of Solomon*

Asch: Essays in cognition and social psychology (pp. 23–38). Hillsdale, NJ: Erlbaum.

Brown, P., & Levinson, S. (1978). Universals in language usage: Politeness phenomena. In E. N. Goody (Ed.), *Questions and politeness: Strategies in social interaction* (pp. 256–289). Cambridge: Cambridge University Press.

Brown, P., & Levinson, S. (1987). *Politeness: Some universals in language usage.* Cambridge: Cambridge University Press.

Buber, M. (1958). *I and thou* (2nd. ed., R. G. Smith, trans.). New York: Harper & Row.

Buber, M. (1963). *Pointing the way* (M. S. Friedman, ed., Friedman & R. G. Smith trans.). New York: Harper & Row.

Buber, M. (1965). *The knowledge of man* (R. G. Smith, ed. & trans.). New York: Harper & Row.

Buchli, V., & Pearce, W. B. (1974). Listening behavior in coorientational states. *Journal of Communication, 24*(3), 62–70.

Burleson, B. R., & Denton, W. H. (1992). A new look at similarity and attraction in marriage: Similarities in social-cognitive and communication skills as predictors of attraction and satisfaction. *Communication Monographs, 59,* 268–287.

Burleson, B. R., & Samter, W. (1990). Effects of cognitive complexity on the perceived importance of communication skills in friends. *Communication Research, 17,* 165–182.

Burleson, B. R., & Samter, W. (1996). Similarity in the communication skills of young adults: Foundations of attraction, friendship, and relationship satisfaction. *Communication Reports, 9,* 127–139.

Burleson, B. R., & Waltman, M. (1988). Cognitive complexity: Using the Role Category Questionnaire measure. In C. Tardy (Ed.), *A handbook for the study of human communication: Methods and instruments for observing, measuring, and assessing communication processes* (pp. 1–36). Norwood, NJ: Ablex.

Canary, D. J., Brossman, B. G., & Seibold, D. R. (1987). Argument structures in decision-making groups. *Southern Speech Communication Journal, 53,* 18–37.

Canary, D. J., & Stafford, L. (1994). Maintaining relationships through strategic and routine interaction. In D. J. Canary & L. Stafford (Eds.), *Communication and relational maintenance* (pp. 3–22). New York: Academic Press.

Carbaugh, D. (1994). Personhood, positioning, and cultural pragmatics: American dignity in cross-cultural perspective. In B. Burleson (Ed.). *Communication Yearbook 17* (pp. 159–186). Newbury Park, CA: Sage.

Chesebro, J. W., Cragan, J. F., & McCullough, P. W. (1973). The small group technique of the radical revolutionary: A synthetic study of consciousness-raising. *Communication Monographs, 40,* 136–146.

Clark, R. A., & Delia, J. G. (1976). The development of functional persuasive skills in childhood and early adolescents. *Child Development, 47,* 1008–1014.

Clark, R. A., & Delia. J. G. (1977). Cognitive complexity, social perspective-taking, and functional persuasive skills in second- to ninth-grade children. *Human Communication Research, 3,* 128–134.

Cline, R. J. W. (1994). Groupthink and the Watergate cover-up: The illusion of unanimity. In L. R. Frey (Ed.), *Group communication in context: Studies of natural groups* (pp. 199–223). Hillsdale, NJ: Erlbaum.

Comadena, M. E. (1984). Brainstorming groups: Ambiguity, tolerance, communication apprehension, task attraction, and individual productivity. *Small Group Behavior, 15,* 251–254.

Contractor, N. S., & Seibold, D. R. (1993).Theoretical frameworks for the study of structuring processes in group decision support systems: Adaptive structuration theory and self-organizing systems theory. *Human Communication Research, 19,* 528–563.

Coon, A. M. (1957). Brainstorming—A creative problem-solving technique. *Journal of Communication, 7,* 111–118.

Cragan, J. F., & Shields, D. C. (1995). Using SCT-based focus group interviews to do applied communication research. In L. Frey (Ed.), *Innovations in group facilitation: Applications in natural settings* (pp. 233–256). Cresskill, NJ: Hampton Press and the Speech Communication Association.

Cragan, J. F., Shields, D. C., & Wright, D. H. (1996). A unified theory of small group communication. In J. F. Cragan & D. W. Wright (Eds.), *Theory and research in small group communication* (2nd. ed., pp. 69–91). Edina, MN: Burgess.

Cragan, J. F., & Wright, D. W. (1980). Small group communication research of the 1970s: A synthesis and critique. *Central States Speech Journal, 31,* 197–213.

Cragan, J. F., & Wright, D. W. (1990). Small group communication research of the 1980s: A synthesis and critique. *Communication Studies, 41,* 212–236.

Cragan, J. F., & Wright, D. W. (1993). The functional theory of small group decision-making: A replication. *Journal of Social Behavior and Personality, 8,* 165–174.

Cragan, J. F., & Wright, D. W. (1995). *Small group communication: Theory, process, and skills* (4th ed.). St. Paul, MN: West.

Crockett, W. H. (1965). Cognitive complexity and impression formation. In B. A. Maher (Ed.), *Progress in experimental personality research* (vol. 2, pp. 47–90). New York: Academic Press.

Crockett, W. H., Press, A. N., Delia, J. G., & Kenny, C. T. (1974). *The structural analysis of written impressions.* Lawrence, KS: Department of Psychology, University of Kansas (mimeo).

Cronen, V. E., Chen, V., & Pearce, W. B. (1988). Coordinated management of meaning: A critical theory. In J. Y. Kim & W. Gudykunst (Eds.), *Theories in intercultural communication* (pp. 66–98). Beverly Hills, CA: Sage.

Cronen, V. E., Johnson, K. M., & Lannamann, J. W. (1982). Paradoxes, double binds, and reflexive loops: An alternative theoretical perspective. *Family Process, 2,* 91–112.

Cronen, V. E., Pearce, W. B., & Harris, L. M. (1979). The logic of the coordinated management of meaning: A rules-based approach to the first course in interpersonal communication. *Communication Education, 28,* 22–38.

Cronen, V. E., Pearce, W. B., & Harris, L. M. (1982). The coordinated management of meaning: A theory of communication. In F. E. X. Dance (Ed.), *Human communication theory* (pp. 61–89). New York: Harper & Row.

Crowell, L., & Scheidel, T. M. (1961). Categories for analysis of idea development in discussion groups. *Journal of Social Psychology, 54,* 155–168.

Cupach, W. R. (1994). Social predicaments. In W. R. Cupach & B. H. Spitzberg (Eds.), *The dark side of interpersonal communication* (pp. 159–180). Hillsdale, NJ: Erlbaum.

Cupach, W. R., & Imahori, T. (1993a). Identity management theory: Communication competence in intercultural episodes and relationships. In R. L. Wiseman & J. Koester (Eds.), *International and intercultural communication annual 17: Intercul-tural communication competence* (pp. 112–131). Newbury Park, CA: Sage.

Cupach, W. R., & Imahori, T. (1993b). Managing social predicaments created by others: A comparison of Japanese and American facework. *Western Journal of Communication, 57,* 431–444.

Cupach, W. R., & Metts, S. (1990). Remedial processes in embarrassing predicaments. In J. A. Anderson (Ed.), *Communication Yearbook 13* (pp. 323–352). Newbury Park, CA: Sage.

Cupach, W. R., & Metts, S. (1992). The effects of type of predicament and embarrassability on remedial responses to embarrassing situations. *Communication Quarterly, 40,* 149–161.

Cupach, W. R., & Metts, S. (1994). *Facework.* Thousand Oaks, CA: Sage.

Cupach, W. R., Metts, S., & Hazelton, V. (1986). Coping with embarrassing predicaments: Remedial strategies and their perceived utility. *Journal of Language and Social Psychology, 5,* 181–200.

Delia, J. G. (1977). Constructivism and the study of human communication. *Quarterly Journal of Speech, 63,* 66–83.

Delia, J. G., & Clark, R. A. (1977). Cognitive complexity, social perception, and the development of listener-adapted communication in six-, eight-, and twelve-year-old boys. *Communication Monographs, 44,* 326–345.

Delia, J. G., Clark, R. A., & Switzer, D. E. (1979). Cognitive complexity and impression formation in informal social interaction. *Communication Monographs, 41,* 199–308.

Delia, J. G., & Crockett, W. H. (1973). Social schemas, cognitive complexity, and the learning of social structures. *Journal of Personality, 41,* 413–429.

Delia, J. G., O'Keefe, B., & O'Keefe, D. (1982). The constructivist approach to communication. In F. Dance (Ed.), *Human communication theory* (pp. 147–191). New York: Harper & Row.

Dennis, A. R., Nunamaker, J. F., & Vogle, D. R. (1990–91). A comparison of laboratory and field research in the study of electronic meeting systems. *Journal of Management Information Systems, 7,* 107–135.

Dewey, J. (1910). *How we think.* New York: Heath.

Dickens, M., & Hefferman, M. (1949). Experimental research in group discussion. *Quarterly Journal of Speech, 35,* 23–29.

Dickson, G. W., Poole, M. S., & DeSanctis, G. (1992). An overview of the GDSS research project and the SAMM system. In R. P. Bostrom, R. T. Watson, & S. T. Kinney (Eds.), *Computer augmented teamwork: A guided tour* (pp. 163–179). New York: Van Nostrand Reinhold.

Dindia, K., & Baxter, L. A. (1987). Strategies for maintaining and repairing marital relationships. *Journal of Social and Personal Psychology, 4,* 143–158.

Emmers, T. M., & Hart, R. D. (1996). Romantic relationship disengagement and coping rituals. *Communication Research Reports, 13,* 8–18.

Fairhurst, G. T., Green, S. G., & Snavely, B. K. (1984). Face support in controlling poor performance. *Human Communication Research, 11,* 272–295.

Fisher, B. A. (1968). *Decision emergence: A process model of verbal task behavior for decision-making groups.* Unpublished Ph.D. dissertation, University of Minnesota.

Fisher, B. A. (1970a). Decision emergence: Phases in group decision-making. *Speech Monographs, 37,* 53–66.

Fisher, B. A. (1970b). The process of decision modification in small discussion groups. *Journal of Communication, 20,* 136–149.

Fisher, B. A. (1971). Communication research and the task-oriented group. *Journal of Communication, 21,* 136–149.

Fisher, B. A. (1974). *Small group decision-making.* New York: McGraw–Hill.

Fisher, B. A. (1980). *Small group decision-making* (2nd ed.). New York: McGraw–Hill.

Fisher, B. A., & Ellis, D. (1990). *Small group communication* (3rd ed.). New York: McGraw–Hill.

Fisher, B. A., & Hawes, L. C. (1971). An interact system model: Generating a grounded theory of small groups. *Quarterly Journal of Speech, 42,* 444–453.

Forston, R. (1968). *The decision-making process in the American civil jury: A comparative methodological investigation.* Unpublished Ph.D. dissertation, University of Minnesota.

Frey, L. R., (Ed.). (1994a). *Group communication and context: Studies of natural groups.* Hillsdale, NJ: Erlbaum.

Frey, L. R. (1994b). The naturalistic paradigm: Studying small groups in the postmodern era. *Small Group Research, 25,* 551–577.

Frey, L. R., (Ed.). (1995). *Innovations in group facilitation: Applications in natural settings.* Cresskill, NJ: Hampton Press and the Speech Communication Association.

Frey, L. R. (1996). Remembering and "re-remembering": A history of theory and research on communication and group decision-making. In R. Y. Hirokawa & M. S. Poole (Eds.), *Communication and group decision-making* (2nd ed., pp. 19–51). Newbury Park, CA: Sage.

Fromm, E. (1956). *The art of loving.* New York: Bantam Books.

Geier, J. (1963). *A descriptive analysis of an interaction pattern resulting in leadership emergence in leaderless group discussion.* Unpublished Ph.D. dissertation, University of Minnesota.

Geier, J. (1967). A trait approach in the study of leadership in small groups. *Journal of Communication, 17,* 316–323.

Giddens, A. (1976). *New rules of sociological method: A positive critique of interpretive sociologies.* New York: Basic Books.

Giddens, A. (1979). *Central problems in social theory: Action, structure and contradiction in social analysis.* London: Macmillan.

Giddens, A. (1984). *The constitution of society: Outline of the theory of structuration.* Berkeley: University of California Press.

Giffin, K., & Patton, B. R., (Eds.). (1971a). *Basic readings in interpersonal communication.* New York: Harper & Row.

Giffin, K., & Patton, B. R. (1971b). *Fundamentals of interpersonal communication.* New York: Harper & Row.

Goffman, E. (1959). *The presentation of self in everyday life.* New York: Overlook.

Goffman, E. (1967). *Interaction ritual: Essays on face-to-face behavior.* Garden City, NY: Anchor Books.

Goffman, E. (1971). *Relations in public.* New York: Basic Books.

Goldsmith, D. J., & Baxter, L. A. (1996). Constituting relationships in talk: A taxonomy of speech events in social and personal relationships. *Human Communication Research, 23,* 87–114.

Gouran, D. S. (1970a). Conceptual and methodological approaches to the study of leadership. *Central States Speech Journal, 21,* 217–223.

Gouran, D. S. (1970b). Response to 'The paradox and promise of small group research'. *Speech Monographs, 37,* 218–219.

Gouran, D. S. (1973). Group communication: Perspectives and priorities for future research. *Quarterly Journal of Speech, 59,* 22–29.

Gouran, D. S. (1982). *Making decisions in groups: Choices and consequences.* Glenview, IL: Scott, Foresman.

Gouran, D. S., & Hirokawa, R. Y. (1986). Counteractive functions of communication in effective group decision-making. In R. Y. Hirokawa & M. S. Poole (Eds.), *Communication and group decision-making* (pp. 81–90). Beverly Hills, CA: Sage.

Gourd, W. (1977). Cognitive complexity and theatrical information processing: Audience responses to plays and characters. *Communication Monographs, 44,* 136–151.

Hale, C. (1980). Cognitive complexity–simplicity as a determinant of communication effectiveness. *Communication Monographs, 47,* 304–311.

Hale, C., & Delia, J. G. (1976). Cognitive complexity and social perspective-taking. *Communication Monographs, 43,* 195–203.

Harris, L. M. (1979). *Communication competence: An argument for a systemic view.* Unpublished Ph.D. dissertation, University of Massachusetts.

Harris, L. M. (1980). Analysis of a paradoxical logic: A case study. *Family Process, 19,* 19–34.

Harris, L. M., & Cronen, V. E. (1979). A rules-based model for the analysis and evaluation of organizational communication. *Communication Quarterly, 27,* 12–28.

Hart, R. P., & Burks, D. M. (1972). Rhetorical sensitivity and social interaction. *Communication Monographs, 39,* 75–91.

Hewitt, J., & Stokes, R. (1975). Disclaimers. *American Sociological Review, 40,* 1–11.

Hirokawa, R. Y. (1985). Discussion procedures and decision-making performance: A test of a functional perspective. *Human Communication Research, 12,* 203–224.

Hirokawa, R. Y. (1987). Why informed groups make faulty decisions: An investigation of possible interaction-based explanations. *Small Group Behavior, 18,* 3–29.

Hirokawa, R. Y. (1988). Group communication and decision-making performance. *Human Communication Research, 14,* 487–515.

Hirokawa, R. Y. (1990). The role of communication in effective group decision-making: A task contingency perspective. *Small Group Behavior, 21,* 190–204.

Hirokawa, R. Y., Gouran, D. S., & Martz, A. E. (1988). Understanding the sources of faulty group decision-making: A lesson from the Challenger disaster. *Small Group Behavior, 19,* 411–433.

Hirokawa, R. Y., Ice, R., & Cook, J. (1988). Preference for procedural order, discussion structure, and group decision performance. *Communication Quarterly, 36,* 217–226.

Hirokawa, R. Y., & Pace, R. (1983). A descriptive investigation of the possible communication based reasons for effective and ineffective decision-making. *Communication Monographs, 50,* 363–379.

Hirokawa, R. Y., & Scheerhorn, D. R. (1986). Communication in faulty group decision-making. In R. Y. Hirokawa & M. S. Poole (Eds.), *Communication and group decision-making* (pp. 63–80). Beverly Hills, CA: Sage.

Ho, D. Y. F. (1976). On the concept of face. *American Journal of Sociology, 81,* 867–884.

Illardo, J. A. (1972). Why interpersonal communication? *Speech Teacher, 21,* 1–6.

Jablin, F. (1981). Cultivating imagination: Factors that enhance and inhibit creativity in brainstorming groups. *Human Communication Research, 7,* 245–258.

Jablin, F., Seibold, D. R., & Sorenson, R. L. (1977). Potential inhibitory effects of group participation on brainstorming performance. *Central States Speech Journal, 28,* 113–121.

Jablin, F., Sorenson, R. L., & Seibold, D. R. (1978). Interpersonal perception and group brainstorming performance. *Communication Quarterly, 26,* 36–44.

Janis, I. L. (1971, November). Groupthink. *Psychology Today, 5,* pp. 43–46 & 74–75.

Janis, I. L. (1972). *Victims of groupthink: Psychological studies of foreign policy decisions and fiascoes.* Boston: Houghton Mifflin.

Janis, I. L. (1983). *Groupthink: Psychological studies of policy decisions and fiascoes* (2nd ed.). Boston: Houghton Mifflin.

Janis, I. L. (1989). *Crucial decisions.* New York: Free Press.

Jenkins, D. H. (1961). Prediction in interpersonal communication. *Journal of Communication, 11,* 129–135.

Johannesen, R. L. (1971). The emerging concept of communication as dialogue. *Quarterly Journal of Speech, 57,* 373–382.

Jourard, S. (1967). *The transparent self.* New York: Van Nostrand Reinhold.

Kasch, C. R. (1996). Computer-mediation and group communication: A selective review of theory and research. In J. F. Cragan & D. W. Wright (Eds.), *Theory and research in small group communication* (pp. 133–146). Edina, MN: Burgess.

Kelley, H. H. (1950). The warm–cold variable in first impressions of persons. *Journal of Personality, 18,* 431–439.

Kelly, G. A. (1955). *The psychology of personal constructs.* New York: Norton.

Kelly, G. A. (1963). *A theory of personality.* New York: Norton.

Keltner, J. (1961). Communication in discussion and group processes: Some research trends of the decade 1950–59—Part II. *Journal of Communication, 11,* 27–83.

Keltner, J. W. (1970). *Interpersonal speech-communication.* Belmont, CA: Wadsworth.

Kline, S. L., & Ceropski, J. M. (1984). Person-centered communication in medical practice. In J. M. Phillips & J. T. Wood (Eds.), *Emergent issues in human decision-making* (pp. 120–141). Carbondale, IL: Southern Illinois University Press.

Knapp, M. L., Stafford, L., & Daly, J. (1986). Regrettable messages: Things people wish they hadn't said. *Journal of Communication, 36,* 40–58.

Kraemer, K. L., & Pinsonneault, A. (1990). Technology and groups: Assessments of the empirical research. In J. Galegher, R. E. Kraut, & C. Egido (Eds.), *Intellectual teamwork: Social and technological foundations of cooperative work* (pp. 373–405). Hillsdale, NJ: Erlbaum.

Larson, C. E. (1971). Speech communication research on small groups. *Speech Teacher, 20,* 89–107.

Larson, C. U. (1971). The verbal response of groups to the absence or presence of leadership. *Speech Monographs, 38,* 199–181.

Lewin, K. (1951). *Field theory in social science.* New York: Harper & Brothers.

Lim, T. S. (1990). Politeness behavior in social influence situations. In J. P. Dillard (Ed.), *Seeking compliance: The production of interpersonal influence messages* (pp. 75–86). Scottsdale, AZ: Gorusuch Scarisbrick.

Lim. T. S., & Bowers, J. W. (1991). Facework: Solidarity, approbation, and tact. *Human Communication Research, 17,* 415–450.

Maslow, A. (1962). *Toward a psychology of being.* Princeton, NJ: Van Nostrand.

Maslow, A. (1970). *Motivation and personality.* New York: Harper & Row.

May, R. (1967). *Man's search for himself.* New York: Signet Books.

McBurney, J. H., & Hance, K. G. (1939). *The principles and methods of discussion.* New York: Harper & Brothers.

McCroskey, J., Larson, C., & Knapp, M. (1971). *Introduction to interpersonal communication.* Englewood Cliffs, NJ: Prentice-Hall.

McLaughlin, M. L., Cody, M. J., & O'Hair, H. D. (1983). The management of failure events: Some contextual determinants of accounting behavior. *Human Communication Research, 9,* 208–224.

McPhee, R. D., Poole, M. S., & Seibold, D. R. (1982). The valence model unveiled: A critique and reformulation. In M. Burgoon (Ed.), *Communication yearbook 5* (pp. 259–278). New Brunswick, NJ: ICA-Transaction Press.

Metts, S. (1992). The language of disengagement: A face-management perspective. In T. L. Orbuch (Ed.), *Close relationship loss: Theoretical approaches* (pp. 111–127). New York: Springer– Verlag.

Metts, S. (1997). Face and facework: Implications for the study of personal relationships. In S. Duck (Ed.), *Handbook of personal relationships* (2nd ed., pp. 373–390). New York: John Wiley and Sons.

Metts, S., & Cupach, W. R. (1989a). The role of communication in human sexuality. In K. McKinney & S. Sprecher (Eds.), *Human sexuality: The societal and interpersonal context* (pp. 139–161). Norwood, NJ: Ablex.

Metts, S., & Cupach, W. R. (1989b). Situational influence on the use of remedial strategies in embarrassing predicaments. *Communication Monographs, 56,* 151–162.

Montgomery, B. M. (1992). Communication as the interface between couples and culture. In S. A. Deetz (Ed.), *Communication yearbook 15* (pp. 475–507). Newbury Park, CA: Sage.

Mortensen, C. D. (1966). Should the discussion group have an assigned leader? *Speech Teacher, 15,* 34–41.

Mortensen, C. D. (1970). The status of small group research. *Quarterly Journal of Speech, 56,* 304–309.

O'Keefe, B. J. (1984). The evolution of impressions in small working groups. Effects of construct differentiation. In H. Sypher & J. Applegate (Eds.), *Communication by children and adults: Social cognitive and strategic processes* (pp. 262–291). Beverly Hills, CA: Sage.

O'Keefe, B. J. (1988). The logic of message design: Individual differences in reasoning about communication. *Communication Monographs, 55,* 80–103.

O'Keefe, B. J. (1990). The logic of regulative communication: Understanding the rationality of message designs. In J. Dillard (Ed.), *Seeking compliance: The production of interpersonal influence messages* (pp. 87–106). Scottsdale, AZ: Gorusuch-Scarisbrick.

O'Keefe, B., & Delia, J. G. (1982). Impression formation in message production. In M. E. Roloff & C. R. Berger (Eds.), *Social cognition and communication* (pp. 33–72). Beverly Hills, CA: Sage.

O'Keefe, B. J., & McCornack, S. A. (1987). Message design logic and message goal structure: Effects on perceptions of message quality in regulative communication situations. *Human Communication Research, 14,* 68–92.

Osborn, A. (1959). *Applied imagination: Principles and procedures of creative thinking* (revised ed.). New York: Scribner's.

Pearce, W. B. (1977a). Naturalistic study of communication: Its function and form. *Communication Quarterly, 25,* 51–56.

Pearce, W. B. (1977b). Teaching interpersonal communication as a humane science: A comparative analysis. *Communication Education, 26,* 104–112.

Pearce, W. B. (1989). *Communication and the human condition.* Carbondale, IL: Southern Illinois University Press.

Pearce, W. B., & Conklin, F. (1979). A model of hierarchical meaning in coherent conversation and a study of 'indirect responses'. *Communication Monographs, 46,* 76–87.

Pearce, W. B., & Cronen, V. E. (1980). *Communication, action, and meaning: The creation of social realities.* New York: Praeger.

Pearce, W. B., Cronen, V. E., Johnson, K., Jones, G., & Raymond, R. (1980). The structure of communication rules and the form of conversation: An experimental simulation. *Western Journal of Speech Communication, 44,* 20–34.

Pearce, W. B., Littlejohn, S. W., & Alexander, A. (1987). The new Christian right and the humanist response: Reciprocated diatribe. *Communication Quarterly, 35,* 171–192.

Pearce, W. B., Wright, P. H., Sharp, S. M., & Slama, K. M. (1974). Affection and reciprocity in self-disclosing communication. *Human Communication Research, 1,* 5–14.

Peterson, L. W., & Albrecht, T. L. (1996). Message design logic, social support, and mixed-status relationships. *Western Journal of Communication, 60,* 291–309.

Petronio, S. (1984). Communication strategies to reduce embarrassment: Differences between men and women. *Western Journal of Speech Communication, 48,* 28–38.

Petronio, S. (1991). Communication boundary management: A theoretical model of managing disclosure of private information between marital couples. *Communication Theory, 1,* 311–335.

Petronio, S. (1994). Privacy binds in family interactions: The case of parental privacy invasion. In W. R. Cupach & B. H. Spitzberg (Eds.), *A dark side of interpersonal communication* (pp. 241–257). Hillsdale, NJ: Erlbaum.

Petronio, S., Olson, C., & Dollar, N. (1988). Relational embarrassment: Impact on relational quality and communication satisfaction. In H. D. O'Hair & B. R. Patterson (Eds.), *Advances in interpersonal communication research: Proceedings of the Western Speech Communication Association Interpersonal Communication Interest Group* (pp. 195–206). Las Cruces: New Mexico State University, Communication Resources Center.

Petronio, S., Reeder, H. M., Hecht, M. L., & Ros–Mendoza, T. M. (1996). Disclosure of sexual abuse by children and adolescents. *Journal of Applied Communication Research, 24,* 181–199.

Phillips, G. M. (1966). *Communication and the small group.* New York: Bobbs-Merrill.

Poole, M. S. (1981). Decision development in small groups I: A comparison of two models. *Communication Monographs, 48,* 1–24.

Poole, M. S. (1983a). Decision development in small groups II: A study of multiple sequences in decision-making. *Communication Monographs, 50,* 206–232.

Poole, M. S. (1983b). Decision development in small groups III: A multiple sequence model of group decision development. *Communication Monographs, 50,* 321–341.

Poole, M. S., & DeSanctis, G. (1990). Understanding the use of group decision support systems: The theory of adaptive structuration. In J. Fulk & C. Steinfield (Eds.), *Organizations and communication technology* (pp. 173–193). Beverly Hills, CA: Sage.

Poole, M. S., & DeSanctis, G. (1992). Microlevel structuration in computer-supported group decision-making. *Human Communication Research, 19,* 5–49.

Poole, M. S., Holmes, M., & DeSanctis, G. (1991). Conflict management in a computer-supported meeting environment. *Management Science, 37,* 926–953.

Poole, M. S., & Jackson, M. H. (1993). Communication theory and group support systems. In L. M. Jessup and J. S. Valacich (Eds.), *Group Support Systems* (pp. 281–293). New York: Macmillan.

Poole, M. S., McPhee, R. D., & Seibold, D. R. (1982). A comparison of normative and interactional explanations of group decision-making: Social decision schemes versus valence. *Communication Monographs, 49,* 1–19.

Poole, M. S., & Roth, J. (1989a). Decision development in small groups IV: A typology of group decision paths. *Human Communication Research, 15,* 323–356.

Poole, M. S., & Roth, J. (1989b). Decision development in small groups V: Test of a contingency model. *Human Communication Research, 15,* 549–589.

Poole, M. S., Seibold, D. R., & McPhee, R. D. (1985). Group decision-making as a structurational process. *Quarterly Journal of Speech, 71,* 74–102.

Poole, M. S., Seibold, D. R., & McPhee, R. D. (1986). A structurational approach to theory-building in group decision-making research. In R. Y. Hirokawa & M. S. Poole (Eds.), *Communication and group decision-making research* (pp. 237–264). Beverly Hills, CA: Sage.

Poulakos, J. (1974). The components of dialogue. *Western Speech, 38,* 199–212.

Powell, J., S.J. (1969). *Why am I afraid to tell you who I am?* Chicago: Argus Communications.

Propp, K. M., & Julian, K. M. (1994). Enhancing accurate information processing: An investigation of verbal information probes in decision-making. *Communication Reports, 7,* 145–152.

Putnam, L. (1979). Preference for procedural order in task-oriented small groups. *Communication Monographs, 46,* 193–218.

Putnam, L. L., & Stohl, C. (1990). Bona Fide Groups: A reconceptualization of groups in context. *Communication Studies, 41,* 248–265.

Rawlins, W. K. (1983a). Negotiating close friendship: The dialectic of conjunctive freedoms. *Human Communication Research, 9,* 255–266.

Rawlins, W. K. (1983b). Openness as problematic in ongoing friendships: Two conversational dilemmas. *Communication Monographs, 50,* 1–13.

Rawlins, W. K. (1989). A dialectical analysis of the tensions, functions, and strategic challenges of communication in young adult friendships. In (Ed.), *Communication yearbook 12* (pp. 157–189). Newbury Park, CA: Sage.

Rawlins, W. K. (1992). *Friendship matters: Communication, dialectics, and the life course.* New York: Aldine de Gruyter.

Richmond, J. F., & Buehler, R. E. (1962). Interpersonal communication: A theoretical formulation. *Journal of Communication, 12,* 3–10.

Rogers, C. (1961). *On becoming a person.* Boston: Houghton Mifflin.

Rogers, C. (1965). *Client-centered therapy: Its current practice, implications, and theory.* Boston: Houghton Mifflin.

Ross, R. S. (1974). *Speech communication: Fundamentals and Practice* (3rd ed.). New York: McGraw–Hill.

Sabourin, T. C., & Stamp, G. H. (1995). Communication and the experience of dialectical tensions in family life: An examination of abusive and nonabusive families. *Communication Monographs, 62,* 213–242.

Salazar, A. J., Hirokawa, R. Y., Propp, K. M., Julian, K. M., & Leatham, G. B. (1994). In search of true causes: Examination of the effect of group potential and group interaction on decision performance. *Human Communication Research, 20,* 529–559.

Sargent, J. F., & Miller, G. R. (1971). Some differences in certain communication behaviors of autocratic and democratic leaders. *Journal of Communication, 21,* 233–252.

Scheidel, T. M., & Crowell, L. (1964). Idea development in small groups. *Quarterly Journal of Speech, 50,* 140–145.

Schutz, W. (1958). *Firo: A three-dimensional theory of interpersonal behavior.* New York: Holt, Rinehart and Winston.

Seibold, D. R., & Meyers, R. A. (1986). Communication and influence in group decision-making. In R. Y. Hirokawa & M. S. Poole (Eds.), *Communication and group decision-making* (pp. 133–155). Beverly Hills, CA: Sage.

Sharkey, W. F., & Stafford, L. (1990). Responses to embarrassment. *Human Communication Research, 17,* 315–342.

Shields, D. C. (1981a). Dramatistic communication based focus group interviews. In J. F. Cragan & D. C. Shields (Eds.), *Applied communication research: A dramatistic approach* (pp. 313–319). Prospect Heights, IL: Waveland.

Shields, D. C. (1981b). Feed dealer focus group interviews on Shell's gestation litter conditioner. In J. F. Cragan & D. C. Shields (Eds.), *Applied communication research: A dramatistic approach* (pp. 335–349). Prospect Heights, IL: Waveland.

Shields, D. C. (1981c). Hog producer focus group interviews on Shell's gestation litter conditioner. In J. F. Cragan & D. C. Shields (Eds.), *Applied communication research: A dramatistic approach* (pp. 321–333). Prospect Heights, IL: Waveland.

Shields, D. C. (1981d). The St. Paul firefighters' *dramatis personae:* Concurrent and construct validation for the theory of rhetorical vision. In J. F. Cragan & D. C. Shields (Eds.), *Applied communication research: A dramatistic approach* (pp. 235–270). Prospect Heights, IL: Waveland.

Shields, D. C. (1988, November). *Communication-based focus group interviews: A speech communication association short-course manual.* Speech Communication Association annual meeting, Chicago, IL. (Available from D. C. Shields, Department of Communication, University of Missouri—St. Louis, 63121.)

Shields, D. C., & Kidd, V. V. (1973). Teaching through popular film: A small group analysis of *The Poseidon Adventure. Speech Teacher, 22,* 201–207.

Shimanoff, S. B. (1988). Degree of emotional expressiveness as a function of face-needs, gender, and interpersonal relationship. *Communication Reports, 1,* 43–53.

Simon, E. P., & Baxter, L. A. (1993). Attachment-Style differences in relationship maintenance strategies. *Western Journal of Communication, 57,* 416–430.

Sinclair-de-Zwart, H. (1969). Developmental psycholinguistics. In D. Elkind & J. H. Flavell (Eds.), *Studies in cognitive development: Essays in honor of Jean Piaget* (pp. 315–336). New York: Oxford University Press.

Stafford, L., & Canary, D. J. (1991). Maintenance strategies and romantic relationship type, gender, and relational characteristics. *Journal of Social and Personal Relationships, 8,* 217–242.

Stamm. K. R., & Pearce, W. B. (1971). Communication behavior and coorientational relations. *Journal of Communication, 21,* 208–220.

Stamm, K. R., & Pearce, W. B. (1974). Message locus and message content: Two studies in communication behavior and coorientational relations. *Communication Research, 1,* 184–203.

Stewart, J. (1972). An interpersonal approach to the basic course. *Speech Teacher, 21,* 7–14.

Stewart, J. (1973). *Bridges not walls: A book about interpersonal communication.* Reading, MA: Addison-Wesley.

Ting–Toomey, S. (1988). Intercultural conflict styles: A face-negotiation theory. In Y. Y. Kim & W. B. Gudykunst (Eds.), *Theories in intercultural communication* (pp. 213–235). Newbury Park, CA: Sage.

Ting–Toomey, S. (1993). Communication resourcefulness: An identity negotiation perspective. In R. L. Wiseman & J. Koester (Eds.), *Intercultural communication competence* (pp. 72–111). Newbury Park, CA: Sage.

Ting–Toomey, S. (1994). *The challenge of facework: cross-cultural and interpersonal issues.* Albany, NY: State University of New York Press.

Tracy, K. (1990). The many faces of facework. In H. Giles & W. P. Robinson (Eds.), *Handbook of language and social psychology* (pp. 209–223). Chichester, Eng: John Wiley.

Tracy, S., & Baratz, S. (1994). The case for case studies of facework. In S. Ting–Toomey (Ed.), *The challenge of facework: Cross-cultural and interpersonal issues* (pp. 287–305). Albany, NY: State University of New York Press.

VanLear, C. A., Jr. (1991). Testing a cyclical model of communicative openness in relationship development: Two longitudinal studies. *Communication Monographs, 58,* 337–361.

VanLear, C. A., Jr., & Zeitlow, P. H. (1990). Toward a contingency approach to marital interaction: An empirical integration of three approaches. *Communication Monographs, 57,* 202–218.

Werner, C. M., & Baxter, L. A. (1994). Temporal qualities of relationships: Organismic, transactional, and dialectical views. In M. L. Knapp & G. R. Miller (Eds.), *Handbook of interpersonal communication* (2nd ed., pp. 323–379). Thousand Oaks, CA: Sage.

White, R. K., & Lippett, R. (1960). *Autocracy and democracy: An experimental inquiry.* New York: Harper & Row.

Wilson, S. R., Cruz, M. G., & Kang, K. H. (1992). Is it always a matter of perspective? Construct differentiation and variability in attributions about compliance gaining. *Communication Monographs, 59,* 350–367.

Wise, C. N. (1972). A prolegomena to a study of the antecedents of interpersonal communication. *Today's Speech, 20*(4), 59–64.

Wolfson, K., & Pearce, W. B. (1983). A cross-cultural comparison of the implications of self-disclosure on conversational logics. *Communication Quarterly, 31,* 249–256.

Wood, J. T. (1995). *Relational communication: Continuity and change in personal relationships.* Belmont, CA: Wadsworth.

Wood, J. T., Dendy, L., Dordek, E., Germany, M., & Varallo, S. (1994). Dialectic of difference: A thematic analysis of intimates' meanings for differences. In K. Carter & M. Presnell (Eds.), *Interpretive approaches to interpersonal communication* (pp. 115–136). New York: SUNY Press.

Zima, P. (1971). Self-analysis inventory: An interpersonal communication exercise. *Speech Teacher, 20,* 108–114.

Zimmermann, S. (1994). Social cognition and evaluations of health care team communication. *Western Journal of Communication, 58,* 116–141.

Zimmermann, S., & Applegate, J. (1992). Person-centered comforting in the hospice interdisciplinary team. *Communication Research, 19,* 240–263.

Zorn, T. (1995). Bosses and buddies: Constructing and performing simultaneously hierarchical and close friendship relationships. In J. T. Wood & S. W. Duck (Eds.), *Understanding relationship process, 6: Off the beaten track: Understanding relationships* (pp. 122–147). Thousand Oaks, CA: Sage.

Chapter 9 *Public Speaking and Organizational Communication Context Theories*

Adams, H. M. (1938). Listening. *Quarterly Journal of Speech, 24,* 209–211.

Adams, J. Q. (1810). *Lectures on rhetoric and oratory: Delivered to the classes of senior and junior sophisters in Harvard University; In two volumes.* Cambridge: Hilliard and Metcalf. Reproduced with an introduction by J. J. Auer & J. L. Banninga (1962). New York: Russell & Russell.

Addington, D. W. (1965). The effect of mispronunciations on general speaking effectiveness. *Speech Monographs, 32,* 159–163.

Addington, D. W. (1968). The relationship of selected vocal characteristics to personality perception. *Speech Monographs, 35,* 492–503.

Allen, M., Hale, J., Mongeau, P., Berkowitz–Stafford, S., Stafford, S., Shanahan, W., Agee, P., Dillon, K., Jackson, R., & Ray, C. (1990). Testing a model of message sidedness: Three replications. *Communication Monographs, 57,* 275–291.

Anderson, J. A. (1991). The social action of organizing: Knowledge, practice and morality. *Australian Journal of Communication, 18,* 1–18.

Appel, E. C. (1987). The perfected drama of Reverend Jerry Falwell. *Communication Quarterly, 35,* 26–38.

Arnold, W. E., & McCroskey, J. C. (1967). The credibility of reluctant testimony. *Central States Speech Journal, 17,* 97–103.

Atwood, E. (1966). The effects of incongruity between source and message credibility. *Journalism Quarterly, 43,* 90–94.

Bach, B. W. (1990). 'Moving up' on campus: A qualitative examination of organizational socialization. *Journal of the Northwest Communication Association, 18,* 53–71.

Bantz, C. R. (1995). Organizing and enactment: Karl Weick and the production of news. In S. R. Corman, S. P. Banks, C. R. Bantz, & M. E. Mayer (Eds.), *Foundations of organizational communication: A reader* (2nd ed., pp. 151–160). West Plains, NY: Longman.

Bantz, C. R., & Smith, D. H. (1977). A critique and experimental test of Weick's model of organizing. *Communication Monographs, 44,* 45–68.

Bantz, C. R., McCorkle, S., & Baade, R. C. (1980). The news factory. *Communication Research, 7,* 45–68.

Barker, J. R., & Cheney, G. (1994). The concept and the practices of discipline in contemporary organizational life. *Communication Monographs, 61,* 19–43.

Baskerville, D. (1952). The vice-presidential candidates. *Quarterly Journal of Speech, 38,* 406–408.

Bassett, R. E., Stanton–Spicer, A. Q., & Whitehead, J. L. (1979). Effects of source attire on judgments of credibility. *Central States Speech Journal, 30,* 282–285.

Beatty, M. J., & Behnke, R. R. (1980). Teacher credibility as a function of verbal content and paralinguistic cues. *Communication Quarterly, 28,* 55–59.

Beebe, S. A., & Beebe, S. J. (1991). *Public Speaking: An Audience-Centered Approach.* Englewood Cliffs, NJ: Prentice-Hall.

Bennett, W. L. (1978). Storytelling in criminal trials: A model of social judgment. *Quarterly Journal of Speech, 64,* 1–22.

Bennett, W. L. (1979). Rhetorical transformation of evidence in criminal trials: Creating grounds for legal judgment. *Quarterly Journal of Speech, 65,* 311–323.

Benoit, W. L. (1982). Richard M. Nixon's rhetorical strategies in his public statements on Watergate. *Southern Speech Communication Journal, 47,* 192–211.

Benoit, W. L. (1988). Senator Edward M. Kennedy and the Chappaquiddick tragedy. In H. R. Ryan (Ed.), *Oratorical encounters: Selected studies and sources of Twentieth Century political accusations and apologies* (pp. 187–200). Westport, CT: Greenwood.

Benoit, W. L. (1995a). *Accounts, excuses, and apologies: A theory of image restoration strategies.* Albany, NY: SUNY Press.

Benoit, W. L. (1995b). Sears's repair of its auto service image: Image restoration discourse in the corporate sector. *Communication Studies, 46,* 89–105.

Benoit, W. L., & Brinson, S. (1994). AT&T: Apologies are not enough. *Communication Quarterly, 42,* 75–88.

Benoit, W. L., Gulllifor, P., & Panici, D. A. (1991). President Reagan's defensive discourse on the Iran-Contra affair. *Communication Studies, 42,* 272–294.

Benoit, W. L., & Hanczor, R. S. (1994). The Tonya Harding controversy: An analysis of image repair strategies. *Communication Quarterly, 42,* 416–433.

Benoit, W. L., Lindsey, J. J. (1987). Argument strategies: Antidote to Tylenol's poisoned image. *Journal of the American Forensic Association, 23,* 136–146.

Berlo, D. K. (1960). *The process of communication: Introduction to theory and practice.* San Francisco: Rinehart.

Berlo, D. K., & Gulley, H. E. (1957). Communication in producing attitude change and learning. *Speech Monographs, 24,* 10–20.

Berlo, D. K., & Lemert, J. B. (1961). A factor analytic study of the dimension of source credibility. A paper presented at the annual meeting of the Speech Association of America, New York, NY. Also reported in J. C. McCroskey, *An introduction to rhetorical communication* (6th ed., 1993, p. 81). Englewood Cliffs, NJ: Prentice-Hall.

Birdsell, D. S. (1987). Ronald Reagan on Lebanon and Grenada: Flexibility and interpretation in the application of Kenneth Burke's pentad. *Quarterly Journal of Speech, 73,* 267–279.

Bitzer, L. F. (1968). The rhetorical situation. *Philosophy and Rhetoric, 1,* 1–14.

Black, E. (1965). *Rhetorical criticism: A study in method.* New York: Macmillan.

Blankenship, J., Fine, M. G., & Davis, L. K. (1983). The 1980 Republican primary debates: The transformation of actor to scene. *Quarterly Journal of Speech, 69,* 25–36.

Blankenship, J., & Robson, D. C. (1995). A 'feminine style' in women's political discourse: An exploratory essay. *Communication Quarterly, 43,* 353–366.

Bock, E. H., & Pitts, J. H. (1975). The effect of three levels of black dialect on perceived speaker image. *Communication Education, 24,* 218–225.

Bormann, E. G. (1972). Fantasy and rhetorical vision: The rhetorical criticism of social reality. *Quarterly Journal of Speech, 58,* 396–407.

Bormann, E. G. (1980). *Communication theory.* New York: Holt, Rinehart and Winston.

Bormann, E. G. (1982). The symbolic convergence theory of communication: Applications and implications for teachers and consultants. *Journal of Applied Communication Research, 10,* 50–61.

Bormann, E. G. (1983). Symbolic convergence: Organizational communication and culture. In L. Putnam & M. E. Pacanowsky (Eds.), *Communication and organizations: An interpretave approach* (pp. 99–122). Beverly Hills, CA: Sage.

Bormann, E. G. (1985). Symbolic convergence theory. *Journal of Communication, 35,* 128–138.

Bormann, E. G., Howell, W. S., Nichols, R. G., and Shapiro, G. L. (1969). *Interpersonal communication in the modern organization.* Englewood Cliffs, NJ: Prentice-Hall.

Bostdorff, D. M. (1987). Making light of James Watt: A Burkean approach to the form and attitude of political cartoons. *Quarterly Journal of Speech, 73,* 43–59.

Bostrom, R. N. (1996). Memory, cognitive processing, and the process of 'listening': A reply to Thomas and Levine. *Human Communication Research, 23,* 298–305.

Bostrom, R. N., Basehart, J. R., & Rossiter, Jr., C. M. (1973). The effects of three types of profane language in persuasive messages. *Journal of Communication, 23,* 461–475.

Bostrom, R. N., & Kemp, A. P. (1969). Type of speech, sex of speaker, and sex of subject as factors influencing persuasion. *Central States Speech Journal, 20,* 245–251.

Bowers, J. W. (1963). Language intensity, social introversion, and attitude change. *Speech Monographs, 30,* 345–352.

Bowers, J. W., & Osborn, M. M. (1966). Attitudinal effects of selected types of concluding metaphors in persuasive speeches. *Speech Monographs, 33,* 147–155.

Bradac, J. J., Bowers, J. W., & Courtright, J. A. (1979). Three language variables in communication research: Intensity, immediacy, and diversity. *Human Communication Research, 5,* 257–269.

Bradac, J. W., Konsky, C. C., & Davies, R. A. (1976). Two studies of the effects of linguistic diversity upon judgments of communicator attributes and message effectiveness. *Speech Monographs, 43,* 70–79.

Brembeck, W. L., & Howell, W. S. (1952). *Persuasion: A means of social control.* Englewood Cliffs, NJ: Prentice-Hall.

Brinson, S. L., & Benoit, W. L. (1996). Attempting to restore a public image: Dow Corning and the breast implant crisis. *Communication Quarterly, 44,* 29–41.

Brock, B. L. (1988). Gerald R. Ford encounters Richard Nixon's legacy: On amnesty and the pardon. In H. R. Ryan (Ed.), *Oratorical encounters: Selected studies and sources of twentieth-century political accusations and apologies* (pp. 227–240). Westport, CT: Greenwood.

Brown, M. H. (1985). That reminds me of a story: Speech action in organizational socialization. *Western Journal of Speech Communication, 49,* 27–42.

Brummett, B. (1981). Burkean scapegoating, mortification, and transcendence in presidential campaign rhetoric. *Central States Speech Journal, 32,* 254–264.

Brummett, B. (1984). The representative anecdote as a Burkeian method, applied to evangelical rhetoric. *Southern Speech Communication Journal, 50,* 1–23.

Bryant, J., & Comisky, P. W. (1978). The effect of positioning a message within differentially cognitively involving portions of a television segment on recall of the message. *Human Communication Research, 5,* 63–75.

Buck, J. F. (1968). The effects of Negro and white dialectical variations upon attitudes of college students. *Speech Monographs, 35,* 181–186.

Bullis, C. A. (1993). Organizational socialization research: Enabling, constraining, and shifting perspectives. *Communication Monographs, 60,* 10–17.

Bullis, C. A., & Bach, B. W. (1989). Socialization turning points: An examination of change in organizational identification. *Western Journal of Speech Communication, 53,* 273–293.

Bullis, C. A., & Tompkins, P. K. (1989). The forest ranger revisited: A study of control practices and identification. *Communication Monographs, 55,* 287–306.

Burke, K. (1939). The rhetoric of Hitler's battle. *Southern Review, 5,* 1–21.

Burke, K. (1945). *A grammar of motives.* New York: Prentice-Hall.

Burke, K. [1935] (1965). *Permanence and change* (2nd ed.). New York: Bobbs-Merrill.

Burke, K. (1966). *Language as symbolic action: Essays on life, literature, and method.* Berkeley, CA: University of California Press.

Burke, K. (1968). Dramatism. *International encyclopedia of the social sciences, 7* (pp. 445–452). New York: Macmillan and Free Press.

Burke, K. [1945] (1969a). *A grammar of motives* (3rd ed.). Berkeley, CA: University of California Press.

Burke, K. [1950] (1969b). *A rhetoric of motives* (3rd ed.). Berkeley, CA: University of California Press.

Burke, K. [1962] (1970). *The rhetoric of religion: Studies in logology* (2nd ed.). Berkeley, CA: University of California Press.

Burke, K. (1972). *Dramatism and development.* Barre, MA: Clark University Press.

Bygrave, S. (1993). *Kenneth Burke: Rhetoric and ideology.* London: Routledge.

Calas, M. B., & Smircich, L. (1991). Voicing seduction to silence leadership. *Organization Studies, 12,* 567–602.

Cardillo, L. L., Ray, E. B., & Pettey, G. R. (1995). The relationship of perceived physician communicator style to patient satisfaction. *Communication Reports, 8,* 27–37.

Carlson, A. C. (1992). Creative casuistry and feminist consciousness: The rhetoric of moral reform. *Quarterly Journal of Speech, 78,* 16–32.

Cathcart, R. S. (1978). Movements: Confrontation as rhetorical form. *Central States Speech Journal, 31,* 267–273.

Cheney, G. E. (1983a). On the various and changing meanings of organizational membership: A field study of organizational identification. *Communication Monographs, 50,* 342–362.

Cheney, G. E. (1983b). The rhetoric of identification and the study of organizational communication. *Quarterly Journal of Speech, 69,* 143–158.

Cheney, G. E. (1991). *Rhetoric in an organizational society.* Columbia, SC: University of South Carolina Press.

Cheney, G. E., & Tompkins, P. K. (1987). Coming to terms with organizational identification and commitment. *Central States Speech Journal, 38,* 1–15.

Chesebro, J. W. (1984). The media reality: Epistemological functions of media in cultural systems. *Critical Studies in Mass Communication, 1,* 111–130.

Chesebro, J. W. (1989). Text, narration, and media. *Test and Performance Quarterly, 9,* 1–23.

Cicero, M. T. (1891). *De Oratore* (J. S. Watson, trans.). London: George Bell and Sons.

Clair, R. P. (1993). The use of framing devices to sequester organizational narratives: Hegemony and harassment. *Communication Monographs, 60,* 113–136.

Clair, R. P. (1994). Resistance and oppression as a self-contained opposite: An organizational communication analysis of one man's story of sexual harassment. *Western Journal of Communication, 58,* 235–262.

Clark, A. J. (1974). An exploratory study of order effect in persuasive communication. *Southern Speech Communication Journal, 39,* 322–332.

Clark, K. B. (1951). Wanted: Skilled communicators in the air force. *Journal of Communication, 1,* 30–33.

Coombs, W. T. (1995). Choosing the right words: The development of guidelines for the selection of the 'appropriate' crisis-response strategies. *Management Communication Quarterly, 8,* 447–476.

Cooper, L. (Tr. and Ed.). (1932). *The rhetoric of Aristotle.* New York: Appleton-Century-Crofts.

Cragan, J. F., & Shields, D. C. (1992). The use of symbolic convergence theory in corporate strategic planning: A case study. *Journal of Applied Communication Research, 20,* 199–218.

Cromwell, H. (1950). The relative effect on audience attitude of the first versus the second argumentative speech of a series. *Speech Monographs, 17,* 105–122.

Cromwell, H. (1954). The persistency of the effect on audience attitude of the first versus the second argumentative speech of a series. *Speech Monographs, 21,* 280–284.

Cullen, S. R. (1951). Teamwork and productivity. *Journal of Communication, 1,* 5–11.

Dahle, T. L. (1954). An objective and comparative study of five methods of transmitting information to business and industrial employees. *Communication Monographs, 11,* 21–28.

Daniels, T. D., Spiker, B. K., & Papa, M. J. (1997). *Perspectives on organizational communication.* Madison, WI: Brown & Benchmark.

Daniels, T. D., & Whitman, R. F. (1981). The effects of message introduction, message structure, and verbal organizing ability upon learning of message information. *Human Communication Research, 7,* 147–160.

Della–Piana, C. K., & Anderson, J. A. (1995). Performance community: Community service as cultural conversation. *Communication Studies, 46,* 187–200.

Dervin, B. (1989). Audience as listener and learner, teacher and confidante: The sense-making approach. In R. Rice & C. Atkins (Eds.), *Public com-

munication campaigns (2nd ed., pp. 67–86). Newbury Park, CA: Sage.

Dervin, B. (1992). From the mind's eye of the user: The sense-making qualitative-quantitative methodology. In J. D. Glaser & R. R. Powell (Eds.), *Qualitative research in information management* (pp. 61–84). Englewood, CO: Libraries Unlimited.

Dickens, M. (1945). Discussion method in war industry. *Quarterly Journal of Speech, 31,* 144–150.

Dickenson, B. (1932). The influence of the press in labor affairs. *Journalism Quarterly, 9,* 269–280.

Dionisopoulos, G. N., & Vibbert, S. L. (1988). CBS vs. Mobil Oil: Charges of creative bookkeeping in 1979. In H. R. Ryan (Ed.), *Oratorical encounters: Selected studies and sources of twentieth-century political accusations and apologies* (pp. 241–251). New York: Greenwood.

DiSanza, J. R. (1993). Shared meaning as a sales inducement strategy: Bank teller responses to frames, reinforcements, and quotas. *Journal of Business Communication, 30,* 133–160.

DiSanza, J. R. (1995). Bank teller organizational assimilation in a system of contradictory practices. *Management Communication Quarterly, 9,* 191–218.

Eisenberg, E. M. (1986). Meaning and interpretation in organizations. *Quarterly Journal of Speech, 72,* 88–96.

Eisenberg, E. M. (1990). Jamming: Transcendence through organizing. *Communication Research, 17,* 139–164.

Eisenberg, E. M., & Goodall, Jr., H. L. (1993). *Organizational communication: Balancing creativity and constraint.* New York: St. Martin's Press.

Eisenberg, E. M., & Riley, P. (1988). Organizational symbols and sense-making. In G. Goldhaber & G. Barnett (Eds.), *Handbook of organizational communication* (pp. 131–150). Norwood, NJ: Ablex.

Elwood, W. N., Dayton, C. A., & Richard, A. J. (1995). Ethnography and illegal drug users: The efficacy of outreach as HIV prevention. *Communication Studies, 46,* 261–275.

Estes, C. T. (1946). Speech and human relations in industry. *Quarterly Journal of Speech, 32,* 160–169.

Estes, C. T. (1951). Communication in industry. *Journal of Communication, 1,* 53–56.

Ewbank, H. L. (1996). The Constitution: Burkeian, Brandeisian and Borkian perspectives. *Southern Communication Journal, 61,* 220–232.

Ewing, W. H. (1945). Finding a speaking-listening index. *Quarterly Journal of Speech, 36,* 368–370.

Fisher, W. R. (1973). Reaffirmation and subversion of the American dream. *Quarterly Journal of Speech, 59,* 160–167.

Fisher, W. R. (1984). Narration as human communication paradigm: The case for public moral argument. *Communication Monographs, 51,* 1–22.

Fisher, W. R. (1987). *Human communication as narration: Toward a philosophy of reason, values, and action.* Columbia, SC: University of South Carolina Press.

Freeley, A. J. (1953). Speech among the bankers. *Today's Speech, 1,* 8–9.

Garko, M. G. (1993). The effect of perceived subordinate communicator style on physician-executives' choices of compliance-gaining strategies. *Communication Reports, 6,* 61–70.

Geertz, C. (1973). *The interpretation of cultures.* New York: Basic Books.

Gibson, C. C. (1970). Eugene Talmadge's use of identification during the 1934 gubernatorial campaign in Georgia. *Southern Speech Communication Journal, 35,* 342–353.

Giles, H. (1978). Communicative effectiveness as a function of accented speech. *Speech Monographs, 40,* 330–331.

Gilkinson, H., Paulson, S. F., & Sikkink, D. E. (1954). Effects of order and authority in an argumentative speech. *Quarterly Journal of Speech, 40,* 183–192.

Goldhaber, G. M. (1993). *Organizational communication.* Dubuque, IA: Brown.

Goodall, H. L., Jr. (1989). *Casing a promised land: The autobiography of an organizational detective as cultural ethnographer.* Carbondale, IL: Southern Illinois University Press.

Goodhall, H. L., Jr. (1991). *Living in the rock 'n' roll mystery: Reading context, self, and others as clues.* Carbondale, IL: Southern Illinois University Press.

Goss, B., & Williams, L. (1973). The effects of equivocation on perceived source credibility. *Central States Speech Journal, 24,* 162–167.

Greenberg, B. S., & Razinsky, E. L. (1966). Some effects of variations in message quality. *Journalism Quarterly, 43,* 486–492.

Griffin, L. M. (1964). The rhetorical structure of the 'new left' movement: Part I. *Quarterly Journal of Speech, 50,* 113–135.

Griffin, L. M. (1969). A dramatistic theory of the rhetoric of movements. In W. Rueckert (Ed.), *Critical responses to Kenneth Burke* (pp. 456–478). Minneapolis, MN: University of Minnesota Press.

Gruner, C. R. (1967). Effect of humor on speaker ethos and audience information gain. *Journal of Communication, 17,* 228–233.

Gumpert, G., & Cathcart, R. (1985). Media grammars, generations, and media gaps. *Critical Studies in Mass Communication, 2,* 23–35.

Gunderson, D. F., & Hopper, R. (1976). Relationships between speech delivery and speech effectiveness. *Communication Monographs, 43,* 158–165.

Haiman, F. S. (1949). An experimental study of ethos related to the introduction in the persuasive speaking situation. *Speech Monographs, 16,* 190–202.

Hample, D. (1979). Motives in law: An adaptation of legal realism. *Journal of the American Forensic Association, 15,* 156–160.

Hart, R. P., & Burks, D. M. (1972). Rhetorical sensitivity and social interaction. *Speech Monographs, 39,* 75–91.

Hart, R. P., Carlson, R. E., Eadie, W. F. (1980). Attitudes toward communication and the assessment of rhetorical sensitivity. *Communication Monographs, 47,* 1–22.

Harte, T. B. (1976). The effects of evidence in persuasive communication. *Central States Speech Journal, 27,* 42–46.

Hawes, L. C. (1972). The effects of interviewer style on patterns of dyadic communication. *Speech Monographs, 39,* 114–123.

Haynes, W. L. (1988). Of that which we cannot write: Some notes on the phenomenology of media. *Quarterly Journal of Speech, 74,* 92–99.

Haynes, W. L. (1989). Shifting media, shifting paradigms, and the growing utility of narrative as metaphor. *Communication Studies, 40,* 109–126.

Haynes, W. L. (1990). Public speaking pedagogy in the media age. *Communication Education, 39,* 89–102.

Hess, J. A. (1993). Assimilating newcomers into an organization: A cultural perspective. *Journal of Applied Communication Research, 21,* 189–210.

Hewgill, M. A., & Miller, G. R. (1965). Source credibility and response to fear arousing communications. *Speech Monographs, 32,* 95–101.

Howell, W. S. (1982). *The empathic communicator.* Belmont, CA: Wadsworth.

Huesca, R. (1995). Subject-authored theories of media practice: The case of Bolivian tin miners' radio. *Communication Studies, 46,* 149–168.

Hunt, E. L. (1915). The scientific spirit in public speaking. *Quarterly Journal of Public Speaking, 1,* 185–193.

Innis, H. A. (1972). *Empire and communications* (Revised by M. Q. Innis; Foreword by M. McLuhan). Toronto, Canada: University of Toronto Press.

Ivie, R. L. (1974). Presidential motives for war. *Quarterly Journal of Speech, 60,* 337–345.

Jablin, F. M. (1982). Organizational communication: An assimilation approach. In M. E. Roloff & C. R. Berger (Eds.), *Social cognition and communication* (pp. 255–286).

Jablin, F. M. (1984). Assimilating new members into organizations. In R. N. Bostrom (Ed.), *Communication yearbook 8* (pp. 594–626). Newbury Park, CA: Sage.

Jablin, F. M. (1985). An exploratory study of vocational organizational communication socialization. *Southern Speech Communication Journal, 20,* 261–282.

Jablin, F. M. (1987). Organizational entry, assimilation and exit. In F. M. Jablin, L. L. Putnam, K. H. Roberts, & L. W. Porter (Eds.). *Handbook of organizational communication: An interdisciplinary perspective* (pp. 679–740). Newbury Park, CA: Sage.

Jablin, F. M., & Krone, K. J. (1987). Organizational assimilation. In C. R. Berger & S. H. Chaffee (Eds.), *Handbook of communication science* (pp. 711–746). Beverly Hills, CA: Sage.

Jablin, F. M., & McComb, K. B. (1984). The employment screening interview: An organizational assimilation and communication perspective. In R. N. Bostrom (Ed.), *Communication Yearbook 8* (pp. 137–163). Newbury Park, CA: Sage.

Jameson, F. R. (1978). The symbolic inference: Or, Kenneth Burke and ideological analysis. *Critical Inquiry, 4,* 507–523.

Jordan, W. J., & McLaughlin, M. L. (1976). Figurativeness as an independent variable in communication research. *Communication Quarterly, 24,* 31–37.

Kelly, C. E. (1987). The 1984 campaign of Representative George Hansen: A pentadic analysis. *Western Speech Communication Journal, 51,* 204–217.

Kelly, J. W. (1985). Storytelling in high tech organizations: A medium for sharing culture. *Journal of Applied Communication Research, 13,* 45–58.

Kibler, R. J., & Barker, L. L. (1968). An experimental study to assess the effectiveness of three levels of mispronunciation on comprehension for three different populations. *Speech Monographs, 35,* 26–38.

Klumpp, J. A., & Hollihan, T. A. (1979). Debunking the resignation of Earl Butz: Sacrificing an official racist. *Quarterly Journal of Speech, 42,* 116–123.

Klumpp, J. A., & Lukehart, J. K. (1978). The pardoning of Richard Nixon: A failure in motivational strategy. *Western Journal of Speech Communication, 42,* 116–123.

Knower, F. (1929). A suggestive study of public-speaking rating scale values. *Quarterly Journal of Speech, 15,* 30–41.

Kraus, S., El-Assal, E., & DeFleur, M. L. (1966). Fear threat appeals in mass communication: An apparent contradiction. *Speech Monographs, 33,* 23–29.

Kreps, G. L. (1980). A field experimental test of Weick's model of organizing. In D. Nimmo (Ed.), *Communication Yearbook 4* (pp. 389–398). New Brunswick, NJ: Transaction Books.

Kreps, G. L. (1990). *Organizational communication: Theory and practice.* New York: Longman.

Larson, C. U. (1973). *Persuasion: Reception and responsibility.* Belmont, CA: Wadsworth.

Ling, D. A. (1970). A pentadic analysis of Senator Edward Kennedy's address to the people of Massachusetts, July 25, 1969. *Central States Speech Journal, 21,* 81–86.

Luchok, J. A., & McCroskey, J. A. (1978). The effect of quality of evidence on attitude change and source credibility. *Southern Speech Communication Journal, 43,* 371–383.

Matthews, J. (1947). The effect of loaded language on audience comprehension of speeches. *Speech Monographs, 14,* 176–186.

McCroskey, J. C. (1966). Scales for the measurement of ethos. *Speech Monographs, 33,* 65–72.

McCroskey, J. C. (1968). *An introduction to rhetorical communication.* Englewood Cliffs, NJ: Prentice-Hall.

McCroskey, J. C. (1993). *An introduction to rhetorical communication* (6th ed.). Englewood Cliffs, NJ: Prentice-Hall.

McCroskey, J. C., & Combs, W. H. (1969). The effects of the use of analogy on attitude change and source credibility. *Journal of Communication, 19,* 333–339.

McCroskey, J. C., & Mehrley, R. S. (1969). The effects of disorganization and non-fluency on attitude change and source credibility. *Speech Monographs, 36,* 13–21.

McCroskey, J. C., Young, T. J., & Scott, M. D. (1972). Special reports: The effects of message sidedness and evidence on inoculation against counter-persuasion in small group communication. *Speech Monographs, 39,* 205–212.

McEwen, W. J., & Greenberg, B. S. (1970). The effects of message intensity on receiver evaluations of source, message, and topic. *Journal of Communication, 20,* 340–350.

McLuhan, M. (1964). *Understanding media: Extensions of man* (2nd ed.). New York: Signet.

McLuhan, M., & Fiore, Q. (1967). *The medium is the massage: An inventory of effects.* New York: Bantam Books.

Messner, B. A. (1996). 'Sizing up' codependency recovery. *Western Journal of Communication, 60,* 101–123.

Miller, G. R. (1963). Studies on the use of fear appeals. *Central States Speech Journal, 14,* 117–124.

Miller, G. R., & Basehart, J. (1969). Source trustworthiness, opinionated statements, and response to persuasive communication. *Speech Monographs, 36,* 1–7.

Minnick, W. C. (1957). *The art of persuasion.* Boston: Houghton Mifflin.

Montgomery, C. L., & Burgoon, M. (1977). An experimental study of the interactive effects of sex and androgyny on attitude change. *Communication Monographs, 44,* 130–135.

Mulac, A. (1976). Effects of obscene language upon three dimensions of listener attitude. *Communication Monographs, 43,* 300–307.

Mullican, J. A. (1971). Kenneth Burke's comic attitude: Corrective to propaganda analysis. *Continuing Education, 4,* 89–92.

Nichols, A. C. (1965). Effects of three aspects of sentence structure on immediate recall. *Speech Monographs, 32,* 164–168.

Nichols, M. H. (1952). Kenneth Burke and the 'new rhetoric'. *Quarterly Journal of Speech, 38,* 133–141.

Nichols, R. G. (1948). Factors in listening comprehension. *Speech Monographs, 15,* 154–163.

Norton, R. (1978). Foundation of a communicator style construct. *Human Communication Research, 4,* 99–112.

Norton, R. (1983). *Communicator style: Theory, applications, and measures.* Newbury Park, CA: Sage.

Norton, R., & Miller, L. D. (1975). Dyadic perception of communication style. *Communication Research, 2,* 50–67.

Norton, R., & Warnick, B. (1976). Assertiveness as a communication construct. *Human Communication Research, 3,* 62–72.

Olsen, K. M. (1989). The controversy of President Reagan's visit to Bitburg: Strategies of definition and redefinition. *Quarterly Journal of Speech, 75,* 129–151.

Ong, W. J. (1980). Literacy and orality in our times. *Journal of Communication, 30,* 197–204.

Ong, W. J. (1982). *Orality and literacy: The technologizing of the word.* London: Metheun.

Pacanowsky, M. E. (1983). A small-town cop: Communication in, out, and about a crisis. In L. L. Putnam & M. E. Pacanowksy (Eds.), *Communication and organizations: An interpretive approach* (pp. 261–282). Newbury Park, CA: Sage.

Pacanowsky, M. E. (1988a). Communication in the empowering organization. In J. A. Anderson (Ed.), *Communication Yearbook 11* (pp. 356–379). Beverly Hills, CA: Sage and the International Communication Association.

Pacanowsky, M. E. (1988b). Slouching toward Chicago. *Quarterly Journal of speech, 74,* 453–467.

Pacanowsky, M. E. (1989). Creating and narrating organizational realities. In B. Dervin, L. Grossberg, B. J. O'Keefe, & E. Wartella (Eds.), *Rethinking communication, II: Paradigm exemplars* (pp. 250–257). Newbury Park, CA: Sage.

Pacanowsky, M. E., & O'Donnell–Trujillo, N. (1982). Communication and organizational cultures. *Western Journal of Speech Communication, 46,* 115–130.

Pacanowsky, M. E., & O'Donnell–Trujillo, N. (1983). Organizational communication as cultural performance. *Communication Monographs, 50,* 126–147.

Parry–Giles, S. J. (1996). 'Camouflaged' propaganda: The Truman and Eisenhower administrations' covert manipulation of news. *Western Journal of Communication, 60,* 146–167.

Pearce, W. B. (1971). The effect of vocal cues on credibility and attitude change. *Western Journal of Speech Communication, 35,* 176–184.

Peterson, T. R. (1986). The will to conservation: A Burkeian analysis of dust bowl rhetoric and American farming motives. *Southern Speech Communication Journal, 60,* 1–21.

Pfau, M., & Parrott, R. (1993). *Persuasive communication campaigns.* Boston, MA: Allyn and Bacon.

Phillipsen, G. (1976). Places for speaking in teamsterville. *Quarterly Journal of Speech, 62,* 15–25.

Phillipsen, G. (1992). *Speaking culturally: Explorations in social communication.* Albany, NY: SUNY Press.

Plato. (1871). *Gorgias* (W. H. Thompson, tran.). London: George Bell and Sons.

Pokorny, G. F., & Gruner, C. R. (1969). An experimental study of the effect of satire as support in a persuasive speech. *Western Journal of Speech Communication, 33,* 204–211.

Powell, F. A. (1965). The effect of anxiety arousing messages when related to personal, familial, and impersonal referents. *Speech Monographs, 32,* 102–106.

Preston, C. T., Jr. (1984). Reagan's 'new beginning': Is it the 'new deal' of the eighties? *Southern Speech Communication Journal, 49,* 198–211.

Procter, D. E. (1995). Placing Lincoln and Mitchell counties: A cultural study. *Communication Studies, 46,* 222–233.

Puls, E. (1917). Speech training for businessmen. *Quarterly Journal of Public Speaking, 3,* 332–337.

Putnam, L. L. (1983). The interpretive perspective: An alternative to functionalism. In L. Putnam & M. E. Pacanowsky (Eds.), *Communication and organizations: An interpretive approach* (pp. 31–53). Beverly Hills, CA: Sage.

Putnam, L. L. (1986). Contradictions and paradoxes in organizations. In L. Thayer (Ed.), *Organizational communication: Emerging perspectives* (pp. 151–167). Norwood, NJ: Ablex.

Putnam, L. L., & Pacanowsky, M. E. (Eds.), (1983). *Communication and organizations: An interpretive approach* (pp. 31–53). Beverly Hills, CA: Sage.

Putnam, L. L., & Sorenson, R. (1982). Equivocal messages in organizations. *Human Communication Research, 8,* 114–132.

Quintilian, M. F. (1856). *Institutes of Oratory* (J. S. Watson, tran.). London: Henry G. Bohn.

Ragsdale, J. D. (1968). Effects of selected aspects of brevity on persuasiveness. *Speech Monographs, 35,* 8–13.

Ralston, S. M. (1993). Applicant communication satisfaction, intent to accept second interview offers, and recruiter communication style. *Journal of Applied Communication Research, 21,* 53–65.

Reinsch, N. L. (1971). An investigation of the effects of the metaphor and simile in persuasive discourse. *Speech Monographs, 38,* 142–145.

Ried, P. E. (1988). The first and fifth Boylston professors: A view of two worlds. *Quarterly Journal of Speech, 74,* 229–240.

Ritter, K. (1985). Drama and legal rhetoric: The perjury trials of Alger Hiss. *Western Journal of Speech Communication, 49,* 83–102.

Roberts, W. R. (Tr. and Ed.). (1954). *Rhetoric of Aristotle.* New York: Modern Library.

Rogers, C. E. (1934). The social justification of the business press. *Journalism Quarterly, 11,* 235–245.

Rosenfeld, L. B., & Christie, V. R. (1974). Sex and persuasibility revisited. *Western Journal of Speech Communication, 38,* 244–253.

Rosenfield, L. W. (1968). A case study in speech criticism: The Nixon–Truman analog. *Speech Monographs, 35,* 435–450.

Rosnow, R. L. (1966). Whatever happened to the 'law of primacy'? *Journal of Communication, 16,* 10–31.

Rushing, J. H. (1986). Ronald Reagan's 'Star Wars' address: Mythic containment of technical reasoning. *Quarterly Journal of Speech, 72,* 415–433.

Ruud, G. (1995). The symbolic construction of organizational identities and community in a regional symphony. *Communication Studies, 46,* 201–221.

Ryan, H. R. (1982). *Kategoria* and *apologia:* On their rhetorical criticism as a speech set. *Quarterly Journal of Speech, 68,* 256–261.

Sass, J. S., & Canary, D. J. (1991). Organizational commitment and identification: An examination of conceptual and operational convergence. *Western Journal of Speech Communication, 55,* 275–293.

Schiappa, E. (1989). The rhetoric of nuke-speak. *Communication Monographs, 56,* 253–272.

Schockley–Zalabak, P. (1995). *Fundamentals of organizational communication: Knowledge, sensitivity, skills, values.* New York: Longman.

Schockley–Zalabak, P., & Morley, D. D. (1994). Creating a culture: A longitudinal examination of the influence of management and employee values on communication rule stability and emergence. *Human Communication Research, 20,* 334–355.

Schunk, J. F. (1969). Attitudinal effects of self-contradiction in a persuasive communication. *Central States Speech Journal, 19,* 20–29.

Seibold, D. R., Kudsi, S., & Rude, M. (1993). Does communication training make a difference? Evidence for the effectiveness of a presentation skills program. *Journal of Applied Communication Research, 21,* 111–131.

Seiler, W. J. (1971). The effects of visual materials on attitudes, credibility, and retention. *Speech Monographs, 38,* 331–334.

Sereno, K. K., & Hawkins, G. J. (1967). The effects of variations in speakers' nonfluency upon audience ratings of attitudes toward the speech topic and speakers' credibility. *Speech Monographs, 34,* 58–64.

Shields, D. C. (1993). Drug education and the communication curricula. In S. H. Decker, R. B. Rosenfeld, & R. Wright (Eds.), *Drug education across the university curriculum* (pp. 44–90). Saratoga Springs, CA: R&E Publishers.

Shields, D. C., & Cragan, J. F. (1981). A communication based political campaign: A theoretical and methodological perspective. In J. F. Cragan & D. C. Shields (Eds.), *Applied communication research: A dramatistic approach* (pp. 177–196). Prospect Heights, IL: Waveland Press.

Siltanen, S. A. (1981). The persuasiveness of metaphor: A replication and extension. *Southern Speech Communication Journal, 47,* 67–83.

Simons, H. W., Chesebro, J. W., & Orr, C. J. (1973). A movement perspective on the 1972 presidential campaign. *Quarterly Journal of Speech, 59,* 168–179.

Smith, L. D., & Golden, J. L. (1988). Electronic storytelling in electoral politics: An anecdotal analysis of the television advertising in the Helms–Hunt senate race. *Southern Speech Communication Journal, 53,* 244–258.

Smith, M. J. (1977). The effects of threats to attitudinal freedom as a function of message quality and initial receiver attitude. *Communication Monographs, 44,* 196–206.

Smith, R. G. (1951). An experimental study of the effects of speech organization upon college students. *Speech Monographs, 18,* 292–301.

Smythe, M.-J. (1995). Talking bodies: Body talk at Bodyworks. *Communication Studies, 46,* 245–260.

Sponberg, H. (1946). The relative effectiveness of climax and anti-climax order in an argumentative speech. *Speech Monographs, 13,* 35–44.

Sussman, L. (1973). Ancients and moderns on fear and fear appeals: A comparative analysis. *Central States Speech Journal, 24,* 206–211.

Talley, M. A., & Richmond, V. P. (1980). The relationship between psychological gender orientation and communicator style. *Human Communication Research, 6,* 326–339.

Taylor, P. M. (1973). An experimental study of humor and ethos. *Southern Speech Communication Journal, 39,* 359–366.

Thomas, L. T., & Levine, T. R. (1996). Further thoughts on recall, memory, and the measurement of listening: A rejoinder to Bostrom. *Human Communication Research, 23,* 306–308.

Thonssen, L., & Baird, A. C. (1948). *Speech criticism.* New York: Ronald Press.

Tompkins, P. K., & Cheney, G. (1983). Account analysis of organizational decision-making and identification. In L. L. Putnam & M. E. Pacanowsky (Eds.), *Communication and organizations: An interpretive approach* (pp. 123–146). Beverly Hills, CA: Sage.

Tompkins, P. K., & Cheney, G. (1985). Communication and unobtrusive control in contemporary organizations. In R. D. McPhee & P. K. Tompkins (Eds.), *Organizational communication: Traditional themes and new directions* (pp. 179–210). Beverly Hills, CA: Sage.

Tompkins, P. K., Fisher, J. Y., Infante, D. A., Tompkins, E. L. (1975). Kenneth Burke and the inherent characteristics of formal organizations: A field study. *Speech Monographs, 42,* 135–142.

Vanderford, M. L. (1989). Vilification and social movements: A case study of pro-life and pro-choice rhetoric. *Quarterly Journal of Speech, 75,* 166–182.

Violanti, M. T. (1996). Hooked on expectations: An analysis of influence and relationships in the tailhook reports. *Journal of Applied Communication Research, 24,* 67–82.

Ware, B. L., & Linkugel, W. A. (1973). They spoke in defense of themselves: On the generic criticism of apologia. *Quarterly Journal of Speech, 59,* 273–283.

Weick, K. E. (1969). *The social psychology of organizing.* Reading, MA: Addison-Wesley.

Weick, K. E. (1979). *The social psychology of organizing* (2nd ed.). New York: Ransom House.

Wendt, R. F. (1994). Learning to 'walk the talk': A critical tale of the micropolitics at a total quality university. *Management Communication Quarterly, 8,* 5–45.

Wendt, R. F. (1995). Women in positions of service: The politicized body. *Communication Studies, 46,* 276–296.

Whately, J. (1828). *Elements of rhetoric.* London: George Bell and Sons.

Wheeless, L. R. (1973). Effects of explicit credibility statements by more credible and less credible sources. *Southern Speech Communication Journal, 39,* 33–39.

Wheeless, L. R., Jones, S., & King, L. (1974). Effect of waiting time on credibility, attraction, homophily, and anxiety-hostility. *Southern Speech Communication Journal, 39,* 367–378.

Whitehead, J. L., Jr. (1971). Effects of authority-based assertion on attitude and credibility. *Speech Monographs, 38,* 311–315.

Wichelns, H. A. (1925). The literary criticism of oratory. In A. M. Drummond (Ed), *Studies in rhetoric and public speaking in honor of James Albert Winans.* New York: Century. Also appearing in R. L. Scott & B. L. Brock (Eds., 1972), *Methods of rhetorical criticism: A twentieth century perspective* (pp. 27–60). New York: Harper & Row.

Widgery, R. N. (1974). Sex of receiver and physical attractiveness of source as determinants of initial credibility perception. *Western Journal of Speech Communication, 38,* 13–17.

Williams, D. E., & Treadaway, G. (1992). Exxon and the Valdez accident: A failure in crisis communication. *Communication Studies, 43,* 56–64.

Winans, J. A. (1915). The need for research. *Quarterly Journal of Public Speaking, 1,* 17–23.

Witte, K. (1992). Putting the fear back into fear appeals: The extended parallel process model. *Communication Monographs, 59,* 329–349.

Witte, K. (1993). Message and conceptual confounds in fear appeals: The role of judgment methods. *Southern Communication Journal, 58,* 147–155.

Witte, K. (1994). Fear control and danger control: A test of the extended parallel process model (EPPM). *Communication Monographs, 61,* 113–134.

Witte, K., & Morrison, K. (1995). Using scare tactics to promote safer sex among juvenile detention and high school youth. *Journal of Applied Communication Research, 23,* 128–142.

Wolvin, A. D. & Coakley, C. G. (1985). *Listening* (2nd ed.) Dubuque, IA: Brown.

Woolbert, C. H. (1917). Suggestions as to methods in research. *Quarterly Journal of Public Speaking, 3,* 12–26.

Chapter 10 Mass and Intercultural Communication Context Theories

Asante, M. K., & Gudykunst, W. B. (1989). Preface. In M. K. Asante & W. B. Gudykunst (Eds.), *Handbook of International and intercultural communication* (pp. 7–13). Newbury Park, CA: Sage.

Austin, B. A. (1986). Motivation for movie attendance. *Communication Quarterly, 34,* 115–126.

Austin, E. W. (1993). Exploring the effects of active parental mediation of television content. *Journal of Broadcasting & Electronic Media, 37,* 147–158.

Austin, E. W., & Meili, H. K. (1994). Effects of interpretations of televised alcohol portrayals on children's alcohol beliefs. *Journal of Broadcasting and Electronic Media, 38,* 417–435.

Austin, E. W., & Nelson, C. L. (1993). Influences of ethnicity, family communication, and media on adolescents' socialization to U.S. Politics. *Journal of Broadcasting & Electronic Media, 37,* 419–435.

Barrow, A. S. (1989). An expectancy-value analysis of the student soap opera audience. *Communication Research, 16,* 155–178.

Barrow, A. S., & Swanson, D. L. (1988). Disentangling antecedents of audience exposure levels: Extending expectancy-value analysis of gratifications sought from television news. *Communication Monographs, 55,* 1–21.

Becker, S. L., & Roberts, C. L. (1992). *Discovering mass communication* (3rd ed.). New York: Harper-Collins.

Berkowitz, D. (1990). Refining the gatekeeping metaphor for local television news. *Journal of Broadcasting & Electronic Media, 34,* 55–68.

Blumler, J. G. (1979). The role of theory in uses and gratifications studies. *Communication Research, 6,* 9–36.

Blumler, J. G., & Katz, E. (Eds.). (1974). *The uses of mass communications: Current perspectives on gratifications research.* Beverly Hills, CA: Sage.

Brosius, H.–B., & Kepplinger, H. M. (1990). The agenda-setting function of television news: Static and dynamic views. *Communication Research, 17,* 183–211.

Brosius, H.–B., & Kepplinger, H. M. (1992a). Beyond agenda-setting: The influence of partisanship and television reporting on the electorate's voting intentions. *Journalism Quarterly, 69,* 893–901.

Brosius, H.–B., & Kepplinger, H. M. (1992b). Linear and nonlinear models of agenda-setting in television. *Journal of Broadcasting end Electronic Media, 36,* 5–23.

Brosius, H.–B., & Weimann, G. (1996). Who sets the agenda?: Agenda-setting as a two-step flow. *Communication Research, 23,* 561–580.

Brown, D. (1970). *Bury my heart at wounded knee: An Indian history of the American West.* New York: Bantam Books.

Canary, D. J., & Spitzberg, B. H. (1993). Loneliness and media gratifications. *Communication Research, 20,* 800–821.

Chen, G.–M., & Starosta, W. J. (1996). Intercultural communication competence: A synthesis. In B. Burleson (Ed.), *Communication yearbook 19* (pp. 353–383). Thousand Oaks, CA: Sage.

Christ, W. G., & Biggers, T. (1984). An exploratory investigation into the relationship between television program preference and emotion-eliciting qualities: A new theoretical perspective. *Western Journal of Speech Communication, 48,* 293–307.

Cocroft, B. K., & Ting–Toomey, S. (1994). Facework in Japan and the United States. *International Journal of Intercultural Relations, 18,* 469–506.

Coffin, T. E., & Tuchman, S. (1972/73). Rating television programs for violence: A comparison of five surveys. *Journal of Broadcasting and Electronic Media, 17,* 3–20.

Cohen, B. C. (1963). *The press and foreign policy.* Princeton, NJ: Princeton University Press.

Comstock, J., & Strzyzewski, K. (1990). Interpersonal interaction on television: Family conflict and jealousy on prime-time. *Journal of Broadcasting and Electronic Media, 34,* 263–282.

Demers, D. P., Craff, D., Choi, Y.–H., & Pessin, B. M. (1989). Issue obtrusiveness and the agenda-setting effects of national network news. *Communication research, 16,* 793–812.

Doob, A. N., & Macdonald, G. E. (1979). Television viewing and fear of victimization: Is the relationship causal? *Journal of Personality and Social Psychology, 37,* 170–179.

Edelstein, A. S. (1993). Thinking about the criterion variable in agenda-setting research. *Journal of Communication, 43*(2), 85–99.

Eleey, M. F., Gerbner, G., & Tedesco, N. (1972/73a). Apples, oranges, and the kitchen sink: An analysis and guide to the comparison of 'violence ratings'.

Journal of Broadcasting and Electronic Media, 17, 21–31.

Eleey, M. F., Gerbner, G., & Tedesco, N. (1972/73b). Validity indeed! *Journal of Broadcasting and Electronic Media, 17,* 34–35.

Fan, D. P., Brosius, H.–B., & Kepplinger, H. M. (1994). Predictions of the public agenda from television coverage. *Journal of Broadcasting and Electronic Media, 38,* 163–177.

Fortner, R. S. (1995). Excommunication in the information society. *Critical Studies in Mass Communication, 12,* 133–154.

Gerbner, G. (1980, January). Death in prime-time: Notes on the symbolic functions of dying in the mass media. *Annals of the American Academy of Political and Social Science, 447,* 64–70.

Gerbner, G. (1990). Advancing on the path of righteousness (maybe). In N. Signorielli & M. Morgan (Eds.), *Cultivation analysis: New directions in media effects research* (pp. 249–262). Newbury Park, CA: Sage.

Gerbner, G., & Gross, L. (1976). Living with television: The violence profile. *Journal of Communication, 26*(2), 173–199.

Gerbner, G., & Gross, L. (1979). Editorial response: A reply to Newcomb's 'humanistic critique'. *Communication Research, 6,* 223–230.

Gerbner, G., Gross, L., Eleey, M., Jackson–Beeck, M., Jeffries–Fox, S., & Signorielli, N. (1977a). One more time: An analysis of the CBS 'final comments on the violence profile'. *Journal of Communication, 21*(3), 297–303.

Gerbner, G., Gross, L., Eleey, M., Jackson–Beeck, M., Jeffries–Fox, S., & Signorielli, N. (1977b). 'The Gerbner violence profile': An analysis of the CBS report. *Journal of Broadcasting, 21,* 280–286.

Gerbner, G., Gross, L., Jackson–Beeck, M., Jeffries–Fox, S., & Signorielli, N. (1978). Cultural indicators: Violence profile No. 9. *Journal of Communication, 28*(3), 176–207.

Gerbner, G., Gross, L., Morgan, M., & Signorielli, N. (1979a). On 'Wober's televised violence and paranoid perception: The view from Great Britain'. *Public Opinion Quarterly, 43,* 123–124.

Gerbner, G., Gross, L., Morgan, M., & Signorielli, N. (1980a). The 'mainstreaming' of America: Violence profile No. 11. *Journal of Communication, 30*(3), 10–29.

Gerbner, G., Gross, L., Morgan, M., & Signorielli, N. (1981). A curious journey into the scary world of Paul Hirsch. *Communication Research, 8,* 39–72.

Gerbner, G., Gross, L., Morgan, M., & Signorielli, N. (1982). Charting the mainstream: Television's contributions to political orientations. *Journal of Communication, 32*(2), 100–127.

Gerbner, G., Gross, L., Morgan, M., & Signorielli, N. (1986). Living with television: The dynamics of the cultivation process. In J. Bryant & D. Zillman (Eds.), *Perspectives on media effects* (pp. 17–40). Hillsdale, NJ: Erlbaum.

Gerbner, G., Gross, L., Signorielli, N., & Morgan, M. (1980b). Aging with television: Images on television drama and conceptions of social reality. *Journal of Communication, 30*(1), 37–47.

Gerbner, G., Gross, L., Signorielli, N., Morgan, M., & Jackson–Beeck, M. (1979b). The demonstration of power: Violence profile No. 10. *Journal of Communication, 29*(3), 177–196.

Gibson, R., & Zillmann, D. (1994). Exaggerated versus representative exemplification in news reports: Perception of issues and personal consequences. *Communication Research, 21,* 603–624.

Gudykunst, W. B. (1985). A model of uncertainty reduction in intercultural encounters. *Journal of Language and Social Psychology, 4,* 79–98.

Gudykunst, W. B. (1988). Uncertainty and anxiety. In Y. Y. Kim & W. B. Gudykunst (Eds.), *Theories in intercultural communication: International and intercultural communication annual, vol. 12* (pp. 123–156). Newbury Park, CA: Sage.

Gudykunst, W. B. (1993). Toward a theory of effective interpersonal and intergroup communication: An anxiety/uncertainty management perspective. In R. L. Wiseman & J. Koester (Eds.), *Intercultural communication competence: International and intercultural communication annual, vol. 17* (pp. 33–71). Newbury Park, CA: Sage.

Gudykunst, W. B. (1995). Anxiety/uncertainty management (AUM) theory: Current status. In R. L. Wiseman (Ed.), *International and intercultural communication annual, vol. 19: Intercultural communication theory* (pp. 8–58). Thousand Oaks, CA: Sage.

Gudykunst, W. B., & Hammer, M. R. (1988). Strangers and hosts: An uncertainty reduction based theory of intercultural adaptation. In Y. Y. Kim & W. B.

Gudykunst (Eds.), *Cross-cultural adaptation: Current approaches* (pp. 106–139). Newbury Park, CA: Sage.

Gudykunst, W. B., Hammer, M. R., & Wiseman, R. L. (1977). An analysis of an integrated approach to cross-cultural training. *International Journal of Intercultural Relations, 2,* 99–110.

Gudykunst, W. B., & Nishida, T. (1986). The influence of cultural variability on perceptions of communication behavior associated with relationship terms. *Human Communication Research, 13,* 147–166.

Gudykunst, W. B., & Nishida, T. (1989). Theoretical perspectives for studying intercultural communication. In M. K. Asante & W. B. Gudykunst (Eds.), *Handbook of international and intercultural communication, vol. 13* (pp. 17–46). Newbury Park, CA: Sage.

Gudykunst, W. B., & Ting–Toomey, S. (1988). Affective communication across cultures. *American Behavioral Scientist, 31,* 384–400.

Gudykunst, W. B., Ting–Toomey, S., & Wiseman, R. L. (1991). Taming the beast: Designing a course in intercultural communication. *Communication Quarterly, 40,* 272–286.

Hall, E. T. (1959). *The silent language.* Garden City, NY: Doubleday.

Hall, E. T. (1966). *The hidden dimension.* Garden City, NY: Doubleday.

Hall, E. T. (1976). *Beyond culture.* Garden City, NY: Doubleday.

Hall, E. T. (1984). *The dance of life: The other dimension of time.* Garden City, NY: Doubleday.

Hall, E. T., & Trager, G. L. (1953). *Human nature at home and abroad: A guide to the understanding of human behavior.* Washington, D.C.: Foreign Service Institute.

Hammer, M. R., & Martin, J. N. (1992). The effects of cross-cultural training on American managers in a Japanese-American joint venture. *Journal of Applied Communication Research, 20,* 162–183.

Hansen, C. H., & Hansen, R. D. (1991). Constructing personality and social reality through music: Individual differences among fans of punk and heavy metal music. *Journal of Broadcasting and Electronic Media, 35,* 335–350.

Hawkins, R. P., & Pingree, S. (1980). Some processes in the cultivation effect. *Communication Research, 7,* 193–226.

Hawkins, R. P., & Pingree, S. (1981a). Uniform messages and habitual viewing: Unnecessary assumptions in social reality effects. *Human Communication Effects, 7,* 291–301.

Hawkins, R. P., & Pingree, S. (1981b). Using television to construct social reality. *Journal of Broadcasting, 25,* 347–364.

Herbst, S. (1991). Classical democracy, polls, and public opinion: Theoretical frameworks for studying the development of public sentiment. *Communication Theory, 1,* 225–238.

Herzog, H. (1944). What do we really know about daytime serial listeners? In P. E. Lazarsfeld & F. N. Stanton (Eds.), *Radio research 1942–1943* (pp. 3–33). New York: Duel, Sloan, and Pearce.

Hirsch, P. M. (1980). The 'scary world' of the nonviewer and other anomalies: A re-analyzis of Gerbner et al.'s findings on cultivation analysis. Part I. *Communication Research, 7,* 403–456.

Hirsch, P. M. (1981). On not learning from one's mistakes: A re-analysis of Gerbner et al.'s findings on cultivation analysis. Part II. *Public Opinion Quarterly, 44,* 287–302.

Hoffner, C., & Haefner, M. J. (1994). Children's news interest during the Gulf War: The role of negative affect. *Journal of Broadcasting and Electronic Media, 38,* 193–337.

Hofstede, G. (1980). *Culture's consequences: International differences in work-related values.* Beverly Hills, CA: Sage.

Hofstede, G. (1983). National cultures in four dimensions: A research-based theory of cultural differences among nations. *International Studies of Management and Organizations, 13,* 46–74.

Hughes, M. (1980). The fruits of cultivation analysis: A re-examination of some effects of television watching. *Public Opinion Quarterly, 44,* 287–302.

Iyengar, S., & Simon, A. (1993). News coverage of the Gulf crisis and public opinion: A study of agenda-setting, priming, and framing. *Communication Research, 20,* 365–383.

Jacobs, R. (1995). Exploring the determinants of cable television subscriber satisfaction. *Journal of Broadcasting and Electronic Media, 39,* 262–274.

Katz, E. (1957). The two-step flow of communication: An up-to-date report on an hypothesis. *Public Opinion Quarterly, 21,* 61–78.

Katz, E. (1959). Mass communication research and the study of popular culture. *Studies in Public Communication, 2,* 1–6.

Kielwasser, A. P., Wolf, M. A. (1992). Mainstream television, adolescent homosexuality, and significant silence. *Critical Studies in Mass Communication, 9,* 350–373.

Kim, Y. Y. (1977a). Communication patterns of foreign immigrants in the process of acculturation. *Human Communication Research, 4,* 66–77.

Kim, Y. Y. (1977b). Inter-ethnic and intra-ethnic communication: A study of Korean immigrants in Chicago. *International and Intercultural Communication Annual, 4,* 53–68.

Kim, Y. Y. (1978). A communication approach to acculturation processes. *International Journal of Intercultural Relations, 2,* 197–224.

Kim, Y. Y. (1979). Toward an interactive theory of communication–acculturation. In B. Ruben (Ed.). *Communication yearbook 3* (pp. 435–453). New Brunswick, NJ: Transaction.

Kim, Y. Y. (1984). Searching for creative integration. In W. B. Gudykunst & Y. Y. Kim (Eds.), *Methods for intercultural communication research* (pp. 13–30). Beverly Hills, CA: Sage.

Kim, Y. Y. (1986a). Understanding the social context of intergroup communication: A personal network approach. In W. Gudykunst (Ed.), *Intergroup communication* (pp. 86–95). London: Edward Arnold.

Kim, Y. Y. (Ed.). (1986b). *Interethnic communication: Current research.* Newbury Park, CA: Sage.

Kim, Y. Y. (1987). Facilitating immigrant adaptation: The role of communication and interpersonal ties. In T. Albrecht & M. Adelman (Eds.), *Communication and social support: Process in context* (pp. 192–211). Newbury Park, CA: Sage.

Kim, Y. Y. (1988a). *Communication and cross-cultural adaptation: An integrative theory.* Clevedon, England: Multilingual Matters.

Kim, Y. Y. (1988b). On theorizing intercultural communication. In Y. Kim & W. Gudykunst (Eds.), *Theories in intercultural communication* (pp. 11–21). Newbury Park, CA: Sage.

Kim, Y. Y. (1989). Personal, social, and economic adaptation: The case of 1975–1979 arrivals in Illinois. In D. Gaines (Ed.), *Refugees as immigrants: Survey research on Cambodians, Laotians, and Vietnamese in America* (pp. 86–104). Totowa, NJ: Rowman & Littlefield.

Kim, Y. Y. (1990). Communication and adaptation of Asian Pacific refugees in the United States. *Journal of Pacific Rim Communication, 1,* 191–207.

Kim, Y. Y. (1991). Intercultural communication competence. In S. Ting–Toomey & F. Korzenny (Eds.), *Cross-cultural interpersonal communication* (pp. 259–275). Newbury Park, CA: Sage.

Kim, Y. Y. (1994a). Beyond cultural identity. *Intercultural communication studies, 4,* 1–24.

Kim, Y. Y. (1994b). Cross-cultural comparisons of the perceived importance of conversational constraints. *Human Communication Research, 21,* 128–151.

Kim, Y. Y. (1994c). Intercultural personhood: An integration of Eastern and Western perspectives. In L. A. Samovar & R. E. Porter (Eds.), *Intercultural communication: A reader* (6th ed., pp. 415–425). Belmont, CA: Sage.

Kim, Y. Y. (1994d). Interethnic communication: The context and the behavior. In S. A. Deetz (Ed.), *Communication yearbook 17* (pp. 511–538). Thousand Oaks, CA: Sage.

Kim, Y. Y. (1995). Cross-cultural adaptation: An integrative theory. In R. L. Wiseman (Ed.), *International and intercultural communication annual, vol. 19: Intercultural communication theory* (pp. 170–193). Thousand Oaks, CA: Sage.

Kim, Y. Y. (1996). *Becoming intercultural: An integrative theory of cross-cultural adaptation.* Thousand Oaks, CA: Sage.

Kim, Y. Y., & Gudykunst, W. B. (Eds.) (1988). *Theories in intercultural communication: International and intercultural communication annual, vol. 12.* Newbury Park, CA: Sage.

Kim, Y. Y., & Paulk, S. (1994). Intercultural challenges and personal adjustments: A qualitative analysis of the experiences of American and Japanese coworkers. In R. L. Wiseman & R. Shuter (Eds.), *Communicating in multinational organizations: International and intercultural communication annual, vol. 18* (pp. 117–140). Thousand Oaks, CA: Sage.

Kim, Y. Y., & Ruben, B. (1988). Intercultural transformation: A systems theory. In Y. Y. Kim & W. B. Gudykunst (Eds.), *Theories in intercultural communication* (pp. 299–321). Newbury, Park, CA: Sage.

Klapper, J. T. (1963). Mass communication research: An old road resurveyed. *Public Opinion Quarterly, 27,* 515–427.

Koester, J., & Olebe, M. (1988). The behavioral assessment scale for intercultural communication effectiveness. *International Journal of Intercultural Relations, 12,* 233–246.

Kosicki, G. M. (1993). Problems and opportunities in agenda-setting research. *Journal of Communication, 43*(2), 100–127.

Kramer, M. W. (1993). Communication and uncertainty reduction during job transfers: Leaving and joining processes. *Communication Monographs, 60,* 178–198.

Krugman, D. M., & Johnson, K. F. (1991). Differences in the consumption of traditional broadcast and VCR movie rentals. *Journal of Broadcasting & Electronic Media, 35,* 213–232.

Lasorsa, D. L., & Wanta, W. (1990). Effects of personal, interpersonal and media experiences on issue saliences. *Journalism Quarterly, 67,* 804–813.

Leeds–Hurwitz, W. (1990). Notes in the history of intercultural communication: The Foreign Service Institute and the mandate for intercultural training. *Quarterly Journal of Speech, 76,* 262–281.

Lowery, S. A., & DeFleur, M. L. (1995). *Milestones in mass communication research: Media effects* (3rd ed.). White Plains, NY: Longman.

Lustig, M. W., & Koester, J. (1996). *Intercultural competence: Interpersonal communication across cultures.* New York: HarperCollins.

Massey, K. B. (1995). Analyzing the uses and gratifications concept of audience activity with a qualitative approach: Media encounters during the 1989 Loma Prieta earthquake disaster. *Journal of Broadcasting and Electronic Media, 39,* 328–349.

McCombs, M. E., & Shaw, D. L. (1972). The agenda-setting function of mass media. *Public Opinion Quarterly, 36,* 176–187.

McCombs, M. E., & Shaw, D. L. (1993). The evolution of agenda-setting research: Twenty-five years in the marketplace of ideas. *Journal of Communication, 43*(2), 58–67.

McLeod, D. M. (1995). Communicating deviance: The effects of television news coverage of social protest. *Journal of Broadcasting and Electronic Media, 39,* 4–19.

McLuhan, M. (1962). *The Gutenberg Galaxy: The making of typographic man.* New York: Mentor.

McLuhan, M. (1965). *Understanding media: The extensions of man.* New York: McGraw-Hill.

McLuhan, M. (1967). *The medium is the message.* New York: Bantam Books.

McLuhan, M. (1973). At the moment of Sputnik the planet became a global theater in which there are no spectators but only actors. *Journal of Communication, 24*(1), 48–58.

McLuhan, M., & Fiori, Q. (1967). *The medium is the message.* New York: Random House.

McLuhan, M., & McLuhan, E. (1988). *Laws of media: The new science.* Toronto, CA: University of Toronto Press.

McLuhan, M., & Powers, B. R. (1989). *The global village: Transformations in world life and media in the 21st Century.* New York: Oxford University Press.

Morgan, M. (1980). Television and reading: Does more equal better? *Journal of Communication, 30*(1), 159–165.

Morgan, M. (1982). Television and adolescents' sex role stereotypes: A longitudinal study. *Journal of Personality and Social Psychology, 43,* 947–955.

Morgan, M. (1983). Symbolic victimization and real world fear. *Human Communication Research, 9,* 146–157.

Morgan, M. (1984). Heavy television viewing and perceived quality of life. *Journalism Quarterly, 61,* 499–504, 740.

Morgan, M. (1986). Television and the erosion of regional diversity. *Journal of Broadcasting and Electronic Media, 30,* 123–139.

Morgan, M., & Signorielli, N. (1990). Cultivation analysis: Conceptualization and methodology. In N. Signorielli & M. Morgan (Eds.), *Cultivation analysis: New directions in media effects research* (pp. 13–34). Newbury Park, CA: Sage.

Morisaki, S., & Gudykunst, W. B. (1994). Face in Japan and the United States. In S. Ting–Toomey (Ed.), *The challenge of facework: Cross-cultural and interpersonal issues* (pp. 47–93). Albany, NY: SUNY Press.

Mosley, W. (1990). *Devil in a blue dress.* New York: Pocket Books.

Noelle–Neumann, E. (1973). Return to the concept of powerful mass media. *Studies of Broadcasting, 9,* 67–112.

Noelle–Neumann, E. (1974). The spiral of silence: A theory of public opinion. *Journal of Communication, 24*(2), 43–51.

Noelle–Neumann, E. (1977). Turbulences in the climate of opinion: Methodological applications of the spiral of silence theory. *Public Opinion Quarterly, 41,* 143–158.

Noelle–Neumann, E. (1979). Public opinion and the classical tradition: A re-evaluation. *Public Opinion Quarterly, 43,* 143–156.

Noelle–Neumann, E. (1980). Mass media and social change in developed societies. In G. C. Wilhoit & H. de Beck (Eds.), *Mass communication review yearbook, vol. 1* (pp. 657–678). Beverly Hills, CA: Sage.

Noelle–Neumann, E. (1983). The effect of media on media effects research. *Journal of Communication, 33*(3), 157–165.

Noelle–Neumann, E. (1984). *The spiral of silence: Public opinion–our social skin.* Chicago: University of Chicago Press.

Noelle–Neumann, E. (1985). The spiral of silence: A response. In L. L. Kaid & D. Nimmo (Eds.), *Political communication yearbook, 1984* (pp. 66–94). Carbondale, IL: Southern Illinois University Press.

Noelle–Neumann, E. (1991). The theory of public opinion: The concept of the spiral of silence. In J. A. Anderson (Ed.), *Communication yearbook 14* (pp. 256–287). Newbury Park, CA: Sage.

Noelle–Neumann, E., & Mathes, R. (1987). The 'event as event' and the 'event as news': The significance of 'consonance' for media effects research. *European Journal of Communication, 2,* 391–414.

Olaniran, B. A., & Williams, D. E. (1995). Communication distortion: An intercultural lesson from the visa application process. *Communication Quarterly, 43,* 225–240.

Olebe, M., & Koester, J. (1989). Exploring the cross-cultural equivalence of the behavioral assessment scale for intercultural communication. *International Journal of Intercultural Relations, 13,* 333–347.

Oliver, M. B. (1994). Portrayals of crime, race, and aggression in 'reality-based' police shows: A content analysis. *Journal of Broadcasting and Electronic Media, 38,* 179–192.

Oliver, M. B. (1996). Influences of authoritarianism and portrayals of race on Caucasian viewers' responses to reality-based crime dramas. *Communication Reports, 9,* 141–150.

Palmgreen, P., & Rayburn, II, J. D. (1985). A comparison of gratification models of media satisfaction. *Communication Monographs, 52,* 334–346.

Palmgreen, P., Wenner, L. A., & Rayburn, II, J. D. (1980). Relations between gratifications sought

and obtained: A study of television news. *Communication Research, 7,* 161–192.

Perse, E. M. (1986). Soap opera viewing patterns of college students and cultivation. *Journal of Broadcasting and Electronic Media, 30,* 175–193.

Perse, E. M., Ferguson, D. A., & McLeod, D. M. (1994). Cultivation in the newer media environment. *Communication Research, 21,* 79–104.

Perse, E. M., & Rubin, A. M. (1990). Chronic loneliness and television use. *Journal of Broadcasting and Electronic Media, 34,* 37–53.

Pfau, M., Mullen, J. J., & Garrow, K. (1995). The influence of television viewing on public perceptions of physicians. *Journal of Broadcasting and Electronic Media, 39,* 441–458.

Potter, W. J. (1986). Perceived reality and the cultivation hypothesis. *Journal of Broadcasting and Electronic Media, 30,* 159–174.

Potter, W. J. (1988). Three strategies for elaborating the cultivation hypothesis. *Journalism Quarterly, 65,* 930–939.

Potter, W. J. (1991). The linearity assumption in cultivation research. *Communication Research, 17,* 562–583.

Potter, W. J. (1993). Cultivation theory and research: A conceptual critique. *Human Communication Research, 19,* 564–601.

Potter, J. P., & Chang, I. C. (1990). Television exposure measures and the cultivation hypothesis. *Journal of Broadcasting and Electronic Media, 34,* 313–333.

Rafaeli, S., & LaRose, R. J. (1993). Electronic bulletin boards and 'public goods' explanations of collaborative mass media. *Communication Research, 20,* 277–297.

Rogers, E. M., & Dearing, J. W. (1988). Agenda-setting research: Where has it been, where is it going? In J. A. Anderson (Ed.), *Communication Yearbook 11* (pp. 555–594). Newbury Park, CA: Sage.

Rogers, E. M., Dearing, J. W., & Bregman, D. (1993). The anatomy of agenda-setting research. *Journal of Communication, 43*(2), 68–84.

Rubin, A. M. (1984). Ritualized and instrumental television viewing. *Journal of Communication, 34*(3), 67–77.

Rubin, A. M. (1993). Audience activity and media use. *Communication Monographs, 60,* 98–105.

Rubin, A. M., & Rubin, R. B. (1985). Interface of personal and mediated communication: A research agenda. *Critical Studies in Mass Communication, 2,* 36–53.

Rubin, A. M., & Windahl, S. (1986). The uses and dependency model of mass communication. *Critical Studies in Mass Communication, 3,* 184–199.

Schmitz, J., & Fulk, J. (1991). Organizational colleagues, media richness, and electronic mail: A test of the social influence of media technology. *Communication Research, 18,* 487–523.

Shapiro, M. A. (1991). Memory and decision processes in the construction of social reality. *Communication Research, 18,* 3–24.

Shapiro, M. A. & Lang, A. (1991). Making television reality: Unconscious processes in the construction of social reality. *Communication Research, 18,* 685–705.

Shaw, D. L., & Martin, S. E. (1992). The function of mass media agenda-setting. *Journalism Quarterly, 69,* 902–920.

Shrum, L. J., & O'Guinn, T. C. (1993). Processes and effects in the construction of social reality: Construct accessibility as an explanatory variable. *Communication Research, 20,* 436–471.

Signorielli, N. (1989). Television and conceptions about sex roles: Maintaining conventionality and the status quo. *Sex Roles, 21,* 341–360.

Signorielli, N., & Morgan, M. (Eds.) (1990). *Cultivation analysis: New directions in media effects research.* Newbury Park, CA: Sage.

Simpson, C. (1996). Elisabeth Noelle–Neumann's 'spiral of silence' and the historical context of communication theory. *Journal of Communication, 46*(3), 149–173.

Smith, K. A. (1987a). Effects of newspaper coverage on community issue concerns and local government evaluations. *Communication Research, 14,* 379–395.

Smith, K. A. (1987b). Newspaper coverage and public concern about community issues: A time-series analysis. *Journalism Monographs, 101,* 1–34.

Sparks, G. G., & Ogles, R. M. (1990). The difference between fear of victimization and the probability of being victimized: Implications for cultivation. *Journal of Broadcasting and Electronic Media, 34,* 351–358.

Spitzberg, B. H. (1988). Communication competence: Measures of perceived effectiveness. In C. H. Tardy (Ed.), *A handbook for the study of human communication* (pp. 67–105). Norwood, NJ: Ablex.

Spitzberg, B. H., & Cupach, W. R. (1984). *Interpersonal communication competence: Sage series in interpersonal communication, vol. 4.* Beverly Hills, CA: Sage.

Stewart, L., Gudykunst, W. B., Ting–Toomey, S., Nishida, T. (1986). The effects of decision-making style on openness and satisfaction within Japanese organizations. *Communication Monographs, 53,* 236–251.

Sullivan, D. B. (1991). Commentary and viewer perception of player hostility: Adding punch to televised sports. *Journal of Broadcasting and Electronic Media, 35,* 487–504.

Swanson, D. L. (1977). The uses and misuses of uses and gratifications. *Human Communication Research, 3,* 214–221.

Tamborini, R., & Choi, J. (1990). The role of cultural diversity in cultivation research. In N. Signorielli & M. Morgan (Eds.), *Cultivation analysis: New directions in media effects research* (pp. 157–180). Newbury Park, CA: Sage.

Tapper, J. (1995). The ecology of cultivation: A conceptual model for cultivation research. *Communication Theory, 5,* 36–57.

Ting–Toomey, S. (1983a). An analysis of verbal communication patterns in high and low marital adjustment groups. *Human Communication Research, 9,* 305–319.

Ting–Toomey, S. (1983b). Coding conversation between intimates: A validation study of the intimate negotiation coding system (INCS). *Communication Quarterly, 31,* 68–77.

Ting–Toomey, S. (1985). Toward a theory of conflict and culture. In W. Gudykunst, L. Stewart, & S. Ting–Toomey (Eds.), *Communication, culture, and organizational processes* (pp. 71–86). Beverly Hills, CA: Sage.

Ting–Toomey, S. (1988a). Intercultural conflict styles: A face-negotiation theory. In Y. Y. Kim & W. Gudykunst (Eds.), *Theories in intercultural communication* (pp. 213–235). Newbury Park, CA: Sage.

Ting–Toomey, S. (1988b). Rhetorical sensitivity style in three cultures: France, Japan, and the United States. *Communication Studies, 39,* 28–36.

Ting–Toomey, S. (1990). Intergroup diplomatic communication: A face-negotiation perspective. In F. Korzenny & S. Ting–Toomey (Eds.), *Communicating for peace* (pp. 75–95). Newbury Park, CA: Sage.

Ting–Toomey, S. (1993). Communicative resourcefulness: An identity negotiation perspective. In R. L. Wiseman & J. Koester (Eds.), *Intercultural communication competence* (pp. 71–111). Newbury Park, CA: Sage.

Ting–Toomey, S. (Ed.) (1994). *The challenge of facework: Cross-cultural and interpersonal issues.* Albany: SUNY Press.

Ting–Toomey, S., & Cocroft, B.-A. (1994). Face and facework: Theoretical and research issues. In S. Ting–Toomey (Ed.), *The challenge of facework: Cross-cultural and interpersonal issues* (pp. 307–340). Albany: SUNY Press.

Ting–Toomey, S., Gao, G., Trubisky, P., Yang, Z., Kim, H. S., & Nishida, T. (1991). Culture, face maintenance, and styles of handling interpersonal conflict: A study in five cultures. *International Journal in Conflict Management, 2,* 275–296.

Trevino, L. K., & Webster, J. (1992). Flow in computer-mediated communication: Electronic mail and voice mail evaluation and impacts. *Communication Research, 19,* 539–573.

Vande Berg, L. R., & Streckfuss, D. (1992). Prime-time television's portrayal of women and the world of work: A demographic profile. *Journal of Broadcasting and Electronic Media, 36,* 195–208.

Wanta, W., & Foote, J. (1994). The president–news media relationship: A time-series analysis of agenda-setting. *Journal of Broadcasting and Electronic Media, 38,* 437–448.

Wanta, W., Stephenson, M. A., Turk, J. V., & McCombs, M. E. (1989). How President's State of the Union talk influenced news media agendas. *Journalism Quarterly, 66,* 537–541.

Watt, J. H., Mazza, M., & Snyder, L. (1993). Agenda-setting effects of television news coverage and the effects decay curve. *Communication Research, 26,* 408–435.

Weaver, D. (1984). Media agenda-setting and public opinion: Is there a link? In R. N. Bostrom (Ed.), *Communication Yearbook 8* (pp. 680–691). Beverly Hills, CA: Sage.

Weaver, J., & Wakshlag, J. (1986). Perceived vulnerability to crime, criminal victimization experience, and television viewing. *Journal of Broadcasting and Electronic Media, 30,* 141–158.

Witte, K. (1993). A theory of cognition and negative effect: Extending Gudykunst and Hammer's theory of uncertainty and anxiety. *International Journal of Intercultural Relations, 17,* 197–216.

Wober, J. M. (1978). Televised violence and paranoid perception: The view from Great Britain. *Public Opinion Quarterly, 42,* 315–321.

Yum, J. O., & Kendall, K. E. (1995). Sex differences in political communication during presidential campaigns. *Communication Quarterly, 43,* 131–141.

Zillmann, D., Gibson, R., Ordman, V. L., & Aust, C. F. (1994). Effects of upbeat stories in broadcast news. *Journal of Broadcasting and Electronic Media, 38,* 65–78.

Zhu, J. H., Watt, J. H., Snyder, L. B., Yan, J., & Jiang, Y. (1993). Public issue priority formation: Media agenda-setting and social interaction. *Journal of Communication, 43*(1), 8–29.

Chapter 11   Communication Microtheories

Aida, Y. (1993). Communication apprehension and power strategies in marital relationships. *Communication Reports, 6,* 116–121.

Alberts, J. K., Miller–Rassulo, M. A., & Hecht, M. L. (1991). A typology of drug resistance strategies. *Journal of Applied Communication Research, 19,* 129–151.

Allen, D. S. (1995, November). Communicative ethics and public journalism: A movement in search of an ethical standard. Speech Communication Association annual meeting. San Antonio, TX.

Ashcraft, K. L., & Pacanowsky, M. E. (1996). 'A woman's worst enemy': Reflections on a narrative of organizational life and female identity. *Journal of Applied Communication Research, 24,* 217–239.

Ayres, J., Wilcox, A. K., & Ayres, D. M. (1995). Receiver apprehension: An explanatory model and accompanying research. *Communication Education, 44,* 223–250.

Baran, S. J., & Davis, D. K. (1995). *Mass communication theory: Foundations, ferment, and future.* Belmont, CA: Wadsworth.

Bateson, G. (1957). *Naven.* Stanford, CA: Stanford University Press.

Baxter, L. A. (1984). An investigation of compliance-gaining as politeness. *Human Communication Research, 10,* 427–456.

Baynes, K. (1994). Communicative ethics, the public sphere and communication media. *Critical Studies in Mass Communication, 11,* 315–326.

Bell, R. A., Cholerton, M., Fraczek, K. E., Rohlfs, G. S., & Smith, B. A. (1994). Encouraging donations to charity: A field study of competing and complementary factors of tactic sequencing. *Western Journal of Communication, 58,* 98–115.

Berger, C. R. (1994). Power, dominance, and social interaction. In M. L. Knapp & G. R. Miller (Eds.), *Handbook of interpersonal communication* (pp. 450–507). Thousand Oaks, CA: Sage.

Bledstein, B. (1976). *The culture of professionalism.* New York: Norton.

Booth–Butterfield, M., & Booth–Butterfield, S. (1994). Communication anxiety and signing effectiveness: Testing an interference model among deaf communicators. *Journal of Applied Communication Research, 22,* 273–286.

Booth–Butterfield, M., & Thomas, C. C. (1995). Communication apprehension among secretarial students. *Communication Reports, 8,* 38–44.

Boster, F. J. (1995). Commentary on compliance-gaining message behavior research. In C. R. Berger & M. Burgoon (Eds.), *Communication and social influence processes* (pp. 91–113). East Lansing, MI: Michigan State University Press.

Bowers, J. W. (1974). Beyond threats and promises. *Speech Monographs, 41,* ix–xi.

Buller, D. B., & Aune, R. K. (1987). Nonverbal cues to deception among intimates, friends, and strangers. *Journal of Nonverbal Behavior, 11,* 269–290.

Buller, D. B., & Aune, R. K. (1988). The effects of vocalics and nonverbal sensitivity on compliance: A speech accommodation theory explanation. *Human Communication Research, 14,* 301–332.

Buller, D. B., & Burgoon, J. K. (1994). Deception: Strategic and non-strategic communication. In J. A. Daly & J. M. Wiemann (Eds.), *Strategic interpersonal communication* (pp. 191–224). Hillsdale, NJ: Erlbaum.

Buller, D. B., & Burgoon, J. K. (1996). Interpersonal deception theory. *Communication Theory, 6,* 203–242.

Buller, D. B., Burgoon, J. K., Buslig, A., & Roiger, J. (1996). Testing interpersonal deception theory: The language of interpersonal deception. *Communication Theory, 6,* 268–288.

Buller, D. B., Burgoon, J. K., White, C. H., & Ebesu, A. S. (1994). Interpersonal deception: VII. Behavioral profiles of falsification, concealment, and equivocation. *Journal of Language and Social Psychology, 13,* 366–395.

Buller, D. B., Comstock, J., Aune, R. K., Strzyzewski, K. D. (1989). The effect of probing on deceivers and truth-tellers. *Journal of Nonverbal Behavior, 13,* 155–170.

Buller, D. B., Stiff, J. B., & Burgoon, J. K. (1996). Behavioral adaptation in deceptive transactions: Fact or fiction: Reply to Levine and McCornack. *Human Communication Research, 22,* 589–603.

Buller, D. B., Strzyzewski, K. D., & Comstock, J. (1991). Deceivers' reactions to receivers' suspicions and probing. *Communication Monographs, 58,* 1–24.

Burgoon, J. K. (1978). A communication model of personal space violations: Explication and an initial test. *Human Communication Research, 4,* 129–142.

Burgoon, J. K. (1986). Communicative effects of gaze behavior: A test of two contrasting explanations. *Human Communication Research, 12,* 495–524.

Burgoon, J. K. (1992). Applying a comparative approach to nonverbal expectancy violations theory. In J. Blumler, K. E. Rosengren, & D. M. McLeod (Eds.), *Comparatively speaking* (pp. 53–69). Newbury Park, CA: Sage.

Burgoon, J. K. (1993). Interpersonal expectations, expectancy violations, and emotional communication. *Journal of Language and Social Psychology, 12,* 30–48.

Burgoon, J. K. (1995). Cross-cultural and intercultural applications of expectancy violations theory. In R. L. Wiseman (Ed.), *Intercultural Communication Theory: International and intercultural communication annual, 19* (pp. 194–214). Thousand Oaks, CA: Sage.

Burgoon, J. K., & Aho, L. (1982). Three field experiments on the effects of violations of conversational distance. *Communication Monographs, 49,* 71–88.

Burgoon, J. K., & Buller, D. B. (1994). Interpersonal deception III: Effects of deceit on perceived communication and nonverbal behavior dynamics. *Journal of Nonverbal Behavior, 18,* 155–184.

Burgoon, J. K., & Buller, D. B. (1996). Reflections on the nature of theory building and the theoretical status of interpersonal deception theory. *Communication Theory, 6,* 311–328.

Burgoon, J. K., Buller, D. B., Ebesu, A., & Walther, J. (1995). Interpersonal deception IV: Effects of suspicion on perceived communication and nonverbal behavior dynamics. *Human Communication Research, 22,* 163–196.

Burgoon, J. K., Buller, D. B., Ebesu, A., & Rockwell, P. (1994). Interpersonal deception V: Accuracy in deception detection. *Communication Monographs, 61,* 303–325.

Burgoon, J. K., Buller, D. B., Ebesu, A. S., White, C. H., & Rockwell, P. A. (1996a). Testing interpersonal deception theory: Effects of suspicion on communication behaviors and perceptions. *Communication Theory, 6,* 243–267.

Burgoon, J. K., Buller, D. B., Guerrero, L. K., Afifi, W., & Feldman, C. M. (1996b). Interpersonal deception XII: Information management dimensions underlying types of deceptive messages. *Communication Monographs, 63,* 50–69.

Burgoon, J. K., & Hale, J. L. (1988). Nonverbal expectancy violations theory: Model elaboration and application to immediacy behaviors. *Communication Monographs, 55,* 58–79.

Burgoon, J. K., & Jones, S. B. (1976). Toward a theory of personal space expectations and their violations. *Human Communication Research, 2,* 131–146.

Burgoon, J. K., & Le Poire, B. A. (1993). Effects of communication expectancies, actual communication, and expectancy disconfirmation on evaluation of communicators and their communication behavior. *Human Communication Research, 20,* 67–96.

Burgoon, J. K., Newton, D. A., Walther, J. B., & Baesler, E. J. (1989). Nonverbal expectancy violations and conversational involvement. *Journal of Nonverbal Behavior, 12,* 97–120.

Burgoon, J. K., & Walther, J. B. (1990). Nonverbal expectancies and the evaluative consequences of violations. *Human Communication Research, 17,* 232–265.

Burke, J. A. (1989). A comparison of methods for eliciting persuasive strategies: Strategy selection versus message construction. *Communication Reports, 2,* 72–82.

Burleson, B. R., & Kline, S. L. (1979). Habermas's theory of communication: A critical explication. *Quarterly Journal of Speech, 65,* 412–428.

Buzzanell, P. M. (1994). Gaining a voice: Feminist perspectives in organizational communication. *Management Communication Quarterly, 7,* 339–383.

Buzzanell, P. M. (1995). Reframing the glass ceiling as a socially constructed process: Implications for understanding and change. *Communication Monographs, 62,* 327–354.

Buzzanell, P. M., Burrell, N. A., Stafford, R. S., & Berkowitz, S. (1996). When I call you up and you're not there: Application of communication accommodation theory to telephone answering machine messages. *Western Journal of Communication, 60,* 310–336.

Campbell, K. K. (1973). The rhetoric of women's liberation: An oxymoron. *Quarterly Journal of Speech, 59,* 74–86.

Campbell, K. K. (1986). Style and content in the rhetoric of early Afro-American feminists. *Quarterly Journal of Speech, 72,* 434–445.

Campbell, K. K. (1989a). *Man cannot speak for her: A critical study of early feminist rhetoric, vol. 1,* New York: Praeger.

Campbell, K. K. (1989b). The sound of women's voices. *Quarterly Journal of Speech, 75,* 212–220.

Campbell, K. K. (1991). Hearing women's voices. *Communication Education, 40,* 33–48.

Campbell, K. K. (Ed.). (1994). *Women public speakers in the United States, 1925–1993: A bio-critical source-book.* Westport, CT: Greenwood Press.

Campbell, K. K. (1995). Gender and genre: Loci of invention and contradiction in the earliest speeches by U.S. women. *Quarterly Journal of Speech, 81,* 479–495.

Chesebro, J. W. (1995). Communication technologies as cognitive systems. In J. T. Wood & R. B. Gregg (Eds.), *Toward the 21st Century: The future of speech communication* (pp. 15–46). Cresskill, NJ: Hampton Press.

Chesebro, J. W., & Cragan, J. F. (Eds.). (1971). Special issue: The rhetoric of women's liberation. *Moments in Contemporary Rhetoric and Communication, 1*(2), 22–54.

Cody, M. J., & McLaughlin, M. L. (1980). Perceptions of compliance-gaining situations: A dimensional analysis. *Communication Monographs, 47,* 132–148.

Comadena, M. E. (1984). Brainstorming groups: Ambiguity tolerance, communication apprehension, task attraction, and individual productivity. *Small Group Behavior, 15,* 251–264.

Coupland, N., Coupland, J., Giles, H., & Henwood, K. (1988). Accommodating the elderly: Invoking and extending a theory. *Language and Society, 17,* 1–41.

Coupland, N., Henwood, K., Coupland, J., & Giles, H. (1990). Accommodating troubles talk: The young's management of elderly self-disclosure. In

G. M. McGregor & R. White (Eds.), *Reception and response: Hearer creativity and analysis of spoken and written texts* (pp. 112–144). London: Croom Helm.

Courtright, J. A., Millar, F. E., & Rogers–Millar, L. E. (1979). Domineeringness and dominance: Replication and expansion. *Communication Monographs, 46,* 179–192.

Courtright, J. A., Millar, F. E., Rogers, L. E., & Bagarozzi, D. (1990). Interaction dynamics of relational negotiation: Reconciliation versus termination of distressed relationships. *Western Journal of Speech Communication, 54,* 429–453.

Craig, R. T., Tracy, C., & Spisak, F. (1986). The discourse of requests: Assessment of a politeness approach. *Human Communication Research, 12,* 437–468.

Daly, J. A., & Stafford, L. (1984). Correlates and consequences of social communicative anxiety. In J. A. Daly & J. C. McCroskey (Eds.), *Avoiding communication: Shyness, reticence, and communication apprehension* (pp. 124–144). Beverly Hills, CA: Sage.

Daly, J. A., Vangelisti, A. L., & Weber, D. J. (1995). Speech anxiety affects how people prepare speeches: A protocol analysis of the preparation processes of speakers. *Communication Monographs, 62,* 383–397.

Darwin, C. [1872] (1955). *The expression of emotion in man and animals.* New York: Philosophical Library.

deTurck, M. A., & Miller, G. R. (1990). Training observers to detect deception: Effects of self-monitoring and rehearsal. *Human Communication Research, 16,* 603–620.

deTurck, M. A., Harszalak, J. J., Bodhorn, D. J., & Texter, L. A. (1990). The effects of training social perceivers to detect deception from behavior cues. *Communication Quarterly, 38,* 1–11.

Dillard, J. P., & Burgoon, M. (1985). Situational influences on the selection of compliance-gaining messages: Two tests of the predictive utility of the Cody–McLaughlin typology. *Communication Monographs, 52,* 289–304.

Dow, B. J. (1995). Feminism, difference(s), and rhetorical studies. *Communication Studies, 46,* 106–117.

Dow, B. J., & Tonn, M. B. (1993). 'Feminine style' and political judgment in the rhetoric of Ann Richards. *Quarterly Journal of Speech, 79,* 286–303.

Ekman, P. (1985). *Telling lies.* New York: Norton.

Ekman, P., & Friesen, W. V. (1969). Nonverbal leakage and clues to deception. *Journal of Personality and Social Psychology, 29,* 288–298.

Ellis, D. G. (1978). Trait predictors of relational control. In B. Ruben (Ed.), *Communication Yearbook 2* (pp. 231–240). Edison, NJ: Transaction Press.

Ellis, D. G. (1979). Relational control in two group systems. *Communication Monographs, 46,* 153–166.

Ellis, D. G. (Ed.). (1996). Special issue, interpersonal deception: Theory and critique. *Communication Theory, 6,* 203–328.

Ellis, D. G., & McCallister, L. (1980). Relational control sequences in sex-typed and androgynous groups. *Western Journal of Speech Communication, 44,* 35–49.

Engler–Parish, P. G., & Millar, F. E. (1989). An exploratory relational control analysis of the employment screening interview. *Western Journal of Speech Communication, 53,* 30–51.

Ferrara, K. (1991). Accommodation in therapy. In H. Giles, J. Coupland, & N. Coupland (Eds.), *Contexts of accommodation: Developments in applied sociolinguistics* (pp. 187–222). Cambridge: Cambridge University Press.

Fink, C. C. (1988). *Media ethics in the newsroom and beyond* (Appendix 3). New York: McGraw-Hill.

Fitzpatrick, M. A. (1977). A typological approach to communication in relationships. In B. Rubin (Ed.), *Communication Yearbook 1* (pp. 263–275). Rutgers, NJ: Transaction Press.

Fitzpatrick, M. A. (1981). A typological approach to enduring relationships: Children as audience to parental relationships. *Journal of Comparative Family Studies, 12,* 81–94.

Fitzpatrick, M. A. (1983). Predicting couples' communication from couples' self-reports. In R. N. Bostrom & B. H. Westley (Eds.), *Communication Yearbook 7* (pp. 49–82). Beverly Hills, CA: Sage.

Fitzpatrick, M. A. (1984). A typological approach to marital interaction: Recent theory and research. In L. Berkowitz (Ed.), *Advances in experimental social psychology, 18* (pp. 1–47). Orlando, FL: Academic Press.

Fitzpatrick, M. A. (1988). *Between husbands and wives.* Beverly Hills, CA: Sage.

Fitzpatrick, M. A. (1991). A microsocietal approach to marital communication. In B. Dervin & M. J. Voigt (Eds.), *Progress in communication sciences, 10* (pp. 67–101). Norwood, NJ: Ablex.

Fitzpatrick, M. A., & Badzinski, D. (1986). All in the family: Communication in kin relationships. In M. Knapp & G. R. Miller (Eds.), *Handbook of interpersonal communication* (pp. 687–736). Beverly Hills, CA: Sage.

Fitzpatrick, M. A., & Best, P. (1979). Dyadic adjustment in relational types: Consensus, cohesion, affectional expression, and satisfaction in enduring relationships. *Communication Monographs, 46,* 167–178.

Fitzpatrick, M. A., & Indvik, J. (1982). The instrumental and expressive domains of marital communication. *Human Communication Research, 8,* 195–213.

Fitzpatrick, M. A., & Ritchie, L. D. (1994). Communication schemata within the family: Multiple perspectives on family interaction. *Human Communication Research, 20,* 275–301.

Foss, K. A., & Foss, S. K. (1983). The status of research on women and communication. *Communication Quarterly, 31,* 195–204.

Foss, K. A., & Foss, S. K. (1991). *Women speak: The eloquence of women's lives.* Prospect Heights, IL: Waveland Press.

Foss, S. K., & Griffin, C. L. (1992). A feminist perspective on rhetorical theory: Toward a classification of boundaries. *Western Journal of Communication, 56,* 330–349.

Foss, S. K., & Griffin, C. L. (1995). Beyond persuasion: A proposal for an invitational rhetoric. *Communication Monographs, 62,* 2–18.

Foss, S. K., Foss, K. A., & Trapp, R. (1991). *Contemporary perspectives on rhetoric* (2nd ed.). Prospect Heights, IL: Waveland Press.

Fox, S., & Giles, H. (1993). Accommodating intergenerational contact: A critique and theoretical model. *Journal of Aging Studies, 7,* 423–451.

Gallois, C., Franklyn–Stokes, A., Giles, H., & Coupland, N. (1988). Communication accommodation in intercultural encounters. In Y. Y. Kim & W. B. Gudykunst (Eds.), *Theories in intercultural communication* (pp. 157–185). Newbury Park, CA: Sage.

Giles, H., Coupland, N., & Coupland, J. (1991). Accommodation theory: Communication contexts and consequences. In H. Giles, N. Coupland, & J. Coupland (Eds.), *Contexts of accommodation: Developments in applied sociolinguistics* (pp. 1–68). Cambridge: Cambridge University Press.

Giles, H., Mulac, A., Bradac, J. J., & Johnson, P. (1987). Speech accommodation theory: The first decade and beyond. In M. L. McLaughlin (Ed.),

Communication Yearbook 10 (pp. 13–48). Beverly Hills, CA: Sage.

Giles, H., & Powesland, P. F. (1975). *Speech style and social evaluation.* London: Academic Press.

Giles, H., & Williams, A. (1992). Accommodating hypercorrection: A communication model. *Language & Communication, 12,* 343–356.

Giles, H., & Williams, A. (1994). Intergenerational patronizing: Young people's evaluations of older people's patronizing speech. *International Journal of Aging & Human Development, 39,* 33–53.

Gonzalez, H. (1989). Interactivity and feedback in third world development campaigns. *Critical Studies in Mass Communication, 6,* 295–314.

Grant, J. A., King, P. E., & Behnke, R. R. (1994). Compliance-gaining strategies, communication satisfaction, and willingness to comply. *Communication Reports, 7,* 99–108.

Greene, J. O. (1984). A cognitive approach to human communication: An action assembly theory. *Communication Monographs, 51,* 289–306.

Greene, J. O. (1989). Action-assembly theory: Metatheoretical commitments, theoretical propositions, and empirical applications. In B. Dervin, L. Grossberg, B. J. O'Keefe, & E. Wartella (Eds.), *Rethinking communication: Paradigm exemplars* (pp. 117–128). Newbury Park, CA: Sage.

Greene, J. O. (1995). An action-assembly perspective on verbal and nonverbal message production: A dancer's message unveiled. In D. E. Hewes (Ed.), *The cognitive bases of interpersonal communication* (pp. 51–85). Hillsdale, NJ: Erlbaum.

Greene, J. O., & Geddes, D. (1988). Representation and processing in the self-system: An action-oriented approach to self and self-relevant phenomena. *Communication Monographs, 55,* 287–314.

Greene, J. O., & Geddes, D. (1993). An action assembly perspective on social skill. *Communication Theory, 3,* 26–49.

Greene, J. O., & Lindsey, A. E. (1989). Encoding processes in the production of multiple-goal messages. *Human Communication Research, 16,* 120–140.

Greene, J. O., Lindsey, A. E., & Hawn, J. J. (1990). Social goals and speech production: Effects of multiple goals on pausal phenomena. *Journal of Language and Social Psychology, 9,* 119–134.

Greene, J. O., McDaniel, T. L., Buksa, K., & Ravizza, S. M. (1993). Cognitive processes in the production of multiple-goal messages: Evidence from the temporal characteristics of speech. *Western Journal of Communication, 57,* 65–86.

Greene, J. O., & Ravizza, S. M. (1995). Complexity effects on temporal characteristics of speech. *Human Communication Research, 21,* 390–421.

Grice, H. P. (1975). Logic and conversation. In P. Cole & J. L. Morgan (Eds.), *Speech acts* (pp. 41–58). New York: Academic Press.

Grice, H. P. (1989). *Studies in the way of words.* Cambridge, MA: Harvard University Press.

Habermas, J. (1964). The public sphere: An encyclopedia article (D. Lennox & F. Lennox, Trans.). *New German Critique, 3*(Fall), 49–55.

Habermas, J. (1970a). Towards a theory of communicative competence. *Inquiry, 13,* 360–375.

Habermas, J. (1970b). Towards a theory of communicative competence. In H. P. Dreitzel (Ed.), *Recent sociology 2* (pp. 114–148). London: Collier-Macmillan.

Habermas, J. (1976a). *Communication and the evolution of society* (T. McCarthy, Trans.). Boston: Beacon Press.

Habermas, J. (1976b). Some distinctions in universal pragmatics: A working paper. *Theory and Society, 3,* 155–167.

Habermas, J. (1984). *The theory of communicative action* (T. McCarthy, Trans.). Boston: Beacon Press.

Habermas, J. (1989). *The structural transformation of the public sphere* (T. Burger & F. Lawrence, Trans.). Cambridge, MA: MIT Press.

Habermas, J. (1990). *Moral consciousness and communicative action* (C. Lenhardt & S. W. Nicholsen, Trans.). Cambridge, MA: MIT Press.

Habermas, J. (1993). *Justification and application: Remarks on discourse ethics* (C. Cronin, Trans.). Cambridge, MA: MIT Press.

Hall, E. T. (1959). *The silent language.* New York: Doubleday.

Hardt, H. (1992). *Critical communication studies: Communication, history and theory in America.* London: Routledge.

Hiltz, S. R., & Turoff, M. (1978). *The network nation: Human communication via computer.* Reading, MA: Addison-Wesley.

Hogg, M. (1985). Masculine and feminine speech in dyads and groups: A study of speech style and gender salience. *Journal of Language and Social Psychology, 4,* 99–112.

Hopper, R., & Bell, R. A. (1984). Broadening the deception construct. *Quarterly Journal of Speech, 70,* 288–300.

Ifert, D. E., & Roloff, M. E. (1996). Responding to refusals of requests: The role of requester sex on persistence. *Communication Reports, 9,* 119–126.

Innis, H. A. (1950). *Empire and communication.* Toronto: University of Toronto Press.

Innis, H. A. (1951). *The bias of communication.* Toronto: University of Toronto Press.

Jacobs, S., Dawson, E. J., & Brashers, D. (1996). Information manipulation theory: A replication and assessment. *Communication Monographs, 63,* 70–82.

Johnson, F. L., & Buttny, R. (1982). White listeners' responses to 'sounding black' and 'sounding white': The effects of message content on judgments about language. *Communication Monographs, 49,* 33–49.

Kidd, V. (1971). A study of images produced through the use of the male pronoun as the generic. *Moments in Contemporary Rhetoric and Communication, 1*(2), 25–30.

Knapp, M. L., & Comadena, M. E. (1979). Telling it like it isn't: A review of theory and research on deceptive communications. *Human Communication Research, 5,* 270–285.

Kondo, D. S. (1994). Strategies for reducing public speaking anxiety in Japan. *Communication Reports, 7,* 20–26.

Kramer (now Kramarae), C. (1974). Women's speech: Separate but unequal? *Quarterly Journal of Speech, 60,* 14–24.

Kramarae, C. (1981). *Women and men speaking: Frameworks for analysis.* Rowley, MA: Newbury House.

Kramarae, C., & Treichler, P. (1992). *Amazons, bluestockings, and crones: A feminist dictionary* (2nd ed.). London: Pandora.

Levine, T. R., & McCornack, S. A. (1996). A critical analysis of the behavior adaptation explanation of the probing effect. *Human Communication Research, 22,* 575–588.

Lindsey, A. E., Greene, J. O., Parker, R. G., & Sassi, M. (1995). Effects of advance message formulation on message encoding: Evidence of cognitively based hesitation in the production of multiple goal messages. *Communication Quarterly, 43,* 320–331.

Linell, P. (1991). Accommodation on trial: Processes of communicative accommodation in courtroom interaction. In H. Giles, J. Coupland, & N. Coupland (Eds.), *Contexts of accommodation: Developments in applied sociolinguistics* (pp. 103–130). Cambridge: Cambridge University Press.

Mark, R. L. (1971). Coding communication at the relationship level. *Journal of Communication, 21* (3), 221–232.

Marwell, G., & Schmidt, D. R. (1967). Dimensions of compliance-gaining behavior: An empirical analysis. *Sociometry, 30,* 350–364.

McCornack, S. A. (1992). Information manipulation theory. *Communication Monographs, 59,* 1–15.

McCornack, S. A., & Levine, T. R. (1990a). When lies are uncovered: Emotional and relational outcomes of discovered deception. *Communication Monographs, 57,* 119–138.

McCornack, S. A., & Levine, T. R. (1990b). When lovers become leery: The relationship between suspicion and accuracy in detecting deception. *Communication Monographs, 57,* 219–230.

McCornack, S. A., Levine, T. R., Solowczuk, K. A., Torres, H. I., & Campbell, D. M. (1992). When the alteration of information is viewed as deception: An empirical test of information manipulation theory. *Communication Monographs, 59,* 17–29.

McCornack, S. A., & Parks, M. R. (1986). Deception detection and relationship development: The other side of trust. In M. L. McLaughlin (Ed.), *Communication Yearbook 9* (pp. 377–389). Beverly Hills, CA: Sage.

McCornack, S. A., & Parks, M. R. (1990). What women know that men don't: Sex differences in determining the truth behind deceptive messages. *Journal of Social and Personal Relationships, 7,* 107–118.

McCroskey, J. C. (1970). Measures of communication-bound anxiety. *Speech Monographs, 37,* 269–277.

McCroskey, J. C. (1971). The implementation of a large-scale program as systematic desensitization for communication apprehension. *Speech Teacher, 21,* 255–264.

McCroskey, J. C. (1977a). Classroom consequences of communication apprehension. *Communication Education, 26,* 27–33.

McCroskey, J. C. (1977b). Oral communication: A summary of recent theory and research. *Human Communication Research, 4,* 78–96.

McCroskey, J. C. (1978). Validity of the PRGA as an index of oral communication apprehension. *Communication Monographs, 45,* 192–203.

McCroskey, J. C. (1984). The communication apprehension perspective. In J. A. Daly & J. C. McCroskey

(Eds.), *Avoiding communication: Shyness, reticence, and communication apprehension* (pp. 13–38). Beverly Hills, CA: Sage.

McCroskey, J. C. (1993). *An introduction to rhetorical communication* (6th ed.). Englewood Cliffs, NJ: Prentice-Hall.

McCroskey, J. C., Ralph, D. C., & Barrick, J. E. (1970). The effect of systematic desensitization on speech anxiety. *Speech Teacher, 19,* 32–36.

McGuire, W. J. (1964). Inducing resistance to persuasion: Some contemporary approaches. In L. Berkowitz (Ed.), *Advances in experimental social psychology, 1* (pp. 191–229). New York: Academic Press.

McLuhan, M. (1962). *The Gutenberg Galaxy: The making of typographic man.* New York: Mentor.

McLuhan, M. (1964). *Understanding media: The extensions of man.* New York: McGraw–Hill.

McLuhan, M. (1974). At the moment of Sputnik the planet became a global theater in which there are no spectators but only actors. *Journal of Communication, 1,* 48–58.

McLuhan, M. (1975). Communication: McLuhan's laws of the media. *Technology and Culture, 16*(1), 74–78.

McLuhan, M. (1977). Laws of the media. *Et cetera, 34*(2), 173–179.

McLuhan, M., & Fiore, Q. (1967). *The medium is the massage: An inventory of effects.* New York: Random House/Bantam Books.

McLuhan, M., & McLuhan, E. (1988). *Laws of media: The new science.* Toronto, CA: University of Toronto Press.

McLuhan, M., & Powers, B. (1981). *The living McLuhan,* Ma Bell minus the Nantucket Gam: Or the impact of high-speed data transmission. *Journal of Communication, 31*(3), 191–199.

McLuhan, M., & Powers, B. R. (1989). *The global village: Transformations in world life and media in the 21st Century.* New York: Oxford University Press.

Metts, S., Cupach, W. R., & Imahori, T. (1992). Perceptions of sexual compliance-resisting messages in three types of cross-sex relationships. *Western Journal of Communication, 56,* 1–17.

Miles, D. (1996). The CD-ROM novel *Myst* and McLuhan's fourth law of media: *Myst* and its "retrievals." *Journal of Communication, 46*(2), 4–18.

Millar, F. E., & Rogers, L. E. (1976). A relational approach to interpersonal communication. In G. R.

Miller (Ed.), *Explorations in interpersonal communication* (pp. 87–103). Beverly Hills, CA: Sage.

Millar, F. E., & Rogers, L. E. (1987). Relational dimensions of interpersonal dynamics. In M. E. Roloff & G. R. Miller (Eds.), *Interpersonal processes: New directions in communication research* (pp. 117–139). Newbury Park, CA: Sage.

Millar, F. E., Rogers–Millar, L. E., & Courtright, J. A. (1979). Relational control and dyadic understanding: An exploratory predictive regression model. In D. Nimmo (Ed.), *Communication Yearbook 3* (pp. 213–244). New Brunswick, NJ: Transaction Books.

Miller, G. R., Boster, F. J., Roloff, M. E., & Seibold, D. R. (1977). Compliance-gaining message strategies: A typology and some findings concerning effects of situational differences. *Communication Monographs, 44,* 37–51.

Neer, M. (1987). The development of an instrument to measure classroom apprehension. *Communication Education, 36,* 154–166.

Neer, M. (1990). Reducing situational anxiety and avoidance behavior associated with classroom apprehension. *Southern Communication Journal, 56,* 49–61.

Neer, M., & Kircher, W. F. (1989). Apprehensives' perception of classroom factors influencing their participation. *Communication Research Reports, 6,* 70–77.

Newton, D. A., & Burgoon, J. K. (1990). The use and consequences of verbal influence strategies during interpersonal disagreements. *Human Communication Research, 16,* 477–518.

O'Hair, H. D., & Cody, M. J. (1994). Deception. In W. R. Cupach & B. H. Spitzberg (Eds.), *The dark side of interpersonal communication* (pp. 181–213). Hillsdale, NJ: Erlbaum.

Olaniran, B. A., & Stewart, R. A. (1996). Instructional practices and classroom communication apprehension: A cultural explanation. *Communication Reports, 9,* 193–203.

Reardon, K. K. (1981). *Persuasion: Theory and context.* Beverly Hills, CA: Sage.

Reardon, K. K. (1987). *Interpersonal communication: Where minds meet.* Belmont, CA: Wadsworth.

Reardon, K. K., Sussman, S., & Flay, B. R. (1989). Are we marketing the right message: Can kids "Just say No" to smoking? *Communication Monographs, 56,* 307–324.

Richmond, V. P. (1984). Implications of quietness: Some facts and speculations. In J. A. Daly & J. C. McCroskey (Eds.), *Avoiding communication: Shyness, reticence, and communication apprehension* (pp. 145–155). Beverly Hills, CA: Sage.

Richmond, V. P., & McCroskey, J. C. (1992). *Communication: Apprehension, avoidance, and effectiveness* (2nd ed.). Scottsdale, AZ: Gorsuch Scarisbrick.

Robinson, A. T. (1915). The faith-cure in public speaking. *Quarterly Journal of Public Speaking, 1,* 221–228.

Rogers, L. E., & Bagarozzi, D. A. (1983). An overview of relational communication and implications for therapy. In D. A. Bagarozzi, A. P. Jurich, & R. W. Jackson (Eds.), *Marital and family therapy: New perspectives in theory, research and practice* (pp. 48–78). New York: Human Sciences Press.

Rogers, L. E., Courtright, J. A., & Millar, F. E. (1980). Message control intensity: Rationale and preliminary findings. *Communication Monographs, 47,* 201–219.

Rogers, L. E., & Farace, R. V. (1975). Analysis of relational communication in dyads: New measurement procedures. *Human Communication Research, 1,* 239.

Rogers–Millar, L. E., & Millar, F. E. (1979). Domineeringness and dominance: A transactional view. *Human Communication Research, 5,* 238–246.

Sabourin, T. C. (1995). The role of negative reciprocity in spouse abuse: A relational control analysis. *Journal of Applied Communication Research, 23,* 271–283.

Schenck–Hamlin, W. J., Wiseman, R. L., & Georgacarakos, G. N. (1982). A model of properties of compliance-gaining strategies. *Communication Quarterly, 30,* 92–100.

Segrin, C., & Fitzpatrick, M. A. (1992). Depression and verbal aggressiveness in different marital types. *Communication Studies, 43,* 79–91.

Shields, D. C. (1971). Focus on the rhetoric of women's liberation—A review. *Moments in Contemporary Rhetoric and Communication, 1*(3), 73–75.

Shields, D. C. (1993). Drug education and the communication curricula. In S. H. Decker, R. B. Rosenfeld, & R. Wright (Eds.), *Drug and alcohol education across the curriculum* (pp. 43–90). Saratoga, CA: R&E Publishers.

Shimanoff, S. B. (1987). Types of emotional disclosures and request compliance between spouses. *Communication Monographs, 54,* 85–100.

Speech Communication Association. (1975). Credo for free and responsible communication in a democratic society. Annandale, VA: Speech Communication Association.

Spitzack, C., & Carter, K. (1987). Women in communication studies: A typology for revision. *Quarterly Journal of Speech, 73,* 401–423.

Steeves, H. L. (1987). Feminist theories and media studies. *Critical Studies in Mass Communication, 4,* 95–135.

Street, R. L., Brady, R., & Lee, R. (1984). Evaluative responses to communicators: The effects of speech rate, sex and interaction context. *Western Journal of Speech Communication, 48,* 14–27.

Thompson, J. B. (1981). *Critical hermeneutics: A study in the thought of Paul Ricoeur and Jurgen Habermas.* Cambridge: Cambridge University Press.

VanLear, C. A., & Zietlow, P. H. (1990). Toward a contingency approach to marital interaction: An empirical integration of three approaches. *Communication Monographs, 57,* 202–218.

Vonnegut, K. S. (1992). Listening for women's voices: Revisioning courses in American public address. *Communication Education, 41,* 26–39.

Watzlawick, P., Beavin, J. H., & Jackson, D. D. (1967). *Pragmatics of human communication: A study of interactional patterns, pathologies, and paradoxes.* New York: Norton.

Wheeless, L. R. (1975). An investigation of receiver apprehension and social context dimensions of communication apprehension. *Speech Teacher, 24,* 261–268.

Wilder, C. (1979). State of the art: The Palo Alto group: Difficulties and directions of the interactional view for human communication research. *Human Communication Research, 5,* 171–186.

Williams, A., & Giles, H. (1996). Intergenerational conversations: Young adults' retrospective accounts. *Human Communication Research, 23,* 220–250.

Wiseman, R. L., & Schenck–Hamlin, W. J. (1981). A multidimensional scaling validation of an inductively-derived set of compliance-gaining strategies. *Communication Monographs, 48,* 251–270.

Witteman, H., & Fitzpatrick, M. A. (1986). Compliance-gaining in marital interaction: Power bases, processes, and outcomes. *Communication Monographs, 53,* 130–143.

Wood, J. T. (1993). Gender and moral voice: Moving from woman's nature to standpoint epistemology. *Women's Studies in Communication, 15,* 1–24.

Wood, J. T. (1995a). Feminist scholarship and the study of relationships. *Journal of Social and Personal Relationships, 12,* 103–120.

Wood, J. T. (1995b). *Relational communication: Change and continuity in personal relationships.* Belmont, CA: Wadsworth.

Zeitlow, P. H., & VanLear, C. A. (1991). Marriage duration and relational control: A study of developmental patterns. *Journal of Marriage and the Family, 53,* 773–785.

Theory Glossary

Action Assembly Theory (AAT)   AAT is a communication microtheory. AAT centers on the message structure of communication. It explains the generative mechanisms of action involved in creating coordinated speech. AAT explains how we develop and store memory organization packets or scripts that can be recalled and used in the same manner again and again. AAT argues that speech practice is the only successful way to store and recall communicative scripts.

Adaptive Structuration Theory (AST)   AST is a small group communication context theory. AST explains how work groups incorporate communication technologies into their work on a group problem. AST posits that small groups create and recreate problem-solving systems through the application of generative rules and resources that incorporate ever-evolving communication technologies.

Agenda-Setting Theory (AT)   AT is a mass communication context theory. AT explains the effect of the mass media in shaping what issues people think about. AT argues that people's beliefs about the importance of an issue correlate with the amount of attention that the mass media gives to that issue.

Anxiety/Uncertainty Management Theory (AUMT)   AUMT is an intercultural communication context theory. AUMT explains effective communication in the intercultural context. AUMT seeks to minimize communication error that might occur when a stranger approaches a person or group from an-

other culture by optimizing the social information that is provided.

Artistic Ethnography Theory (AET)   AET is an organizational communication context theory. AET explains organizations as cultures. AET critiques the organization as a symbolic place with an identity and boundaries with each organization being a unique symbolic construction.

Burke's Dramatism Theory (BDT)   BDT is a public speaking communication context theory. BDT explains the cyclical and hierarchical nature of human relations as moving symbolically from order to pollution to guilt, then victimhood, and finally redemption. BDT argues the rhetor describes this purification ritual in terms of the dramatistic hexad to elicit identification with the audience.

Communication Apprehension Theory (CAT)   CAT is a communication microtheory. CA is a communication construct that explains a most important communicator attribute across all contexts. CA is both a communicator trait and a situational state of anxiety. People that exhibit *high* communication apprehension appear to be communicatively incompetent across one or more of the communication contexts.

Communication Boundary Management Theory (CBMT)   CBMT is a communication microtheory that explains how couples regulate dialectical tension by relying on disclosure boundary management strategies.

Communication Metatheory, The (TCM)   TCM is a theory of theories that allows you to classify, anatomize (flesh-out or dissect), and evaluate communication theories. TCM's five *classifying elements* are determined by asking, Is a particular theory a general, contextual, micro, special, or symbiotic theory?. TCM's *anatomical elements* are origin, roots, and assumptions; communicative force and paradigm; theoretical technical concepts; modeling and relating concepts; and theory–method complex. Finally, TCM's *evaluative elements* are power and scope; heuristic and isomorphic; elegance and parsimony; validity and utility; and withstanding the critics.

Communication microtheories Communication microtheories are powerful, thin-banded theories that illuminate some important aspect of communicators communicating in a medium. Microtheories explain this thin band of communication across the various communication contexts. Communication microtheories, although anatomically correct, tend to feature one of the six metatheoretical metaconcepts of The Communication Metatheory (TCM) used throughout this book.

Communication Theory A *communication theory* is a set of concepts and relationship statements that help describe, explain, evaluate, predict, and control communication events. Communication theories (Level 2 talk) are why explanations of the phenomena occurring at Level 1 talk (actual communication).

Compliance-Gaining/Resisting Theory (CGRT) CGRT is a communication microtheory. CGRT concentrates on the basic concept of communication known as compliance-gaining and -resisting. It possesses two theoretical research strains, one coercive and one non-coercive. The non-coercive compliance-gaining/resisting research shows the most promise as a communication theory with practical, persuasive applications. CGRT explains the effect of several types of reasoned-based requests and reasoned-based denials.

Constructivist Theory (CT) CT is an interpersonal communication context theory. CT explains the relationship between *cognitive complexity* and interpersonal communication *competency*. CT argues that people with *high* cognitive complexity are generally more communicatively competent than people who are cognitively simple.

Contextual communication theories Contextual communication theories explain communication within the confines of the traditional contexts of interpersonal, small group, public speaking, organizational, mass, and intercultural communication. There are two types of contextual communication theories. Type 1 contextual theories use one or more theoretical concepts that tie them forever to the context. Type 2 contextual theories are fermenting and evolving and may prove broader in scope and thus become either a general communication theory or a communication microtheory.

Coordinated Management of Meaning Theory (CMM) CMM is an interpersonal communication context theory. CMM explains how people co-create meaning in and through communication and use semantic and pragmatic meanings to choreograph joint human action. CMM argues that three classes of rules—constitutive, regulatory, and authoritative— guide communication interaction as communicators co-create their hierarchically based scripted reality.

Cross-Cultural Adaptation Theory (CCAT) CCAT is an intercultural communication context theory. CCAT explains how an immigrant or sojourner adapts and assimilates to a new culture. CCAT posits that the person new to a culture moves back and forth between the original culture and the new culture to achieve successful acculturation.

Cultivation Effects Theory (CET) CET is a mass communication context theory. CET posits that heavy exposure to television's images and messages leads viewers to see the real world as consistent with those mediated portrayals. CET reports that heavy viewers of television are more fearful and distrustful of others than they would otherwise be.

Decision Emergence Theory (DET) DET is a small group communication context theory. DET explains the complex communicative process that problem-solving groups go through in reaching consensus about a decision. DET argues that over time small groups go through a four stage communicative process of orientation, conflict, decision emergence, and reinforcement.

Dialectical Relationship Theory (DRT) DRT is an interpersonal communication context theory. DRT explains the dyadic communication strategies necessary for coping with the inherent dialectical tensions that are endemic to close personal relationships. DRT posits that the primary dialectical tensions include autonomy-connection, predictability-novelty, openness-closedness.

Diffusion of Innovations Theory (DIT) DIT is a general communication theory that explains the effect of the communicative force of diffusing innovation talk on producing change in social systems. With DIT the communicative force flows from communicators (change agents and agencies; opinion leaders, gatekeepers, and agenda-setters; and adopters, resisters, and rejecters) communicating (engaging in the innovation decision process) by presenting messages (awareness, opinion, practice, advocacy, and resistance talk) propagated through a medium (authoritative versus collectivist versus individualist social system attuned to interpersonal, mass, or mixed communication channels).

Expectancy Violation Theory (EVT) EVT is a communication microtheory. EVT explores the message structure of nonverbal messages. It explains a narrow band of communicative interaction grounded primarily in the arena of nonverbal communication messages. EVT indicates that when communicative norms are violated non-verbally or verbally, the violation may be regarded by receivers as excusable or inexcusable depending upon the esteem within which they hold the violator.

Face Management Theory (FMT) FMT is an interpersonal communication context theory. FMT explains the communicative rules for maintaining and repairing public face in communicative interaction. FMT argues that facework contains four classes of communicative strategies: Defensive, protective, preventative, and corrective facework.

Face Negotiation Theory (FNT) FNT is an intercultural communication context theory. FNT explains how people in individualistic and collectivist cultures negotiate face and deal with conflict. FNT stitches together elements of Face Management Theory to explain how two or more people from different cultures adjust their negotiation styles to maintain face.

Feminist Genre Theory (FGT) FGT is a communication microtheory. FGT evaluates communication by identifying feminist speakers and re-framing their speaking qualities as models for feminist liberation. FGT seeks to eliminate the ideology of male dominant rhetoric. It seeks to replace it with feminist principles of safety, values, and freedom that are available for both men and women.

Functional Decision-Making Theory (FDT) FDT is a small group communication context theory. FDT explains the relationship between competently performed communication behaviors and the quality of group decisions. FDT argues that faulty decision-making can be avoided if at least four communication behaviors are performed competently. These four behaviors are understanding the problem, assessing the requirements for acceptable solutions, assessing the positive consequences of each proposal, and assessing the negative consequences of each proposal.

General communication theories General communication theories are valid, powerful, why-explanations of communicators communicating over time in a medium that hold across the traditional six contexts of interpersonal, small group, public speaking, organizational, mass, and intercultural communication. Each general communication theory's basic concept locates a fundamental communicative interaction or communicative force that accounts for human action.

Habermas's Critical Theory (HCT) HCT is a communication microtheory. HCT is an ideal, moral, competency-based, communication theory for human action. HCT creates this ideal through shared knowledge, mutual trust, and accord with each other represented by an idealized speech situation. HCT is an evaluative communication microtheory because it seeks to throw-off and replace repressive ideologies so that communicators may engage in emancipated communication in the public sphere. The idealized speech situation in the public sphere assumes unrestricted free speech, equal opportunity to speak, the legitimization of competing perspectives, and power-parity with respect to money and status.

Image Restoration Theory (IRT) IRT is a public speaking communication context theory. IRT explains the image restoration strategies necessary to repair the good name of individuals and/or organizations. IRT offers several image repair strategies, such as denial, evasion of responsibility, reduction of the offensiveness of the act, correction of the wrong, and mortification.

Information Manipulation Theory (IMT) IMT is a communication microtheory. IMT concentrates on explaining a basic concept of communication as it illustrates four ways of deceiving and manipulating information: fabrication, concealment, distortion, and equivocation. IMT explains how listeners are covertly mislead. IMT features the basic concept of information manipulation.

Information Systems Theory (IST)   IST is a general communication theory that explains the effect of the communicative force of information-sharing on the creation and maintenance of order, structure, and control for coordinated human action. With IST, the communicative force flows from communicators (senders, receivers, and observers) communicating (sharing syntactic, semantic, and pragmatic information) by presenting messages (information bits that are coded and sequenced) propagated through a medium (closed, open, or mixed systems).

Interpersonal Deception Theory (IDT)   IDT is a communication microtheory. IDT concentrates on a basic concept of communication as it views the receiver as the active communicator who attempts to detect deception. IDT posits that deceptive messages encompass three basic concepts: the central deceptive message (verbal), the bolstering ancillary message (verbal and nonverbal), and inadvertent leakage behaviors (mostly nonverbal) that point-up deception.

Marital Communication Theory (MCT)   MCT is a communication microtheory. MCT also explores the realm of the communication dynamic of communicative interaction. It explains the warring marital communication schema known as traditional, independent, separate, and mixed. Marital participation in specific schema predict both functional and dysfunctional communicative behaviors in both dyads and the family group.

Mathematical Theory of Communication   There are two that led to the development of Information Systems Theory. Norbert Wiener's mathematical theory of communication concerns the circular causality of feedback in which A causes B, B causes C, and C causes A, so that A causes itself. Claude Shannon's mathematical theory of communication appeared first in two issues of the *Bell System Technical Journal* (1948a, 1948b). Shannon's mathematical theory dealt with the syntactical problem of optimizing the amount of information that could flow through a given channel capacity when transmitted from a source to a self-correcting receiver. The theory operationalized information as an *information bit* sent by an appropriate processor called an encoder that reduced uncertainty by 50 percent. The information bit was received by another processor called a decoder that contained a self-correcting feedback device. Shannon's theory provided the world with a mathematical formula for determining the maximum amount of information bits that could be sent nearly error free through any given channel with a minimum of power.

McLuhan's Media Law Theory (MLT)   MLT is a communication microtheory. MLT argues that the medium is the message, that is, that new forms of mass media transform the message so that ultimately the medium is more important than its specific content. MLT argues that four laws govern the media's impact on society. They are the laws of acceleration, obsolescence, synthesis, and retrieval.

Muted Group Theory (MGT)   MGT is a communication microtheory. MGT focuses on an evaluative metaconcept of The Communication Metatheory. MGT posits that women are marginalized, muted, and oppressed by male-gendered, sexist language. MGT explains that traditional language possesses an inherent male bias because our men, almost exclusively, created our public language.

Narrative Paradigm Theory (NPT)   NPT is a general communication theory that explains the effect of the communicative force of narration (storytelling) as contributing the value–justification for human action. With NPT, the communicative force flows from communicators (storytellers and audience) communicating (storytelling) by presenting messages (stories containing emplotments, characterization, and a place of presentation) propagated through a medium (an open, democratic society).

Neo-Aristotelian Theory (NAT)   NAT is a public speaking communication context theory. NAT explains the force of persuasive speeches on the attitudes, beliefs, values, and behaviors of audiences. NAT argues that rhetorical syllogisms are used to make three important artistic proofs—ethos, pathos, and logos—to persuade audiences.

Organizational Assimilation Theory (OAT)   OAT is an organizational communication context theory. OAT explains the communicative process that mediates the individual-organizational relationship. OAT explains why newcomers become or fail to become organizational members—they complete or fail to complete a stagic process of assimilation.

Problematic Integration Theory (PIT) PIT is a special communication theory that explains the role of comforting and supportive communication in the treatment of illness in applied health communication.

Rational Argumentation Theory (RAT) RAT is a general communication theory that explains the effect of the force of rational argument as justifying conviction and spurring human decision-making. With RAT, the communicative force of argument-making flows from communicators (arguers, audience, and critic) communicating (making argument through contentions and cases) in a medium (field invariant or field dependent situation).

Relational Control Theory (RCT) RCT is a communication microtheory. RCT explores the realm of the communication dynamic of communicative interaction. It argues that relational control, a communication dynamic concept, is the most important concept in explaining relational satisfaction. RCT argues that couples continually negotiate their dominant-submissive relationship to one another across a host of issues, with *domineering* (both competing for and not resolving dominance) as a major source of relationship dissatisfaction.

Role Emergence Theory (RET) RET is a small group communication context theory. RET explains the formation of group roles as a product of the perceptions and expectations shared by the group members about the communicative behaviors of an individual in both the task and social dimensions of group interaction. RET argues that people compete for group roles and these roles evolve through a two stage process of primary and secondary tension.

Special communication theories Special communication theories are "how-to-do-it" theories that advise the communication practitioner about preparing certain types and forms of communication in the agreed-upon style of the day. Examples of special theories are Monroe's Motivated Sequence for public speaking or Dewey's Five Steps of Reflective Thinking for group problem-solving.

Speech/Communication Accommodation Theory (SCAT) SCAT is a communication microtheory. SCAT centers on the message aspect of communication. SCAT explains the tendency for communicators to experience convergence (a linguistic strategy whereby individuals accommodate vocal differences between themselves and others) of their speech and communication styles. SCAT argues that communicators engage in convergence to increase efficiency, gain approval, and maintain a positive social identity.

Spiral of Silence Theory (SST) SST is a mass communication context theory. SST explains the long-term effect of the mass media on public opinion and human action and inaction. SST explains how the mass media work in conjunction with majority opinion to silence minority beliefs on political issues and engender conformity.

Symbiotic (interdisciplinary) theories Symbiotic theories flow from the allied disciplines like linguistics, English, psychology, and sociology. They often exist in a close relationship with the theories from the communication discipline. This relationship exists on a continuum ranging from common ontological assumptions to cooperative interdisciplinary research on the same theory.

Symbolic Convergence Theory (SCT) SCT is a general communication theory that explains the effect of the communicative force of fantasy-chaining as providing meaning, emotion, and motive for human action. With SCT, the communicative force flows from communicators (fantasizers and rhetorical communities) communicating (fantasy-chaining) by presenting messages (fantasy themes, symbolic cues, fantasy types, sagas, and rhetorical visions) propagated through a medium (group-sharing or public-sharing).

Uncertainty Reduction Theory (URT) URT is a general communication theory that explains the effect of the communicative force of social information-sharing on interpersonal relationships. With URT, the communicative force of social information-sharing flows from communicators (co-interactants, strategic communicators and targets) communicating (seeking and giving passive, active, and interactive social information) by presenting messages (drawn from message organization packets, plans, and contingency plans and presented in phases) propagated through a medium (high context collectivist culture or low context individualist culture).

Unobtrusive Control Theory (UCT) UCT is an organizational communication context theory. UCT explains how organizations exert power over their employees by using organizational identification to foster conformity to organizational decision-making patterns, policies, and procedures. UCT argues that a tension occurs between an individual's symbolic identification and the organization's symbolic identification structure.

Uses and Gratifications Theory (UGT) UGT is a mass communication context theory. UGT explains why people choose, use, and receive benefits from attuning to the mass media. UGT argues that the media actually have limited effects on audiences because the individual audience member exerts control over media selection and information processing.

Vid-Oral Theory (VOT) VOT is a public speaking communication context theory. VOT emphasizes the oral preparation and presentation of talks over the written. It calls for the use of arguments and proofs drawn from the influence of contemporary media. VOT is compatible with the use of Burke's Dramatism Theory, Symbolic Convergence Theory, and Narrative Paradigm Theory as contemporary communication theories that bring the symbols of these vid-oral times to life.

Weick's Organizing Theory (WOT) WOT is an organizational communication context theory. WOT explains the organizing process as an attempt to optimize the amount of equivocality faced by humans. WOT posits three message structure concepts—enactment, selection, and retention—that characterize the collective activity of organizations as embodied in talking, interpreting, and remembering.

Name Index

Abrahams, M. F., 135, 136, 349
Adams, H. M., 238, 373
Adams, J. B., 327, 355
Adams, J. Q., 235, 237, 373
Addington, D. W., 330, 373
Adelman, M. B., 126, 131, 143, 325, 351, 386
Aden, R. C., 167, 325, 343, 352
Afifi, W. A., 143, 348, 392
Agee, P., 373
Aho, L., 332, 391
Aida, Y., 294, 390
Alberts, J. K., 170, 220, 287, 352, 363, 390
Albrecht, T. L., 200, 211–212, 327, 355, 370, 386
Alexander, A., 328, 370
Allen, D. S., 303, 390
Allen, I. L., 326, 355
Allen, J., 324, 338
Allen, M., 87–88, 330, 340, 373
Allen, R. R., 354
Aloimonos, Y., 324, 338
Altman, I., 135, 325, 348
Alperstein, N. M., 143, 348
Andersen, J. F., 325, 351
Andersen, P. A., 323, 334
Anderson, B. D., 33, 340
Anderson, J. A., 253–254, 340, 366, 373, 376, 388
Anderson, J. C., 58, 88, 339
Antola, L., 327, 355, 361
Antonelli, C., 327, 355
Appel, E. C., 241, 373
Applegate, J., 212, 373

Appleton, H., 356
Aristotle, 68, 156, 235, 237, 239, 259, 340, 352
Arnett, R. C., 209, 363
Arnold, W. E., 330, 373
Asante, M. K., 274, 383, 385
Ashcraft, K. L., 299–300, 390
Ashcroft, J. R., 326, 327, 361
Atkins, C., 362, 376
Atkinson, J. M., 55, 337
Atwood, E., 330, 373
Aune, R. K., 288, 332, 391
Aust, C. F., 332, 390
Austin, B. A., 332, 383
Austin, E. W., 332, 383
Aydin, C., 327, 360
Ayres, D. M., 294, 390
Ayres, H. J., 51, 58, 337
Ayres, J., 294, 325, 348, 390

Baade, R. C., 331, 374
Baaske, K. T., 326, 354
Babrow, A. S., 12, 87, 334, 335, 343
Bach, B. W., 179, 250, 331, 355, 373, 375
Badzinski, D., 333, 394
Baesler, E. J., 167, 352, 392
Bagarozzi, D. A., 333, 393, 397
Bahniuk, M. H., 59, 324, 337, 339
Baird, A. C., 235, 382
Bakee, K. L., 339
Baker, G. P., 68, 172, 340, 352
Baker, R., 339
Bales, R. F., 44, 95, 224, 226, 337, 343, 363

Ball, M. A., 325, 329, 343, 363
Ball-Rokeach, S., 51, 338
Balthrop, B., 90, 340
Banks, S. P., 373
Bantz, C. R., 87, 249, 324, 325, 326, 331, 340, 344, 355, 373, 374
Baran, S. J., 296, 390
Baratz, S., 328, 372
Barclay, R. O., 199, 327, 355, 358, 360
Bardini,T., 326, 327, 355
Barker, J. R., 194, 331, 355, 374
Barker, L. L., 330, 379
Barnes, A. M., 327, 356
Barnett, G. A., 324, 326, 327, 339, 355–356, 377
Barnland, D. C., 209, 223, 363
Barrick, J. E., 333, 396
Barrow, A. S., 332, 383
Barton, S. N., 115, 344
Basehart, J., 330, 375, 379
Basil, M. D., 51, 59, 178, 337, 356
Baskerville, D., 244, 374
Bass, F. M., 179, 186, 189, 198, 356, 359
Bass, J. D., 326, 352
Bassett, R. E., 330, 374
Bateson, G., 55, 290, 339, 390
Bavelas, J. B., 323, 334
Baxter, L. A., 132–133, 215–218, 325, 328, 332, 348, 363, 364, 367, 372, 390
Baynes, K., 301–303, 390
Beach, W. A., 45, 55, 323, 334, 337

Subject Index